Reader's Digest

SCENIC
WONDERS
OF
AMERICA

Reader's Digest

SCENIC WONDERS

The Reader's Digest Association, Inc., Pleasantville, New York
The Reader's Digest Association Ltd., Montreal, Canada

OF AMERICA

Contents

7 Finding Your Way to the Wonders

10 Introduction: Our Country, Our Heritage

18 Acadia National Park, Maine
Acadia Area Map 24   Surrounding Scenic Places 24–25   Campgrounds 529

26 Mount Washington, New Hampshire
Mount Washington Area Map 32   Surrounding Scenic Places 32–35   Campgrounds 529

36 Niagara Falls, New York
Niagara Falls Area Map 43   Surrounding Scenic Places 43–45   Campgrounds 530

46 Cape Cod National Seashore, Massachusetts
Cape Cod Area Map 52   Surrounding Scenic Places 52–55   Campgrounds 530

56 Hudson Valley, New York and New Jersey
Hudson Valley Area Map 63   Surrounding Scenic Places 63–65   Campgrounds 531

66 Shenandoah National Park, Virginia
Shenandoah Area Map 72   Surrounding Scenic Places 72–75   Campgrounds 531

76 Mammoth Cave National Park, Kentucky
Mammoth Cave Area Map 81   Surrounding Scenic Places 81–83   Campgrounds 532

84 Great Smoky Mountains National Park, North Carolina and Tennessee
Great Smoky Mountains Area Map 89   Surrounding Scenic Places 89–93   Campgrounds 533

94 Outer Banks, North Carolina
Outer Banks Area Map 100   Surrounding Scenic Places 100–101   Campgrounds 534

102 Okefenokee Swamp, Georgia
Okefenokee Area Map 107   Surrounding Scenic Places 107–109   Campgrounds 534

110 Everglades National Park, Florida
Everglades Area Map 118   Surrounding Scenic Places 118–121   Campgrounds 534

122 Boundary Waters Canoe Area, Minnesota
Boundary Waters Area Map 129   Surrounding Scenic Places 129–131   Campgrounds 535

132 St. Croix River, Wisconsin and Minnesota
St. Croix Area Map 139   Surrounding Scenic Places 139–141   Campgrounds 536

142 Sleeping Bear Dunes, Michigan
Sleeping Bear Area Map 147   Surrounding Scenic Places 147–149   Campgrounds 536

150 Mississippi Palisades, Iowa, Illinois and Wisconsin
Mississippi Palisades Area Map 155   Surrounding Scenic Places 155–157   Campgrounds 537

158 Flint Hills, Kansas
Flint Hills Area Map 165   Surrounding Scenic Places 165–167   Campgrounds 538

168 Ozark National Scenic Riverways, Missouri
Ozark Riverways Area Map 174   Surrounding Scenic Places 174–177   Campgrounds 538

178 Wichita Mountains National Wildlife Refuge, Oklahoma
Wichita Mountains Area Map 185   Surrounding Scenic Places 185–187   Campgrounds 539

188 Bayou Country, Louisiana
Bayou Country Area Map 194   Surrounding Scenic Places 194–195   Campgrounds 539

196 Padre Island National Seashore, Texas
Padre Island Area Map 203   Surrounding Scenic Places 203–205   Campgrounds 540

206 Devils Tower National Monument, Wyoming
Devils Tower Area Map 213   Surrounding Scenic Places 213–215   Campgrounds 540

216 Badlands National Monument, South Dakota
Badlands Area Map 224   Surrounding Scenic Places 224–227   Campgrounds 540

228 Scotts Bluff National Monument, Nebraska
Scotts Bluff Area Map 234   Surrounding Scenic Places 234–235   Campgrounds 541

236 Rocky Mountain National Park, Colorado
Rocky Mountain Park Area Map 243   Surrounding Scenic Places 243–247   Campgrounds 541

248 Black Canyon of the Gunnison National Monument, Colorado
Black Canyon Area Map 253   Surrounding Scenic Places 253–257   Campgrounds 542

258 Great Sand Dunes National Monument, Colorado
Great Sand Dunes Area Map 262   Surrounding Scenic Places 262–263   Campgrounds 542

264 Carlsbad Caverns National Park, New Mexico
Carlsbad Area Map 272   Surrounding Scenic Places 272–275   Campgrounds 542

276 Big Bend National Park, Texas
Big Bend Area Map 283   Surrounding Scenic Places 283–285   Campgrounds 543

286 Glacier National Park, Montana
Glacier Area Map 294   Surrounding Scenic Places 294–297   Campgrounds 543

298 Hells Canyon, Idaho and Oregon
Hells Canyon Area Map 304   Surrounding Scenic Places 304–307   Campgrounds 543

308 Yellowstone–Grand Teton National Parks, Wyoming
Yellowstone-Teton Area Map 320   Surrounding Scenic Places 320–323   Campgrounds 544

324 Craters of the Moon National Monument, Idaho
Craters of the Moon Area Map 329   Surrounding Scenic Places 329–333   Campgrounds 544

334 Great Salt Lake Desert, Utah
Great Salt Lake Area Map 342   Surrounding Scenic Places 342–345   Campgrounds 544

346 Arches–Canyonlands National Parks, Utah
Arches–Canyonlands Area Map 355   Surrounding Scenic Places 355–359   Campgrounds 545

360 Bryce Canyon–Zion National Parks, Utah
Bryce Canyon–Zion Area Map 369   Surrounding Scenic Places 369–373   Campgrounds 545

374 Grand Canyon National Park, Arizona
Grand Canyon Area Map 383   Surrounding Scenic Places 383–387   Campgrounds 545

388 Petrified Forest National Park, Arizona
Petrified Forest Area Map 394   Surrounding Scenic Places 394–397   Campgrounds 546

398 Saguaro National Monument, Arizona
Saguaro Area Map 403   Surrounding Scenic Places 403–405   Campgrounds 546

406 Olympic National Park, Washington
Olympic Area Map 415   Surrounding Scenic Places 415–417   Campgrounds 547

418 Mount Rainier National Park, Washington
Mount Rainier Area Map 426   Surrounding Scenic Places 426–429   Campgrounds 547

430 Columbia River Gorge, Washington and Oregon
Columbia Gorge Area Map 437   Surrounding Scenic Places 437–439   Campgrounds 547

440 Oregon Coast, Oregon
Oregon Coast Area Map 449   Surrounding Scenic Places 449–451   Campgrounds 548

452 Crater Lake National Park, Oregon
Crater Lake Area Map 457   Surrounding Scenic Places 457–459   Campgrounds 548

460 Redwood National Park, California
Redwood Area Map 466   Surrounding Scenic Places 466–469   Campgrounds 549

470 Yosemite National Park, California
Yosemite Area Map 478   Surrounding Scenic Places 478–481   Campgrounds 549

482 Big Sur Coast, California
Big Sur Area Map 487   Surrounding Scenic Places 487–489   Campgrounds 550

490 Sequoia–Kings Canyon National Parks, California
Sequoia–Kings Canyon Area Map 495   Surrounding Scenic Places 495–497   Campgrounds 550

498 Death Valley National Monument, California
Death Valley Area Map 505   Surrounding Scenic Places 505–507   Campgrounds 551

508 Mount McKinley National Park, Alaska
Mount McKinley Area Map 515   Surrounding Scenic Places 515–517   Campgrounds 551

518 Waimea Canyon, Kauai, Hawaii
Waimea Canyon Area Map 524   Surrounding Scenic Places 524–527   Campgrounds 551

528 Campground Directory

552 Geological Time Chart   Index 554   Picture Credits 574

Finding Your Way to the Wonders–Large and Small

On the pages that follow there are descriptive essays, color photographs and, in most cases, informative drawings to help you appreciate and enjoy 50 of the most scenic natural wonders in America.

These major wonders are indicated on a map at the end of each essay; and, as revealed on these maps, each wonder is surrounded by many other places of exceptional interest. Each map, in fact, shows some 20 other scenic places within a day's drive of the major wonder—for a total of more than 1000 beauty spots in all, including some from every state in the nation.

These area maps, prepared specially for this book, have unique features to make them more interesting and useful. These features are indicated by the following symbols.

☐ The main scenic wonder is outlined in red, and its name is lettered in red. If the area is small it is simply marked with an open red square, as shown here; if it is a large area, the red outline encloses the entire shape.

■ Other places of outstanding scenic interest are marked with a solid red square, with the names alongside in capital letters. These places are described in alphabetical order immediately following the map, and some are illustrated in color photographs as well.

🏛 This symbol indicates the location of a museum or other permanent exhibit that will help you better understand and enjoy the scenery and natural life of the area. At the end of each feature, the museums are listed alphabetically under the name of their nearest town or national park.

▲² Campgrounds are indicated by this tent symbol and an accompanying number. The number identifies the campground in a Campground Directory beginning on page 529. Look in the Contents to find the page numbers for each section of the directory. There is a list of campgrounds for each of the major wonders, and the information here includes the campground name, season, size, utilities provided, and special amenities such as swimming, boating, horseback riding and so on.

✈ Airports that offer regular commercial service are designated by the airplane symbol. This is to help those who may want to fly to a chosen area and rent a car on the spot.

The small brown square on the miniature map of the United States shows the general location of the region covered by each map. On the opening page of each feature the wonder is located on an outline of its state.

Exceptionally scenic roads are marked in green: solid green if they are U.S. or state highways, in green dashed lines if they are unpaved roads, and with green borders if they are part of the Interstate system.

National Forest land is marked in light green, and national parks, monuments and seashores in darker green.

Turn the page to see how the entire United States is covered by the 50 area maps. The name of each scenic wonder appears in red, and its location is marked with a symbol: ✸ The page number on which each area map appears is indicated by the number in the lower-right-hand corner of each square.

Where the Wonders Are

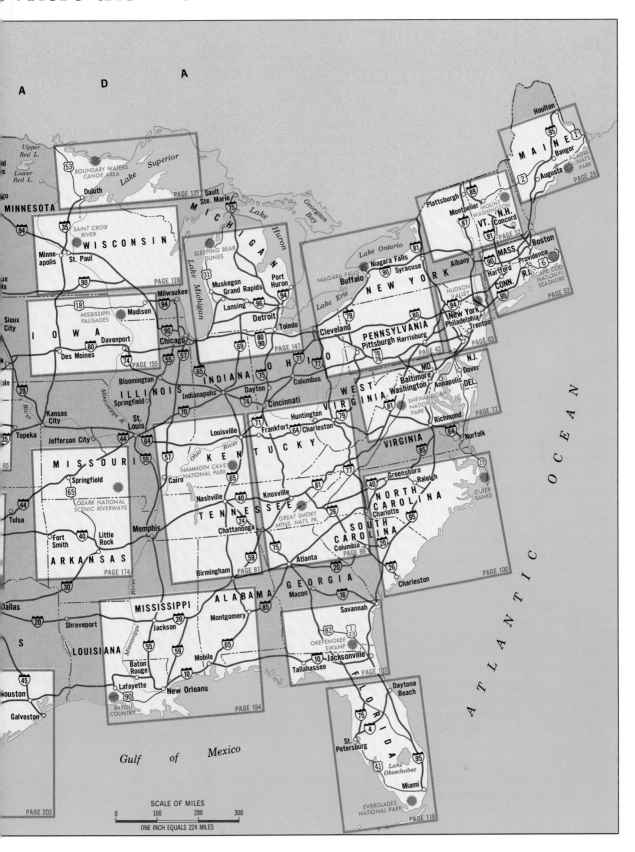

A

D

A

A

MINNESOTA

Upper Red L.
Lower Red L.

53 BOUNDARY WATERS CANOE AREA
Duluth
Lake Superior
PAGE 129
Sault Ste. Marie

94

35 SAINT CROIX RIVER
WISCONSIN
Minne-apolis
St. Paul
90
PAGE 139

Sioux City

18 MISSISSIPPI PALISADES
Madison
94
Milwaukee

IOWA
80 Davenport
Des Moines
74 PAGE 155
55 57
Chicago

29

oln

Kansas City
Topeka

35

65

Tulsa

44

MISSOURI
Springfield
65
OZARK NATIONAL SCENIC RIVERWAYS
Jefferson City
44 55
64

Fort Smith
40 Little Rock
ARKANSAS
PAGE 174

30

Dallas

20

S

Shreveport

LOUISIANA
Baton Rouge
55 59
Mobile
Lafayette
90 BAYOU COUNTRY
New Orleans
10
PAGE 194

45

ouston

Galveston

Gulf of Mexico

MICHIGAN
SLEEPING BEAR DUNES
Lake Huron
Georgian Bay
75
Lake Michigan
31
Muskegon Grand Rapids
Port Huron
94
Lansing
96
Detroit
Toledo
80 90
PAGE 147
69

INDIANA
Bloomington
Indianapolis
Springfield
70
75
Dayton
74
Cincinnati

ILLINOIS
Mississippi R.
St. Louis
57
65

Louisville
71 Frankfort
64 Charleston
KENTUCKY
Ohio River
MAMMOTH CAVE NATIONAL PARK
Cairo
65
Huntington
79

Memphis
TENNESSEE
Nashville
40 Knoxville
81
24
Chattanooga
GREAT SMOKY MTNS. NAT'L PK.
26
75
59 Atlanta
PAGE 81

Birmingham

ALABAMA
Montgomery
65
85
GEORGIA
Macon
16

MISSISSIPPI
Jackson
20

Mississippi River

OHIO
Cleveland
71 77
Columbus
20

Lake Erie
Lake Ontario
NIAGARA FALLS
Niagara Falls
Buffalo
79
Syracuse
81

NEW YORK
Albany
90
84
HUDSON VALLEY
New York
Philadelphia
Trenton

PENNSYLVANIA
Pittsburgh Harrisburg
70
76
PAGE 43

WEST VIRGINIA
20
SHENANDOAH NATIONAL PARK
81
Richmond
64

VIRGINIA
85

MD.
Baltimore
Washington
Annapolis
DEL.
Dover
N.J.

PAGE 72

Norfolk

Plattsburgh
Montpelier
89
MOUNT WASHINGTON
VT. N.H.
87
91 Concord
PAGE 32

MASS.
Hartford
CONN.
90
R.I. Providence
6 CAPE COD NATIONAL SEASHORE
Boston
95
PAGE 52

MAINE
Houlton
95
Bangor
2
Augusta
1
ACADIA NATL PARK
PAGE 24

Greensboro
Raleigh
40
12
OUTER BANKS
NORTH CAROLINA
Charlotte
95
SOUTH CAROLINA
Columbia
20
PAGE 89
26
Charleston
PAGE 100

Savannah
82
1 23
OKEFENOKEE SWAMP
10 Jacksonville
Tallahassee
FLORIDA
PAGE 107

Daytona Beach

75
4
St. Petersburg
41
Lake Okeechobee
95
Miami

EVERGLADES NATIONAL PARK
PAGE 118

ATLANTIC OCEAN

PAGE 203

SCALE OF MILES
0   100   200   300
ONE INCH EQUALS 224 MILES

9

Our Country, Our Heritage— the Triumph of the American Landscape

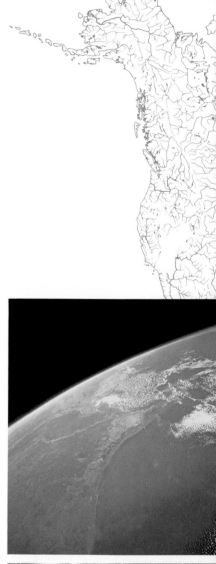

This book celebrates America's most magnificent scenery. Some of it—like Yellowstone and the Grand Canyon—is world famous, while other places—Kent Falls in Connecticut, for example, or Cloudland Canyon in Georgia—may be known only to those who live close by. In style, too, the wonders shown here reflect the enormous variety of the American landscape, ranging from the ferocious grandeur of the Rockies to the soft green forms of the Nebraska Sand Hills. Each state has its share of natural beauty, and this book will help you to seek it out, as well as to appreciate the awesome forces that created it over eons of time.

How the Continent Was Slowly Shaped

As more and more of us fly at 40,000 feet over this country, and become familiar with relief maps and globes, and marvel at the photographs sent back by the Apollo and Gemini flights, we are learning to think of America as a country of mountains and rivers and river valleys and not just as a collection of cities linked by concrete. We notice how rivers have carved their valleys through the mountains, and how the mountains form chains; we see, perhaps, how the White Mountains or the Adirondacks of the Northeast are "old" mountains, their crowns worn smooth with age, in contrast to the jagged, "young" peaks of the Rockies. And the pictures from space are a revelation—although, for example, we might have thought the mapmaker exaggerated the scimitar-smooth curve of Padre Island in Texas, the space photo puts the indisputable proof before us.

While the astronauts concentrated on the broadest of views, covering tens of thousands of square miles in one photograph, and revealing even the curvature of the earth and the band of dark blue that is the lower part of the earth's atmosphere, the geologist closes in on the details of the landscape and the reason for them. He seeks answers to hard questions, some buried so deep in rock and time that they may never be found. Indeed, the geologist has something in common with the naturalist. Searching the rocks, he discovers the hidden signatures of the living earth and learns from them, much as a naturalist learns from the tracks in mud or snow of animals that are too shy to be seen.

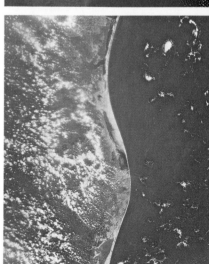

Water is the prime shaper of landscape; the drainage map of North America, above, shows our complex web of waterways. Today, photos taken from space help to fill out this geological story. On the left, the Red River cuts a lighter swath across the dark forests of Louisiana on its way to the Gulf of Mexico. Below, the sea shapes the outer edge of Texas' Padre Island as precisely as though smoothed with a trowel.

Geology might be called the elemental science, after the four elements of the ancients: earth, air, fire and water. The latter three are the forces that shape the earth. In reality our earth is mostly rock. You can see this clearly when you drive through a deep highway cut, where dynamite has been used to blast through a hill. Beneath the softening green cloak of vegetation the rocks are exposed, the bare bones of the earth, surprisingly close to the surface. So an understanding of the three main types of rocks (igneous, sedimentary and metamorphic) is the first step toward understanding the landscape.

Igneous rocks (from the Latin word for fire) form when molten materials squeezed up from the mantle (the deep semiliquid layer that lies below the thin shell of the earth's crust) cool and solidify. Two famous examples of basalt, the most common igneous rock, are Devils Postpile in California and Devils Tower in Wyoming, both tall structures composed of five- or six-sided columns that formed when the molten material fractured as it cooled. Granite, the other common igneous rock, is widely distributed in North America. It forms Yosemite's Half Dome and El Capitan, as well as the rounded summits of the Hudson Highlands in New York and of the nearby Adirondacks.

Sedimentary rock (from the Latin word for settling) covers 70 percent of the continent. These rocks had their origin in the succession of shallow inland seas that once covered much of North America. Mud, sand and shells sank to the bottom of the seas, layer on layer over eons of time, and eventually the layers solidified. Shale and sandstone are the most common types of sedimentary rock. Shale is solidified mud; sandstone, cemented sand. Limestone, another sedimentary rock, often contains the shells of marine organisms that lived in the prehistoric seas. Known as fossils, these are an excellent guide to the age of the rocks that surround and contain them.

Metamorphic rocks (from the Greek, meaning changed) can be of either igneous or sedimentary origin but at some stage they have been changed by heat, pressure or other means. Schist, slate (derived from shale) and gneiss are the most common types; marble, which comes from limestone, is perhaps the best known. Some of the valleys in the Green Mountains of Vermont are made of weak, coarse-grained marbles.

Two forces are constantly at work on the earth's rock surface: erosion and uplift. The two processes counterbalance each other: before the Colorado River could cut its mighty chasm, it was necessary that the land be uplifted. Otherwise there would have been no downward gradient to start the river on its cutting course. And mountains are constantly being eroded, boulders worn down, rocks ground into sand.

Erosion itself is a catchall term, used loosely to include three basic processes: weathering, mass wasting and true erosion. Weathering is the effect of chemical and physical processes on rock; mass wasting is the force of gravity in action, as in landslides and avalanches; and erosion, strictly defined, is the mechanical action of water, wind and ice on rock. But erosion is the master sculptor of the land, and water wields the biggest hammer. The old legend of a contest among the rock, the sun, the wind and the rain as to which was strongest (the rain won) comes to mind when we study erosion. Wind can be important as an erosion agent, blowing sand that abrades the rock; and in the north glaciers still have some of the grinding power that has changed a third of the world's land surface. But river drainage is the single most important factor in land formation—a greater force by far in its steady, scouring persistence than the abrupt violence of earthquakes or volcanic eruptions.

The Mississippi, 2350 miles long, is this continent's "master river." Its tributaries drain about one third of the continental United States, excluding Alaska, an area of over a million square miles. The Mississippi transports almost a million and a half tons of sediment a day into the Gulf of Mexico. Its major tributaries, like the Missouri, itself 2300 miles long, are fed by smaller rivers, and these smaller streams by creeks, dwindling down to the merest brooks and rivulets. A map of America showing only drainage looks like the bare branches and delicate veinlike twigs of a dozen gigantic trees pressed against the land.

Where does all the water come from? First, from the spring or glacier at which the stream itself starts; then from rainfall, snowfall, but also, and most important, from the massive reservoirs of underground water stored by millions of years of precipitation. The earth's crust contains about two million cubic miles of water that has percolated down between grains of rock and soil, through layers of rock and cracks in the bedrock. As a stream, with its load of sediment, cuts down its valley ever deeper, it receives fresh infusions when it taps this constantly replenished source of water that lies in the saturated zone.

The most obvious results of uplift are the mountains, which dominate the east and west coasts of this country, and rise to magnificent heights in the confusion of ranges in the Rockies. Many Indian legends center on mountains as the dwelling places of gods and demons. And, in fact, our modern science has still not solved all the mysteries of mountains, particularly as to their origin. Present-day theories of mountain-building remain just theories. The simplest of them goes something like this. Convection currents (rising warm currents and descending cooler currents) in the semiliquid mantle below the surface have created troughs in the earth's crust (called geosynclines) hundreds and sometimes thousands of miles long. Sediments accumulating miles deep in these troughs forced the troughs farther down, and other forces squeezed the sides inward, folding and breaking the layers of sediment. At the bottom of the trough the heat was intense; here the sediments melted, and in some places the molten rock burst through the crust in the form of volcanic eruptions. A general uplift of the crust occurred in response to the trough-building. And it is this crustal balancing act, so the theory goes, that has given us mountains.

These are the changes, of uplift and weathering and deposit and collapse, that form a landscape, over periods of time almost beyond the imagination's grasp. Some of the forces involved are explained in drawings throughout the book, and the drawings that appear on pages 552–553 will give you an idea of the role of geologic time in the formation of the majestic American landscape.

What Happened When the People Came

Mankind had little effect on this landscape until quite recent times. If we could look back at the face of North America through a time machine, the only changes we would see for thousands of centuries would be geological, even though man was present for some of this time. But with the coming of industrialization, change occurred at an increasingly rapid rate. In the last 50 years or so, with the development of technology, we have seen the rate of change increase dramatically each year. New words for what has happened to the land—megalopolis, urban sprawl, Northeast Corridor—have become part of our vocabulary. But all this change has been concentrated into a very short time, hardly a drop in the bucket of the ages.

The human history of this continent began about 50,000 years ago, during the most recent Ice Age, when the first of successive waves of the people we now call Indians moved down across the ancient land bridge that linked Alaska with Siberia. As the ice gradually melted, these people spread out of Alaska down a corridor east of the Rocky Mountains.

These men of the Paleo-Indian period were hunters—of mammoth, giant bison, ground sloth and mastodon. Around 6000 years ago the animals began to die out, and men turned to other sources of food, hunting smaller mammals and gathering berries. On the east and west coasts they found great beds of shellfish and began harvesting them, and invented weirs to trap the plentiful fish. By the time European settlers reached Massachusetts the Indians were well equipped to demonstrate how to cultivate corn and other crops.

America's earliest inhabitants, the Indians, took from the land what they needed—above, Plains Indians stampede buffalo to death over a cliff. Otherwise they left the face of America comparatively unchanged, apart from the rich legacy of their buildings and arts to be seen in the Southwest: left, the Cliff Palace at Mesa Verde, a maze of more than 200 rooms; below, a stone jar from New Mexico that predates Columbus by 400 years.

The ancient Indians of whom we know the most are those of the Southwest desert, since they constructed dwellings of such excellent masonry and workmanship that many show few signs of deterioration six centuries after they were abandoned to bake in the desert sun. The Indians of the Mesa Verde in the southwestern corner of Colorado progressed from pit houses, which were little more than caves with roofs, through pueblos or villages grouped around an open court, to the apartmentlike cliff dwellings we see today.

Their flourishing fields and vegetable gardens were what made it worthwhile for these Western Archaic people, as anthropologists call them, to build permanent dwellings. They had first learned to cultivate corn, and then to grow beans, which furnished a source of protein in addition to meat. At the same time they were developing the arts of basket and pottery making, so food and grain could be stored when harvests were abundant and supplies laid in for lean times.

Water was precious in the dry Southwest; the Indians of the Colorado plateau must have been skilled in nursing along their crops with a carefully hoarded water supply. A Navajo myth conveys the sense of wonder inspired by a river at flood: "That flowing water! That flowing water! My mind wanders across it . . ."

Indians of all cultures had a different attitude toward the land from that of the white European settlers who eventually came to North America. Unlike the Europeans, the Indians had no idea of claiming ownership of the land, only of using it. To them the land was a provident mother. They belonged to the land, rather than the land to them. And despite occasional contrary indications—Plains Indians, for example, set fire to the woods and prairies to force buffalo into a circle, thus making them easier to kill, and also used fire to clear land for farming and settlement—this instinctive feel for the inviolability of nature held true throughout most of Indian history. But that history, which had endured for so many centuries, could not survive the onslaught of war, persecution and disease that followed the arrival of the European settlers.

The 16th and 17th centuries were the great ages of New World exploration by Europeans. Christopher Columbus, seeking a westward route to the Indies, explored most of the Caribbean and reached as far as Panama on his four voyages between 1492 and 1504. But he did not realize he had discovered a great new continent until, on the third voyage, he sighted the northeast coast of South America. He never dreamed of the continent to the north.

The Spaniards, concentrating on the South and the Southwest, gained a tremendous advantage when Hernando Cortes conquered Mexico in 1521. The gold sent back from this treasure house financed more expeditions and eventually helped make it possible for many explorers and settlers to leave the Old World for the adventure of the New.

Early in the 16th century Ponce de Léon explored Florida; de Soto crossed the Mississippi and journeyed as far west as Oklahoma. In 1673 Marquette and Joliet explored the Mississippi down to the mouth of the Arkansas River—far enough for them to conclude that the Mississippi emptied into the Gulf and not into the Pacific, which was one of the erroneous ideas of the day.

Daniel Boone, the epitome of the independent, self-reliant frontiersman, blazed trails through the Kentucky woods in the mid-18th century, opening up more new territory to settlement by way of the Wilderness Road. A different type of pioneer, Father Junípero Serra, toiled up and down the California coast in the 1770s, building adobe missions in the Spanish style, oases of peace and harmony that survive to this day.

The Louisiana Purchase in 1803 was the incentive for President Thomas Jefferson to charge Meriwether Lewis and William Clark with one of the most tremendous tasks of exploration ever commissioned: to explore the vast, mostly unknown lands obtained by the Purchase via the Missouri and Columbia rivers, and to follow the Columbia to its outlet in the Pacific Ocean. The three-year saga ended in 1806, and after the journals of Lewis and Clark were published, the West could no longer be considered unknown territory.

The most important contribution to the opening up of the West was the discovery of gold in California in 1848. The rumor and the fact of gold had the effect of almost literally lifting men up out of their chairs, out of their homes, to leave their farms, their jobs and their families behind for the dangers and hardships of

Early white explorers were aided by Indians on their great journeys of discovery. Right, Sacagawea, the only woman on the Lewis and Clark Expedition, often served as a guide and interpreter; and below, the Frenchmen Joliet and Marquette, who traveled much of the Mississippi, also depended on Indian guides

Daniel Boone, the great frontiersman, lived to be 86. One of his greatest achievements was opening up the Wilderness Road, one of the highways westward that eventually led to the sort of boom psychology seen in the poster, right

the Gold Rush. The Santa Fe and Oregon trails they followed became major highways through the Rockies to the Pacific.

Settlement of the rest of America was assured when the Homestead Act was passed in 1862. It offered 160 acres of land free and clear to anyone, including immigrants, who would farm it and make certain improvements. Only a few decades after Lewis and Clark had made their arduous way across the country, rail service was opened to the Pacific Coast. The virgin continent had been breached; now even the remnants of the 500 Indian tribes who were living here in the time of Columbus were doomed.

It is ironic that only a century or two after our ancestors virtually exterminated these "primitive" peoples in the name of progress, we have finally come around to an Indian point of view: that the land is precious, a resource valuable for more than what can immediately or next year be extracted from it; that it should not be violated; that it "belongs" to no one; and that we hold it in trust for the future and our children.

Such realization was a long time coming, but this book bears eloquent witness to its importance. For with it was born a concept of national trusteeship that has kept much of our finest scenery away from the most intensive exploitation and development.

The Future Is in Our Hands

The majority of the 50 scenic wonders in this book have the word "National" in their names: National Park or Monument, National Scenic Riverway, National Wildlife Refuge. This is no accident. It reflects a program of preservation of our natural wonders under the National Park System, which now encompasses 27 million acres. This is still only about one percent of all the land in America, and when you look at the areas under Park Service administration on a map it seems that we have set aside a pitifully small proportion of land. But the selection is choice. Visit one of the great western parks, or even any of the smaller, more crowded eastern parks during an off-season, and you can still experience solitude; the wilderness does indeed seem to stretch for hundreds of square miles all around. The more remote parks—Big Bend, for example, down near the Texas–Mexico border, or Olympic, far off in the northwest corner of Washington—are especially rewarding in their reminders of natural solitude and grandeur. And almost always, if you step back from the scenic overlook and let a trail lead you away from the road for a mile or two, you travel back in time to an earlier, more primitive America.

A New Yorker, the well-traveled, wilderness-loving Frederick Law Olmsted, the landscape architect who designed Central Park (and many other city parks), provided the impetus for the first step toward a national park system. After a pleasure trip to Yosemite Valley more than a century ago, he and a group of associates persuaded Congress to pass a bill, which President Lincoln signed in 1864, preserving Yosemite Valley "for public use, resort and recreation." A few years later, in 1872, President Grant signed the Yellowstone Park bill, which provided that over two million acres surrounding the marvels at Yellowstone be set aside as "a public park or pleasuring ground for the benefit and enjoyment of the people."

But others were interested in these pleasuring grounds more for their own benefit than for "the people." Commercial encroachments by lumbermen and sheep ranchers, for example, were a constant threat to Yosemite Valley. A Scot, John Muir, became the valley's champion. Muir was a passionate and articulate spokesman for conservation before either the term or the idea were fashionable, and his pleas for the wilderness led to the establishment of a "forest reservation" of a million acres in Yosemite Valley. But it was not until 1903, when Muir and President Theodore Roosevelt camped together in the valley, and Roosevelt became enthralled both with the scenery and with Muir's point of view, that the conservation movement found an ally powerful enough to ensure its survival.

In 1906 Congress passed the Antiquities Act. Although its main purpose was to protect ancient Indian dwellings, it ultimately gave President Roosevelt the authority to declare the Grand Canyon a national monument without having to wait for an Act of Congress. This prompt action prevented a promoter from carrying out his plan to stake mining claims on the canyon rims, with the aim of developing the canyon itself as a tourist attraction.

In 1916 Congress passed the National Park Service Act. Under the imaginative leadership of Stephen Mather, the first director, the 14 de facto "national parks" were officially designated and their number soon increased to 21. These parks were served by a dedicated group of rangers united by a common ideal: to preserve America's wilderness and natural wonders, and to interpret and present them to the public to whom they belong.

The words "national parks" conjure up many different images in the minds of those who have visited them: to a backpacker, the memory of aching muscles at the end of a hard day's hike softened by the warmth and companionship found around a campfire; to a camping family, a father's delight in his child's pleasure at discovering the green world; and to all who see such unforgettable sights as the Grand Canyon or Mount Rainier, an enhanced appreciation of America's true marvels.

The range of educational experiences in the national parks, for young and old, is vast. A recent visitor to Olympic's Hoh Rain Forest, drinking from an icy stream clouded gray with particles of glacial debris carried in suspension, tasted the odd but not unpleasant grittiness of glacial dust. The ranger-naturalist leading the nature walk had drunk the water first, pronounced it potable, and a few in the group found it impossible to resist the once-in-a-lifetime experience of such a close contact with the ages. At Kalaloch, on the Pacific Coast side of the park, ranger-naturalists lead daily walks at high tide to the fascinating tide pools, depressions hollowed out in the rocks, in which crabs, barnacles and flower-like green sea anemones live. Again the naturalist led the way, showing the group how the anemone's food-gathering tentacles gently closed around his finger. Soon most of the group, men, women and children, were squatting on the barnacle-covered,

wave-splashed rocks, sticking their fingers in the pools and allowing themselves to communicate, however queasily, with the grasping anemones.

National parks statistics can be misleading. Yellowstone, one of the most popular parks, had 2.1 million visitors in 1971; Olympic, 1.8 million. But most people go to Yellowstone in the summer, to see Old Faithful and the mud pots and Yellowstone Falls, so the impression is one of great crowds at those areas and the approaches to them. Olympic, on the other hand, has mild, if rainy, winters, except in the mountains, and its attractions are widely separated. So even though almost as many people visit Olympic as Yellowstone, at Olympic they are spread out over space and time and the park seems relatively uncrowded.

The strain on the national parks grows as Americans become more affluent and more mobile and highways open up once-remote areas. In 1960, 79 million of us visited a national park; by 1970 this figure had more than doubled: 160 million visits were recorded. Seven-square-mile Yosemite Valley was jammed with nearly 55,000 automobiles one recent Fourth of July. Even Mount McKinley National Park in Alaska has been opened up to an influx of travelers with the completion of the highway linking Fairbanks and Anchorage.

The solution to the Mount McKinley problem has been to limit the number of cars allowed into the park to about 80 (which is the total number of campsites available), to require reservations for these and to provide frequent free bus service into the park on the 87-mile road over the tundra.

In Yosemite Valley, private cars are now banned east of Curry Village, but free shuttle buses make frequent loop tours through scenic areas. In Everglades National Park you can pay a $2 entrance fee, park your car off the Tamiami Trail and board a tram that goes to the Shark Valley Observation Tower, with its views of the teeming birdlife.

These sort of measures, and others still being developed, will alleviate at least part of the parks' people and car problems, and offer visitors a more pleasurable way of seeing the national parks than simply driving through them.

The national park movement has been the salvation of America's natural wonders. It came along in the nick of time, and the men who carried out its aims have done a superb job of preservation and interpretation. Comparatively little of America's magnificent natural heritage is still unclaimed, and the major thrust among conservationists today is not so much to preserve more as to ensure that the scenery already preserved is not spoiled by careless use and utterly unrestricted access. The challenge faced by most park officials comes less these days from the forces of commercial exploitation than from the thoughtlessness and untidiness of far too many park visitors, who litter, carve their names on trees and often frighten the animals.

The 500 pages that follow show how beautiful America still is, how much there is in every state to enjoy and admire. We hope the book will inspire you to go out and explore its scenic highlights and byways—and as you do so, to remember that this land is *your* land and should be treated accordingly.

Great figures who opposed reckless 19th-century overdevelopment included John Muir, shown above bringing Teddy Roosevelt under his spell at Yosemite, and landscape architect Frederick Law Olmsted, left. They and their followers were the ancestors of the extensive group of public agencies now charged with preserving the American wilderness. Some of their emblems and signs appear below.

Acadia National Park

MAINE

Sunrise from Cadillac Mountain is often America's first look at the light.

America's Earliest Sunrise
Lights an Ancient Drowned Shore

Before sunrise on a cloudless midsummer day, there is a feeling almost of presumption at being atop Cadillac Mountain on Maine's Mount Desert Island. For what you are awaiting are the first rays of sunlight to touch the United States.

Here, too, at any time of day is the heart of Acadia National Park—and the place from which to survey its 41,000 acres. It is an eagle's-eye preview of all the natural splendors of coastal Maine. To the east, across Frenchman Bay, lies Schoodic Point, a windswept headland of huge granite ledges that turn Atlantic waves into lofty geysers. On the southwest horizon, far out to sea, is Isle au Haut, a primitive, one-village island, almost completely forested, and laced with hiking trails. Below you, the largest section of Acadia spreads out over 40 percent of Mount Desert Island. Here are more than a dozen ancient granite mountains, smoothed by time and wrapped in dark green forests of spruce, hemlock, fir and pine; glacial lakes and ponds are cupped in the uplands, which plunge steeply to seaside cliffs and rockbound coves.

For a more down-to-earth, close-up introduction to Acadia, visit the park headquarters, just south of Hulls Cove. Maps available here show the island's two main scenic loops, as well as hiking and bicycling trails; and schedules outline summer nature walks, mountain

Crashing surf slowly wears away at the coastline below Ocean Drive, Mount Desert Island. Faults and joints cause granite to break in blocks.

hikes and fine boat cruises. Acadia also offers a tape-recorded tour you can play in your car.

Heading south on Route 3 from headquarters you come to Bar Harbor, with its many tourist amenities. Beyond the town it is important to head south on Route 3, for the famous Ocean Drive ahead is one way south. Near the start of the drive, there is a worthwhile detour to Sieur de Monts Spring, to sip the cool waters and admire the wildflower gardens —and especially to see the exhibits of Acadia's natural history in the Nature Center.

Once on Ocean Drive, a series of spectacular vistas of sea, forest and mountain dramatize every turn. There are frequent overlooks, trails and a picnic area. A rough path descends to Anemone Cave, where at low tide you can see thousands of colorful sea anemones clinging to the walls. Swimmers hardy enough to brave 55-degree water can take a dip at Sand Beach, a strand of quartz sand and fragmented seashells. Everyone stops at Thunder Hole, where an ocean-carved chasm slaps back the tidal rush with a mighty boom. On Otter Point, a trail through thick spruces winds along the edge of crags that drop a hundred feet to ledges and offshore reefs, the feeding grounds of gulls and cormorants.

Turning inland now, the road crosses streams running through birch and pine woodlands that are home to foxes and deer, and reaches Jordan Pond, one of Acadia's great natural amphitheaters. Penobscot Mountain and Pemetic Mountain cradle the deep glacial lake between them. The surrounding hills, glens and

Acadia's ponds and lakes were formed when mile-thick glacial ice scooped out hollows in the granite hills. Those seen in this aerial view are Jordan Pond (in foreground) and Eagle Lake.

Tide pools left behind in the rocks by the retreating tide are a constant source of wonder at Acadia; they shelter colorful plants and creatures that are adapted to life in water and air.

Acadia's Past: Ice and Granite

The Maine coast around Acadia has passed through many complex geological processes. Hundreds of millions of years ago this region was covered by the sea. Ocean-floor deposits hardened into rock layers. These were folded and lifted into mountains, which were worn down by erosion, then again flooded by the sea. After eons of erosion, with intermittent uplifts, low hills of granite—the once-molten "root" rock of the ancient mountains—remain. During the Pleistocene Epoch, beginning about two million years ago, glacier ice a mile thick covered the area. Its gradual melting exposed smoothed highlands and deepened valleys, which the rising sea flooded to form today's Acadia.

meadows can be explored on horseback or by horse and buggy along 40 miles of carriage paths. (Nearby Wildwood Stable rents both.) Bikers should continue north along the road to Eagle Lake, circled by a spectacular four-mile cycle trail. (Rent cycles in Bar Harbor.)

Backtracking to the coast, the road now enters Northeast Harbor, where the yachts crowded at anchor tell eloquently of the well-to-do community that summers here and sails these waters. On the far side of town Sargent Drive begins to unfold its magnificent vistas of Somes Sound, the deepest fjord on the eastern coast of the United States. (A true fjord is the seaward segment of a valley cut by glacial ice and later "drowned.") The sound, which is six miles long and flanked by bluffs that plunge sheerly into 150 feet of water, is probably the most vivid memento of the Ice Age that shaped Mount Desert Island.

Somesville, the village at the head of the sound, straddles Route 102, which runs around the western part of Acadia. Driving south from here, you can stop at Echo Lake for a fresh-water swim, or hike up trails to the surrounding hills, where eagles are sometimes seen. The village of Southwest Harbor is another center for the summer people. There is a park campground and picnic area at Seawall, a good place to bird-watch or ramble.

The most southerly point of the island is Bass Harbor Head, where the lighthouse, perched on a cliff and framed by spruces, is perhaps the most photographed in Maine. Also a visual pleasure are nearby Bass Harbor and Bernard, typical Down East fishing villages that share a long, protected harbor. Their waters are decorated with colorful fishing boats, and piers are stacked with bright tangles of lobster traps and buoys. From here the road turns north, running past deeply indented coves and tranquil ponds, along the flank of Western Mountain and across the top of Long Pond, largest of Acadia's lakes.

Even such a comparatively brief sampling of Acadia's natural wonders—its sparkling visions of sea and mountain, its sturdy mixture of rock and evergreens, its teeming marine life and wave-smashed shore—converts most of the two and a half million annual park visitors into strong partisans of the place. As such, they are members of a long tradition. Since the Civil War, vacationers have been coming here, and many families—including Fords, Rockefellers and other powerful names —have built summer homes. In fact, the 8000-odd year-round residents are heavily outnumbered by summer people.

But it was summer residents who so loved the island that they wanted to preserve it for public as well as private enjoyment. In 1901 a small group was organized to acquire and protect the land, and by 1913 they had 6000 acres. Their holdings became a national park in 1919, the first actually donated to the government, and the first east of the Mississippi.

So today's visitors, as they drive up Cadillac Mountain at dawn, or cross the causeway back to the mainland at the end of their tour, have much to be grateful for. They have experienced a welcome contradiction of the cliché that tourists and summer people tend to love a place to death. At Acadia, these were the people whose love helped it to live for everyone.

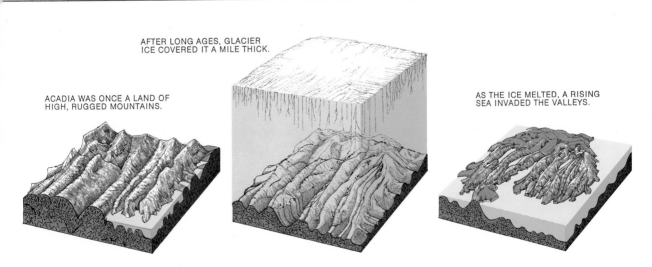

ACADIA WAS ONCE A LAND OF HIGH, RUGGED MOUNTAINS.

AFTER LONG AGES, GLACIER ICE COVERED IT A MILE THICK.

AS THE ICE MELTED, A RISING SEA INVADED THE VALLEYS.

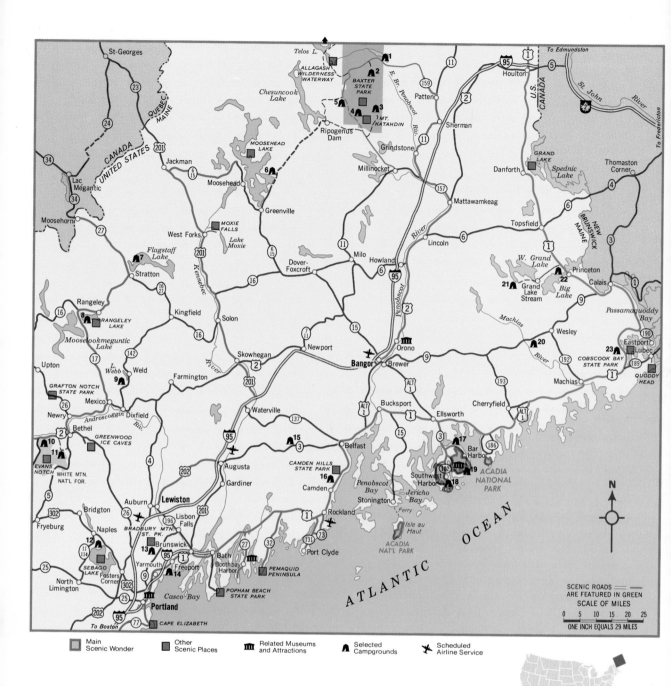

WITHIN A DAY'S DRIVE:

Maine's Wild Mixture of Forests, Lakes and Rocky Shores

Allagash Wilderness Waterway.
(*Picture appears on facing page*)

Baxter State Park. This 200,000-acre area of coniferous forests, mountains and glacial lakes is almost untouched by civilization. Baxter's only concession to the auto is three narrow, unpaved

roads; most of the park can only be seen from 75 miles of rustic, wooded hiking trails.

Bradbury Mountain State Park. A gentle hike up the granite slopes of Bradbury leads to a panoramic view of inland lakes, the White Mountains and Casco Bay.

Camden Hills State Park. Forests and glacier-smoothed mountains come down to the sea at Camden. From the top of Mount Battie and Mount Megunticook are splendid vistas of Penobscot Bay.

Cape Elizabeth. Two Lights State Park, a steep, exposed Atlantic overlook, is a great place to watch stormy surf; Crescent Beach State Park has a good sandy beach.

Cobscook Bay State Park. A reverse saltwater falls is produced as the Atlantic tide rushes over the rocks in Denys and Whiting bays.

Evans Notch. On one side of the road through this narrow mountain pass are spectacular views of surrounding peaks. On the other, steep cliffs rise above the valley.

Grafton Notch State Park. Grafton has a surprising amount of scenery in a small area: a mountain, two falls, a cave and a stretch of Appalachian Trail.

Grand Lake. Straddling the U.S.-Canadian border, these forest-lined waters are crowded with salmon, trout and perch.

Greenwood Ice Caves. Large glacial boulders, reached by an easy hiking trail, hide the entrance to these caves, named for the ice that lingers until late summer.

Moosehead Lake. Hundreds of miles of thick forest extend beyond the twisting shores of Maine's largest lake. Only the southwestern shore is accessible by public road, but private toll roads cover the rest of the area.

Mount Katahdin.
(*Picture appears on this page*)

Moxie Falls. This spectacular cataract is on the Kennebec River, off scenic U.S. 201.

Pemaquid Peninsula. The cliffs of Pemaquid are some of the most rugged in a state famous for them. The tidal Damariscotta River here teems with spawning alewives every spring.

Popham Beach State Park. There are fine sandy beaches here, and surfing is popular offshore.

Quoddy Head. Quoddy Head caps a peninsula at the northeastern tip of the United States, and a variety of seabirds are seen round its sheer cliffs. A state park here also contains an isolated example of arctic tundra.

Mount Katahdin. *The highest point in Maine, at 5267 feet, is in Baxter State Park. It shares America's first sunrise with Cadillac Mountain. The Appalachian Trail to Georgia begins nearby.*

Allagash Wilderness Waterway. *Canoeists treasure the 92-mile chain of lakes connected by the Allagash River as it winds through virgin northwestern Maine. Cars can drive to the start at Telos Lake.*

Rangeley Lake. This is actually a series of five interconnected lakes, beautifully spread out in a chain beneath the Longfellow Mountains.

Sebago Lake. The state's second biggest lake is a spectacular one. Sebago Lake State Park, on the north shore, has especially good sand beaches, and nature trails through the forest.

RELATED MUSEUMS AND ATTRACTIONS

Acadia National Park. Nature Center.

Boothbay. U.S. Fish Hatchery and Aquarium.

Orono. University of Maine Herbarium.

Portland. Portland Society of Natural History.

Mount Washington
NEW HAMPSHIRE

Glacier-scoured Mount Washington, as seen from Bretton Woods.

Mount Washington

NEW HAMPSHIRE

New England's Everest Creates Its Own Winter

Leaving Route 16 in New Hampshire and driving up Mount Washington is like leaving New England for Labrador, or summer for winter. The trip up may have begun in sunny July weather, but at the top it's darker and colder, perhaps down around 45 degrees. The wind, which has been gradually increasing, is now blowing hard. Fog swirls about and a cloudcap may blot out the view. The trees are gone; only lichens and an occasional low-lying plant cling to the glacier-scrubbed ground. The whole atmosphere is likely to be one of fierceness and gloom, the forces of nature barely held in balance.

Yet on this peak, famous for having what is probably the worst weather at any perma-

nently occupied place in the world, there are buildings, roads, cars, even crowds. About a dozen people live and work here during the summer, staffing the Summit House restaurant and the cog railway. Hardy men live all year long at the noted Mount Washington Observatory and the radio and TV transmitter building.

Mount Washington, the heart of this paradox, is one of the White Mountains, which in turn are part of the Appalachian chain that runs through eastern North America. The most prominent of the several White Mountain ranges is the Presidential Range, about 15 miles long and five miles wide. Mount Washington, its tallest peak at 6288 feet, lies roughly at the center of the range, with mounts Clay,

Jefferson, Adams and Madison to the north, and Monroe, Franklin, Eisenhower, Clinton, Jackson and Webster to the south.

As you stand on the summit of Mount Washington all these giants heave up their mighty shoulders around you: old, rounded peaks flowing off into the far horizon, blending with neighboring ranges in an incredibly complex topography. When the sun shines, and cloud shadows pass over the mountains and valleys, it is like being in another world.

For the nonhiking tourist, there are three ways of getting to the top of Mount Washington: on the toll road, in your own car; on the toll road, but riding in a chauffeured station wagon hired at the base; or on the colorful, Toonerville Trolley-like cog railway with its chugging steam engine.

Most noticeable on the way up is the striking contrast between the vegetation at the upper and lower levels. At the mountain's base and up to about 3500 feet is hardwood forest, predominantly birch and maple, dense enough to block most views of the surrounding mountains. Above 3500 feet, coniferous trees—red spruce, white pine, hemlock—appear among the hardwoods. Soon the hardwoods thin out and the forest is mostly conifers—spruce and balsam fir. All the time the trees are getting smaller and smaller, as if crouching against the force of the wind. Soon they look more like bushes than trees. Near the top even the low-lying plants are mostly gone, and the barren, rocky ground is strewn with huge boulders.

Among the few creatures that can live in this hostile environment is a species of arctic butterfly called the White Mountain butterfly. During the last Ice Age the ancestors of this butterfly, together with other arctic species of animals and plants, migrated southward in advance of the ice sheet which covered even the highest peaks of the Presidential Range. As the ice retreated most of these plants and animals moved north again, but a few species, like the White Mountain butterfly, remained.

But Mount Washington is famous more for its rigorous weather than for its plant and ani-

The deep, bowl-shaped area dropping away to the left of the solitary hiker in this picture is the Great Gulf Wilderness, a natural amphitheater, or cirque, carved out ages ago by glacial action. The view is from the summit of Mount Jefferson, looking southeast toward Mount Washington.

Mount Monroe, Mount Washington's neighbor to the south, rears up beyond one of the Lakes of the Clouds. Arctic lichens cover the rocks that border the lake. A mountain climbers' hut near here serves as a base for hikers who brave the mile-and-a-half climb to Mount Washington's summit.

mal life. The constant threat of bad weather is the most important factor about the mountain as far as safety is concerned. To quote a Forest Service pamphlet: "The needless loss of life in the areas above timberline has been largely due to the failure of hikers to realize that storms of incredible violence occur during the summer months." Forty-three climbers have died on Mount Washington in the past 80 years, mostly from exposure after becoming lost on the misty heights.

Mount Washington's bad weather is a deadly mixture of high winds, low temperatures and frequent fog. The average wind velocity throughout the year is 35 miles per hour, and the average yearly temperature is 27 degrees. Snow may fall every month of the year, and fog occurs 90 percent of the time.

In view of the almost constant high winds,

the wind chill factor is important. The stronger the wind the more body heat lost, so if the wind is 40 mph and the temperature 45 degrees, a person *feels* as cold as if it were 19 degrees on a day with no wind.

One reason for the extraordinarily strong winds is that the peak lies in a zone where several storm tracks meet and mingle. Typical storm tracks crossing northern New England come from the northern Great Plains or southern Canada, the southwestern U.S. and the Atlantic Ocean. Coastal storms often produce the most severe weather. It was during such a storm, on April 12, 1934, that the highest gust of wind ever recorded on earth—231 mph— was registered. Although this top speed lasted for only a few moments, the *average* wind speed that day was an amazing 129 mph.

Another reason for the wild weather is that

Mount Washington is both the highest point (wind speed usually increases with height) and near the center of a long range of mountains. If the peak stood alone, air could pass around as well as over it, with reduced velocity.

Obviously the top of Mount Washington is a perfect place for a weather station. The Mount Washington Observatory, founded in 1932, is considered one of the world's outstanding mountain weather research stations. It may also be the world's strongest wooden building. The frame is made of huge beams retired from the cog railway bed and bolted either into concrete or into the bedrock itself. Other buildings are chained down. In winter, ice and hard-packed snow add their weight and help keep the buildings together in winds of superhurricane force.

There are three places of special interest near the top of Mount Washington. The Great Gulf Wilderness, visible from the toll road, is a deep glacial valley filled with a magnificent forest. At the head of Great Gulf is Spaulding Lake, an exquisite cirque pond scoured out by glacial action.

The Alpine Garden, east of the summit, is an area where delicate, colorful alpine plants grow in abundance. Plants like these are usually found much farther north—in Greenland, Labrador or even the Brooks Range in northern Alaska, which is within the Arctic Circle.

Finally, Tuckerman's Ravine, high on Mount Washington's eastern slopes, is a glacial cirque, or natural amphitheater, a catch basin for the snow that blows off the tops of nearby mountains. Intrepid skiers climb the steep slopes without benefit of lifts or tows, but are rewarded for their efforts by snow that may last into July. The less athletic can walk close enough to the ravine to see the famous Headwall and the trough carved by ancient glaciers.

For anyone who goes up Mount Washington, no matter how, the trip is above all an adventure. In the sense of desolation and chaotic natural forces at the summit the meaning of the word "wilderness" sinks in. The violent extremes of weather possible in this high, strange world, which test the limits of survival for all forms of life, are real and meaningful.

When the hikers come "off the top of the mountain," as they say, into the warmth of the restaurant, the spirit of adventure that moves them touches everyone else. And stories about the skiers and climbers who lost their lives on the mountain take on the quality of legend.

Even the less hardy visitor, who breathes a sigh of relief when he returns to the familiar world of green-leaved trees and sun-warmed air at the base of the mountain, may later find himself strangely eager to go up again.

A Lofty Magnet for Harsh Weather

The map at left illustrates why winds of superhurricane force occur on Mount Washington. A storm coming out of western Canada, for example, roars over the plains unimpeded by high mountain ranges until it hits the White Mountains. Mount Washington, highest of the White Mountains, forces the already strong winds up over its peak, as shown in the diagram. As the winds rise they accelerate. The picture at right shows the Mount Washington Observatory in midwinter, under its burden of ice and snow.

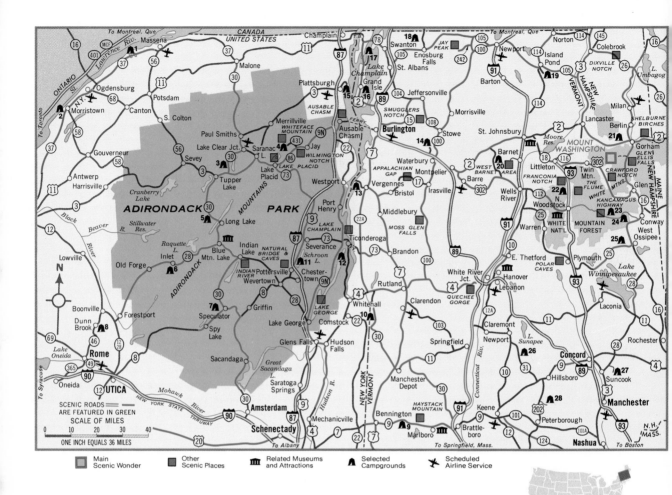

WITHIN A DAY'S DRIVE:

New England's Mountain Country: Great Riches in Small Space

Appalachian Gap, Vt. A superbly engineered road twists up the gap between Stark and Molly Stark mountains. There are scenic overlooks at every bend, with views of tumbling mountain streams, cliffs, forests and deep ravines. On the gap's eastern slope is the famous Mad River Glen ski area.

Ausable Chasm, N.Y. Carved out by the Ausable River about 500 million years ago, Ausable Chasm is a gorge up to 200 feet deep cut through sharply defined sandstone layers. There are walkways along the river banks, and boat trips through the chasm.

Crawford Notch, N.H. This majestic pass was named for Abel Crawford, an early New Hamp-

shire innkeeper. In Crawford Notch State Park is Arethusa Falls, 200 feet high and accessible via a mile-and-a-half trail, and an interesting outdoor exhibit of native wild animals and waterfowl. Two more waterfalls, Silver and Flume cascades, are seen from the road at the notch's northern end.

Dixville Notch, N.H. Experts say the best way to see New Hampshire's mountains is to drive through their notches, or gaps, and Dixville Notch is one of the wildest and most beautiful of all —a narrow, winding, very rugged gorge surrounded by the jagged spurs of the Dixville Mountains.

The Flume, N.H. Located in Franconia State Park, the Flume is

a long (800 feet), narrow gorge through which Flume Brook flows in a series of cascades. Trees and shrubs form a canopy overhead, and catwalks and paths permit easy access. A side trail (under a mile) leads to lesser-known but equally striking Liberty Gorge, the Cascades and the Pool, a deep basin on the Pemigewasset River surrounded by high cliffs.

Franconia Notch, N.H. In this heavily forested eight-mile gorge, filled with sheer cliffs and fast-flowing streams, is a concentration of natural wonders. Among them are the Old Man of the Mountains, a 40-foot-high head, carved out of Cannon Mountain by erosion, which towers over Profile Lake; the Basin, a deep

32

glacial pothole at the foot of a waterfall (one of several in the notch); and mountain-ringed Echo Lake, noted for its good swimming and fishing.

Glen Ellis Falls, N.H. This attractive 65-foot waterfall in Pinkham Notch is easily reached by footpaths and walkways right off the highway. One mile south is the Appalachian Mountain Club base camp at the foot of Mount Washington, where hardy climbers rest up for their ascent.

Haystack Mountain, Vt. A one-mile hike up Haystack Mountain on Vermont's famous Long Trail leads to the Natural Area, covering about 10 acres, where rare arctic and alpine plants grow. Hazens Notch, also on the mountain, has several overlooks from which to view the surrounding Green Mountain ranges.

Indian River, N.Y.
(*Picture appears on page 34*)

Jay Peak, Vt. From the summit, reached by an aerial tramway, is one of the most sweeping and varied views in the East. On a clear day it encompasses the towers of Montreal to the north, the peaks of the Presidential Range to the east, and Lake Champlain and the Adirondacks to the west.

Kancamagus Highway, N.H. This extraordinarily scenic route, named after a 17th-century Indian chief, cuts through the White Mountain National Forest. Sights along the way include Loon Mountain, Sabbaday Falls and the Rocky Gorge and Lower Falls scenic areas. Cathedral Ledge in Echo Lake State Park, a few miles north of the highway's eastern end, is a broad rock table 700 feet high with a panoramic view of the Presidential Range.

Lake Champlain, N.Y. Although less scenic in setting than Lake George, Lake Champlain as seen on a ferry trip between Vermont and New York (from Burlington to Port Kent or Grand Isle to Cumberland Head) is impressive. The best view from the New York shore is at Crown Point.

Quechee Gorge, Vt. A deep (165 feet), *narrow ravine cut by the Ottau-quechee River, the gorge can be viewed from the highway bridge that crosses it at midpoint. The more adventurous can walk along the rock ledges above the rushing stream, near the ravine's lower end. Ferns and mosses add a touch of green to the dark and dripping walls.*

Indian River, N.Y. *This Adirondack river, noted for its sporty white-water canoeing, flows out of Indian Lake and joins the Hudson a few miles north. The lake, dotted with small wooded islands, makes an ideal vacation spot—one family can reserve a whole island.*

Lake George, N.Y.
(Picture appears on facing page)

Lake Placid, N.Y. A boat trip from Grote's Landing offers the most exciting view of the lake. Nearby Mount Marcy is the highest of the Adirondack High Peaks. Superb views will reward those willing to hike to the top, but the *shortest* trail is seven miles long. The Lake Placid area has long been noted for winter and summer sports and for the many hiking trails through the rugged Adirondack country.

Moss Glen Falls, Vt. Located in the five-mile-long Granville Gulf area at the edge of the Green Mountain National Forest, the falls has one large drop and several smaller ones. Nearby Texas Falls, in the national forest, has a nature trail and an observation platform for viewing the falls.

West Barnet Area, *Vt. Lush green valleys, the deeper green of coniferous trees and the glowing foliage of fall oaks and maples combine to paint a* scene typical of pastoral eastern Vermont, in the Connecticut River Valley. Farmers around here grow strawberries and vegetables—and raise cows as well.

Lake George, N.Y. *Thirty miles long and dotted with nearly 200 tree-covered islands, Lake George lies in the heavily wooded foothills of the* eastern *Adirondacks. The mountainous area between Bolton Landing and Hague is one of the most attractive stretches of its shoreline.*

Natural Bridge and Caves, N.Y. There is a variety of geological curiosities on view in this commercially operated but worthwhile exhibit, including a natural stone arch about 175 feet long, five caves, huge potholes, a gorge, several waterfalls and an underground river.

Polar Caves, N.H. Fifty thousand years ago a mile-high glacier scoured the area, and veins of glacial ice still remain in the enormous boulder caverns that form Polar Caves. When the 80-ton Hanging Boulder fell off a cliff, eons ago, it wedged in so tightly that it seems unlikely to fall again, even though 75 percent of it hangs free.

Quechee Gorge, Vt.
(*Picture appears on page 33*)

Shelburne Birches, N.H. Old-growth white birches line both sides of the highway for about a mile in one of the handsomest stands in the country. White birches have always inspired poetry; they have been called, among other things, "the cap-

tured souls of druids that danced too long, one summer's night."

Smuggler's Notch, Vt. The notch is a deep, rugged, winding gorge, supposedly the route of smugglers from Boston during the War of 1812 and the Civil War. It has many unusual rock formations. Bingham Falls is at the notch's southern entrance. Mount Mansfield, just south of the notch, is the center of a highly developed ski area, and helped make the town of Stowe famous. A toll road leads from the ski area to Mansfield's summit, and yields sweeping views.

West Barnet Area, Vt.
(*Picture appears on facing page*)

Whiteface Mountain, N.Y. Memorial Highway leads to the top of Whiteface, with its encompassing view of all 46 of the Adirondack High Peaks (those over 4000 feet). These mountains are the surviving roots of the oldest geological formations in North America. Symmetrical evergreen spires cloak the upper slopes. Look for the scars made by ava-

lanches and rock slides on the surrounding peaks; some of the more dramatic ones extend all the way down the mountain from summit to base.

Wilmington Notch, N.Y. The road through the notch follows the west branch of the Ausable River, with nearly vertical cliffs shadowing the route. Birch, pine and spruce grow to great size here, and waterfalls thunder off steep cliffs into deep pools in nearby High Falls Gorge.

**RELATED MUSEUMS
AND ATTRACTIONS**

Blue Mountain Lake, N.Y. Adirondack Museum; nature and canoeing lore.

Hanover, N.H. Dartmouth College Natural History Museum.

Marlboro, Vt. Luman Nelson Museum of New England Wildlife.

North Woodstock, N.H. Lost River Nature Garden.

St. Johnsbury, Vt. Fairbanks Museum of Natural History.

Niagara Falls
NEW YORK

Horseshoe Falls (foreground) *and American Falls* (background) *share this aerial panorama.*

Niagara Falls

NEW YORK

The Falling Water That All the World Comes to See

Other waterfalls, even here in the United States, are higher, and many are more ethereally beautiful. But none has the sheer bulk and massive mesmerizing force of Niagara. Ever since the French missionary-explorer Louis Hennepin first gazed awestruck upon it in 1678, it has inspired wonder and amazement among visitors. More than four million people a year come to stare, to photograph, to peer down from above or up from below at the stupendous cataract. Whatever else it may be, this is beyond question the world's most accessible, and visited, waterfall.

Such a status brings delights and drawbacks in about equal measure. On the one hand it offers a unique opportunity for Niagara visitors to get to the very heart of the great

spectacle: by donning oilskins and riding the *Maid of the Mist* through the seethe of white water, or by clambering about the walkways below Prospect Point and Goat Island to see the falls in towering profile. But the lure of Niagara has also drawn more than a fair share of tawdry commercialism, and no great American scenic resource is so disfigured in its approaches—by the stench and fume of chemical industry, the shrill carnival atmosphere and the proliferation of catchpenny "attractions" that seem to go with a honeymoon resort.

Such excess is nothing new at Niagara. Right from the start it has inspired exaggeration; Father Hennepin himself reported its height at 600 feet and published with his account of his travels an engraving of the falls

far more remarkable for imagination than accuracy. A traveler 10 years later increased the height to 800 feet (it is actually 186 feet), and it was not until the more calm and rational 18th century was well advanced that Niagara visitors began to measure the waters by scientific rather than poetic standards. As the frontier of the young American nation began to move westward, the falls at Niagara became the most widely admired and frequently depicted of the scenic marvels that lay across the Atlantic from Europe.

Probably more ink has been expended in attempting to describe the falls than upon any other natural scene in America; rather than add to the flow, let a brief quotation from the ecstasies of the Irish poet Thomas Moore, who visited Niagara in 1804, suffice: "I have seen the falls, and am all rapture and amazement . . . I felt as if approaching the very residence of the Deity. Oh! Bring the atheist here and he cannot return an atheist! . . . It is impossible by pen or pencil to convey even a faint idea of their magnificence."

With such a press, it was no wonder that curiosity to see the falls waxed with the 19th century. And soon, with the construction of the first railroad to the falls—from Buffalo, in 1837—the foundation was laid for the development of a tourist industry. Later trains were helped on their way by the construction of the Niagara Suspension Railway Bridge, completed in 1855, which became a wonder all on its own. Built by John Roebling, who later went on to even greater fame with the Brooklyn Bridge, it was by far the longest and most successful railway suspension bridge in the world. The shell of Roebling's bridge still carries trains and cars across the Niagara River, though the suspension system has been replaced with a steel arch.

As more and more visitors began to find their way to the falls, so the urge to turn a dollar from the sightseers increased—and to supplement the natural spectacle, there began a procession of odd and daring entrepreneurs. The time of the stuntmen had come. Sam Patch, later widely celebrated in song and legend for his daring leaps, was the first to hazard life and limb in the churning waters. In

A telephoto lens draws Niagara's great cascades close together in a multilayered torrent of smashing water. Land in the middle is Goat Island.

1829 he made two leaps from a platform built out from Goat Island—and survived both of them (he later perished leaping into the Genesee River at Rochester). But the French tightrope walker Blondin established for himself perhaps the most enduring Niagara legend. In 1859 and 1860 he crossed the gorge below the falls on a number of occasions, each time with added encumbrances to test his skill and terrify the thousands of watchers who jammed the shores. Perhaps his worst moment came the time he was carrying his manager across on his back and a guy rope broke. Blondin died in his bed, however, as did all but one of the tightrope walkers who followed him.

Other daredevils were not so lucky. Captain Matthew Webb, fresh from swimming the English Channel, drowned in an 1883 attempt to swim the rapids in the gorge below the falls; and although several of the people who tried for quick notoriety by going over the falls in a barrel lived to tell about it, as many perished. It became clear that even the tawdry glamour of such a feat was dying when Mrs. Anna Taylor survived a barrel stunt in 1901: the riches she had hoped for did not come, and for the next 20 years she made a pathetic figure as she sat in the street beside a copy of her barrel, offering to autograph pictures of herself. The final change on Niagara stunts was rung by Lincoln Beachey, who in 1911 flew a Curtiss biplane under the Falls View Bridge.

The daredevils were not the only ones to see Niagara as a source of instant riches. Whatever the visitor's impressions of today's commercialization of the falls, he would have been astounded by the sleazy atmosphere that prevailed in the mid-19th century. Every scrap of land from which the falls could be seen was in the hands of entrepreneurs who charged heavily for the privilege; and in 1837 a report on conditions on the Canadian side said that "the difficulty of escape from the organized band of cabmen, fancy and variety store keepers, guides, sight showers, picture takers, oil clothes furnishers, hotel keepers and runners, all working to plunder . . . has been so great as to elicit the comments of travelers and the criticisms of the public press throughout the civilized world."

Ultimately such excesses bred the obvious remedy. In 1885 the state established a reservation to protect the New York side of the falls from further private despoliation, and

Getting Wet at Niagara

Visitors to Niagara have always liked to dare the power of the falls by getting as close to the cataract as possible—even if it meant getting wet. There was a time when they could actually walk right behind the American Falls, through the Cave of the Winds; but falling rock that killed three tourists in 1920 put an end to that. Further collapses of rock have since eliminated the cave, though it still gives its name to a spray-drenched promenade along wooden walkways near the base of the falls. Another sure way of getting wet is to take the

How Niagara Began —and Could End

Niagara Falls cuts its way upstream because it runs over hard limestone covering a layer of softer shale. The water soon wears away the shale; then the limestone, undercut, collapses at intervals. Thus the falls move slowly back, to become a series of rapids.

Maid of the Mist *boat ride. There has been a* Maid of the Mist *to take people into the rapids right below the Horseshore Falls ever since 1885, though today's boats are less than 20 years old. The Maid's passengers are required to wear slickers, and they certainly need them. These days, commercial helicopter trips over the falls are available for those who want the best of all possible views without the slightest danger of a dash of spray in the face. For those who just want to gaze, and stay dry, Prospect Point is probably the most spectacular overlook—particularly the observation tower that is built out from the base of the cliff.*

A ride on Maid of the Mist *is a splashy experience.*

The little boat noses close to the Horseshoe Falls.

A Cave of the Winds walk yields an awesome closeup.

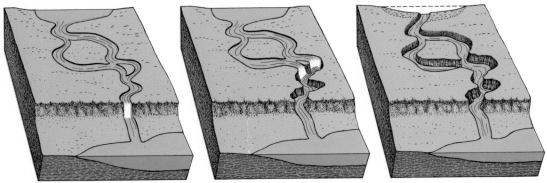

FALLS FIRST FORMED OVER BLUFF.   RIVER CUTS BACK TO PRESENT SPOT.   LIMESTONE ENDS; FALLS EVEN OUT.

the Ontario government followed suit on the Canadian side three years later. It was probably just in time, for in the following decades the villages on both sides of the falls, swollen by the huge power projects that began to tap the energies of the rushing river, and by the coming of the auto, grew into one huge metropolitan area that now lines both banks for many miles. For countless thousands of people today the falls, as a source of power to draw industry, and as a magnet to tourist multitudes, are the center of their livelihood. Yet the river will not always be roaring its way down its rocky gorge.

As the incredible time spans of geology go, the falls are quite young. They are there because on its hurrying journey downhill from Lake Erie to Lake Ontario the Niagara River runs over a steep limestone bluff lying on top of a layer of softer shale. The power of the water cascading over the bluff constantly gnaws away at the softer rock, and the limestone above, undercut, collapses at intervals. In this way the falls have moved seven miles

upstream since they began. This movement, as well as the ultimate fate of the falls, is shown in preceding sketches. The end will not come in the lifetime of any of our imaginable descendants; but in an eon or two the thunder will be gone, the turbulent history, the poets' exclamations, the honeymooners' sighs—all vanished, a moment in time.

And perhaps man, in his reckless domination of nature, will bring them to an end himself. It can be done. Only three years ago engineers turned off the American falls for a season to investigate ways of moving the talus, or piled rocks, from beneath them. And every day the amount of water the power stations allow over the falls varies (twice as much during the summer, for the tourists). So perhaps it is as well to see as much as we can of the great waterfall while it is still at its awesome best. Fortunately —along with a few other great sights in this book—Niagara can be enjoyed at night too, its waters bathed in a rainbow of lights they generate themselves in their headlong plunge between lakes Erie and Ontario.

Even at night Niagara does not cease to be a mighty spectacle. Dozens of searchlights are switched on to illuminate the water in ever-shifting patterns of bright color *(above, the lighted American Falls). Power from the rushing water, harnessed by huge hydroelectric turbines nearby, runs the lights.*

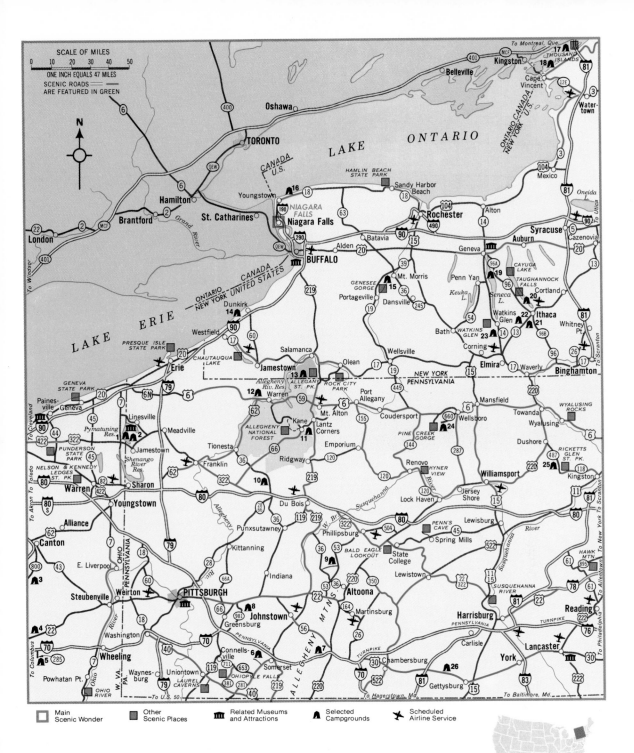

Map legend:

- □ Main Scenic Wonder
- ■ Other Scenic Places
- 🏛 Related Museums and Attractions
- ▲ Selected Campgrounds
- ✈ Scheduled Airline Service

WITHIN A DAY'S DRIVE:

Lakes, Hills—and More Waterfalls

Allegany State Park, N.Y. This is one of the largest state parks in New York: 60,000 acres of unspoiled forests and lakes.

Allegheny National Forest, Pa. One of the finest forest preserves in the East, Allegheny still contains much primitive woodland.

Tionesta and Hearts Content scenic areas have notable stands of hemlock and hardwoods.

Bald Eagle Lookout, Pa. From this vantage point on U.S. 322 there is an extensive view over the valley of Bald Eagle Creek and its surrounding hills.

Cayuga Lake, N.Y. All of New York's Finger Lakes have their attractions, but Cayuga, with its sinuous, hilly shoreline and scenic flanking highway, is one of the most striking of them.

Chautauqua Lake, N.Y. This sparkling 22-mile lake in the un-

Hyner View, Pa. A setting sun lights the winding course of the West Branch of the Susquehanna in this celebrated view from a point above one of Pennsylvania's most scenic highways—Route 120 through the Bucktail wilds that stretch eastward from the edge of the Allegheny National Forest.

spoiled western corner of the state is a favorite of boatsmen and fishermen.

Genesee Gorge, N.Y. The state's "Grand Canyon," a 600-foot sandstone gorge carved out by the Genesee River, includes three fine waterfalls. Letchworth State Park contains the most spectacular stretch of the gorge.

Geneva State Park, Ohio. There are very few good public beaches along this reach of Lake Erie, and Geneva's half mile of firm sand is one of the best.

Hamlin Beach State Park, N.Y. The wooded southern shoreline of Lake Ontario is well represented in Hamlin's three miles of smooth beach.

Hawk Mountain, Pa. For keen bird watchers in the Northeast, this is the place to be in early fall, to watch the annual flyby of migrating hawks.

Hyner View, Pa.
(Picture appears on this page)

Laurel Caverns, Pa. Southern Pennsylvania offers a large number of caves. Laurel, set in a hilltop with a commanding view, is one of the more colorful, with picturesque lighting effects.

Nelson and Kennedy Ledges State Park, Ohio.
(Picture appears on facing page)

Ohiopyle Falls, Pa. These are rapids rather than falls (the Youghiogheny River drops about 100 feet in a turbulent mile and a half) and are a favorite with white-water canoeists who enjoy a real wilderness setting.

Ohio River, Ohio. Despite the industrial ravages on its upper and lower reaches (Cincinnati and Pittsburgh), the Ohio is a sweetly pastoral stream where it forms the boundary with West Virginia in southeast Ohio.

Penn's Cave, Pa. This is claimed to be America's "only all-water cavern." The boat ride on underground Lake Nitanee is an intriguing experience.

Pine Creek Gorge, Pa. Another "Grand Canyon" claim is staked by this 50-mile gorge, 1000 feet deep in places. The most impressive viewing points are in Colton Point and Harrison state parks.

Presque Isle Peninsula, Pa. Most of this curving spit of land jutting into the lake above Erie is a state park, a haunting place of dunes and marshy lakes.

Punderson State Park, Ohio. The lake at the heart of Punderson is a natural glacial one, surrounded by the typical gentle hills of moraine country. The lake margins are a wildlife haven.

Ricketts Glen, Pa. Kitchen Creek tumbles through the glen in a series of waterfalls—33 in all— that can be followed along a charming waterside trail.

Rocky City Park, N.Y. The fantastic blocks and slabs of rock strewn here were once at the bottom of a prehistoric sea. They show clearly the effects of jointing in quartz conglomerate.

44

Susquehanna River, Pa. The mighty river is spectacular along most of its course, but particularly unspoiled in the reaches above Harrisburg. At Sunbury a vast man-made lake is produced each summer by the use of an inflatable rubber dam.

Taughannock Falls, N.Y. The 215-foot leap Taughannock Creek takes over a sheer cliff here makes it 50 feet higher than Niagara. A mile-long forest trail leads to it from Lake Cayuga.

Thousand Islands, N.Y. Where Lake Ontario enters the great St. Lawrence, green islands crowd the water in myriad shapes and sizes. Wellesley Island State Park is a good place to start exploring.

Watkins Glen, N.Y.
(Picture appears on this page)

Wyalusing Rocks, Pa. From this point overlooking a grand sweep of the Susquehanna and the Endless Mountains country, the Iroquois Indians were supposed to have prayed to their gods. It is still a profoundly inspiring spot.

RELATED MUSEUMS AND ATTRACTIONS

Buffalo, N.Y. Buffalo Museum of Science; local flora and fauna.

Geneva, N.Y. Hobart and William Smith Colleges Museum; flora and fauna.

Lancaster, Pa. Franklin and Marshall College North Museum; natural history and mineralogy.

Linesville, Pa. Pymatuning Waterfowl Museum.

Mentor, Ohio (near Painesville). Holden Arboretum.

Pittsburgh, Pa. Carnegie Institute Natural History Museum.

Watkins Glen, N.Y. A stream draining into Seneca Lake has cut a dramatically deep and narrow gorge in which the water drops 700 feet in two miles.

Nelson and Kennedy Ledges State Park, Ohio. The abrupt and towering rock formations here— softened in the picture above by a thick carpet of russet fall leaves—are a striking example of how rock outcrops can be carved and molded by millions of years of weather and glacial action.

Cape Cod National Seashore
MASSACHUSETTS

Pilgrim Lake, on the cape's bay side, shines beyond the dune grasses.

MASSACHUSETTS — Cape Cod National Seashore

Man and Ocean Do Battle for Endangered Dunes

"The bared and bended arm of Massachusetts" was Henry David Thoreau's metaphor for Cape Cod, the peninsula that thrusts bravely out into the Atlantic breakers from the eastern edge of the continent, then hooks back toward the mainland.

Today the Cape Cod National Seashore protects much of the landscape that Thoreau surveyed with an inlander's curiosity and a poet's eye on his visits 125 years ago. It stretches for 35 miles along what Thoreau would have described as the cape's forearm, from the elbow north to the fisted hand. But if you ask more conventional directions of a local citizen—a Yankee who locates Maine "Down East" in defiance of the compass—he will call this outer part of the arm the "lower cape" and point

your way northward "down" to the seashore.

The land you find—once you cross the Cape Cod Canal and head down Route 6, the Mid-Cape Highway—is very different from the mainland at your back. From the canal to the cape's elbow, the road follows what geologists call a moraine—a spinal ridge made of a mix of coarse sand and stones, known as "till"—left by the retreating glacier as the icy Pleistocene melted into the modern age some 10,000 years ago. From the crest of the moraine the land drops gently away on both sides to the shores. The clearly defined hollows pocking these sloping outwash plains are "kettles," formed by ice blocks left by the receding glacier to melt under an insulating blanket of sand.

As the road curves northward at Chatham,

the cape's elbow, carrying you toward the National Seashore Visitors' Center at Eastham, the landscape changes again. The moraine that originally formed this north-south extension breasted the stormy Atlantic, and most of it has been blasted away by sea and wind. The remaining high bluffs that front the beach—most spectacularly at Truro's Highland Light, 130 steep feet above the waves—are still losing ground at a rate averaging several feet per year.

Your route now descends to the less-threatened lowland. Here the kettles often penetrate into the reservoir of groundwater that underlies the cape, forming hundreds of steep-sided ponds. At Truro the moraine ends in an escarpment, High Head. All the land beyond—the spectacular dunes around Pilgrim Lake, the roll-

A treasure house for students of geology and ecology, Cape Cod is also rich in birdlife; nature trails and sanctuaries abound. This boardwalk is through a cedar swamp at Marconi Station.

The vivid green of salt marsh grass spreads a textured carpet over wide areas of the cape's inner shore. In the background the yellower field has already dried out into salt marsh hay.

Over glowing moorland reminiscent of the Scottish Highlands, an old track leads toward the high bluffs that tower above the beach at Truro.

This landscape, near Higgins Hollow, shows how spreading vegetation has helped to anchor the shifting cape sand in areas inland from the sea.

Why Cape Cod Began to Blow Away, and How It Is Being Restored

Early settlers on Cape Cod overgrazed the land with their cattle; in order to build ships they cut down most of the trees. As a result the soil, which the vegetation helped to hold together, loosened and

blew away. Great dunes were then piled up by the cape's powerful winds. The dunes increased the devastation by burying some of the remaining trees, thus depriving the loose surface of the firm

ing moors and Provincetown's expensive real estate—was originally plundered by the sea from the broad beaches of Wellfleet and Truro and brought here grain by grain in an endless exercise of creation followed by destruction.

In spite of its comparatively mild temperatures and plentiful moisture, the cape offers little encouragement to vegetation. Its sandy soil, scoured and leached clean of nourishment, inhibits growth: a pine no more than 20 feet tall and six inches in diameter may boast 50 rings of hard-won annual growth.

After centuries of man's abuse, nothing remains of the hardwood forests and fertile topsoil the Pilgrims found when they stopped at Provincetown in 1621. Only a few suggestions of the primeval landscape persist: the Massachusetts Audubon Society sanctuary in Wellfleet; the stately, ancient elms and maples in a few towns; the resurgent wilderness of Paradise Valley, on the Wellfleet-Truro line.

In much of the outer cape the erosion encouraged by careless human exploitation is worsening. Within the protected borders of the National Seashore, however, plant life is making a comeback. The land wears a tenuous stubble of green. Stunted pines and oaks reclaim the hills; ground-hugging plants and low shrubs blanket the moors; and deep-rooted grasses help hold the dry and shifting dunes.

Especially in springtime, the wildflowers—dusty miller, rugosa rose, Mayflower, lady's slipper and the rest—fleck the cape's subtle and austere complexion with sequins of bright color. Birds in their season select their habitat: redwing blackbirds in the cattail marshes; warblers and other songbirds in the woods; gulls, terns and sandpipers along the shore.

Indeed, this apparently naked sandspit teems with life; but it is life at the margin, neither lush nor flamboyant. Yet when taken on its own honest terms, the understated cape landscape exerts a quiet influence, and you may well respond to its stark and elemental beauty.

You will not be alone. Thoreau loved Cape Cod as a refuge where he could "put all America behind him"; come to Cape Cod now, especially in August, and you may feel that all America is at your elbow. The roads are jammed; the most accessible beaches are shingled with sun seekers, the narrow streets of Provincetown are awash with tourists.

In June, September and October, however, the population pressure is off, prices are lower and the natives regain their off-season good nature. Then the cape is more likely to reveal to you that special character of light and space and air, that sense of being at one with the sea and wide sky, which is its most enduring gift to its visitors.

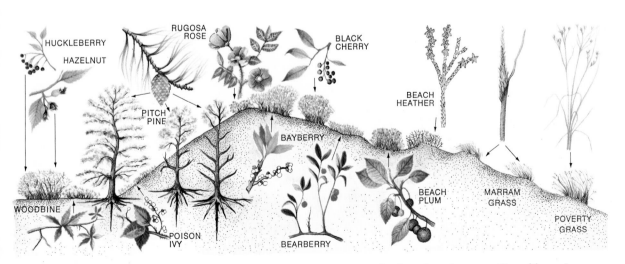

anchorage of tree roots. Overdevelopment in many areas of Cape Cod continues to promote remorseless erosion by the wind and the bruising winter tides. Too much asphalt, and the destruction of beach vegetation by dune buggies, are still problems. In the protected National Seashore, however, careful planting of appropriate dune cover, like the hardy species above, helps stabilize the damaged shore.

51

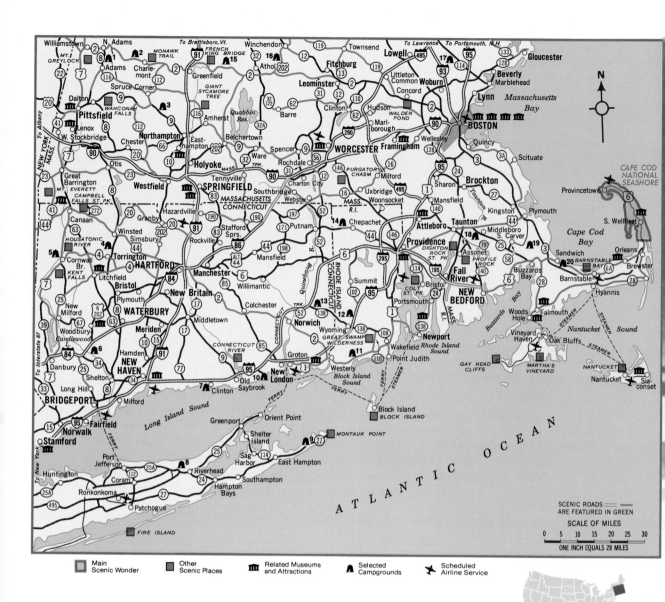

Map legend:

■ Main Scenic Wonder	■ Other Scenic Places	🏛 Related Museums and Attractions	▲ Selected Campgrounds	✈ Scheduled Airline Service

SCENIC ROADS ARE FEATURED IN GREEN

SCALE OF MILES

0 5 10 15 20 25 30

ONE INCH EQUALS 28 MILES

WITHIN A DAY'S DRIVE:

Fine Beaches, Rolling Hills and Pastoral Loveliness

Barnstable Bay, Mass. The sharp edges of glaciers carved Barnstable Bay into the north shoreline of Cape Cod. Miles of uncluttered beach line its outer rim.

Block Island, R.I. (*Picture appears on page 55*)

Campbell Falls State Park, Conn. A waterfall that's actually in Massachusetts pours over a gentle rock incline into a stream surrounded by evergreen forest in Connecticut. The park is idyllic for quiet walks, and the more energetic will enjoy climbing around the rock ledges.

Colt State Park, R.I. The former Colt family estate now has picnic areas and playing fields beside a scenic three-mile drive overlooking Narragansett Bay.

Connecticut River, Conn. One of the best river vistas is from Route 9A by Haddam Meadows

State Park. Another extensive view may be had from a surviving car ferry, at the intersection of 9A and 80.

Dighton Rock State Park, Mass. Probably chiefly of interest to archeologists, both amateur and professional, the rock itself contains one of New England's oldest examples of prehistoric carving. However, the park is on the Sakonnet River and also has attractive picnic grounds.

Fire Island, N.Y. This narrow, 32-mile barrier beach is a roadless National Seashore, although there are summer homes at the western end. Soft beaches of quartz and magnetite sand line the Atlantic shore, and the mixed terrain of the bay side is a haven for wildlife. The Sunken Forest is a hollow filled with thick stands of low-growing serviceberry, black gum and holly.

French King Bridge, Mass. Perhaps the best vista of the northern stretch of the Connecticut River and its gently rolling valley is the one north from this bridge on Route 2, which offers a sidewalk for viewing.

Gay Head Cliffs, Mass. (*Picture appears on page 55*)

Giant Sycamore Tree, Mass. In a state known for its magnificent trees, this remarkable specimen at Sunderland deserves a special word. It would take five or six adults with outstretched arms to span the trunk, and the limbs are as thick as the trunks of mature elm trees.

Great Swamp Wilderness, R.I. For those who crave wild solitude in a heavily populated area—and don't mind swarms of insects—this is the place. A third of its 2700 acres is actually dry land, from which visitors can observe game birds and animals and a variety of vegetation that ranges from arctic moss to semitropical orchids. The quiet waters of Worden Pond, good for waterbirds, comprise another third of the reservation.

Housatonic River, Conn. The shallow, rippling Housatonic is lined in the Kent area with one of the finest pine groves in the East. Route 7, which flanks the river through Housatonic Meadows State Park from West Cornwall to Cornwall Bridge, offers superb views of the river.

Kent Falls, Conn. (*Picture appears on page 54*)

Martha's Vineyard, Mass. This small resort island, 20 miles by 10, has an amazingly varied land-

Mount Greylock, *Mass. Dense groves of pine and birch give the Berkshires their soft gray-green cover. Mount Greylock, at 3491 feet the highest peak in the state, has an observation tower and lodge on top. Note the bald eagle soaring above the slopes.*

scape for its size. There are soft sand beaches, scrub country, rolling farmland, trout streams, cliffs, coves, dunes and tidal flats.

Mohawk Trail, Mass.
(*Picture appears on this page*)

Montauk Point, N.Y. The stark coastline at the extreme eastern tip of Long Island is marked by a lighthouse on a cliff above a rocky promontory. The crashing surf attracts beachcombers and fishermen; bird watchers find the point rewarding for seabirds. Hither Hills State Park preserves some of the point's finest scenery.

Mount Everett, Mass. A steep, narrow road leads to the top of Mount Everett for a sweeping view of the Berkshires. Two

thirds of the way up is a delightful rest area beside a pond. Hiking trails wind through the rest of the area, which in spring is bright with rhododendrons.

Mount Greylock, Mass.
(*Picture appears on page 53*)

Nantucket Island, Mass. Once the whaling capital of the world, Nantucket today is a popular summer resort. The sea, warmed to 70 degrees by the Gulf Stream, washes up on miles of beaches. Inland are extensive areas of bayberry, heather and beach plum.

Profile Rock, Mass. A remarkably detailed natural cliff profile of a man's head, Profile Rock is as striking as New Hampshire's Old Man of the Mountains.

Purgatory Chasm, Mass. This half-mile-long gorge is an unusual feature in an area noted mostly for gentle hills. Strange, contorted rock formations jut from the cliffsides.

Wahconah Falls, Mass. A state park surrounds this charming if unspectacular cascade deep in the Berkshire Hills. Picnic tables are scattered among a handsome stand of hemlocks and beeches near the falls.

Walden Pond, Mass. The pond where Thoreau built his cabin and lived in the woods away from his fellowman is a great deal closer to urban civilization today. The pond may be used for swimming (there's a beach and a bathhouse), fishing and boating;

Mohawk Trail, *Mass. State Route 2 follows the trail originally blazed by the Mohawk Indians centuries ago. At every turn there are stunning vistas of mountains, woods and water— like this Deerfield River view.*

Kent Falls, *Conn. A woodland path follows this waterfall as it cascades 200 feet in a series of steps, pausing in shallow pools along the way. In the broad meadow at the foot of the falls is a splendidly located picnic area.*

forest trails have been cut through the woods. A monument marks the spot where the great naturalist's cabin stood.

RELATED MUSEUMS AND ATTRACTIONS

Attleboro, Mass. Bronson Museum; natural history.

Boston, Mass.
Arnold Arboretum.
Harvard University Geological Museum.
Museum of Science.
New England Aquarium.

Brewster, Mass. Brewster Natural History Museum.

Canaan, Conn. (near). Bartholomews Cobble, Ashley Falls, Mass.; wildlife sanctuary.

East Falmouth, Mass. Ashumet Holly Reservation.

Easthampton, Mass. Arcadia Bird Sanctuary.

Framingham, Mass. Garden in the Woods.

Lenox, Mass. Pleasant Valley Wildlife Sanctuary.

Litchfield, Conn. Litchfield Nature Center and Museum.

Nantucket, Mass. Nantucket Maria Mitchell Association; natural science.

New Haven, Conn. Peabody Museum of Natural History.

Pittsfield, Mass. Berkshire Museum; natural science.

Portsmouth, R.I. (near). Norman Bird Sanctuary.

Providence, R.I. Providence Natural History Museum.

Springfield, Mass.
Springfield Science Museum.
Trailside Museum; natural science.

Stamford, Conn. Stamford Museum and Nature Center.

Wellfleet, Mass. Wellfleet Bay Wildlife Sanctuary.

Woodbury, Conn. Flanders Nature Center.

Woods Hole, Mass. Biological Laboratory Aquarium.

Worcester, Mass. Worcester Science Museum; natural history.

Block Island, *R.I. Over 300 ponds, some excellent for fishing, are scattered on this small island. Mohegan Bluffs, on the east shore, are spectacular clay cliffs. A good time to visit the island is in spring and fall, when thousands of migrating birds descend.*

Gay Head Cliffs, *Mass. These bluffs overlook a boulder-strewn shore on the southwest tip of Martha's Vineyard. Waves beating against the base of the bluffs have exposed the clay inside, which comes in many colors: red, yellow, brown, black and white.*

Hudson Valley

NEW YORK AND NEW JERSEY

From Bear Mountain the Hudson sweeps toward the south, and New York City, in shining curves.

NEW YORK

Hudson Valley

NEW JERSEY

A Great River Heavy with History Marches Proudly to the Sea

On Mount Marcy, the highest mountain in the Adirondacks, nestles a small, gleaming body of water known as Lake Tear of the Clouds. From here flows a trout stream called the Hudson. As it winds its way through the hills, the tumbling stream is joined by others. Three miles above Troy its largest tributary, the Mohawk River, cuts in, and the stream becomes the mighty Hudson River—a river often compared to Germany's Rhine, a river whose surroundings sweep from ruggedly picturesque to depressingly industrial, a river once of strategic importance in war, in commerce—and lately in battles for conservation.

Despite its importance in American history the Hudson is not very long—only 300 miles from its source to its meeting with the sea in New York Harbor. And the stretch with the most striking and celebrated scenery—the Hudson Highlands lining each shore, the great open reaches around Tappan Zee and the triumphal finish between the cliffs of the Palisades on one side and Manhattan on the other —is less than 100 miles long.

Once the Hudson was much longer. For eons it ran for another 150 miles out beyond what is now the shore, carving an ever-deepening canyon. That river channel still exists, but now it is covered by the Atlantic Ocean. During or shortly after the last glacial period the seas rose and covered a third of the river and shore.

The Palisades tower steeply above the river along the New Jersey shore in this view looking north from the George Washington Bridge.

The ocean still dominates the Hudson: twice a day the tides rush up the river, to make it in effect an arm of the sea. The tides are felt as far as Troy, where the river usually rises about four and a half feet. As the tide recedes, the waters rush back downstream to fill the breach, producing a powerful downstream current. This two-way current was of great advantage to sailors in the days when sloops carried passengers and produce up and down the Hudson; with the right wind, sailing ships leaving New York on the tide could make Albany in 24 hours—and in fact, oceangoing vessels still go up the river as far as the state capital.

The Hudson's salinity line, marking the farthest reach of the ocean's salt water, is generally around Newburgh, 60 miles upstream from New York. This means that despite its current level of pollution the river teems with a remarkable variety of fish. In the same stretch of river, saltwater and freshwater fish can be found living side by side.

Below Kingston, in the lower, more dramatic reaches of the Hudson Valley, the river flows between gently rounded mountains—the Catskills on the west and the older Taconic mountains on the east, collectively known as the Hudson Highlands. The highlands are not so very high, but they rise abruptly from the water and loom over the narrow river. The winds that blow through the gaps in these hills make sailing treacherous, and one of the region's many legends offers a fanciful reason for this. A goblin was said to sit on top of Dunderberg, just south of Bear Mountain.

Sloops failing to bow their sails to him as they entered the narrow channel below were forced to acknowledge him master by the violent winds he sent down upon them.

From the overlooks at Storm King or Bear Mountain, with the river winding far below and the frowning mountains across the bend, the scenery looks almost alpine, and far more dramatic than actual statistics of height or width would lead you to expect. Fortunately, most of the forested hillsides of the highlands are protected. Bear Mountain is now a section of the Palisades Interstate Park, and has been beautifully laid out for public enjoyment. In fact, all sections of Palisades Interstate Park accommodate both hiker and motorist. The Bear Mountain and Harriman sections in particular are laced with hiking trails of varying length and degree of difficulty, and a number of lakes offer swimming beaches and picnic areas. Bear Mountain Inn, open all year, has food and lodging in rustic surroundings. But majestic Storm King, a few miles upstream, is less well guarded from exploitation. Here conservationists have fought a long drawn out battle to prevent New York's Consolidated Edison Company from building a mammoth hydroelectric plant in the mountainside.

Nearby West Point (where the United States Military Academy was established in 1802), however, has had neither its security nor its beauty threatened since Benedict Arnold's day: that infamous traitor tried to betray the strategic spot to the British during the Revolutionary War. West Point overlooks a sharp, often turbulent bend of the river, and here during the same war enormous chains were stretched across the river to prevent the British from sailing northward. Had the redcoats succeeded in their attempt to control the Hudson, the New England colonies would have been cut off from the others and the Revolution might have failed for this lack of communication.

Below the highlands the river turns placid; its banks become pastoral. The Hudson gradually widens like a sea until it reaches its maximum width of about three and a half miles at Haverstraw. The best place to view this immense reach of the river is from the top of High Tor, south of Haverstraw: spread out below you here is a vast panorama of water and marshy shore.

Just south of here, at Tarrytown, the Hudson is still so wide that the Dutch called it a

A Changing Profile Over Millions of Years

Here is the Hudson as it appears today in a view to the north from above Anthony's Nose— and an artist's reconstruction of the changes time and ice have made beneath the visible surface. During the last Ice Age, glaciers pushing down out of the north carved a deep gorge into an old valley: the river floor was then 800 feet below where it is now, though most of that depth has since been filled by silt and sediment. The floor of the Hudson gorge has always been below sea level, however, which means that ocean tides sweep in and out, creating a fjord. In the diagram, note how the strong current has deepened the riverbed.

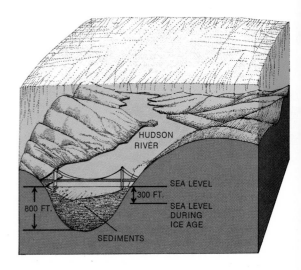

sea, Tappan Zee (Tappan was the Dutch version of the name of a nearby Indian tribe). The Tappan Zee Bridge was built here at this wide point because the shallow water made it easier to build the bridge foundations.

Though the river narrows somewhat from this point on, it continues on a broad and quiet course, with spreading, low banks, until the lava walls of the Palisades erupt suddenly along the western shore. Named for their resemblance to the wooden stockades settlers built for protection, the Palisades were formed from molten rock which boiled up into faults in the sandstone long ago. As the lava cooled, it fractured into columns, and long centuries of weather eroded away the sandstone and exposed them. The cliff we see today ranges from about 350 to 550 feet high, but actually this is only the edge of a 900-foot-high layer that

slopes gradually westward into New Jersey.

One of the best views of the Hudson and the Palisades is from the Cloisters, a medieval art branch of New York's Metropolitan Museum of Art, perched high on the rocky ridge of Fort Tryon Park at the northwestern tip of Manhattan. From the other side of the river the overlooks along the top of the Palisades offer dramatic views of New York City. Tall apartment buildings rise atop the Jersey Palisades now, but north of the George Washington Bridge the columns themselves, plus a margin of land along the Palisades Parkway, are maintained by the Interstate Park Commission to prevent further commercial development. Stone steps lead down from the top of the Palisades at the New Jersey end of the bridge to the beginning of a mostly level 12-mile shore path that skirts the Hudson. This shore path can also be reached by car via winding road descents at the Englewood and Alpine exits from the parkway and Route 9W.

People have always liked building close to the river. During the 19th century the construction of large houses overlooking the Hudson became something of a fad, and many of the great mansions that sprang up at this time themselves became part of the river scenery. Apparently believing that the existence of castles along its banks would increase the Hudson's proud resemblance to the Rhine, wealthy men put up imitations of French châteaus, Italian villas, Greek temples and buildings in a style that later became known as Hudson River Gothic. Romantic ruins were erected and carefully landscaped into picturesque wildness to evoke melancholy thoughts appropriate to the grandeur of the river.

The air of romanticism that developed here was also reflected by the Hudson River school of painters, the first American artists to concentrate on landscapes instead of portraits. From the Hudson, too, came the inspiration for the first American literature taken seriously in Europe—Washington Irving's stories based on the folklore of the region, "Rip Van Winkle" and "The Legend of Sleepy Hollow."

But the 18th- and 19th-century Hudson was in fact far from sleepy; it was a scene of constant bustle and activity. In the early days of settlement it was a frontier, and as such attracted men as rough as those often found on frontiers. And later, farmers of the Hudson Valley, hoping to wrest land of their own from the large land-grant holders who reigned almost feudally, were among the first to rebel against Great Britain.

In the 19th century came the great transportation boom along the river. Although there are now four tunnels under the Hudson, and numerous bridges across it, there were no bridges at all until 1889; the first tunnel came nearly 40 years later than that. So ferries plied the river. There were fishing boats and pleasure boats, and industries sprang up along the banks. Picturesque river towns like Peekskill, Garrison and Cold Spring grew up around industries and as landing stations for people and goods. In 1825 the Erie Canal was inaugurated with much rejoicing up and down the river; the highway of the Hudson now reached all the way to the Middle West by way of the Great Lakes.

But the era of the canals and the steamboats is over now. Most of the great houses are derelict, although some have been restored or belong to institutions. The little self-contained river towns have turned into suburban communities, their rotting docks the only souvenir of another time. Because of pollution, the fish are no longer as safe to eat as they were. There are fewer birds. The last steamboat, taking tourists on river excursions, sailed in 1971.

But the river still lives. Much of the scenery remains magnificent and surprisingly unspoiled—and dedicated people are fighting to keep it so. No longer necessary as a highway of commerce, the Hudson has become a perhaps even more vital public resource as a place of recreation and beauty.

In the Hudson's heyday as a major trade link between New York City and the Great Lakes, many towns grew up along its shores and prospered.

Today the most neglected parts of towns like Garrison, above, are the waterfront areas— wistful and decaying reminders of busier times.

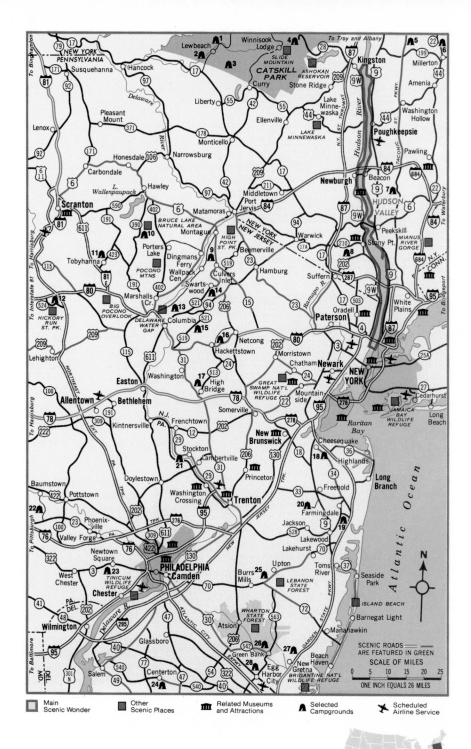

WITHIN A DAY'S DRIVE:

Scenery Around the Metropolis

Ashokan Reservoir, N.Y. A drive through picturesque countryside leads visitors to this attractive reservoir surrounded by pine groves, in a setting like a miniature Switzerland.

Big Pocono Overlook, Pa. On a clear day you can see to the Cats-

kills from the top of Pocono Mountain (2131 feet), which has a highway and many hiking trails to the summit.

Brigantine National Wildlife Refuge, N.J. Mostly coastal marsh with open bays and channels, Brigantine is one of the finest

bird refuges in the East. It was established for the protection of the 250 or more species of birds that migrate through here each year along the Atlantic flyway.

Bruce Lake Natural Area, Pa. Hiking trails connect Promised Land State Park to this roadless wilderness area. Backpackers may camp by glacial Bruce Lake.

Delaware Water Gap, Pa. and N.J. (*Picture appears on facing page*)

Great Swamp National Wildlife Refuge, N.J. (*Picture appears on this page*)

Hickory Run State Park, Pa. In this park is Boulder Field, a collection of enormous boulders deposited by a retreating glacier.

Hawk Falls, also in the park, has a particularly attractive setting.

High Point State Park, N.J. The park includes the highest point in the state—thus its name. There are well-marked trails, and scenic roads with sweeping views over the Delaware Valley.

Island Beach State Park, N.J. Most of the shoreline of this state-owned 10-mile barrier beach is open to the public. There is

good surf fishing and walkways for bird watchers.

Jamaica Bay Wildlife Refuge, N.Y. The largest wildlife refuge of any city in the world, it is a major haven for shorebirds and waterfowl migrating along the Atlantic flyway.

Lake Minnewaska, N.Y. This lake is within Awosting State Park, in the Shawangunck Mountains. There are fine views of the Catskills to the north and across the Hudson to the Taconic Mountains.

Lebanon State Forest, N.J. Here in the heart of the extensive Pine Barrens, wild orchids and abundant wildlife, including bald eagles, mink and beaver, flourish. The area was named in colonial days, when land was deemed barren if it could not sustain traditional crops. Pitch pine still dominates, but today about one third of U.S. cranberry crops are grown here.

Mianus River Gorge, N.Y. This unspoiled wilderness area has well-marked nature trails canopied by stately hemlocks. The river runs a varied course through the gorge, sometimes serene, sometimes busy with rapids.

Pocono Mountains, Pa. Twenty-four hundred square miles of lush forests, mountains, 100 lakes, cascading waters and nature trails await visitors to this popular resort area. Among the outstanding waterfalls are Bushkill, Dingmans, Buck Hill and Winona.

Slide Mountain, N.Y. The highest peak in the Catskills, Slide Mountain has a network of trails that are popular with climbers.

Tinicum Wildlife Refuge, Pa. This marshland, within the city limits of Philadelphia and fed by tidewaters of the Delaware River, is a favorite of bird watchers. Migrating waterfowl are abundant during spring and fall.

Wharton State Forest, N.J. Here, only two hours from mid-Manhattan, canoeists can paddle along the 55 miles of the Mullica River, enjoying its quiet beauty. Penn

Great Swamp National Wildlife Refuge, N.J. *In recent years threats of a jetport here have awakened strong public interest in this wild area so close to the metropolis. It is a mixture of marsh, meadow and virgin timber—and therefore a bird watcher's delight.*

Delaware Water Gap, *Pa. and N.J. The Delaware River has carved a valley through the Kittatinny Mountains at this celebrated spot. The gap itself is crowded by a highway and a railroad, but the broad sweep of the river and the steep profile of its valley remain impressive. Perhaps the best views of the gap are from overlooks at Kittatinny Point, N.J., and Point of Gap, Pa.*

State Forest nearby has an observation tower for magnificent woodland panoramas.

RELATED MUSEUMS AND ATTRACTIONS

Bear Mountain, N.Y. Bear Mountain Trailside Museum.

Cornwall-on-Hudson, N.Y. Museum of the Cornwall Countryside.

Greenwich, Conn. Audubon Center of Greenwich.

Mountainside, N.J. Trailside Nature and Science Center.

New Brunswick, N.J. Rutgers University Geology Museum.

New York, N.Y. American Museum of Natural History. New York Aquarium. New York Botanical Garden, Bronx Park. William T. Davis Wildlife Refuge, Staten Island.

Oradell, N.J. Hiram Blauvelt Wildlife Museum.

Pawling, N.Y. Gunnisonian-Quaker Hill Museum of Natural History.

Philadelphia, Pa. Academy of Natural Science of Philadelphia. University of Pennsylvania Herbarium and Arboretum.

Princeton, N.J. University Museum of Natural History.

Rye, N.Y. Rye Nature Center.

Scranton, Pa. Everhart Museum of Natural History, Science and Art.

Trenton, N.J. New Jersey State Museum; natural history.

Washington Crossing, Pa. Bowman's Hill State Wildflower Preserve.

Shenandoah National Park

VIRGINIA

Subtle and brilliant fall colors blend on the Appalachian ridges.

A Lofty Highway Commands Vast Panoramas of Blue

This view, looking west over the peaceful farms of the Shenandoah Valley, was shot from the wind gap through Massanutten Mountain in Shenandoah

The overwhelming view the visitor takes away with him from Shenandoah National Park is of the vast blue distances—the folds of the Appalachians succeeding each other to the far horizon beyond the pastoral patchwork of fields, farms and woods in the peaceful Shenandoah Valley.

There are two ways of experiencing Shenandoah, one active, the other passive. The passive way is simply to stand and gaze out from one of the 66 scenic overlooks along Skyline Drive, the parkway that runs the length of the park. The view of the Appalachian ridges from these vantage points is one of the most magnificent in the East, equally inspiring in spring, summer or fall. Mist gathers in the hollows and valleys between the ridges, and the farthest ridge trembles against the sky in a blue-gray haze.

But to those willing to hike a mile or more, the real Shenandoah is off the road, in the woods, by the clear mountain runs and waterfalls where the speckled trout hide, and where the wonderfully various shrubs and flowering plants are left to grow as they will.

The park area on both sides of Skyline Drive adds up to a total of 303 square miles, about 95 percent of which is wooded. The road follows the crest of the Blue Ridge, the southeasternmost of the great series of parallel ridges that form the central section of the Appalachian mountain system. This section of the Blue Ridge consists largely of very ancient lavas (some rocks are estimated to be 1.1 billion years old) which have been metamorphosed, or changed, by heat, pressure and infiltration into a rock known because of its color as greenstone schist.

In the 18th century, when the area that is now Shenandoah National Park began to be settled, it was common practice for the residents to set fire to the forest in order to clear land for pasture and homesteads and to permit wild blueberries and other cash crops to grow. By the time the park was dedicated, in 1936, what forest remained was predominantly second growth—that is, trees that had grown from seedlings after the original, virgin trees had been burned or cut down.

Now, after some 30 years of protection, the once bare slopes are covered with trees, grasses and shrubs. The hardy "pioneer" trees typical

National Park. The gap, called New Market Gap, was created because the waters of the stream that once flowed here were diverted, or captured, by another, stronger stream running on higher ground. The highway leading west from Luray to the town of New Market makes good use of the gap.

of the eastern forest—sassafras, tulip poplar, persimmon and black locust—were the first to flourish. These species are now giving way to the oaks and hickories typical of the mature, or "climax," forest. But there are still a few stands of virgin trees left in the park. In the Limberlost section of Whiteoak Canyon is a grove of about 100 large virgin hemlocks, and some white oaks estimated to be as much as 500 years old.

When the park was established the mountain folk were resettled outside park boundaries, and the animals came under protection. Deer have multiplied to the point where they are commonly glimpsed from the road. Bear, although not so numerous, are increasing. (The best time to spot these larger mammals is during late fall and winter, when trees are bare of leaves.) Gray fox, skunk, raccoon and bobcat are common in the woods, and chipmunks, woodchucks and squirrels will sometimes come boldly up to humans, looking for handouts—a practice which can be dangerous and unhealthy. Turkey vultures, crows and ravens, all relatively large black birds, are common, as are the sharp-shinned hawk, ruffed grouse, mourning dove, a variety of warblers in season and three species of woodpeckers.

Most trees in Shenandoah are of the broad-leaved deciduous type (they lose their leaves). When the autumn foliage is at its height—with its subtly complex blending of shades of red, brown, yellow and orange flecked with the green of conifers—the human visitor population also reaches its peak. So rather than becoming part of the traffic jam on an October weekend, it might be wiser to visit the park at other times.

There are plenty of summer pleasures at Shenandoah. In Big Meadows, for instance, the Park Service has interfered with the natural tendency of trees to take over grassland, so that the meadow, mowed once a year to keep larger shrubs and small trees from gaining a foothold, breaks forth in a spectacular annual burst of flowers. Eighteen different kinds of violets grow in Shenandoah, for example, and 17 wild orchids; many of them blossom in Big Meadows. All kinds of ferns and small shrubs also grow unimpeded there.

The amateur geologist, as well as the botanist, will find many rewards. At Franklin Cliffs, Crescent Rocks, on Stony Man Mountain and in Whiteoak Canyon, massive greenstone lava layers form a series of cliffs up to 150 feet high. Columnar jointing—columns that separated out from the rest of the cliff when the lava cooled and contracted—is common. A striking example of columnar jointing can be seen about 200 feet south of the Little Stony Man parking area. Almost every greenstone outcrop is spotted with amygdules—formed by gas bubbles in the lava that have filled with concentric circles of differently colored minerals until they bear a strong resemblance to fried eggs.

For the hiker, Shenandoah National Park offers a great variety of trails, ranging from short, easy walks of under a mile to much longer and more rugged hikes that may involve scrambling up sheer rock faces. There are 370 miles of foot trails, including a 95-mile section

The Blue Ridge in an unusual mood: at sea level, where the James River crosses the Blue Ridge Parkway. The mirrorlike surface of the water reflects a cloud-flecked autumn sky. The parkway, a continuation of Shenandoah National Park's Skyline Drive, runs all the way to the Smoky Mountains.

of the Appalachian Trail, which runs 2000 miles down the Appalachian crest all the way from Maine to Georgia.

One of the easiest and most interesting walks is the Swamp Trail, near Big Meadows. A leaflet describing the highlights of the trail is available at the parking area. In two miles of nearly level walking (there and back) one passes through a variety of habitats: forest, meadow and mountaintop swamp. These "edge" environments, where forest shades into meadow, meadow into swamp, are ideal for spotting many bird and animal species.

The Dark Hollow Trail, over greenstone cliffs, involves a fairly strenuous climb on the way back, but the view of Dark Hollow Falls is worth it: a series of cascades tumbling over great boulders, set in a ravine surrounded by deep forest. An alternate route to the falls, starting at Fisher's Gap, passes the sites of several old mountain homesteads. A mile of the trail is on the Gordonsville Turnpike, which was used by Civil War soldiers crossing the Blue Ridge on their campaigns.

Hawksbill Mountain is the highest in Shenandoah (4049 feet). The three-mile trail to the top and back is the route followed by the park's ranger-naturalists in their guided summer hikes. On the trail, the forest occasionally opens up to reveal the surrounding mountains and valleys. On Hawksbill's summit grow a few balsam fir and red spruce—trees typical of far more northerly latitudes, but seen here because of the relative coolness on the mountain.

In April or May the hardwood trees along Skyline Drive are often still leafless. But down in the hollows the waterfalls run with springtime fullness, and flowers bloom on the forest floor. The redbud and the dogwood blend their pink and white colors late in April, and mountain laurel blooms in early June.

So go to Shenandoah late in the fall to spot deer through the naked branches, or early in spring to catch the first freshness of the blooming earth. Hike through cool glades away from a sizzling summer day, or take your chances with the crowds to enjoy the color burst of autumn. The park closes only when ice and snow make it too dangerous to drive. Each season has its own beauty, and no two visits will ever be the same. Shenandoah (which means "Daughter of the Stars" in a long-forgotten Indian language) is a refreshing return to America's pristine past.

The Chemistry of Fall Color

In fall the shorter, cooler days slow down the production of chlorophyll in leaves. The disappearance of the green chlorophyll exposes granules of pigments called carotenoids, which tint leaves orange and yellow. Further cold weather causes sugar to accumulate in leaves, leading to the production of a group of red and purple pigments called anthocyanins. As all of these pigments combine, they give the fall foliage palette its enormous variety. Tannins, common in oaks, hickories and walnuts, are waste products that turn leaves brown.

RICH IN CHLOROPHYLL, LEAVES STAY GREEN IN SUMMER.

COLD WEATHER EXPOSES RED AND YELLOW PIGMENTS.

TANNINS MAY CAUSE SOME LEAVES TO TURN BROWN.

SPECIAL CELLS AT BASE WEAKEN STEM; THE LEAF FALLS.

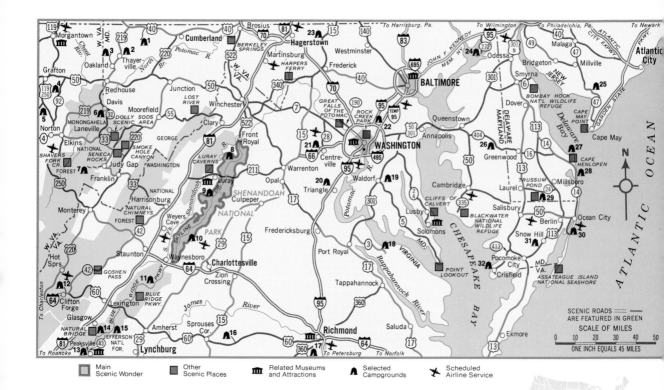

Main Scenic Wonder | Other Scenic Places | Related Museums and Attractions | Selected Campgrounds | Scheduled Airline Service

SCENIC ROADS ARE FEATURED IN GREEN
SCALE OF MILES
0 10 20 30 40 50
ONE INCH EQUALS 45 MILES

WITHIN A DAY'S DRIVE:

Wooded Hills and Swampy Shores Are Mid-Atlantic Highlights

Assateague Island National Seashore, Md. and Va.
(*Picture appears on facing page*)

Berkeley Springs, W.Va. George Washington surveyed the springs in 1748, later took his family there for the waters. The three springs in Berkeley Springs State Park flow 2000 gallons per minute at a constant temperature of 74 degrees—enough water to supply the town of Bath and fill the town pool. Nearby Prospect Peak offers a panoramic view of the Potomac River valley and its surrounding hills.

Blackwater National Wildlife Refuge, Md. Blackwater is one of the most interesting of the chain of waterfowl refuges on the Atlantic Flyway. Among its unusual features are the dark stands of loblolly pine that often rise abruptly from its extensive marshes. Wildlife exhibits are featured at the refuge's visitor center.

Blue Ridge Parkway, Va. A continuation of Skyline Drive in Shenandoah National Park, the parkway connects Shenandoah with Great Smoky Mountains National Park in North Carolina. The Appalachian Trail roughly parallels the parkway for about 100 miles, and there are many other, shorter trails leading off its scenic overlooks.

Bombay Hook National Wildlife Refuge, Del.
(*Picture appears on page 75*)

Cape Henlopen, Del. Seen from the air, the cape resembles a long, sandy finger crooking out into the Atlantic. In addition to fine beaches, Cape Henlopen State Park has nature trails leading past rare plants and wind-stunted trees that grow in the high dunes.

Cape May Point, N.J. Travel west from the charming old town of Cape May to reach this southern-

most tip of New Jersey. A largely deserted beach stretches for miles along the shores of Delaware Bay, and among the ponds and bushy slopes of the dunes behind, hosts of birds roost during spring and fall migrations.

Cliffs of Calvert, Md. Fossil hunters have been picking over the cliffs since the 17th century, when the first Miocene Age (10 to 25 million years ago) snail shell was discovered. The cliffs, up to 120 feet high, stretch for 30 miles along the western shore of Chesapeake Bay. The neighborhood of the Calvert Cliffs Nuclear Plant offers the best view over them.

Dolly Sods Scenic Area, W.Va. This section of the Monongahela National Forest is an unusual mix of upland bogs and windswept plains 4000 feet above sea level. Azalea and rhododendron bloom here in spring, but much of the 10,000-acre tract has a somber arctic look. A number of plants native to the Arctic Circle itself are found growing here.

Goshen Pass, Va. Indians and migrating buffalo were the first to use Goshen Pass, a four-mile gap through the Appalachians cut by the Maury River. Several waterfalls mark the river's course. Hikers along the nature trails bordering the river can cross to the other side via old-fashioned swinging bridges.

Great Falls of the Potomac, Md. and Va.
(*Picture appears on page 75*)

Harpers Ferry, W.Va. The view from Jefferson Rock (Thomas Jefferson pronounced the sight worth the voyage across the Atlantic) encompasses two rivers —the Shenandoah and the Potomac, which meet in the valley below—and three states—West Virginia, Virginia and Maryland. The Blue Ridge Mountains surround the much-restored historic town, which was the scene of John Brown's Civil War raid.

Lost River, W.Va. Underground streams in high limestone country often cut extensive tunnels through the underlying rock. Where a river on the surface approaches such an underground watercourse, the latter captures the water supply, and the surface river dips underground. Lost River is one of many disappearing rivers to be seen in this part of the country.

Luray Caverns, Va. Of all the caverns in this cave-rich area, Luray is perhaps the most rewarding. It is Virginia's largest cave: 64 acres, of which 27 are open to the public. Wide natural corridors and tasteful indirect lighting make it a pleasure to explore. Stalactites and stalagmites come in rainbow hues; huge fluted columns and cascades of frozen stone are massed together in hall after stunning hall. There are big pools of crystal-clear water, up to 15 feet deep, which apparently support no forms of life.

Natural Bridge, Va. Arching 215 feet over Cedar Creek, this fa-

Assateague Island National Seashore, *Md. and Va. A magnificent 35-mile barrier beach, the National Seashore has over 10 miles of shell-strewn public beaches. The famous Chincoteague ponies, seen here grazing a marshy meadow, actually live on Assateague.*

Natural Chimneys, *Va. These seven huge limestone towers stand in a near circle against a hill, rising 120 feet above the surrounding plain. Each rock layer is clearly visible, and a stream has cut smooth tunnels in some of the chimney bases.*

mous limestone arch is believed to have been the roof of an underground tunnel through which the creek once flowed. So strong and thick is the span that it carries a modern highway on top. Thomas Jefferson once owned Natural Bridge, and George Washington carved his initials on it.

Natural Chimneys, Va.
(*Picture appears on page 73*)

Point Lookout, Md. In the cross-rips and currents where the Potomac flows into Chesapeake Bay, striped bass, bluefish and white perch await the fisherman. One of the best fishing areas in the country, Point Lookout is also known for the abundant and easily caught blue crabs on its three-mile stretch of beach.

Rock Creek Park, Washington, D.C. This wooded tract, about four miles long and one mile wide, preserves a jumbled mass of rocks and ledges along Rock Creek, all that remains of an ancient mountain range. The park is rich in wildlife, considering its city location, but most of its

mammals—opossum and flying squirrel, for example—are nocturnal, and rarely seen by day. Its Nature Center, designed primarily for the young, is first rate.

Seneca Rocks, W.Va. So popular with climbers that it is nicknamed the "Face of 1000 Pitons," Seneca Rocks is a jagged outcrop of quartzite (one of the strongest of all rocks) that rises 1000 feet above the North Fork Valley. Spruce Knob, a few miles south, is the highest point in West Virginia, a rugged area of windblown red spruce. There is an observation tower on the summit.

Shavers Fork Creek, W.Va.
(*Picture appears on this page*)

Smoke Hole Canyon, W.Va. Here the South Branch of the Potomac has cut a gorge through the mountains so deep that the sun shines on the river only at midday. The North Fork River, a few miles to the west, drops an average of 32 feet per mile, culminating in a rush of water through the five-mile mountain gorge known as Hopewell Gap.

Trussum Pond, Del. Millions of years ago much of this area was covered with bald cypress swamp. Now almost all that remains of the northernmost stand lies within the 4500 acres of Trussum Pond. Orchids and swamp magnolia grow here, and the roots of cedar and cypress color the water amber.

RELATED MUSEUMS AND ATTRACTIONS

Baltimore, Md. Cylburn Park Natural History Museum.

Luray, Va. Shenandoah National Park Visitor Center.

Morgantown, W.Va. West Virginia University Arboretum and Natural Wildlife Museum.

Peaks of Otter, Va. Blue Ridge Parkway Visitor Center.

Richmond, Va. Maymont Park Wildlife Exhibit.

Solomons, Md. Chesapeake Biological Laboratory; natural history museum, aquarium.

Washington, D.C. Smithsonian Institution Natural History Museum.

Shavers Fork Creek, *W.Va. This lovely creek in the Monongahela National Forest is typical of many in West Virginia's Potomac Highlands. The forest, one of the few remaining wilderness areas within range of the eastern seaboard, has hundreds of miles of trails, and its fishing is famous.*

Bombay Hook National Wildlife Refuge, *Del. Salt marsh hay and other food plants attract as many as 20,000 Canada geese like these to Bombay Hook during the fall migration. Many other land and shore birds, notably the osprey, flourish here. Wildlife can be seen from observation towers.*

Great Falls of the Potomac, *Md. and Va. At Great Falls the broad Potomac drops 76 feet, foaming and rushing among the huge boulders strewn in its path. The picturesque Chesapeake and Ohio Canal, surveyed by George Washington, parallels the river. Great Falls Park has overlooks.*

Mammoth Cave National Park

KENTUCKY

A Fantasy World
That Is Still
Being Explored

The astonishing thing about Mammoth Cave is the vastness of its labyrinthine depths. As Billy Sunday, the noted evangelist, said years ago, "There is only one word in the language to describe Mammoth Cave, and that is mammoth." Both the longest and the third longest cave systems in the world are here. Some of the rooms themselves are enormous; there are 150 miles of explored passages, several very wide, and hundreds of miles (no one really knows how many) of unexplored passages. A geologist has described the Mammoth Cave ridge as a "limestone mass literally honeycombed with openings." Nearby ridges may contain even bigger caves.

Judging from the artifacts found there, humans have known about Mammoth Cave for about 3000 years. Woodland Indians lived in the Mammoth area from 1000 B.C. to A.D. 900, and apparently went through the cave looking for gypsum—a mysterious quest, since scientists still haven't figured out why they wanted it. Various theories are still under investigation. Among them are that the gypsum was used as a salt substitute, as medicine, as a paint base, or even perhaps for fertilizer, since this was a time of change in the Indian way of life, from fishing, hunting and food-gathering to the cultivation of crops.

The partially preserved remains of an "Ancient Gypsum Miner," as the Park Service calls him (also, more familiarly, Lost John), are on

ammoth Cave's vast Rotunda, site of old saltpeter mines.

display in Mammoth Cave in a glass case. This Indian, discovered accidentally in 1935, was killed by a five-ton boulder that crashed down on him as he was chipping minerals from the walls, unaware that he was also digging his own grave. When first discovered, Lost John was quite well preserved, but when the 2370-year-old corpse was brought out into the sunlight a thick, furry fungus began to grow on him. He was rushed back into the more hospitable atmosphere of the cave.

During the War of 1812, slaves were put to work digging up the cave floor to get at the nitrate, or saltpeter, which was needed for making gunpowder. The presence of large amounts of nitrates was an important factor in winning the war. The nitrate pits and the old wooden pipes remain, remarkably preserved after 160 years in the unchanging air.

During 1842 and 1843 a Dr. John Croghan, who had bought the Mammoth Cave property to develop it, decided to put a theory of his into action. He believed that tuberculosis victims might benefit by living in the constant temperature of the cave. He had some evidence for this, improbable as it seems now, in the remarkable health said to have been enjoyed by the nitrate miners several decades earlier. Dr. Croghan had brick and wooden structures built to house and feed 15 patients. Of this number apparently at least two died rather quickly and the rest emerged sicker. To quote an 1890 account: "The experiment was an utter failure; as was also the pitiful attempt on the part of these poor invalids to make trees and shrubbery grow around their dismal huts." The majority of those patients who stayed the longest died within three weeks of emerging.

Local people, who have been poking around these caverns for generations, still tell the story of Floyd Collins, a Kentucky cave explorer who discovered nearby Crystal Cave. Searching for another entrance to Mammoth Cave nearly 50 years ago, he became trapped in a narrow opening in Sand Cave when a boulder fell on his foot. The efforts to rescue Collins, which went on for 18 days, captured the imagination of the country, fed by breathless stories filed by newspaper reporters. People flocked by the thousands to Sand Cave and had to be held back by state troopers. But in spite of all the best efforts of several brave men, no one could extricate Collins, and the explorer finally was declared dead on February 16, 1925.

Two factors have made Mammoth Cave what it is today: water and time. About 240 million years ago, during the geological era called the Mississippian period, the succession of seas that covered this area were depositing mud, shells and sand in layers. The shells and ooze hardened into limestone, the sand into sandstone. Upward movements of the earth's crust drained the sea away. Then mildly acidic groundwater dissolved the limestone along cracks, enlarging small openings and finally hollowing out caves. As further earth movements lowered the water table, the upper cave passages dried out and at least five overlapping and interlinked cave levels evolved.

The decoration of Mammoth Cave comes from groundwater percolating through the limestone ceiling. Here it evaporates, leaving a carbonate deposit called travertine. More water, more travertine, until stalactites grow downward. Water dripping to the floor of the cave gradually duplicates the process upward, to form stalagmites. However, there are relatively few of these in Mammoth Cave.

The eons are piled on top of each other, the floor of one sea overlying that of another. Flowerlike gypsum crystals bloom on the walls, and little helictites turn and twist in directions that defy the laws of gravity. The formations are surprisingly colorful: some of the flowstone is like a cascade of rippling water, reflecting the browns, oranges and yellows of dissolved minerals. Many visitors come to the cave with preconceived ideas of how the formations will look from having seen color photographs which cannot really do the cave justice.

The solution of the limestone underground weakens the strata supporting the surface, and

Piled up in layer after intricate layer like a frozen stone drip castle, this massive flowstone formation has been named the Chinese Temple.

How Caves Are Formed

Surface water picks up carbonic acid from decaying vegetation. This solution drains down through fractures in the limestone, then begins to move horizontally toward the river. The solution dissolves the rock, making chambers and passageways. As the water table (blue section of rock) lowers, the process is repeated on a lower level, leaving the original cave network dry.

the surface begins to sink. This part of the state is permeated with sinkholes that lead to common caves. Steam rises in winter from these warm earthen nostrils, and cool drafts breathe out from the caves in summer. (In Mammoth Cave the temperature is always 54 degrees, the humidity a high 87 percent.)

Three main cave tours are offered by the Park Service. The easiest is the Frozen Niagara, which covers three quarters of a mile, takes a little over an hour and features Frozen Niagara, one of the most impressive formations in the cave. The Historic Tour covers about two miles and takes two hours. Features include the largest cave rooms, Lost John the mummy, the remains of the nitrate mining operations, and Mammoth Dome, highest dome in the cave. The Scenic Tour is a strenuous four-mile walk with many hills to climb. But walking through the long, winding passages gives a visitor an inkling of the vastness and complexity of the cave. This tour ends up at Frozen Niagara and includes a lunch stop in the Snowball Room, whose ceiling is covered with gypsum flowers.

Aboveground there are self-guiding nature trails, and a one-hour cruise-with-nature-talk on *Miss Green River II*, a replica of a steamboat that plies the pellucid Green River.

Many visitors neglect the north side of Mammoth Cave National Park. This is a mistake. Even getting there is exciting: one crosses the Green River on a car ferry run by a paddlewheel and guided by cables. The best time to go is in spring, when the hills burst with bloom and the light purple of redbuds blends with the smudgy white of dogwood, and all the streams are flowing with winter melt and spring rain. Although trails on this northern side are few, the stream beds themselves are easy to follow. There are waterfalls and natural bridges, and tree roots clinging to the sides of steep bluffs. In summer maples, hemlocks and towering beeches shade the cool hollows; in fall the flaming reds and burning yellows of hardwoods consume the forest and delight the eye. This side of the park, which seems almost reluctant to be discovered, is a fit cover for the marvels that lie beneath.

This view of the rolling Kentucky hills in their glowing autumn foliage shows a side of Mammoth Cave National Park that many visitors miss.

The Cave Island nature trail leads to the Green River bottomlands, where "lost" underground rivers emerge among huge sycamores and beeches.

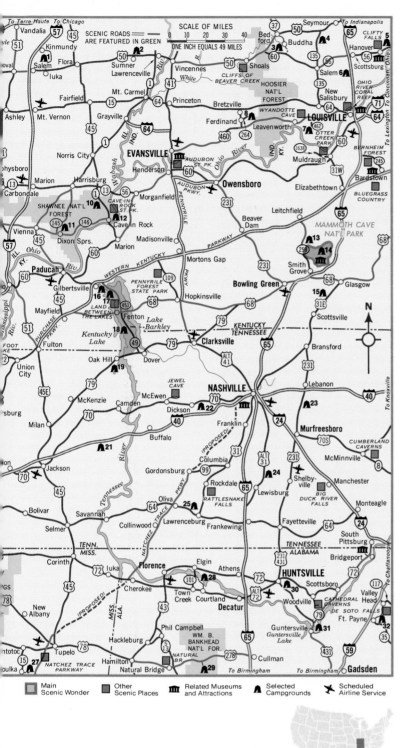

SCALE OF MILES
ONE INCH EQUALS 49 MILES
SCENIC ROADS ══════
ARE FEATURED IN GREEN

N

Main Scenic Wonder ▪ Other Scenic Places 🏛 Related Museums and Attractions ▲ Selected Campgrounds ✈ Scheduled Airline Service

Bluegrass Country, Ky.
(Picture appears on page 83)

Cathedral Caverns, Ala. An entrance so large scores of people can stand in it side by side, an appropriately huge stalagmite called Goliath, an immense "frozen waterfall" and an extensive stalagmite forest—all combine to make this one of the most engrossing of the area's many caves.

Cave-in-Rock State Park, Ill. The cave for which this 60-acre park is named is an opening 25 feet high, 40 feet wide and 200 feet long, carved out of a sheer rock bluff overlooking the Ohio River.

Cliffs of Beaver Creek, Ind. The cliffs, ranging from 60 to 100 feet high, extend for more than a mile along Beaver Creek at the point where it flows into the White River. The highest cliff is a honeycombed rock of beautifully blended colors, with a large cavern in its north side.

Clifty Falls, Ind. Over 500 species of flowering plants have been identified in Clifty Falls State Park, a virtually unspoiled nature preserve. Two waterfalls and a deep, boulder-strewn canyon where the sun shines only at midday are the major attractions.

Cumberland Caverns, Tenn. At the western edge of the Cumberland Mountains, Cumberland Caverns is filled with columns and draperies of gracefully frozen stone. Some of its passages are still being explored and mapped.

De Soto Falls, Ala.
(Picture appears on page 82)

Jewel Cave, Tenn. Named for its spectacular, multicolored rock formations, Jewel Cave is Tennessee's smallest commercial cave, but one of its most attractive. The two main rooms are filled with a dazzling variety of stalactites and stalagmites.

John J. Audubon State Park, Ky. The great artist-naturalist spent many years studying and painting the birds, plants and animals of the Kentucky wilderness. The park includes a tract of virgin

WITHIN A DAY'S DRIVE:

Bluegrass and Myriad Caves

Bernheim Forest, Ky. This 14,000-acre woodland wildlife sanctuary is crisscrossed with trails along which hikers may see deer, wild turkey, raccoon and other native animals and birds. Paved roads lead to four fishing lakes.

Big Duck River Falls, Tenn. The Big Duck and the Little Duck spill over a staircase of rocky ledges in a series of waterfalls. On the 100-foot bluff between the two rivers are the ruins of a stone fort built by Indians in A.D. 400.

De Soto Falls, *Ala. In the heart of 5000-acre De Soto Falls State Park, the Little River drops 110 feet at De Soto Falls. In the lower section of the park is the great canyon through which the Little River flows. A five-mile highway follows it along the crest of the canyon.*

was centuries old, worn down by deer, buffalo and Indians, when Hernando De Soto, the Spanish explorer, crossed it 400 years ago. Today's parkway crosses and recrosses the old road; depressions along ridges and across fields mark where it ran. Views from the parkway are often of lovely old plantation houses.

Natural Bridge, Ala. A sandstone arch vaults almost 150 feet across a deep ravine filled with delicate ferns and wildflowers and giant magnolias with blossoms 14 inches across. Stately Canadian hemlocks soar up over the arch from the floor of the ravine.

Ohio River Coral Reef, Ky. The largest exposed coral reef of its type in the country, the formation is visible below the dam at the falls of the Ohio River. Many of the rock layers are coral reef limestone, formed under the shallow sea that covered this area in the dim geological past, and bear fossils of animal life that existed 300 million years ago.

Otter Creek Park, Ky. Perched on a high bluff above the Ohio River, this 3000-acre park has a nature center, 10 miles of hiking trails and three swimming pools. The park is in a region of heavily wooded hills and deep valleys, honeycombed by several large caverns with weird formations.

Pennyrile Forest State Park, Ky. Once an eroded, cutover timberland, Pennyrile Forest is now a model of good forest management—and one the public can enjoy. Pennyrile Park has nature walks leading to scenic overlooks.

Rattlesnake Falls, Tenn. Located in an area of rough, densely wooded terrain trenched by deep valleys, Rattlesnake Falls is a series of cascades spilling from a big cold spring over a high limestone ledge.

Reelfoot Lake, Tenn. A series of spectacular earthquakes in 1811 and 1812 created 14,500-acre Reelfoot Lake. A wildlife refuge attracts over 200 bird species, and the cypress forests are a natural fish hatchery.

forest and a bird sanctuary, as well as a museum of Audubon paintings and one of the famous "Elephant" folios of *The Birds of America.*

Land Between the Lakes, Ky. and Tenn. A heavily wooded 170,000-acre peninsula between Lake Barkley and Kentucky Lake, Land Between the Lakes has over 3000

miles of shoreline and 300 miles of backcountry roads and hiking trails. Numerous coves and bays make for excellent fishing, boating and camping in this recreation area developed by the Tennessee Valley Authority.

Natchez Trace Parkway, Miss. and Tenn. The Trace is actually several trails linked together. It

Wyandotte Cave, Ind.
(*Picture appears on this page*)

**RELATED MUSEUMS
AND ATTRACTIONS**

Bridgeport, Ala. Russell Cave
Natural History Museum.

Carbondale, Ill. Southern Illinois
University Natural History
Museum.

Clermont, Ky. Bernheim Forest
Nature Center and Natural
History Museum.

Evansville, Ind. Natural History
Museum, Evansville Museum of
Arts and Sciences.

Hanover, Ind. Hanover College
Geology Museum.

Louisville, Ky. Museum of Science
and History; natural history,
geology.

Mammoth Cave National Park,
Ky. Natural History Museum.

Nashville, Tenn. Tennessee State
Museum; geology, natural history.

Wyandotte Cave, *Ind. Wyandotte is one of the largest caves in the
country; much of it remains unexplored. Some of the passages are
almost filled with massive dripstone deposits. Little Wyandotte Cave,
a few miles farther to the south, is smaller and easier to explore.*

Bluegrass Country, *Ky. Bluegrass, or June grass, is
both hardy and handsome, widely used for lawns
in temperate climates. Such grasses cover mile
after mile of the gently rolling, fertile hills in the
central part of the state, providing excellent
grazing for the horses at Kentucky's stud farms.*

Great Smoky Mountains
NATIONAL PARK, NORTH CAROLINA AND TENNESSEE

The Smokies' ancient ridges recede hazily in this view from the Blue Ridge Parkway.

Great Smoky Mountains
Nat. Pk.

A Rich Mountain Wilderness Is Our Most Popular Park

Cades Cove, on the Tennessee side of the park, is an oasis of pastoral beauty amid the towering ridges. About a hundred mountain families

One of the remarkable things about the Great Smoky Mountains National Park is that it exists—800 square miles of forest, wild and intact, sitting astride the North Carolina–Tennessee line, much of it a mile in the sky and all of it within an air hour or two of the East's megalopolis. Trees grow here that predate the discovery of America, giants with trunks measuring 25 feet in circumference. Spruce, fir and hemlock reach toward the sky with a majesty equaled only by the redwoods'. Heaths of rhododendron, mountain laurel and flame azalea have run wild. Vegetation everywhere is so varied and so lush that the vapor it gives off, cooling and condensing on its way up the mountains, spreads a blue veil over the land— the "smoke" of the Smokies.

These lands were once privately owned. In the 1920s, paper manufacturers held vast tracts of timber, earmarked for cutting. Elsewhere, bits and pieces belonged to descendants of the original Scots-Irish settlers who had funneled down the Appalachian chain from the north. In time the forests might have fallen had the park not been established to preserve them.

Almost 6600 privately owned parcels of land, large and small, were pieced together to form the Great Smoky Mountains National Park. It took very nearly 20 years, and millions in state, federal and private pledges, before the park was officially dedicated in 1940. Today it is America's most popular national park, with the remarkable number of more than seven million visitors streaming through each year.

There is no single spectacle in the Smokies to draw tourists. No Grand Canyon, Old Faithful or Petrified Forest. There is only *living* forest, hushed mountain wilderness. Within the park's 516,000 acres grow 1400 different species of flowering plants, very nearly as many as in some countries. There is such diversity of plant life, in fact, that it is possible, simply by climbing or driving up a mountain, to move from the dogwood and redbud of the South up through the sugar maples and yellow birches of New England to the balsam, fir and spruce of Canada on the cooler summits.

Rivers and streams slash through the mountain greenery, revealing geological formations as fascinating to scientists as any found in the Rockies. The Smokies are ancient—America's

once lived and tilled their land on this flat, green
valley floor, where some of their rough pioneer
houses remain in a sort of open-air museum.

An 11-mile-loop auto road tours the valley;
there is also a short self-guiding nature trail
through a mature grove of fine pines and oaks.

oldest mountains—with sedimentary rocks
dating back to a time 500 million years ago,
when the area was covered by a shallow sea.
The mountains' actual formation began about
200 million years ago with the Appalachian
Revolution, a gradual buckling and thrusting
upward of the earth's crust that lasted many
millions of years. It took many more millions
of years for the rains and rivers to hone and
shape the gently billowing mountains of today.
The hills and valleys of the Smokies, geologists
explain, are not so much a heaving up of
mountains as a wearing down of valleys.

Because of their age, the Smokies have none
of the rugged drama of the Tetons or Cascades.
They are mountains with an old-shoe sort of
comfort: worn and soothing. To stand atop
Clingmans Dome, at 6643 feet the loftiest peak
in the park, or to hike the trail up Mount Le
Conte (another of the park's 23 peaks above
6000 feet) is to emerge amid a peaceful ocean
of mountains, "to rest easy," the hill folk say.
The wind singing in a spruce or a solitary
woodpecker tapping on the bleached skeleton
of a chestnut tree helps to put the man-made
in perspective.

You can get abundant views of the Smokies
by driving the Newfound Gap Road, which
hairpins across the park from Cherokee, North
Carolina (the Indian reservation adjoins the
park), to Gatlinburg, Tennessee. But the simplest and deepest joys of the park lie deep

87

The Great Smoky Haze: a Brew of Sunlight and Greenery

The haze that lies almost constantly over the Smokies has its origin in the forested hillsides. Trees exude terpenes, which are hydrocarbon molecules derived from their essential oils. Sunlight breaks the molecules down.

The fragmented molecules interact and form new and larger molecules, which begin to refract, or bend, the sun's rays. Terpene production—and therefore haze— is particularly heavy in fall as the leaves begin to decay.

The larger molecules then aggregate with each other, and with the molecules of various forms of air pollution (different colors above). The sunlight able to penetrate without refraction is now limited —and the "smoke" is thick.

---

inside it, on the more than 650 miles of trails.

The Appalachian Trail zigzags for 70 miles along the park's ridge. To hike it is to burst from dense green woodland into sunny, secret meadows tufted with wild flowers; to examine firsthand a cluster of Indian pipes pushing up through fallen leaves; to inspect a yellow lady-slipper or a painted trillium. Equally memorable is the hand-over-hand crawl to the pinnacle of Chimney Tops to see, far below, the silver of Little Pigeon River. Or a late-June stroll across the rhododendron bouquet of Gregorys Bald. Or a pony trek across the northern end of the park in the shadow of Big Cataloochee Knob, to emerge unexpectedly in a pastureland of Shangri-La remoteness and magic. Every park trail promises a delightful surprise—a sudden cascade, a mossy bank by a trout stream, a deer in flight or, perhaps, a glimpse of a rare pileated woodpecker.

The hill folk so loved these mountains that some of them were allowed to remain inside the park, "tucked," as they would say in the Elizabethan dialect of their forefathers, "so far back in them hills we have to keep wiping at the shadows." Most settled in a snug Tennessee valley called Cades Cove (where only two

families now remain), living in humble cabins, farming from "kin see to cain't see." A road circles through, and the lucky visitor may see white-tailed deer foraging in the meadows or wild turkeys sauntering by. There are "b'ars now and again," though most of the park's black bears live in the forests, coming out in warm weather to rifle litter baskets.

Every season casts a spell over the Smokies. Winter drapes the mountains with snow, then pushes woolly cumulus into the coves, making mountaintop islands in swift rivers of clouds. In spring and early summer, dogwood, redbud, laurel, flame azalea and rhododendron paint the mountains red (and purple, orange, pink and white). Midsummer cloaks them with a green of jungle brilliance; then autumn sets them aflame.

Whatever the season, the "smoke" is always there, drifting, shifting according to the time of year or time of day: "valley fog" in the morning flattening the mountains, silhouetting one shoulder against another; mere wisps at noon, sliding through the coves; a pink scrim at sunset, stacking purple mountain layers up against the sun. The Smokies are mountains of infinite mood—and mystery.

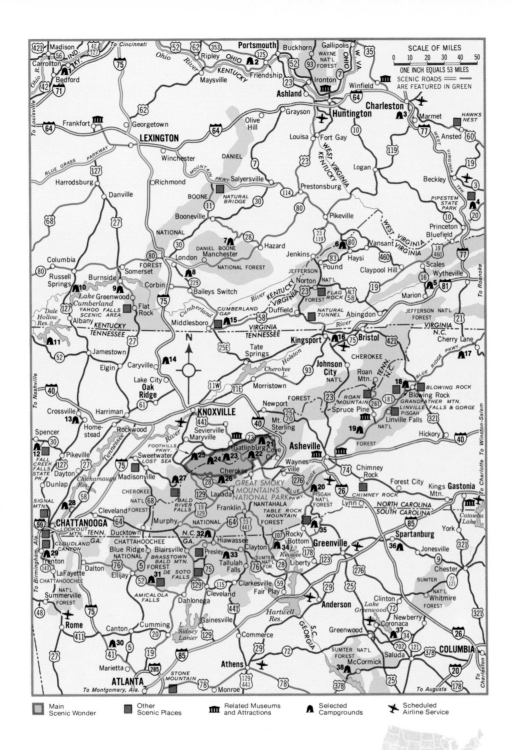

SCALE OF MILES

0 10 20 30 40 50

ONE INCH EQUALS 53 MILES

SCENIC ROADS ═══
ARE FEATURED IN GREEN

▢ Main Scenic Wonder	▪ Other Scenic Places	⎰ Related Museums and Attractions	▲ Selected Campgrounds	✈ Scheduled Airline Service

WITHIN A DAY'S DRIVE:

Rocky Overlooks and River Gorges

Amicalola Falls, Ga. A series of cascades that drop 729 feet comprises Amicalola, the highest falls in Georgia. There is a rough trail to the foot for ambitious hikers; the top can be reached by car. The start of the famous Appalachian Trail, which runs all the way to Maine, is nearby.

Bald River Falls, Tenn. The waters here plunge 70 feet from two upper levels. There are trout in the Bald River itself, and wild Russian boar, Smoky Mountain black bear and deer in the surrounding woods. Modern campgrounds and a beautiful mountain lake add to the appeal of the area.

Blowing Rock, N.C. Snow falls upward at this strange place, and light objects dropped from the rock are blown back. The steep walls of the gorge below it form a flume; strong northwest winds blowing through it force air currents upward. There is an observation terrace above the gorge.

89

Brasstown Bald Mountain, Ga. At nearly 5000 feet, this is the highest point in the state. An observation area at the summit offers a spectacular panoramic view of the Smokies.

Chimney Rock, N.C. A beautiful 75-mile view over Lake Lure and the mountains beyond rewards those who take the elevator inside the mountain or hike the trails to the summit.

Cloudland Canyon, Ga. (*Picture appears on page 92*)

Cumberland Gap, Ky., Va., Tenn. The gap is actually a wind gap— a notch cut by former stream activity into a ridge of rock. Wilderness Overlook provides a view over a stretch of primeval American landscape. The Pinnacle has a sweeping view of seven states. Daniel Boone came through here on his way to Kentucky.

De Soto Falls, Ga. It is an energetic hike to these falls in a mountainous area of the Chattahoochee National Forest. They comprise six beautiful cascades and are named for Spanish conquistador Hernando De Soto, discoverer of the Mississippi, who passed this way around 1540.

Falls Creek Falls State Park, Tenn. Falls Creek Falls, on one of four scenic streams within the

Lookout Mountain, *Tenn. Visitors can ride the steepest passenger incline railroad in the world to the top of this mountain. A view of seven states spreads out below Lover's Leap. The summit's* *attractions include Rock City Gardens, with its natural rock formations, and 10 acres of scenic trails. Reflecting pools and profuse wildflowers border a three-mile drive along the western slope.*

Natural Bridge, *Ky. This is the largest (78 feet long, 65 feet high) of several such arches in the area. A state park has been developed around it, and several nature trails lead to panoramic* *overlooks. Natural bridges are formed by a process of wind and water erosion that cuts away softer rock beneath a vein of hard surface rock; the hard rock is left to form the span.*

park, plunges 256 feet into a shaded pool. Suspension bridges crossing deep ravines, nature trails and scenic overlooks combine to produce a wide choice of walks for the hiker.

Flag Rock, Va. On High Knob Mountain, huge boulders exposed by eons of erosion are prominent on the slopes. From observation points visitors can look down on the town of Norton, where streets are so laid out that they appear to spell its name.

Grandfather Mountain, N.C. The side of this 6000-foot mountain has been eroded into the likeness of an old man's face. Flowers and vines grow in the furrows of the stone face, and red spruce and balsam soften the contours of the mountain peak.

Hawks Nest, W.Va. This overlook offers a view of the New River canyon, one of the most spectacular in the East. Over millions of years the New River cut its way through thousands of feet of sedimentary rock layers, forming the gorge in much the same way as the Colorado River formed the Grand Canyon. Exciting white-water raft trips can be made on the boiling rapids: the two-day, 30-mile journey starts at the village of Prince.

Linville Falls and Gorge, N.C. The steep gorge through which the Linville River rushes is one of the most rugged in the area. Linville Mountain forms one side, and Jonas Ridge, consisting of several oddly shaped rock formations, including Sitting Bear and Hawksbill, the other.

Lookout Mountain, Tenn.
(Picture appears on facing page)

Lost Sea, Tenn. Deep inside a mountain is this underground lake, believed to be the largest in the world. Visitors can reach it by gently sloping walkways (no stairs) and explore it in glass-bottom boats that provide a look at the huge rainbow trout living in the depths. Emerald Falls is a pretty underground cascade.

Natural Bridge, Ky.
(Picture appears on this page)

Natural Tunnel, Va. Water wearing its way through a limestone ridge carved this tunnel, the remnant of a much longer one. It is about 1000 feet long and 100 feet high, with a stream and a railroad passing through.

Cloudland Canyon, *Ga. This spectacular 2000-foot gorge, with its series of striking rock formations, is on the Georgia side of Tennessee's famous Lookout Mountain. It was once the home of Cherokee Indians, and there have been many stories of a lead mine here that was never found. A trail leads to a waterfall in the gorge.*

Pipestem State Park, W.Va. The newest and largest of West Virginia's fine parks, Pipestem surrounds the spectacular 3600-foot Bluestone Gorge. There is a tramway to the bottom of the gorge, and 100 miles of hiking trails.

Roan Mountain, Tenn. and N.C. (*Picture appears on facing page*)

Signal Mountain, Tenn. From Signal Point overlook, visitors can gaze at a beautiful view over the "Grand Canyon" of the Tennessee River, Williams Island and Chattanooga.

Stone Mountain, Ga. The world's largest exposed mass of granite, Stone Mountain appears from a distance to be bare rock, but it is actually covered with plant life—much of it rare. There is a massive sculpture of Confederate leaders carved in the north face. A skylift to the top of the mountain provides a close-up look at the carving, and a sweeping view.

Table Rock Mountain, S.C. (*Picture appears on facing page*)

Yahoo Falls Scenic Area, Ky. Rugged uplands and a gorge through which Yahoo Creek flows form the heart of this section of Daniel Boone National Forest. There are hiking trails and scenic overlooks; wildflowers and rhododendron are abundant.

RELATED MUSEUMS AND ATTRACTIONS

Asheville, N.C.
Craggy Gardens Visitor Center, Blue Ridge Parkway.
Colburn Mineral Museum.

Frankfort, Ky. Kentucky State Game Farm.

Gastonia, N.C. Gaston Museum of Natural History.

Gatlinburg, Tenn. Great Smoky Mountains National Park Museum.

Huntington, W.Va. Marshall University Geology Museum.

Spruce Pine, N.C. Museum of North Carolina Minerals, Blue Ridge Parkway.

Winfield, W.Va. Morgan's Museum of Natural History.

Roan Mountain, *Tenn. and N.C. Mile-high Roan Mountain is belted with firs and crowned with a lush growth of rhododendron that covers 600 acres.* *(In fact, the broad, flat summit is the scene each June of a rhododendron festival.) The Doe River cuts a scenic 25-mile gorge through the mountain.*

Table Rock Mountain, *S.C. The Cherokee Indians believed the gods could use this flat-topped 3200-foot mountain as a table—thus the name.* *There are hiking and nature trails to the top and also up nearby Pinnacle, with its blue lake at the foot. Both are included in a 2000-acre state park.*

Outer Banks
NORTH CAROLINA

The great sandspit runs ruler-straight for miles, dividing Atlantic waves from quiet bay.

NORTH CAROLINA   Outer Banks

A Restless Ocean Shapes a Scimitar of Stormswept Sand

Just below Norfolk, Virginia, a dot-dash string of sandspits splinters off the mainland and aims for an angry, unpredictable part of the Atlantic known as "The Graveyard." Here the warm Gulf Stream thrusting north and the Cold Stream pouring south mingle with a fury that has sunk nearly a thousand ships and disabled as many more.

In the middle of it all lie the flotsamlike sandspits that form North Carolina's Outer Banks. Barely a mile wide in most places, they stretch across 150 miles of ocean from the Virginia line to Cape Lookout, lying 20, sometimes 30 miles at sea—abandoned, it seems, by a retreating mainland. In a way, the Outer Banks *were* abandoned. At the end of the Ice Age, waters from the melting glacier far to the

north infiltrated the coastal lowlands, creating the tidal sounds and rivers that now separate the banks from the mainland.

From the air today the Outer Banks are an awesome sight, a slender golden thread drawn across the ocean, flexed at Cape Hatteras like an outsize Indian bow around North Carolina's tidewater counties. The islands were Indian once: "Out Banks," the Indians called them, because they lay so far from shore. In the Indian days the banks were heavily forested with cedar, pine and live oak. Today they are virtually barren, prey to man more than to sea. The trees were first axed in the days of clipper ships to provide timber for planking and pitch for calking. In recent years they have been bulldozed to make room for vacation villages.

Off Cape Hatteras powerful ocean currents smash together, producing waves that are seldom less than mountainous. These turbulent waters have sunk so many ships that the area is known as "The Graveyard," and bleaching ship skeletons are still seen along the wide beaches. The one in the picture above was once the Laura Barnes.

Scruffy yaupon (Indian holly) and myrtle survive. And a few live oaks struggle along on the sound side of the islands, sculpted by salt spray and trailing tatters of Spanish moss.

Strangely, the death of the forests gave birth to the Outer Banks' most dramatic features: the dunes. With little vegetation to anchor the soil, and with gales of mountain-moving force to loosen it, the dunes *are* mountainous, as though half the Sahara had been dumped there. Jockey Ridge, a towering 138 feet high, isn't a single dune but a series, a crazy Brobdingnagian sandpile in Nags Head's backyard. It is the tallest coastal sand dune on the Atlantic or Gulf coasts, and the view from the top is magical—especially at dawn when the sun makes cotton candy of the ground fog, and at dusk when the sand shines with 24-carat intensity all the way to Hatteras Island, 15 miles south.

To drive south on routes 158 and 12 along the Outer Banks is to travel backward in time. Bodie Island, linked to the mainland by the Wright Memorial Bridge, is today motel row, a 25-mile string of not very attractive beach towns: Kitty Hawk, where the Wright brothers lived while conducting their "scientific kite-

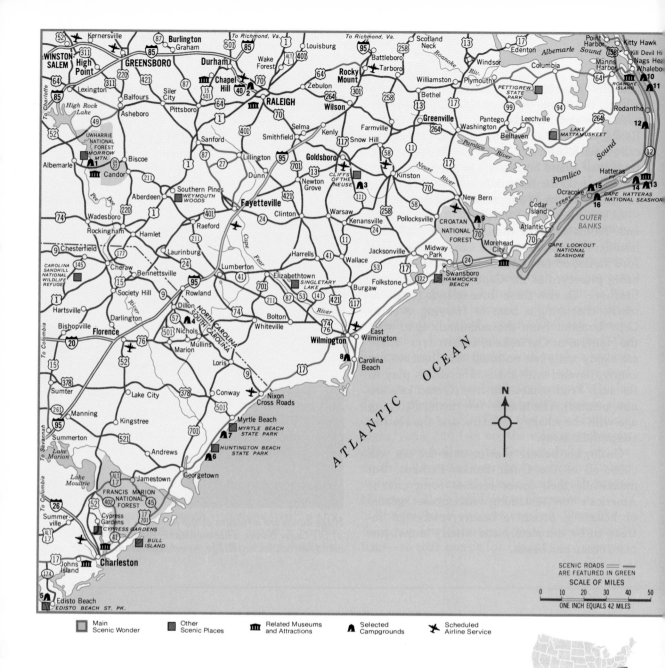

Main Scenic Wonder · Other Scenic Places · Related Museums and Attractions · Selected Campgrounds · Scheduled Airline Service

SCENIC ROADS ARE FEATURED IN GREEN
SCALE OF MILES
0 10 20 30 40 50
ONE INCH EQUALS 42 MILES

Birds and Beaches Crowd the Shores

Bull Island, S.C.
(*Picture appears on facing page*)

Carolina Sandhills National Wildlife Refuge, S.C. Upland game, Canada geese and ducks and over 175 species of songbirds have been spotted here. There are picnic and camping facilities.

Cliffs of the Neuse, N.C. A 90-foot cliff thick with fossils rises above the Neuse River, creating a rewarding place for amateur paleontologists. The surrounding woods contain a mixture of herbaceous plants and Spanish moss.

Cypress Gardens, S.C.
(*Picture appears on facing page*)

Edisto Beach State Park, S.C. Edisto is a state park on a semi-tropical island rich in fossils, seashells and driftwood. Myrtle, yaupon and sabal palms line its two miles of white sand beaches.

Hammocks Beach, N.C. From atop the unusually high sand dunes on this sea island there is a panoramic view of surf washing the Atlantic shore, the marsh-lands along the bay side and the windblown sand beaches that ring the whole island. A free ferry (no cars) operates between Swansboro and Hammocks during the summer months.

Huntington Beach State Park, S.C. Huntington has long stretches of beach and is a particularly inviting place for seaside walks: within its 2500 acres are ponds, marshes, dunes and a considerable variety of wildlife.

Lake Mattamuskeet, N.C. Mattamuskeet is a refuge for thousands of ducks, geese and swans. The fishing is good all year round here, especially for largemouth bass and other game fish.

Morrow Mountain, N.C. This state park is located on the banks of the Pee Dee River in the Uwharrie Mountains, one of the oldest ranges in the United States. From Morrow's summit there is a sweeping view of nearby lakes, rolling hills and thick forests.

Myrtle Beach State Park, S.C. Myrtle Beach has been developed into a major seaside resort, and the state park offers cool forests, smooth sand beaches and deep-sea fishing only minutes from the usual resort amenities.

Pettigrew State Park, N.C. The main attraction in Pettigrew is Lake Phelps, one of the loveliest natural lakes in the state. Thick stands of cypress growing along its shores provide delightful places for picnics.

Singletary Lake, N.C. The impact of a meteorite striking the earth is believed to have produced the crater now filled by this 527-acre lake. The state park surrounding

it offers fishing, boating, group camping and nature study.

Weymouth Woods, N.C. A nature preserve in the heart of the Sandhills country, Weymouth Woods is known for its longleaf pines and temperate year-round climate. A nature study program and a natural history museum add to a visitor's enjoyment of the many animals and birds that are found in the park.

RELATED MUSEUMS AND ATTRACTIONS

Cape Hatteras, N.C. Museum of the Sea.

Chapel Hill, N.C. University of North Carolina, Coker Arboretum.

Charleston, S.C. Charleston Museum; natural history.

Johns Island, S.C. Magnolia Gardens and Nurseries.

Morehead City, N.C. Hampton Museum of Marine Life.

Morrow Mountain State Park, N.C. Park Natural History Museum.

Raleigh, N.C. North Carolina State Museum; natural history.

Whalebone, N.C. (near). Bodie Island Visitor Center; natural history.

Bull Island, *S.C. These tidal flats are part of Cape Romain, the largest wildlife refuge on the East Coast. Seasonal visitors include a spectacular variety of birds following the Atlantic flyway, and giant sea turtles.*

Cypress Gardens, *S.C. The roots of giant cypress trees loom from the freshwater lake at Cypress Gardens. The 250-acre garden may be toured by boat or along footpaths bordered by camellias and azaleas.*

Okefenokee Swamp

GEORGIA

GEORGIA

Okefenokee
Swamp

A Voyage on the
Waters of Time

In south Georgia and north Florida, covering 660 square miles of wilderness—as primeval as any our ancestors ever knew—lies the great Okefenokee Swamp. In places it is a dim world of tannin-stained brown water at the giant bases of bald cypress trees. Other parts are dazzling with subtropical sun. The Okefenokee, its people say, is enchanted. Certainly it is untamed. Processions of biologists have come and gone; nobody yet knows whether one or two species of bears live in the swamp's inner reaches, or if any panthers survive there. The Okefenokee does not yield its mysteries easily.

America has had other swamps, but most of them have been drained for factories, shopping malls and suburbs. The Okefenokee survives because it is far from population centers. The first group of promoters who tried to dry it out went bankrupt, though their canals remain as the realm of pickerel and largemouth bass and bream and killifish. The lumber corporation which began devastating cathedrals of bald cypress soon learned that the wood cost more to cut than it could ever be sold for. When the swamp was finally made a National Wildlife Refuge in 1937, its continuing enchantment was assured. Today the increasing numbers of nature lovers and fishermen who visit here find the richness of its plant and animal life virtually undiminished.

Once the Okefenokee was a churning salt-water sound; Florida was an island then. High

Shallow-draft boats pole silently through the swamp.

An Okefenokee johnboat in a world of spectral cypresses. These boats, which have outboard motors as well as poles for power, carry 8 to 10 passengers on two-hour tours, starting from Okefenokee Swamp Park. They follow cleared canals through the swamp's dense tangles of growth.

Trail Ridge, which today marks the swamp's eastern boundary, was an ocean reef. Gradually Trail Ridge was thrust up from the sea's floor. Simultaneous land upheavals to the north and west and south made the sound an inland lake. Then it began to fill with vegetation until the swamp of modern times was born. To the Creek Indians who once poled its waterways, Okefenokee was "the land of the trembling earth." It still trembles. As vegetable matter decays beneath the water, it forms hydrogen sulfide and methane gases which make it rise to the surface once more. Grasses and smilax vines and bushes begin to grow on its surface, and the resulting island of matter drifts until it is snagged by a tree. Seeds drop; other trees begin to grow. The "blowup" of the gases has produced ground that for years may quiver under the feet of wildcats and bears. When the

island becomes more stable, Okefenokee natives dignify it as a "house"—a place where it is safe to build a cabin. Meanwhile by day and night, blowups continue to occur: the process of land formation and disintegration goes on.

The Okefenokee is not one world but many. There are pine barrens, where the ground is a few inches higher than surrounding land and brown-headed nuthatches stab high trunks for insects. Below them, gray foxes prowl in an understory of bushes, including the lather bush, whose leaves crushed in the hand will foam like soap. Through thick pineland wire grass move the snakes: pigmy and canebrake and diamondback rattlers, harmless king snakes and blue racers. When the wire grass is leaning one way and the wind is blowing another, swamp guides caution, watch out: a snake, not a breeze, is bending the tough blades. At twilight Florida flying squirrels begin to perform their acrobatics in the branches. Sometimes the raw scream of a far-off wildcat rends the ensuing darkness.

The swamp has a language all its own. When the "good God is sitting in the hooraws," the event is not religious. Okefenokeeans mean that a pileated woodpecker is perched in a species of bush that scientists call *Pieris*. Red-headed woodpeckers are "cham-chacks" and bitterns are "thunderpumps" (their croaks pump like thunder). The rabbits of the barrens are "barneys"—the name a relic, probably, of a time when some long-gone tourist told his boatman he saw a bunny.

In the hardwood hammocks stand water oaks festooned with red-berried smilax vines, and jasmine that blooms in yellow cascades every February. The monarchs of the hammocks are the broad live oaks, bearing their eternal burden of Spanish moss, which is not a moss (nor a parasite) but a member of the tropical pineapple family. It draws its nourishment from the abundant moisture in the air.

The older swamp islands, the "houses," bear isolated patches of sand scrub. On river bluffs dogwoods bloom in clouds of white every March, and evergreen myrtles give off a characteristic tangy perfume. Some of the swamp is crowded with soaring cypresses that stand pale in the sun like the columns of Greek temples. In the water, golden clubs send up yellow-tipped spikes from lavender stems. "Never-wets," swamp people call them; the base grows in water but the club remains erect. Smaller pond cypresses and black gums grow in pools that are shallow depressions in surrounding pinewoods. There are also wide bogs of sphagnum moss; early in the morning their spiderwebs become chains of tiny diamonds as they are struck by the rising sun. Raccoons fish at the bogs' edges, and families of skunks often parade before onlookers.

Eighteenth-century naturalist William Bartram marveled at the profusion of environments in what he called the Ouaquaphenogaw. The

Creatures of the Swamp

Okefenokee's dark waters conceal the rich diversity of the life beneath their surface. There is plentiful food here for fish and reptile, part of a complex food chain in which the creatures consume the plant life—and often each other. Yet only the croaking of frogs is likely to give away all this underwater activity.

Creek Indians told him its islands were inhabited by incomparably beautiful women called Daughters of the Sun, "involved in perpetual labyrinths . . . alternately appearing and disappearing." English poet Oliver Goldsmith, reading Bartram's description of the Okefenokee, painted a vividly accurate picture of his own. He conjured up visions of

"Those pois'nous fields with rank luxuriance
 crowned
Where the dark scorpion gathers death
 around:
Where at each step the stranger fears to
 wake
The rattling terrors of the vengeful snake . . ."

Perhaps the most vengeful in the Okefenokee is the cottonmouth moccasin. There are chilling tales of men who have entered the swamp's depths never to leave them, presumed victims of the cottonmouth.

The rivers and creeks of the Okefenokee are full of otters, drumming marsh rabbits, wood rats, opossums, deer and an occasional rare Alabama weasel. Two rivers rise in the swamp: the Suwannee, which flows down to the Gulf of Mexico, and the St. Mary's, which empties into the Atlantic. The swamp's eastern half is covered by watery "prairies" that have lakes and islands of their own. Between lakes and islands stretch the runs down which canoes and swamp boats powered with small weed-shedding outboards can travel.

Most beautiful of the runs, perhaps, is Minnie's, which leads from Billy's Lake in the southern part of the swamp northward to little Minnie's Lake. Minnie's Run is an ever-changing pageant of cypress, water lily—and 'gator holes often so invisible that a boatman finds himself on top of a 'gator nest before he knows where he is. And sometimes, on the edge of some remote prairie past which Minnie's Run flows, dance the Okefenokee's rare sandhill cranes. During their mating season they move in stately minuets that climax in wilder leapings and whirlings until the flock suddenly rises beating into the rosy gold of distant skies. In every corner the swamp is full of life, and yet it can be so noiseless that the smallest crackling of a twig under the foot of some wild creature seems deafening.

There are three ways to enter the Okefenokee. All provide accommodations, guides and boat rentals. One is at the Okefenokee Swamp Park on Cowhouse Island near Waycross, Georgia. At Folkston, on the southeast, there is the Suwanee Canal Recreation Area, with nature trails, a wildlife drive, observation towers, boat tours and wilderness canoeing. At Fargo on the southwest, the Stephen C. Foster State Park provides camping and cabins. Stephen Foster never saw the Suwannee he made immortal, but the people of the Okefenokee know his song and they can take you through groves of blooming white *Itea* bushes to where the headwaters of the Suwannee rise. Here the naturalist's eternal hope of finding one of the last ivory-billed woodpeckers on earth may be realized.

For everyone, from the people born within it to pilgrims from cities of steel and concrete, the swamp is an adventure of perpetual discovery. Civilization and its amenities on the edges are comforting, but few who penetrate the wilderness for any distance are immune to the wonder and subtleties of its abundance or the timelessness of its tangles and savannas. To the unwary it can be dangerous, but to those who respect its treacheries and go equipped to face them the Okefenokee is an unforgettable place, harking back to the world's innocence at the morning of creation.

An open pond area, or "prairie," as it is locally known. These stretches, often surfaced with expanses of water lilies, were created by peat fires.

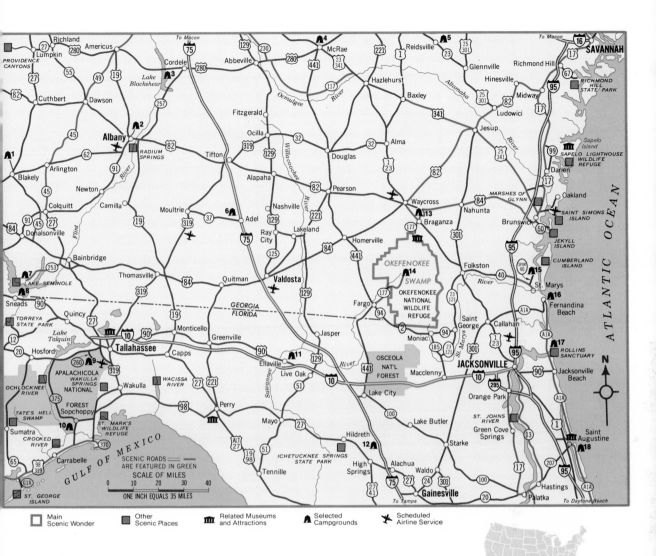

WITHIN A DAY'S DRIVE:

Sea Islands, Bubbling Springs and Wilderness Rivers

Crooked River, Fla. Ospreys and herons share the excellent fishing available on this winding, unspoiled stream overhung with cypress and giant magnolia.

Cumberland Island, Ga. The largest and perhaps the loveliest of Georgia's Sea Islands, Cumberland has a freshwater lake, an area of wild dunes and abundant birdlife. It has recently been purchased as a National Seashore.

Ichetucknee Springs State Park, Fla. The center of this new park is a short river fed by seven springs, one of them the third largest in the state. These keep the water crystal clear, and the river is a favorite of canoeists and snorkelers.

Jekyll Island, Ga. Once a club for multimillionaires, this island has been a state park since 1946. Alongside the resort facilities and the restored "cottages" of the rich are a nine-mile beach and a wildlife refuge.

Lake Seminole, Ga. (*Picture appears on page 108*)

Marshes of Glynn, Ga. (*Picture appears on page 109*)

Ochlockonee River, Fla. A canoeist paddling along this wilderness river might see a panther or a black bear in the dense forests that line its banks.

Providence Canyons, Ga. (*Picture appears on page 109*)

Radium Springs, Ga. For a small fee a summer visitor can swim in a bowl of clear blue water at a constant 68 degrees. The spring flows from an unknown depth at 700,000 gallons every minute.

Richmond Hill State Park, Ga. Although not far from Savannah,

107

Lake Seminole, *Ga. Ducks float in the misty dawn on huge Lake Seminole, created by a dam on the Chattahoochee River. Dotted with islands and fringed with state parks on both the Georgia and Florida sides, the lake is celebrated for the fine quality of its hunting and fishing.*

this new state park is on Georgia's wildest river, the Ogeechee. Lying so near the coast, the park attracts both shore and land birds, and its profuse vegetation includes wild orchids.

Rollins Sanctuary, Fla. Birds on the Atlantic flyway use this area of Fort George Island as a stopping-off place. As a result, trees in spring and fall are alive with migrants, especially warblers. The island also has fine beaches.

St. George Island, Fla. Empty miles of white beach, edged with palms and scented by pines and wild rosemary, line this largely uninhabited island. The sea life is abundant, and at low tide it is possible to wade out and gather oysters and bay scallops.

St. Johns River, Fla. The unusual feature about this lovely river is that it runs from south to north,

paralleling Florida's east coast. On its course it passes through seven lakes. For the most part unspoiled, it is lined with miles of virgin pine or with groves of orange, oak and palm. Perhaps the most picturesque spot on the river is around Picolata Landing.

St. Mark's Wildlife Refuge, Fla. The Canada goose finds its major Florida wintering ground among the 100 square miles of marsh, freshwater pools and woodland that make up the refuge.

Saint Simons Island, Ga. A long beach, brilliant semitropical flowers and picturesque old plantations are the highlights. Spanish moss drapes the island's ancient oaks, which supplied the timber for "Old Ironsides."

Sapelo Lighthouse Wildlife Refuge, Ga. The Marine Institute of the University of Georgia main-

tains a laboratory on Sapelo Island to study the marine food-chain cycle under ideal conditions. Off the island is a reef with excellent fishing and colorful tropical sea life.

Tates Hell Swamp, Fla. Highway 65 now crosses this swamp wilderness named for a hunter who wandered in it for a week after being bitten by a rattlesnake. Panthers are sometimes seen here.

Torreya State Park, Fla. Notable trees are the stars here: the rare *Torreya taxifolia,* which grows only within a 20-mile area, and the Florida yew.

Wacissa River, Fla. A 14-mile canoe trail follows this narrow, swift stream through some of Florida's pristine wilderness. The clear river, its banks melting into wooded swamp, flows south from Wacissa Springs.

Wakulla Springs, Fla. You can take a glass-bottom boat ride over the deepest of Florida's 17 major springs—which is also one of the prettiest and least commercialized. The river and bordering forests form a wildlife sanctuary.

RELATED MUSEUMS AND ATTRACTIONS

Perry, Fla. Forest Capital Center.

St. Augustine, Fla. St. Augustine Alligator Farm.

Sapelo Island, Ga. Sapelo Island Research Foundation; natural history and arboretum.

Tallahassee, Fla. Maclay Gardens State Park; local flora.

Waycross, Ga. (near). Okefenokee Swamp Park Museum.

Providence Canyons, *Ga. This spectacular phenomenon, 30,000 acres of steep-sided and multicolored gullies, some of them 200 feet deep, has been carved by erosion in the course of only the past century. Many of the canyons are still deepening.*

Marshes of Glynn, *Ga. Most of Georgia's coastal marshland looks like this from the air: an often inextricable maze of reeds and water. The lovely*
Marshes of Glynn received their immortality from Sidney Lanier's famous poem about them. The grasses seem to change color in the light.

Everglades National Park
FLORIDA

A cloud of snowy egrets skims above an Everglades cypress swamp.

Water Is the Key
to Survival for
the "River of Grass"

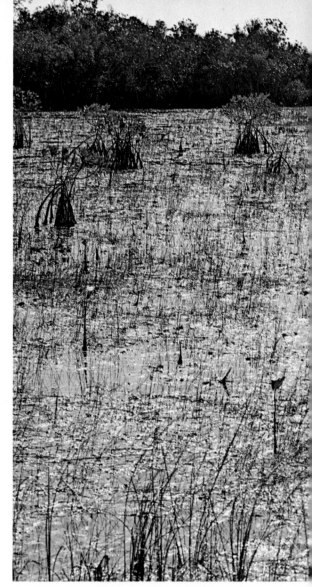

A mangrove swamp, like this one broiling in the semitropical heat, is in a constant state of renewal. The small mangrove roots will soon form

At first sight the Everglades are an unending expanse of tall grass, a wide robin's-egg-blue sky with clouds massed on a distant horizon, and occasional jungles of trees on small islands where the ground rises a few inches above a wet plain. Not exactly a scenic spectacular, yet the Everglades, eight feet above sea level at their highest point, offer spectacles of their own. From a stand of cypresses a flock of a hundred snowy egrets suddenly rises into the air, tiny plumes waving in a gentle tradewind. On the bank of a river there is a sudden plop as a crocodile submerges; he is not round-jawed and brownish like his relative the alligator, but a gray-green, with a pointed mouth full of vicious teeth he uses much more readily than the 'gator.

Slowly, in a clump of hardwoods, a strangler fig vine stifles a West Indian mahogany. Overhead ethereal ghost orchids bloom like snow-white frogs suspended in midair. A black snake slithers across a narrow path; he is familiar, but the West Indian gecko lizard he is about to eat is not.

As increasing numbers of West Indian creatures manage to make the journey from the Caribbean, the glades are becoming more tropical still. The Bahama swallow is a recent migrant, as is the fragile Cuban golden warbler. Mangrove cuckoos and anis have come to stay in coastal forests. White-crowned pigeons feed in plum thickets, and scarlet ibises flock vividly vermilion in Florida Bay. The Everglades are, in reality, a paradox: West Indian life can thrive in them if it manages to reach them, but

so can many North American forms, which find the glades more easily because Florida is attached to the mainland. Raccoons, otters, maple and hackberry trees and wintering robins live in labyrinths of Caribbean devil's-claw vine. Blue jays scream raucously from gumbo-limbo trees.

Geologically the story is simple enough. Southern Florida remained under water until the Pleistocene, or Recent, era. Westward in Collier County there are rock formations of an earlier period, the Pliocene, and these extend down into the Florida Keys, but in the glades themselves the peaty soil covering porous Pleistocene limestone called Miami oolite is less than 5000 years old. When hurricanes sweep mud inland from coastal flats, the soil

*dense thickets and the seeds will continually
germinate and put down more roots. Mangroves
are the only trees that can grow in salt water,*

*and vast stands of them crowd the amorphous
areas where swampland turns into seashore
along the southwest reaches of the Everglades.*

over the oolite is smothered and plants die
by the thousands. Yet new homes for such
plants are constantly being created. In the great
saw-grass marshes, alligator nests are built of
plant materials heaped two or three feet high.
When the alligators abandon them, they become host to colonies of red bay, leather ferns
and myrtle—and a new hammock, as it is
called, is in the making.

Coconut-palm-fringed salt waters are home
to enormous tropical turtles which on hot spring
nights lumber their way up pristine beaches to
deposit their eggs. On summer afternoons tarpons flash silver-green in shallow flats. Deeper
swim the blue parrot fish, barracuda, snook,
mangrove snappers and yellowtails. In the bays
lie huge cigar-shaped sea cows, the manatees

which history credits with originating the mer-
maid legend. The sailor who created it must
have been offshore too long, for the manatee is
anything but beautiful. It is a mammal lacking
external hind limbs; its forelimbs are paddles,
and it moves with the aid of a broad, flat tail.
The pastures it grazes are grassy beds of marine plants. In the bays porpoises frolic too;
when tamed, they are the staple attractions of
Florida marine shows. Porpoises are in fact so
common that sooner or later any fisherman in
the area is bound to see a school of them.
Rarer, though, is the pageant of a baby porpoise's birth. A group encircles the laboring
mother, and when the baby is born they move
inward and begin slapping it and throwing it
into the air until movement and breath are

113

assured, much as a doctor spanks a newborn child—and for the same reason.

Perpetually the geography of the bay islands is being altered. They are thick with mangroves, many of which bear seeds that germinate while attached to the parent branch. The seeds then fall, to grow more breathing roots, which soon become caked with coral, marine skeletons and shells. The caked material and the roots become additional soil. Flocks of seabirds congregate in the mangroves to fish and roost, and even as the birds adorn the mangroves they destroy them, for the guano they drop burns living plant tissue. Mangroves are

steadily in process of birth, accretion and death. They can be killed overnight by hurricanes, but the earth's only saltwater trees are ultimately indestructible because of their easy propagation.

Behind the mangrove forests stretch batis, or saltwort, marshes, which reek with damp decay most of the year, although during man-made or natural droughts they can become dry and in late winter are often ravaged by fire. Then the glades are enveloped in thick palls of smoke, and at night the horizon is red with flames leaping from salt marsh to hammock and occasional pinewoods. When fire strikes

Saw grass is a triple-edged sword: on each of its three sides is a row of sharp, spiny cutting edges, exactly like the teeth of a tiny saw. It is among the oldest plants known, and has grown in the Everglades for perhaps 4000 years. The palms are one of 10 species found in the park.

a manchineel tree, with its poison bark, the smoke can be deadly to inhale.

Today it is possible even for uninitiated visitors to see the most characteristic glades land, flats of saw grass (*Cladium jamaicense*) which can tear human garments—and flesh—to ribbons. Airboats, many of them driven by Seminole Indians, can skim over the saw grass. To many Seminoles in villages along the Tamiami Trail from the west coast to Miami, airboat tours are a living. From airboats, nature lovers can also see at close hand the rock ridges which look like landlocked reefs and are actually the remnants of former shorelines. These reefs, or hogbacks, shelter tropical hardwoods and a bewildering variety of exotic orchids, including mule-orchids, which flower unpredictably pale green or yellowish-brown or reddish and have leaves the shape of mules' ears. These plants are so highly prized by collectors that they were in danger of extinction before the Everglades were made a National Park; slowly they are coming back to something like their former numbers.

Everglades swamps are of many kinds. Some support savannas of cabbage palms. Rarer are the tall paurotis and royal palms of the ponds, and the pop ash and custard apple mazes whose pools are choked with burgeoning water lettuce. The freshwater snails in these places, and the birds that feed on them, tend to disappear when man-made drainage projects dry out their environment; the Florida Flood Control project north of the glades has given America miles of tomatoes and peppers even as it has diminished the wilderness. Men, not nature, now control how much water the Everglades may receive in a season through man-made floodgates bordering south Florida truck farms.

Among the most exquisite of the West Indian colonists in the Everglades are the hammocks' tree snails, which in isolation in Florida have developed new and striking patterns. A *Liguus* grows to a length of two inches; its solid colors are black, orange, lavender and brilliant white, and often it is intricately mottled. More than 50 designs have been discovered, and new combinations of color and pattern are constantly being found.

Visitors may enter the Everglades in one of three ways. Just east of the tiny community of Forty Mile Bend, on the Tamiami Trail, a short loop road with a public tram service leads south to the Shark Valley observation tower

overlooking an area rich in exotic birdlife. At Everglades City there is a ranger station where visitors with boats—canoes or small runabouts powered with outboards—may obtain information about what must surely be one of the most unusual trails in America, the Wilderness Waterway.

The Waterway is rugged, and its campsites are extremely primitive. You can zoom through it in six hours if you are good at following markers and don't care about the scenery, or you can savor it for days. It is remote enough to warrant rangers' cautions about backcountry survival; its reward is the incomparable love-

The Threat to an Ecosystem

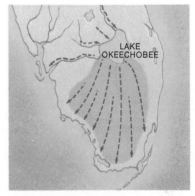

South Florida in 1880.

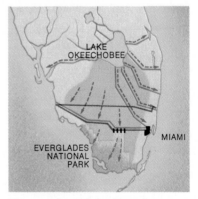

Now, with roads and canals.

The unique character of the Everglades was created by Lake Okeechobee, 70 miles to the north. Spillage from the lake flowed to the sea in a "river of grass" some 50 miles wide and less than a foot deep. The dikes, roads and ditches have diverted and reduced the flow. Sluiceways control the water, and the Everglades are now but a remnant of what they were. The critical balance of water, plants and animals is increasingly endangered.

"Hammocks" are islands of hardwood trees and other vegetation dotting the sea of saw grass that makes up most of the Everglades. Where rainfall is high, the hammock supports a tropical abundance of trees, ferns, air plants and orchids. Yucca and cactus grow on the drier hammocks.

liness of mangrove forests and a handful of sand beaches empty of humanity.

The way most travelers enter the Everglades, however, is by U.S. 27, which leads southwest from Homestead to the main park visitor center. From this center a paved road meanders down to Flamingo, where there are comfortable accommodations for lovers of civilization. Along the way, side roads lead to nature trails; Royal Palm Hammock and the Anhinga Trail, Pineland Trail, Pahayokee and Mahogany hammocks and Paurotis and Nine Mile ponds, where panthers may lurk. Are there flamingos at Flamingo? Only if you are willing to frequent the mud flats where they feed. Everglades country is not one of clipped wings and captivity. Tent and trailer campsites are provided at Long Pine Key and at Flamingo; at Flamingo, boats may be launched and rented.

It is all a wonderland of alternating limitless peace and teeming life, of wind-singing saw grass—and occasional violence. The pinewoods where red-bellied woodpeckers hammer are fragrant with resin. The heat of the summer sun is stark over the marshes, and the rainy season is full of turmoil when silver sheets sweep the glades to leave them glistening like forests and prairies of crystal. Autumn hurricanes hurl in periodically, churning and devastating and destroying and also building. Whole coastal islets are blown inland, and once again a habitat has shifted and new forms arrive.

If initially the Everglades do not amaze, finally they enthrall. For this they require time, patience and keen ears and eyes. Because they are a wilderness imperiled, their fragility is doubly poignant. The expansion of Miami threatens daily, and in recent years they have barely escaped a jetport as a close neighbor. But the miracle of their presence remains. Whatever their ultimate destiny, there is plenty of time to enjoy them now.

Osprey, or fish hawk

Black-crowned night heron

White-tailed deer

Little blue heron (immature)

Anhinga, or water turkey

Alligator

Black skimmer

Roseate spoonbill

Birds and Animals of the Everglades

Early morning, late evening and night are the most likely times to see the park's birds and mammals. Although the numbers of birds and variety of species have declined considerably from the once incredible richness of animal life in south Florida, some wading birds still roost by the tens of thousands at Duck Rock, on the park's Gulf Coast. White ibis, roseate spoonbills and many types of herons converge on this small mangrove island. Panthers and alligators are becoming rare in the glades, but colorful butterflies and other insects are plentiful, as are many species of reptiles and amphibians. Schools of dolphin are often sighted in the coastal waters.

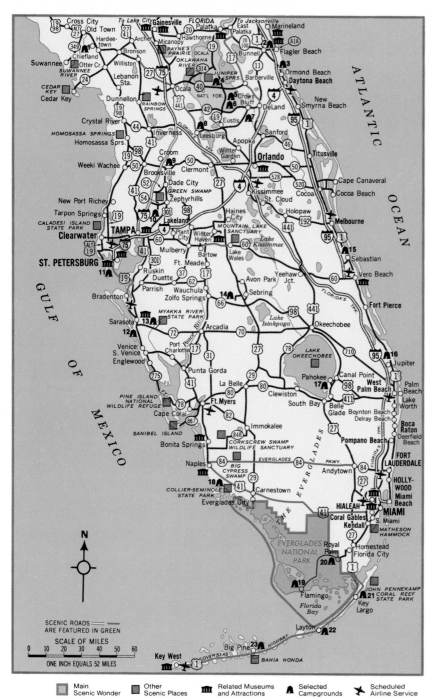

Caladesi Island State Park. An unspoiled white sand beach framed by Australian pines (*Casuarina*) and sea grapes awaits visitors to this tranquil area. It can be reached only by boat: a ferry carries passengers across from Dunedin. The vegetation is transitional between north and south Florida, and the largely undeveloped park is noted for its windswept live oaks.

Cedar Key. The northern limit of the mangrove in Florida is among a group of islands of which Cedar Key is the largest. Shallow launching sites and glittering water make it ideal boating territory, and trout and redfish (plus mackerel, in season) provide outstanding offshore fishing.

Collier-Seminole State Park. A particularly fine royal palm hammock exists in this subtropical wilderness. These trees are the largest and most stately of palms, with a straight, gray trunk that tapers into a smooth, green sheath topped by large, feathery leaves. The park area was the last refuge of the Seminole Indians, and their villages can still be found among the palms.

Corkscrew Swamp Wildlife Sanctuary.
(*Picture appears on page 121*)

Green Swamp. The southernmost true hardwood swamp in Florida, it is a strange mixture of hanging orchids—butterfly and green-fly —strap ferns, air plants and northern trees such as hickory and ash. Five rivers have their source here, and it is an excellent place for observing great flocks of white ibises, among the most spectacular Florida birds.

Homosassa Springs. A leisurely boat ride takes visitors along a jungle-lined creek where monkeys chatter and swing and water birds swim up to be fed. Pink flamingos wander among the trees, and an underwater viewing chamber puts you in the middle of vast swarms of multicolored fish.

John Pennekamp Coral Reef State Park.
(*Picture appears on page 121*)

WITHIN A DAY'S DRIVE:

Sanctuaries and Springs

Bahia Honda.
(*Picture appears on facing page*)

Big Cypress Swamp. Federal acquisition of over 500,000 acres has ensured the preservation of this area and protected it from private development. Along with Lake Okeechobee, Big Cypress Swamp provides the water the Everglades' unique life systems depend upon. It is an open forest of low-lying cypress trees and several unique species of orchids.

Juniper Springs. This recreation area in the heart of the Ocala National Forest is noted for its beautiful springs. The forest has one of the largest deer herds in Florida, the fishing is excellent, and Juniper Springs Run is popular for canoeing.

Lake Okeechobee. "The great liquid heart of Florida," as it has sometimes been called, covers over 700 square miles. (Okeechobee is an Indian word meaning "big water.") Wading birds are visible as much as a mile from shore because of the shallow waters: at its greatest depth the lake is only 22 feet, but it is the major source of water for the entire Everglades system.

Matheson Hammock. An abundance of unusual shrubs, strangler figs, lignum vitae, gumbo-limbo and Madeira mahogany may be seen along the trails in this combination of virgin forest and beach. Adjacent to the hammock (a dense growth of trees, shrubs and vines that takes root on slightly elevated ground) is Fairchild Tropical Garden, a large experimental garden filled with many types of tropical plants.

Mountain Lake Sanctuary. An atmosphere of planned serenity exists in the gardens here, bright with Indian azaleas and other flowering shrubs and trees. The home of publisher Edward Bok's "Singing Tower," the sanctuary has a permanent colony of flamingos and is a refuge for other birds as well.

Myakka River State Park. A boat tour and a nature ride by trackless train provide close-up looks at easily observed wildlife. There is a tower for viewing the great numbers of various species of birds and their large roosts. The park, like all Florida state parks, also serves as a wildlife sanctuary, where animals can roam free and unafraid.

Oklawaha River. Water hyacinths, considered a nuisance by Floridians, bloom in lavender extravagance along this river that runs through the scrubland of the Ocala National Forest. Its shores are lined with oak, holly and magnolia, wild orange and bay trees, flamboyant trumpet vines and clear springs. Fishing is superb, mostly for bream and largemouth bass.

Payne's Prairie. The time to see this relatively treeless stretch of land is in the morning, when its spiderwebs catch the first light of the rising sun. Wild Seminole horses roamed freely at one time; now cattle and their attendant cattle egrets have taken their place. Herons and snowy and American egrets are plentiful, and important fossils have been found here.

Bahia Honda. *Hundreds of islands, large and small, curve out from the southern tip of Florida, and about 50 of these are linked by the famous Overseas Highway from Miami to Key West.*

One of the loveliest of these Florida Keys is Bahia Honda, where the crescent-shaped white beach and alluring tropical palms are all part of a state park. This view is from the causeway.

Pine Island Wildlife Refuge. The shore is lined with coconut palms, and shelling is very good along the white sand beaches. In summer frigate birds are abundant. In autumn the refuge is a good place to see the rare white pelicans, which arrive in spectacular flocks of as many as 200, their sunlit wings beating rhythmically in the sky.

Rainbow Springs.
(*Picture appears on this page*)

Sanibel Island.
(*Picture appears on facing page*)

Suwannee River. The river made famous (although he never saw it) by Stephen Foster's celebrated song rises in Georgia's Okefenokee Swamp and flows down through northern Florida to the Gulf, fed by 55 springs. In its last 50 miles it is a broad stream bordered with cypress.

RELATED MUSEUMS AND ATTRACTIONS

Bonita Springs. Everglades Wonder Gardens.

Gainesville.
Florida State Museum; ornithology, natural history. U.S. Fish Cultural Station; marine exhibits.

Key West. Aquarium and Turtle Kraals.

Marineland.
Marineland of Florida. Washington Oaks Gardens.

Miami.
Museum of Science; nature center. Wometco Miami Seaquarium.

Naples. Caribbean Gardens.

Orlando. Central Florida Museum; natural history.

Palatka. Ravine Gardens.

St. Petersburg.
Aquatarium; marine exhibits. Sunken Gardens.

Sarasota. Sarasota Jungle Gardens.

Tampa. Museum of Science and Natural History.

Vero Beach. McKee Jungle Gardens.

Winter Haven. Cypress Gardens; local flora.

Rainbow Springs. *A little hill, rare in Florida, enables visitors to gaze down on the translucent waters of this beautiful spring. A paddleboat takes them along the winding, peaceful river that flows from the spring, and deep-draft glass-bottom boats give passengers a diver's-eye view of the colorful world underwater.*

John Pennekamp Coral Reef State Park. *Scuba and skindivers can explore the depths here, in the only underwater state park anywhere—and the only living coral reef in continental North America. It is the spawning ground of a myriad of bright tropical fish, which glide among colorful vegetation. Glass-bottom boats are available for those who prefer to stay dry.*

Corkscrew Swamp Wildlife Sanctuary. *America's largest remaining stand of bald cypress is here: many of the trees tower as high as 130 feet, draped with Spanish moss. Swampy ponds fill up with vivid water lettuce. A long boardwalk takes visitors through the refuge on a circle route to see its birds, orchids and alligators.*

Sanibel Island. *The best shelling grounds in the Western hemisphere are found on Sanibel's beaches. The island and its neighbor, Captiva, are linked to the mainland by causeway but remain quiet and unspoiled. The J. N. ("Ding") Darling National Wildlife Refuge is a saltwater marsh preserve for over 200 species of birds and other wildlife.*

121

Boundary Waters Canoe Area

MINNESOTA

Fenske Lake, here paved with water lilies, is one of thousands in Boundary Waters.

A Watery Hideaway That Lies Deep in the North Woods

The great evergreen forest of the north stretches from Alaska across the broad face of Canada to the harsh coasts of Newfoundland. Four thousand miles long and 500 wide, it dips in a huge arc across the northern reach of Minnesota and there spreads itself regally in endless, magnificent stands of black and white spruce, red and white pine, balsam fir, birch and aspen.

Interwoven by waterways, this forest is like none other on earth. Huge lakes, medium-sized lakes, tiny lakes, thousands upon thousands of them are strewn across the landscape in an intricate pattern of sparkling waters. Dotting the lakes are myriad islands, and connecting them is a lacework of streams, here wide and deep and placid, there churning through rocky channels in foaming cascade.

This splendid wilderness has the firmest of foundations. Ancient glaciers scoured the billion-year-old rock that surfaces here, and indeed bulldozed the basins that hold the lakes themselves. So the shores are solid to the step: shelves of polished granite line the islands and fingers of land, and in the coves between are beaches of firm quartz sand. Here and there great vertical cliffs of rock plunge into the limpid water, and spotted among the silent trees that everywhere crowd the shore great truck-size boulders rest. Erratics, geologists call them. They were carried along by the ice and

A thick carpet of pine needles allows even the most citified camper to walk quiet as an Indian through the woods in Superior National Forest.

left behind 10,000 years ago when the climate warmed and the great glaciers slowly melted.

The essence of this wilderness of forest and lakes lies along the Minnesota–Ontario border. Stretching a hundred miles along the American side is the Boundary Waters Canoe Area. Covering 1660 square miles, it is reserved exclusively for canoeists; no motors are allowed on the water. Since there are no roads, cars are out of the question. Even the airspace above is restricted. Lakes attract seaplanes, and after World War II there came a rash of fly-in camps and resorts. Roaring motors and the threat of getting knocked out of a canoe by low-flying planes proved incompatible with the wilderness concept, so airplanes were excluded.

Adjoining the canoe area to the west is the new Voyageurs National Park. Full development is expected by 1976, with all the facilities and activities normal to a national park. Across the border from Boundary Waters, the canoe country extends into Ontario's Quetico Provincial Park, 750 square miles of it, which is managed under the same rules. No border stations exist here. To the visitor, it is all one huge interrelated area.

Today the only sounds to be heard here are the dip of the paddle, the clear whistle of the white-throated sparrow, the scream of eagle or osprey, the clatter of ducks startled into flight, the murmur of distant rapids—and the occasional resounding clang of an aluminum canoe striking a rock.

In the evening the sounds change. As the setting sun turns the lake into a sheet of glit-

125

A hair from a beaver's underfur magnified 3000 times. The fur, an effective insulator, made up into the finest felt for beaver hats; trappers in search of it cut trails that helped to open and settle the Northwest.

tering gold the yodeling laugh of a loon floats across from the jagged silhouette of the opposite shore. Overhead the pines and the spruce sigh in the soft evening breeze, and around the point a beaver slaps the water as he dives. In the early summer, it is true, you will hear another, less desirable sound: the persistent hum of swarming mosquitoes.

And if you are lucky, really lucky, when night settles over the forest and lake, you may hear the grandest and most chilling sound in the American wilderness: the howling of the wolves. Wolves have many voices, and occasionally they gather and burst forth in a sort of harmonic singing.

This Minnesota country is one of the few places in the United States outside of Alaska where wolves still hold out. Once common throughout the country, they have been relentlessly exterminated almost everywhere. Men have always killed wolves, because wolves kill cattle and sheep. But here, where there is little stock raising, a new threat to the wolves has emerged: killing for pelts. A good wolf skin may retail for $100, and it is considered elegant by some to have one hanging on the wall.

Contrary to common belief, wolves are no physical threat to man, probably because, as predators, they recognize through thousands of years of association that man too is a predator and is best avoided. Sigurd Olson, who has lived in these woods all his life, tells of a time he was followed by a pack of wolves while snowshoeing across a frozen lake. He knew that at a point where the lake narrowed they might swing around to intercept him, and he had nothing but a pocket knife for protection. Sure enough, when he reached this point there they were. From 50 feet away the wolves stared at him, motionless. Olson stared right back. After a few minutes the wolves turned and went away. Olson is certain that the only reason they did not attack was because he did not show his fear, thus triggering their attack mechanism.

In the north woods the wolf hunts for moose. During winter, when the lakes are frozen, weak or sick animals fall easily to a pack of hungry wolves, but in summer the moose spends most of its time in or near the water, where it has the advantage. Thus, unlike the human hunter who seeks the best trophies, the wolf actually helps to improve the quality of the moose herd by killing only the weaker members.

A moose is an impressive beast. A large bull may weigh half a ton and stand seven feet tall at the shoulder. To see one browsing the lake bottom, flank deep, and suddenly raise its great bony head with a frond of pondweed hanging from its mouth and water cascading from its glistening palmate antlers is memorable indeed.

Black bears, coyotes, foxes and bobcats share the forest, too. A casual visitor is unlikely to see these animals, for they are shy. But the knowledge of their presence in the surrounding woods may make a city-bred canoe

Beavers made this hole in the forest by damming a small creek (the dam is the straight edge at the pond's lower end). The pond thus formed drowned the evergreens, and the beavers cut down aspens for food as well as dam material. The brown spot near the dam is the beavers' lodge, the sticks in front their winter food supply.

The Beaver's Amazing Abilities

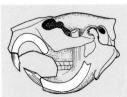

A beaver's strong jaws and curved incisors enable it to cut through trees 12 inches in diameter—a pair of beavers can fell a tree in 15 minutes. Beavers often sample the bark as they cut the tree into manageable lengths.

Inner flaps seal the beaver's mouth as it dives to the pond bottom to store food. Valves shut in ears and nostrils, and a membrane slides over the eyes so it can see underwater. Food is placed close to the lodge for easy access.

Stones, dredged up and carried in the beaver's front paws, form the base of its dam. Twigs and branches are piled on top, matted together with weeds and finally cemented with mud. Dams are repaired and extended year after year.

127

traveler seek out an island campsite, come evening.

White-tailed deer, raccoons, porcupines, cottontails, hares, red squirrels, minks, voles, shrews, white-footed mice, and of course beavers live here too.

The beaver is the most sophisticated of animal engineers: it purposefully alters its environment to suit its needs. A beaver needs aspen buds and bark for food, and deep water for protection of its homesite. Wherever it finds a suitable pond it builds a stick-and-mud lodge. If the water is too shallow it will dam the outlet, and if it can't find an unoccupied pond it will dam a stream and make one. Evidence of the beaver's work is everywhere—in neatly felled aspens on the shore, in a sheltered cove where a lodge stands out of the water high as a man, in a forest stream where one dam succeeds another like rungs on a ladder.

A beaver's fur is unusually fine. Each tiny hair is serrated. Growing densely together, the hairs trap oils and microscopic pockets of air to keep the beaver warm and dry underneath. But the beaver's fine coat was also a liability, because the qualities that kept the beaver cozy were also those that produced fine felt. In the 18th and early 19th centuries the most sought-after felt hats in Europe were made from American beaver fur.

The Hudson's Bay Company opened its first outpost at Churchill, on the west coast of the bay, in 1688 to tap the Canadian fur sources. The Northwest Company at Montreal followed, and set up a remarkable transportation system. Trade goods—axes, pots, needles, knives—were carried in 36-foot birchbark canoes a thousand miles to the western shore of Lake Superior. Here, in mid-July, these were exchanged for the furs brought down from the northwest by other brigades of paddlers in 26-foot canoes. The larger canoes were essential on the often stormy Great Lakes; the smaller ones could be more easily paddled along shallow streams and carried on portages.

Local beavers were cleaned out early, and voyageurs pushed over farther and farther, to Rainy Lake, the Lake of the Woods, up the Winnipeg River to Lake Winnipeg and beyond. And at last they reached Lake Athabasca, 2000 miles by paddle and portage from the fort at Grand Portage on the shore of Lake Superior. These voyageurs wintered in the north at a dozen posts. In spring they traded with the Indians for furs trapped during the winter and then set out, carrying 1500 pounds to each canoe, for the midsummer rendezvous.

The final stretch of their route follows the U.S. boundary through the heart of today's canoe country—Lake La Croix, Crooked Lake, Basswood River, Basswood Lake, Knife Lake.

Near the town of Ely, Minnesota, where outfitters will provide canoes and other equipment, the U.S. Forest Service maintains a visitor center with a full-size replica of a voyageur's birchbark canoe on display. Maps, camping permits and advice are available here. Sample advice: Don't choose the usual routes; pick one with a long portage. You may sweat a bit, but the bonus in solitude will be worth it.

The simple paths at the portage points were old when Rome was young. Indians used them a thousand years before the voyageurs came. This has always been canoe country. God and the United States Forest Service willing, it always will be.

About 350 years ago an Indian painted a moose, a cougar and himself on a rock in Hegman Lake, using the local iron ore mixed with animal fat.

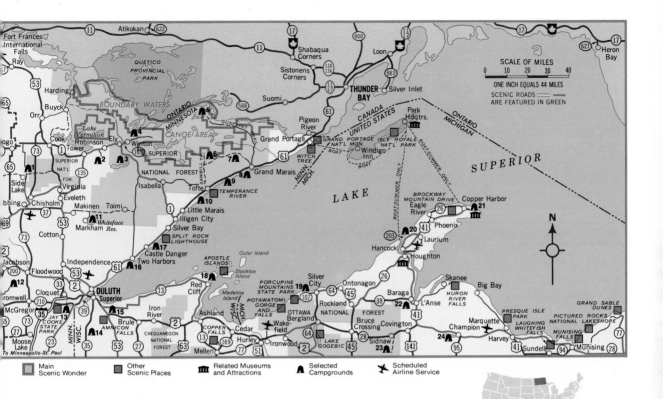

■ Main Scenic Wonder	■ Other Scenic Places	🏛 Related Museums and Attractions	▲ Selected Campgrounds	✈ Scheduled Airline Service

WITHIN A DAY'S DRIVE:

A Land of Waterfalls, Deep Forests and Splendid Lakeshore Vistas

Amnicon Falls, Wis. A state roadside park preserves several waterfalls, including Amnicon, and some unusual rock formations. Amnicon Falls is a series of golden-brown cascades spilling down the steep cliffs that slope toward Lake Superior.

Apostle Islands, Wis. (*Picture appears on page 130*)

Brockway Mountain Drive, Mich. One of the highest roads between the Alleghenies and the Rockies, Brockway Mountain Drive is a revelation to those who think of Michigan as part of the flat Midwest. Panoramic views of Lake Superior and the whole peninsula can be photographed from a scenic overlook.

Copper Falls, Wis. The falls occur at the point where the Bad River flows over the edge of the ancient layers of lava into a deep gorge. A nature trail skirts the area.

Copper Falls State Park offers swimming and fishing.

Grand Portage National Monument, Minn. The monument commemorates the voyageurs and their incredible journeys by canoe through the chain of lakes along the U.S.–Canada border. Nearby sights include the High Falls of the Pigeon River.

Grand Sable Dunes, Mich. Located in the eastern section of Pictured Rocks National Lakeshore, the dunes are piled on top of Grand Sable Banks, which rise steeply to a height of 275 feet above Lake Superior. The dunes cover about five square miles.

Huron River Falls, Mich. At the western edge of the Huron Mountains, Huron River Falls is set in a forest of towering pines and virgin hardwoods. Huron National Wildlife Refuge on the Huron Islands offshore in Lake Superior

attracts big flocks of wintering Canada geese and other birds.

Isle Royale National Park, Mich. (*Picture appears on page 131*)

Jay Cooke State Park, Minn. The park is located on the banks of the St. Louis River, which flows out of Lake Superior's westward-pointing finger. The scenery is typical of the lake's north shore: rugged, rocky and loud with the sound of waterfalls.

Lake Gogebic, Mich. The largest lake (20 square miles) in Michigan's Upper Peninsula, Lake Gogebic is noted for its good fishing, particularly for golden walleyed pike, bass, bluegill and perch. Among the wildlife often seen here are deer, black bear and ruffed grouse.

Laughing Whitefish Falls, Mich. A series of cascades on the Laughing Whitefish River, the falls

129

Apostle Islands, *Wis. A wind- and water-carved rock outcrop on Stockton Island, one of the 23 Apostles, stands out in the fog. The islands were left in the wake of glaciers that ground over this ancient land. Stockton Island, also called Presque Isle, is noted for its agate beaches and "singing" sand.*

drop almost 100 feet in a wooded setting between Hiawatha and Michigamme national forests.

Munising Falls, Mich.
(*Picture appears on this page*)

Pictured Rocks National Lakeshore, Mich. The lakeshore preserves a 15-mile stretch of richly colored sandstone cliffs carved by wind and water into caves, columns, arches and great jutting headlands. The cliffs rise abruptly from Lake Superior up to 200 feet above the water. The best way to see them is from the boats that leave daily in summer from the Munising dock.

Porcupine Mountains State Park, Mich.
(*Picture appears on facing page*)

Munising Falls, *Mich. The falls drop 50 feet over a sandstone bluff, another 25 feet in a steep rapids. Much of the surrounding area is forested, rich in wildlife and spectacularly colorful in fall. Nearby Miner's Falls is the highest cascade in Michigan.*

Potawatomi Gorge and Falls, Mich. The falls, in Ottawa National Forest, are two of several cascades on the Black River. This whole section on the Upper Peninsula abounds with waterfalls. Close to the Superior shoreline the land is veined with countless small rivers. Black River Harbor, on the lake, offers boating.

Split Rock Lighthouse, Minn. Built in 1910 to guide ships on Lake Superior, and retired in 1969 thanks to improvements in electronic navigation, the lighthouse is now the center of a state park. It towers 170 feet above the lake on top of a nearly vertical cliff. There is a superb view over Lake Superior from Palisade Head, a few miles north.

Temperance River, Minn. A series of rapids speeds the Temperance River on its way to Lake Superior. Stands of tall white pines add a wilderness touch to Temperance River State Park.

Witch Tree, Minn. A gnarled old cedar, veteran of countless fierce Lake Superior storms, the tree served as a landmark to voyageurs. Here they would get themselves ready for their grand entrance to the Fur Trading Post at Grand Portage—the culmination of weeks and even months in the wilderness.

**RELATED MUSEUMS
AND ATTRACTIONS**

Copper Harbor, Mich. Fort Wilkins State Park Museum; botany.

Houghton, Mich. Seaman Mineralogical Museum, Michigan Technological University.

Isle Royale, Mich. Isle Royale National Park Museum; nature center.

Porcupine Mountains State Park, *Mich. The shallow, fast-flowing Little Carp River lures fishermen with a promise of trout. The state park, highest land in Michigan, has an alpine air, especially at the jewel-like Lake of the Clouds.*

Isle Royale National Park, *Mich. A roadless wilderness of hardwood and evergreen forests, the island is home to about 60 timber wolves, which prey on the 600 or so moose that browse in the shallow lakes. There is excellent fishing in the island's multitude of lakes and fjordlike inlets.*

131

St. Croix River
WISCONSIN AND MINNESOTA

The river cuts a deep gorge between sheer cliffs at St. Croix Falls.

An Untamed Northern River
That Flows in Beauty

In a quiet and almost empty corner of northwest Wisconsin flows one of America's wildest and loveliest rivers. Its name, the St. Croix, is not nearly as familiar as Hudson, Mississippi, Ohio, Susquehanna or Colorado, but it retains more of the essence of what a river can be than any of these often misused waterways.

The St. Croix runs south for only 164 miles from its source near Solon Springs, Wisconsin, before it merges with the great Mississippi. In that comparatively brief run, however, it passes through a number of startling transformations, from a narrow river with a swift current and plentiful rapids to a final broad and leisurely stream that widens into a lake.

The landscape through which it passes is for the most part amazingly pristine; from the air two thirds of the St. Croix Valley looks as untouched as it was in primitive times. Since most of the St. Croix and its major tributary, the Nemakagan, have been designated by Congress as a National Scenic Riverway, the river may be allowed to retain its unspoiled quality.

The upper river is alive with rapids, and is a mecca for white-water canoeists. Among the most famous and jolting stretches is Kettle Rapids, a seven-mile run full of glacial boulders and ledges that is a challenge to the most skillful paddle. The entire river is fed by a maze of tributaries: the Snake, Sunrise, Apple, Totogatik, Yellow, Clam and Nemakagan, all

The northern reaches of the St. Croix, in Wisconsin, are so unspoiled that a deer is not afraid to make the crossing on a misty morning.

with rapids of their own—as well as countless minor creeks familiar only to local trout fishermen. The whole St. Croix system flows through luxuriant woods of maple, oak and ash, with groves of aspen, white birch and pine. Sometimes it cuts through high sandy banks of glacial moraine, sometimes meanders across rich floodplains colorful with flowers.

The upper valley is largely unsettled as far as the Dalles, the great gorge through which the river flows just above Taylors Falls and St. Croix Falls. Civilization, in the form of farmland on its banks, vacation homes along wide Lake St. Croix, marinas and motorboats and flanking highways, appears only south of here, after the river has broadened and lost its plunging momentum.

To understand why the northern and southern reaches of the St. Croix Valley are so different, one must go back 10,000 years to postglacial times, when melting masses of ice shaped two immense lakes. Glacial Lake Grantsburg extended westward into Minnesota. Its torrential runoff forged its way south, carving out part of the valley of the upper St. Croix as well as the broader valley of the lower river. Later another and much greater impoundment, Glacial Lake Duluth, the ancestor of Lake Superior, was formed as the mass of ice retreated toward the north. Unable to drain east to the St. Lawrence and the Atlantic because of ice blocking its way, the runoff forced a channel south from Superior, through what is now the Brule River Valley east of Duluth, boring its way through everything in

135

How to Recognize a Glaciated Landscape: Signs the Last Ice Age Left Behind

Wisconsin and Minnesota, in which the St. Croix flows, were extensively shaped by the action of great Pleistocene ice sheets. In fact, the most recent Ice Age, which ended about 10,000 years ago, is called "Wisconsin." The imaginary landscape shown here illustrates the plucking and grinding action of glacier ice and the deposition of rock debris as the ice melted.

A drumlin *is a low, stream-lined hill of "till"—rock broken up by glacier action. The drumlin was shaped by the passage of ice over it, and its tail points in the direction the glacier moved. An* esker *is a long, winding ridge of sand and gravel deposited by a stream in an ice tunnel. A* recessional moraine *is an irregular heap of till built up in front of advancing ice. A* kame *is a mound of sand and gravel deposited by meltwater. A* kettle *is a depression formed when sand and gravel settled over melting ice.*

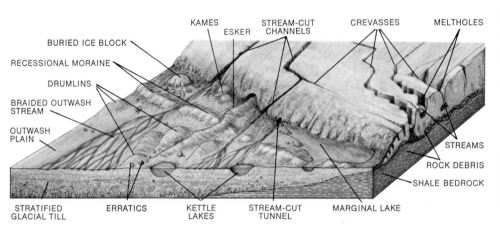

its path: huge deposits of sand, gravel and boulders from the glacial moraines, basic bedrocks. It even sliced through the deep gorge of the Dalles. It was this river that formed the giant kettle holes where churning currents, swirling and rotating stones and gravels over the rock, have dug holes up to 60 feet in depth. Beyond the Dalles the flood followed the broad valley shaped by the Grantsburg River, widening and deepening it even more into what is now Lake St. Croix.

The St. Croix Valley today literally teems with life. Fur bearers such as the beaver, otter, muskrat, mink and raccoon are still there. The big wolves are gone, but coyotes, foxes, hawks and owls keep to their predatory ways. The buffalo are only a memory, but white-tailed deer still live along the river, and on many evenings one can see them in adjoining meadows or along the water's edge. There are black bear, and sometimes even a moose wanders down from the north. Partridge and sharp-tailed

grouse are in the uplands, woodcock on the mud flats, and in the rice lakes and sloughs are mallards and black ducks. Wood ducks nest in old trees above the stream.

A wide variety of fish is found here: small-mouth bass, brown and brook trout, walleyed pike and great northerns, catfish along the lower reaches and even an occasional sturgeon. Great blue herons wing their way when disturbed by canoes. The rattle of kingfishers is a constant sound, and their flash of metallic blue is almost startling as they careen across the river. The great horned owl shrieks at dusk, and the pileated woodpecker loudly pounds away at some dead stub.

No wonder the Sioux and Chippewa Indians loved this river, for in its valley there were always game and fish, and in the north were the stands of wild rice they treasured. For centuries they fought desperately against enemies, both red and white, to hold it as their own. The Dakota, as the Sioux were known before

Near Taylors Falls, in Interstate Park, Wisconsin, the St. Croix has cut a dramatic 200-foot gorge in an ancient lava flow. The vertical jointing of the lava is clearly seen here. This gorge, the Dalles, marks the end of the part of the St. Croix preserved as a National Scenic Riverway.

being renamed by the French, lived in the St. Croix Valley long before the discovery of America. Then, about 1500, the Chippewa moved in from the east, driven out of their ancestral lands by the warlike and powerful Iroquois. A desperate and homeless people, they looked at the rich valley with longing. Hundreds of battles were fought up and down the valley until, in the 1860s, the Sioux were finally driven from the St. Croix. The battlegrounds were legion but are still remembered: Izatys, the Kettle, the Snake, the Dalles, Sunrise and Battle Hollow. Outside of small surviving bands, most of the Sioux moved west or north to escape their Chippewa conquerors, only to be banished at last by the whites.

During the mid-17th century, French voyageurs and explorers arrived in the area. One, Daniel Greysolon, Sieur Dulhut, for whom Duluth is named, came down along the Brule River in 1679 from Lake Superior, crossed the famous portage to the source of the St. Croix and continued to the Mississippi. Others coming up from the Mississippi included Father Louis Hennepin, who discovered Niagara Falls. Under the French regime the entire valley became well known, and trading posts sprouted along its banks.

When the British defeated the French in 1763, the French and Indian Wars came to an end, but the Northwest Company, the XYZ and the Hudson's Bay Company carried on the trade with undiminished vigor. The valley was prime beaver country but had an abundance of other fur bearers as well. With the War of 1812, the United States prohibited all foreign traders from using its territory, thus inaugurating another new era.

By the mid-19th century the fur trade was coming to an end, and white settlers began to occupy the lower valley of the St. Croix. Soon after the Civil War, loggers began moving in to cut the great stands of white pine along the river; for the next few decades the woods resounded with the cry of "*TIMBERRRRRR!*" as the big pines crashed to the ground. Soon the river was choked with logs bound for such mill towns as Marine and Stillwater. During the spring drives, where the river narrowed (as at the gorges of the Dalles), the logs jammed into enormous crisscrossed piles. It took brave men to blast them loose, and many lives were lost when the thundering timber came down. Thousands of men thronged the river towns, and when the drives were over, the loggers and "river pigs" spent their money in wild carousals and senseless battles. Then suddenly the trees were gone, the logs stopped coming down, and the river was as before.

Now, nearly a hundred years later, the violence of the past seems forgotten, and it is sometimes hard to realize all that happened along the St. Croix. There are many places, however, where the past presses in on the visitor so strongly that the old river can be seen and felt. One such spot is at the south end of Upper St. Croix Lake, near Solon Springs, where you can look to the north toward the famous portage into the Brule. One can almost see the birchbark canoes coming down from Lake Superior, or those from the Mississippi going upstream. On some days during the fall, when the shores are a panorama of red and gold and a haze lies over the water, the old wilderness is still there. Or perhaps at the Dalles, when the entire gorge is bathed in moonlight, it seems as if you can hear the banter of the voyageurs, the sound of their canoes, even the soft voices of the Indians above the rushing of the water.

It is good to know that the loveliness of the St. Croix will always be there.

That stretch of the St. Croix River south of the Dalles flows through a broad valley with low, cultivated banks—a very different scene from the wilder, rapids-strewn reaches farther north. Before joining the Mississippi, the river widens into comparatively developed Lake St. Croix.

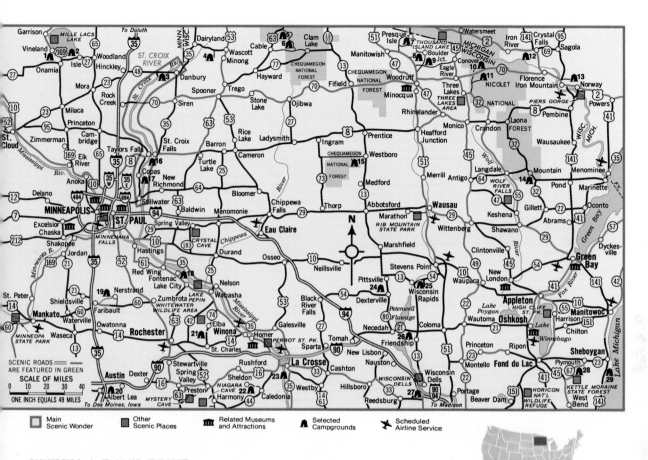

WITHIN A DAY'S DRIVE:

Mississippi Vistas, Myriad Lakes and Reminders of the Ice Age

Crystal Cave, Wis. The colorful limestone formations are illuminated by ultraviolet light in parts of the cave, producing some eerie effects. The cave contains 33 rooms on three levels, carved out by an underground river.

High Cliff State Park, Wis. There is a fine view out over Lake Winnebago from the forested bluffs here. Hiking trails wind among 829 acres of trees. Visitors can also enjoy swimming and boating on the lake.

Horicon National Wildlife Refuge, Wis. Although there are plenty of birds—ducks and other waterfowl—to be seen here, Horicon's chief interest is as a fall stopover for thousands of Canada geese on the way to their southern wintering grounds. Some sections of the largely marshy refuge

are open to hunters and fishermen at the appropriate seasons.

Kettle Moraine State Forest, Wis. A moraine is an accumulation of rock deposited by a retreating glacier, and kettles are the holes left by the melting of great chunks of ice imbedded in the moraine mass. The landscape of this state forest, preserved as part of the Ice Age National Scientific Reserve, is a record of the Pleistocene Ice Age, which ended as recently as 10,000 years ago. Among the other classic glacial features visible here are drumlins, or low, rocky hills smoothed over by glacial action.

Lake Pepin, Minn. Tall limestone bluffs line the banks of the Mississippi where it broadens out into Lake Pepin. The lake was formed by a natural dam thrown up

by the Chippewa River. Maiden Rock is one of the more spectacular cliffs, and there is a fine vista over the lake from Frontenac State Park.

Mille Lacs Lake, Minn. There is a shoreline 150 miles long around this large and beautiful lake, another remnant of the area's glacial age. A small, rocky island in the middle of the lake has been set aside as a refuge for the often elusive purple martin.

Mineopa State Park, Minn. Two waterfalls that roar down a deep gorge are the most spectacular feature of this heavily wooded park. Snowmobiling is a winter pastime here.

Minnehaha Falls, Minn. The "laughing water" falls made famous by Longfellow (who never

139

Wisconsin Dells, Wis. *Where the Wisconsin River passes through a 25-mile stretch of soft sandstone it has carved the rock into fantastic shapes. This view is of the Lower Dells in January; in summer there are boat rides through the Upper and Lower Dells.*

Wolf River Falls, Wis. *There are many attractive falls along the wild Wolf River system, the least harnessed in the whole state: Big Smoky, Keshena, Peavy, Big Eddy, Rainbow and—shown above—Ducknest. A scenic highway follows the river's most picturesque stretch.*

actually saw them) are preserved in a pleasant park in south Minneapolis. The 53-foot falls are surrounded by attractively landscaped trees and flowers.

Mystery Cave, Minn. A river disappears into white cliffs outside the entrance to Mystery Cave, reappearing as a large and beautiful underground lake inside. The cave, which is a commercial operation, is run in conjunction with the larger Minnesota Caverns two miles away.

Niagara Cave, Minn. An underground stream that twists among a maze of passageways, fossil beds and some weirdly shaped rock formations are special features here. There is also a 60-foot waterfall.

Perrot State Park, Wis. *(Picture appears on this page and facing page)*

Piers Gorge, Mich. The Menominee River tumbles over piled rocks

Perrot State Park, Wis. *The view from the top of Trempealeau ("Soaking in Water") Mountain over the Mississippi and Trempealeau rivers is one of the loveliest in the state. Other magnificent river panoramas in this area are from Granddad Bluff in La Crosse, and the summit of Sugar Loaf Mountain.*

between heavily wooded banks at this celebrated beauty spot.

Rib Mountain State Park, Wis. A 60-foot tower atop Rib Mountain yields a magnificent 30-mile panorama over the Wisconsin River and some of the prettiest country in the central part of the state. The mountain itself is the third highest in Wisconsin, at 1940 feet—and also one of the oldest in the world. It is a hard quartzite formation which geologists estimate was formed about a billion years ago.

Thousand Island Lake, Mich. A typical northern lake, ringed by dense evergreen forest, this is the largest in a chain of 15 lakes in Ottawa National Forest.

Three Lakes Area, Wis. Despite its name, the lake system here actually consists of a chain of 27 lakes, said to be the largest inland chain in the country. Most of the area is within the Nicolet National Forest, and the amenities encompass nature trails—including one through an area where nearly every known variety of mushroom is found—wildlife refuges, auto tours and canoe trails.

Whitewater Wildlife Area, Minn. Excellent trout streams winding through narrow valleys among steep wooded hills are plentiful here. At nearby Whitewater State Park, generations of beavers, working without disturbance by man, have built the biggest beaver dam in Minnesota.

Wisconsin Dells, Wis.
(Picture appears on facing page)

Wolf River Falls, Wis.
(Picture appears on facing page)

RELATED MUSEUMS
AND ATTRACTIONS

Excelsior, Minn. University of Minnesota Landscape Arboretum.

Green Bay, Wis. Neville Public Museum; geology, natural history.

Homer, Minn. Liers Otter Sanctuary.

Minneapolis, Minn. Eloise Butler Wildflower Garden, Theodore Wirth State Park. University of Minnesota Museum of Natural History.

Minocqua, Wis. Wisconsin Gardens.

New London, Wis. New London Public Museum; natural history.

Oshkosh, Wis. Oshkosh Public Museum; natural history.

St. Paul, Minn. The Science Museum of the St. Paul Institute; natural history.

Sleeping Bear Dunes
MICHIGAN

Sleeping Bear affords a broad view over Lake Michigan.

America's Biggest Sandpile Rises from Lake Michigan

At the base of Michigan's Leelanau Peninsula, on the eastern shore of Lake Michigan, lies a place of beauty and silence. Rising from a landscape of green forests and shimmering inland lakes, Sleeping Bear is a 37-mile stretch of massive sand dunes whose presence can be sensed long before their softly mounded contours loom into sight: the air seems to change color, and the horizon takes on a lighter hue from the lake waters.

This legacy of unspoiled Great Lakes scenery is one of the most striking sights on Lake Michigan. Steep, rugged slopes tower from broad stretches of flat white beach to a height as much as 460 feet above the sparkling blue water of the lake. In fact, Sleeping Bear knows few peers: it ranks in height among the biggest dunes in the world, exceeded only by some in Colorado, the Sahara and Saudi Arabia.

The Sleeping Bear Dunes are both remote and accessible: remote in the sense that most of their natural features remain untrammeled and wild; accessible because they lie within one day's drive of some 20 million people. They have been called the Cape Cod of the Midwest, the Riviera of the Great Lakes, and a staff biologist of the National Audubon Society was quoted as saying, "I know of nothing like 'The Bear' in the eastern U.S. or Canada."

The ever-changing nature of Sleeping Bear is another exciting facet of its character. Some of the huge dunes have been stabilized by

The Sleeping Bear Dunes rear up steeply from the Lake Michigan beach. Behind this sandy bluff lies a wilderness often more than two miles wide.

vegetation, a few are covered with forests, but the rest are still active. Driven by prevailing westerly winds, they are constantly on the move, inching inland at the rate of more than two feet a year.

As recently as the 1800s, three villages located along Michigan's western shoreline succumbed to the dunes' relentless advance. The villages now lie buried, forgotten by all but historians. Sometimes haunting remnants of ancient forest covered by the onslaught of sand reappear to stand lonely vigil, their ghostly trunks tilting against the horizon.

Before Michigan's first settlers arrived, Sleeping Bear was known only to the Indians and to a few white men who trapped and sailed along the eastern shoreline of Lake Michigan. Legend has it that the Indians gave it this name because the dark vegetation atop the great sand massif resembled a giant bear who had curled up on top of the dunes and gone to sleep. They also depicted the Manitou Islands that lie 12

Wind and Sand Built Sleeping Bear On Top of Ancient Bluffs

The mammoth line of dunes—shown on the right in an aerial view over Sleeping Bear Point— were created by sand that had been ground down by Lake Michigan and then blown on top of steep bluffs that lines the lakeshore. They are thus not normal dunes, composed entirely of sand. The bluffs themselves are part of a huge glacial moraine, a rock pile left by an ice age glacier.

miles offshore as the bear's cubs, on their way to the mainland to join her.

The Sleeping Bear legend is a very appealing one, but it tells us nothing about the true glacial heritage of the dunes. They are the descendants of great piles of debris left behind by retreating glaciers. These glacial moraines were eroded by the waters of Lake Michigan's ancestor lake, forming sheer bluffs. Sand created by the ceaseless pounding of the lake's waters was blown on top of these bluffs to create the huge dune formations found today.

If you want to inhabit another world, hike the wind-graded mesa atop the Sleeping Bear Dunes. Some people climb up the inland side expecting to see Lake Michigan spread out below—only to be faced by a sea of sand. It is two and a half miles across at the widest point before you reach the lake bluffs. The mesa seems a barren place, lonely and empty. Yet the early morning visitor may see evidence of wildlife in the crisscross of tracks on the sand: mice, squirrels, raccoons, even deer make nocturnal sorties here.

The topography of the active dunes is varied. The plateau is sparsely covered with cottonwood trees and beach grass. Scattered about on its surface are limestone rocks and boulders on which strange patterns have been etched by the windblown sand. In other parts of the dunes you will come upon the brilliant yellow blossoms of the Indian puccoon, the tiger lily, the bluebell and the wild sweet pea, all spilling color over the dun slopes.

On the lake side you will find only clumps of low juniper clinging tenaciously to the wind-whipped flanks of the dunes. On the beach lie weird and strangely beautiful formations of driftwood, shaped and polished by the sharp grains of the blowing sand. On its inland side, Sleeping Bear looms like a colossus over the resort village of Glen Haven and Glen Lake. (Glen Lake, incidentally, is one of Michigan's loveliest, with crystal-clear blue water.)

D. H. Day State Park, two miles southwest of Glen Haven, is a fine place to become acquainted with the dunes. Not only does it offer campers a place to stay or to picnic, it provides them with one of the world's greatest sandpiles. Adults and children seem equally to enjoy climbing the dunes and then running or tumbling back down again.

Nonhikers can tour the dunes in two ways. Dune buggies with oversize balloon tires make

Children probably get the most out of the precipitous, leaping scramble down the steep dune slopes—though adventurous adults join in the fun.

frequent trips out of Glen Haven. They take you on a thrilling ride over the dunes to the very brink of the almost perpendicular eastern bluffs. There is also a private park, Sleeping Bear Dunes Park, with a day-use picnic area and a scenic dunes road. You use your own car to travel the more than 14 miles of road cut through the sand and dense forest. Along the way is a lookout platform where you can enjoy a panoramic view over dunes, beach, Lake Michigan and the Manitou Islands.

Dune exploring is not the only attraction around Sleeping Bear. The more energetic can also swim, boat, water-ski or skin-dive. Those who prefer a more leisurely way can take pictures, watch the sunsets at Point Betsie and admire the picturesque lighthouse standing there, sunbathe or study the unusual natural life found on the dunes.

Others may want to canoe or take a float trip down the Platte River. Boat rentals are available where the river crosses State Highway 22; here also is Benzie State Park, popular with fishermen since the Platte River became one of the first Michigan streams to be planted with the famous coho salmon. During the fall run it yields fabulous fishing.

No visit would be complete without driving scenic State Highway 22, the old Manitou trail

over the top of Leelanau Peninsula to Traverse City. Along the way you will come upon the quaint fishing village of Leland and an Indian settlement, and see quiet lakes rimmed with stately resort homes and rolling hills dotted with bright red-and-white farm buildings. Stop off at Sugar Loaf Mountain and take the ski lift that also operates on summer weekends; it offers a superb panoramic view of Lake Michigan, the offshore islands, Lime Lake and miles of scenic countryside.

If your budget runs to boat trips at $4 a person, you may want to visit South Manitou Island. During the summer months a boat makes daily round trips. On the southwest corner of South Manitou you will find dunes similar to Sleeping Bear but on a smaller scale. They afford a striking view back toward the Michigan shoreline. There is also a private bird rookery and the largest stand of northern cedar in the United States.

Festivals and celebrations are another dunes area attraction. There is the March maple syrup festival, when Leelanau's huge stand of maple trees produce thousands of gallons of syrup; a spring cherry blossom festival, when ranks of cherry trees blanket the countryside in pastel pink, and a fall color tour at Glen Arbor.

There should be a final word of warning, however, to potential visitors to Sleeping Bear Dunes. The area became a National Lakeshore in 1970, but officials are planning a minimum of development so as to keep it in as natural a condition as possible.

And although the National Lakeshore boundaries encompass the whole stretch of dunes from Good Harbor Bay to Point Betsie, as well as the offshore islands and part of the Platte River and Glen Lake, most of this land is still in private ownership. It will take several years before Park Service officials are able to offer Sleeping Bear visitors the sort of facilities, in terms of camping, hiking trails and public access, that they would like to.

Meanwhile the existing state park facilities show the strain in high summer, with heavy traffic on approach roads, and regular turnaways from the campgrounds. So those who want to enjoy this great natural wonder are best advised either to bide their time until the National Lakeshore is more ready to accommodate them—or to avoid the height of the summer season. The experience of Sleeping Bear is worth whatever wait is necessary.

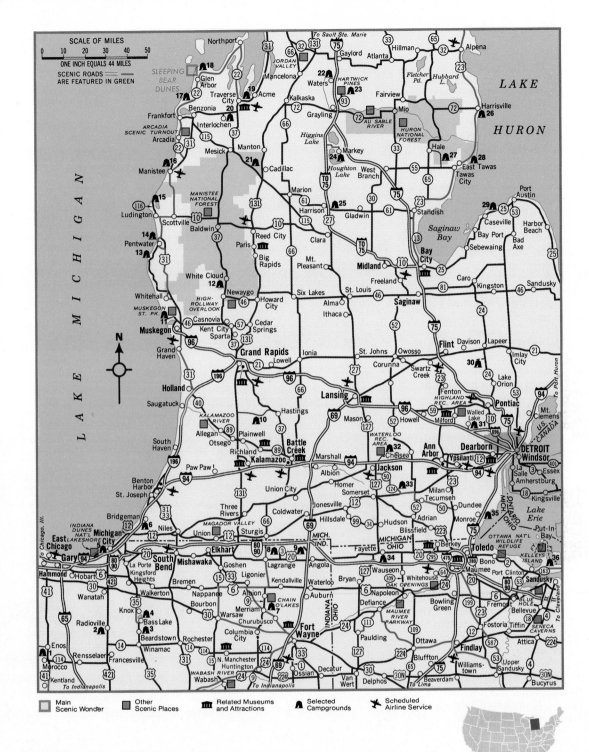

WITHIN A DAY'S DRIVE:

Forest Trails and Some Fine Fishing

Arcadia Scenic Turnout, Mich. Michiganders call this spot, a mile north of the town of Arcadia, one of the most impressive views of Lake Michigan in the state.

Au Sable River, Mich. (*Picture appears on page 148*)

Blue Hole, Ohio. Fed by rain and groundwater, including an underground river from Seneca Caverns, the Blue Hole is a clear blue spring in attractive grounds.

Chain O'Lakes, Ind. In this land of small lakes and wooded hills

and valleys above the Wabash River, Chain O'Lakes State Park makes a good base for a swimming, fishing and boating vacation. Readers of *Girl of the Limberlost* will want to visit the Gene Stratton Porter State Memorial on Sylvan Lake.

Hartwick Pines, Mich. The largest of the virgin red and white pines in this 9000-acre tract measures 150 feet tall and 13 feet wide. The Au Sable River runs through the forest, and the area is popular with sportsmen.

Highland Recreation Area, Mich. Roads wind over the wooded hills in this attractive upland forest. Hikers will appreciate the excellent system of trails. Horseback riding, fishing and boating are available, and Teeple Lake has a fine sandy beach.

High-Rollway Overlook, Mich. The view from the overlook is most rewarding at the height of the fall color season. The deep Muskegon River, which has the longest and narrowest valley in the state, first served as the road into the fur-trapping regions.

Huron National Forest, Mich. Trout fishing is one of Huron's biggest attractions. At the eastern edge of the forest are the fine beaches of Lake Huron. When the nesting ground of the rare Kirtland's warbler was discovered in the forest, a tract was set aside for the tiny bird.

Indiana Dunes National Lakeshore, Ind.
(*Picture appears on this page*)

Jordan Valley, Mich. The Jordan River flows through Pigeon River State Forest, and the Jordan Valley Wilderness Area is noted for its quiet beauty.

Kalamazoo River, Mich. The Island Queen Excursion Line boats leave from Saugatuck in summer for a refreshing cruise up the river through rugged, wooded country, much of which is inaccessible by road.

Kelleys Island, Ohio. Ages ago a mile-thick glacier plucked boulders from Canadian granites to the north and carried them to Kelleys Island, where the six-foot-deep grooves they cut into the island's softer limestone are still visible.

Magador Valley, Mich. A deep, glacier-cut valley extending from

Au Sable River, *Mich. This attractive wild river and its tributaries wind through many miles of northern Michigan's wooded, gently rolling hills, surrounded by campgrounds and ski areas. This view of the river's South Branch is taken from Canoe Harbor campground. The fast-flowing waters are ideal for trout.*

Indiana Dunes National Lakeshore, *Ind. Highways press on it, and Gary and Chicago are not far away, yet here on the southern shore of Lake Michigan the beaches are clean and the dunes roll to the horizon. The Lakeshore, which covers about 8000 acres, is designed to preserve remaining dunes, bogs and marshes as well as to provide lakeside recreation.*

Shavehead Lake four miles southeast to Long Lake, this remote spot has a quiet beauty.

Manistee National Forest, Mich. The town of Manistee was the hub of the white pine lumber industry in the 19th and early 20th centuries. Manistee National Forest (Manistee is the Chippewa word for "spirit of the woods") stands as a symbol of the new age of forest management: close to half a million acres of timbered hills. Loda Lake Scenic Area is noted for its wildflowers.

Maumee River Parkway, Ohio. One section, where North Turkey Foot Creek empties into the Maumee River, offers interesting examples of river geology, such as natural levees and alluvial floodplains and terraces. Missionary Island, across from Farnsworth Park, escaped erosion because its bedrock is highly resistant dolomite, which is exposed at the northern end.

Muskegon State Park, Mich. On the shores of Muskegon Lake and Lake Michigan, the park has about 1200 acres of dunes and woods. Pine and hardwood forests cover much of the dune area.

Oak Openings, Ohio. Famous among botanists, Oak Openings was once the beach of a glacial lake. The mixture of plants is unusual: where the sand is low-lying, swamp vegetation flourishes; but on the hummocks, flowers such as mountain phlox and gentian grow. Picnic areas surround three lakes.

Ottawa National Wildlife Refuge, Ohio. One of the few bald eagle nesting sites left on the Great Lakes, the refuge consists of cattail and sedge marshes, with colorful aquatic plants like pond lilies and spatterdocks that bloom all summer long. Waterfowl are the chief attraction.

Seneca Caverns, Ohio. This cave was formed by an earthquake, not by water, so there are no stalactites or stalagmites. But there is a crystal-clear underground river 147 feet down, which feeds the Blue Hole, 14 miles north.

Wabash River, Ind. The Wabash, subject of the famous song, drains some of the richest grain and livestock farmland in the Midwest. Salamonie River State Forest, near the town of Wabash, is a good place to see typical river scenery, and highway U.S. 24 is a scenic riverside drive.

Waterloo Recreation Area, Mich. Michigan's biggest recreation area, Waterloo spreads over 16,000 acres of rough hills, watered with many lakes and a stretch of the Portage River. Ponds and marshes attract a wide variety of birds and waterfowl, and fishing (mostly for trout) is fine.

RELATED MUSEUMS AND ATTRACTIONS

Ann Arbor, Mich. University of Michigan Exhibits Museum; natural history.

Battle Creek, Mich. Kingman Museum of Natural History.

Bay City, Mich. Jennison Trailside Museum; natural history.

Berkey, Ohio. Secor Park Nature Center.

Detroit, Mich. Nankin Mills Nature Center, Garden City.

East Lansing, Mich. Michigan State University Museum; natural history.

Fort Wayne, Ind. Jack Diehm Museum of Natural History.

Grand Rapids, Mich. Grand Rapids Public Museum; nature center.

Kalamazoo, Mich. Kalamazoo Nature Center.

Milford, Mich. Kensington Park Nature Center.

North Manchester, Ind. Manchester College Natural History Museum.

Paris, Mich. Wildlife Exhibits; mounted specimens of local fauna.

Richland, Mich. Kellogg Bird Sanctuary of Michigan State University.

Toledo, Ohio. Toledo Museum of Health and Natural History.

Traverse City, Mich. Clinch Park Aquarium and Con Foster Museum; natural history.

Mississippi Palisades
IOWA, ILLINOIS AND WISCONSIN

WISCONSIN

Mississippi
Palisades

IOWA

ILLINOIS

Wooded bluffs line the river near McGregor, Iowa.

"Old Man River" Looks His Best 1500 Miles from the Sea

Nowhere else on its long journey from its birth in Minnesota to the Gulf of Mexico is the Mississippi River surrounded by such dramatic scenery as where it follows the borders of Wisconsin, Illinois and Iowa. Here, spaced along its shores, precipitous limestone bluffs loom like giant fortresses, and forested hills roll away to blue horizons.

The ruggedness of the riverbanks is emphasized by the sheer size and the many moods of the "Father of Waters," from its wildness when winds whip it into frothy whitecaps to its more usual slow serenity. Little wonder that this magnificent riverscape, hidden in the flat agricultural heart of America, has been compared to the Rhine and to the Hudson River Palisades. (It was actually for the latter the Mississippi Palisades were named.)

Yet neither comparison—nor any other—is really fair. To its admirers, the beauty of this stretch of the Mississippi and its palisades is unequaled by any other river. And it is certainly unique geologically. Much of it is part of a formidable oasis (twice the size of New Jersey and shaped rather like an arrowhead) that was never invaded by the glaciers that covered most of this part of the United States in the last Ice Age. Geologists call it "the land the glaciers forgot."

The southern tip of this unglaciated region reaches just below 1716-acre Mississippi Palisades State Park near Savanna, Ill., which is

*The great Mississippi bears its burden of barges
past a solitary farm north of Bellevue, Iowa.
Most of the riverbanks here form a wildlife refuge.*

*Magnificent vistas over the river are enjoyed
by visitors to Mississippi Palisades State Park,
perched atop the bluffs near Savanna, Illinois.*

probably the best place to catch the essence of
the palisades. It is here that three miles of
bluffs rise like a great gorge wall, 250 feet
above the river at some places, so steep and
rugged that amateur climbers have died trying
to scale their faces. In piquant contrast, the
park landscape atop the palisades is gently
rolling country, with lookouts over sweeping
vistas of the broad river.

Unlike the glaciers, the wind and rain did
not bypass the palisades, but carved strange
likenesses on their escarpments. Among them
is Sentinel Rock, a 120-foot sheer limestone
pinnacle on which mountain climbers like to
practice; Twin Sisters, a pair of craggy look-
alikes on a single pedestal; and, perhaps most
striking of all, Indian Head, which could easily
be a gigantic stone profile of one of the Miss-

issippi region's earliest inhabitants.

For in ages past, Indian tribes lived, fought
and died on these Mississippi bluffs. The only
vestiges of their existence are arrowheads, pottery and strange prehistoric conical and effigy
burial mounds. While conical mounds occur in
many places along the river bluffs—and there
are some in Mississippi Palisades State Park
—the weird bird and animal effigies are much
rarer. (The largest group of these along the
river is at Effigy Mounds National Monument,
near Marquette in northern Iowa.) Some of the
nature trails in Palisades Park follow Indian
paths which may once have led to sacred burial grounds. Hiking these paths up the tree-
covered slopes with their vistas of the river below is a fascinating way to explore the park.

Another diversion is the fossils. Brachiopods,

pelecypods and corals are plentiful in the exposed rock at the park's entrance and near Indian Head and Twin Sisters—evidence that much of the land close to the river is heavily fossilized. The fossils in the park should be left alone, but others can be picked up by collectors in riverside quarries. However, it is not the fossils but Palisades Park's bubbling spring, with its cool, unpolluted water, that first attracts most visitors. Watercress, plucked crisp and cold from the tiny spring-fed stream winding through Sam's Valley campground, is another fresh pleasure. And spring sprinkles a lush crop of morel mushrooms, eagerly hunted on the bluffs.

Hikers here often startle deer but are seldom lucky enough to catch glimpses of another park resident, the nocturnal flying squirrel.

There is plenty of other wildlife to compensate, however. The river frontage is part of the extensive Upper Mississippi National Wildlife Refuge. Here bald eagles spend the long winter, migrating north only when the ice breaks up in the spring and barge traffic begins to move on the river. In their place male red-winged blackbirds, vanguards of the coming migration, sail in early; the ducks and geese make their courting maneuvers, and gulls call just as they do 1500 miles downstream at the seashore.

Spring brings other, more colorful changes to the palisades. Dainty wildflowers bivouac on sunny slopes and in shaded glens. Lacy ferns carpet the ravines. Along a typical river-bottom nature trail, cardinal flowers bloom in a glorious spread of red velvet, and yellow water

The Story the Fossils Tell: Creatures of Prehistoric Seas

At a time estimated as between 250 and 300 million years ago, the extensive Mississippi Valley area of the central United States lay under the waters of a vast sea; in fact the river has given its name to this period in prehistory, which is known to geologists as the Mississippian. The towering palisades along the riverbanks in Iowa and Illinois are composed of limestone and contain very large numbers of fossils, bony skeletons of tiny creatures that lived in such a sea. These are some more common ones.

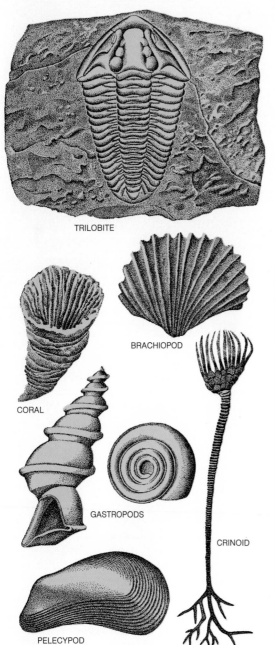

TRILOBITE

BRACHIOPOD

CORAL

GASTROPODS

CRINOID

PELECYPOD

lilies blanket the quiet reaches of the sloughs.

Come fall, the view changes from quiet beauty to a spectacle as exciting as exploding fireworks. The bluffs shimmer with the blood red of maples, the gold of birch, the russet of oaks and the fire of sumac. The colors seem to be intensified by the continuing greenery of the red cedars that cling tenaciously to the rocky crags.

Palisades Park, then, sets the scenic tone of the Mississippi River Palisades, though farther north up the valley the bluffs reach their highest around McGregor, Iowa, and Prairie du Chien, Wis.—more than 500 feet. And always there is the Great River Road, skirting both sides of the river. On the east, north of Palisades Park, it leads to the quaint old town of Galena, Ill., then to the lofty Wisconsin bluff (now part of Wyalusing State Park) where, in 1673, Marquette and Joliet became the first white men to see the grandeur of the Wisconsin River joining the Mississippi.

On the Iowa side, the Great River Road heads past Bellevue State Park, with its scenic bluff, good campground and resident population of rare pileated woodpeckers, to Dubuque, Iowa's oldest town and home of the state's first white settler. Here Eagle Point Park affords a bird's-eye view of three states, and from the waterfront the paddle-wheeler *Julie N. Dubuque II* takes passengers on excursions smacking of riverboat days.

Near McGregor rises Pikes Peak, which General Zebulon Pike climbed long before the famed Colorado peak that also bears his name. Now it is a lovely state park.

All summer long the river is a happy hubbub of barge traffic, water skiers, fishermen, picnickers—and bustling marinas where houseboats can be rented for lazy, relaxing trips on the river. Sometimes the houseboaters moor to one of the many wild islands in midstream, to swim and relax on the natural sandy beaches. Or perhaps they spend the night, and in a world seemingly remote as a South Sea island from the surrounding shore, watch the sun slip down in orange splendor, the stars grow big and bright, and the silhouetted bluffs turn ghostly in the soft moonglow.

Such experiences are all part of the irresistible lure of the great river and its tall cliffs. For many who have come to love this place above all others it is a constant refreshment, to be returned to again and again.

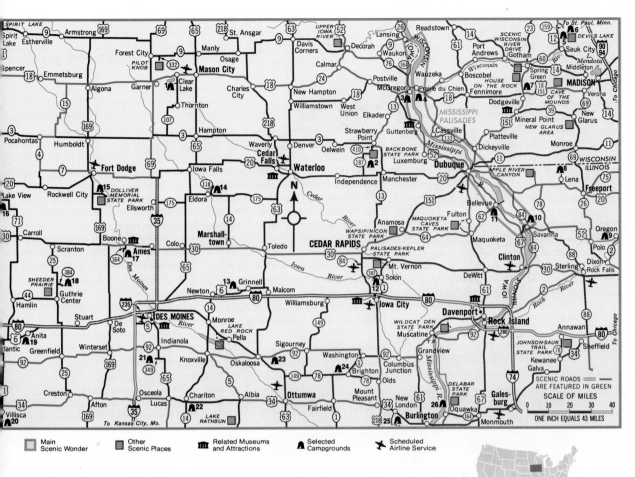

Main Scenic Wonder · Other Scenic Places · Related Museums and Attractions · Selected Campgrounds · Scheduled Airline Service

WITHIN A DAY'S DRIVE:

Peaceful Rivers, Gentle Hills and a Survivor of the Virgin Prairies

Apple River Canyon, Ill.
(Picture appears on page 157)

Backbone State Park, Iowa. A high ridge of rock running for a quarter mile along the center of the park gives it its name. Many marked trails lead through 1600 scenic acres—up rocky staircases, to caverns and along the banks of the Maquoketa River.

Cave of the Mounds, Wis. Cave pearls, or oolites, are among the very rare formations found here. The cave also contains unusual black stalactites.

Delabar State Park, Ill. Delabar is the site of an annual rock swap when rock hounds meet every August to display and trade their fossils and other stones. It is a

long, narrow, heavily wooded park along the bank of the Mississippi River—to which a boat-launching ramp provides access.

Devils Lake, Wis.
(Picture appears on pages 156–157)

Dolliver Memorial State Park, Iowa. The most unusual feature here is the copperas deposits found in a high sandstone bluff; this is an iron compound that was used by Indians for paint and dye. Hiking trails lead up and down steep slopes from Indian mounds to the Des Moines River, and an attractive trail follows Prairie Creek.

House on the Rock, Wis. An imaginative house built on Deer-

shelter Rock (a massive chimney-shaped formation 450 feet high) affords beautiful views. The house overlooks the Wyoming Valley, and off in the distance are the Baraboo Bluffs.

Johnson Sauk Trail State Park, Ill. Indian tribes crossing the Great Plains originally used this trail, surrounded by oak, white pine and maple trees. A state park of more than 800 gently rolling acres has been developed around it; 10 miles of nature trails allow hikers close looks at the spring wildflowers and woodland creatures.

Lake Rathbun, Iowa. The state's newest and biggest lake is also one of its most attractive, with wooded shores that are excellent

155

for bird watching. There is good boating, water skiing and fishing in the lake's 11,000 acres, and a new state park, Honey Creek, has been developed on its northern shore.

Lake Red Rock, Iowa. Red Rock Dam has created a 9000-acre lake. Its name comes from the red sandstone still visible in abandoned quarries at one end of the lake. The open waters provide plenty of room for good boating.

Maquoketa Caves State Park, Iowa. Well-marked, sometimes rugged trails lead to 13 caves, past balanced rocks, under natural bridges and around the tops of cliffs. Up to 75 feet high, these cliffs have overlooks for views of the valley and creek below.

New Glarus Area, Wis. The state's first Swiss settlement, this area is often called America's "Little Switzerland." It is a peaceful, pastoral place, with small farms creating a patchwork landscape. New Glarus Woods and Roadside Park provide 80 acres of hiking trails within an extensive forest of oak trees.

Palisades–Kepler State Park, Iowa. Nature trails follow vertical cliffs along the bank of the Cedar River and wind through beautiful white oaks to a natural stone arch and a honeycomb of caves. Lookout Tower provides a fine view of the area.

Pilot Knob, Iowa. Formed by glacial deposits, Pilot Knob, with an altitude of 1500 feet, is the second highest point in the state. Fertile farmland stretches out in multicolored patterns below the peak, visible as far as 35 miles in any direction.

Scenic Wisconsin River Drive, Wis. A narrow, winding road follows the lovely stretch of river between Gotham and Bridgeport. Canoeists like the river's remote wilderness atmosphere (no river traffic or loud boat motors).

Sheeder Prairie, Iowa. This is one of four areas of virgin prairie set aside by the state as natural monuments to the way it all once was. A spring or summer walk through the fields blazing with wildflowers is a vivid reminder of prairie beauty.

Spirit Lake, Iowa. The Iowa Great Lakes, including West and East Okoboji, Spirit Lake and other smaller lakes, form a popular resort area. Fishing for walleyes and northern pike and bass is good all summer. Plenty of open water provides fine swimming and boating.

Apple River Canyon, *Ill. The sparkling waters of the Apple River flow beneath limestone cliffs and beside flowery meadows. A 300-acre state park includes the most scenic reach; from above the river there are excellent views to nearby Charles Mound and Mount Sumner.*

Devils Lake, *Wis. Sheer quartzite cliffs up to 600 feet high dwarf the small, jewel-like lake, once part of the Wisconsin River gorge. Several striking rock formations can be seen atop the cliffs, including Balance Rock, shown here. A state park offers swimming.*

Upper Iowa River, Iowa. High cliffs and sloping bluffs exposing many layers of rock rise spectacularly above this relatively wild and unpolluted river. It is a fine place for fossil hunters, with some remarkable but currently undeveloped caves. The rapids-strewn river is popular with canoeists.

Wapsipinicon State Park, Iowa. Sandstone and limestone bluffs spotted with columbines and patched with bright green moss tower above the Wapsipinicon River at this favorite local beauty spot. The park also contains a large stand of white pine and several caves, including an ice cave. The fishing in the river is regarded as among the finest in the state.

Wildcat Den State Park, Iowa. "Steamboat Rock," "Devil's Punch Bowl" and other unusual rock formations may be reached by trails leading through thick woods. The undergrowth includes juniper moss, moccasin flowers and a wide variety of ferns and other wildflowers.

RELATED MUSEUMS AND ATTRACTIONS

Boone, Iowa. State Wildlife Exhibits.

Davenport, Iowa. Davenport Public Museum; science, geology.

Des Moines, Iowa. Iowa State Museum; minerals.

Guttenberg, Iowa. Federal Aquarium.

Iowa City, Iowa. State University Museum of Natural History.

Mineral Point, Wis. Mineral Point Historical Society Museum; mineral collection.

Waterloo, Iowa. Museum of History and Science; geology.

157

Flint Hills

KANSAS

Cattle and cowboys seem to be the only living things beneath the vast prairie sky.

An Ocean of Grass to Match the Vastness of the Prairie Sky

Kansas, generally considered one of the flat-test states of the union, actually slopes from more than 4000 feet along the Colorado border to 700 feet on the Missouri line. At the bottom of the slope, in eastern Kansas, lie the Flint Hills, grass-covered escarpments rising 300 to 400 feet above the surrounding plateau. They ripple down much of the length of the state, approximately from Marshall County in the north to Butler County in the south—though Kansans have been known to disagree about where they begin and end.

Modern civilization has not taken root in these hills. Because the flint outcroppings for which they are named make farming impossible, the pioneers traveling west and later the settlers who turned the lowland prairies of Kansas into some of the richest farmland in the country left the Flint Hills untouched. It was only in 1900 that a use was found for them. Farmers discovered that cattle grazing on the slopes quickly grow fat and valuable—in fact, during spring and summer one steer can gain as much as 100 pounds in a month. Agronomists now know that this is because the grass is nourished by deep layers of protein-rich limestone, deposited among the flint when the Permian ocean that once covered Kansas dried up some 250 million years ago. Today cowboys, cattle, wind pumps and an occasional ranch are the only signs of man's presence in

Light and shadow play on the gently molded green velvet of the Flint Hills, changing their apparent contours as the sun makes its way across the sky.

the Flint Hills—and along some remote back roads in Chase and Greenwood counties even these fleeting signs disappear.

Here the rock-strewn surface of the hills is buried under a tall sea of grass arching in the wind. Cloud shadows float across the shimmering surface undistorted by barns, telephone poles, fence posts or trees. While the rocky soil has kept man from littering the hills with his domestic objects, the grass itself helps keep the trees out. The grass roots grow deep (20 feet or more), thick and fast, soaking up all the available water and leaving little space between them for any chance seedling to take root and flourish.

Geologists believe that drought and fire have also contributed to the dominance of grass over trees in the Flint Hills. Trees cannot survive many dry years, but the native grasses—which require less moisture—can and do. For centuries before the white man came, any tree seedlings that managed to sprout were wiped out by the fires that regularly swept across the prairie lands.

The three main species of grass that grow on the Flint Hills are big bluestem, switch grass and Indian grass (see the diagram on page 163). They are called the tallgrasses because when left alone they reach a height of eight feet—though today, in most parts of the hills, grazing cattle keep them much shorter than that. The so-called shortgrasses, two to three feet high, cover the plains farther west.

Below the cliffside of the escarpments, rocky land etched with fast-running streams lies

161

*Cattle wind along a Flint Hills track at dawn.
The rich grass that grows on these limestone hills
provides fine nourishment for the beasts
that graze it—and ultimately, flavorful steaks.*

bleaching in the sun. In these watered gullies wild plum thickets and trees such as the osage, hackberry and walnut have managed to establish themselves. A close inspection of the cliffs reveals marine fossils embedded in the limestone layers. These lay on the floor of the Permian Sea until earth movements thrust the ocean bottom up as cliffs an estimated 200 million years ago.

The Flint Hills are home to a large prairie animal population. The hundreds of thousands of buffalo and pronghorn that lived here two centuries ago are gone now, but the smaller animals—rabbits, skunks, beavers, gray foxes, badgers, weasels—and birds such as the blue heron, horned lark, quail, night hawk and killdeer still abound.

The town of Eureka, on U.S. 54, east of Wichita, makes a good starting point for a 150-mile loop drive through the heart of this virgin prairie land. (At the Eureka airport it is also possible to rent a two- or four-seater plane at a reasonable price for a survey of the hills from above—a remarkable sight.) From Eureka take

The Grasses of Kansas: Tall and Short—and How They Grow

Though Flint Hills, like most of eastern Kansas, looks like a sea of level grass, there is much more variety to it than meets the eye. The tallgrasses (big bluestem, switch grass and Indian grass) thrive in the valleys, or lowland sites, because their long roots can penetrate deep into the rich soil and take up the large amounts of water they need. Tallgrasses grow from 4 to 8 feet above the ground; their roots thrust 6 to 20 feet into the soil. Midgrasses (western wheatgrass and needlegrass), which require less water than tallgrasses, grow to a height of 4 feet on the slopes, or upland sites, of the hills. The diffuse root systems of the 12- to 20-inch-high shortgrasses (side oats grama, blue grama) and midgrasses are adapted to the shallow soil on the hilltops, which cannot hold much water.

All the grasses of the Flint Hills, but especially the big bluestem, have more nutritional value than the same varieties grown elsewhere on the semiarid plains of the central United States —and that is why this is great cattle country. Steers grazing in the hills can gain as much as three pounds in one day. This is because the calcium-rich limestone leaches into the soil, and the grass roots absorb the calcium deposits along with the water, thus providing extra nourishment for the cattle browsing the grass.

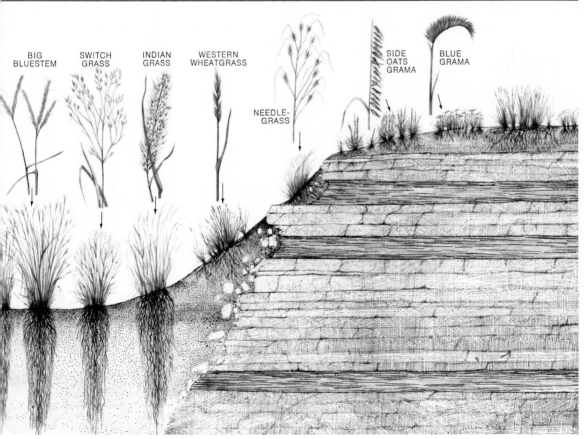

BIG
BLUESTEM

SWITCH
GRASS

INDIAN
GRASS

WESTERN
WHEATGRASS

NEEDLE-
GRASS

SIDE
OATS
GRAMA

BLUE
GRAMA

163

the county road up through Thrall to Cassoday, picking up State Route 177 north just before the Kansas Turnpike intersection. Continue on 177 (or any other county road that takes your fancy) to Cottonwood Falls; the county road from there to Emporia; and State 99 back down to Eureka.

Sunrise or early morning (before nine o'clock) is the best time to start out. Shadows fill the valleys then, leaving the hilltops ablaze with color: red in the fall, deep blue-green in the summer, rich brown or blinding white in winter and multicolored in spring. Colonies of wildflowers spread out across the slopes: wild red roses, Queen Anne's lace, larkspur, wild indigo, cornflowers, prairie clover, bergamot— more than 250 varieties in all. In any season the view across the tops of these hills seems to stretch as far as human sight can reach: from you all the way to infinity.

It is hard to decide which season in the hills surpasses the others in beauty, but fall is definitely the most exciting. This is roundup time. The hardworking cowboys—hats, chaps, boots and all—drive the cattle to stations where the young are separated from the rest of the herd

for eventual return to pasture. Many of these stations straddle the county roads, and the cowboys will not mind you stopping to watch and perhaps take pictures as long as you do not disturb the cattle or horses. If you drive through the hills in October or November, ask around a bit to find out where the next roundup will take place.

Covering this virgin prairie land and its inhabitants like a gigantic ceramic dome is the enormous sky. Usually it is robin's-egg blue in color, spread with soft cloud puffs and burning with a yellow, hot sun. But in the course of a summer storm the Flint Hills can suddenly and dramatically turn into tornado country. The dome cracks and discolors to a rough gray splattered with lurid streaks of light, and the sun disappears. The wind dies as if in fearful expectation of what is about to happen; no animal makes a sound. Then a black mass of cloud twists off from the horizon like a mad genie escaping from a bottle and races across the ground. But nothing disturbs the prairie peace for long. The tornado swirls out of sight in minutes, and the sun reappears, shining over the ancient landscape.

The most exciting time to visit the hills is probably in the fall, which is roundup time. Then cowboys herd the cattle to stations from the rich grazing land where they have been fattening all summer. Older cattle are shipped to market from here; the younger steers are returned to the grassland.

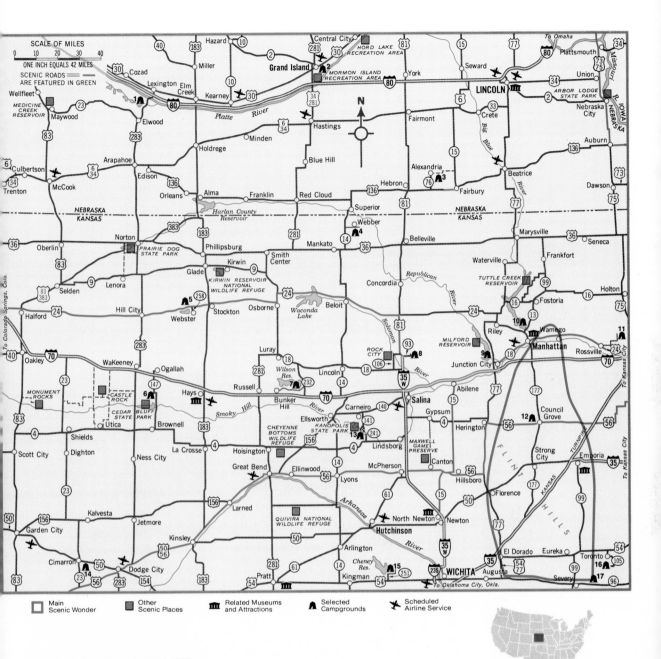

Main Scenic Wonder · Other Scenic Places · Related Museums and Attractions · Selected Campgrounds · Scheduled Airline Service

WITHIN A DAY'S DRIVE:

Carved Rocks and Game Refuges

Arbor Lodge State Park, Neb. J. Sterling Morton, the founder of Arbor Day, planted hundreds of varieties of trees here. Nature walks wind through the 65 acres; from some of the paths are splendid views of the Missouri River.

Castle Rock, Kan. Four chalk spires rise above the Kansas plains, the highest landmark (70 feet) for miles around. Fossils are embedded in the chalk, rem-

nants of the teeming marine life that lived here when Kansas lay at the bottom of the Permian Sea some 250 million years ago.

Cedar Bluff State Park, Kan. Cedar Bluff is an ideal center from which to make explorations into northwest Kansas. The 1400-acre park and reservoir has excellent recreational facilities and is also surrounded by several teeming wildlife refuges.

Cheyenne Bottoms Wildlife Refuge, Kan. Nineteen hundred acres of marshland and lake country provide a home for prairie wildlife and waterfowl here. Excellent hunting and fishing are available in the appropriate seasons.

Hord Lake Recreation Area, Neb. (*Picture appears on pages 166–67*)

Kanopolis State Park, Kan. A well-marked hiking trail leads through

165

Monument Rocks, *Kan. Wind and water have eroded this cluster of 60-foot-high chalk outcroppings into weird shapes. Embedded in the chalk are marine fossils, the remains of tiny creatures that lived in the Permian Sea which covered the Midwest 250 million years ago.*

Hord Lake Recreation Area, *Neb. A series of natural sandpit lakes like this lie along the banks of the Platte River (seen here during the dry season). Many of them have been developed for recreation, and offer excellent facilities for swimming, fishing and picnicking.*

Buffalo Track Canyon, where footprints of the buffalo herds that once used this trail are still visible on the soft sandstone path. Along the way are caves (used by early settlers as homes), and huge boulders fallen from the cliff. On the north shore of Kanopolis Reservoir stands Inscription Rock, a sandstone cliff covered with Indian petroglyphs, some over 1000 years old. Eight miles away is tiny Mushroom State Park, where sandstone rocks have been carved by wind erosion into mushroomlike shapes.

Kirwin Reservoir National Wildlife Refuge, Kan. Bird watchers are attracted to Kirwin's 10,800 acres by the multitude of waterfowl to be found on the reservoir and in the surrounding prairie and bottomlands. It is also a worthwhile spot for fishermen and boatmen.

Maxwell Game Preserve, Kan. Buffalo and elk herds roam this 2500-acre preserve, sometimes within sight of the road. The refuge manager will guide visitors who wish to see them to the best vantage points.

Medicine Creek Reservoir, Neb. County roads north and east from Medicine Creek traverse some of Nebraska's most striking scenery: a rugged terrain of canyons and gorges that have been eroded by wind and water.

Milford Reservoir, Kan. A dam on the Republican River created this lake, which has a 160-mile shoreline. Milford State Park, on the eastern shore, has excellent facilities for camping, fishing and boating.

Monument Rocks, Kan. (*Picture appears on this page*)

Mormon Island Recreation Area, Neb. The high water table in Nebraska feeds a chain of lakes along Interstate 80 from Grand

Island to North Platte. (When highway engineers dug for landfill along the proposed route, the holes filled up with water from below.) Many of these lakes have been developed for recreation; one of them, Mormon Island, is just off the highway, in a delightful roadside park—an ideal place for a picnic and a swim as a break from traveling the highway.

Prairie Dog State Park, Kan. The Prairie Dog River lends its name to this park. (Prairie dog colonies thrived in Kansas before the settlers came, but few remain today.) The park is noted for Norton Reservoir, which boasts some of the best fishing in the state, and for the pheasants and prairie chickens that live among its expanses of long grass.

Quivira National Wildlife Refuge, Kan. Quivira attracts both migrating waterfowl and songbirds, as well as the smaller plains animals—coyotes, badgers, rabbits, mink—that populated the prairie in huge numbers before the white man came.

Rock City, Kan. Erosion in the Solomon River valley has sculpted sandstone rocks into contorted spheres. There are 200 of them, ranging in size from 8 to 30 feet in diameter, dotted around this 15-acre area.

Tuttle Creek Reservoir, Kan. Four separate recreational areas are spread out over 1100 acres of prairie land beside the reservoir, which has excellent fishing, swimming and boating.

RELATED MUSEUMS AND ATTRACTIONS

Emporia, Kan. Kansas State Teachers College Biology Museum; natural history.

Hays, Kan. Fort Hays Kansas State College Museum; natural history, paleontology.

Lincoln, Neb. University of Nebraska Natural Science Museum.

Manhattan, Kan. Kansas State University Herbarium and Zoological Museum.

North Newton, Kan. Kauffman Museum, Bethel College; natural history.

Pratt, Kan. Kansas Forestry, Fish and Game Commission; zoology exhibits and aquarium.

Ozark National Scenic Riverways

MISSOURI

Clear Spring-Fed
Streams That Serve
as Canoe Highways

The broad ribbon of Interstate 44 across southeastern Missouri gives no evidence of the extraordinary country that lies less than a couple of hours' drive to the south: a country of hills and hollows, of quiet streams and deep woods, of names like Jam Up Cave, Pulltite Spring, Jerktail Landing and Powder Mill Ferry.

This is the Big Springs country, whose heart is the Current and Jacks Fork rivers; and 140 miles of these waters, with adjacent buffer-zone land, are now under the jurisdiction of the National Park Service as the Ozark National Scenic Riverways. It forms 113 square miles of a unique and beautiful area that is also the world's largest concentration of springs.

A turn off the Interstate onto Route 19 at Cuba points the visitor in the right direction. Immediately the road is writhing up and along steep ridges. Just south of Salem, signs point you to Montauk State Park, near the headwaters of the Current, and a fine place to begin a sightseeing pilgrimage through this fascinating country. (The traveler farther south, on U.S. 60, can make his start at Van Buren.)

From the opening of the trout fishing season on March 1 until the approach of winter shrivels the flamboyant fall leaves of its forests, there will be people in the wilds of the Scenic Riverways: anglers, campers, and with the budding of the spring foliage in warmer weather, sightseers and canoeists. Near the

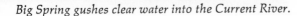
Big Spring gushes clear water into the Current River.

169

Current's source in the springs the water is always too cold for swimming (58 degrees Fahrenheit the year round), but farther downstream it warms up.

From a beginning at Montauk State Park, the traveler can investigate the entire area by car along back roads, by boat or—perhaps best of all—by a combination of road and stream travel. The float-fishing Ozark angler prefers the graceful scow-bow johnboat and reckons on 10 miles as a day's average. Eager canoeists can triple that speed. Slack-water stretches intervene between swift riffles in which the unwary boater can be "dumped." At normal water stage there is little danger of any mishap more serious than getting wet. Except on the lower river, a capsized boatman usually ends up in wadable water or finds it a few swimming strokes away.

Camping on the frequent gravel bars is traditional to the Ozarks. To this has lately been added both improved and primitive riverside campgrounds. Rental canoes and pickup service (at the end of the float) are available from concessionaires.

These Ozarks are ancient, a mountain range raised by uplift and eroded by water, wind and frost. In this region the bluffs are of limestone whose pitted faces tell of eons of weathering. Water erosion here did more than shape the surface; it shaped the subsurface too, in the form of underground stream flows that lace the entire region. These streams carved out vast hidden reservoirs, which are filled by rain sinking through the porous soil. The reservoirs feed the springs. Over the years diminished underground flows or changed courses have left explorable caverns, many of them large, with colorful stalactite and stalagmite formations. One such is at Round Spring, another near Van Buren.

From Pulltite Campground on the upper Current River to Round Spring is an easy day's float to sample the pleasures of the river, with opportunity to savor the scenery of bluffs and remote glens inaccessible except by water. Cross-river from the camping site a trail leads up Pulltite Branch to Pulltite Spring itself, boiling from the base of a bluff at the rate of 20 million gallons a day.

Chances are that the early-waking traveler will find the Current eerily obscured by river mist—the result of condensation caused by nighttime cooling of the air while the river

The spring-fed Current River can be peaceful, as in this stretch, but even at its calmest the river helps to propel its traffic along. Johnboats

temperature remains constant. Those out of bed first may be rewarded with the sight of whitetail deer at their morning watering, or the sound of wild turkey gobbling on the flanking high ridges.

The forest bordering the Current is mixed: predominantly oak and hickory and shortleaf pine, with incursions of maple, sycamore, birch, cedar and others. Birdlife is abundant; more than 200 species are to be seen and heard in season, including many warblers. Passage around a river bend may startle a great blue heron, and that riveting-machine racket could be the rare pileated woodpecker.

At night, raccoon and opossum emerge from their retreats; sleep comes to the sounds of

are usually equal to the challenge of the occasional riffles and rapids. More campsites are now being built on the wooded banks along the streams to meet a growing demand from canoeists and other river travelers, but the Scenic Riverways area still contains some quiet corners.

hoot and screech owls, bobwhite quail, whippoorwills and remorseless forest insects like the cicada. The spine-chilling scream of a bobcat could make for a raucous awakening. Rabbits and squirrels abound, and deer and small-game hunters rendezvous here in late autumn and winter.

Flowering dogwood and redbud first signal the arrival of spring, a spectacular season in these parts; as the dogwood fades, the flowers of high summer begin to bloom. Flowers are abundant here, and the floral season long. Many are indigenous to the waterside meadows, others thrive on the wooded hills. A few, such as some species of sweet William, the Missouri primrose and a species of aster, are unique to this region. Nature trails are marked in the park areas (Round, Big and Alley springs). There are lecturing naturalists here in tourist season.

A leisurely float down the Current will allow time to cast a line for the Ozarks' most famous fighting fish, the smallmouth bass—with red bass ("goggle-eye") and bluegill as alternative prizes. Trout are confined to the stocked area by Montauk Springs.

All along the river the springs are evident, flowing from bluff walls, bubbling from gravel bars, rising from the streambed itself. Round Spring boils up in a great circular hole caused by the collapse of a cavern roof. A path descends to the spring, where the traveler finds

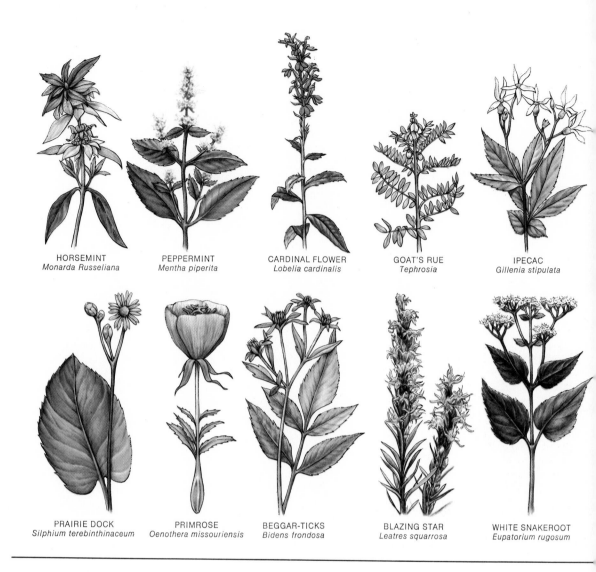

HORSEMINT
Monarda Russeliana

PEPPERMINT
Mentha piperita

CARDINAL FLOWER
Lobelia cardinalis

GOAT'S RUE
Tephrosia

IPECAC
Gillenia stipulata

PRAIRIE DOCK
Silphium terebinthinaceum

PRIMROSE
Oenothera missouriensis

BEGGAR-TICKS
Bidens frondosa

BLAZING STAR
Leatres squarrosa

WHITE SNAKEROOT
Eupatorium rugosum

an air-conditioning effect from the water's cool temperature. Nearby is Sinking Creek, whose waters bore through a massive ridge to form a natural bridge.

Leaving the river for a while, and resuming travel by car, you can follow Route 19 on its twisting course to the south. A scenic turnout offers a breathtaking view of remote folded hills. A bronze marker recounts the history of the region. From here the road continues to the Jacks Fork River crossing at Eminence, a small county seat clinging to a hillside. A short side trip west from here takes you to picturesque Alley Springs, with its historic red mill restored to occasional operation for the edification of visitors. The spring, which surges from the base of a curving bluff, has a flow of nearly 90 million gallons a day.

To the east lies Powder Mill Ferry, a cable ferry once propelled only by the flow of the river, but now augmented by outboard motor. This is the heart of the Scenic Riverways, and a trip across brings one to the interpretive Visitor Center of the Park Service, which plans to restore the ferry to its original current power.

There are more scenic float water, springs, caves and bluffs along the Current and Jacks Fork, but the climax must come at Van Buren's nearby Big Spring. Its awesome flow from a massive bluff face in a setting of huge trees and variegated plant life catches the essence of this Ozark region—an escape from the congestion and pressure of urban life, a friendly corner where beauty, recreation and relaxation are delightfully combined.

A national survey recently reported that the Ozarks region is one of the seven most attractive and pollution-free living areas in the United States. This is a statement a visitor finds easy to believe.

SPRING BEAUTY
Claytonia virginca

SWEET WILLIAM
Phlox pilosa

A Rich Spread of Wildflowers—and Why

The profusion of plant species found in the Ozarks (about 1500 have been identified) is partly because the region was never covered by glaciers. During the last Ice Age, northern plant species spread south to the area of the Ozarks ahead of the glaciers. As the glaciers melted, southern species moved north. They met here. The Ozarks are also a botanical crossroads, at the heart of the continent. So plants have migrated here from east and west.

Watery Caverns that Feed the River

Cave Spring, one of the many to be found in this area, flows into the Current River from the base of a high limestone cliff. In mountainous terrain like the Ozarks system, groundwater quickly filters down through the porous limestone that overlies the mountains' granite base. This action dissolves the limestone and hollows out great systems of underground caverns. Eventually the water inside these caves emerges at a lower level as springs, typically along the sides of river valleys. This is the source of the enormous springs that feed the Current, Jacks Fork and neighboring Eleven Point rivers.

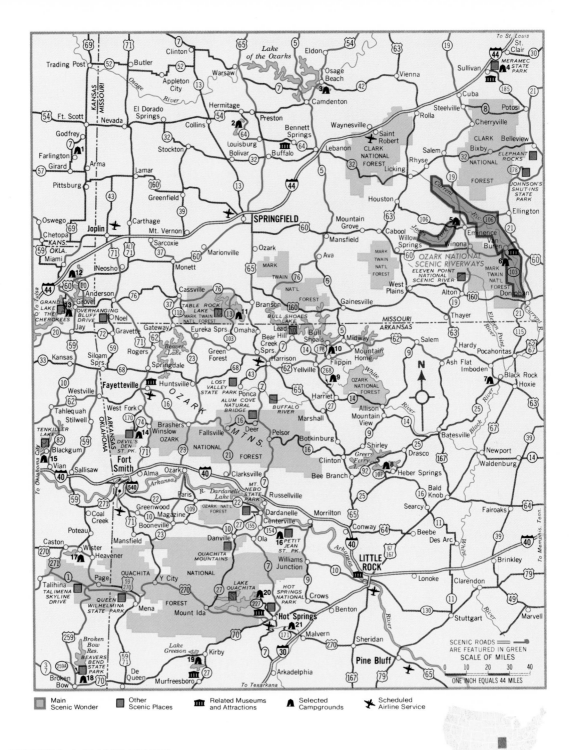

WITHIN A DAY'S DRIVE:

Wild Rivers, Lakes and Lost Valleys

Alum Cove Natural Bridge, Ark. You can walk to the top of this handsome natural bridge, which is 130 feet long and 20 feet wide and located in the heart of the Ozark National Forest. The Natural Bridge Scenic Area, 320 acres surrounding the bridge, is filled with typical Ozark hardwoods: white oak, red and black gum, beech, black cherry and hickory.

Beavers Bend State Park, Okla. The clear waters of the Mountain Fork River run through the park, populated with many species of game fish. A variety of water sports can be enjoyed at nearby Broken Bow Reservoir, with the rugged Kiamichi Mountains as a backdrop.

Buffalo National River, Ark. *(Picture appears on facing page)*

Bull Shoals Lake, Ark. and Mo. Spread out between Missouri and

Arkansas like a dragon with many arms, Bull Shoals Lake is a mecca for fishermen: lunker bass are their commonest catch. Nineteen recreation areas are scattered along the thousand-odd miles of shoreline. The lake is fed by the White River, flowing down from the Ozarks.

Devil's Den State Park, Ark. Gaping cracks and crevices in the high sandstone bluffs have been eroded by wind and water; earth movements have twisted the rocks into weird formations. Hiking paths and bridle trails lead through this rough terrain in the Boston Mountains. Lee's Creek and a small lake provide a choice of good fishing spots within the park.

Elephant Rocks, Mo. These enormous rocks are thought to be the oldest exposed granite rocks in North America. The largest, weighing about 680 tons, is approximately 1.2 billion years old. Some rocks have been rounded and polished by the elements, others eroded into grotesque shapes that resemble animals—including elephants. Visitors can walk a path among the boulders or scramble up on top of them.

Eleven Point National Scenic River, Mo. A 40-mile stretch of clear, spring-fed water in Mark Twain National Forest, the Eleven Point is most famous for Greer Spring, at its upper end. One of the largest in the state, the spring flows for over a mile through a wild forested gorge. At the river's lower end is the Narrows Aquatic Farm, a complex of springs in a bluff-bound valley.

Grand Lake o' the Cherokees, Okla. White bass fishing is excellent in this large impoundment of the Grand River. The lake lies on the western slopes of the Ozarks, which are covered with dogwood and wild cherry, oak, sycamore and maple. With a 1300-mile shoreline and over 46,000 acres of water, Grand Lake deserves its name.

Hot Springs National Park, Ark. Ringed round by five wooded mountains, Hot Springs is both city and park. The 47 springs, which lie along a fault in the

Buffalo River, *Ark. The Buffalo, swinging from one side of its narrow valley to the other, has carved towering limestone bluffs on the outside curve of each bend. This is Roark Bluff, near Ponca, where many float trips begin. The free-flowing Buffalo is a National Scenic Riverway.*

Ouachita Mountains, *Ark. This view of the Oua-chitas, near Danville, shows the deep valleys formed by thrusting earth movements that bent* *and twisted the underlying beds of shale and sandstone. The nearby Ozarks, twice as old, are more rounded, built of limestone and dolomite.*

earth's crust, have a combined flow of more than a million gallons a day at an average temperature of 143 degrees. Two springs are kept open so visitors can see how the waters boil up; the others are sealed and their waters cooled and piped to central reservoirs. Hiking trails and bridle paths lead through nearby woods.

Johnson's Shut-ins State Park, Mo.
(Picture appears on facing page)

Lake Ouachita, Ark. Scuba divers delight in the unusually clear water of this island-studded lake on the Ouachita River. It is also famous for its bass, crappie and bream fishing. A state park on its shore has facilities for fishing, boating and water sports, and the pine-clad Ouachita Mountains beckon nature lovers with miles of hiking trails.

Lost Valley State Park, Ark.
(Picture appears on facing page)

Meramec State Park, Mo. The Meramec River cuts through rugged, forested hills, providing a wilderness setting for fishing, swimming and boating. Deer are often seen from the nature trails in the woods. Fisher's Cave, in the park, is the biggest of about 20 caves in the area. Meramec Caverns, a commercially operated cave, has an underground river, a waterfall that rumbles eerily through the chambers and some impressive formations

Mount Nebo State Park, Ark. The summit of Mount Nebo, at 1800 feet, provides a fine view of the surrounding mountain scenery, which can also be experienced more actively on the many miles of hiking trails. The park's swimming pool is perched on the

mountain crest and has a sweeping view of Lake Dardanelle and the river valley. Boats, including houseboats, can be rented.

Ouachita Mountains, Ark.
(Picture appears on this page)

Overhanging Bluff Drive, Mo. From Noel north to Lanagan on Route 59, this scenic road crosses St. Clair Lake on the Elk River and runs beneath overhanging limestone bluffs that seem about to topple over onto the road.

Petit Jean State Park, Ark. Deep mountain gorges and large tracts of dense forest are the highlights of this spectacular park. There are plenty of trails into remote areas, and Lake Bailey provides fishing and swimming.

Queen Wilhelmina State Park, Ark. The handsome inn here is a relic of the time when this lofty park, nearly 3000 feet up on Rich Mountain, was a retreat for the wealthy. Now it is open to all as one of Arkansas' most popular parks. Mountain slopes are covered with a remarkable variety of plant life, some of which is subtropical. Nature trails and a deer forest, as well as a miniature railroad, are park features.

Table Rock Lake, Mo. Of all Missouri's lakes, Table Rock has the longest and most scenic vistas from the highways that cross and circle it. A state park here offers boating, fishing and swimming.

Talimena Skyline Drive, Okla. Traversing the highly picturesque northern section of the Ouachita National Forest, the road offers motorists a memorable experience as it follows the crest of Winding Stair Mountain through unspoiled wilderness country, with numerous scenic overlooks and hiking trails that lead off them. A popular stopping place along the drive is 90-acre Cedar Lake.

Tenkiller Lake, Okla. Fed by the clear, pure waters of the Illinois River, Tenkiller is a favorite with scuba divers and campers alike. Set in heavily wooded hills, the 12,500-acre lake has many coves that offer a wide choice of fishing and camping sites. A state park has complete facilities for water sports and family recreation.

RELATED MUSEUMS AND ATTRACTIONS

Fayetteville, Ark. University of Arkansas Museum; geology and natural history.

Hot Springs, Ark. Hot Springs National Park Museum.

Lebanon, Mo. Bennett Spring State Park Nature Center.

Little Rock, Ark. Arkansas Game and Fish Commission; wildlife exhibits and natural history museum.

Murfreesboro, Ark. Museum of Rocks and Minerals.

Sullivan, Mo. Meramec State Park Nature Museum.

Van Buren, Mo. Big Spring State Park Museum.

Lost Valley State Park, *Ark. A pleasant hike of three quarters of a mile through a narrow gorge that is hemmed in with high limestone cliffs leads to Cob Cave, with its underground creek and waterfall, and to a nearby massive natural bridge spanning the valley floor.*

Johnson's Shut-ins State Park, *Mo. Shut-ins are narrow stretches along rivers where, as the river cut its way downward, it met resistant volcanic rock. The result, as here, is a tumbled mass of rock and water.*

177

Wichita Mountains
NATIONAL WILDLIFE REFUGE, OKLAHOMA

This peaceful view shows the Wichitas' tamer side. Elsewhere water and trees are nonexistent.

OKLAHOMA

Wichita Mountains

Home on the Range for the Last of the Buffalo Herds

To a visitor driving through the nearly featureless farmland of southwestern Oklahoma, the sudden upthrust of a chain of rugged rocky hills comes as an almost physical shock. Where did they come from, these startling, misplaced mountains? What left them here, like an abandoned battleship afloat in a sea of prairie grass?

The Wichita Mountains were formed some 300 million years ago by a tremendous upheaval, with its vigorous folds and faults. Erosion stripped off the upper parts of the mountains and deposited this material in the intervening flats, leveling out their profile. Today the Wichitas reach less than 3000 feet into the clear Oklahoma skies—though geologists tell us they were once much higher.

Since prehistoric times the Wichitas, with their lush intermountain meadows, small lakes and wooded valleys, have attracted man. Indians followed the game into this bountiful hunting ground and were in turn followed by the white man. Here the mighty buffalo roamed by the millions before white settlers began the systematic slaughter which by 1871 had destroyed the great southern herd. Elk thrived here too, and whitetail deer, along with many other animals. It was to preserve their habitat and restore the endangered species that the Wichita Mountains Wildlife Refuge was created here.

First reserved for public use in 1901 when the Apache, Comanche, and Kiowa Indian Reservation was opened to settlement, the area was made a game preserve in 1905. Thirty

Before the coming of the white man, some 60 million bison (more commonly called buffalo) moved in wide waves across the Great Plains grasslands.

years later it became a wildlife refuge under the Bureau of Sport Fisheries and Wildlife. It is one of the bureau's four fenced big-game areas, and one of the oldest refuges in the country. The bureau aims to maintain the habitat and ecology as near as possible to its natural state.

In 1907, Oklahoma's statehood year, 15 buffalo arrived, donated to the original Wichita game preserve by the New York Zoological Park. It was a dramatic return to the plains from which they had been exterminated by man's greed, and people from all over the countryside flocked to the railway station at Cache

They were efficiently slaughtered for hides and meat and rendered virtually extinct by the early 1900s. Now protected by law and supported on federal refuge areas, a few thousand descendants of the original herds, such as these grazing in a Wichita valley, are still to be seen today.

to see the shaggy beasts. Among them were the great Comanche chief Quanah Parker and many of his braves, come to welcome back the bison that had provided meat, clothing and shelter for generations of their people. By 1962 the herd had grown to 1000, more than twice the total number remaining on the North American continent in 1900. The herd has since been cut back to 475 through donation or public auction of yearlings, but will be rebuilt to 600.

The refuge's herd of longhorn cattle, another relic of the early days of the prairie, is kept to 300 through an annual live auction. Although not native, having been brought here by Spanish explorers, the hardy, cantankerous longhorns were included in the refuge because of the significant role they played in the history and development of the region. It is the steers, not the bulls or cows, that develop the characteristic long curved horns, sometimes measuring as much as six feet across from tip to tip. Several steers are kept in an exhibition pasture at Wichita.

The refuge also harbors an elk herd of 350, which has been controlled in recent years through a limited public hunt for which hunters are selected by drawing. (Except during the

181

Palo Duro Canyon, *Tex. A setting sun paints this magnificent canyon, carved by the Red River in its sweep across the arid panhandle plains.*

Texas' largest state park embraces the canyon, and an aerial tramway to the rim offers the best view of its multicolored spires and towers.

feet). They are covered with layers of gypsum and selenite that sparkle in the sun, thus giving them their name. Erosion has carved strange formations in the gypsum caps, notably 300-foot-high Cathedral Rock, whose gray-green gypsum gives the effect of windows.

Great Salt Plains National Wildlife Refuge, Okla. The 32,000 acres that have been set aside here for wildlife are on the central flyway for migrating geese and ducks, and also serve as a wintering place for bald and golden eagles. An unusual feature within the refuge is a flat, barren expanse called the salt plains. Covering this land is a thin layer of salt, which Indians once swept up with turkey wings. It is possible to dig up selenite crystals here. A state park on the shores of a large reservoir provides facilities for water sports.

Lake Texoma Recreational Area, Tex. and Okla. A dam built on the Red River by the Army Corps of Engineers has backed up a 90,000-acre lake that straddles the state line. Both states have parks on the lake shores, and campgrounds, picnicking facilities and marinas are plentiful. Fishing is excellent here.

Little Sahara State Park, Okla. Large dunes stretch along the banks of the Cimarron River, giving the area a remarkable resemblance to its namesake. Several camels kept in the park add to the illusion. Riding dune buggies is popular here; they can be rented from park headquarters.

Quartz Mountain State Park, Okla. Enormous boulders of red granite contrast with the green of mesquite in the Quartz Mountains, the remains of a chain once as high as the Rockies. They are named for their quartz crystals. Among their dry, rugged slopes lies a 6770-acre lake, popular locally for water sports.

Red Rock Canyon State Park, Okla.
(*Picture appears on this page*)

Sanford (now Lake Meredith) National Recreation Area, Tex. Seven federal recreation areas and a variety of facilities surround the shores of Lake Meredith. A 21,600-acre lake, in the Canadian River Valley, was created in 1964 by the U.S. Bureau of Reclamation.

Tishomingo National Wildlife Refuge, Okla. There are two game refuges on Lake Texoma: Hagerman National Wildlife Refuge on the Texas side of the lake, and Tishomingo on the north arm of the lake in Oklahoma. The Tishomingo refuge is a stopover for migrating ducks and geese. A separate management area provides excellent hunting.

Turner Falls, Okla. Unlike most waterfalls, which result from rock layers being eroded away by a stream, these falls were built up by a stream. Honey Creek has created a 75-foot precipice of spongy-textured travertine over which it now crashes to a quiet pool below. A privately run park here is a favorite picnicking spot.

RELATED MUSEUMS AND ATTRACTIONS

Ada, Okla. East Central State College Museum; mineralogy and geology.

Alva, Okla. Northwestern State College Natural History Museum.

Goodwell, Okla. No Man's Land Historical Museum; mineralogy and geology.

Lawton, Okla. Museum of the Great Plains; plains ecology.

Stillwater, Okla. Oklahoma State University Natural History Museum and Herbarium.

Sulphur, Okla. Platt National Park Museum.

Palo Duro Canyon, Tex.
(*Picture appears on facing page*)

Platt National Park, Okla. Our smallest national park—and unusual also for being in a town—Platt is most visited in summer. When the hot Oklahoma sun beats down, its rippling creek, shaded by trees, provides welcome coolness. The park is noted for its cold mineral springs—over 20 sulfur, iron and bromide springs as well as several freshwater ones that flow through rocks without mineral deposits. A nature center has been built over Travertine Creek. The park is a good place from which to explore Arbuckle Recreation Area.

Red Rock Canyon State Park, *Okla. A winding road leads down into a surprising hidden valley, flanked by towering red rock walls. The fine old trees that grow here are thought to have survived because the canyon sheltered them from the harsh plains weather.*

187

Bayou Country
LOUISIANA

LOUISIANA

Bayou Country

A Maze of Water and Spanish Moss

By the time the mighty Mississippi River reaches Louisiana after a 2000-mile journey from its birthplace in Minnesota it has become what geologists call an old river. This means that it is meandering over a wide floodplain, depositing more material on its way than it picks up. By doing so, it continually changes its own course, because where there is virtually no gradient to determine a river's course, any slight obstacle, which will gather an accumulation of deposited silt, is sufficient to turn the water aside.

As a result, the Mississippi floodplain in Louisiana is a classic study in meanders, a watery maze of cutoffs and oxbow lakes that the river shaped and abandoned on its royal progress to the sea. These little waterways, permanently cut off from the river, have become the placid bayous—barely moving streams and creeks shaded by lush vegetation —that help to give the delta country southwest of New Orleans its special character.

Another element in the personality of bayou country is its people. For this is the land of the Acadians, French-speaking descendants of settlers driven from Nova Scotia by the English more than 200 years ago. Although the soft-spoken Acadians may not gather together for a spirited *fais-do-da* (a local dance) as frequently as before, the atmosphere of the bayou remains distinctly French. The names of the bayous, and the villages scattered among them,

ypress and Spanish moss shadow dim Bayou Courtebleu.

189

Deer wander under the moss-draped trees in Avery Island's Jungle Gardens. The "island" is a dome of solid rock salt rising above surrounding flat land.

Bird City on Avery Island is famous for its numbers of herons and egrets; above, a flock of cattle egrets soars over a bamboo grove in a flutter of

also reflect the beguiling flavor of the local tongue: Teche, Tigre, Soule, Anse, Ile des Cannes, Lafourche, Arnaudville, Jeanerette, Charenton, Courtebleu, Broussard.

Dense forests of cypress, live oak, wild pecan and elm overhang the sun-dappled waters of the lazy, winding bayous, and misty curtains of Spanish moss draped over nearly every branch create a dreamy atmosphere of semi-twilight. In the soft rays of the sun the Spanish moss, an air plant, is chameleonlike in its constant shifts of color, ranging from almost pure silver-gray through gray-green to green and finally, in death, to coal black. (Oddly enough, it is classed botanically as a member of the pineapple family.)

The city of Lafayette serves as an ideal starting point for travel in bayou country. Anyone who can arrange to be there in March should take the 25-mile Azalea Trail through the city. The brilliance and variety of the azaleas' color is an unforgettable introduction to this part of the world. Lafayette is a city of magnificent gardens, and also boasts an annual springtime Mardi Gras celebration which it claims is second only to that of New Orleans.

To the east of Lafayette, and extending southward to the Gulf of Mexico, is the vast Atchafalaya Basin, the last great remaining swamp area of its kind in the United States. So huge that it could accommodate the better-known Okefenokee Swamp in Georgia several

times over, the basin covers 1300 square miles, laced with winding streams and dotted with fish-filled lakes. Birdlife is abundant, and so are alligators (though they can be heard slithering through the water more often than they can actually be seen), and the teeming wildlife also includes those tiny green turtles that are sold in so many novelty shops. They are trapped here in the basin.

Currently there are no guided tours through the swamp; probably the best way to experi-

shining white wings. Snowy egrets were almost extinct half a century ago when the founder of the Avery Island sanctuary discovered seven aban- *doned young birds and began raising them in cages. Although they were later freed they returned here to nest, and there are now over 100,000 of them.*

ence it is to seek out a friendly local fisherman who might take you out in his boat to the parts he knows. Or you can take a plane trip over the swamp from any airfield in the vicinity—the only way to get a real idea of its incredible extent. Ultimately state conservationists hope to get the entire basin designated as a National Recreational Area, which will presumably bring more visitor facilities.

South of Lafayette, the heart of bayou country lies around New Iberia and St. Martinville

(home of the Evangeline Oak, made famous by Longfellow's poem and now in a state park). A short side trip from St. Martinville leads to Pine and Oak Alley, a magnificent mile-long drive lined by stately pine and oak trees. The imaginative visitor can see in his mind's eye how it must have looked one night in 1850 when wealthy plantation owner Charles Durand sprayed the branches of every tree with cobwebs of gold and silver for the double wedding of his daughters.

Another short trip, a few miles to the north, leads to Breaux Bridge, which proclaims itself as "Crawfish Capital of the World." It holds an annual crawfish festival and is also well worth visiting for its charming old Acadian cottages and fine trees.

Just west of New Iberia, off Highway 14, lie Avery and Jefferson islands. These are not islands in the normal sense of land surrounded by water, but are huge salt domes that rise abruptly from the surrounding flat marshland. Both islands are home to splendid gardens: Jef-ferson's are more formal, in the English manner, but Avery's Jungle Gardens contain practically every species of plant and flower native to south Louisiana and are therefore more lush, varied and semitropical.

Also on Avery Island is Bird City, a huge sanctuary that features one of the largest egret rookeries in the country. The whole island abounds with wildlife, and in the profusion of its living things, and the color and variety of its plants, it almost seems to be a miniature Garden of Eden arising like a vision from the

The word "bayou" comes from the French pronunciation of bayuk, *which is the Choctaw Indian word for river or creek. Louisiana's bayou country is a land of muddy, sluggish streams, and standing water left by spring floods of the Mississippi or by the damming up of streams by flood-borne sediments.*

level marshes. The salt which forms the island is mined here, and there is a public tour of the mine. Indians first found this salt, and it supplied the entire South during the Civil War. Avery Island is also the sole source of those small, hot peppers that are transformed, by a heavily guarded secret process, into tabasco sauce, the potent and vital ingredient for so much Creole and other spicy cooking.

It was on Avery Island that a number of nutrias (South American fur-bearing animals of the rodent family) once escaped from their pens during a hurricane and spread out through the marshes. They multiplied so rapidly that their pelts now help Louisana to lead the country in fur production. Nutrias (also known locally as coypus) can often be seen alongside the country roads in marshy parts of bayou country.

This area, seemingly so casual and lazy, actually teems with industry of many kinds. It is rich in oil, for one thing, and oil wells can frequently be seen along the winding back roads. It is also sugar country, and fields of tall sugarcane surround the splendid old plantation houses to which they once brought riches. Every fall New Iberia is host to a jolly extravaganza in its Sugar Cane Festival. This is the time of year, too, when visitors can stop by one of the sugar refineries to see juice pressed from the cane stalks and turned magically into sparkling mountains of sugar.

Fall is also probably the best time to enjoy the huge coastal bird refuges. Here, where the delta country shades imperceptibly into the ocean in a great wilderness of marsh grass and lakes, threaded by the Intracoastal Waterway, lies a chain of refuges that are home to millions of wintering waterfowl. Much of the refuge country is spread over a series of coastal islands, virtually inaccessible except by boat. But if you head southwest on Highway 82 beyond Abbeville you will come to the vast Rockefeller refuge along the Gulf Coast where there is every type of marsh and shore habitat, and a great variety of birds—and bird watchers seeking them out.

These are some of the highlights of bayou country. But the essence of its appeal lies not so much in its actual sights as in its pervading atmosphere of relaxed charm and the placid beauty of the quiet waterways that give it its name. It is like nowhere else at all—an experience unique in the world.

The Meandering Mississippi Leaves a Lake Behind

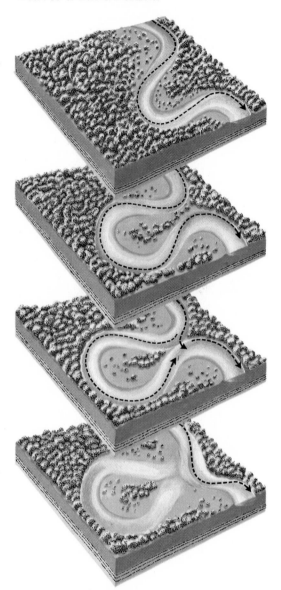

Geologically "mature" rivers like the Mississippi, which traverse a flat floodplain, wander from side to side in great loops in a process called meandering. (Young rivers, actively cutting their way downward, do not meander.) A meander starts because of a slight irregularity in the stream bed. Sediment is deposited on the inside curve of the developing meander. On the outside curve, where the water flows faster, the riverbank is eroded. (The dotted lines in the diagram above indicate the area of strongest flow.) When the loop becomes sufficiently exaggerated, the force of the water causes the river to shorten its course by cutting clear across the neck of the meander. The abandoned arc thus produced is known as an oxbow lake.

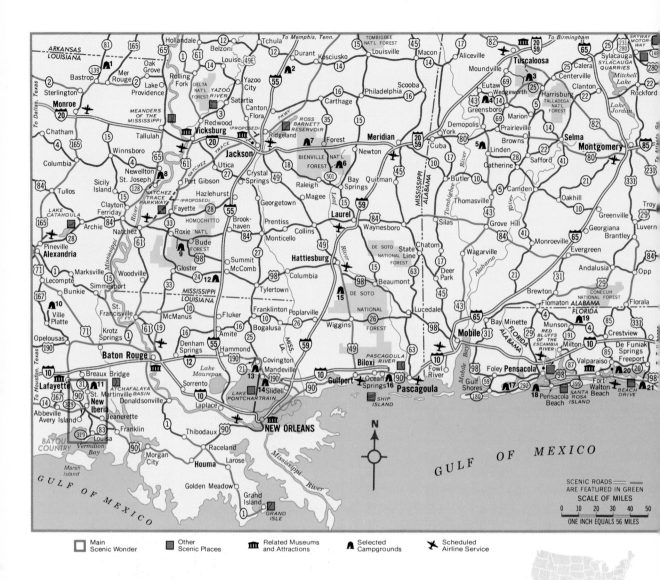

Main Scenic Wonder · Other Scenic Places · Related Museums and Attractions · Selected Campgrounds · Scheduled Airline Service

SCENIC ROADS ARE FEATURED IN GREEN
SCALE OF MILES
0 10 20 30 40 50
ONE INCH EQUALS 56 MILES

GULF OF MEXICO

WITHIN A DAY'S DRIVE:

Gulf Beaches, River Meanders and an Ancient Indian Highway

Atchafalaya Basin, La. The largest expanse of swampland in the country, the basin is probably best seen from the air. Its bayous, rivers, lakes and overflow swamp offer superb fishing and hunting.

Beach Drive, Fla. From Destin to Panama City, the drive parallels dazzling white beaches washed by Gulf waters that are a rich blend of blues and greens.

Grand Isle, La. In the 19th century Grand Isle was the base of the legendary smuggler and sol-

dier of fortune Jean Laffite. Record sailfish, marlin, tuna and dolphin are taken from the adjacent Gulf waters.

Lake Catahoula, La. The Atakapa Indians dipped their amulets and arrows in Lake Catahoula's waters to make them more effective. Vast stretches of the Atchafalaya Swamp east of the lake attract many bird and animal species to a wildlife refuge.

Lake Pontchartrain, La.
(*Picture appears on facing page*)

Meanders of the Mississippi, Miss.
(*Picture appears on facing page*)

Natchez Trace Parkway, Miss. The most rewarding stretch of this scenic parkway in Mississippi is south from Port Gibson to Natchez. Emerald Mound, a large Indian temple mound, is close to the road, which follows the Trace, an ancient Indian route.

Pascagoula River, Miss. You can hire a boat and guide to explore the marshes, bayous and islands along the upper reaches of the

Pascagoula, a land of cypress, live oak and palmetto.

Red Bluffs of the Escambia River, Fla. Rose- and beige-colored bluffs sprawl along the shore where the Escambia empties into the west branch of Pensacola Bay.

Ross Barnett Reservoir, Miss. Bass, crappie and bluegill are the prizes sought by fishermen in this large impoundment of the Pearl River.

Santa Rosa Island, Fla. A 50-mile barrier island, Santa Rosa offers a string of beautiful beaches.

Ship Island, Miss. Boats sail to Ship Island from Gulfport and Biloxi. It is a place of beautiful beaches and abundant birdlife, one of the finest Gulf islands.

Skyway Motorway, Ala. The scenic drive traverses the ancient Cumberland Mountains in the Tallegega National Forest.

Sylacauga Quarries, Ala. Visitors here can watch open-pit quarrying in a bed of solid marble 32 miles long and over a mile wide.

Yazoo River, Miss. The Yazoo, a tributary of the Mississippi, runs parallel to it for miles because the Mississippi has built up its own natural levee, preventing the Yazoo from joining it.

RELATED MUSEUMS AND ATTRACTIONS

Baton Rouge, La. Louisiana State University Museums of Geoscience and Natural Science and Herbarium.

Fort Walton Beach, Fla. Florida's Gulfarium; marine exhibits.

Jackson, Miss. State Wildlife Museum.

Lafayette, La. Lafayette Natural History Museum.

New Orleans, La. Louisiana Wildlife Museum.

Tuscaloosa, Ala. University of Alabama Museum of Natural History.

Vicksburg, Miss. Corps of Engineers Mississippi River Test Mockups.

Lake Pontchartrain, *La. New Orleans occupies much of the southern shore of this large and shallow lake, and it is crossed by the world's longest overwater highway bridge. But it also contains many quiet and peaceful corners like the one in this sunset view.*

Meanders of the Mississippi, *Miss. Above Vicksburg the Mississippi is serpentine with meanders (see diagram on page 193). The large loop of water in the foreground might become an abandoned oxbow lake if the river cuts across the meander neck.*

195

Padre Island National Seashore

TEXAS

Dunes separate the ocean and the beach from vast lagoon mudflats on Padre Island.

Surf Fishermen and Seabirds
Share a Great Wild Beach

All through the coastal plains of southwest Texas you are conscious of the vast reach of the sky—a limitless dazzling vault that dwarfs every sign of human habitation. It seems impossible that light and space and air could be more overwhelming. But south of Corpus Christi, where one of the world's great barrier islands sits low in the Gulf of Mexico, the impact is even greater. Here, on Padre Island, is a seemingly endless world of beach, surf, marsh and blue sky that is all but unaffected by the existence of man.

Padre Island is 113 miles long, pointing like a long sandy finger toward Mexico. Only the extreme northern and southern ends are developed with roads, gas stations, motels and the other human encroachment that inevitably accompanies a great beach in a sunny climate. The rest, approximately 80 miles of it, is virtually as nature made it; there are some places where the only people ever seen are park rangers on their daily patrols by jeep or helicopter. For this central expanse is the Padre Island National Seashore, one of the newest members of the National Park Service's great family of parks, monuments, refuges and seashores. Already, only five years after it was opened, it is heading toward a million visitors a year, and park officials are working on plans to preserve its wilderness character before a mounting demand for recreation facilities.

Camping by the sea is popular at Padre. This is the official campground, but campers can also drive along the beach and set up below the dunes.

Although the extremities of the huge beach will become increasingly crowded, the central section is likely to remain a comparatively lonely place for years to come. For the road runs out only 10 miles from the start of National Seashore territory, at Malaquite Beach, and after that the wide beach itself is the only highway down Padre Island. At first it seems to make little difference to the crowds. Intrepid drivers take to the sand, and for the first few miles after the road ends there are still a number of campers' tents and trailers nestling below the slope of the dunes. But they soon thin out, and travelers safe in four-wheel-drive vehicles begin to come upon conventional cars stranded like beached whales in the shifting sands, wheels spinning furiously as they try to pull out. Helping stalled cars is one of the rangers' chief duties along this stretch; it is a long way to a towing service.

After about five miles of beach (the distance varies according to the weather and the condition of the sand) the Park Service puts out its warning signs that only four-wheel-drive vehicles can go farther—and then the human presence dwindles remarkably. For those with the right sort of vehicle, a steady hand at the wheel and an ability to absorb an endless succession of bumps and jolting swerves, there are more than 50 miles of wilderness beach still ahead before Mansfield Channel divides the island. It is a highly exhilarating drive, twisting and turning to avoid the soft patches where new loose sand is sifting in, evading sudden watery dropouts, lurching over pieces

199

of driftwood, now racing along on the flat, smooth sand near the creamy advance of the ocean, now hugging the edge of the tawny dunes. And any time you stop—choosing your ground carefully to be sure you can get under way again—only the earth's own sounds can be heard: the roar of the surf, the cry of the seabirds and the rustle of the wind among the dune grasses.

Climb one of the dunes—there are some tall ones behind Big Shell Beach—and from a height of only 40 feet or so the view seems infinite. North and south the beach stretches into a haze of blue distance. Eastward a sparkling expanse of water reaches, unruffled by land, out into the Gulf and the Caribbean. And to the west, beyond miles of grassland, lie the endless mudflats and shallow waters of the Laguna Madre that separates Padre from the Texas mainland.

In all this great panorama the only sign of human life is probably a distant jeep crawling along the beach or a tanker far out to sea beating up the coast toward Corpus Christi or Galveston. Lost in a sea of grass inland lie the ruined wooden buildings and tumbledown fences of the old Dunn Ranch, established nearly 100 years ago. Cattle have been grazed on the island for generations; in fact, past overgrazing is responsible for the present coarse and sparse vegetation, though little by little, under the protection of the National Seashore, grazing has been phased out and the green is creeping back.

The island has not always been as empty and unexploited as it is today. Like so much else in this corner of Texas, most of its history is Spanish. It was discovered in 1519 and originally named Las Islas Blancas (The White Islands). It was the doom of many Spanish galleons sailing these waters in the 16th and 17th centuries, including a fleet of treasure ships that broke up here during a hurricane in 1553. Not until later was the island named Padre—after Padre Nicholas Balli, who received it as part of a land grant in 1800 and began running cattle on it.

Legends persist of lost treasure still buried on Padre Island, and current regulations forbid the use of metal detectors anywhere in National Seashore territory—a blow to eager treasure seekers who may imagine there are still chests of Spanish gold lying around unclaimed beneath the sand.

This panoramic view of Padre Island looks south toward Mexico. Four-wheel-drive vehicles can go for 50 miles along this beach (note the tracks

WILLET 13½"

BLACK SKIMMER 17"

Birds That Find Padre Island a Haven—Plus One Rare Neighbor

All the birds shown here can be found quite readily on Padre Island except the large and rare whooping crane, which winters at the nearby Aransas refuge (see page 205.) Two species here are increasingly threatened: the great blue heron and the white pelican, whose eggs are becoming thinner and more fragile as a result of the pesticides they consume in their fish diet. The willet and the graceful avocet are usually to be seen at the edge of the water, while the black skimmer, true to its name, skims the surface, beak wide ajar, in search of food.

in the sand), though few venture all that way
into the wilderness. On the right, behind the line
of dunes, grassy flatlands once grazed by cattle
stretch off toward Laguna Madre, a broad shallow
lagoon that separates Padre from the mainland.
Snakes, including rattlers, inhabit these tawny flats.

GREAT BLUE HERON 38″

WHITE PELICAN 50″

WHOOPING CRANE 45″

MARSH HAWK 17″

AVOCET 15″

But there are plenty of other treasures, both natural and man-made, to be found along the strand. The ranger station at the entrance has a display of them: shells, pieces of driftwood, the beautiful glass Japanese fishing floats. And Padre is one of the best places for surf fishing in the country; most of the men who take the long drive out to the farthest reaches of the beach do so to set up their rods on the edge of the ocean and fight the big ones—including sharks, whose powerful bodies, threatening even in death, are sometimes washed up on the beach after a storm.

And Padre is rich in birdlife. Nearly 300 species have been recorded here as either permanent residents or transients, coming up in the spring from their wintering grounds in Mexico and Central America and returning in the fall. Great blue herons, willets, black skimmers, flocks of knots and hosts of little scurrying sanderlings are common along the beach. Inland, on the lagoon flats and the grasslands, there are avocets, meadowlarks, marsh hawks, purple martins and occasional great horned owls and rare peregrine falcons. And less than two hours' drive to the north, at the extensive Aransas National Wildlife Refuge, is the sole American wintering ground of the nearly extinct whooping crane (see picture on page 205).

Coyotes, gophers, ground squirrels and kangaroo rats share the dunes and grasslands with no less than 12 species of snakes, including two types of rattlesnake; caution is therefore advised before stepping too far off the beaten track.

One of the best beaten tracks on Padre is the Grasslands Trail, a nature trail that leads three quarters of a mile off into the dunes not far from Malaquite Beach. It shows how dunes look in differing stages of stabilization, introduces the visitor to such typical plants as sea oats, railroad vines, croton, the spring-blooming white-stem wild indigo, and the only remaining stand of the Virginia live oaks that were once common on the island.

And for those who come to Padre not so much for solitude or nature study as simply to enjoy sunning and swimming, the first five miles of broad white beach, with easy access from the road and well-designed facilities for eating, changing and showering, rank among the best anywhere. So the island has something for every visitor—and not the least of its gifts are the precious ones of peace and solitude.

The great Intracoastal Waterway that hugs close to most of America's southern and eastern coasts passes along the broad Laguna Madre behind Padre Island, and the dredging for its construction threw up vast spoil banks that remain as low-lying islands in the shallow water. Some have fishing shacks.

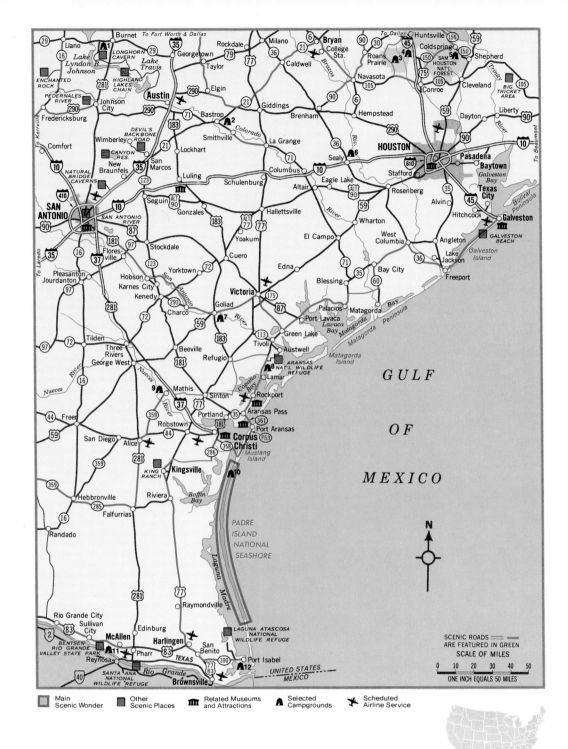

WITHIN A DAY'S DRIVE:

Hill Country and Bird Refuges

Aransas National Wildlife Refuge. (*Picture appears on page 205*)

Bentsen-Rio Grande Valley State Park. A drive through fragrant citrus orchards leads to this heavily wooded park on the banks of the Rio Grande. Nature trails wind among dense sub-tropical woods, and the bird-watching is outstanding. One of the best of several campsites overlooks the river and Mexico.

Big Thicket Area. A huge stretch of dense forest covering hundreds of square miles, Big Thicket has thick stands of pine, American holly and yaupon. The Sam Houston National Forest contains part of it, including the Big Thicket Scenic Area near Cold Spring, and local roads anywhere in the area offer forest drives. On the Alabama-Coushatta Indian Reservation, tours in swamp buggies are available.

Galveston Beach. *More than 30 miles of clean and sandy beach stretch westward from the city along Galveston Island. Many fishing piers are built well out into the water, the surf fishing is highly rated, and deep-water catches from boats offshore include sailfish, marlin, king mackerel and red snapper.*

Canyon Reservoir. Blue waters surrounded by steep evergreen-clad hills make this one of the most attractive lakes in Texas. The excellent fishing includes rainbow trout along the Guadalupe River below the dam.

Devil's Backbone Road. Follow winding routes 12 and 32 along a razorback ridge between San Marcos and Wimberley for fine views over the hill country.

Enchanted Rock. Strange creaking and groaning sounds that emerge from this broad 500-foot granite rock at night are explained as the results of cooling after the heat of the day. Early Indians worshiped and performed sacrifices here. Another stone phenomenon, Balanced Rock, can be found in a roadside park a few miles away.

Galveston Beach.
(*Picture appears on this page*)

Highland Lakes Chain. Dams on the lower Colorado River have created this series of six large lakes set amid steep hills. Inks and Lyndon B. Johnson lakes are probably the most attractive of them; all offer good fishing.

King Ranch. A 12-mile loop route leads tourists past the headquarters, stables and several departments of America's biggest ranch. Covering about 820,000 acres— bigger than some Eastern states —it stretches most of the way from Kingsville to Raymondville and out to the coast. The public entrance is west of Kingsville.

Laguna Atascosa National Wildlife Refuge. Bird watchers can walk or drive along mapped trails through this 44,000-acre area of coastal marsh, lakes and scrub forest. Among the rarities to be seen here are the caracara, the reddish egret and the white-tailed kite, as well as countless ducks and geese in migration.

Longhorn Cavern. Sparkling displays of calcite crystals and a "Hall of Marble" are the special features of this huge cave, administered as a state park.

Natural Bridge Caverns. Four college boys exploring an underground passage in 1960 came upon this enormous cave system, with its lavish formations, entered below a 60-foot natural bridge.

Pedernales River. The Texas hill country surrounding the river looks remarkably like Africa, with its low hills and scattered, stunted trees and bushes. Pedernales Falls State Park encloses a series of picturesque cascades.

San Antonio River. In the heart of a bustling city, the walk along the river comes as a delightful surprise. Beautifully planted with trees and tropical flowers, the River Walk meanders for several miles below street level.

Santa Ana National Wildlife Refuge. You can gaze across the placid Rio Grande into Mexico from one of the many trails through this area of semitropical forest, one of the last remnants of the kind of vegetation that once covered the river valley. Expect to find rare birds here, like chachalacas and green jays, not normally seen north of Mexico.

RELATED MUSEUMS AND ATTRACTIONS

Corpus Christi. Corpus Christi Museum; natural history, shells.

Galveston. Sea Arama Marine World; local marine life.

Houston. Museum of Natural Science. University Geological Museum.

Luling. Palmetto State Park; botanical garden, tropical plant life.

Port Aransas. University of Texas Marine Science Institute; local marine life.

Rockport. Texas Parks and Wildlife Departments Marine Laboratories; local marine life.

San Antonio. Witte Memorial Museum; natural history.

Aransas National Wildlife Refuge. *The whooping crane, now almost extinct, has chosen this vast coastal refuge as its wintering ground (it breeds in northern Canada). Shown above is a crane family; young one is in the middle. A boat tour from Lamar takes visitors closest to the cranes.*

Devils Tower

NATIONAL MONUMENT, WYOMING

Nature's Skyscraper Stands Tall Above the Plains

Standing sentinel above the forest-patched hills and the rolling, broken grasslands of northeastern Wyoming is a mysterious, fluted rock pyramid that slants steeply nearly 1300 feet above the river near its base. It changes color and character strangely with the shifting light: now dark and brooding, now shining like a city skyscraper. On clear days it can be seen for 100 miles.

This strange phenomenon, the largest rock formation of its kind in the United States, is the Devils Tower. Its cluster of spectacular columns rise 800 feet above a base of varicolored sedimentary rocks—shale, gypsum, sandstone and limestone, the consolidated deposits of prehistoric seas. The mighty pillar of igneous (once molten) rock, 1000 feet across the bottom, has a flat summit surface of an acre and a half.

Geologists continue to search for more clues to the origin of the monolith, but some basic explanations are widely accepted. The ancient rock is estimated to be about 50 million years old. Eons ago a mass of molten material oozed up into deep sedimentary beds that kept the hot, liquid rock covered until it had solidified. The curious polygonal columns were formed during this cooling process: the cooling caused the rock to contract, creating a series of joints, or cracks, as it did so. The shape and size of the tower's columns is determined by the number and width of these joints.

Devils Tower looms mysteriously in a morning mist.

Thousands of feet of sedimentary beds have since been worn away by the agents of erosion —wind, frost, rain and the running water of the Belle Fourche River at the tower's base— to expose the hard, resistant core of solidified magma. Gravity, pulling down pieces of the columns broken by the effects of freezing and thawing of water in joints and crevices, formed the talus slopes at the tower's base.

Historically, Devils Tower has played an important role in the lives of millions of people, from prehistoric natives to present-day tourists. Some of the early Indians called it Mateo Tepee, meaning Grizzly Bear Lodge. Others called it the Bad God's Tower, a name adopted, with slight modification, by the U.S. Geological Survey party of 1875.

Several enchanting Indian legends describe the origin of Mateo Tepee. According to the Kiowas, the fluted rock formations resulted from the scratching by bears' claws as they vainly reached for seven little Kiowa girls. The girls were saved when the Great Spirit elevated a rock on which they had sought refuge to its present great height. The bears finally died from exhaustion, and the seven little maidens became the seven stars of the Pleiades. Another legend claims that during summer storms thunder is created by the Bad God. Satan himself beats his drum on the summit of the Bad God's Tower, and the surrounding land trembles in fear.

The tower was a guiding beacon to early explorers of the Black Hills region. The first settlers appreciated its uniqueness, and although it was difficult to reach over the rough trails by horse and wagon, it became a favorite camping and picnicking spot. In 1906 popular and scientific interest inspired President Theodore Roosevelt to make Devils Tower the country's first national monument.

In his 1876 book *The Black Hills*, Col. Richard I. Dodge, commander of the military escort of the 1875 U.S. Geological Survey party, described the tower as "one of the most remarkable peaks in this or any country," and added:

The great columns of which the tower is formed show clearly in this closer view. Many of them, fragmented by eons of weathering, have fallen.

The tower is easier to climb than at first appears, and increasing numbers try it. The record time for an ascent is now less than an hour and a half.

best picture of the main attraction. But there is no "best" time to shoot Devils Tower. It changes endlessly in lighting and perspective from dawn to dusk, and in the course of just an easy walk along the trail. For campers, sites are available for trailers and tents only from May 15 through September 30. A museum at headquarters has exhibits explaining the geology, history and natural environment of the monument region, and a full-time ranger is on duty to answer visitors' questions and supply information on the unique and engrossing features of this natural skyscraper.

Because of the way it looms over the surrounding landscape, Devils Tower is one of those places you see long before you reach it, thrusting into the wide prairie sky off to the side of Interstate 90 on the route between the high plains and the Rockies. Equally, it retains its powerful image in your mind—as well as in your rearview mirror—long after you have left it behind: an austere and brooding milepost on the westward pioneer trail.

The Belle Fourche River, which was named by early French explorers, flows along the base of the Devils Tower, softening the stern landscape.

In this distant view of the tower as viewed from the south, it is easy to see why it became a landmark to early settlers on their great journey westward.

The tallest formation of its kind in the United States, it is clearly visible for many miles across the prairie and became an early gathering place.

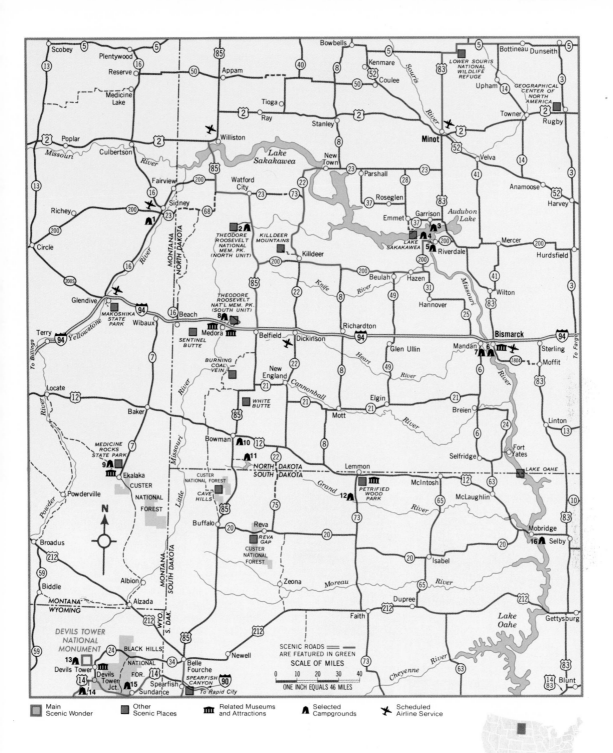

Map legend:

Main Scenic Wonder
Other Scenic Places
Related Museums and Attractions
Selected Campgrounds
Scheduled Airline Service

SCENIC ROADS ARE FEATURED IN GREEN
SCALE OF MILES
0 10 20 30 40
ONE INCH EQUALS 46 MILES

WITHIN A DAY'S DRIVE:

Badlands and Inland Oceans

Burning Coal Vein, N.D.
(*Picture appears on page 215*)

Cave Hills, S.D. You can drive on rather rough roads through this remote section of Custer National Forest, and it is well worth the effort. The rugged country is like a combination of badlands, with its weird erosion shapes, and the spectacular wooded Black Hills farther south. A number of small caves give the area its name.

Geographical Center of North America, N.D. A stone cairn beside the road in open prairie country marks this spot—a curio for travelers. (The geographical center of the United States is in neighboring South Dakota.)

Killdeer Mountains, N.D. From the top of the Killdeer Mountains there is a vast panorama of miles of prairie. The 51-mile "Lost Bridge Road" leading there has

213

Theodore Roosevelt National Memorial Park (South Unit), *N.D. This unit includes a burning coal vein, petrified trees and several overlooks for surveying* *the colorful badland territory. The country and its wildlife are substantially unchanged from the time President Theodore Roosevelt ranched in this area.*

observation points along the way for views over the badlands, Little Missouri Bay on Lake Sakakawea, and the surrounding prairie.

Lake Oahe, S.D. and N.D. A huge earthen dam near Pierre, S.D., created an enormous lake with hundreds of miles of shoreline reaching north into North Dakota. The lake has many recreational facilities, and fishing is excellent (in fact, Mobridge, S.D., describes itself as "the pike capital of the world").

Lake Sakakawea, N.D. There is a guided tour of towering Garrison Dam, a key structure in the control of the Missouri River for irrigation, recreation and power. The huge lake provides prime fishing for northern pike, walleyes and sauger.

Lower Souris National Wildlife Refuge, N.D. Once a favorite breeding ground for ducks, the marshes along the Souris River,

inadequately drained for agricultural use, were returned to the waterfowl in 1935. There is a fantastic variety of birds here, even saltwater ones: a dozen kinds of ducks, Wilson's phalaropes, cormorants, various gulls, pelicans, bobolinks, upland plover and many others.

Makoshika State Park, Mont. The Sioux word *makoshika* is translated as "hell cooled over," and it is a graphic description of these 800 acres of colorful, twisted erosion formations.

Medicine Rocks State Park, Mont. (*Picture appears on facing page*)

Petrified Wood Park, S.D. This small park, preserving the remains of enormous petrified trees, has an excellent museum that includes local geological specimens.

Reva Gap, S.D. The 40-mile-long red rock escarpments of Reva Gap and Slim Buttes are of inter-

est historically as well as scenically. They were the site of a famous Indian battle in 1876.

Sentinel Butte, N.D. From the top of this butte, seven miles south of the town of the same name, is a beautiful scenic panorama over the rolling rangeland.

Spearfish Canyon, S.D. In the northern Black Hills a road follows trout-filled Spearfish Creek along this shadowy canyon. Occasionally the forest opens up to show towering cliffs above, and there are two spectacular waterfalls along the way.

Theodore Roosevelt National Memorial Park (North Unit), N.D. The park is divided into three sections: the main South Unit, Roosevelt's Elkhorn Ranch, and this one. Here, from a series of overlooks along a 13-mile scenic drive, the visitor can see the rock formations carved by the Little Missouri River.

Theodore Roosevelt National Memorial Park (South Unit), N.D.
(Picture appears on facing page)

White Butte, N.D. The highest point in North Dakota at more than 3000 feet, White Butte rears abruptly from the level plains. White Lake Wildlife Refuge sits at its foot.

RELATED MUSEUMS AND ATTRACTIONS

Bismarck, N.D. Dakota Zoo.

Devils Tower, Wyo. Devils Tower National Monument Park Museum.

Ekalaka, Mont. Carter County Museum; natural history, geology.

Lemmon, N.D. Petrified Wood Park Museum.

Medora, N.D.
Fur Trade, Wildlife and Indian Museum.
Theodore Roosevelt National Memorial Park Visitor Center.

Burning Coal Vein, *N.D. A vein of lignite coal began burning in 1880 and since then has traveled a quarter of a mile to reach its present site. The stand of columnar cedars nearby, a formation unique to this spot, apparently owe their shape to the effects of the sulfur fumes.*

Medicine Rocks State Park, *Mont. These weird formations carved into the sandstone by centuries of wind and rain stand out from a surrounding terrain of rolling prairie. The Indians named them medicine rocks, made them into a subject of legend and performed their ritual dances here.*

Badlands National Monument

SOUTH DAKOTA

Bright grass and eroded rock create a weirdly beautiful landscape below Pinnacles Overlook.

Nature Sculpts a Spectacularly Strange World in Rock and Grass

Near Cactus Flats, just below Interstate 90, the rolling flow of South Dakota's grassland erupts in a jagged row of sawtooth peaks. They serve as signposts to the jumble of windblasted rock and gutted canyons that sprawl southward to form the White River Badlands —one of the most awesome and forbidding landscapes known to man, and world famous as a classic example of erosion.

Bordered on the north by the Cheyenne River and on the south by the waters of the White, the Big Badlands, as they are also known, cut an arid swath through the southwestern quarter of the state. U.S. Highway 16A, dropping from the interstate, twists for 27 miles along the edge of naked scarps and knife-edged ridges that separate the upper and lower grasslands. In the heart of this area 111,530 acres are set aside as the Badlands National Monument.

Approaching the northeast entrance of the monument, the sharp spires become turrets of finely stratified rock, banded in narrow parallels of pink, white and yellow. With almost shocking suddenness the land falls away beneath the road into twisted gullies and fluted towers of varicolored stone. Gray mud rocks, marked by the trailings of prehistoric worms, bulge from the earth. Between them rise pink pyramids of siltstone, capped by table-flat patches of green prairie grass.

The different layers of rock in the badlands buttes are clearly highlighted in this dramatic view of Cedar Pass. Shades of brown are due to iron oxide.

The badlands began some 80 million years ago as layers of muddy sediment on the floor of a shallow inland sea. Deposited over a span of 20 million years, the layers of ocean slime were uplifted and drained by the same forces that raised the Rocky Mountains. Over the eons, plant forms covered the old sea floor and local streams carved it into rolling hills and broad valleys. Quite recently, as geologic time passes (a mere 35 million years ago), raging rivers, charged with tons of rocky debris, cascaded from the western mountains. These torrents dumped hundreds of feet of new sediments, leveling the area into a vast floodplain. Its marshes became grasslands from which, in due course, the slow wearing of wind, water and frost carved the fantastic badlands.

The area is richly studded with fossil remains. In the lowest sections, snail-like ammonites share space with the stone bones of monster alligators and giant sea turtles. Overlying these marine shales, the Chadron formation yields up the remains of the awesome titanothere—a rhinoceroslike mammal slightly smaller than an elephant. And the Brule sediments bristle with the bones of the oreodont, a pig-shaped animal with the sheeplike teeth of a ruminant. It roamed the once lush country with small saber-toothed tigers, fox-sized horses and our earliest camels. Judging from the remains, the badlands were at once a haven and a graveyard for these creatures. But their story ended three million years ago.

Much briefer is man's history in the area. We know that night fires of nomad hunters

These smoother mounds of bentonite—volcanic ash compacted into clay—are in stark contrast to the sharp spires. Winds brought quantities of ash from volcanic eruptions in the Yellowstone and Bighorn areas millions of years ago. The veins are cut by water draining down the mounds' sides.

flickered in the badland darkness of A.D. 900. By A.D. 1000, forebears of present-day Indian tribes camped on the bordering plains. French trappers, pushing down from Canada, were the first Europeans to visit the area. They called the country *les mauvaises terres*, which, like the Indian *mako sica*, translates as "badlands."

In 1823 the mountain man Jedediah Smith and his band of American trappers challenged this arid land. It almost destroyed them. With their water supply exhausted in midcrossing, their situation was desperate. Two of the weakest members were buried to their necks in the sand to preserve their body moisture until others found water. But all survived.

Early reports of fossil wealth brought in col-

lectors by 1843 and a government geologist in 1849. General Custer saw the badlands and described them as "Hell with its fires burned out." By the turn of the century, tourists were packing out fossil souvenirs by the wagonload. It was not until 1929 that Congress authorized the national monument to preserve the area.

At first sight, the starkness of the badlands is almost grotesque, seemingly empty and barren. Yet in many areas erosion has undercut the cliffs, tumbling masses of mud and stone into the ravines, and these slump blocks, ranging in size from a few yards to several acres, hold moisture for a flourishing plant and animal life. Here bloom the bright, yellow clusters of the rubber rabbit brush mixed with the

drooping white sprays of the chokecherry. Silvery leaves of the buffalo berry mingle with the darker green skunkbrush. Both offer shade for the pink blossoms of the meadow rose. And everywhere there is the sun-warmed scent of juniper and red cedar. The badlands invade the prairie and are surrounded by it, so that nearly half the national monument is grassland. In spring a multitude of wildflowers color these plains like a bright Indian blanket.

The patient watcher may also find that this seemingly empty land has more wildlife than he would have dreamed at first sight. Within the eroded canyons mule deer may suddenly appear, silent silhouettes, huge ears erect, staring in frozen curiosity at the traveler. A buff-colored coyote slips along the canyon wall. His movement startles a tiny chipmunk into furious circles of panic. Overhead, the darting flight of cliff swallows relieves the monotony of a cloudless sky. The black hulks of buffalo loom on the grasslands. White dots, spotted against the prairie, mark a band of antelope. Startled by some intruder, they erect the white hairs of their rump patch, flashing a warning semaphore across the plains. Life and spectacle is everywhere in the apparently dead land.

Though the badlands are open all year round, the best seasons are spring and fall. Then the climate is ideal, the colors are at their best and crowds are small. A visit should begin in early morning, provide for a long noon

Indians made knives from slabs of translucent chalcedony like these. The mineral forms in cracks, and remains after the softer silts and clays that surround it have all been eroded away.

Fossils found in the badlands are evidence of long-extinct creatures that lived here millions of years ago. This is the skull of a type of oreodont, a hoofed mammal that was ancestor to ruminants.

break and continue through late afternoon. Both viewing and photography are best when the sharper angle of the sunlight makes deep shadows on the towers and buttes.

The highway through the badlands, designed for leisurely driving, contains many scenic turnouts and each of them offers information on the area. But the best way to appreciate this bizarre country is to take one of the short, self-conducted walks. Door Trail, one of the most impressive, is only a three-quarter mile round trip. It is best seen around sunrise. At midtrail, you are surrounded by jagged towers and scalloped ridges, sharp against the sky as paper cutouts. Beneath your feet you can feel the strange softness of the stone. Watching the sun tint the eerie shapes with its shifting light is like an experience of some strange planet.

Near Cedar Pass, a visitor center provides information and a small museum. From early June through early September the center offers naturalist-conducted hikes during the day, and

The spires and turrets seen in the badlands have been sculptured largely by the short, heavy rains of the area; each downpour creates tiny changes.

Ultimately the forces of erosion will wear these strange shapes down to a vast and level plain. The badlands are at their most striking in the

evening programs in the amphitheater. In addition to the large public campground at Cedar Pass, there is primitive camping on Sage Creek Rim Road.

Today, even as the visitors enjoy the wild scenery of the badlands, the forces of erosion are working to destroy it; eventually all of its strange beauty will be leveled to a vast plain. But for now and the foreseeable future the badlands will remain to cast their spell over all who see this macabre place.

sort of half-light seen here, when their weird outlines stand like cutouts against the sky. Walking the Door Trail at sunrise is a good introduction.

A Way of Life That Was Built Around the Bison

The bison was the mainstay of the Plains Indian's existence. From it he obtained not only food but the utensils to cook and eat it, not only winter and summer clothing but needle and thread to sew them. From hide and bone he fashioned shelter, tools, weapons, even boats in some areas. His cooking pots were made from the beast's stomach. The bison's extermination ended a whole way of life; after that the Indian depended increasingly on manufactured goods.

CARRYALL
(HIDE)

TEPEE
(HIDE)

THONG
OR ROPE
(RAWHIDE)

LADLE (HORN)

SCRAPER (BONE)

SHIELD
(RAWHIDE)

POUCH
(HIDE)

BULLBOAT (RAWHIDE)

BLANKET OR ROBE
(HIDE)

COOKING POT
(STOMACH)

223

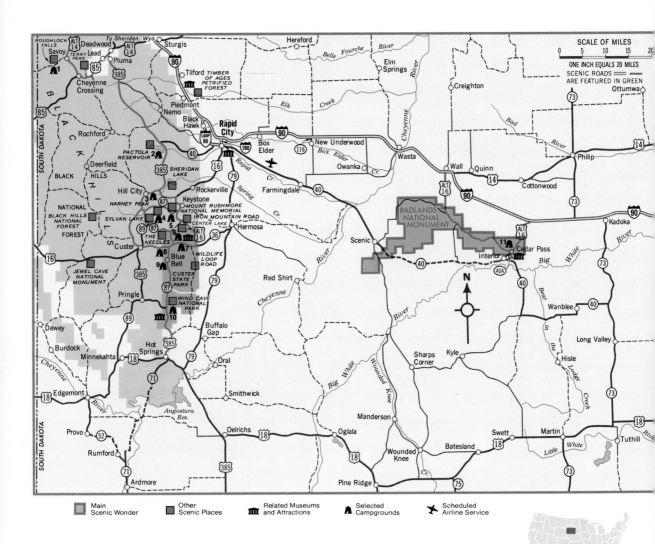

WITHIN A DAY'S DRIVE:

High Lakes and Evergreen Mountains

Black Hills National Forest.
(*Picture appears on page 226*)

Center Lake. Although one of the smaller lakes in the area, it is one of the most beautiful, hidden in the deep shadows of majestic pines and screened by the ragged forms of aromatic cedars. The Wilderness Fishing Trail that begins at the inlet offers three miles of rugged hiking and excellent trout fishing.

Harney Peak. The highest mountain (7242 feet) east of the Rockies has been altered by erosion so that its trails are relatively easy to climb. The lichen-covered summit is a rugged granite dome

that provides an unequaled view of the entire Black Hills area and surrounding states.

Iron Mountain Road. The southern approach to Mount Rushmore is one of the most scenic in the Black Hills. It is an exciting drive down a corkscrew road through dense evergreen forests. It cuts its way through solid rock tunnels that frame the distant carvings on Mount Rushmore, offering one of the most photogenic views of that famous memorial.

Jewel Cave National Monument. A wildlife sanctuary where deer, elk and other native animals are often seen surrounds Jewel Cave.

Inside are formations unique in the United States: combinations of stalactites, flowstone and crystal-covered walls occur together in several places; and hydromagnesite "balloons" that have a shell only about one thousandth of an inch thick cover one of the cave rooms.

Mount Rushmore National Memorial.
(*Picture appears on facing page*)

Pactola Lake. Slopes covered with stands of pine, patches of scrub oak and clusters of stark white birches surround the lake on three sides. To the east, the land opens on a lush valley. It is this break in the encircling hills that makes Pactola one of the most scenic lakes in the area, giving the impression of a cirque lake in a mountain setting.

Roughlock Falls. Ancient cottonwoods form a solid green canopy over a lush and deep-shaded forest grove, and not until the visitor walks out on a narrow wooden bridge are the 30-foot falls actually visible—as prettily composed as a Japanese print.

Sheridan Lake. Tall pines screen this irregularly shaped lake from the highway. Boating and fishing are both popular summer activities, and several small campgrounds line the south shoreline.

Sylvan Lake.
(Picture appears on page 227)

Terry Peak. A road leads up to a chair lift (open all year), and continues up to a parking area from which there is a long, steep climb to the summit. For most visitors it is easier to take the chair lift to within a few hundred

Mount Rushmore National Memorial. *Over 1000 acres of parkland surround the granite mountain on which sculptor Gutzon Borglum carved the faces of Presidents Washington, Jefferson, Theodore Roosevelt and Lincoln. Observation points provide a variety of views.*

Wind Cave National Park. *The cave itself is most noted for its delicate calcite boxwork formations, resembling honeycombs. The park outside, seen above, preserves part of the original prairie grassland dotted with ponderosa pine, where herds of bison and other animals can roam freely.*

feet of the top for a panoramic view of the Black Hills and a five-state area.

The Needles.
(Picture appears on facing page)

Timber of Ages Petrified Forest.
Upright stumps of fossilized trees and huge logs up to 80 feet in length form this phenomenon. A museum has displays of minerals, polished wood and fossils found in the area, and guided walks can be taken through part of the weirdly stunted forest.

Wildlife Loop Road.
Winding southeastward along the Lame Johnny Creek in Custer State Park, the road threads its way at first through deer country; at a later point, where the road turns north, small herds of bison are within easy view of anyone driving by. A host of smaller animals, including foxes, bobcats and rabbits, inhabit the area and are best seen during early morning and late evening.

Wind Cave National Park.
(Picture appears on page 225)

RELATED MUSEUMS AND ATTRACTIONS

Custer. Custer State Park Historical Museum and Zoo;

Hot Springs. Wind Cave National Park Museum; natural history.

Interior. Badlands National Monument Museum.

Piedmont. Timber of Ages Wood Museum; natural history.

Rapid City. South Dakota School of Mines and Technology Geology Museum.

The Needles. *The lofty spires that rear skyward in a jagged row are all that remain of the original granite plateau. Erosion has carved them into their present shape and is still continuing the disintegration process. The Needles Highway winds and curves through these giant monoliths for 14 spectacular miles.*

Black Hills National Forest. *The thick evergreen covering gives a dark appearance to the mountainous 1,327,000 acres that comprise this vast forest. It abounds in high lakes, spectacular canyons with waterfalls, caves and beautiful streams—such as the quiet birch-lined brook seen here.*

Sylvan Lake. *The surface of this body of water smooth as a mirror reflects the colors and patterns of its beautiful surroundings. It is nestled on the top of a ridge in a peaceful setting of pines interspersed with several oddly shaped rock formations.*

227

Scotts Bluff

NATIONAL MONUMENT, NEBRASKA

A modern highway parallels the historic Oregon Trail through Mitchell Pass.

For the Pioneers, a Beacon Welcoming Them to the West

Like a medieval castle, turreted and golden in the sun, Scotts Bluff rises out of the monotonous flatlands of southwestern Nebraska to dominate the valley of the North Platte River—and to stir man's imagination.

For today's auto travelers on Route 92, the towering monolith, 800 feet high and half a mile long, is likely to come as a sightseeing bonus along their route: a freak of nature to be wondered at, admired and explored. To buffalo-hunting plains Indians, it was "Me-a-pa-te," the-hill-that-is-hard-to-go-around. For covered wagon trains, lumbering westward on the North Platte River branch of the Oregon Trail, it was a welcome landmark. Here was wood for campfires, spring water—and best of all, Mitchell Pass, a gap leading behind the bluff and skirting river badlands too rough for wagons to cross.

In this bottleneck, where wagons had to go single file—a rare happening—the Oregon Trail was cut so deep that even now it resembles a country road. Erosion has erased most of the ruts, but time has not dimmed the story of the 150,000 emigrants who came through during the 1850s and '60s, many walking to save wear and tear on the wagon teams.

From the pass today's visitor too can walk the Oregon Trail, clearly defined for almost a mile. Along the way currant bushes offer berries in the fall. In summer, wild prairie roses

The half-mile escarpment of Scotts Bluff, rising 800 feet above the valley of the North Platte River, offers views as far as 125 miles on very clear days.

bloom. Rugged Scotts Bluff barricades the eastern horizon. Although seldom seen, rattlesnakes lurk in the rocks. Dust often swirls in the angry winds that sweep the prairies, causing eyes to smart and hair to blow. The sun burns relentlessly. And, when the pioneer Jackson campsite is reached, you have experienced only a tiny fraction of what the emigrants endured every day.

Some of their strength might have come from Scotts Bluff itself, which seems to emanate an almost mystic power to move those who see it. Early travelers felt this fascination. One of them noted: "It has the appearance of castles, forts . . . It seemed as if the wand of a magician had passed over a city, and like that in the *Arabian Nights*, had converted all living things to stone." A Mormon emigrant recorded that it was "highly beautiful, almost approaching the sublime."

Today Scotts Bluff is a national monument that helps to preserve the story of one of the greatest migration corridors in American history. Not only the lurching prairie schooners came through Mitchell Pass; so did the Overland Stage, the Pony Express and the first transcontinental telegraph.

In the monument area, encompassing five square miles, today's visitors have the advantage over the emigrants of easy access to the summit of Scotts Bluff. Taking off from monument headquarters at the base is a paved toll road. It snakes 1.7 miles up the sheer west side of the bluff, swinging through three man-made tunnels to the summit parking lot. For

231

The Making of the Oregon Trail

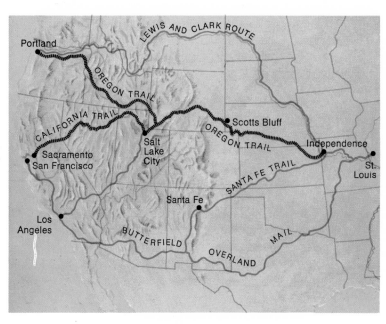

Animals and wagons following the Oregon Trail were forced to go single file through Mitchell Pass, which accounts for the unusual depth of the ruts there (right). During 1852, at the height of the great California Gold Rush, an estimated 50,000 men, women and children stopped here on their way west. The westward trails started at Independence, Missouri, and followed the Platte River to the mountains (see map on left, in which each dash on the trail represents a day's journey). It took most of the wagon trains at least five months to get from Independence to California or Oregon; each of them had to be outfitted and provisioned as though embarking for a lengthy ocean voyage.

the sturdy of foot there is the steep and spectacular Saddle Rock Hiking Trail, switchbacking up the eastern side.

On top of the bluff the appearance is that of a pretty little park. Gnarled, stunted ponderosa pines and sturdy Rocky Mountain junipers offer shade. Yucca sends up its delicate creamy white blooms. Lichens cling to the rocks. Despite the shallow soil, wildflowers and native grasses are abundant. Pencil-like tracks across the western cliffs reveal the travel patterns of mule deer. Occasionally a red fox slinks by. Overhead sparrow hawks soar, showing off rusty red tails that glint in the sun.

From overlooks linked by a half-mile summit trail, you can see for an amazing distance. On a clear day, 125 miles away in Wyoming, snowcapped Laramie Peak looms on the horizon. Out of the northwest swings the historic North Platte River, guideline of the emigrants, and rising 500 feet from its banks is the slender spire of Chimney Rock, a striking Oregon Trail landmark. Between the river and the face of the bluffs are the tortuous badlands that blocked the wagon trains—but yielded the fossils displayed in the monument museum.

On the summit trail stands the marker to

Covered wagons swayed westward over the plains like ships under full sail, bearing settlers and prospectors and all their goods to the golden lands.

unfortunate Hiram Scott, for whom the bluffs were named. A fur trader, Scott became ill and, cruelly abandoned by his companions, is said to have died in this vicinity. Fur traders were the first known white men to see Scotts Bluff.

When violent winds and occasional torrential rains lash at the bluff, as if trying to erase it from the landscape, park rangers order visitors off the summit and sometimes close the toll road. Furious storms can loosen rocks, which fall like giant hailstones on the road. Keeping the record of Scotts Bluff erosion on top is a steel pipe: in 1933 it was embedded flush in a rock, but now it is exposed for the 18 inches that have been worn away since then.

The tremendous impact of Scotts Bluff can best be experienced by hiking down the zigzagging blacktopped Saddle Rock Trail—but stay on the path. Leaving it causes erosion and is also dangerous, for the soft, crumbling edges give way easily.

One of the most thrilling spots on the trail is where it moves along a precipitous ledge out to the grotesque spires on the rocky front porch of Scotts Bluff. Exposed here in the top sandy strata are the hard, tubular concretions that keeps the bluffs from completely eroding away. Obvious too are the interlacing layers of white volcanic ash, blown here from ancient volcanoes. The highway tunnel on the way up is cut through such ash strata.

Box Canyon, a secluded place halfway down, is a contrast to the rocky slopes. Here pines and wildflowers thrive, and during rains, torrents of water race madly through the canyon's rocky throat. A few yards farther, a pause at Scotts Bluff spring to observe birds and other wildlife is often rewarding.

Now, with the hiker almost back on the valley floor and out of the buffeting wind, the quieter sounds of nature reassert themselves: the cooing of rock doves, the throaty chorus of meadowlarks from their perches on yucca plants, perhaps the cry of the rare prairie falcon as it flies to its nest high in the rock walls.

Few places in America offer such a stirring mixture of history, scenery and natural life as Scotts Bluff. Even without the knowledge of its place in the lives of the pioneers it would be a magnificent phenomenon. But it has meant so much to our forebears—as a landmark on their great journey, as a resting place, as an inspiration to carry on westward—that it has become a powerful symbol of the pioneer spirit.

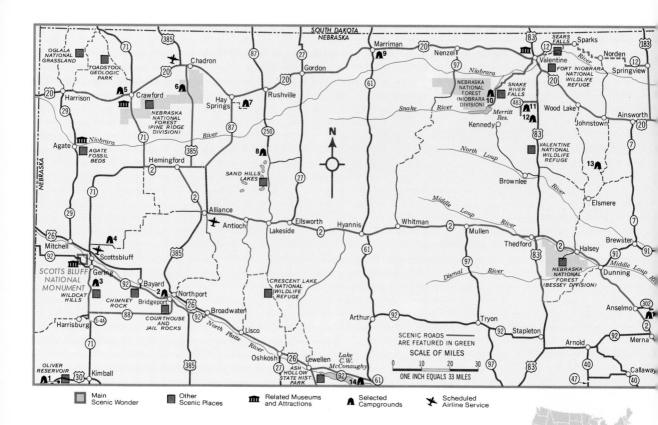

■ Main Scenic Wonder	■ Other Scenic Places	⛪ Related Museums and Attractions	▲ Selected Campgrounds	✈ Scheduled Airline Service

WITHIN A DAY'S DRIVE:

A Variegated Landscape of Buttes, Lakes and Grassy Hills

Agate Fossil Beds. A treasure trove of animal fossils from the Miocene Age (25 to 13 million years ago), these beds are now designated as a national monument. The most common mammal represented was a rhinoceros a bit smaller than a Shetland pony, but one aggressive, piglike creature stood seven feet tall. A self-guiding trail leads to an area of exposed fossils.

Ash Hollow State Historical Park. Guides printed for pioneers in the mid-19th century praised Ash Hollow's springs as the best water on the Oregon Trail. Ash and cedar provided firewood.

Chimney Rock. The most frequently described landmark on the route of westward migration, Chimney Rock is a slender column on a conical base rising about 300 feet above the North Platte River. An easy half-mile hike from a gravel road takes you to the base, and there is a good view from U.S. 26.

Courthouse Rock.
(Picture appears on facing page)

Crescent Lake National Wildlife Refuge. May to October is the best time to visit this lake-dotted 46,000-acre refuge bordering one of the country's few undisturbed tallgrass prairies. Sandhill cranes, long-billed curlews, grouse, geese and pronghorn antelope are among the wildlife to be seen.

Fort Niobrara National Wildlife Refuge. This is one of the two places in the country where big herds of buffalo, elk and longhorn cattle graze in the same practically undisturbed environment. Upland game birds are present all year long. Five miles of auto trails lead through areas where animals roam at will; more are planned.

Nebraska National Forest (Bessey Division). Almost a quarter of this 90,000-acre Sand Hills forest is covered with pine and cedar, all planted by man in a vast reforestation project.

Nebraska National Forest (Pine Ridge Division). Deer and wild turkey roam the pine-studded bluffs, and about 90 bird species have been identified here. Guided horseback trail rides are conducted at Chadron State Park, which is located inside the forest.

Oglala National Grasslands. Named for a Sioux Indian tribe, the land has been reclaimed from what was once misused and drought-stricken farmland to its present lush state. Pronghorn antelope graze on the rolling hills.

Oliver Reservoir. Located near the highest point in Nebraska (5424 feet), this impoundment of Lodgepole Creek is popular with campers and fishermen.

Sand Hills Lakes.
(Picture appears on this page)

Sears Falls. On the Niobrara River, just outside the wildlife refuge, this is one of several attractive cascades in the area.

Snake River Falls. The Snake, a tributary of the Niobrara, spills over in Nebraska's largest waterfall above the dam that forms Merritt Reservoir. Sometimes, in late summer, it dries up.

Toadstool Geologic Park. The most fascinating aspect of Nebraska's badlands, the toadstools, some weighing hundreds of tons, are made of sharp-edged layers of sandstone, balanced on pillars of sunbaked soil. Fossils, agates and Indian arrowheads can still be found. The toadstools themselves are a short walk from a sheltered picnic area.

Valentine National Wildlife Refuge. Peak populations of over 300,000 ducks have appeared at this Sand Hills refuge during October, a prime migration month. Abundant underground water feeds the lakes and marshes, which cover about 11,000 acres.

Wildcat Hills. The hills are actually two ranges separated by Pumpkin Creek Valley. North of the Wildcat Hills Recreation Area is a stunning view of the butterimmed valley. Elk, buffalo and turkey wander through the Wildcat Hills State Game Refuge.

RELATED MUSEUMS AND ATTRACTIONS

Agate. Agate Fossil Beds National Monument; fossil exhibits.

Crawford. University of Nebraska Trailside Museum; natural history.

Scotts Bluff. Scotts Bluff National Monument Visitor Center; geology and paleontology.

Valentine. Fort Niobrara National Wildlife Refuge Natural History Museum.

Courthouse Rock. *Courthouse and Jail Rocks, twin landmarks on the Oregon Trail, mark the beginning of the long ridge that broadens into the Wildcat Hills before it terminates abruptly at Scotts Bluff.*

Sand Hills Lakes. *The vast and lake-pocked, rolling Nebraska sand hills cover an area of 24,000 square miles, mostly blanketed with prairie grasses. Some of these grassy hills rise to hundreds of feet.*

Rocky Mountain National Park

COLORADO

The east face of the Rocky Mountains' Front Range rises abruptly behind Bear Lake.

An Uplifting Introduction
to America's Mountain Roof

The air is suddenly cool and sweet with the aroma of pine and spruce as you head westward out of the neat, quiet town of Loveland, Colorado. Even if the mountains were not visible, you would know the Rockies are near. For the first few miles highway U.S. 34 stretches between hayfields, cherry orchards and pastures dotted with cattle. Suddenly it enters the chasm gouged out by the rushing Big Thompson River, winding steadily upward between towering precipices.

Thirty miles west of Loveland, and 2500 feet higher, the highway emerges from a grove of slender lodgepole pine into a broad alpine valley. This is Estes Park, named after Joel Estes, who chanced this way in 1859 and was so entranced by its beauty that he returned to settle the following year and gave the area its name. Today it serves as the gateway to one of America's great scenic experiences, Rocky Mountain National Park.

At the far end of Lake Estes, which now fills part of the valley, is Estes Park Village, 7522 feet above sea level, a bustling tourist center in summer and a drowsy alpine town in winter. Here the road divides. The north fork leads five miles to the Fall River entrance of Rocky Mountain National Park. The south fork takes you four miles to Park Headquarters and the Beaver Meadows gate. The headquarters, at 8000 feet, incidentally, is the *lowest* point in

The rugged, sun-warmed walls of the Rock Cut frame this dizzying view of Forest Canyon and the snowy ridges of the Continental Divide beyond.

the park. Because it would take weeks to explore the park's 410-square-mile wilderness of jagged peaks, alpine lakes and valleys, forests, glaciers and perpetual snowfields, it is only prudent to seek guidance at the visitor center in the handsome stone headquarters building. A large relief map in the lobby helps you orient yourself, and a free movie shown in the spacious downstairs auditorium gives a quick overview of the park's features.

Among other things, it tells you that many millions of years ago mountains began to emerge from the vast inland sea that covered the area now occupied by the park. As millions more years passed, canyons widened into valleys and erosion reduced the once towering peaks to a rolling plain.

Sixty million years ago, at the end of the Mesozoic era, the mountain-building process was repeated. Once more many of the high peaks were worn down, creating the undulating uplands above timberline today. Finally, in fairly recent times—only a million or so years ago—the climate changed drastically and ice and snow covered the land. Enormous drifts were compacted into glaciers which, in their inexorable fashion, ground out the U-shaped valleys visible in many parts of the park. Five small glaciers are all that remain of the Ice Age—one of them, Andrews Glacier, can be reached by a rugged four-mile trail.

Rocky Mountain National Park can be traversed east to west in a few hours by highway, but the best way to get to *know* it is by hiking over some of the 300 miles of trails and per-

Eternal snows patch the high peaks of the Front Range, and a few small glaciers, remnants of the Ice Age, persist at the heads of sheltered gorges. Views like this are common along the Trail Ridge Road.

haps spending a night or two camping out. The trails range from brief and easy strolls to strenuous climbs. Undoubtedly the stiffest one-day hike is the 16-mile walk from Longs Peak Campground to the summit of 14,256-foot Longs Peak (the highest point in the park) and back. It is a trip that taxes even hikers in excellent physical condition, but as many as 200 men and women a day make it to the top at the height of the summer season.

The park's regular campsites can accommodate about 2500 persons a night on a first-come basis. There is room for another 1200 in designated "back-country" campsites for hikers. To prevent overcrowding and damage to the ecology these sites are available only on a permit basis; when the day's quota is reached, no more permits are issued.

Even the most sedentary, however, can en-

The Great Convulsions That Raised the Rockies over Millions of Years

A great mountain range always has a long history; that of America's rocky spine is complex as well. Around 150 million years ago a geosyncline, or trough, was formed in the area of the present Rocky Mountains by disturbances in the plastic mantle rock beneath the earth's crust. A sea filled this trough, and layers of sediment accumulated in it, gradually becoming rock strata. About 60 million years ago the strata were slowly folded and heaved up to elevations as great as 20,000 feet. Erosion wore down these mountains to mere hills. Some 25 million years ago new uplifts started another cycle of erosion. Since then most of the Rockies from Colorado southward have been eroded down to the granite cores formed in the original mountain building. But along their flanks are stumps of the old sedimentary strata, steeply tilted. The great red sandstone slabs seen in Colorado's Garden of the Gods, near Colorado Springs (see page 244) and at Red Rocks Park, west of Denver, are both clear examples of such tilted stumps.

joy a leisurely half-mile stroll around Bear Lake, one of a series of crystalline lakes strung out like jewels against green velvet at the end of a pleasant nine-mile drive from the Beaver Meadows entrance.

For the average visitor the most spectacular part of the park is the automobile trip over Trail Ridge Road, the nation's highest continuous highway, with 11 breathtaking miles winding over the tundra above timberline. Once this route was the migration trail of Ute and Arapaho Indians traveling from winter to summer grounds. At its highest point, between Iceberg Lake View and Fall River Pass, the road reaches 12,183 feet—nearly two and a half miles above sea level.

There are several ways to make this trip, but one of the best is to start at Moraine Park Visitor Center with a quick look at the exhibits. From there it's a five-mile drive through Beaver Meadows and Horseshoe Park to the start of the Fall River Road. This is a graded but unpaved, one-way road along the banks of tumbling, brawling Fall River. Ponderosa pine and Douglas fir give way to thick stands of lodgepole pine and aspen as the road climbs. In the moist, shady areas are handsome blue spruce and a host of wildflowers—pasqueflower, penstemon, Rocky Mountain iris, Indian paintbrush. Above 9000 feet, Engelmann

Generations of lichens slowly make a place for humus to collect and hold soil on granite, so that wildflowers like these bluebells can flourish.

spruce and limber pine take over. It is at these altitudes that the columbines, reflecting the delicate blue of the sky, are at their best.

At timberline, about 11,000 feet, even the gnarled, wind-twisted trees disappear and arctic tundra holds sway. The climate here is comparable to that of the Arctic Circle—a region of fearsome gales and numbing cold in winter. Summer is but a few brief weeks in July and August, with dwarfed wildflowers blooming in profusion among the hardy grasses, moss

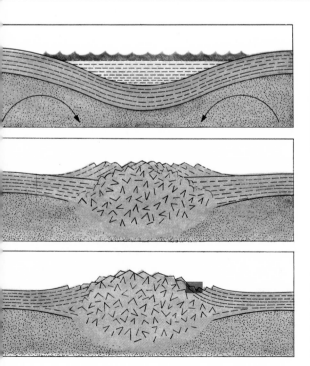

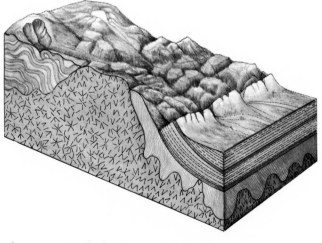

Three stages in the building of the Rockies are illustrated here. The first shows the trough, the second the upheaval that produced the mountains, the third the effects of later erosion on the sedimentary strata. The detail above, enlarged from the third drawing, shows the structure of the tilted sedimentary stumps seen in the Rockies' foothills.

and lichen that are part of the tundra ecology.

Fall River Road joins Trail Ridge Road at Fall River Pass (11,796 feet), where the Alpine Visitor Center interprets the tundra country. A few miles farther west is 10,758-foot Milner Pass over the Continental Divide, followed by Farview Curve Overlook with a splendid view of the Never Summer Mountains. Far below is the birthplace of the Colorado River, the prime creator of Arizona's Grand Canyon on its way to the Gulf of California.

Farview Curve is the logical spot for a family conference. You can continue downhill and leave the park at the Grand Lake entrance, driving through the lake country of Shadow Mountain National Recreation Area before joining U.S. Highway 40 at the ranch town of Granby. Or, if you choose, you can turn around and head back to Estes Park via Trail Ridge all the way.

Be sure to pick up a free guide to Trail Ridge Road at one of the visitor centers. Some of the highlights it lists are Rock Cut, from which there is a spectacular view of Forest Canyon 2000 feet below; Rainbow Curve, overlooking

Wildflowers run rampant in the Rockies, carpeting whole meadows with bloom and splashing bright patches of color in secluded forest glades like this.

a dizzying drop to the silver horseshoe bends of Fall River; and Hidden Valley, a lovely winter sports area. Despite its altitude, Trail Ridge Road is remarkably safe, the chief problem being overheated engines. Rangers patrol the road frequently.

While the park is open the year around, Trail Ridge understandably is only a summer attraction. Deep snow on "the roof of the nation" usually closes the road from late in October until the traditional opening on Memorial Day, when hardy athletes follow the snow-plows over the divide, to ski on snow at the summit and water-ski an hour later on summery Grand Lake on the western side.

Because of the more than 6000 feet between the park's lowest and highest points, there is a wide variety of wildlife. It includes several hundred species of birds ranging from eagles and hawks to tiny hummingbirds and the astonishing ouzel, which walks underwater along stream bottoms in search of food. Beaver are found in numerous watercourses. About sunset they can be seen surfacing in their ponds and setting out to cut aspen and willows whose bark is their food. If you are quiet, they won't even notice you. Mule deer, named for their long ears, frequent the meadows, particularly in early morning and at dusk. Shy bighorn sheep share the lofty crags with ptarmigan, marmots—a high-altitude relative of the woodchuck—and the rabbitlike pika, which harvests hay for its winter meals.

Early autumn visitors have a special excitement in store. Snows drive the majestic elk down from timberline meadows and the great antlered bulls bugle at sundown to assemble their harems. Wait silently in your car in Horseshoe Park when the moon is full and frost is on the grass to hear the hair-raising sounds of this drama of nature.

Autumn, in fact, is the best time of year to visit Rocky Mountain National Park. After Labor Day, most of the tourists are gone. The air is crisp but the Indian summer sun is warm. The aspen leaves turn golden, transforming entire hillsides into waves of color. Snows frost the topmost peaks and each week the line of white slips a little lower. On an autumn day when the sky is an incredibly deep blue and the trout are rising to feed on the season's last insects, it is easy to understand why Joel Estes came back to live out his days in these mountain ridges and valleys.

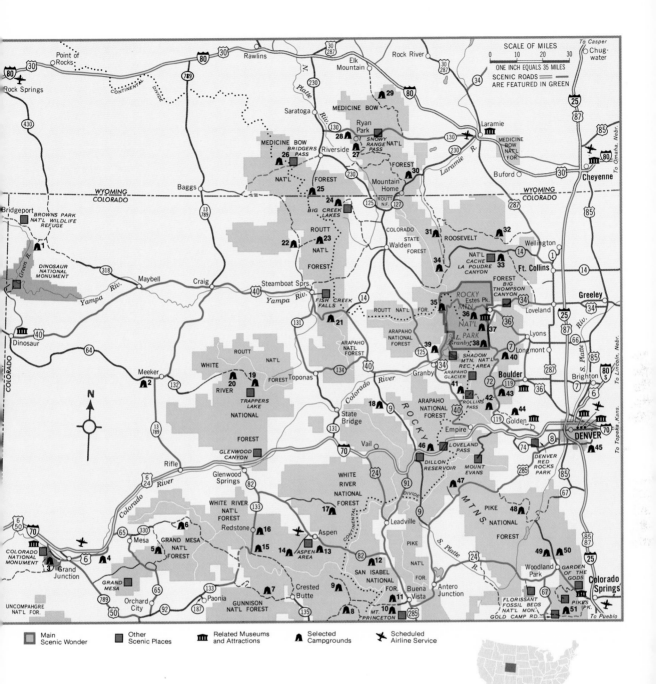

WITHIN A DAY'S DRIVE:

Lofty Passes Through a Dizzying Divide

Arapaho Glacier, Colo. Arapaho, which is one of the sources of Boulder's water supply, is probably the most accessible American glacier—a three-mile hike from the Peak-to-Peak Highway that runs below the Continental Divide.

Aspen Area, Colo.
(*Pictures appear on pages 244, 245 and 247*)

Big Creek Lakes, Colo. The "parks" of Colorado are flat, treeless, mountain-ringed grasslands —cattle country—and the drive to Big Creek Lakes, up near the Wyoming line below the Continental Divide, gives a good idea of the scenery of North Park. These lakes are surrounded by splendid forests sloping toward the high country.

Big Thompson Canyon, Colo. A spectacular introduction to Rocky Mountain National Park for travelers from the east, the canyon is traversed by a road that leads steadily upward alongside the rushing Big Thompson River between ever steeper, towering forested precipices. Estes Park, gateway to the mountains, is at the head of the canyon.

243

Bridger's Pass, Wyo. Straddling the Continental Divide in Medicine Bow National Forest, the pass is a high desert land of desolate grandeur. Saddle and pack trips open up the high wilderness.

Brown's Park National Wildlife Refuge, Colo. This area was known as Brown's Hole in the 1840s, when it was the gathering place of beaver-trapping "mountain men," and later of cattle thieves and bank robbers. Now the refuge attracts Canada geese and other waterfowl.

Cache la Poudre Canyon, Colo. The Cache la Poudre (hide the powder) River has cut a narrow valley through Roosevelt National Forest. With its quiet pools, the river has superb trout fishing.

Colorado National Monument, Colo.
(Picture appears on pages 246–247)

Denver Red Rocks Park, Colo. A natural amphitheater walled on two sides by massive sandstone formations, Red Rocks in summer is the setting for concerts, square dances and other events. The red Cambrian sandstone walls provide almost perfect acoustics for the music.

Dillon Reservoir, Colo. The Blue River feeds this large lake near Colorado's Middle Park. A full range of facilities for water sports are available in a peaceful, mountain-ringed setting. A 23-mile tunnel carries water from the reservoir underneath the Rockies to Denver, on the opposite side of the Continental Divide.

Dinosaur National Monument, Colo. and Utah.
(Picture appears on page 247)

Fish Creek Falls, Colo. The lofty falls, which tumble 260 feet over sheer rock walls, are easily accessible by road. Picnic grounds surround the area, and Mount Werner ski area is close by.

Florissant Fossil Beds National Monument, Colo. A series of eruptions in the Florissant area preserved many types of plant and insect life beneath layers of volcanic ash. Nearby, in the Colorado Petrified Forest, are the stumps of petrified sequoias, some as big as 10 feet across.

Garden of the Gods, *Colo. Tall, fantastically eroded rocks in every shade of red, brown and orange lie within easy walk of the road that traverses this magnificent park near Colorado Springs. Groves of fragrant juniper and piñon pine add green life to the arid landscape.*

Aspen Area, *Colo. A cloud plume flies off Pyramid Peak, near the historic mining town of Aspen in the Roaring Fork Valley. The Maroon Bells, symmetrical pyramid-shaped mountains, are nearby. Aspen is now as noted for culture as for splendid skiing and scenery.*

Garden of the Gods, Colo.
(*Picture appears on facing page*)

Glenwood Canyon, Colo. The sheer walls of Glenwood Canyon, an 18-mile gorge west of the Continental Divide, rise over a thousand feet. A two-mile trail leads to Bridal Veil Falls and Hanging Lake, which seems to hang on a sheer cliff 1200 feet above the canyon floor.

Gold Camp Road, Colo. A 36-mile gravel road on the old bed of the Colorado Springs and Cripple Creek Railroad, Gold Camp Road traverses some startling mountain scenery to the site of what were, 70 years ago, the richest gold workings in the world. Tourists can go down into the Mollie Kathleen mine for a

glimpse into the past and the hard life of the miner.

Grand Mesa, Colo. A 10,000-foot-high tableland 30 miles long, covered with lush meadows and spruce forests, riven by deep canyons and dotted with sparkling lakes, Grand Mesa is the world's largest flattop mountain.

Loveland Pass, Colo. Even though a Colorado visitor may cross the Continental Divide again and again, it remains a thrill. Loveland Pass, at almost 12,000 feet, is one of several mighty passes leading to the forests and ski areas of the high country. Unlike some others, it is open all winter.

Mount Evans, Colo. Mount Evans Highway, the highest road in the

United States, climbs to 14,264 feet. Two contrasting views, equally extraordinary, await the hardy driver: the Great Plains rolling far eastward, and the peaks of the Continental Divide, 20 miles or so to the west, looking almost close enough to touch in the clear, thin air.

Mount Princeton, Colo. Mounts Princeton, Yale and Harvard in the Collegiate Range are all over 14,000 feet. Thirteen additional peaks in the area, including Mount Elbert, Colorado's highest, also top 14,000 feet. The ghost town of St. Elmo lies at Mount Princeton's base, beneath the pale Chalk Cliffs.

Pikes Peak, Colo. Pikes Peak, the easternmost of all Colorado's high

Colorado National Monument, *Colo. Water, frost and wind carved the light red sandstone of Independence Monument into the striking monolith seen* *here. The same forces created delicate spires, open caves, "coke ovens" and other formations, all of them visible in a trip along 22-mile Rim Rock Drive.*

peaks, was the first to be discovered and became the most famous of her mountains. "Pikes Peak or bust" was the slogan of many hopeful 19th-century prospectors. The ascent is easy: by car over a toll road up Ute Pass or by cog railway from Manitou Springs.

Rollins Pass, Colo. A graded but unpaved highway follows the pass along the right-of-way of a defunct railroad past Yankee Doodle Lake and over the divide. It is a hair-raising but highly spectacular drive.

Shadow Mountain National Recreation Area, Colo. Three large lakes, surrounded by mountains, are linked together like beads on a string: Shadow Mountain, Grand Lake and Lake Granby. Five species of trout live in the lakes, and there are complete facilities for all water sports, plus a number of scenically located campgrounds.

Snowy Range Pass, Wyo. The paved, 70-mile Snowy Range Pass road carries you right through the heart of the breathtaking Snowy Range peaks, rising to a

height of 12,000 feet from such clear, sparkling alpine lakes as Silver, Mirror and Marie.

Trappers Lake, Colo. The lake, in the flattops country of the White River National Forest, is noted equally for its beauty and its splendid trout fishing.

RELATED MUSEUMS AND ATTRACTIONS

Boulder, Colo. University of Colorado Museum; natural history.

Cheyenne, Wyo. Wyoming State Museum; mineralogy.

Dinosaur National Monument, *Colo. and Utah. These sheer, color-ful cliffs rising above the Green River at Island Park, in Utah, are a typical example of Dinosaur's dramatic scenery. Boat trips down the Green or Yampa River canyons offer white-water thrills.*

Colorado Springs, Colo. Colorado College Museum; natural history.

Denver, Colo.
Denver Botanic Gardens.
Denver Museum of Natural History.

Dinosaur, Colo. Dinosaur National Monument Quarry Visitor Center.

Estes Park, Colo. Rocky Mountain National Park Natural History Museum.

Fruita, Colo. Colorado National Monument Natural History Museum.

Golden, Colo. Colorado School of Mines Geology Museum.

Laramie, Wyo. University of Wyoming Geological Museum.

Aspen Area, *Colo. Water-loving cottonwoods border the Crystal River, near Redstone, under the tall ramparts of Chair Mountain. Farther along the Crystal is the ghost town of Marble, whose quarries supplied the stone used in Washington's Lincoln Memorial.*

247

Black Canyon of the Gunnison
NATIONAL MONUMENT, COLORADO

Black Canyon's Painted Wall drops a sheer 2250 feet.

A Dark, Forbidding Cleft in Colorado's Mighty Mountains

Other western canyons are as sheer, some are deeper, narrower or longer—but no canyon in the whole of North America is at once as deep, narrow and darkly forbidding as the Black Canyon of the Gunnison River.

Deriving its name from the darkness of its gloom-shrouded walls, this wild chasm starts near Colorado's Blue Mesa Dam and carries the turbulent Gunnison River plunging 2150 feet on its journey to its confluence with the North Fork River, some 50 miles westward.

From the canyon's sunny rim, the visitor looks off into a world of wild desolation that has been locked in for eons by sheer lichen-covered walls of black-stained schist, coarsely banded gneiss and crystalline-textured granite. The imperceptible but relentless downcutting action of the Gunnison River has been gnawing at the hard Precambrian rock for some two million years. Differential weathering and erosion on rocks of varying degrees of hardness have sculptured pinnacles and block "islands" on the floor of the canyon. The powerful carving action of the Gunnison River, more rapid than that of its smaller tributaries, has left hanging canyons where the mouths of streams were sliced off—though some side canyons extend to the main canyon floor.

In places the canyon is deeper than it is wide, with depths ranging from 1730 to 2425 feet. The width is as narrow as 1300 feet at the rim and a mere 40 feet at the bottom. The

249

rapid downcutting of the river, combined with the extreme resistance of the granitic walls, accounts for the sheerness; Chasm Wall, for instance, has an almost vertical drop of 1800 feet, and Colorado's greatest cliff, the Painted Wall, is a sheer 2250 feet from rim to river.

The Black Canyon may seem like a singularly inhospitable place, but the canyon area shelters a much greater variety of wildlife than the visitor might expect. Many of its creatures are nocturnal, however, so that their presence is more often sensed than observed.

The cougar sometimes prowls the canyon's lonelier reaches. More rarely, a golden shaft of sunlight probing the shadowy recesses will pick out a Rocky Mountain bighorn sheep clinging to the precipitous canyon wall like a hairy apparition as it browses on the small plants growing from cracks in the rock. An occasional black bear wanders along the canyon rim in search of small rodents such as ground squirrels or perhaps to savor the berries of the abundant chokecherry, gooseberry or wax currants.

Golden eagles tilt over the canyon depths in quest of rabbits and small rats. Red-tailed hawks skillfully ride the air currents, and turkey vultures survey the scene on motionless wings. Mountain chicadees, juncos and titmice inhabit the denser woodlands, piñons and scrub jays scream from exposed boughs, and the canyon may be Colorado's last stronghold for the endangered peregrine falcon.

On the upper slopes of the canyon are stands of piñon juniper and gambel oak; in the cooler dampness of the north-facing slopes Douglas fir and quaking aspen flourish. In summer there are bright splashes of wild rose, mock orange and rock spiraea. Beneath the damp overhangs grow oak fern and woodsia.

The most spectacular reach of the canyon is within the Black Canyon of the Gunnison National Monument, whose overlooks and trails offer the most striking views into the canyon's depths. Gunnison Point, Chasm View, Sunset View, and the place called High Point, on the South Rim Drive, are all likely to take your breath away. The south rim is open all year, by a five-mile drive from U.S. 50 east of Montrose. The north rim, reached by a 14-mile graded

The prospect from Black Canyon's north rim is even more dramatic than that from the south rim; it is also harder to reach, by a 14-mile graded road.

dirt road, is accessible by car only from early spring to late autumn.

There are no established trails to the bottom of the gorge, and trips down should be undertaken only by people with good scrambling experience and in top physical condition; for casual ramblers it is a risky business. Park rangers must be notified before any descent is made. Passage along the bottom of the canyon, alongside the water, must be made with care, though the river, tamed by the Curecanti dams, has a relatively constant flow these days. Float trips are not possible.

For those who dare the journey, the canyon floor is a different world: a place of frothy rapids, emerald pools, eternal shadow and a solitude almost unknown in the brighter world above. Beavers live down here, and rainbow and German brown trout.

But whether the visitor is on the canyon floor looking up at the narrow slit of sky, or on the rim peering into the dark abyss below, the Black Canyon is a place of wonder and awe.

The joints (fractures in the rock) seen in this view from a dizzy overlook on the canyon's south rim are caused by internal stresses, not by weathering.

Mammals of the Rockies: Telling Look-Alikes Apart

The Rocky Mountain scenery is so spectacular that it is easy to overlook one of the other great attractions of the high country: its remarkable variety of wild creatures. This spotter's guide will help you to distinguish between some of the more common mammals to be seen in the mountains—and which may seem confusingly alike in the quick first glance that is often all you can get at shy wild animals. How can you tell a black bear from a grizzly, for instance? Or a yellowbellied marmot from a badger? There are nearly always important differences in size, coloring or habits to help you.

BLACK BEAR
Straight nose, face always brown, no hump, two-inch claws. Color: black in East, cinnamon in West

GRIZZLY BEAR
Nose turns up, face same color as body, hump above shoulders, four-inch claws. Color: pale yellow to dark brown, grizzled back. This is our largest bear.

YELLOWBELLIED MARMOT
Diurnal. Color: yellowish brown, white between eyes. Feet: beige to dark brown.

BADGER
Nocturnal. Color: yellowish gray, white stripe over head. Feet black, long claws.

GOLDEN-MANTLED SQUIRREL
Coppery-colored head. Stripes on body only. Tail fairly short.

LEAST CHIPMUNK
Yellowish gray. Stripes on face and body. Long tail, which is carried erect when running.

COYOTE
Color: gray or reddish gray. Feet, ears and legs rusty. Tail held in downward position when running.

RED FOX
There are several color variations, but the feet and legs are always black, and the tail is always tipped with white.

MULE DEER
Reddish in summer, blue-gray in winter, light rump, black-tipped tail, large ears.

ELK
Larger than mule deer. Reddish-brown body, neck brown, rump yellowish, no black on tail.

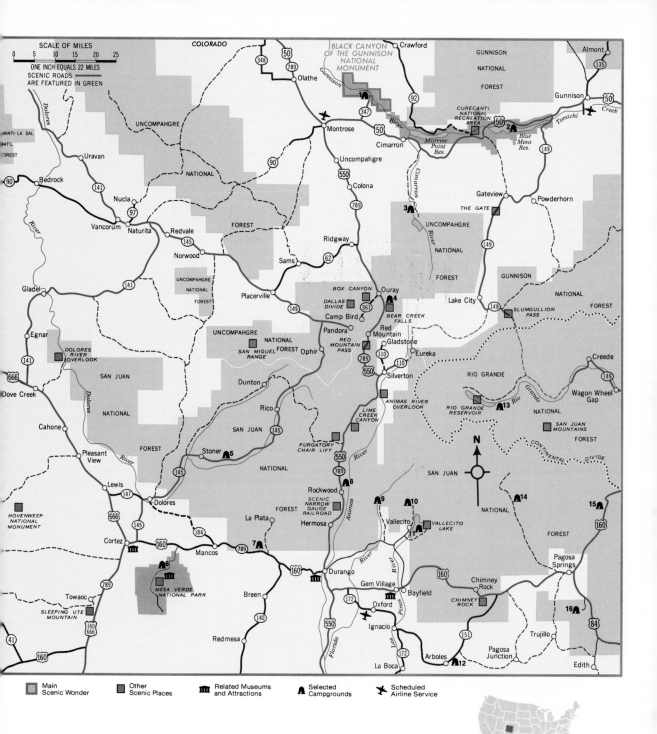

SCALE OF MILES
0 5 10 15 20 25
ONE INCH EQUALS 22 MILES
SCENIC ROADS
ARE FEATURED IN GREEN

COLORADO

Legend:
■ Main Scenic Wonder
■ Other Scenic Places
🏛 Related Museums and Attractions
▲ Selected Campgrounds
✈ Scheduled Airline Service

WITHIN A DAY'S DRIVE:

Canyons, Mesas and Shining Peaks

Animas River Overlook. The Rio de las Animas Perdidas (river of lost souls) received its name because of the rugged country through which it flows. This overlook is one of the best places for the driver on U.S. 550, one of the state's most scenic roads, to admire its steep side canyons, waterfalls, cliffs and forests.

Bear Creek Falls. These lofty falls cascade 227 feet down precipitous gorge walls. The so-called Million Dollar Highway crosses above the falls and has a parking overlook from which motorists can take good pictures. This section of highway U.S. 550 was named for the gold ore gravel with which it was surfaced, not for

the spectacular scenery through which it passes.

Box Canyon. Within the city limits of Ouray lies this deep gash in granite, only 20 feet wide but 221 feet deep. Hike the trail to the bottom of the canyon for a view of the spectacular Canyon Creek Falls. For a sweeping view

253

of the small valley in which Ouray nests, hike up Bear Creek to American Flats.

Chimney Rock. Rising from the flat tableland of a high mesa above the Piedra River is this striking rock formation. Nearby are some of the easternmost pueblo ruins to be found.

Curecanti National Recreation Area. Three dams, each producing a separate lake, have given Curecanti the largest total body of water in the state. It is popular for water recreation, and also offers excellent fishing. Blue Mesa, largest of the three lakes, has a particularly scenic drive along its mountainous northern shore.

Dallas Divide.
(*Pictures appear on this page and facing page and page 257*)

Dolores River Overlook. The Dolores River is one of Colorado's least known and most primitive, and this remote viewpoint offers a sweeping vista of the river. It is a challenge for canoeists and runs through a number of canyons with towering sandstone walls.

Hovenweep National Monument. This monument, reached by way of rather primitive roads leading into the Utah border country, is worth visiting for the unique masonry towers and other ruins of the Classic Pueblo period of

Indian culture—and for the remarkable views to Sleeping Ute Mountain, Shiprock in New Mexico, and the snowcapped summits in the high country of Colorado and Utah.

Lime Creek Canyon. Among the many canyons bringing mountain creeks down to join the Animas River, Lime Creek is one of the most spectacular. It is short, but its depth of 2000 feet creates a powerful effect.

Mesa Verde National Park. About 2000 years ago Indians were first attracted to the forested slopes of the "green table." The many deep sandstone canyons and overhanging cliffs provided shel-

San Juan Mountains. *Scattered among the rocky canyons and lofty peaks of this area of Colorado are many abandoned ghost towns and derelict gold and silver mines. This skeleton of a silver mine is near Creede, which was the center of a rich silver strike back in 1890.*

Dallas Divide. *The pastoral valleys that lie below the lofty Uncompahgre Plateau help to emphasize the dramatic lift of this line of superb snowcapped peaks. Mount Sneffels is the highest among the mountains in this lyrical view, shot by late afternoon sun that lingered on after a clear moonrise.*

ter, and the top made fertile farmland. For 1300 years people lived there and developed many skills. Then, probably because of drought, they left. All that remains now are their remarkable cliff dwellings, in magnificent settings of wooded canyons. In the summer, park rangers give conducted tours of these ancient Indian buildings—man's earliest apartment houses.

Purgatory Chair Lift. One of Colorado's newer ski areas in winter, and a magnificent overlook in summer, Purgatory is named for the death of some Spanish explorers, not for any terrors engendered by the ride. The chair lift, up the flanks of 13,000-foot Engineer Mountain, spreads below the visitor some of the state's finest scenery.

Red Mountain Pass. A spectacular section of the Million Dollar Highway leads up to this pass, the boundary between Uncompahgre and San Juan national forests. The three Red Mountains get their name and color from the iron pyrite in their rock.

Rio Grande Reservoir. This beautiful lake at the headwaters of the Rio Grande is surrounded on three sides by the lofty peaks of the Continental Divide.

San Juan Mountains.
(*Picture appears on facing page*)

San Miguel Range.
(*Picture appears on page 256*)

Scenic Narrow Gauge Railroad.
(*Picture appears on page 257*)

Sleeping Ute Mountain. A legendary giant Ute Indian guards a Ute reservation here, and his imaginary shape is seen in the outline of this striking mountain near Towaoc. The high, flat uplands of this area afford magnificent views of distant mountains. Several miles to the southwest of the Sleeping Ute landmark is the only place where the corners of four states meet: Colorado, Utah, New Mexico and Arizona.

Slumgullion Pass. Beginning in 1879, an ore trail used to go through here. Miners would stop in the pass and cook themselves a mess of stew called slumgullion.

The Gate. A few miles south of Curecanti Recreation Area, towering granite walls on either side of the Lake Fork of the Gunnison frame the entrance to a gorge with steep, multicolored cliffs—a smaller version of Black Canyon.

Vallecito Lake. The second largest lake in Colorado is in the San Juan Basin, and is a center for pack trips up to Windom Park and the high San Juan country that towers above it.

RELATED MUSEUMS AND ATTRACTIONS

Bayfield. Gem Village Museum; mineralogy.

Cortez. Four Corners Museum; natural history, fossils (including dinosaurs).

Durango. Durango Public Library Museum; natural history, geology, herbarium.

Mesa Verde National Park. Park Museum.

Scenic Narrow Gauge Railroad.
The "Silverton" makes a daily
trip in summer over the stunning
route between Durango and the
old mining town of Silverton.
The 45-mile trip along the Animas
River gorge was once a necessary
link between mining communities,
but is now run just for tourists.
Reservations for it are advised.

San Miguel Range. *Nearly every
road in the area around Ophir and
Telluride offers a superlative
view; this one is from State Highway 145, and shows the quaking
aspen in its brilliant fall color
of shimmering gold. According to
Indian legend, the aspens quiver
eternally because they once failed
to do so before the Great Spirit.*

Dallas Divide. *Snowdrifts along
State Highway 62, and plumes of
snow blowing off the 13,000-foot
summit of Mount Hayden, in the
Sneffels Range, present the magnificent scenery of the Uncompahgre area at its most severe. Some
of these mountains have been sufficiently tamed for skiing: the
Dallas ski area is along this road.*

257

Great Sand Dunes
NATIONAL MONUMENT, COLORADO

Sunrise colors the dunes below the Sangre de Cristos.

Wind at a Mountain Wall Creates a Mirage Landscape

Like a mirage, Colorado's Great Sand Dunes rise from the almost treeless San Luis Valley. They run 10 miles along the flank of the towering Sangre de Cristo Mountains, many of whose peaks are snow-topped the year around —a fantastic visual blend of Sahara and Switzerland. In everyone who sees them, from the Spanish explorer who first discovered them nearly 200 years ago to today's tourists, the dunes inspire unbelieving surprise and awe.

Since 1932 these Sahara-like dunes have been part of the Great Sand Dunes National Monument, a region covering 36,000 acres and supervised by the National Park Service. Although close to 200,000 people visit them each year, the dunes remain one of America's lesser known natural wonders.

For eons, prevailing southwesterly winds have swept across the flat San Luis Valley— an area three times the size of Delaware—and picked up sand anchored only by sparse rabbit brush, sagebrush and bunchgrass. As the winds rise over the Sangre de Cristos, they lose velocity and rain sand at the foot of the range. Then they rush through Mosca, Medano (Dune) and Music passes—the last named for eerie sounds created by gusts whistling through dead spruces at the crest.

Man has long been associated with the Great Sand Dunes. Archeological finds suggest the region was occupied 10,000 years ago by nomadic hunters. Excavations have uncovered

259

Wind constantly shifts sand from the windward to the leeward side of a dune, causing the pile to advance. As it does, it slowly engulfs any vegetation. Tree skeletons are later uncovered again.

The shadows created by the early morning and late afternoon sun emphasize the fluid contours of the wind-sculpted dunes and the knife edge sharpness of the ridges. The steep side is the leeward side.

ancient spear points as well as evidence of an early basketmaking culture. For centuries Ute Indians controlled the valley, and hunting parties that passed through included Apaches, Comanches, Cheyennes and Arapahoes. In an expedition during the winter of 1806–07, U.S. Army Lieutenant Zebulon Pike (for whom nearby Pikes Peak is named) led a party over Medano Pass into the dunes. Today, passes east of the dunes are open only to foot and horse travel, except for one four-wheel-drive track leading over Medano Pass.

Most tourists arrive at the monument, 37 miles northeast of Alamosa, by way of Colorado Route 150. Some take the more scenic gravel road off U.S. 160 to the south: this graded road extends 13 miles around the base of 14,363-foot Mount Blanca. Only camping and picnic facilities are available at the monument; each year about 50,000 campers stay overnight at the 120 campsites.

The visitor center is the focal point for new arrivals. From here many visitors take a leisurely stroll along the half-mile Montville Trail: a booklet identifies flowers and shrubs along the way and tells where to look for signs of the toll road through Mosca Pass, once a highway for westbound pioneers. There is a picnic area at the edge of the dunes, and another trail to the so-called Ghost Forest.

Hiking into the dunes in midsummer is probably most rewarding during the early morning and late afternoon. At these times the slanting rays of the sun create shadows that intensify dune contours, and photographers can get spectacular dune pictures (camera expo-

Sunflowers are among the wildflowers that grow in moisture-retaining pockets in the sand. The wind-rippled sand in the distance looks as if it has been formed by the action of waves washing on a beach.

sures should be the same as for seascapes and snow scenes). A round-trip hike to the crest of dunes nearest the monument headquarters takes about three hours.

Although winds constantly alter the dunes' shape, shifting the sand into fresh patterns daily, photographs taken half a century ago show that the major formations have changed little. Storms from the northeast periodically create temporary sand ledges, but a return of the prevailing southwest winds restores ridge contours. Strong winds create sand plumes rising over ridges, curling onto downward slopes.

And dunes slowly encroach upon nearby stands of trees, elsewhere uncovering skeleton forests smothered years ago.

Along the eastern and southern fringes of the dunes, Medano Creek flows before slowly sinking into the sand. After a heavy rain or snowmelt the stream may be up to 600 feet wide, but only six inches deep, its surface rippled by small waves. Within hours it will be a trickle. Willows thrive along the watercourse, but except in low pockets that trap moisture to nurture dwarf sunflowers and low-lying pea plants, vegetation is absent from the dunes. Next to the dunes, however, grow cottonwood, piñon, mountain mahogany and chokecherry.

Animals abound in the area, but it is likely the visitor will see only tracks of most of them, though deer are often seen in the monument. Weasels, coyotes, porcupines, bobcats, cottontail rabbits, kangaroo rats and jumping mice are residents of the neighborhood. Elk move through outlying regions, and during winter months mountain lions kill deer within the monument. Rare bighorn mountain sheep winter in the area, and antelope graze nearby. Golden eagles, sparrow hawks, great horned owls and screech owls all hunt their prey here.

At any season, sunset at the monument invariably reminds visitors of their first impression—that Great Sand Dunes is a mirage floating in front of the mountains: copper-colored foothills, smooth as clouds, below the crimson peaks of the Sangre de Cristos.

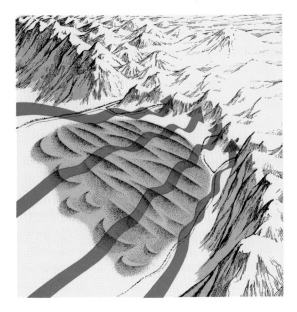

Wind, Sand and Mountains

The Sangre de Cristo range curves like the crook of an elbow around the San Luis Valley's eastern end. The prevailing winds blowing across the valley are trapped in this bend (shown at left). As they reach the mountain barrier they rise to flow through the low passes in the range. Sand is too heavy to be carried up, so it is dropped just where the winds sweep upward. The resulting sand accumulation has produced dunes 700 feet high.

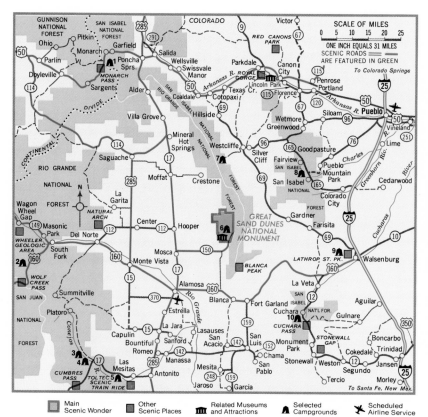

Main Scenic Wonder | **Other Scenic Places** | **Related Museums and Attractions** | **Selected Campgrounds** | **Scheduled Airline Service**

WITHIN A DAY'S DRIVE:
Mountain Vistas Abounding

Blanca Peak.
(Picture appears on facing page)

Cuchara Pass. The pass is closed in winter, but in summer the motorist has a magnificent view of the Sangre de Cristo range and the Spanish Peaks. Nearby is Devil's Stair Steps, a massive lava wall that subsequently split in two and resembles an enormous stairway.

Cumbres Pass. The road through Cumbres from Chama, New Mexico, into Colorado is no major highway; but any difficulty in driving is more than compensated for by the remarkable scenery it offers. Forested slopes of the Continental Divide soar on the west side of the road, varied by flowery mountain meadows and small valleys carved by rushing creeks.

Lathrop State Park. The all-encompassing view of the distant Spanish Peaks is the highlight of this small park centered around two lakes near Walsenburg. The Indians called these peaks "huajatollas," meaning "breasts of the world," and believed they were the home of gods. The park houses a buffalo herd.

Monarch Pass.
(Picture appears on facing page)

Natural Arch. Near Del Norte in Saguache (blue earth) County, the "arch" can be reached by a dirt road and a trail. It is actually a hole, 20 feet wide and 40 feet tall, in a mountain ridge of conglomerate rock which was laid down millions of years ago when the entire region was covered by an inland sea.

Red Canons Park. A series of small canyons and red sandstone formations give this undeveloped park near Canon City its name. Nearby is a site where a sign announces that fossils of five dinosaurs have been unearthed here.

Royal Gorge. Sheer walls of red granite, whose color changes with the sun, rise 1000 feet above the Arkansas River in this dizzyingly steep and narrow canyon. The gorge can be viewed from the suspension bridge that crosses it —said to be the world's highest— and from an aerial tramway, cable car or walkway. The gorge is operated commercially, and there is an admission charge.

Stonewall Gap. A granite barrier reaching heights of over 200 feet stretches across the Stonewall Valley and gives it its name. A similar "wall" appears elsewhere in the Rockies, thrown up by the same volcanic activity that created the Sangre de Cristo range, but only here does the formation reach such a height. Near the town of Stonewall is a natural gap in the huge barrier, traversed by the Purgatoire River.

Blanca Peak. *The jagged peaks of Blanca and Lindsey (formerly Old Baldy), visible all over the San Luis Valley, actually form one mountain, connected by a saddle. They are part of the Sangre de Cristo range, which includes eight mountains over 14,000 feet high.*

Toltec Scenic Train Ride. This narrow-gauge railroad has been recently reestablished for scenic tourist rides on weekends in summer between Chama, New Mexico, and Antonito, Colorado. It crisscrosses the state line many times on its trip through spectacularly rugged terrain.

Wheeler Geologic Area. Set in a canyon with towering cliffs are weird formations of sandstone carved by erosion. This is a difficult spot to reach even in summer, but well worth the effort. It is best to ride in on horses rented at Wagon Wheel Gap.

Wolf Creek Pass. This fine pass through the Continental Divide is surrounded on both sides by stirring vistas of the Rio Grande and San Juan national forests. Colorado's heaviest snows fall here, but the pass is open all year.

RELATED MUSEUMS AND ATTRACTIONS

Canon City. Canon City Municipal Museum; natural history.

Great Sand Dunes National Monument. Park Museum.

Monarch Pass. *The 11,312-foot altitude of this pass on the Continental Divide makes it one of the highest in the Rockies. A journey through it is like being on top of the world: clouds often enfold the magnificent panorama of mountains stretching in all directions.*

263

Carlsbad Caverns
NATIONAL PARK, NEW MEXICO

The Temple of the Sun glows with subtly placed light in Carlsbad's subterranean blackness.

Dazzling Chambers That Shelter
a Fascinating Army of Bats

The landscape of the Texas-New Mexico border region is startlingly empty. Under the high-intensity sunlight, the endless undulations of the Chihuahuan desert conceal nothing and reveal nothing; after a while, its overpowering vastness numbs the mind. The level horizon leads your eye almost full circle, obstructed only by the low ridge of the Guadalupe Mountains, which trespass a few miles into Texas before terminating abruptly in the sheer stone brow of El Capitan.

But just above the level of the desert floor, buried under the foothills on the eastern flank of the mountains, lies a sight as different from the arid landscape as you can imagine: the Carlsbad Caverns, soaring like a cathedral entombed in the heart of a rock. Yet these caverns are beyond the most exalted geometry of Gothic architects; even Jules Verne, who could imagine a journey to the center of the earth, could scarcely find anything as utterly fantastic in his dreams.

Man had nothing to do with this monumental edifice. The rock that holds the caverns in its heavy embrace is limestone, laid down 250 million years ago as a living reef in the offshore shallows of a vast inland sea. In the course of millennia, this sea dried up; eventually seabed, reef and shoreline were obscured under a blanket of sediment several thousand feet deep. Thus protected, the buried reef spent

The Left Hand Tunnel is a beautifully decorated cleft that is located close to an underground cafeteria where 1000 cave visitors an hour can be fed.

well over half of its total existence almost totally unaffected by the constantly altering shape of the earth surface above.

Something less than 20 million years ago, during a period of mountain-building activity, a massive fault split the reef and thrust a great block upward to become the Guadalupe Mountains. Erosion commenced to strip away the tremendously thick blanket of sediment overlying the ancient reef. Groundwater seeped through the tiny fractures in the limestone mass, carrying carbon dioxide absorbed from the soil. The water was actually a weak carbonic acid solution, capable of changing the limestone into calcium bicarbonate, which could be dissolved and carried away. The reef became a rocky sponge, saturated with the corrosive fluid that slowly ate away its tissues.

As the water table gradually lowered, creating great cavities ever deeper within the rock, air filled the upper caverns. Massive blocks of porous rock, denied the buoyant support of water, began to collapse under their own weight, further increasing the size of these chambers.

Exposed to the air for the first time after ages underwater, the cavern walls began to grow a stone stubble. Surface rain and melted snow, percolating through the earth and porous rock, carried with it dissolved limestone, which solidified again inside the caves as the water evaporated drop by drop.

As the slow seepage went on for centuries, each drop of water adding a minute limestone deposit, stone icicles called stalactites grew down from the ceilings. Excess water accumu-

Carlsbad's Strange Nightly Spectacle: The Great Flight From Bat Cave

Many caves have bats, but only at Carlsbad has their nightly exodus become a major spectacle for visitors. The entrance to Bat Cave has even been provided with a steeply raked amphitheater, as if for an audience at some primitive drama. Each night, from April to October (most of the bats migrate to warmer places in winter), millions of them emerge in a black cloud of wings from the depths of Bat Cave and set off for an all-night insect hunt in the valleys of the Black and Pecos rivers to the south. They return at first light. There are 14 species of bats in the park, none of them harmful to man—though ladies have been known to scream when they emerge. As many as nine million bats have been estimated to hang in Bat Cave at one time. When they come out, it is at the rate of more than a million an hour —which means about 300 of them every second.

---

lated at their tips to rain eternally on the floor below, building stalagmites of waxen stone like grotesquely melted candles. These two formations are the caverns' most common speleothems—the term for stone accretions built up by chemical action.

The Carlsbad visitor can choose between two routes into this nether world. From the natural entrance—a huge cave under a hilltop —you can, if you are really energetic, follow a steep, zigzag trail to the caverns more than 800 feet below. After a strenuous mile-and-three-quarter hike through a series of spooky antechambers, you arrive at a welcome, if incongruous, underground cafeteria.

Or, if you prefer, a high-speed elevator will drop you straight from the visitor center to the cafeteria level. Either way, the cafeteria is your jumping-off place for the conservatively named Big Room—the 14-acre main cavern whose ceiling soars 285 feet into the subterranean night. A loop trail leads you around the circumference of this incredible chamber—a distance of a mile and a quarter—past a succession of artfully illuminated stone formations like the small antechapels around the perimeter of a great cathedral.

In the vast empty spaces of this underground fastness, even the muffled, awed voices of your fellow visitors may seem inappropriate. The best way to experience Carlsbad is to start early, descending in the first elevator in the morning, or walking in with the day's first group, and skipping the lunch break. If you can manage to move on ahead of the crowd to explore the Big Room on your own, you can enjoy for a while the eerie illusion of being the first astronaut to arrive in *inner* space. You feel completely cut off from the world above, as indifferent to it as it is to you. Your senses seem superacute in the odorless, silent darkness. The loudest noise you hear is the regular rhythm of your own breathing, punctuated by the sound of water dripping from the stalactites above, each drop adding its tiny burden of limestone to the endless construction. In the constant 56-degree dampness, you may fancy that you are the only warm, mortal being in a world of cold and silent stone.

But huddled in a chamber at the other end of the caverns, their hearts beating faster than yours, hundreds of thousands of warm-blooded fellow creatures share the Stygian gloom. They are the famous Carlsbad bats—mostly Mexican freetails—that have summered here, generation after generation, for at least 1700 years. They sleep away the days packed in tight masses—300 of them to the square foot —on the ceiling of their chamber, coming to life at nightfall to fly abroad in search of food.

It was their nightly exodus that first attracted local settlers to the caverns' entrance cave. Then, just after the turn of this century, the bats' sanctuary was invaded for the nitro-

The Natural Radar System Bats Fly—and Eat—By

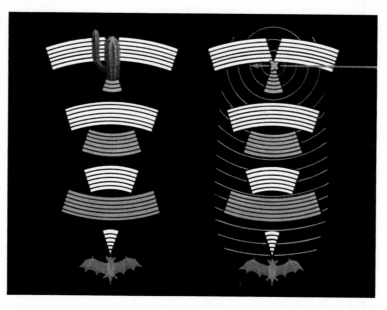

Bats, as nocturnal creatures, have to be able to "see" in the darkness of cave and nocturnal desert. They do so with a remarkable echo-location system that works like a radar network. They emit pulses on ultrasonic frequencies (far beyond the range of human ears) that bounce off other objects in their path, enabling them to sense the presence of obstacles —and to catch the flying insects that are their food. In the drawings at right, bats bounce their pulses off a stationary object and a moving insect. The insect emits a pulse of its own which the bat receives, enabling it to sense motion.

gen-rich guano—or bat droppings—that had accumulated over centuries to a depth of many feet. More than 200 million pounds of guano from the Bat Cave were sold as commercial fertilizer before the caverns were afforded the protection of national monument status in 1923. They were finally dedicated as a national park in 1930.

Though the Bat Cave is off limits to visitors —for your protection as well as the bats', as conditions in their private chamber are hardly sanitary—their regular evening flights during the summer months offer a fascinating spectacle and make Carlsbad a double attraction of natural marvels.

Without quite knowing what to expect, you take your seat just before sunset, at the hour posted by a park ranger, in a small amphitheater built on a slope opposite the entrance cave. The setting, appropriate for a Greek tragedy, the fast-gathering night and the atavistic human fear of bats combine to amplify your

sense of rather anxious anticipation. As you stare into the immense, shadowed mouth of the cave, agile swallows wheel and skim perilously close to the face of the rock, then dive headlong into the caverns' depth, sending their excited, shrill voices echoing to the surface.

Then silence. Finally, from deep in the earth, your straining ears hear the whisper of moving air. The bats come, a few at first, then more, spiraling counterclockwise out of the dark opening in a living tornado. So fast is their flight—up to 30 miles per hour—that individual bats blur into gray shadows in the dim twilight. Their wings—thin membranes stretched taut between long, delicate finger bones—beat furiously, making the very air alive.

Climbing steeply, sometimes flying so close that the wind of their passage grazes your face,

they veer southward over the crest of the hill and are gone. All night they will sweep the air above the Texas plains and river valleys to the south, broadcasting high-frequency sonar signals to help them zero in on the insects they capture and eat on the wing. In a night's hunting, each bat may consume half its own weight in insects; the caverns' population of several million rids local farmers of several tons of flying pests each night.

Long before the bats return unerringly at dawn, diving with folded wings into the mouth of the cave, you will have followed the winding road back down to the familiar world below. But after a single day at Carlsbad Caverns, you will return to that world with a deeper understanding of the mysteries that lie far beneath the earth.

Water Created Carlsbad's Elaborate Chambers

The underground wonderland of the Carlsbad Caverns offers an astounding range and variety of colorful effects. In the Queen's Chamber (on facing page), great masses of stalactites have grown together until they look like voluminous golden draperies. The Totem Pole (on the right) is the tallest—40 feet—of a number of similar formations at Carlsbad. Although it looks as if it must have grown downward from the ceiling, it is in fact a tall and skinny stalagmite, which grew up from the cave floor to this remarkable height because the water that formed it was dripping off the ceiling too fast to produce a parent growth of any size. It is tempting when looking at such formations to try and measure their growth in terms of human history; but although we can tell the exact age of a tree by counting its annual growth rings, there is no reliable method of aging limestone cave formations, for their rate of growth can be affected by so many factors— rainfall, limestone solution, degrees of temperature and humidity. Some stalactites take millennia to grow an inch; others grow so fast that Carlsbad's elevator shaft already sprouts some.

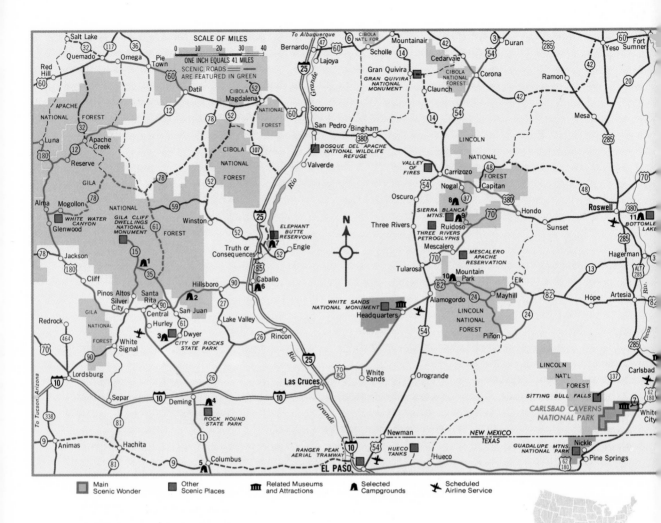

Ancient Lava Beds, Indian Relics and a Mecca for Rock Hounds

Bosque del Apache National Wildlife Refuge, N.M. For avid bird watchers, this is the spot to be any time from November to March. During these winter months the refuge is the southern home of many ducks and geese—and most of this continent's greater sandhill cranes.

Bottomless Lakes, N.M. Seven crystal-clear lakes make this area an oasis in the desert, a place to picnic, swim and boat. They were named by cowboys who were unable to touch bottom with a string of weighted lariats. Geologists believe the lakes were formed when underground water forced the ground above to cave in.

City of Rocks State Park, N.M. Flat desert runs into colossal rock outcroppings here, scenic oddities that attract picnickers and campers. Another bonus is an outstanding botanical garden that specializes in varieties of cactuses from all over the Southwest.

Elephant Butte Reservoir, N.M. Below Elephant Butte, a volcanic promontory, a dam holds back the Rio Grande and creates a finger lake about thirty miles long in the arid surrounding desert. This provides a popular playland for swimming, boating, water skiing and fishing. There is a marina with boat rentals and tackle to lure bass and catfish.

Gila Cliff Dwellings National Monument, N.M. About 600 years ago an Indian community lived in this cliffside apartment house. Protected from above by cliffs, it is carved out of stone 150 feet aboveground. The rock caves once held 35 to 40 rooms, walled with stone and adobe.

Gran Quivira National Monument, N.M. About A.D. 1000 Pueblo Indians built houses here and, on nearby fields, farmed corn, beans and squash. By 1600, Spanish gold-seekers and missionaries had found the village. Their legacy is the ruins of a church 140 feet long with stone walls five feet thick.

Sitting Bull Falls, *N.M. A spring is the source of the creek that falls 180 feet here, creating pools below big enough to swim in. The water is so full of various minerals that when it splashes and then quickly evaporates in the hot, dry air, odd mineral formations, like mushroom-shaped rocks, build up.*

Guadalupe Mountains National Park, Tex.
(Picture appears on this page)

Hueco Tanks, Tex. For centuries, rock basins have stored rainwater here, and the site became a crucial landmark for those who journeyed across this arid land. Some travelers left behind vivid proof of their passing: rocks show names of gold-rushers bound for California in 1849 and 2000-year-old Indian carvings.

Mescalero Apache Reservation, N.M. Of the 3400 Apaches who live in New Mexico, about half, known as Mescaleros, live on 460,000 lavishly scenic acres. They have pioneered recreation enterprises, including a ski area on Sierra Blanca, a mountain sacred to the Apaches. Visitors can go fishing for trout and see the state's largest mule deer herd.

Ranger Peak Aerial Tramway, Tex. For those who like to climb mountains effortlessly, this is the way to do it. The glass and steel gondola glides up to Ranger Peak, more than a mile high, offering views of Texas, New Mexico and Mexico.

Rock Hound State Park, N.M. Unlike most parks where visitors are asked to leave things as they find them, this one encourages you to take away—at least in limited numbers—stones. Agate, amethyst, jasper and carnelian are among the finds for keen-eyed rock hounds among the volcanic rock. It is a picnic and camping ground too, all in view of the lofty Florida Mountains.

Guadalupe Mountains National Park, *Tex. Sun yellows the cliffs of Guadalupe Peak, at 8751 feet the highest point in Texas. This is part of a spectacular fossil reef, once underwater, that was built about 250 million years ago. Now canyons shelter cactuses, hardwoods, evergreens—and animals like raccoons, elks and bobcats.*

White Sands National Monument, *N.M. Sunrise strikes the world's largest gypsum desert. Winds out of the southwest ripple low-lying sands, picking up fine grains to make huge dunes like snowdrifts. Tough plants like yucca and cottonwood survive among dunes, and some lizards and mice turn white to camouflage themselves.*

Sierra Blanca Mountains, N.M. Splendid views are the rule in this White Mountain region, part of the Lincoln National Forest. In winter it is popular with skiers, and in summer it is a cool refuge from desert heat; tourists come especially for the gondola ride to an 11,400-foot peak.

Sitting Bull Falls, N.M.
(*Picture appears on page 273*)

Three Rivers Petroglyphs, N.M. About 500 Indian carvings, some a thousand years old, cover stones along a quarter-mile ridge here. The carvings—like others in the Southwest—keep their secrets. Strollers along the asphalt trail can only guess whether they record ancient games, religious rites or hunting triumphs.

Valley of Fires, N.M. About a thousand years ago rivers of lava flowed from Little Black Peak and spread southward; according to Indian legend, volcanic eruptions made a valley of fires. It is a strange and fascinating terrain, where stone bubbles, ridges, arches and tunnels forever record the many shapes of congealed lava. The Mal Pais lava beds stretch for miles to the south.

White Sands National Monument, N.M.
(*Picture appears on facing page*)

Whitewater Canyon, N.M. Most canyon explorations require special skills or equipment. But here a catwalk—anchored to rock walls and two and a half miles long—enables the visitor to venture out on the cliff face. He can linger over signs that identify plants, and enjoy in close-up the colors in the canyon walls.

RELATED MUSEUMS AND ATTRACTIONS

Carlsbad, N.M. Carlsbad Municipal Museum; minerals, archeological relics.

White Sands, N.M. White Sands National Monument Park Museum.

Big Bend National Park
TEXAS

The rugged Chisos Mountains, heart of the Big Bend country, glow in the clear desert air.

Mountain Grandeur and Solitude in a Remote Curve of the Rio Grande

There is so much red rock piled up in the Big Bend country that it seems as if the boundary between Mexico and the United States must sag southward here to accommodate its mass. The "big bend" is a curve in the Rio Grande, and the national park that bears its name is located far from any major route between east and west. And Big Bend has another reason besides its remoteness for not being heavily visited: it's just too hot down there during summer vacation time.

People who come to this awesomely rugged land at different seasons of the year might think they are visiting entirely different parks. The July visitor heading south from Marathon, Texas, on highway U.S. 385 drives through Persimmon Gap to find that the only moving things are the dust devils, tortured writhings of air almost too hot to breathe. When he comes upon the park it is at its worst, sere and brown. In July it is easy to understand why a Texas rancher referred to a pasture of 80,000 acres as being overstocked when it fed two mules; that same July heat inspired the story about the Big Bend coyote chasing the Big Bend jackrabbit, and "they wuz both walking."

But the March visitor who arrives 48 hours after one of the infrequent rains sees a different Big Bend entirely. Then the red of the twisted and folded layers of sandstone glows even more brightly next to the new-minted

Sunlight penetrates into the dim, frowning depths of Santa Elena Canyon for a couple of hours after sunrise each day. It can only be entered on foot.

green leaves that followed the rain. Spanish dagger covers the slopes with mounds of creamy white flowers, and an explosion of crimson spreads along the stalks of ocotillo. Tasajillo is in bloom and the mesquite is shiny and bright beside the dry watercourses. There is even a cactus bud that tastes like cold, juicy strawberries—once you strip off its spines.

Barren or flowery, the tortured mountains of Big Bend record the cataclysmic upheavals of a distant geologic past. Its striated layers of sedimentary rock were deposited on the bottom of a primeval sea—although today it is difficult to visualize this land ever having enough water to swim in. It took millennia for the sandstone to be deposited, and in some areas it is over a thousand feet thick. Later the Rio Grande carved its deep ditch through the sandstone as though with a knife.

The weather provides most of the remarkable contrasts of Big Bend. Ninety-three degrees was officially recorded in February at Presidio; six days later a five-inch blanket of snow covered a ranch downstream. Temperatures can vary as much as 50 degrees between sunup and four o'clock in the afternoon. Animal life that can survive this extreme diurnal range must be tough and adaptable. This wide temperature fluctuation means that at every part of the day the weather is just right for some species. So each species is active during its particular period and waits, with the patience of the desert, during the rest of the day.

Degrees of comfort are closely related to the elevation figures for different parts of Big Bend

The Rio Grande—no longer a very grand river at this stage of its long journey—forms the frontier with Mexico in this corner of Texas. Here

Mexicans from the neighboring village of Boquillas are crossing the water below the rugged ramparts of the Sierra del Carmen. This crossing is in

National Park. Chisos Basin is more than a mile high. It is the location of the park's biggest and best campground, where you will sleep under blankets even in July. Spring or fall temperatures will move the campers down a little, perhaps to Castolon. When winter nights drop below freezing, the camper will probably choose Rio Grande Village, warmest spot in the park.

It is the spectacular if austere beauty of the Chisos Mountains that lures most visitors to Big Bend; but many also enjoy the good fishing for catfish in Boquillas or Santa Elena canyons. Here the Rio hardly justifies its "Grande." Sucked almost dry by a thousand miles of irrigation ditches between its cradle in the snows of Colorado and the arid rock of the bend, it is placid, slow-moving and serene.

For the best experience of the park, visitors should enter through the north gate, cross Tornillo Creek and stop 3800 feet high at park headquarters for maps and informational brochures. There is a gradual climb as you head for Chisos Basin, and the slow change in elevation reveals a succession of different life zones, including the varied vegetation of high mountain desert, and some unusual wildlife.

Whitetail deer are common in the park and often stroll tamely through the campgrounds. Not too many years ago campers witnessed the savage spectacle of a cougar chasing, catching and killing a whitetail buck right in the Chisos Basin campground. Usually the park lions are secretive, and it is a lucky visitor who catches sight of the tawny cat. Other deer in the park includes the mule deer in the lower areas. Coy-

Boquillas Canyon, which is much longer (25 miles) and wider than Santa Elena, Big Bend's other celebrated canyon. It is particularly lovely at sunset.

WESTERN
COLLARED
LIZARD

ALLIGATOR
LIZARD

REGAL
RINGNECK SNAKE

BLACK-TAILED
RATTLESNAKE

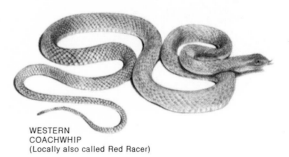

WESTERN
COACHWHIP
(Locally also called Red Racer)

Secretive Denizens of Big Bend Country

Lizards and snakes—both in the same reptile family—are cold-blooded: their body temperature depends on that of the surrounding air. They like warmth but above 105 degrees they may suffer heat prostration and die; so they have learned to seek out shade—the small regal ringneck snake, for instance, lives under rocks and logs. A high level of heat tolerance allows the red racer to chase its prey even in midday sun. The western collared lizard adapts to the temperature by lightening or darkening its skin to reflect or absorb heat; it can run surprisingly fast on its hind legs. The alligator lizard, like some others, can slip out of its tail to escape enemies. But snakes and lizards alike shed their skins, lizards in sections, snakes all at once.

281

otes, bobcats, badgers and skunks are often seen, and the little javelina, or wild pig.

Big Bend is a bird watcher's delight at any time of the year. Black and turkey vultures ride the ever-present thermal currents on motionless wings. This is a mixing ground, a meeting place between U.S. and Mexican bird zones. Roadrunners lope along through the stunted nopal (prickly pear cactus), and the tiniest of our doves, the little ground dove, nods its head as if proud of itself as it walks among the tumbled red boulders. The cactus wren is the bird heard most often, but you should also catch sight of pyrrhuloxia and painted buntings. (Park rangers like to tell of the American who could not identify a bird he had seen, and called on a Mexican to give him the Spanish name. The Mexican truthfully said it was a "pajarito" in Spanish. The birder was chagrined to find the translation in the dictionary: "little bird.")

Good advice to the visitor in any language is to get supper out of the way in the Chisos Basin in time to watch the magnificent pageant that is sunset in this clear air and high altitude. The steep sides of Casa Grande glow red in the late afternoon sun, slowly turn to purple and then dim into darkness as if a light were lowered inside them. Deer move out of their daytime lairs and fan out to feed over the long slope which leads to La Ventana (The Window), the huge gap in the wall of this natural amphitheater. Birds that have been silent since morning suddenly make themselves heard.

The plaintive, querulous wailing of coyotes marks the transition between dusk and night. The towering rock walls echo their howling until it seems that you must be surrounded by coyotes. Then the coyote falls silent to go about its nocturnal business and only rarely sings again. It is now pitch dark, and the bass hooting of the great horned owl seems eerily loud as you get ready for bed. The stars are very close here, in the clear air.

Morning is the best time of all, so get up early and enjoy a hike up to the South Rim, where you can easily toss a rock across to bounce on the foreign rock of another nation. Mornings, before the sun is too high, is also the time to explore the high desert, so full of unexpected activity. Rattlesnakes are rare, though present. Most often, the sudden movement in the shade of a huisache tree reveals a skink, which is a fast-running member of the lizard family.

The Big Bend is a land of tremendous distances, scorching heat and bitter cold. It is a land almost without rainfall, but filled with bustling animal life. It is a land of cruel beauty that expands to the immensity of deep canyons and contracts to the sudden flash of color of a warbler flitting into the shade of a mesquite. It is a land of brooding silences broken by the lilting song of a wren. It is a land where a man can get off by himself and take his measure against the colossal backdrop of the Dead Horse Mountains, and breathe the air no one else is breathing for a dozen miles in every direction. And perhaps that alone is well worth the long detour to this curve of the Rio Grande.

At Castolon Peak, one of the most striking formations along the Rio Grande, the volcanic rocks common in this area of the park are clearly seen.

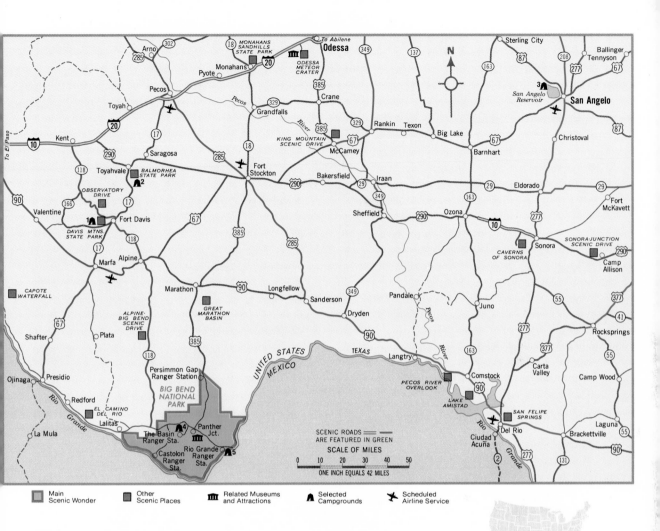

Main Scenic Wonder | Other Scenic Places | Related Museums and Attractions | Selected Campgrounds | Scheduled Airline Service

WITHIN A DAY'S DRIVE:

Dunes, Oases, a Meteor Crater—and Infinite Views in Clear Desert Air

Alpine—Big Bend Scenic Drive.
(Picture appears on page 284)

Balmorhea State Park. The huge San Solomon Springs, which gush from this dry land at a remarkable 26 million gallons a day, have created a small river, a sizable lake and a surrounding oasis of greenery here. The springs also fill one of the world's largest swimming pools.

Capote Waterfall.
(Picture appears on page 284)

Caverns of Sonora. Discovered and opened to the public (for an admission charge) only a few years ago, these caves are slowly

becoming better known as some of the most beautiful in the country. Despite their remoteness, on a back road southwest of the little desert town of Sonora, they are well worth the effort to reach them. Delicate crystalline formations grow in remarkable profusion, and shimmer in a rainbow of colors.

Davis Mountains State Park. The rolling Davis Mountains, less spectacularly rugged than the towering Chisos farther south, are at their spacious best in this 1870-acre park. There are several hiking trails, and observation stations to watch birds and wildlife. The 5000-foot altitude of the

Davis range and the prevailingly clear, sunny weather makes it a popular recreation area. Hunting is good for deer and antelope.

El Camino del Rio.
(Picture appears on page 285)

Great Marathon Basin. Amateur rock hounds as well as professional geologists are drawn to this rugged area full of large outcroppings of varied rocks and minerals. One particularly striking series of jagged formations is known as Hell's Half Acre.

King Mountain Scenic Drive. The drive across King Mountain, a 3000-foot mesa towering above

Alpine–Big Bend Scenic Drive. *State Highway 118 down to the western entrance of Big Bend National Park passes through wide plains and past a series of isolated, dramatically shaped mountains and mesas, which include Bee Mountain (shown here), Packsaddle and Cathedral.*

Capote Waterfall. *A rough, unpaved road out of the tiny hamlet of Candelaria leads to this unique phenomenon. The evaporation of a 160-foot-high double fall has left a towering travertine deposit rather like a giant stalactite. Impurities in the water have colored it.*

McCamey, offers sweeping vistas over miles of surrounding ranch country and the Pecos Valley.

Lake Amistad. The United States and Mexico joined forces to create this colossal (67,000 acres) impoundment on the Rio Grande, the Devils River and the Pecos River, and the sight of this vast expanse of blue water in the middle of desert country is like a mirage. The international boundary across the lake is marked by buoys. The American shore is controlled by the National Park Service, and extensive boating facilities are available; more are under construction.

Monahans Sandhills State Park. Like a stretch of the Sahara Desert dumped in the middle of Texas, the Monahans Sandhills cover thousands of acres. The dunes are host to a vast "forest" of miniature oak trees, which send down roots as far as 90 feet to maintain themselves at the height of small shrubs. Dune buggy rides are available in the state park area.

Observatory Drive. Named after the University of Texas McDonald Observatory, which is perched in the clear air at the summit of Mount Locke, this 74-

mile loop drive embraces most of the highlights of the scenic Davis Mountains. After skirting Mount Locke it passes through Madera Canyon and then past the remarkable Rockpile Roadside Park, where colossal boulders as tall as three-story houses stand beside the highway.

Odessa Meteor Crater. The outline of the impact made by a giant meteor striking the earth an estimated 20,000 years ago is still apparent here, though subsequent silting has almost filled it level with the surrounding plain.

A museum on the site exhibits meteor fragments.

Pecos River Overlook. Today highway U.S. 90 crosses the canyon carved by the Pecos River on a fine bridge; but to pioneers passing this way the canyon was a major obstacle. The overlook, on the east rim, yields an impressive view; Indian caves are visible in the canyon walls.

San Felipe Springs. Another in the chain of springs that once provided watering stops in this arid land, San Felipe's 65 million gallons a day create a lush oasis. Moore Park offers swimming.

Sonora-Junction Scenic Drive. Heading east out of Sonora, highway U.S. 290 gradually climbs into the hills along the Llano River. Several ruined forts dot this forbidding landscape.

RELATED MUSEUMS AND ATTRACTIONS

Odessa. Odessa Meteorite Museum; meteor fragments.

Panther Junction. Big Bend National Park Museum.

El Camino del Rio. *The Spanish-named "River Road" hugs the American shore of the Rio Grande between the ghost town of Lajitas and Presidio. It is an eye-filling drive, with mountain walls and steep canyons on one side and the wide bends of the river below. Desert blooms brighten it in spring.*

285

Glacier National Park
MONTANA

St. Mary Lake lies below (left to right) Mahtotopa, Little Chief, Citadel and Fusillade mountains.

Mountains, Lakes and Forests Blend in a Wilderness Shaped by Ice

The towering mountain wilderness of Glacier National Park is as majestic a natural composition as any place on earth. Like a great work of art, its design is faultless: the juxtaposition of lake and mountain, of forest and ice field, of sweeping upcurve and jagged skyline, of sharp color and muted shade.

A half-dozen large lakes, five miles or more long, stretch from the park's lowland edges into the mountainous interior. Several hundred other lakes, large and small, line deep canyons and nestle in gigantic cups of lofty valleys, forests sloping up from their shores. On the eastern mountainsides are stands of subalpine fir, limber pine, Engelmann spruce and Douglas fir. The western slopes are more heavily blanketed with red cedar, hemlock, larch and lodgepole pine. Meadows starred with summer wildflowers cling to the steep pitches above the forests, and beyond the meadows the faces of the mountains rise sheer to jutting peaks.

On the heights, snowfields drape every ledge and pocket, about 60 of them big enough to qualify as glaciers. (A glacier can be defined as a permanent snow mass, deep enough to compact the lower levels into ice and heavy enough to creep downhill.) Grinnell, the largest, covers 300 acres and contains ice 400 feet thick; many others are almost as big. From every glacier and snowfield streams of water flow in summer, forming a lacework of glistening cascades

The glacier on Mount Oberlin carved out this steep-sided basin, known as a cirque. Above Bird Woman Falls is a spectacular example of a hanging valley.

on the mountainsides. Gathering volume as they join, the waters rush down the cobbled creek beds and finally tumble, a froth of white, into deep cold lakes.

Approached from the west, Glacier National Park comes as a lovely climax to a disordered series of sometimes forbidding ranges. From the east the effect is more emphatic. As you top the low rises of U.S. Route 2 or 89, the peaks seem to grow and come at you, like the prows of a fleet of ships driving out over the rolling sea of Montana prairie. And geologically speaking, this is exactly the case; for the crust of the earth has been compressed here, and the top layers, like a scuffed rug, have been folded over.

But a rock is not a rug, and these rocks, in layers originally 20,000 feet thick, broke along the fold. During the last 50 million years or so the severed edge has been shoved more than 30 miles east. This is the famous Lewis overthrust, an extraordinary geological phenomenon. What the visitor sees today is the intricately sculptured remnant, perhaps one fifth, of the original rock mass.

Such a complex of lake, stream, forest, meadow and rocky height would seem a good home for wildlife, and so it is. Fifty-seven species of mammals and more than 200 species of birds live here.

Coyotes and a few wolves sometimes enter the lower meadows from the adjacent plains. Beaver, muskrat, mink, otter, fisher and marten live along the lakes and streams. Ground squirrels burrow in the meadows and badgers

289

Clements Mountain, with its high, steep sides and roughly pyramidal shape, is a typical example of a glacial horn, or matterhorn, and dramatic testi- *mony to the power of glacial erosion. It was formed by the action of at least three glaciers, which "plucked" boulders from the ground, thus greatly*

dig right in after them. White-tailed and mule deer browse around forest clearings. Elks, five feet tall at the shoulder, graze in the meadows. Moose favor the lake shallows, where they nose around for underwater plants. Black bears shuffle through the forest and clearings. These bears will eat almost anything: plant shoots, grasses, berries, lily bulbs, grubs, ants, ground squirrels, fish, garbage, salami sandwiches, Tootsie Rolls and occasionally a finger of some park visitor foolish enough to think feeding them is fun.

Above the timberline little pikas busily put up hay for the winter. Marmots sun themselves on alpine meadows. Bighorn sheep seek tender grasses on rocky slopes. And the very symbol of Glacier is the mountain goat (not really a goat but an antelope). Its agility is legendary, but no amount of hearsay quite prepares you for the sight of one casually skipping up a sheer cliff face.

And then there is the grizzly bear. This hunch-shouldered, dish-faced, gray-backed bear is extremely shy, and a good thing too—at 500 pounds it is the second largest carnivore on earth, surpassed only by the Alaskan brown bear. Generally grizzlies stay away from the trails and avoid people and their habitations. But there are a thousand miles of trails in Glacier. To avoid chance encounters with these

Pressures That Toppled the Order of the Ages

FIFTY MILLION YEARS AGO—FOLDING BEGINS.

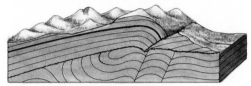

THE FOLD BREAKS; ROCK LAYERS OVERLAP.

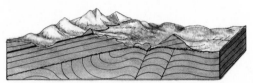

PRESENT—OVERTHRUST ROCKS HEAVILY ERODED.

Tremendous pressures beneath the earth's crust west of Glacier compressed and uplifted its layers of sedimentary rock, in an age of mountain-building that continued for millions of years. Finally the rocks were squeezed into one great fold. Pressure eventually toppled the fold and caused the layers to break. The western leg of the fold was forced up and over the eastern, reversing the order of the layers, so that older rocks lay over younger. Then the rocks were eroded into the rugged mountains you see today.

increasing their scouring power. These glaciers, grinding their way back through narrow, stream-cut valleys, left the sharply faceted horn behind.

very dangerous beasts, experienced hikers make plenty of noise: some carry bells or rattle-cans containing a few pebbles tied to their belts.

Don't expect to see all these animals during even an extended visit. But you will see goats, sheep, black bears and perhaps even an elk or moose. Hawks and eagles soar overhead, and grouse explode underfoot. And if you look into the swift-flowing streams, you may spy an ouzel, or dipper, flitting about for food, using its wings as a fish uses fins.

Stop at the visitor center at St. Mary and ask where animals are most likely to be. And look at the exhibits, which explain that the park was named not for existing glaciers but

for the ancient massive ice sheets that during the last million years carved the valleys and peaks and dug the lake beds, then finally melted away 10,000 years ago. Find out about the campgrounds, ranger-guided hikes, horse trips and boat excursions.

Then drive over the spectacular Going-to-the-Sun Highway. Fifty miles long, it is the only road that crosses the park. Starting from St. Mary, it skirts the north shore of St. Mary Lake, heading west toward a sea of peaks. After about five miles you come to the first of 17 parking turnouts, with a superb view of Triple Divide Peak, whose waters flow to three oceans: the Pacific by the Columbia River, the Arctic by Hudson Bay, the Gulf of Mexico via the Mississippi system.

At the narrows of St. Mary Lake the road crosses the Lewis overthrust fault line. Beyond and overhead the rocks are several hundred

Mosses and lichens carpet the rocky ground of Glacier's higher slopes. This alpine zone occurs above timberline, the elevation (about 7500 feet at Glacier) above which trees are both less frequent and considerably smaller than at lower elevations, rarely growing higher than 10 or 15 feet.

million years older than the rocks below. Here the valley road starts to climb, clinging to the face of the precipitous cliffs. Viewpoints open onto vast panoramas of glaciers and pinnacles, among them Mount Jackson, at 10,080 feet one of the park's highest.

From 6650-foot Logan Pass the Continental Divide winds north along the Garden Wall to Swiftcurrent Mountain and beyond. Naturalists at a visitor center answer questions and will probably suggest taking the self-guiding nature trail to Hidden Lake. This mile-and-a-half trail, partly a boardwalk, wanders across icy brooks, through gardens of wildflowers and along a glacial moraine to an unsurpassed view 800 feet above the shining blue lake.

To the north a trail traverses the foot of the Garden Wall, far above the timberline, to Granite Park Chalet, eight miles distant. The chalet supplies meals and rustic sleeping accommodations, and is a good place to spot grizzly bears—from a distance.

Beyond the pass the road winds down the mountain faces toward Lake McDonald. Near the bottom, just beyond a switchback, a roadside exhibit points out a bed of fossil algae, primitive plants that grew in an ancient sea a half-billion years ago. Another 10 miles brings you to the lake, McDonald Lodge and three large campgrounds.

Other roads from the east side lead to other lodges and campgrounds. Pick one and settle down. Hiking is the thing at Glacier, and a visit should not be entirely spent driving around in a car. There is a trail for every degree of stamina, from short, easy walks to week-long, backpacking treks into remote high country. Don't expect to find amusement concessions or golf courses.

"What am I supposed to do?" one man snorted. "Look at the scenery?"

Yes, that's it. Bring a warm jacket and some good walking shoes and take a long, affectionate, inquiring look at that scenery.

White mountain goat

Hoary marmot

ull moose

Bighorn ram

Grizzly yearling

Black bear

Glacier's Creatures, Fierce and Gentle

Of Glacier's bigger mammals, the agile mountain goat is the most tolerant of park visitors—even interested in them. Not a true goat at all, but a goat antelope, it is related to the chamois of the Alps. Its soft-centered, splayed hooves enable it to scamper over almost sheer rock faces and cling to the most precarious perches. The fearsome grizzly bear is best glimpsed from a distance. Sharing the forest with the bears are elks, deer, moose, cougars and wolves. The marmot, pika and wolverine prefer the cliffside habitat of the mountain goat. Among the 210 species of birds found in the park is the golden eagle. Bighorn ewes and lambs can often be seen in the meadow grazing near the Many Glacier Hotel.

293

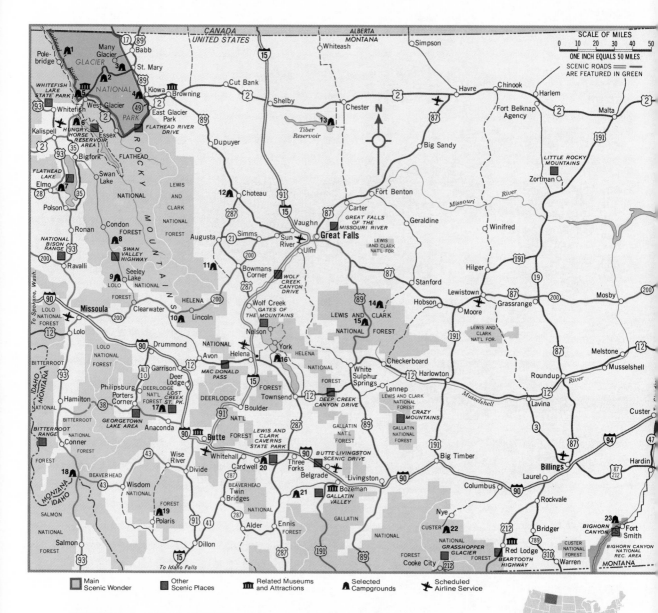

Main Scenic Wonder | Other Scenic Places | 🏛 Related Museums and Attractions | ▲ Selected Campgrounds | ✈ Scheduled Airline Service

Breathtaking Highways Through the Heart of the Mountains

Beartooth Highway. Superb views —including one from Beartooth Plateau of several gleaming mountain lakes and fields of alpine flowers—are found all along the 70-mile route leading southwest from Red Lodge. Open in summer only, the road climbs from 5000 feet to a height of 10,942 feet at Beartooth Pass.

Bighorn Canyon.
(*Picture appears on facing page*)

Bitterroot Range. Dramatic, snow-capped peaks crown the mountains that form the core of the Selway–Bitterroot Wilderness. An easily traveled gravel road follows along the West Fork of the Bitterroot River through a peaceful valley lined with evergreen forests and past Painted Rocks Lake, with its multicolored shores.

Butte–Livingston Scenic Drive.
(*Picture appears on page 297*)

Crazy Mountains. A drive along highway U.S. 89 provides sweeping views of these impressive peaks, lofty harbingers of the Rockies. Crazy Peak rises to over 11,000 feet in the middle of the range. Side roads from the Shields River valley lead up into the mountains, as well as into the neighboring Bridger Range.

Deep Creek Canyon Drive. Winding its way along the creek, U.S.

294

12 takes travelers through part of the Helena National Forest for glimpses of deer, elks and other wildlife.Scenic side roads permeate the lower Canyon Ferry Reservoir area; wooded trails for hikers branch off them.

Flathead Lake.
(Picture appears on pp. 296–297)

Flathead River Drive. Highway 2 follows the Middle Fork of the Flathead through rugged mountains and coniferous forests for views of the wild river below. Mountain goats, clinging to the rocky crags, can be seen from some of the overlooks.

Gallatin Valley. Fertile land, abundant with crops in spring and summer, forms variegated patterns of blues, purples, tans and greens, with brilliant wild flowers adding splashes of white

National Bison Range. *A herd of bison that roams freely over the 18,000-acre range is easily seen from a self-guided 20-mile drive on a gravel road that winds up to a point overlooking the entire Flathead Valley. The Mission Range forms a majestic backdrop to the view.*

Bighorn Canyon. *Yellowtail Dam has backed up the Bighorn River into a huge lake more than 70 miles long below sheer cliffs almost half a mile high. A primitive National Recreation Area of 63,000 acres surrounds this remarkable canyon, which reaches into Wyoming. Boating and fishing are available.*

and yellow. It is a striking contrast to the wild mountains above.

Gates of the Mountains. The dramatically scenic gorge of the Missouri River was discovered and named by Lewis and Clark, and is reached by boat from Clark Landing. The river snakes its way between 2000-foot limestone cliffs of the Big Belt Range. There are two-hour cruises through the canyon in summer.

Georgetown Lake Area. A spectacular pass leads through the Sapphire Mountains to this sparkling lake. There are several campgrounds in the area, which is one of the finest fishing spots in the state.

Grasshopper Glacier. One of the largest ice fields in America gets its name from the millions of grasshoppers imbedded in its depths. The frozen insects form layers of black lines across the face of the ice. The glacier is reached by hiking, horseback or jeep and is frequently inaccessible because of snow. Granite Peak, the highest point in Montana (12,799 feet), is nearby.

Great Falls of the Missouri River. The scenic falls, on the edge of the city named after them, were discovered by Lewis and Clark in 1805. Nearby is Giant Springs, one of the largest freshwater springs in the West, which flows at 388,800,000 gallons a day.

Hungry Horse Reservoir Area. A winding gravel road affords stunning views of the picturesque lake and surrounding mountain

ranges. Well-developed campgrounds provide a variety of facilities. Wildlife in the area includes whitetail deer and elks.

Lewis and Clark Caverns State Park. Montana's best-known state park features the largest-known limestone caverns in the Northwest. The intricate passageways are a fantasy of color and variety. Guided tours are conducted May through September.

Little Rocky Mountains. For the traveler weary of the seemingly

Butte–Livingston Scenic Drive. *Green valleys such as the one here, crowned with a rainbow near Manhattan, alternate with lofty mountain vistas along the 110 miles of scenic switchback highway that connects these towns. Bozeman Pass is one of the journey's highlights.*

Flathead Lake. *The snowcapped Mission Range lines the eastern horizon in this view over the largest (nearly 200 square miles) natural freshwater lake west of the Mississippi. Cutthroat, Dolly Varden and lake trout and kokanee salmon are among its prize catches.*

endless monotony of the high plains, these low green mountains come as a welcome relief and a stirring hint of the mountain splendors to come.

Lost Creek State Park. Aspens, willows and evergreens form a shadowy setting for Lost Creek Falls, which cascade down over sheer rock as the creek flows through a deep limestone canyon.

MacDonald Pass. The Continental Divide west of Helena is only 6400 feet high, but this pass is still a magnificent drive among wooded mountain slopes. Another striking drive out of Helena is along the Forest Service "Scenic Figure 8 Route," which climbs into the Big Belt Mountains on the east of Canyon Ferry Reservoir.

National Bison Range.
(Picture appears on page 295)

Swan Valley Highway. Dense forests give a wilderness atmosphere to this road passing between the Swan and Mission ranges. The million-acre Bob Marshall Wilderness, reachable only by trails, lies just to the east.

Whitefish Lake State Park. The park is located on the southwest shore of the lake in a heavily wooded area. The fishing is excellent, and big game animals abound in the nearby mountains. The double chair lift at nearby Big Mountain Ski Resort has breathtaking Rockies views.

Wolf Creek Canyon Drive. Interstate 15, with its recreation frontage road, gives access to almost 40 miles of outstanding fishing and scenery. A section follows the Missouri River and includes a length of Prickly Pear Creek, which is shaded by aspen and cottonwood trees and lined by multicolored canyon walls.

RELATED MUSEUMS AND ATTRACTIONS

Bozeman. Montana State University Herbarium.

Browning. Scriver's Wildlife Museum.

Butte. Montana College of Mineral Science Museum.

Red Lodge. See 'Em Alive Zoo.

West Glacier. Glacier National Park Museum.

Hells Canyon
IDAHO AND OREGON

Hells Canyon

OREGON | IDAHO

The Snake River Cut a Gorge Deeper Than Grand Canyon

The Snake River has carved America's deepest gorge.

In a remote and mountainous corner where Idaho meets Oregon lies the deepest gorge in the Western hemisphere—even deeper than the much more accessible and visited Grand Canyon. Hells Canyon of the Snake River is a dizzying gash 75 miles long and with an *average* depth of 5500 feet from rim to river; at its deepest, from the summit of flanking He Devil Peak in the Seven Devils range to the bottom of the gorge it is an impressive 7900 feet. (In comparison, the highest point on the Grand Canyon's rims is 5650 feet above the Colorado.)

What makes Hells Canyon even more striking is its narrowness—it is also this country's narrowest major gorge. The river is often less than 100 feet wide; yet the views along the gorge and to the flanking mountains are remarkably spacious, and the visitor never gets the feeling of being hemmed in as he would, for example, at the bottom of the Black Canyon of the Gunnison, in Colorado.

From the depths of the canyon the land rears upward so steeply that in places the walls are nearly vertical. For many miles, as the Snake surges northward to meet the mighty Columbia, it is imprisoned between rough walls of basalt. The eastern wall rises more than a mile high in a lateral distance of only two miles. Its sheer rise is interrupted by a natural bench at 3500 feet, from which circular promontories of rock jut out into the canyon, providing a

Some Canyon Profiles and What They Mean

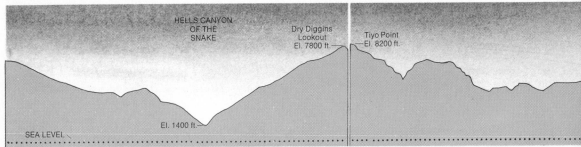

HELLS CANYON
OF THE
SNAKE

Dry Diggins
Lookout
El. 7800 ft.

Tiyo Point
El. 8200 ft.

El. 1400 ft.

SEA LEVEL

Rivers cut their canyons with incredible slowness, but in the long life of the earth they have cut them deep—and sometimes, as in Grand Canyon, wide. The drawing shows the profiles of seven American

canyons, indicating both their depth and the height of the riverbed above sea level. In general, canyons cut in sedimentary rock, such as Grand Canyon, tend to have a stair-step profile, while canyons cut

series of panoramic natural observation points.

One of these, Dry Diggins Lookout, on the Idaho side, is 7828 feet above the river. Just 2.2 miles away, where Saddle Creek flows into the Snake, the elevation is a mere 1408 feet. The canyon terrain is characterized by deep jagged side canyons. Its lower slopes are mostly grass-covered, interspersed with sheer canyon walls. Few trees grow below 4000 feet, except beside the river itself.

Petroglyphs and artifacts found along the Snake indicate that the area has been inhabited for a hundred centuries or more. Archeologists estimate that there are about 200 separate archeological sites here, only a handful of which have as yet been explored. Since the Hells Canyon area was the meeting place of two early American cultures, the Columbia Plateau and the Great Basin, further exploration could supply some of our answers to the mystery of the first men who migrated to North America.

Hells Canyon and the Snake River were always a formidable obstacle to explorers, fur traders and boatmen. Donald McKenzie, a bear of a man weighing over 300 pounds, an agent for the Northwest Company of Montreal, may have been the first white man to ascend the Snake by boat. McKenzie and his party of six rowed, pushed and finally pulled a barge from the junction of the Snake and the Clearwater at Lewiston all the way through Hells Canyon. In 1895 the 165-foot stern-wheeler *Norma* also

The vertical scale in this Hells Canyon view is an amazing 8000 feet, from river level to the snowy summits in the Seven Devils range far above.

made it all the way through the canyon.

Twenty-five years ago the canyon and the Snake became more accessible with the development of outboard motors with greater horse-power. Where daredevils used to shoot rapids in rubber rafts, visitors may now travel in lightweight, strongly built, jet-propelled boats. Today several operators carry passengers through the foaming rapids.

Most river trips through Hells Canyon begin either at Lewiston, Idaho, or at Clarkston, Washington. (The towns are named for Lewis and Clark.) You can take a six-and-a-half-hour jet boat trip up the river from Lewiston and stop along the way to pan for gold along the sandy beaches. Or you can take a one-day round trip to the lower end of the canyon on the mailboat from Lewiston—an unforgettable experience. Trips of two or three days and even longer are made possible by comfortable camps strategically located along the Snake. Many a harassed city-dweller has experienced the profound refreshment of being lulled to sleep by the sound of rushing water, awakening relaxed and ready for a breakfast of pancakes, eggs and trout fresh from the stream.

Access to any part of Hells Canyon by car was difficult, if not impossible, until the Idaho Power Company began building Brownlee Dam in 1955. Next came Oxbow Dam and finally, in 1968, Hells Canyon Dam. Now a drive of 60 miles over hard-surfaced roads from Cambridge, Idaho, puts a visitor deep within the canyon walls. The Idaho Power Company also maintains several fine campgrounds, complete with electricity and trailer

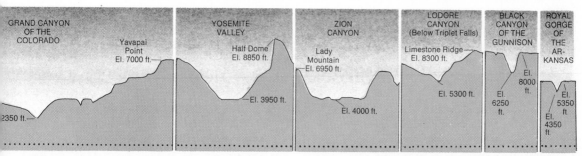

in dense volcanic rock, like the Black Canyon of the Gunnison, develop a steeper, V-shaped profile. People wonder how a river can cut a deep canyon, when a normal rate is no more than one hundredth of an inch a year, the thickness of a sheet of paper. But in a century it will cut one inch, in 1000 years 10 inches, and in a million years—not long in geological terms—an 800-foot canyon will have formed.

hookups, all furnished free of charge.

And the viewpoints in the canyon area are worth any trouble to reach. Just south of White Bird, Idaho, a bridge crosses the Salmon River. From there a gravel road winds upward to the Pittsburg Saddle, where there is an overwhelming view of Hells Canyon and of the Snake and Salmon rivers almost a mile below. A rough road continues down to the Snake at Pittsburg Landing, which is as far as you can take your car. From Riggins, Heaven's Gate Observation Point is also accessible by car; this provides one of the outstanding views of the whole Seven Devils Scenic Area, 130,000 acres extending for 22 miles along the Snake. Dry Diggins Lookout, another fine vantage point, is another nine miles by trail. From the Oregon side there are splendid views from Hat Point, reached by a hair-raising drive on a rough road from Joseph and Enterprise. Also on the Oregon side, a paved road goes to the Oxbow Dam, and after that continues as a rough track that actually crosses the canyon on a bridge. Try this only with a four-wheel-drive vehicle.

A single trail on the Idaho side traverses the length of the canyon and may be traveled by foot or horseback. Other trails lead up into the Wallowa Mountains and the Seven Devils range. Many high lakes, at elevations above 7000 feet, nestle in the mountains, providing a cool contrast to the canyon below. In the summer the temperature may hit 115 degrees at water level while the higher peaks of the Seven Devils are still covered with snow.

Hells Canyon contains a wide variety of wildlife. Songbirds are abundant, and bald and golden eagles, ospreys, hawks and owls make their homes here, while Canada and Steller's jays and Clark's nutcrackers make their noisy presence known. Game birds include blue, ruffed and Franklin grouse, wild turkey, Hungarian partridge, mountain and California quail. The chukar, a partridge imported from the high steppes of India, provides unlimited sport for upland game hunters, but it takes a stout-hearted athlete to pursue these birds along the canyon walls.

Bigger animals include bears, cougars, mountain goats, white-tailed deer and bobcats. Close to 30,000 mule deer and over 5000 elk were counted in a recent census. On the trail or along the riverbank a hiker might see raccoon, beavers, badgers, skunks, coyotes, mink, otter

The Snake was known as the "Accursed Mad River" in the early days, and certainly in parts of Hells Canyon's gloomy depths, where it rushes wildly from

or porcupines. These animals are so comparatively unaccustomed to man that they may often be approached at close range.

Some of the finest smallmouth black bass fishing in the country is possible in the Snake. Other fish abounding in the river and in the mountain lakes are rainbow, cutthroat, Dolly Varden and brook trout, perch, crappie, chinook salmon and steelhead. The white sturgeon, a survivor from prehistoric times, is now completely protected, but may be caught and

one rapids to another, it seems to deserve the name. But there are surprisingly lush pockets along the river valley, where ferns and shrubs, wildflowers and ponderosa pines grow, nourished by mist and rain, and protected from the high winds of the surrounding mountains by the steep canyon walls.

then released unharmed. These big fish may weigh from 200 to 300 pounds.

In fact, the canyon area offers a variety and uniqueness of wildlife habitats unmatched elsewhere in the country. But Hells Canyon, so recently opened up to the average tourist, faces an uncertain future. Conservation groups have been fighting for years to keep the Snake free of any more dams, but power advocates stress the area's growing need for more electric power, which additional dams would supply.

They want to harness other stretches of the 100 remaining, free-flowing miles of the Snake between Hells Canyon Dam and Lewiston.

It is impossible to guess the outcome of the battle at this stage. But the increasing numbers of visitors who come to see the Snake and who inevitably go away profoundly impressed by its wild and primitive beauty would probably incline to the view once eloquently propounded by Oliver Wendell Holmes: "A river is more than an amenity. It is a treasure."

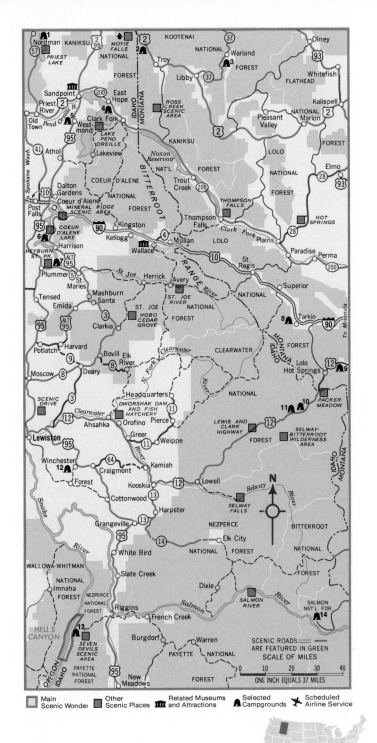

Main Scenic Wonder · Other Scenic Places · Related Museums and Attractions · Selected Campgrounds · Scheduled Airline Service

SCENIC ROADS ARE FEATURED IN GREEN
SCALE OF MILES
0 10 20 30 40
ONE INCH EQUALS 37 MILES

ery can produce more than eight million baby steelheads a year. Both dam and hatchery have observation areas for visitors.

Heyburn State Park, Idaho. Idaho's largest state park occupies a mountain-ringed basin so lush with forest and meadow that it looks almost like a sunken garden. Over 2000 of its approximately 8000 acres are water, embracing Lake Chatcolet, part of Coeur d'Alene, and several others. Chatcolet has been called Idaho's most beautiful lake. Bowl-shaped, it clings to the side of a mountain, its waters colored dark green from the reflection of evergreens that grow right down to the shoreline.

Hobo Cedar Grove, Idaho. Located in the St. Joe National Forest, the 240-acre grove is dominated by a dense canopy of large western red cedar. Some of the giant trees are more than eight feet in diameter. Timber has never been harvested from the area, and as a result the ground beneath the trees is carpeted with a luxuriant growth of ferns.

Hot Springs, Mont. Mountains rise on three sides of this celebrated health resort, whose natural mineral water springs flow at a constant temperature of 120 degrees. You can take a dip in a hot "plunge," or relax in a hot mud bath. The springs are located on the Flathead Indian reservation in the valley of the Little Bitterroot River; nearby Rainbow Lake is noted for water sports.

Lake Pend Oreille, Idaho. (*Picture appears on page 306*)

Lewis and Clark Highway, Idaho. (*Picture appears on page 307*)

Mineral Ridge Scenic Area, Idaho. Plants are marked for easy identification along the 3.3 miles of trails in this scenic area in Coeur d'Alene National Forest. Seven ridgetop overlooks offer the hiker magnificent views across Lake Coeur d'Alene.

Moyie Falls, Idaho. The highway bridge on U.S. 2 near Bonners

WITHIN A DAY'S DRIVE:

Lovely Lakes and Noble Forests

Coeur d'Alene Lake, Idaho. (*Picture appears on facing page*)

Dworshak Dam and Fish Hatchery, Idaho. One of the nation's highest dams is being constructed on the North Fork of the Clear-

water River. Near it is the world's largest hatchery for steelhead trout, which migrate to the Pacific for a two-year period after spawning, and return to the stream of their birth when they reach 10 to 20 pounds. The hatch-

Ferry affords an impressive view of the Moyie River and Falls. The river rushes over a dam and large boulders in a series of steep cascades, hemmed in between narrow, dark rock walls. Rugged mountains ring the horizon, and forested hills border the river.

Packer Meadow, Idaho. The explorers Lewis and Clark rested here at Lolo Pass with their party before beginning the trek across Idaho to the Snake River. The meadow is brilliant with wildflowers in spring and summer, the deep green conifers contrast with the lush meadow grasses, and on the horizon to the southeast the peaks of the Bitterroot Range run for 80 miles.

Priest Lake, Idaho. With its pale, sandy beaches shaded by pine and fir, and high, forest-clad mountains rising in the background, Priest Lake makes an ideal setting for boating, fishing and water sports. Mackinaw trout of over 50 pounds have been taken from these waters. A meandering river connects Lower Priest and Upper Priest lakes, to create a strikingly scenic boating trip.

Ross Creek Scenic Area, Mont. There is an easy half-hour self-guiding trail through this grove of giant ancient cedars, whose thick trunks rise over the fern-carpeted forest floor.

St. Joe River, Idaho. This is the highest navigable stream in the world, and its tree-lined banks and still, deep waters have earned it the nickname "Shadowy St. Joe." A Forest Service road parallels the stream for more than a hundred miles, through the St. Joe National Forest. The St. Joe is noted for its fishing.

Coeur d'Alene Lake, *Idaho. The generally wild scenery of northern Idaho becomes tamer around the 108-mile shoreline of this lovely lake. Its hilly shores are deeply indented with bays, and a* *promenade at Coeur d'Alene offers water sports facilities. The name comes from French fur traders, who joked that hard-bargaining local Indians were so tough they had the "heart of an awl."*

Lake Pend Oreille, *Idaho. Mountain goats clamber over the crags that rise above Pend Oreille's clear waters. The lake, an ideal combination of scenic* *beauty and good fishing, is noted for its trout and landlocked salmon. The world record Kamloops, a rainbow trout of 37 pounds, was taken in this lake.*

Salmon River, Idaho.
(Picture appears on facing page)

Scenic Drive, Idaho. Highway U.S. 95 from New Meadows north to Bonners Ferry offers one of the most varied and scenic drives to be found anywhere in the country. North of New Meadows great herds of beef cattle graze in summer on pastures reminiscent of the Alps. At Riggins the highway meets the Salmon River and follows it for 30 miles, through deep canyons and beside abandoned mines, to White Bird. Beyond the rich farmlands of Camas Prairie the highway dips again to the Clearwater River. North of Lewiston the road passes through some of the world's richest wheatlands, nourished by volcanic soil, in the rolling Palouse prairie country.

Lovely Coeur d'Alene and Pend Oreille lakes and the Kootenai River make a memorable ending to this drive.

Selway–Bitterroot Wilderness Area, Idaho. The largest such area in the United States, with over 1.2 million acres, Selway–Bitterroot straddles the Idaho–Montana border. Great herds of elk roam through the meadows and forest. Roads, open during summer only, lead into the wilderness, and riding and backpacking trails take you farther, to superb trout streams and to haunts of the moose, elk and mountain goat.

Selway Falls, Idaho. In spring a loud roar of cascading water greets the visitor when the falls are heavy with the runoff of ac-

cumulated snow water from the high mountains. You can drive right up to the falls, which were formed when a landslide blocked the Selway River ages ago.

Seven Devils Scenic Area, Idaho. The volcanic Seven Devils range rises 8000 feet above the canyon of the Snake River. From natural rock overlooks jutting out over the canyon you can see for miles into Oregon, Idaho, Washington and Montana. Graded roads and a system of trails permit all types of wilderness recreation: hunting, boating, fishing, hiking and camping. He Devil Mountain rears up to 9393 feet, highest in the area, and jagged canyons and terraced ridges interrupt the grassy plateaus. Roads lead in from Riggins, New Meadow Council, Weiser and Cambridge. Heavens

Gate, one of the most dramatic Hells Canyon overlooks, is accessible from Riggins by car; Dry Diggins Lookout is another nine miles by trail. Mirror Lake has one of the prettiest settings in the area: a perfect glacial cirque ringed by granite crags.

Thompson Falls, Mont. The Thompson Falls Recreation Area, on the upper reaches of Noxon Reservoir, is surrounded by rugged mountains. Boating facilities are located along the shore. Fishing is good here, and the area is becoming increasingly popular with picnickers.

RELATED MUSEUMS AND ATTRACTIONS

Sandpoint, Idaho. Bonner County Museum; geology, mineralogy, natural history.

Wallace, Idaho. Chamber of Commerce Museum; natural history.

Lewis and Clark Highway, *Idaho. This part of the great explorers' westward journey took them nine days—though today a car can cover the spectacular 133-mile stretch along the Lochsa River in just a few hours. Trails and Forest Service roads lead off into untouched wilderness areas.*

Salmon River, *Idaho. The Salmon is called "River of No Return" because its current is so strong upstream that navigation was impossible until the age of jet-powered boats. It drops over 7000 feet in its 425-mile, rapids-filled journey through primitive wilderness to join the Snake at Hells Canyon.*

Yellowstone–Grand Teton

NATIONAL PARKS, WYOMING

Beavers have dammed this Snake River tributary into a mirror for the magnificence of the Tetons.

A Magnificent Mountain Wall Is Neighbor to Nature's Boiler Room

The Grand Tetons and Yellowstone are neighbors on the map—but far apart in spirit. Both parks are heavily forested, certainly, and shelter the same animals; both are spectacularly endowed with mountains, lakes and river valleys. But it is the solidity and mass of the jagged Tetons, rearing up like the remotest peaks of the Himalayas, that linger in the mind, in sharp contrast to the steaming fumaroles and bubbling mud pots of Yellowstone, with Old Faithful flinging up its snowy white plume against the blue. Form and mass oppose action and motion; fixity stands against fluidity. Change has already taken place in the Tetons; the results are frozen into stone. But at Yellowstone the turmoil of creation continues.

Grand Teton National Park is much smaller than Yellowstone, only 500 square miles compared to nearly 3500. But within its bounds is a concentration of scenic grandeur almost unmatched in the country. The Tetons themselves —13,766-foot Grand Teton, and its neighbors, mounts Owen and Moran and the South and Middle Tetons, their snow-streaked spires reflected in Jackson Lake—are almost overpoweringly splendid. Jackson Lake, an impoundment of the Snake River, fills much of Jackson Hole, and Jackson Hole ("hole" was what the old-time mountain men called a valley), almost flat, and lush with wildflower meadows, makes a perfect theater from which to view the Tetons.

In this soaring Teton closeup, Grand Teton looms in the left background, Mount Teewinot's jagged east face fills the foreground. Mount Owen is at right.

The larger lakes all lie close to the foot of the range, surrounded by dense coniferous forest and reflecting in their waters a wonderland of mile-high peaks. The Snake River winds through the valley, its tributaries dammed here and there into placid ponds by the work of beavers. Wild creatures—pronghorn, elk, moose, bald eagle and white pelican—are so plentiful that visitors are much more likely to see them here than in other parks.

The view that greets motorists driving south from Yellowstone along the Lewis River Canyon is unique because it embraces the entire width of a great mountain range at a glance. The twisting road emerges suddenly from thick forest and straightens out into a tree-lined avenue 800 feet above the sparkle of Jackson Lake, and there before you is the soaring east face of the Tetons, 20 to 30 miles away.

The Teton Range is short and narrow, about 40 miles long and 10 to 15 miles wide, with no foothills on the eastern side to soften and blur the pyramid-shaped peaks. In contrast to folded mountains of volcanic origin like the Shenandoah and Rocky mountains and the Cascade Range, the Grand Tetons are fault-block mountains. The fault block formed about 60 million years ago, when stresses beneath the surface sheared the earth's crust to form the Teton Fault, and two huge segments were displaced to the east and west along it. A block more than 40 miles long and about 13 miles wide was thrust roughly 20,000 feet upward to the west. The block to the east of the fault was depressed, forming the valley now

311

Even from a distance the abruptness with which the Tetons rise above Jackson Hole is striking. Grand Teton, mounts Owen and Teewinot are on the left in this view above the meadows; the big mountains on the right are Mount St. John and Rockchuck Peak. Grand Teton has much in common with Switzer-

known as Jackson Hole. All this occurred gradually, over a long period of time, not like a sudden earthquake. Later, glaciers carved the flat surface of the block into the sharp-pointed, faceted peaks you see today.

One of the most all-encompassing views of the Tetons is from the top of 7730-foot Signal Mountain, reached by a five-mile scenic drive: a parade of jagged peaks lines up against the sky, their reflections trembling in Jackson Lake. Skillet Glacier shines on Mount Moran, and the deep, U-shaped valleys linking the mountains testify to the sculpting power of glaciers of old. The dark streak running down the whole east face of Mount Moran is the outcropping edge of what geologists call a dike, formed from molten rock that welled up into fissures in the mountain. The dike on Mount Moran is about 150 feet wide near the summit, and has been traced westward all the way out of the park for more than seven miles.

Grand Teton National Park offers a full range of facilities and accommodations. There are campgrounds, trailer villages, dude ranches and luxuriously rustic lodges. The visitor center at Colter Bay provides the best orientation for a first-time visitor. The museum at Moose documents the history of the early fur traders' role in opening up the Teton area, while the Jenny Lake one stresses mountain climbing.

more than 200 miles of hiking trails. You can, of course, drive through the park; the Jackson Hole Highway follows the course of the Snake River, keeping the Tetons constantly in view.

Grand Teton, with its memorable mountains looming through clear, glittering air and its great variety of wildlife, scenery and activity, combines all the elements of a perfect vacation. It is not too rugged or desolate; some of its highest peaks can be climbed in one day (by experts) and there are magnificent rambles for every degree of energy. It is a splendid example of a national park.

land's Matterhorn: their shapes are remarkably similar, and both rise about 7000 feet above their valleys, which in turn are about 6000 feet above sea level.

Among the variety of hiking opportunities in the Tetons is a 14-mile round-trip, all-day hike into the high elevations, departing from this museum. It is worth getting into shape beforehand for it. The Tetons are respected even by veteran alpine mountain climbers, and this hike gives a novice a glimmering of the allure of high mountains.

Even if you've never climbed a mountain or even a rock before, the Exum School of Mountaineering can teach you enough to make a practice climb the very day you arrive. To prepare yourself for such a project, start out with a short, easy nature walk and then progress to a slightly longer self-guiding trail. There are

Schoolroom Glacier may be a remnant of the huge tongue of ice that cut Cascade Canyon. The glacier has built up a terminal moraine, a wall of glacial debris, which borders a small, cold lake at its tip.

An Eerie World of Hot Mud and Tall Geysers

Yellowstone is like a vision in some pictur-esque legend. Sulfurous fumes fill the air, steam hisses somewhere out of sight, a geyser announces an impending eruption with a boom-ing whoosh, mud belches up in a viscous pool from the bowels of the earth and great mud bubbles break open in slow motion. Board-walks crisscross the perilous, steaming earth like adhesive tape holding together the thin cover over a subterranean hell. All the ele-ments of a childhood dream are there—mud, strange smells, danger and a magic path on which to walk, the only place where you are safe, and off which you must not step.

Surely this is the most intriguing of all parks to visit. Its thermal effects are always surpris-ing, no matter how often we have seen them happen; and they are created by forces that are extremely complex. Nothing is as predict-able as it seems. Old Faithful does go off pretty regularly, it is true; but the exact time and duration of its eruption are up to the forces of nature, not to park officials working with a computer. Geysers are said to play, and this word captures the sense of surprise and free-dom so typical of Yellowstone.

The word "geyser" comes from the Icelandic *geysa*, meaning to gush. (Iceland, New Zealand and Siberia are the three other areas in the world in which a concentration of geysers oc-curs.) Yellowstone has over 200 active geysers —the greatest concentration in the world—and around 3000 hot springs.

Essentially, Yellowstone is a dying volcanic area. The mountains surrounding it are the eroded remnants of piled-up lava flows and pyroclastic materials. Pyroclastic means fire-broken: the molten rock and gases hurled out of an erupting volcano that cooled and hard-ened in the air and fell to the ground as solid particles of dust, ash and cinders.

The cooler air of early morning thickens the steam from some of the 27 geysers in the Norris Geyser Basin. The boardwalks protect the fragile crust.

Old Faithful signals an eruption with a splash of water above its crater. Then it surges up to a height of 130 feet for anywhere from two to five minutes.

The first men to see Minerva Terrace at Mammoth Hot Springs described it as a mountain that was turning itself inside out. They were close: hot water seeping through rock rich in calcium carbonate evaporates and builds up travertine terraces. The subtly blended colors come from algae.

In many parts of the park the ground is hot or warm to the touch, from heated water or gases. The magma, or molten rock, probably lies less than three miles below the earth's crust. Rainwater and melted snow from the surrounding mountains supply the groundwater that charges the geysers, and the magma heats it up. These two ingredients, water and heat, must be present for geysers to occur. Most of Yellowstone's geysers occur in three well-defined basins—Upper, Lower and Norris—along faults, or fractures, in the earth's crust, where one section of rock has been displaced in relation to another, adjacent section.

Geysers are the most obvious form of thermal activity in the park. No one has climbed down into one to see how it works, but the most plausible explanation is that groundwater, heated either by the molten magma itself, or by gases given off by the magma, moves upward through underground passages, always under pressure from more groundwater entering the system (see drawing on facing page for a more detailed explanation).

Geyser predictions are posted at the Old Faithful Visitor Center, but there are so many geysers in the Upper Geyser Basin, and such variety in their frequency of eruption and the length of time they play, that the permutations are endless. The range is remarkable: Old Faithful erupts for from two to five minutes, while little Grotto blows for six to ten *hours;* Old Faithful goes off roughly every hour, others three times a day, and still others, like Giantess, have one or two active phases a year, with five-minute eruptions every 30 to 60 minutes; some are not predictable at all. But with a little patience and a little luck, even a short visit can net you the sight of several erupting geysers, in addition to Old Faithful's high, memorable plume.

Riverside Geyser, perched at the edge of the Firehole River, is Yellowstone's most graceful geyser, and even more regular than Old Faithful. At approximately seven-hour intervals it arches its column of water and steam out over the river, reaching a height of about 75 feet and playing for five minutes.

Clepsydra Geyser (from a Greek word meaning water clock) has four vents on its cone. In one phase it plays only from the highest vent, and water jets up 10 to 15 feet high at three-minute intervals. Its "wild phase" lasts from three to six hours and is much more forceful. Water plays from all four vents, accompanied by the deafening roar of steam.

There are three other types of thermal activity at Yellowstone: hot springs, fumaroles and mud pots. Hot springs are similar to geysers, but their plumbing is such that the underground water circulates freely enough to avoid actual eruption. The interesting thing about hot springs is the algae and bacteria that can live in them, or in the cooler runoff channels. Orange, dark green and brown bands appear in the channels flowing out of hot springs: these are caused by the different types of algae that live at different temperatures. Strands of pink, yellow or white seen undulating in the bubbling waters of the springs themselves are microscopic bacteria.

Fumaroles, the third type of thermal activity, are hot springs with almost no supply of water at all. The little groundwater that does seep down the vent into the plumbing is immediately converted to steam.

Mud pots form where fumaroles eject their steam into muddy cauldrons on the ground surface. Sometimes, as in the Fountain Paint Pots, minerals tint the mud pink, orange and cream. In late summer, when the mud gets very thick, bursting bubbles are quite likely to toss dollops of mud onto unwary visitors.

But all is not mud and steam at Yellowstone; the geyser basins cover less than two percent of the park. The Grand Canyon of the Yellowstone River, for instance, would warrant a national park or monument all to itself. It is an awe-inspiring gorge with a narrow bottom and steep walls, mostly golden, but with shades of orange, brown, red, gray, pink and white blended in. The Lower Falls are higher than Niagara, over 300 feet, and the Upper Falls, at 109 feet, mark the beginning of the canyon.

Why Does a Geyser Play? And a Mud Pot Boil?

Groundwater seeping down into and through cracks in the lava flows that surround Yellowstone's geyser basins becomes heated by the underlying molten lava. This heated water rises up through vents and rock tubes by convection. In the case of a geyser, water collects in pockets and becomes superheated, but boiling is delayed by the weight of the overlying water. Temperatures as high as 450° F. have been recorded. Eventually this water starts to boil, forcing some of it up and out. As the pressure drops, the superheated water flashes into steam, causing an eruption. Hot springs are simpler; the water circulates freely enough to avoid superheating and simply emerges at the surface. A fumarole is a kind of hot spring without enough water to flow out, but with ample heat to convert available water to steam. A mud pot is found on top of a fumarole whose steam contains acid gases that decompose rocks into clay and mud.

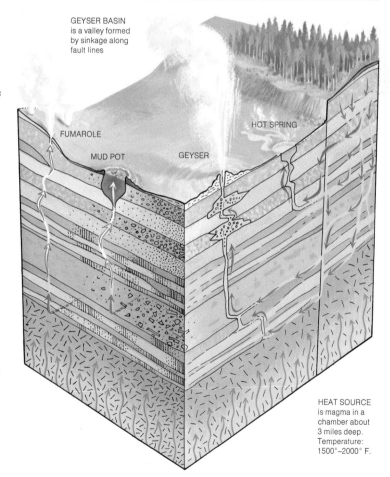

GEYSER BASIN is a valley formed by sinkage along fault lines

FUMAROLE

MUD POT

GEYSER

HOT SPRING

HEAT SOURCE is magma in a chamber about 3 miles deep. Temperature: 1500°–2000° F.

There are many spectacular viewpoints from which to admire it.

Yellowstone is so huge and has so much to offer that a visitor must choose between staying long enough to do it justice and severely limiting what he sees. The Grand Loop Road, the park's Main Street, which passes close to most of the major attractions, plus the mileage in and out of the park, add up to about 200 miles. But help for the harassed tourist faced with a multitude of choices and a perennial summer shortage of accommodation has come in the form of transmitters located at strategic spots like entrances and campgrounds. Signs tell motorists to tune their car radios to a certain frequency, where they hear recorded messages giving information about fees, availability of campsites, scenic walks in the area— and the dangers of boiling mud and bears.

Most people think of bears right after Old Faithful when they think of Yellowstone—and it is true that there are about 500 black bears in the park. But there are also between 10,000 and 15,000 elk, 1000 moose, 150 pronghorn and 600 bighorn sheep.

Yellowstone's bears used to be famous for holding up traffic on the Grand Loop Road, begging for food from tourists who were all too willing to stop their cars to photograph the animals and feed them whatever they happened to have on hand. Not only were "bear jams" becoming frequent but also, far more serious, the bears were changing their eating habits and becoming spoiled by bread and sweets, neglecting their own natural food. There were incidents of people teasing the bears, and some bears reacted by taking a swipe at the hand that withheld food. The situation became so dangerous for humans and so injurious to bears that park officials cracked down. The prohibition against feeding the bears is now strictly enforced. Fines are levied against offenders, and roadside begging has been greatly reduced. In fact, the question visitors ask most frequently is: "Where are all the bears?" The answer is, in the forest where they belong, foraging for themselves.

To see more animals and fewer people, hit the trails. At Yellowstone, as at Grand Teton, there are plenty of well-marked hiking trails— over 1000 miles of them. And some lead close to the wilderness heart of the park, crossing the Continental Divide, the Gallatin Range, and following the Lamar River with its re-

Grand Prismatic, Yellowstone's largest hot spring, shades from deep blue to green, yellow, orange and red. Steam often reflects the rainbow hues.

markable Fossil Forest. This forest, like so much in Yellowstone, is unique. Other fossilized tree trunks—in the Petrified Forest, for example—were transported by rivers, and so we see them lying on their sides. But Yellowstone's petrified forests were caught by blankets of volcanic material in an upright position, and they have remained standing.

Successive periods of volcanic activity, in eruptions that could last for years, buried generations of forests, which would grow up again as each eruption died down. It took hundreds of years for a forest to regrow, then eventually the old volcano would erupt once more, bury the new green forest, eventually petrify it, and the whole cycle would begin anew. This cycle took place 27 times, and the side of the valley has been cut away to show the forests one on top of the other. The Fossil Forest is accessible via a vigorous hike.

It's an incredible sight—like so much else at this most amazing of national parks.

The Lower Falls of the Yellowstone drop more than 300 feet into a golden gorge, where ospreys nest on rock pinnacles and several small geysers spout.

You can hike to the brink for a breathtaking view of the plunge into Grand Canyon of the Yellowstone, 24 miles long and with sheer, 1000-foot-high walls.

319

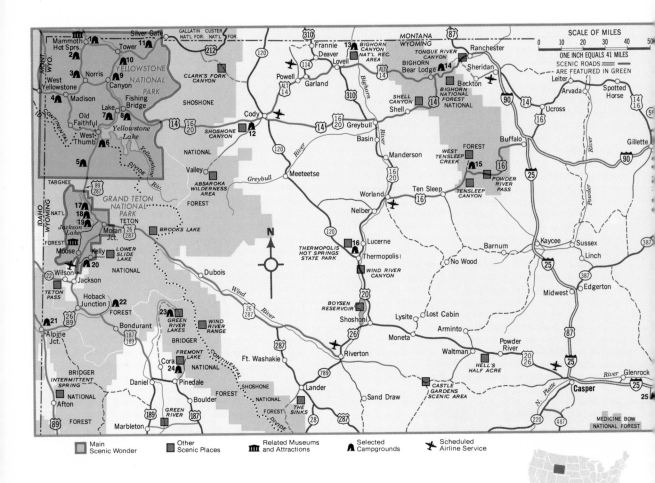

Main Scenic Wonder · Other Scenic Places · Related Museums III and Attractions · Selected ▲ Campgrounds · Scheduled ✈ Airline Service

WITHIN A DAY'S DRIVE:

Wilderness Highways and Lakes

Absaroka Wilderness Area. Some of the most rugged and spectacular country in the West is protected within this vast area east of Yellowstone. It ranges in elevation from 4600 to 13,140 feet and includes, in the southernmost part, the impressive Shoshone River canyons and the upper reaches of the Yellowstone River.

Bighorn Canyon National Recreation Area. Most of the 96,000 acres here are covered by 71-mile-long Bighorn Lake Reservoir, which stretches into Montana. And more than half of this huge lake—excellent for swimming, boating and fishing—lies cradled by canyon walls. In some places, sheer cliffs nearly a mile high loom over the water, revealing layers of colored stone that span 500 million years of geo-

logic time. Wildlife that roams in the neighborhood of the canyon includes one of the last surviving herds of wild horses in America —a thrilling sight.

Bighorn National Forest. A sweeping high mountain country of open valleys and broad alpine meadows, the forest is edged on the north by a jagged line of barren granite peaks. The openness of the country makes it easy to spot the abundant wildlife, including mule deer, whitetails, elk, moose, bears and bighorn sheep. Part of the forest includes the Cloud Peak Primitive Area, open to hikers and horseback riders.

Boysen Reservoir. An unusual setting enhances the impact of this lake. It is surrounded on three sides by rolling sagebrush hills

and rocky desert plains typical of the high desert plateau country. The fourth side is rimmed by wind-smoothed cliffs of reddish sandstone, their soft pastel colors contrasting sharply with the dark blue waters of the lake. This is a fine place to swim, boat and fish.

Brooks Lake. An alpine lake at an altitude of more than 9000 feet, Brooks has an imposing backdrop of granite palisades. On two sides, pine-covered slopes rise to form weirdly shaped barren peaks. The lake has excellent fishing for rainbow and other species of trout and mackinaw.

Castle Gardens Scenic Area. (*Picture appears on page 322*)

Clarks Fork Canyon. A Forest Service road offers a scenic drive

320

of 36 miles that is among the most memorable in the West. From the summit of Dead Indian Hill there is a chilling vista of the jumbled peaks of the Absaroka Wilderness contrasting with the deep, ragged gash of Clarks Fork Canyon. The road zigzags down from this 9000-foot overlook, losing 1500 feet in a few miles.

Fremont Lake. This lovely 5000-acre lake lies in the foothills of the Wind River Range. It is on that dividing line where the rolling sagebrush prairies end and the mountain slopes begin, so that half the lake is edged with sagebrush and golden-green aspen groves, the rest with steep banks covered with pine and spruce. There is a large campground, boating and fishing.

Green River.
(*Picture appears on page 322*)

Green River Lakes.
(*Picture appears on page 323*)

Hell's Half Acre. A startling ruggedness is the hallmark of this fantastic miniature badlands. Wind and water have carved dramatic towers, caverns, spires and fortresses out of highly colored shale and sandstone formations.

Intermittent Spring. An unusual spring erupts from a hole in one of the walls of Swift Creek Canyon. For about 18 minutes at a time, water cascades over moss-covered rocks to the canyon floor. Then it stops for about 18 minutes; during this pause you can hear the sound of air being sucked into the cavern. Scientists cannot explain this phenomenon which appears to be a sort of cold-water geyser.

Lower Slide Lake. The beautiful 1100-acre lake in Teton National Forest was formed by a huge landslide from the Gros Ventre Range above; the scars of the slide are still visible on the hillside leading down to the lake.

Powder River Pass. Once known to pioneers as Muddy Pass, the present route winds through alpine meadows, bright with flowers. At 9666 feet it crosses the Sheep Mountain range where jagged granite peaks thrust up from timbered slopes to create a grand panorama of high-mountain beauty. Nearby Meadowlark Lake, seemingly held in place by smooth mountain slopes, is the place to linger for swimming, boating or fishing for trout.

Shell Canyon. A spectacular highway through the V-shaped canyon edges steep cliffs hundreds of feet high. A turnout provides a view of the lovely Shell Falls, where foaming waters of the creek cascade over a series of small drops to reach the main falls. There the stream plunges 75 feet down a sheer granite face.

Shoshone Canyon. The narrow valley is lined with fantastic rock formations, stone sculptures with

Wind River Range. *These perpetually snow-tipped peaks lie along the Continental Divide, and include Wyoming's loftiest—Gannett Peak (13,875 feet).*

Their rugged beauty, lavish with alpine lakes and streams, makes the area ideal for hiking, fishing— or riding wilderness trails, like the group seen here.

Green River. *Beneath these towering bluffs was a famous pioneer river crossing on the historic Overland Trail. The Oregon Trail and the Pony Express route are other early ways westward that took advantage of the great gap through the Rockies in this southwestern corner of Wyoming.*

Castle Gardens Scenic Area. *Like the ruins of a Greek temple this sandstone sculpture reaches magnificently into the sky. It is part of a badlands region that contains a number of rocks chiseled by wind and water. Long ago Indians carved pictures on the many towers here.*

fitting names like Laughing Pig, Chinese Wall and Holy City. At the canyon's east end is Buffalo Bill Reservoir, a place to boat, swim and fish for record mackinaw. Walled on the south by the slopes of Cedar Mountain, it has for a backdrop the splendidly rugged beauty of the Absaroka Wilderness.

Tensleep Canyon. As highway U.S. 16 slides into the canyon, it seems it must be blocked by reddish-gray walls of massive granite. But it threads between the blocks of stone that lean over from both sides like the turrets of some ancient fortress; then, leveling for a moment at Tensleep Creek, the road suddenly plunges through red stone cliffs, dropping several hundred feet in less than a mile. The canyon ends abruptly in a prairie basin.

Teton Pass. At 8431 feet the summit of this lofty pass above Jackson offers a vista of jagged snow-covered peaks. The melting of the snows in summer creates a profusion of wildflowers that brighten the alpine slopes surrounding the pass.

Thermopolis Hot Springs State Park. Here is the largest mineral hot spring in the world, yielding water at 135 degrees at the rate of 18,600,000 gallons a day. These thermal waters have created highly colored mineral formations; most famous is the Rainbow Terrace. In the park is a public bathhouse where visitors can sample the waters.

The Sinks. In a towering mountain canyon, the Popo Agie River, a glacier-fed waterway, suddenly vanishes into a gaping cave. Half a mile away it reappears in the form of fast-flowing springs. Fat rainbow trout can be seen feeding in the crystal-clear pools.

Tongue River Canyon. The eerie shapes of eroded sedimentary rock form the walls of this picturesque canyon. Directly below the formation known as the Castle of the Gods, a large grove of ancient cottonwoods shades a picnic area and campground.

West Tensleep Creek. A Forest Service road to West Tensleep Lake follows the creek, one of the most scenic wild mountain streams that can be seen from a car. Public campgrounds are set at intervals, each site selected for its particular beauty. From the lake a trail gives access to the Cloud Peak Primitive Area.

Wind River Canyon. Long, wide and deep, the canyon cuts through the Owl Creek Mountains east of the Grand Tetons. At some points black diorite cliffs tower half a mile above the road, the grimness of the scene relieved only by the sparkling waters of the fast-flowing Wind River.

Wind River Range.
(*Picture appears on page 321*)

**RELATED MUSEUMS
AND ATTRACTIONS**

Moose. Grand Teton National Park Museum.

Yellowstone Park. Yellowstone National Park Museums.

Green River Lakes. *A pair of alpine lakes that form the headwaters of the Green River are set as prettily as jewels in the richly forested slopes near Gannett Peak. Flattop Mountain, pocketed with snowfields, forms a tall backdrop in this view, one of the state's most photogenic.*

Craters of the Moon
NATIONAL MONUMENT, IDAHO

Rugged, 300-foot-high Big Craters is strikingly lunar.

IDAHO

Craters
of the
Moon

Bursts of Fiery Lava Created a Stark Lunar Landscape

Sprawled over the broad valley of the Snake River in central Idaho is a landscape so harsh, desolate and lifeless that American astronauts training for Apollo moon flights were taken there to give them an idea of what they would find on the lunar surface. Seldom has a place been so aptly named as the strangely fascinating Craters of the Moon.

Vast fields of black, jagged lava stretch in all directions, with cinder cones rising abruptly to heights of 800 feet above them, and a multitude of smaller spatter cones at their feet. Here and there, where trees were caught in the flowing lavas, only molds of them remain. Beneath the surface lie spectacular ice caves. Big Southern Butte, a monument to volcanic eruptions, rears its summit, stark and lonely, on the eastern horizon, and to the northwest the barrenness is softened by the green slopes of the Pioneer Mountains.

Unique among Idaho's many lava flows for its comparative youth (some of its more recent flows took place within recorded human history), Craters of the Moon was formed during three separate epochs of eruption. Many of the more recent flows covered earlier lavas, but today a visitor can see evidence of volcanic activity from each of these epochs. A massive fissure in the earth, known as the Great Rift, opened up to produce the original eruptions. Lava gushed forth at temperatures up to 2000 degrees, forming a long line of cinder cones

This tunnel is the longest of the many lava tubes found in the monument; it was formed by cooling and hardening of the top and sides of a lava stream.

Cinder cones such as these range from 120 to 800 feet high; the greater height indicates that they were created by several fiery lava eruptions. They

where gas had blown it sky-high in fountains of fire. As the liquid magma welled up from as far as 25 miles below the earth's surface, there is evidence that it sometimes pushed chunks of the granite layer above it to the surface. The Devils Orchard and the crags south of Big Cinder Butte contain the oldest lavas.

During the second and third epochs the Great Rift was reopened several times; the second epoch saw the creation of many of the more prominent cinder cones, but the barren black lavas so common throughout Craters of the Moon were all emitted during the final period of eruption, which probably occurred as recently as 1600 to 2100 years ago.

Man's links with the area are unrecorded until the 19th century, though there is evidence that the Shoshone Indians were familiar with it. Crescent-shaped piles of rocks, obviously man-made, can be seen near Indian Tunnel, but their purpose is obscure; they may have been windbreaks. Stone artifacts and mounds made as trail markers are further evidence of Indian habitation.

A party led by Captain Benjamin Bonneville visited the area in 1833, and he described it as "a desolate and awful waste, where no grass grows nor water runs, and where nothing is to be seen but lava." John Powell, a rancher, explored the lava fields in 1879 while searching for water for cattle, and a marker he built still stands in Vermilion Chasm. In 1921 Craters was officially surveyed, and a recommendation

made that it be preserved; three years later 39 square miles were set aside as a national monument; this has since been expanded to 83 square miles.

Visitors to the monument area should call first at the visitor center, where there is an informative display of the volcanic features and the plants and wildlife of Craters of the Moon. A seven-mile loop drive leads past most of the points of particular interest, and self-guiding trails provide access to the heart of this bizarre country. Always take water with you when leaving the highway, particularly in mid-

are conical in shape, with loose, cindery surfaces. The steeper-sided spatter cones, which are less than 50 feet high, were formed by the spray

from smaller fire fountains. The majority of cones of both types are aligned along the Great Rift, thus clearly indicating the position of that deep fissure.

summer, when the sun is at its highest and bakes the sere landscape.

The more adventurous who wish to strike out on their own should obtain a special permit from the visitor center that allows them to explore the wilderness area between the end of the road and the southeastern boundary of the monument. There are nearly 10 miles of seldom-explored lava flows here—both the ropelike coils of the pahoehoe lava and the rough, jagged aa type. There are long caves that were once the tubes in which the lava flowed; you can crawl down into a number of

these, but be sure to take a flashlight with you.

Despite the apparently lifeless look of Craters of the Moon, there are some remarkable examples of adaptation, by plant and animal life, to a seemingly hostile environment. About 300 species of plants are found here, though only a few can be easily seen: dwarf buckwheat, for instance, whose silvery leaves nearly blanket some cinder cones, and which sends down deep roots to locate moisture. A self-guiding trail at Devils Orchard has markers explaining how plant life develops after volcanic activity—and the different kinds of vegetation that takes hold in lava dating from several different epochs.

Birds live here, too, among the rabbit brush, bitterbrush and limber pine that grow on the moister north cinder slopes. Idaho's state bird, the mountain bluebird, is often seen, along with red-shafted flickers, nighthawks, violet-green swallows and Say's phoebes. Recordings of bird songs along the Devils Orchard Nature Trail help visitors identify the various species.

Larger creatures include mule deer, coyotes and bobcats, though these can generally only be seen at dusk or dawn along the more remote trails. Dusk and dawn, too, are the best hours for photographers to catch the extraordinary shadows that low light creates in the grotesque lava formations.

The first impression of Craters of the Moon can be a forbidding one—death and destruction once reigned here. But a closer acquaintance leads to awe at the adaptability of life, which has managed to gain a foothold even in so difficult an environment. A comment in the visitor's book sums up neatly what many visitors come to feel upon closer acquaintance with the marvels of Craters of the Moon: "I have passed by several times before but never stopped—I wish now that I had."

Strange Landscapes of Frozen Lava

Craters of the Moon has only one type of lava, in chemical terms: iron-rich basalt, which gleams blue-black in the sun. There are two kinds of flows, though: pahoehoe and aa (Hawaiian for smooth and rough), which show several aspects. The pahoehoe surface cools so quickly that one can walk on it while the molten lava beneath still flows sluggishly. The final effect is of ropy billows. The combination of gas and heat can change so that pahoehoe turns into jagged aa; less often the reverse can happen too.

Pahoehoe lava flows like a river at Big Craters.

Lava gleams at Vermilion Chasm.

A lava-enveloped tree rots, leaving mold of its shape.

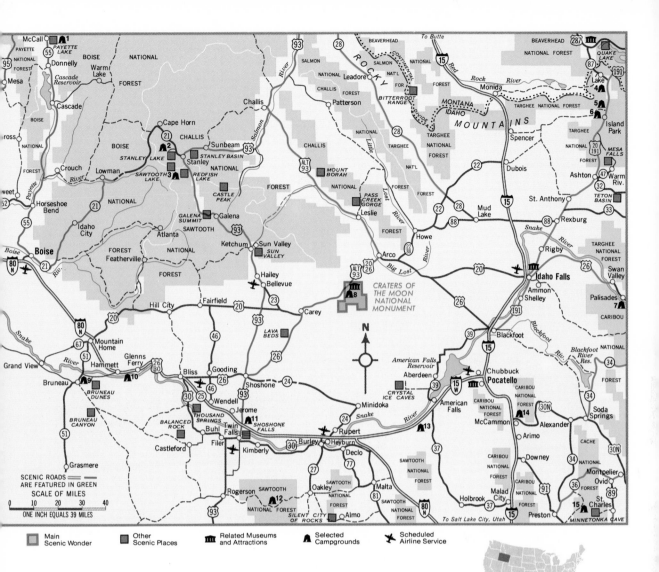

WITHIN A DAY'S DRIVE:

Hidden Valleys and an Earthquake's Legacy

Balanced Rock, Idaho. The colorful formations of the Salmon Falls Creek gorge climax with Balanced Rock. Shaped like a mushroom, it is 40 feet high and rests on a small block of igneous stone. It looks as if a strong wind could topple it at any moment.

Bitterroot Range, Idaho. Highway 28 from Mud Lake to Salmon is a scenic drive through a broad, flat, startlingly high valley flanked on both sides by national forest. The Bitterroot Range soars far above the valley floor to form the Continental Divide.

Bruneau Canyon, Idaho. A crack in the earth comes as a shock in flat, sagebrush-covered desert country. The steep walls of the 67-mile-long canyon reach a depth of 2000 feet and are so close together that in places a stone can be thrown across the gorge from one rim to the other.

Bruneau Dunes, Idaho. (*Picture appears on page 333*)

Castle Peak, Idaho. (*Picture appears on page 332*)

Crystal Ice Caves, Idaho. (*Picture appears on page 331*)

Earthquake Lake, Mont. On August 17, 1959, eight states felt the shock of one of the strongest quakes recorded in North America. West of Yellowstone National Park, 80 million tons of mountain fell into the Madison River valley, damming the river and forming Earthquake Lake. Houses and roads were submerged as the basin of nearby Hebgen Lake tilted. To see geology in action, visit the slide area in Madison Canyon and look at the visitor center exhibits.

Galena Summit, Idaho. At 8701 feet the pass between Sun Valley and Stanley Basin is one of Idaho's highest. It provides a view of the Sawtooth Peaks, and parts of the White Cloud Mountains, with many lovely valleys below.

Lava Beds, Idaho. After learning about volcanic activity at Cra-

329

ters of the Moon, visitors will enjoy seeing the many other lava beds throughout the Snake River plains. South of Highway 20 between Idaho Falls and Arco two ancient volcanoes, Twin Buttes, rise several hundred feet. Farther west is Big Southern Butte, the remainder of a volcano that predates the Craters eruptions.

Mesa Falls, Idaho. In Targhee National Forest, in a canyon bordered by conifers and birches, the Henry's Fork of the Snake River cascades in two impressive waterfalls. The upper falls drop around 100 feet, while the lower falls, with a greater concentration of water, plunge about 45 feet. A road leads to each fall.

Minnetonka Cave, Idaho. A short trail, as well as a highway, lead up to a sheer wall of rock and to the entrance of an astonish-ing mountain cave, perched at a height of more than 7500 feet. There is a small fee to enter the huge chambers of the cave to see its formations and the fossils from a prehistoric sea.

Mount Borah, Idaho. Idaho has six mountains over 12,000 feet. Four of them are in the Lost River range, including Mount Borah, at 12,655 feet Idaho's tallest peak. An excellent view of this mighty

range can be obtained from the valley road, Highway 93A, north of Mackay.

Pass Creek Gorge, Idaho. Compared with some other gorges in the state, a narrow, mile-long canyon may seem insignificant, but it is a remarkable sight. Sheer walls rise in dark-blue limestone, and there are colorful rock formations before and within the canyon. Trees shade picnic spots.

Payette Lake, Idaho. The waters of this magnificent horseshoe-shaped lake are a many-spangled blue. At an altitude of 5200 feet the climate is comfortable in summer, when many visitors come to enjoy the lake.

Redfish Lake, Idaho.
(*Picture appears on page 333*)

Sawtooth Lake, Idaho.
(*Picture appears on facing page*)

Shoshone Falls, Idaho. Pouring over a 1000-foot-wide horseshoe rim, the Snake River plunges 212 feet, higher than Niagara. The falls, torrential in spring, may be less so in high summer, when waters are diverted for irrigation.

Silent City of Rocks, Idaho. From a distance, the 10-square-mile area resembles a city. Closer, some of the granite formations look like great fortresses and

Crystal Ice Caves, *Idaho. Among Idaho's hundreds of caves, this one is unusual: it is a fissure cave instead of a lava tube, with stalactites and columns of ice instead of stone. When it is a summery 90 degrees outside, the formations inside the cave remain rigidly frozen.*

Sawtooth Lake, *Idaho. No roads lead to this lake, at the base of Mount Regan on the edge of the Sawtooth Primitive Area. But there are many fine trails to the cirque, and hikers who make the effort will find some good camping spots as well as spectacular scenery.*

cathedrals, others like animals and humans. Long ago California-bound travelers scratched names and messages on the rocks, and treasure hunters still search for gold from an 1878 stagecoach holdup said to be buried here.

Stanley Basin, Idaho. The basin is the essence of alpine beauty. Snowy peaks of the Sawtooth Mountains flank a broad, grass-covered valley dotted with primitive lakes and old homesteads.

Stanley Lake, Idaho. A beautiful lake in the Stanley Basin lies among meadows where wildflowers sway brightly in spring and summer. A mountain slope thick with evergreens provides a backdrop, beyond which rise the lofty and jagged peaks of the Sawtooth Mountains.

Sun Valley, Idaho. Famous as a vacation spot, the valley is a sheltered basin surrounded by national forest land. Although it provides many resort facilities—for both summer and winter activities—it has been developed carefully to protect and maintain the natural beauty which has drawn people to the area for so many years.

Teton Basin, Idaho. For spectacular views of mountain peaks, drive along highways 32 and 33 from Ashton to Victor. The Teton range in Wyoming seems so close that you must almost crane your neck to see the summits.

Thousand Springs, Idaho. Gushing from many different spots on a canyon wall, thousands of gallons of clear water pour into the Snake River. One of the sources of the springs is thought to be the Lost River, which disappears into the lava northeast of Craters of the Moon.

RELATED MUSEUMS AND ATTRACTIONS

Arco, Idaho. Craters of the Moon National Monument Museum.

Earthquake Area Visitor Center, Mont.

Idaho Falls, Idaho. Sportsman's Park Museum; natural history.

Pocatello, Idaho. State University Museum; natural history.

Castle Peak, *Idaho (facing page).* Motorists driving over the pass between Sun Valley and the Stanley Basin can see the White Clouds range in the distance. A dirt road off Highway 93 brings them even closer, where 11,820-foot Castle Peak looks what it is: the tallest point in the range. But it is the backpacker who can truly be in touch with this wilderness.

Redfish Lake, *Idaho (right).* The rising sun gilds peaks of the Sawtooth Range, leaving the lake still shadowy. The lake is already sky-high at 6500 feet, but its mountain backdrop reaches up another 3000 feet. A good road leads to the lake, located near the Sawtooth Primitive Area, and the U.S. Forest Service maintains an information center here.

Bruneau Dunes, *Idaho (below).* Snow-white sands cover about four square miles; two main dunes rise to about 450 feet. No motorized vehicles are permitted on the dunes, which make an oversize playground for walking, sliding and sand skiing. For those who tire of beach-bound sports, there is lake swimming, boating and fishing for bluegills.

Great Salt Lake Desert

UTAH

Wind creates a delicate tracery on the dazzling surface of the Salt Lake Desert flats.

Great
Salt Lake
Desert

UTAH

A Dazzling Wasteland Born
of Burning Sun and Bitter Water

In the American West it is often true that the less hospitable a place seems outwardly, the more interesting it turns out to be. The Great Salt Lake region is such a case. The area is barren, dry and at times the bleakest piece of real estate in the United States. The lake seems a cruel joke in the arid West: the largest west of the Mississippi—75 miles long and 50 miles wide—it is unfit to drink and not ideally comfortable for swimming.

And for all the impressive statistics, the lake you see today is virtually a drop in the bucket compared to the original. Thousands of years ago freshwater Lake Bonneville stretched from east of Salt Lake City across into Nevada and north into Idaho. The lake stood 1000 feet above its present level, held 500 times as much water and covered 20,000 square miles. (You can still see the wave-cut terraces marking its former shorelines high on the flanks of the Wasatch Mountains.)

Today's lake has 8 billion tons of salt worth around $50 billion. There is magnesium, lithium, gypsum, potash, boron, and sulphur and chloride compounds. They have come from the rivers that fed ancient Lake Bonneville and then concentrated in this depression as the lake evaporated over the centuries.

A fine introductory glimpse of the lake is in the vicinity where it was first seen and tasted by white men: at the mouth of the Bear River.

An aerial view from high over the sere hills of the Great Salt Lake's eastern shore shows the railroad crossing the water to Promontory Point.

A paved road follows the Bear River west from Brigham City, past fishermen sitting in chairs waiting for catfish to bite, to Bear River Migratory Bird Refuge, a 64,000-acre marsh with some two million birds in late summer. This is the country's biggest refuge, and its huge marshy wastes blend into the lake's shallow waters on the far horizon.

You can spot at least a dozen different species of birds by the time you reach the refuge headquarters with its high lookout tower. Black coots are common, as are great blue herons, seagulls and various ducks. Use the checklist available at headquarters and bring along binoculars and a good bird book.

A different look at the lakeshore is from Willard Bay State Park, south of Brigham City. Turn west below the steep, bare Willard Peaks, drive past fields with sleek horses and white beehives, cross the railroad tracks and arrive at a marina and campgrounds. Boating and fishing are both popular here.

A more adventurous approach to the lake is by way of Syracuse, west of Layton. Drive through the farming community's main street and continue west. Where the mainland ends, a gravel road leads across the lake to Antelope Island. If the gate is open and the road clears the water by a foot, proceed carefully, watching for soft road shoulders.

Great Salt Lake State Park, on the north end of Antelope Island, is the ideal place to begin a boat trip around the southern part of the lake. But first, see if there is movement in the shallow water by the ramp. Often you can find

337

The railroad causeway that crosses the lake changes the color of the water; that to the south, being fresher, is bluer than that to the north.

A herd of bison still roams on privately owned land south of Antelope Island State Park, and cowboys ride the range against a dazzling backdrop.

the flat, rust-colored, one-quarter-inch-long brine shrimp with their centipedelike legs. These invertebrates are collected, packaged and sold as tropical fish food.

Just beyond Antelope Island is Egg Island, teeming with birdlife. As you approach, thousands of California gulls climb into the air, dive-bomb and scream. Signs forbid landing during the nesting months, when the presence of humans can disturb the birds.

As your boat goes farther away from Antelope Island, you begin to get an idea of the lake's size: it is really a small sea, and the first taste of spray sharply reminds you of this. As you skirt Fremont Island, look for herds of wild horses galloping along the hill crests. On its west coast are crude loading chutes for

sheep that are brought to and from the island for the summer grasses.

Ahead are Promontory Point and two railroad lines. The southernmost is the famous Lucin Cutoff, built in 1903. It saved a long, tough 102 miles over the Promontory Mountains from the West Coast to Ogden, but cost $8 million, took 38,000 trees and left headaches for those who have since tried to maintain the trestles. The other is a rock-fill causeway, just a stone's throw to the north. The Southern Pacific completed it in 1959 at a cost of $50 million, and it too has problems: periodically the wave action shifts the rocks.

The causeway has brought about a marked change in the lake. The water to the south appears bright blue: it contains only about 15

percent salt because it is fed with fresh water from the Bear, Weber, Ogden and Jordan rivers. The north side is pinkish and the salt concentration is about 25 percent: it receives only a slight freshwater runoff from the low-lying hills to the north.

One island north of the causeway is worth seeing but it means putting a boat in at the village of Lakeside. Gunnison Island is a nesting site for the great white pelican, a magnificent bird but a messy housekeeper. Its rookeries are strewn with malodorous fish lying half eaten among the unfledged youngsters.

Other islands in the lake have had nesting colonies of great blue herons, Caspian terns and the ubiquitous California seagulls. Bird Island, despite its name, harbors only a family of

ravens on its hilly part, while a small colony of gulls nests on its sand spit.

Stansbury Island, at the south end of the lake, is really a peninsula jutting northward over 11 miles. Its 3000-foot peaks provide habitat for black-tailed jackrabbits, cottontail rabbits, mule deer and occasionally a coyote or mountain lion.

Cutting across the lake east from Stansbury, Antelope Island now comes back into view. Look for a herd of bison—it has roamed the island since 1890—often seen by boaters along the west shore, south of the state park. And this same 15-mile coast offers some splendid vistas for camera buffs. The wind-fluted and water-eroded rocks rival the most unusual formations in the West. Watch for an area that has tan rocks containing bands of snake-like green and orange.

For a glimpse of the lake's history of recreation, head west of Salt Lake City to Saltair, the once-great "Coney Island West" that drew thousands of fun seekers during the days of the big dance bands. It died as the lake receded, then burned. But with high water in recent years, interest has revived in this south end of the lake, and old-timers speak nostalgically of rebuilding Saltair. Today Sand Pebble, Silver Sands and Sunset Beach offer boat rentals, cruises and showers for those who want to sample the salty swimming. This is a strange recreation in Great Salt Lake. The swimmer feels himself unable to sink; and on occasions it can be dangerous, for waves are big, and heavy with salt (on average the lake is four times as salty as the ocean).

Another era is recorded at the Golden Spike National Historic Site, west of Brigham City. This was where the country's first transcontinental railroad tracks from the East met those from the West. A golden spike was driven into the last tie in 1869, and the small visitor center, with its slide-sound show and reenactment of

A setting sun throws long shadows from stunted desert bushes near the major highway—Interstate 80—that leads westward across the Great Salt Lake Desert. The low mountains that rise on the horizon everywhere in this arid desert once lay beneath the waters of enormous Lake Bonneville.

the meeting ceremonies, brings it vividly to life.

History is made every year near Wendover, at the Bonneville Salt Flats. Cars scream across the glistening salt raceway, their drivers pushing for new world land speed records. What began in 1911 with W. D. Rishel driving a Packard at 50 incredible miles per hour has progressed to today's daredevil drivers reaching for 1000 mph with jet cars.

But however people get to know this desert salt region—as a challenge, a curiosity, a wildlife refuge, a recreation spot—it determinedly belies its bleak appearance.

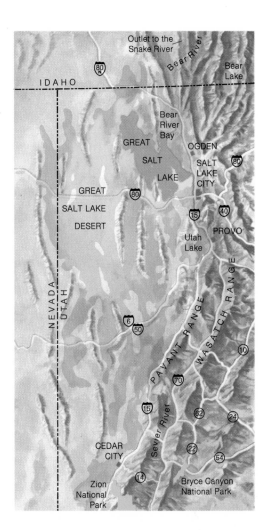

The highway also passes through the Bonneville Salt Flats, where many successful attempts at the world land speed record are made on a desert track.

Great Salt Lake Is a Tiny Remnant of Prehistoric Lake Bonneville

Although Great Salt Lake seems impressively huge even today, it is only a puddle compared to its vast ancestor, Lake Bonneville, which at 20,000 square miles was almost as big as Lake Michigan. Formed by melting snows in successive ice ages, this huge body of water once covered the entire area shown in pale blue above, including much of western Utah and parts of Idaho and Nevada. At one time its waters were 1000 feet above where Great Salt Lake is today, and the benches cut by its waves on the flanks of the Wasatch Mountains can still be seen. At its peak level, Lake Bonneville drained through the Red River Canyon into Idaho's Snake River basin. As the climate gradually changed, however, and the last ice age gave way to a hot climate, evaporation exceeded the freshwater input, and the lake shrank, becoming more and more salty as it receded from its outlet. Now only Great Salt Lake and Utah Lake (still fresh because the water flows through) remain, their levels virtually stabilized in recent years.

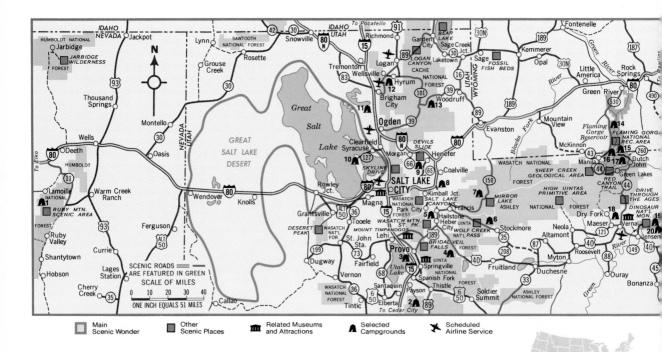

| Main Scenic Wonder | Other Scenic Places | Related Museums and Attractions | Selected Campgrounds | Scheduled Airline Service |

WITHIN A DAY'S DRIVE:

Cool Trout Streams, Sunbaked Desert –and Some Geological Trails

Bear Lake, Utah and Idaho. The best way to come upon this mountain-ringed lake is from the head of Logan Canyon, at an overlook that opens up a splendid panorama of clear, dark blue waters. There are lakeside picnic spots, swimming beaches and a state marina; fishermen come from far around to net its cisco.

Bridal Veil Falls, Utah. (*Picture appears on facing page*)

Deseret Peak, Utah. It is about a three-hour hike up the trail to the 11,031-foot peak, but the summit perch amply rewards the effort: the Skull Valley salt flats run to the edge of Great Salt Lake, which stretches out in blinding whiteness northward as far as the eye can see.

Devil's Slide, Utah. Weber Canyon cuts through gentle farmland and narrows down at Devil's Gate, an appropriate prelude to the Devil's Slide that follows. Years of erosion have designed a rock chute fit for the recreation

of a giant—it is several hundred feet long, with sides 40 feet high.

Dinosaur National Monument, Utah and Colo. (*Picture appears on pages 344-45*)

Drive Through the Ages, Utah. A billion years of history unfold like a geological newsreel on the 30-mile road up to the summit of the Uinta Mountains. Layers of rock exposed by erosion are marked by roadside signs, each recording the eras when substances like coal, petrified wood, uranium, sandstone, shale and quartz crystal were formed.

Flaming Gorge National Recreation Area, Utah and Wyo. (*Picture appears on page 345*)

Fossil Fish Beds, Wyo. Catfish, bowfins, perch, herring, stone gar and a turtle are among the remarkable fossil finds near Diamondville, where Carl Ulrich and his family display these ancient treasures and instruct fossil-hunting sightseers and students.

High Uintas Primitive Area, Utah. (*Picture appears on page 345*)

Jarbidge Wilderness, Nev. This remote and little-known place features eight peaks higher than 10,000 feet, magnificent alpine scenery and Wild Horse Reservoir.

Logan Canyon, Utah. Despite ever-increasing use, the canyon has withstood civilization and is easily the loveliest throughway of the Wasatch range, particularly when its trees turn in the fall. Shaded campsites and picnic areas dot the canyon.

Mirror Lake, Utah. Forested slopes and alpine peaks are the background for this tranquil mountain lake, with its campsites and picnic grounds. This is the jumping-off spot for the High Uintas Primitive Area.

Red Canyon Trail, Utah. A trail winding for about a half hour's hike through a ponderosa pine forest is a primer in forest lore. Fifteen numbered stops give visi-

Bridal Veil Falls, *Utah. Like fine white wedding lace, the two cataracts fall gracefully down the rocky Provo Canyon. The waterfalls can be admired from below or from an aerial tramway a lofty 1700 feet overhead. This is one of several beauty spots in the Mount Timpanogos Scenic Area: others are Timpanogos itself (the summit is a hard day's hike away) and a cave full of fascinating formations.*

343

tors clues on how to see lichens create soil, how to guess the age of trees and to spot wildlife.

Ruby Mountain Scenic Area, Nev. More than 40,000 acres of glacier-carved canyon country attract hikers and campers to this wilderness. Sheer walls of U-shaped canyons rise 2000 feet, some laced with waterfalls fed by high pools.

Salt Lake Canyons, Utah. Mill Creek, Big Cottonwood and Little Cottonwood canyons are splendid mountain passes just east of Salt Lake City. This is a ski area in winter, but for other seasons there are hiking trails, picnic places and spectacular alpine scenery.

Sheep Creek Geological Area, Utah. A geological spectacle: an immense break in the surface of the earth has exposed billions of years of history, with giant twisted walls of multicolored stone towering above the road.

Skyline Drive, Utah. Interstate 15, edging the foothills of the Wasatch Mountains, is a reward-ing drive. The levels of old Lake Bonneville are revealed, and there are magnificent views of Great Salt Lake, especially at sunset.

Wasatch Mountain State Park, Utah. Campsites lie alongside one of the prettiest public golf courses in the state. There is hiking and horseback riding, and in Deer Creek Reservoir and the Provo River fishing for trout.

Wolf Creek Pass, Utah. The 9450-foot-high pass is a summit view-point about midway along an out-

standing mountain drive. The road follows the Provo and Duchesne rivers, excellent for fishing.

RELATED MUSEUMS AND ATTRACTIONS

Provo, Utah. Brigham Young University Geology Museum.

Salt Lake City, Utah. University of Utah Earth Science Museum.

Timpanogos Cave National Monument, Utah. Park museum.

Vernal, Utah. Utah Field Museum of Natural History.

Flaming Gorge National Recreation Area, *Utah and Wyo. Wedged into a stone corridor, the Flaming Gorge Reservoir hosts all the popular water sports. Its rocky pinnacles serve as aeries for rare golden eagles.*

High Uintas Primitive Area, *Utah. King's Peak, at 13,528 feet the highest point in the state, overlooks a plateau where no motor vehicle may enter: backpackers and horseback riders enjoy primeval beauty.*

Dinosaur National Monument, *Utah and Colo. The Green River winds below Split Mountain. Downstream it passes near a working quarry that has yielded ancient bones of crocodiles and 14 species of dinosaurs.*

Arches–Canyonlands

NATIONAL PARKS, UTAH

Grandview Point at Canyonlands overlooks Monument Basin, 2000 feet below, and the White Rim.

Fantastic Desert Cities
Carved from Red Sandstone

The Colorado River flows west out of the Rockies and the Green River runs south from the mountains of Wyoming. As they cut through ever-deepening canyons, they join in southeastern Utah amid a fantasy of sculptured rock 50 miles wide and 100 miles long. This is the red-rock region of that huge space between the high ranges of Colorado and the great basin of Nevada which geographers call the Colorado Plateau. Although it contains nothing as deep as the stupendous maw of the Grand Canyon 200 miles to the southwest, this land of canyons and mesas is infinitely more varied and widespread—and the innermost reaches are somewhat more accessible.

It has been called Standing Up Country because more rocks are standing up than lying down. It has also been described as a rock jungle. Both are fitting. There are a dozen major canyons and hundreds of minor ones. There are tens of thousands of mesas, buttes, spires, pinnacles, domes, fins, knobs and towers. And there are hundreds of natural arches and bridges, countless caves and overhangs. (The rock of which they are all composed is sandstone, uniform grains of 99-percent-pure quartz, cemented by infiltrated iron oxide. The red color is in the cement alone, not in the clear grains.) Then there is the Colorado River. In digging its canyons this noble river was primarily responsible for today's landscape.

In this view of some of the White Rim formations, the thick cap of erosion-resistant white sandstone which covers the underlying rock is clearly visible.

This is harsh country in some ways. It has none of the lush charm of mountain parks, with fragrant meadows and sparkling streams. The canyonlands are semidesert: summer days are hot and the sun glares relentlessly. The colors are hot too: reds, brown and buff, mostly untempered by green. Sand gets into your shoes. Water is rare and what little is available usually tastes bitter.

But the land can be benign too. The air is absolutely clear: a 40-mile view is not unusual. Insects are scarce. At sundown the harsh colors turn to muted violets. Nights are cool, and the Milky Way gleams across the limpid sky as you have seldom seen it before. Campers prepare for bed simply by spreading a small tarpaulin, throwing down their sleeping bags and sliding inside for the night.

Beyond all this is the stunning beauty of shape everywhere. Stripped of topsoil and vegetation, the stones are the bare, chiseled bones of the earth. It is peculiarly satisfying simply to walk over the sterile and massively undulating sandstone forms or to clamber to a lofty alcove and sit quietly looking out across the bizarre landscape.

Canyonlands National Park is at the heart of this area. A rough rectangle 35 miles long and 20 miles wide, it consists of four principal sections: the Island in the Sky, a 6000-foot mesa that dominates the region between the Colorado and Green rivers; the rivers with their canyons, the Needles area in the southern portion and the remote Maze District to the west of the rivers. Arches National Park nearby

Landscape Arch, 291 feet long and thought to be the world's longest, seems to stretch for an incredible distance when you stand beneath its thin, *flattened span, as attenuated as a hank of taffy pulled to the snapping point. Like most of the features in Arches National Park, Landscape Arch*

contains an incomparable collection of natural sandstone arches.

Most visitors arrive by car, and the spot to head for is Moab on U.S. Route 163, 30 miles south of Interstate 70. Moab has good motels, all supplies, jeep rentals and guide service. Park headquarters for Canyonlands is here, right on Main Street.

Arches is the closest park and the place to visit first. Rangers and exhibits at its visitor center explain much about the nature of the country, and the road is paved and excellent, a rarity here off the principal highways. There is also a campground with water. (Wherever you go, carry lots of water. The air is dry and thin at 6000 feet, and a supply of one gallon a day per person is an absolute minimum.)

The greatest concentration of natural arches in the world—about 88, plus a large assortment of other sandstone formations—awaits the visitor to Arches. A bird's-eye view best shows how the arches were formed: the earth humped and cracked a 300-foot layer of sandstone in regular rows 10 to 20 feet wide, clear to the bottom. The lower levels, containing moisture, eroded first, and occasional rockfalls speeded the process (see diagram on page 351).

Probably the most remarkable single formation is called Landscape Arch. With a span of 291 feet, it is the largest arch in the world. It is unusually flat, is bulkiest at the middle, and at one end is only six feet thick. As a mathema-

Water in the Desert Is the Principal Arch Builder

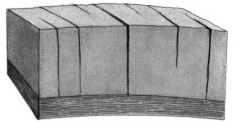

BULGING EARTH CRACKS SURFACE

FURTHER BULGING
AND EROSION WIDENS JOINTS

UNDERCUTS PIERCE "FINS," FORMING ARCH

is quite accessible: an easy, one-mile hike from the Devils Garden campground, which is an 18-mile drive on a paved road from the park visitor center.

tician can prove that a ladybug cannot fly because its wings are too small and its shape is ridiculous, so a structural engineer can prove that Landscape, weighing thousands of tons, just cannot be supported by such widespread legs, however sturdy looking.

Delicate Arch is not as big, but with its spraddle-legged stance on the rim of a smooth and spotless natural amphitheater it is an extraordinary sight. The trail leading to the arch is itself remarkable—a long ascending ledge transversing a steep declivity.

For a different kind of experience go north from Moab 10 miles, then southwest 31, checking in at the Canyonlands National Park ranger station, to Grandview Point. Here the

Natural bridges and arches are among the most eye-catching of erosional forms, but they are created in quite different ways. A bridge results from the cutting power of a deeply entrenched and meandering stream. Occasionally the stream will break through the divide between two wide loops to form a hole, which is then enlarged by weathering into a bridge. Arches, however, are formed by the erosion of a narrow "fin," or sandstone wall, as shown here. In the first phase the earth upwarps, cracking (or jointing) the sandstone. In phase 2 the cracks are widened by rain and other weathering agents, while at lower levels alternate frost and thaw flake away the damp surfaces. In phase 3 these processes cut through a fin to form a hole, which is enlarged by rockfalls until an arch is formed. Surface weathering rounds the shapes. (Contrary to popular belief, the effects of sandblasting have little to do with arches.) Eventually an arch will collapse, leaving only the end buttresses. Arches in all stages of development exist in Arches National Park, and several natural bridges share a Monument.

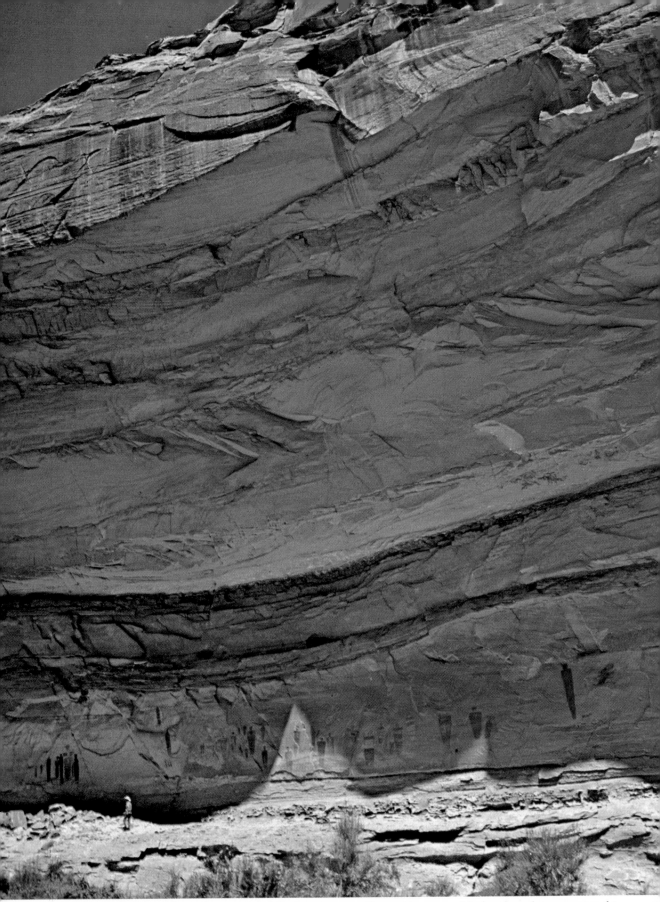

In remote Horseshoe Canyon, west of the Green River, is the country's largest gallery of Indian pictographs, spread for 175 feet along the cliff face.

Over 1000 years old, they have been preserved in perfect condition by the dry desert atmosphere, but the people who painted them remain an enigma.

Delicate Arch, perhaps the most famous feature in the Arches park, perches on the rim of a giant sandstone bowl, framing the distant La Sal Mountains.

The Tooth, typical of the geological flukes found at Canyonlands, is 20 miles by jeep up the Salt Creek Bed. Angel Arch is just a half-hour hike beyond it.

tip of a gnarled finger of land points out from the Island in the Sky toward the confluence of the Colorado and Green rivers. Grand indeed is the view. Sixty miles to the southwest the Henry Mountains joggle the horizon. Thirty-five miles to the east the snowcapped La Sals— Tomaski, Tukuhnikivatz and Mount Peale— glare in the sun. There, across the Green River, is the Land of Standing Rocks, Ernie's Country and the Maze. To the south, far across the terraced walls of the Colorado, lie the Needles, looking like a sprawling, crenellated city. Beneath your feet the wall drops a vertical 1000 feet to the White Rim, a broad shelf of creamy sandstone, and beyond it another cliff plummets another 1000 feet to the river.

On the return to Moab, take the side road to Upheaval Dome, a mile-wide, 1500-foot-deep crater near the edge of the Island in the Sky. How can a crater be called a dome? A vast half-mile-thick bed of salt—from the ancient seas—underlies the visible layers of sandstone and shale. Salt is lighter and more pliable than the rocks of the overburden and tends to rise, like bubbles, in zones of weakness. Here a giant salt dome ballooned and cracked open the top layers of the earth.

Driving back, you may see a cow or two. This country has been rangeland for a century, though it can take 1000 acres to feed a cow. A rancher here once said that to get enough to eat, a cow had to have a mouth six feet wide and graze at a gallop.

Back at Moab the Colorado River is swift and shallow as it passes under the town bridge. It flows evenly for 70 miles south to its meeting with the Green River, though the channel is tricky and there are frequent hidden bars. The Green River also flows serenely through its sheer-walled, winding canyons to the meeting point. Beyond the junction the Colorado runs unruffled three more miles. Then, at a bowl in the canyon called Spanish Bottom, the river turns sharp left and enters Cataract Canyon. For 16 miles it rushes through a rapid succession of severe, rock-strewn rapids and then debouches into the placid waters of Lake Powell. Commercial operators take rafting parties down the smooth stretches, or on down through the rapids on occasion. Jet boats leave from Moab on day-long or overnight excursions—but only on the calm waters.

The highway to the southern part of Canyonlands National Park runs 40 miles south of Moab, then 35 miles west to Squaw Flat. From here you can explore the Needles area, roughly 10 square miles of startling, almost grotesque beauty. The Needles themselves climax at Chesler Park, a lofty mile-wide circular meadow ringed by an exquisite assortment of 300-foot towers and minarets. To some they look like a conference of giants turned to stone, to others like a ring of soaring buildings not so much ruined as simply worn into smooth and sensuous shapes.

To the west of Chesler are the Grabens—long, grass-carpeted parallel valleys bounded by high vertical walls. These too are a result of the underlying salt bed. Groundwater dissolved sections of the salt, and the crust sank into the resulting underground chambers. To the east are Salt Creek Canyon and Horseshoe Canyon with their ruins of ancient Indian dwellings and their pictographs, and Angel Arch. You can hike up and sit beneath Angel Arch: the going is rough—be sure to pass the Tooth—but the reward is considerable.

You cannot take your car beyond Squaw Flat campground. A rough jeep trail continues over Elephant Hill, into the Needles and beyond, through Bobby's Hole, Pappy's Pasture and Ruin Park. Another jeep trail winds 20 miles up Salt Creek, with a turnoff to Angel Arch. You can hire a jeep with driver at Moab or Monticello. It's expensive but a fine wilderness experience. Pack trips are also available and hiking is always in style.

The remote Maze District, west of the Colorado River, is a long desert drive, strictly for those who like wild places where few people have been before. And that is the essence of the appeal of the whole Canyonlands area: a place to see nature at its most intransigent—and spectacular.

The diagonal streaks in this sandstone formation were the faces of a series of sand dunes. When the dunes were covered by a sea, iron oxide percolated through and cemented the sand grains into stone. Later, after the land rose above the sea, desert rains sculpted the undulating forms seen now.

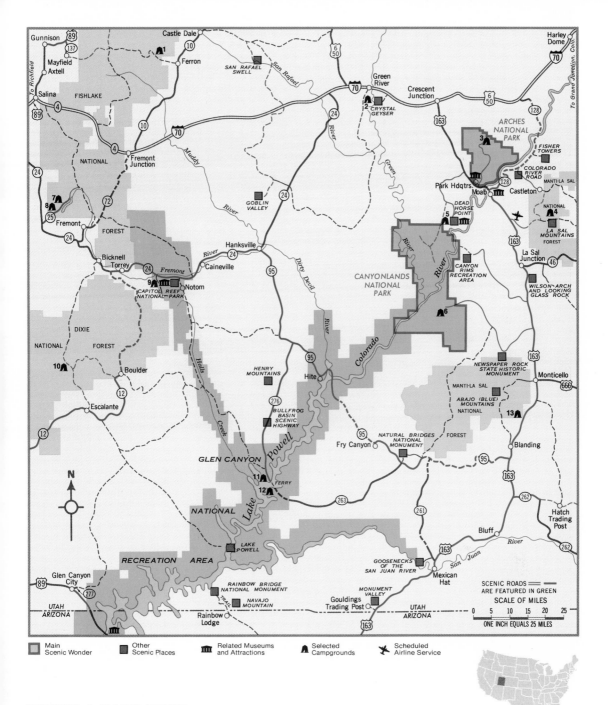

WITHIN A DAY'S DRIVE:

Natural Bridges and a Big Desert Lake

Abajo (Blue) Mountains. These are rare laccolithic mountains, one of only three such ranges in America. (The others, both in southeastern Utah, are the Henry and La Sal mountains.) They formed underneath thousands of feet of rock, never broke the surface but were exposed by erosion. Scenic dirt roads and jeep trails lace the Abajos, and there are good views from U.S. 163.

Bullfrog Basin Scenic Highway. The road goes through the Henry Mountains, past Mount Hillers, then crosses the vivid desert canyon country of Bullfrog Basin. The Waterpocket Fold cliffs rise near the end of the highway.

Canyon Rims Recreation Area. A 20-mile-long mesa, Hatch Point, surveys Canyonlands National Park from the east. Here are two developed viewpoints which offer fantastic vistas: Needles Overlook and Anticline Overlook.

Capitol Reef National Park. (*Picture appears on page 356*)

Colorado River Road. Utah routes 279 and 128 follow the Colorado River gorge for a spectacular 60 miles. Vertical sandstone cliffs wall in the river, which is lined

355

Capitol Reef National Park. *Buttes of the Water-pocket Fold, an enormous wrinkle in the earth's crust, tower above a colored landscape. The massive 90-mile wall of ancient rock has slowly eroded into a vivid maze of cliffs, towers, domes, deep canyons, rock pinnacles and natural bridges.*

with willow, tamarisk and cottonwood trees. Some rocks along the roadway reveal Indian petroglyphs and dinosaur tracks.

Crystal Geyser. Cold, odorous water, clear as crystal, erupts at about four-hour intervals to startling heights. The main geyser is surrounded by minor spouts and brightly hued mineral terraces.

Dead Horse Point. A wide-angle panorama unfolds from this state park overlook: vast red-rock canyonlands to the south, the La Sal mountain range in the east and an enormous bend in the Colorado River gorge 1700 feet below.

Fisher Towers. A group of tall, monolithic spires of dark red stone are visible for many miles. The tallest tower, Titan, rises 900 feet. There is a picnic site here, as well as the beginning of an outstanding hiking trail.

Goblin Valley. Unusually weathered rocks in the valley especially delight photographers and children. Thousands of monoliths have eroded into eerie shapes resembling people, animals and grotesque fantasies.

Goosenecks of the San Juan River. A state reserve protects an undeveloped canyon rim that towers over several gooseneck loops of the deep San Juan River gorge. A foot trail leads from the rim down into the gorge.

Henry Mountains. Like the Abajo Mountains, the range is of laccolithic origin. Stupendous slabs of red and white sandstone lie on the dark lower flanks of the peaks, and knife-thin igneous rocks soar skyward for several hundreds of feet.

Lake Powell.
(*Picture appears on pages 358–59*)

La Sal Mountains. A splendid loop road climbs into the La Sals, the area's highest but most accessible range—and the one most developed for recreation. Scenic jeep trails lace the heights.

Monument Valley.
(*Picture appears on page 359*)

Natural Bridges National Monument. *Owachomo Bridge, the oldest of three huge stone spans, is worn flat and thin. Visitors can survey the bridges from overlooks or follow trails that go underneath them.*

Rainbow Bridge National Monument. *Appropriately called Rainbow-Turned-to-Stone by Navajo Indians, this massive bridge of weathered pink sandstone is the largest known natural span in the world.*

357

Natural Bridges National Monument.
(*Picture appears on page 357*)

Navajo Mountain. This isolated mountain decorated with enormous sandstone slabs is so massive that it sometimes generates storms all by itself. It is on Navajo land and sacred to the Indians, who restrict access. The best way to view it is from the air or from a boat on a nearby arm of Lake Powell.

Newspaper Rock State Historic Monument. The single panel of ancient Indian petroglyphs is aptly called Newspaper Rock. The crowded "writings" show humans, animals and abstract designs.

Rainbow Bridge National Monument.
(*Picture appears on page 357*)

San Rafael Swell. The remains of a 30-mile-long oval "blister" on the earth's crust is a geological curiosity. Massive upswelling caused the earth to bulge and break. Most of the original surface rock has eroded, leaving multicolored canyons, plateaus and buttes. At the edges of the swell are gigantic walls of sharply tilted rock.

Wilson Arch and Looking Glass Rock. These two large natural arches are unusual because they stand near a main highway. Both are colorful picture subjects.

**RELATED MUSEUMS
AND ATTRACTIONS**

Arches National Park. Visitor
Center.

Capitol Reef National Park. Visitor Center.

Dead Horse Point State Park.
Visitor Center.

Glen Canyon Dam. Visitor
Center; lake geography.

Moab. Moab Museum; natural
history, mineralogy.

Monument Valley. *A dying sun lights the Yebechei Rocks in the Navajo Indians' immense valley. Dunes and sand flats erupt into solitary buttes and towers, walls and escarpments, all in glowing red sandstone. The valley, on the Utah-Arizona border, is most striking in half-light.*

Lake Powell. *Bodies of water in desert regions are always spectacular, and this reservoir set in red rock, nearly 200 miles long and with 1800 miles of shoreline, is a playground for every kind of water sport. It was formed by massive Glen Canyon Dam backing up the Colorado River.*

359

Bryce Canyon–Zion
NATIONAL PARKS, UTAH

Bryce's Inspiration Point unfolds a world of carved ocher pinnacles lightly glazed with snow.

UTAH

Bryce
Canyon-Zion
National Parks

Extraordinary Stone Visions Shaped Out of Space and Color

The southwest corner of Utah has been so richly blessed with outstanding scenery that it seems almost unfair to the rest of the country. The two national parks that preserve Bryce and Zion canyons lie only about 90 miles apart, over roads marked, appropriately enough, scenic highways; they could hardly be otherwise in this part of the world.

Just as Zion and Bryce are within a short drive of each other, so they stand close together in the geologic scheme of things. In fact, tracing a line southwest to northeast, Grand Canyon provides the best-known record of ancient geologic history, Zion Canyon records most clearly the events of middle (Mesozoic) time, while Bryce reveals much of the most recent age. The story of Zion begins where

Grand Canyon's ends, and ends where Bryce Canyon's begins. From 50 miles above the earth, astronauts in a spacecraft would see a series of escarpments or steps leading slowly upward from Grand Canyon onto Zion and through to Bryce—a grand stairway of varying colors and formations. Once a large shallow sea and later a windswept desert, the Zion area today shows stunning effects of its varied past: enormous, unscalable frozen dunes; canyons, buttes and mesas laid down in orderly layers; veiled nooks green and dripping with mossy life facing dry, sun-splashed cliffs on which grow scrub oak and juniper.

Zion has been called a Yosemite painted in oils. It makes much the same impression: massive forms and sheer rock faces towering over a flat valley. But here, instead of the dark or neutral rocks at Yosemite, the vertical sandstone walls are shades of red, blending upward into white. The shales beneath them are the most brilliantly colored rocks known: purple and lilac, pink and yellow.

Zion Canyon was cut by the Virgin River. There is some dispute about the origin of the name: it might have been called after Thomas Virgin, one of Jedediah Smith's men who was wounded by Indians, or the Spanish might have called it after the Virgin Mary. And there was once dispute about how the canyon was cut. Some theorized that it resulted from a fissure or fracture along a fault line, others that glacial action scoured out the valley. But we know now that the steady—and occasionally

Leisurely exploration from the many trails down into Bryce Canyon brings into sharp focus close-up color portraits in stone, each seemingly fashioned by an ambitious, superhuman artist. At the left, looking exactly like a mammoth hollowed-out tree stump, stone towers balance above a gallery of gracefully fluted fingers and pinnacles. Above, oversize mushrooms, fitted with shapely peaked caps, cluster among the evergreens.

flashing—waters of the Virgin River did the job, aided by the erosional effects of wind, rain and frost, and the downward pull of gravity.

All the ingredients necessary for rapid erosion are present at Zion. The Virgin River, the Colorado's largest tributary in southern Utah, gathers water from a large area; it is a fast moving river flowing over extremely soft rock which disintegrates quickly, and the thin soil of this area does not support enough vegetation to significantly slow down the river's course. The Virgin today drops 50 to 70 feet per mile and carries away hundreds of thousands of tons of rock a year.

The first white men to venture into this southwest corner of Utah were two Spanish priests, Dominguez and Escalante, in 1776. Frustrated by earlier efforts to ford the Colorado River, Dominquez and Escalante were searching for an easier passage from the Spanish settlements at Santa Fe, New Mexico, to Monterey on the California coast. If they saw Zion and Bryce canyons at all, they left no written record.

Fifty years later the intrepid fur trader Jedediah S. Smith took 16 men from the American Fur Company headquarters on Great Salt Lake, following a series of rivers in pursuit of the beaver pelts they knew awaited them. But the vast canyons of Zion and the hundreds of brilliant stone pinnacles of Bryce escaped them and do not figure in accounts of their journey. It may have been seen first by Mormons who settled Utah during the mid-19th century; one was sufficiently moved to name the canyon Zion, meaning the heavenly resting place.

Ebenezer Bryce, the man who gave Bryce Canyon its name and one of the first settlers to explore it, wryly remarked that Zion was "a helluva place to lose a cow." But many of the names the Mormons gave to the park's features reflect the reverence the scenery inspired in them: there are temples, patriarchs, thrones and cathedrals. The massive forms and sheer walls seemed to call for weighty names. One of the most charming examples is the tableland called Angels Landing.

In 1871–72 Major John Wesley Powell, the one-armed Civil War veteran and first explorer of Grand Canyon, threaded Zion's steep canyons and gave it the Indian name Mukuntuweap. Years later local pressure caused it to be rechristened with the Mormons' name: Zion. In 1872 C. K. Gilbert explored that part

Caught in a winter storm, the snow-seamed Towers of the Virgin rear their peaks forbiddingly in the center of Zion National Park. Like many other lofty

of Zion where the canyon floor narrows to 20 feet, with sheer walls rising 2000 feet on either side. He named it the Narrows and said it was "the most wonderful defile it has been my fortune to behold."

Gilbert no doubt encountered the Narrows under favorable weather conditions. Today even experienced hikers are warned to notify the Chief Ranger's Office if they plan to walk it; hikes are virtually forbidden during the thunderstorm season, from mid-July through early September. During these months a sudden storm can turn the normally placid Virgin

cliffs in the region, the stones offer a lesson
in earth history. In various ages seas and
broad rivers covered the area, each depositing

its layers of sediment. Today the narrow Virgin
River cuts an ever-deeper channel, but wind and
rain remain the most powerful canyon architects.

River into a raging torrent. "It seethes like a thing alive, a serpent devouring red watery tons of mud and sand from countless tributaries," writes park naturalist Allen Hagood. "We stand awestruck as enormous boulders crash and split asunder. Uprooted cottonwoods tumble and upend like jackstraws." At its best, though, the Narrows provides man—adventurous man—with a 13-mile trek into a darkening void broken only now and then by thin shafts of sunlight, slanting down between the towering banks, glinting on green water. Hikers in the Narrows sometimes hear the thump-

ing of cobbles colliding in hollows on the channel floor, driven by swirling backwashes of the river.

One of the glories of Zion is that much of it is downright impenetrable. Indeed, Zion was not completely mapped until 1930, when it was photographed from an airplane. In the same year the remarkable Zion–Mt. Carmel Highway was completed, at the cost of a million dollars and three years of tunnel-blasting, offering an ideal access from the east. Pine Creek Tunnel, more than a mile long, descends toward the canyon floor, a series of lookouts through

Zion's Great White Throne, a flattop stool fit for giants, towers behind rugged rock precipices (above), while aspens, aglow with sunlight, glitter beneath it. From Observation Point (left), the Throne and its neighboring tall stone bluffs stand guard on either side of the Virgin River, which winds through Zion Canyon like a snake.

"windows" in the tunnel wall providing welcome light and spectacular views of the East Temple, Sentinel Mountain, Great West Wall and the Great Arch.

Driving the Zion–Mt. Carmel Highway, even though it is laced with switchbacks, may be too easy a way to see the park; a slogging hike through the Narrows may be too tough. In between, however, are a variety of hikes, walks and climbs to take you nearer to Zion's splendor. You can trek two miles round trip (from the Zion Lodge parking area) to Emerald Pool, set between two waterfalls. On foot or by horse, you can traverse the east- and west-rim trails by leaving the valley floor at the foot of the Great White Throne and climbing half a mile along a zigzag path, up talus slopes, through cool, dark, slitlike canyons, emerging among the

pines of Kabob Terrace. So diverse are Zion's habitats that you may see wildlife ranging from desert dwellers like roadrunners, golden eagles and Gambel quail to water creatures such as blue herons and water ouzels. Mule deer are common, cougars rare. Here and there a rattlesnake may cause a stir. But the most unusual tenants are the invertebrates—the Zion snails, found only here, which have become adapted to the moist niches along the dim reaches of the Narrows.

Zion is open year-round (though the park's lodging facilities are closed in winter). In summer there is the bonus of hardwoods in leaf—aspen, cottonwood, ash and willow; ferns and mosses at their greenest; and a procession of wildflowers: prince's-plume, poppy, buttercup, larkspur, columbine—the list is surprisingly long and varied.

Northwest of Zion lies Bryce Canyon National Park—which is not actually a canyon but a horseshoe-shaped basin carved from white and pink limestone, shale and sandstone. Bryce's presence is signaled by the Pink Cliffs, which run almost 150 miles from Cedar City to the Paria River and north beyond the Fremont River—"the glory of all rock work," according to Major C. E. Dutton, who surveyed the area in 1880. Standing at the edge of the basin—two miles wide, three miles long and several hundred feet deep—you peer into a wonderland of spires, pinnacles, walls, arches and windows, all the more arresting for their vivid coloring: iron compounds of red and brown, limonite yellows, manganese purple and lavender.

The knobby, angular pinnacles at Bryce, some of which bear a startling resemblance to cardboard cutouts of human figures, have always inspired men to flights of fancy in naming them. Both the familiar and the exotic are invoked. On the park's most popular nature walk, the Navajo Loop Trail, which descends 521 feet in a two-hour hike, are Wall Street, the Temple of Osiris, Thor's Hammer, the Camel and Wise Man. On the five-mile Peekaboo Loop there are views of the Wall of Windows, Hindu Temples and Three Wise Men. On the Fairyland–Tower Bridge–Bryce Trail—five and a half strenuous miles—formations are so numerous and varied that most of them have not yet been named.

These 36,010 acres also invite endless picture-taking, though one is advised to observe the exposure, for the tendency is to over-expose in the belief that the landscape is less bright than it really is. The light will be flat from 10 A.M. to 3 P.M.—but shots taken early in the morning or late in the afternoon may come out so well as to make an amateur dream of turning professional.

Plant and animal life varies markedly at different levels. Traveling from top to bottom you may think you are shifting worlds. At 7000 to 8500 feet grow Douglas fir, Rocky Mountain juniper, ponderosa, bristlecone and limber pine. Piñons and junipers dot the slopes below the rim, while grasses and sagebrush flourish on the open valley floors. Wild flowers further color the already painted landscape: yellow evening primrose, blue columbine, Indian paintbrush and sego lily.

Those 19th-century trappers and traders found plenty of beaver around Bryce—in fact they named the area Paunsaugunt, home of the beaver. The beaver has been trapped out of existence for its fur, but there are 30 mammals, nine carnivores and 20 rodents that still live in the canyons, including skunks, gray foxes, bobcats, and rockchucks, or yellow-bellied marmots. Also: hawks, doves, owls and a variety of songbirds. Chipmunks and ground squirrels, scampering along the Rim Drive, seemingly unaware of the no-feeding rules, somehow steal the spotlight from the more exotic creatures.

Despite the splendor of the scenery in the clear light, there is a very real threat to Bryce and Zion. A park naturalist concerned with the area's future has noted that during the past decade an increasingly intense pall has been noted in the skies above Zion, along with many other western desert places, and that in the upper stretches of the Virgin River, "much of the water, poisoned by human wastes, is now unfit to drink without treatment." Jedediah Smith, Ebenezer Bryce and the 19th-century surveyors found the air above Zion and Bryce pure and the streams clean. It will be a sorry legacy of our century if those who follow us can no longer marvel at the clarity and freshness of these magnificent scenes.

Checkerboard Mesa is a classic example of crossbedded sandstone. Shallow horizontal creases indicate the levels of the ancient dunes, which piled one on another to a depth of 1000 feet to form this mountain of rock. The vertical grooves were made by the scouring effect of rainfall on the steep slope.

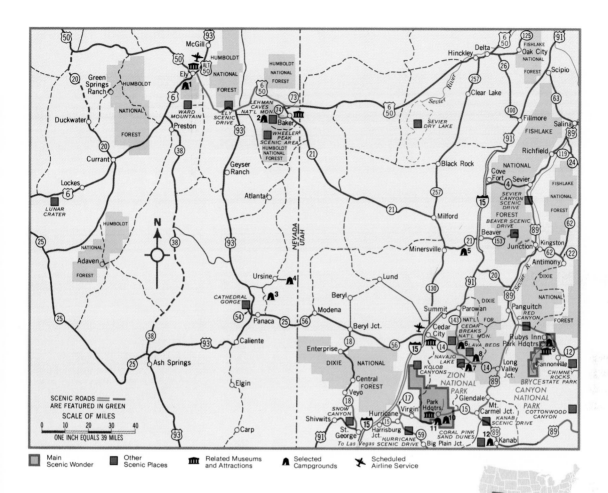

■ Main Scenic Wonder	■ Other Scenic Places
血 Related Museums and Attractions	▲ Selected Campgrounds
✈ Scheduled Airline Service	

Red Rock Drives, Pink Sand Dunes
–Plus a Disappearing Lake

Beaver Scenic Drive, Utah. One of the highest roads in Utah loops through alpine country of quiet aspen groves and lakes. Where the road cuts through the Tushar Mountains, the altitude is 10,000 feet, but Mount Belknap and Delano Peak to the north are taller yet, rearing up 2000 feet more above Puffer Lake.

Cathedral Gorge State Park, Nev. (*Picture appears on page 372*)

Cedar Breaks National Monument, Utah. (*Picture appears on page 373*)

Chimney Rocks State Park, Utah. The approach to the park is a fine prelude to it: sweeping ranchlands lie among sandstone buttes,

walls and escarpments. Once inside, the road passes tall red and white sandstone fingers before arriving at Kodachrome Basin, the star attraction: a broad, wooded meadow here is surrounded by steep pastel-hued walls hundreds of feet high.

Coral Pink Sand Dunes, Utah. (*Picture appears on page 373*)

Cottonwood Canyon, Utah. A road rough enough to be avoided in wet weather but rewarding on bright days heads north along Cottonwood Creek and runs through remote red rock country. Grosvenor Arch, a sandstone span, rises in the east just before the road reaches the stone sculpture of Chimney Rocks.

Ely Scenic Drive, Nev. The highway squeezes through high ranges with wooded slopes, then travels along immense, semiarid valleys carpeted with ranchlands. Connors Pass is the highest point at 7723 feet, but just east of Sacramento Pass is the scenic highlight: a fine view of Wheeler Peak, 13,061 feet tall.

Hurricane Scenic Drive, Utah and Ariz. From a lushly green farming valley, the road climbs up through deep black lava gorges. Then it breaks through ranges of brilliantly colored cliffs, buttes, escarpments and terraces. Before reaching Fredonia, Ariz., it crosses painted desert as vivid and brightly colored as any to be found in the country.

369

Kanab Scenic Drive, Utah. The road is only a short 40 miles, but its sights—most of which prompt leisurely stops—ensure a slow drive. As the highway climbs uphill about 3000 feet between Kanab and Long Valley Junction, it passes red rock stream gorges, gigantic caves, tiny lakes and colored walls of various mineral outcroppings.

Kolob Canyons, Utah. A paved road about five miles long hooks into the northwest corner of Zion National Park, an undeveloped region that is largely ignored by park visitors. There are many pullouts for viewing the sweeping red canyons, and hikers can

Lehman Caves National Monument, *Nev. While the centerpiece of the park is the caves and their elaborate interior displays, the 640 acres also harbor trees like this ancient bristlecone pine. These are the longest-lived trees on earth; some of them reach 4500 years.*

Wheeler Peak Scenic Area, *Nev. Flat plateau country, lying well above the desert valleys that dominate this corner of Nevada, rises to a mighty procession of snow-crested peaks. The highest of them, lofty Wheeler Peak, reaches up into the sky more than 13,000 feet.*

walk two miles alongside Middle Fork to a monumental double-arch amphitheater.

Lava Beds, Utah. Between Duck Creek and Navajo Lake is the region to explore some relatively recent (1000 to 2000 years old) lava beds. One immense flow has no vegetation on it at all. Elsewhere aspen and evergreen forests are slowly spreading across the lichen-encrusted lava, and the raw lava folds, ridges and cinders form picturesque outcrops between the forested patches.

Lehman Caves National Monument, Nev.
(*Picture appears on facing page*)

Lunar Crater, Nev. The neighborhood south of Black Rock Summit looks like a moonscape strangely come to earth. Cinder cones pockmark the land, and the 400-foot-deep Lunar Crater is an enormous reminder of the volcanic upheavals that disturbed the region just yesterday in geological time.

Navajo Lake, Utah. A gigantic lava dam creates the barrier that locks in these mountain waters high in a wooded valley. The lake's only outlets are sinkholes into the underlying limestone and seepage beneath the lava. It is a popular setting for water-based activities, including fishing.

Red Canyon, Utah. A fitting introduction to Bryce Canyon National Park is the stretch of highway that leads to it from the west. The road winds through several miles of the wooded Red Canyon, a lively series of red-orange terraces, spires, ridges and tunnels.

Sevier Canyon Scenic Drive, Utah. The highway roughly parallels the Sevier River as it twists down a narrow wooded valley walled with sheer mountains. Years of erosion have exposed brightly colored and wildly distorted rock outcroppings, including the original Big Rock Candy Mountain, which is colored a

sharp yellow shot through with softer pastel hues.

Sevier Dry Lake, Utah. The huge flats here seldom hold any water, but they produce mirages of startling reality. When weather conditions are right—and they often are—viewers see a gigantic, calm body of water, with gentle wavelets lapping at a shoreline near the highway.

Snow Canyon, Utah. The highway through the canyon starts in semi-desert land, winding between rounded red sandstone domes and walls bordering Snow Canyon State Park, a recreation area with overlooks, campgrounds and hiking trails. Then the route rises to cross a volcanic landscape of compelling strangeness.

Ward Mountain, Nev. More than two miles high, the mountain is the towering landmark of a large recreational area in high desert country. Nearby are gigantic rock kilns once used to make charcoal.

Wheeler Peak Scenic Area, Nev. (*Picture appears on pages 370–371*)

RELATED MUSEUMS AND ATTRACTIONS

Bryce Canyon National Park, Utah. Visitor Center.

Cedar City, Utah. College of Southern Utah, Museum of Natural History.

Ely, Nev. Chamber of Commerce and Mines Museum; local geology and mineralogy.

Lehman Caves National Monument, Nev. Visitor Center.

Zion National Park, Utah. Visitor Center.

Cathedral Gorge State Park, *Nev.* *(facing page). Some of the fluted shapes here look just like ruined towers. This is one view of a long bluff that has weathered into a labyrinth of sharp spires, ridges and deep, winding canyons, some ending in cathedral-like caves.*

Cedar Breaks National Monument, *Utah (right). The majestic rock outcroppings shown are part of a gigantic natural amphitheater whose walls, spires, ridges and terraces are a fantasyland of rainbow colors. The rocks here are about 55 million years old.*

Coral Pink Sand Dunes, *Utah (below). Wildflowers grip soft sand hills, a coral-colored velvet that carpets one side of an unspoiled high valley. Elsewhere in the park here, woods and meadows flourish, the whole basin surrounded by low, evergreen-studded slopes.*

Grand Canyon National Park

ARIZONA

Rocks over a billion years old are bared by massive erosion in the mile-deep gorge.

The Mile-Deep Chasm Called "A Landscape Day of Judgment"

To one-armed Civil War veteran Major John Wesley Powell, whose expedition a century ago conquered the swirling, silt-choked Colorado River in Arizona, the Grand Canyon's music was "the orchestra of wind in the pines at dusk, the call of the coyote, the celestial song of the hermit thrush" and the echoing trills of canyon wrens in "amphitheaters fit for Gods." It was the roar of canyon waterfalls like Cheyava and Havasu, the cawing of ravens and the buzzing of bees in white Jimsonweed blossoms on the canyon's floor. The music is still there; crowds who come today as pilgrims can hear it in the unchanging silence of their own amazement. In all the world there is only one Grand Canyon, and to Major Powell and the millions who followed him it was not the world's eighth wonder but the first.

It has inspired some notably eloquent tributes. The American naturalist and writer Donald Culross Peattie described the canyon as "the grandest and most boldly stated fact on earth . . . Through the beholder surges a sense of the power of the divine will. The Grand Canyon is a sight with the impact of revelation." The noted English writer J. B. Priestley, overcome after his first visit, rhapsodized: "Those who have not seen it will not believe any possible description. Those who have seen it know that it cannot be described. . . . In fact, the Grand Canyon is a sort of landscape

The mighty Colorado, carrying thousands of tons of silt and abrasive rock, cuts through the Kaibab Plateau at the puny rate of 6.5 inches each 1000 years.

Day of Judgment. It is not a showplace, a beauty spot, but a revelation. The Colorado River made it; but you feel when you are there that God gave the Colorado River its instructions."

Stand on either the North or South Rim, and the trees below you tumble downward in billowing clouds of gray-green. Sandstone and limestone walls fall under them in curtains of cream and dusty rose. From the South Rim you can see the red Colorado and the black mysteries of gneiss and schist rocks in the Inner Gorge half as old as the earth itself, grotesque faces of goblins twisted into them by ancient heat and thrust. Here and there canyon gardens climb up into the rocks in fragile tendrils. At sunset, massive buttes glow gold against turquoise skies, the sandstone turns russet, and the limestone near the surface begins to pale into silver. Perhaps you will see, then, the curves of a bighorn sheep silhouetted against some distant rocky bastion or hear the scream of a mountain lion. At dawn the landscape is all birdsong and pastels, pale blues and pinks and whites, peach and gold.

It is not impossible to come to an early understanding of the canyon, though it takes a lifetime to know it. What is needed is a frame of reference. Perhaps the simplest is that of broad areas: South Rim, North Rim and canyon bottom. The three worlds are close, but spectacularly dissimilar.

The rims, as little as four miles apart as the crow (or should it be the eagle?) flies at certain points, are 21 miles apart by the strenuous

Kaibab hiking trail that links them—and over 200 miles apart by automobile.

The South is the populous rim; but still the delicate fragrance of its cliff roses lingers after dusk, its tiny Gunnison's prairie dogs bark at such places as Pasture Wash, and open fields beyond piñon and juniper forests are covered with yellow wild buckwheat, purple asters, a species of blue lupine unique to Arizona and a white prickly poppy found only within a few thousand feet of the chasm. Violet-green swallows and white-breasted nuthatches hover at the edge; paperflowers nod gracefully. Large campgrounds, an imposing hotel, cabins and a lodge provide accommodations for a steady flow of visitors, but, paradoxically, you can have plenty of company or, just a few feet down into the canyon, solitude. Canyon hikers should go armed with information as well as backpacks; the elementary lesson that it is easier to descend than to climb up is learned by eager beginners every year, and mule or helicopter rescues are expensive. (A single mule sent down on a rescue mission may cost a hapless hiker 40 dollars.)

The North Rim is quieter. It is a country of high blue-green firs, scarlet gilias, ruddy golden-mantled ground squirrels—and crashing summer thunderstorms, with black mists rolling inland from the abyss. To wander in the woods after such a storm is to walk through a cool paradise heady with the scent of resin. Campgrounds and cabins and lodge are informal. The North Rim is farther from major highways and cities, and in winter a thick blanket of snow (as much as 200 inches a season) shuts it off with blinding drifts.

The North Rim's devotees find it very special. From Bright Angel Point you can see at close hand the bulking stone sculptures of Deva, Brahma and Zoroaster Temples—exotically named, perhaps, because their size and shifting colors seemed to early canyon explorers so outrageously far from the commonplace as to require Eastern mystery in their labels. From Bright Angel Point, too, you can see high Humphreys Peak, visible also on the Flagstaff, Arizona, skyline. Humphreys Peak is the tallest of the San Francisco Mountains at 12,670 feet, and at the mountains' bases has solidified layer upon layer of volcanic lava.

There are panoramas both far and near on the North Rim: the great gape of Cape Royal and the jutting platform of limestone into which the elements have eroded a hole in the rock known as Angel's Window. You may walk along a nature trail adorned by carmine thistles which bloom all summer long, the brilliant yellow rays of the broom snakeweed and the pallid petals of cliff fendlerbushes in which mule deer love to browse. Point Imperial, 10 miles from the North Rim Lodge by a well-paved road, is the highest point in the Grand Canyon itself at 8801 feet. When summer storms are brooding over the canyon, Point Imperial can be eerily isolated; it alone is visible, and the tumult you hear is a series of majestically crashing echoes, their reverberations magnified a thousandfold by the unseen depths that roll away beneath.

A Grand Staircase That Reveals the Earth's Geological Past

If you could stack Zion and Bryce canyons on top of Grand Canyon, you would see the ancient history of the world told in stone. At the lowest levels of Grand Canyon are rocks from the early Precambrian era, formed nearly two billion years ago—so old that they bear no trace of fossils. In the later Precambrian layers above the Inner Gorge are algal reefs. All the remaining layers were formed during the Paleozoic era. The yellowish sandstone is a reminder of the sand dunes it once was. The layer nearest the rim was the floor of an ancient sea, and the gray limestone walls are full of marine fossils. The two later eras, both eroded away from the canyon's rims, are the Mesozoic, found at Zion, and the Cenozoic, prevalent at Bryce.

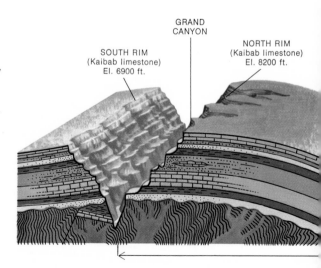

GRAND CANYON

SOUTH RIM
(Kaibab limestone)
El. 6900 ft.

NORTH RIM
(Kaibab limestone)
El. 8200 ft.

Sun backlighting a summer thunderstorm spills a
flood of liquid gold over the color-glowing rock.
So little rain (almost always less than 10 inches per
year) reaches the canyon floor that it qualifies as
a true desert, although the Kaibab Plateau above
receives 26 inches and the canyon rims about 16.

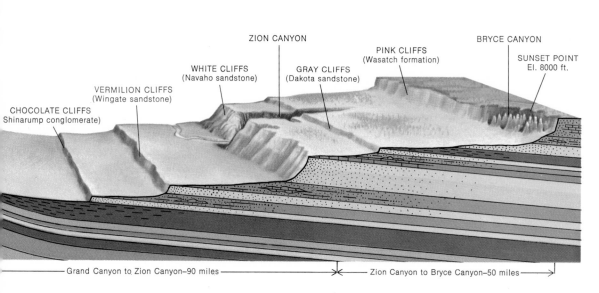

CHOCOLATE CLIFFS
Shinarump conglomerate)

VERMILION CLIFFS
(Wingate sandstone)

WHITE CLIFFS
(Navaho sandstone)

ZION CANYON

GRAY CLIFFS
(Dakota sandstone)

PINK CLIFFS
(Wasatch formation)

BRYCE CANYON

SUNSET POINT
El. 8000 ft.

Grand Canyon to Zion Canyon—90 miles

Zion Canyon to Bryce Canyon—50 miles

379

Fighting the Colorado in a Small Wooden Boat: It Takes Nerve to Try It

Many tourists have made all or part of the 277-mile Colorado River trip through Grand Canyon on huge rubber rafts powered by outboard motors. These relatively stable craft offer plenty of excitement and a sense of the river's power, as well as superb views of the canyon from the bottom up. But riding the Colorado in a small wooden dory that carries only two to four passengers and an

oarsman, and that moves silently at the river's own pace, is a far different and more rugged experience. The rapids above are at Lava Falls, toward the lower end of the canyon, where spills are almost to be expected. John Wesley Powell, the famous explorer, had bigger but less stable boats, and he and his men had to "line" them around most rapids. But these dories run them all, and only at

The canyon floor is arid subtropics: mesquite and cat's-claw and yucca and blackbrush; the jointed ephedra or "Mormon tea" given for colds long before the commercial pharmaceutical production of ephedrine. Canyon depths have their own lizards and pocket mice, desert sparrows and sage thrashers and the unique pink Grand Canyon rattlesnake. In summer, the heat is torrid.

A more elaborate frame of reference with which to approach the Grand Canyon is as a series of life zones. At the bottom, there is the Lower Sonoran Arizona desert. Above this, the Upper Sonoran is full of evergreen oaks, piñons in which bright blue jays scream ceaselessly and rock squirrels scramble. In the succeeding Transition zone the characteristic tree is the ponderosa with its choruses of Steller's jays, and on each rim the Transition zone has its own tassel-eared squirrel. On the South Rim it is the Abert, its head, parts of its back, sides and the top of its tail blue-gray. Its back has reddish glints, and its belly is white. On the North Rim the Kaibab squirrel looks like the Abert except for a white tail and black underparts. It is the canyon's most distinctive

mammal, for its entire range is the rocky edge and only a few miles north of that. Though you may see Kaibab squirrels in the national park area if you are lucky, the best place to look for them is in the ponderosa pines at Jacob Lake as you drive down toward the North Rim from Kanab, Utah. For some reason the Kaibabs here have little fear of man, and do not scurry away at his approach.

The highest life zone, at an altitude of 10,000 feet, is the Hudsonian forest immediately north of the North Rim itself. It is a wilderness of spruces and Douglas firs and quivering aspens and brilliant mountain flowers that bloom in brief opulence. Each drop of a thousand feet in canyon elevation equals 300 to 400 miles of level land; subtropics and northern Canada are all, figuratively, within a day's mule trip. And the canyon's mules are as much a part of it as its native animals. Riders may get dizzy, but the mules never falter on the slenderest of twisting outcrops as they thread their way down to the Colorado. From the South Rim, overnight trips stop to rest at privately operated Phantom Ranch in the canyon's Inner Gorge, where there are

a few of the worst, such as Lava Falls, are passengers urged to get out to avoid a probable dunking. (Rapids form when rare flashfloods roar down side canyons carrying boulders sometimes as big as houses into the channel.) The full 18-day dory trip starts at Lee's Ferry, where all boat trips begin, and ends near Lake Mead. Actual time on the water averages about four hours a day, with frequent stops to explore the side canyons. Boats at right are moored at the mouth of Havasu Creek.

cabins, a large dining room, even the ultimate luxury of an improbable swimming pool.

It is impossible not to catch a contagion of adventure as your mule train prepares for the steep journey down. The animals amble slow and sleek from their corral; whimsical guides have given them names ranging from the romanticism of Posy to the clowning of Schlitz. The mules may look as sleepy and act as stubborn as other mules while they are being readied for the trek, but once on the trail each animal becomes a paragon of coordination and intelligence. The canyon has never lost a mule rider. It is a reassuring statistic to keep in mind as you begin jogging down from the security of the rim to the hazards of the snaking paths bordered by cacti and yucca. Mule etiquette is unfailing; the mules know how to stand on the path's rim to let other mule trains going in the opposite direction pass, and they also know the easy gait which makes the journey painless for any rider in reasonably good physical condition. You do not have to know much about riding to make the journey down; the train leader gives the orders. But you ought to know everything about not merely looking at wil-

derness but seeing it—the record of the rocks, the meaning of the piñons and cacti and wildflowers. You ought too to know not only how to listen but to hear: the tiny scurries of squirrels, the lilting of warblers, the poignant cries of coyotes in a rosy dusk. For Grand Canyon visitors in search of its essence, a mule trip down is a necessary beginning.

Geology provides still another way of assimilating the canyon's miracles. The greatest miracle is the very simplicity of the canyon's origin. No more than two million years ago the earth across which the Colorado meandered rose in a series of upheavals. When the land was high, the river with its abrasive cargo of rocks from dry regions to the north began cutting through the raised ground until it had carved the canyon as we know it. The river's work goes on, though more slowly now that man has impounded its waters above the Grand Canyon National Park at Glen Canyon dam. But Grand Canyon is only the end of the story. Its formations had to take shape before they could be revealed by water.

In the beginning the land was flat. The Inner Gorge with its darkly chaotic surfaces was laid down something like two billion years ago as sand and mud were sculptured by water and wind, then contorted by heat and pressure into high mountains. Then rivers and rains began widening mountain valleys through succeeding millennia until the mountains were worn down. The oldest fossil the Grand Canyon has ever yielded is the imprint of a 500 million-year-old primitive sea plant found in the Proterozoic stratum directly above the dark, mysterious Vishnu schist of the Inner Gorge itself.

There were deserts, as the eons went on; there were more mountains, and more erosion, more rivers and more storms. The Tonto Platform, which slopes gradually upward from the Inner Gorge, bears witness to them in its sandstone and mud-born shale and its limestone that reveals fossils of prehistoric sea animals,

among them the crablike trilobite, the undisputed lord of creation for hundreds of millions of years. Then it vanished utterly, though a shrimplike cousin, *Apus aequalis*, occasionally turns up in canyon rain pools.

On top of the Tonto Platform, the vermilion Redwall limestone is the canyon's amphitheaters and temples and curving tunnels. Over it, in Supai sandstone, have been found the tracks of large primitive four-footed creatures. The Hermit Shale above contains outlines of giant ferns and horsetails, cone-bearing plants, insect wings four inches long and a variety of salamanders. Then sands blew in to create the Coconino formation, and after them swept warm, shallow seas represented in the Toroweap and Kaibab layers. The latter is directly beneath your feet as you stand on either rim. In its pale gray limestone have been found horn corals, sponges, sharks' teeth and bivalves approximately 200 million years old. Here time stops in the canyon. Later earths have all been washed away. The Colorado began cutting its way downward from Kaibab to Inner Gorge only geologic seconds ago when its valley was pushed up. Thus the canyon is like an afterthought in its own huge history.

The canyon drama begins northeast of the park at Lee's Ferry, where the Colorado is a flat and gentle stream. Lee's Ferry has a music of its own, and only some of it is the kind Major Powell heard—for in addition to the singing birds and winds and trees there is the bustle of river trips being outfitted for the canyon's 277 miles of swift current and thundering rapids. Tourists haven't stilled the music; the music has stilled the tourists. Most of them probably share the feelings of John Wesley Powell as he prepared to enter the canyon. In his journal he wrote: "We are now ready to start our way down the Great Unknown . . . We have but a month's rations left. We are imprisoned three quarters of a mile in the depths of the earth and the great unknown river shrinks into insignificance . . . With some eagerness and some anxiety we enter the canyon below and are carried along by the swift waters through walls which rise from its very edge." As you watch his 20th-century successors climb into one of the huge rubber rafts or small wooden dories, you will long more than anything else in the world to be going along, to hear all of the music in all of the castles of rock for yourself.

Hikers weary from the eight-mile trip down to Havasu Falls, at the bottom of Grand Canyon, can rest and cool off on natural travertine terraces.

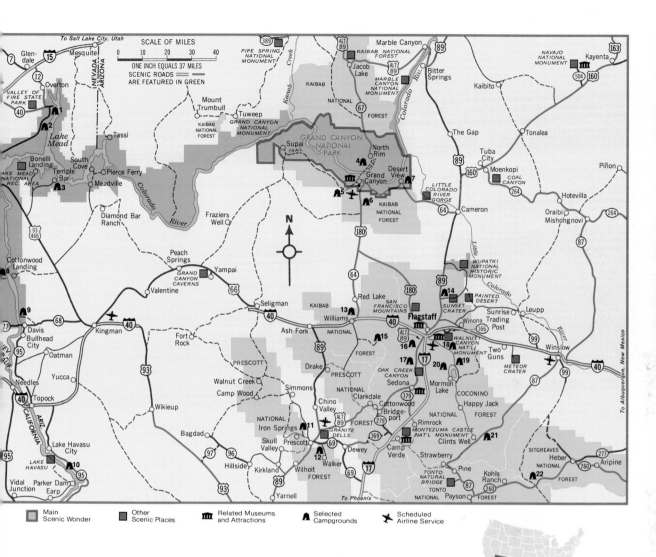

■ Main Scenic Wonder	■ Other Scenic Places	⛬ Related Museums and Attractions	▲ Selected Campgrounds	✈ Scheduled Airline Service

WITHIN A DAY'S DRIVE:

A Painted Desert, Colorful Gorges and Two of America's Mightiest Craters

Coal Canyon, Ariz. Eons ago fire, perhaps set by lightning, ignited the vein of soft coal that lies between the shale and sandstone layers of these weirdly eroded pinnacles and buttes and baked the overlying formations a deep red. On moonlit summer nights the skirtlike lower strata of one of the spires seems to shimmer, which has given rise to the local legend of a dancing ghost that haunts the canyon.

Grand Canyon Caverns, Ariz. Here an elevator plummets you 21 stories down below the earth. The first stop is a cavern 18,000

feet square in which have been found the bones of prehistoric humans and a giant ground sloth, mummified coyotes and bobcats, and marine fossils over a quarter of a million years old. Tours are conducted through the caverns over paved, lighted trails.

Granite Dells, Ariz. High granite spires tower over the lakes that line the scenic highway north of Prescott. The resort of Granite Dells offers visitors both lake and pool swimming.

Kaibab National Forest, Ariz. For people planning a trip to Grand

Canyon's North Rim the Kaibab National Forest—an impressive stand of ponderosa pine, spruce and aspen—is the best possible introduction. The Grand Canyon National Game Preserve in the forest is famous for its Kaibab deer herd, and for the beautiful Kaibab squirrel that is found only here and around the canyon's North Rim: it has a striking white tail, long ears and black markings. Forest headquarters is at Jacob Lake, where an inn provides accommodation.

Lake Havasu, Ariz.
(Picture appears on pages 386–87)

Pipe Spring National Monument, *Ariz. (left). The Mormons who discovered this oasis built a fort with walls of sandstone blocks three feet thick to protect settlers from Indians. Many of the original furnishings have been preserved in the building.*

Sunset Crater, *Ariz. (right). In 1065, volcanic eruptions covered an 800-square-mile area with cinder and ash and built up Sunset Crater's 1000-foot-high cone. It is worth climbing to the top to see the lava snaking away from the base and in the distance the superb San Francisco Mountains.*

Valley of Fire State Park, *Nev. (below). The brilliant red sandstone formations make the park a photographer's delight, particularly during the hours around sunrise and sunset. Here, prickly pear cactus blooms add further color.*

Lake Mead National Recreation Area, Nev. and Ariz. Hoover Dam, one of the highest in the world, backs up the Colorado River to form Lake Mead, 115 miles long and covering an area of 229 square miles. The lake is surrounded by colorful desert country, high plateaus and deep canyons. Wide sandy beaches and steep, dark canyon walls make it a pleasure to explore by boat. Complete facilities for all water sports are available, including well-equipped marinas.

Little Colorado River Gorge, Ariz. Steep, winding Route 64 leaves Desert View at the eastern boundary of Grand Canyon and skirts the Grand Canyon of the Little Colorado. The gorge is very narrow, and as much as 2000 feet deep, with walls ranging from buff to rust and black. The view from the rim is not for anyone nervous about heights.

Marble Canyon National Monument, Ariz. The only way to see this 52-mile stretch of the wild, rapids-filled Colorado River is by boat. In places the gorge is only 75 feet wide and the rapids are very turbulent. The river has polished the Redwall limestone so smooth that in places it resembles marble, hence the name. A highlight of the trip is Vaseys Paradise, where streams gush down from crevices in canyon walls covered with vines and ferns.

Meteor Crater, Ariz. About 20,000 years ago a meteor spun out of the northern sky toward the Arizona desert, weighing at least a million tons and traveling at several miles a second. It drove nearly a mile through solid rock, and its impact was so great that much of the mass probably exploded and hurtled back into the atmosphere. The rim of the crater rises 150 feet above the plain, and as you approach it looks like nothing more than a flat-topped mountain. But the crater's depth (570 feet) and diameter (4000 feet) are staggering: the footpath circling the rim, for example, is a strenuous three-mile hike. Fragments of the meteor are displayed in a museum on the rim.

Montezuma Castle National Monument, Ariz. The castle, named by white settlers in the mistaken belief that the Indians who lived there were Aztecs, is five stories high and has one section with 20 rooms, another with 45, filling a large natural cave 145 feet up the face of a perpendicular cliff. The Pueblo Indians could safeguard their fortress home by hauling in the access ladders. Montezuma Well, about four miles north, is a large limestone sink ringed by cliff dwellings.

Navajo National Monument, Ariz. The Anasazi (Navajo for ancient ones) who lived here centuries ago were skilled artisans and builders. Three of their cliff dwellings are preserved here. Tours are conducted to Betatakin, the most accessible, a 135-room complex in a 500-foot-high cave. Dirt roads and a trail lead to smaller Inscription House. Keet Seel, the third ruin, may be reached only by an eight-mile trail down a canyon; the trip takes a full day.

Oak Creek Canyon, Ariz.
(*Picture appears on facing page*)

Painted Desert, Ariz. Stretching 300 miles across northeastern Arizona, the buttes and cones of the Painted Desert are the eroded remnants of vast beds of sedimentary clay mixed with volcanic ash—the same mixture that buried the trees of the Petrified Forest. Black rain clouds darken the desert into a somber, forbidding place; the puffy white clouds of a summer day create a shifting kaleidoscope of colors. Sunrise and sunset stain the sand red.

Pipe Spring National Monument, Ariz.
(*Picture appears on page 384*)

San Francisco Mountains, Ariz. Arizona's highest mountains, the San Francisco peaks rise over 12,000 feet above the ponderosa pines in 1.8 million-acre Coconino National Forest. The peaks are of volcanic origin; the huge cinder cones among them are extinct volcanoes. On a clear day you can see an amazing panorama of surrounding mountains from the Snow Bowl chair lift.

Sunset Crater, Ariz.
(*Picture appears on page 385*)

Oak Creek Canyon, *Ariz. In some places the buff sandstone walls of the canyon tower 2500 feet above Oak Creek. The canyon, 16 miles long, is unusual in Arizona for its placid river and relatively lush green vegetation. It often supplies the background for Western movies.*

Lake Havasu, *Ariz. This desert lake, behind Parker Dam on the Colorado River, is noted for its bass fishing. Lake Havasu City, a year-round resort with the emphasis on water sports, is the sunny new home of London Bridge, transported here stone by stone in 1971.*

Tonto Natural Bridge, Ariz. The largest travertine bridge in the world is 150 feet wide, 393 feet long and 181 feet high—big enough to accommodate a small farm on top. It spans Pine Creek and a 40-foot-deep pool that is popular with swimmers. Below the bridge are several large caves, some still unexplored.

Valley of Fire State Park, Nev. *(Picture appears on page 384)*

Walnut Canyon National Monument, Ariz. The long limestone ledges of this small canyon made it easy for Indians to transform them into cliff dwellings by walling up the fronts and partitioning the ledges into rooms. A self-guiding trail leads past about 100 rooms. The masonry, over 700 years old, is still solid and well made; drought probably drove out the ancient Sinaguan Indians who lived here.

Wupatki National Historic Monument, Ariz. Eighteen miles north of Sunset Crater by a paved road, the monument preserves the villages of Indians who farmed here in the 12th century. More than 800 ruins remain, some with a view over the Painted Desert. Near the biggest structure is an amphitheater and a ball court where the Indians played a game of Mayan origin similar to the basketball of today.

RELATED MUSEUMS AND ATTRACTIONS

Flagstaff, Ariz.
Museum of Northern Arizona; natural history.
Walnut Canyon National Monument; natural history, herbarium, wildlife refuge.

Grand Canyon, Ariz. Grand Canyon National Park Tusayan Museum; geology, archaeology.

Sedona, Ariz. American Meteorite Museum.

Tonalea, Ariz. Navajo National Monument Park Museum; natural history.

387

Petrified Forest

NATIONAL PARK, ARIZONA

Time Fashions Stone
Logs like Jewels

As you cross the dry, mile-high grasslands of eastern Arizona, any thoughts you may have of green forests and flowing rivers must be inspired—like a desert mirage—by their very absence. During much of the year the sun burns mercilessly out of a limitless sky, baking the earth. The scant nine inches of annual rain are concentrated in brief summer downpours, leaving the earth inhospitable to all but the most tenacious plants.

Yet if there had been no floods to deposit the earth in layers, no torrents to sculpt landforms of intricate fantasy, there would be no Painted Desert here. And if there had been no stands of green trees, the monumental, gem-studded stone logs strewn over the desert in the adjoining Petrified Forest might well be—as the Paiute Indians once thought they were—the arrow shafts of Shinuav, the thunder god, or what the Navajo saw as the bones of Yietso, the Great Giant of their mythology.

In fact, the unique landscape you see in the Petrified Forest National Park—really two parks in one, with the adjoining Painted Desert—is the cumulative record of evolutionary events that began 200 million years ago. Then, in what geologists call the Late Triassic period of the Early Mesozoic era, the high arid grassland you now drive across was a low-lying, swampy semijungle. Giant amphibious reptiles, armor-plated phytosaurs with the long, sharp-toothed jaws and muscular tails of crocodiles, ruled the

A stone tree lies like a fallen pillar at Blue Mesa.

389

ferny undergrowth. Above, the crowns of 200-foot conifers formed a green canopy. The waters teemed with clams, snails and fish.

Today your 27-mile route through the park takes you through the graveyard of this time-lost jungle, whose appearance scientists can only infer from its geological bones. For the same ancient water that carried nutrients to support life here also transported the material to bury it. Over millions of years, flowing rivers and inland seas laid down layer upon layer of sediment. Soft blue and gray clay stone, mudstone and siltstone, harder sandstone and conglomerate, all alternated to make a geological layer cake, baked firm during interludes of dry weather. Mineral compounds, percolating through the layers, stained the lighter-colored sediments into an earthy rainbow. The Painted Desert owes its predominant rusty pink hue to iron oxides.

Yellow and red from iron, black from manganese or carbon, and white and gray from quartz, all combine to create a color kaleidoscope in a petrified log.

A landslide of logs: these stumps in the Blue Mesa section tumbled into a gully after their 150 million-year-old clay covering had eroded away.

After tens of millions of years, the Triassic jungle lay beneath as much as 3000 feet of overburden, topped by a vast inland sea that flooded much of the Southwest. Then, about 70 million years ago, the sea gradually withdrew as the land reared up into our western mountain ranges. The blanket of earth smothering the primordial jungle was no longer thickened by sedimentation, but eroded—fractions of inches in a season, year in, year out, eon after eon.

As though time were running backward, the overburden was stripped away by wind and rain. The lower deposits of the Triassic period were exposed one after another. Armed with abrasive sands, rainwater sluiced through every crevice, cutting deep wounds that ran rust-red with silt. The wind made a cutting edge of the dust and dirt to erode the soft strata of clay and mud. Only where a layer of harder sandstone or conglomerate armored the underlying earth could it resist, rising in sharp ridges and flat-topped mesas above the plain.

Even these highlands are temporary, for the wind still blows and the brief summer rains still fall. As you stand on the high ground overlooking the vast badlands of the Painted Desert, the ever-changing light alters the apparent form and color of the landscape, giving you an intimation of the endless changes the elements will work in ages to come.

You get a close-up view of the ongoing geological processes that have formed the Painted Desert at Blue Mesa, midway along the park road. A one-mile loop of paved trail takes you along the ridge formed of blue-gray clay carved into intricate sculptures. More extended expeditions into the vast surrounding wastelands must be arranged with the park rangers; without roads or water, they are not for casual or unprepared exploration.

South of the Painted Desert area of the park, you get your first look at the most striking souvenirs of the geological past. At first they appear to be simply giant logs, left behind by some prodigal Paul Bunyan. On closer inspection they prove to be stone replicas of all sizes, from the smallest twig on the surface to massive tree trunks still rooted in the rock matrix like unfinished sculptures.

Though they are known as "petrified wood," they are more properly described as tree fossils. They were formed when trees dying in the Triassic jungle became buried in the accumu-

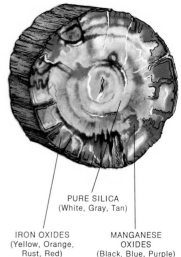

PURE SILICA
(White, Gray, Tan)

IRON OXIDES
(Yellow, Orange,
Rust, Red)

MANGANESE
OXIDES
(Black, Blue, Purple)

The Chemistry of Time: How Volcanoes and Rain Petrified Wood

The logs you see at Petrified Forest once stood as tall trees in a dense forest that grew in this part of Arizona 200 million years ago. Covered up by hundreds of feet of later sediment, the trees were preserved by an unusual combination of factors. Volcanoes in the area produced deep layers of ash, and rainwater sinking down through this dissolved silica from it. As the water penetrated into the logs, the silica precipitated, replacing the logs' organic materials with glasslike deposits of silicon dioxide. Impurities in the water have colored the logs in various ways, as shown above.

lating sediments. By a process scientists do not fully understand, many of these trees did not simply break down into their constituent elements. Groundwater, rich in dissolved silica, infiltrated the tissues of the trees. As the silica came out of solution, it formed deposits of quartz crystals, which replaced the soft organic material, turning the trees to stone. Other trace minerals in the water added colors: yellow and red from iron; blacks from manganese and carbon (as shown above).

In the larger cavities near the hearts of the trees the quartz crystals sometimes grew into giant gemstones—amethyst, rose quartz, smoky quartz and others. In the 19th century, collectors and fortune hunters dynamited a great many logs into tiny fragments in search of their rockbound treasure. Thousands of other logs were carted away to nearby mills to be crushed into commercial abrasives. Such depredations aroused support for protection of the area, and it was designated a national monument in 1906 and a national park in 1962. Even the smallest toothpick of petrified wood is now under federal protection. If you want to take a souvenir home, the park gift

shop sells samples (collected from outside the park). However, more than 12 tons of petrified wood are still taken from the park each year: nature is not the only force that is eroding the Petrified Forest.

Men have lived here, leaving behind the petroglyphs and ruins of their successive civilizations that you see at the well-marked stopping points along the road. But the untenanted villages and indecipherable symbols seem only to emphasize the inhumanity of the landscape. The animals that live here now—gopher and king snakes, rattlers, small rodents and lizards, rabbits, bobcats, foxes—are furtive, invisible to the casual observer. The wildflowers that make a sudden show of color in the spring, decorating the desert like an impressionist canvas, surrender quickly to the less flamboyant but better adapted plants—cacti and yucca and homely desert grasses. Even with a piece of the Petrified Forest in the palm of your hand, or purchased as a keepsake, you may feel out of place in this hard, rocky land, out of scale with the monumental forms. But at the same time you will be a privileged witness to the continuing creation of the world.

A large area of northeastern Arizona is covered by multicolored sedimentary layers known as the Chinle Formation. Iron oxides and other mineral elements have tinted the clay with a remarkable range of shades, and the resulting Painted Desert is seen at its best in the park, along a loop drive.

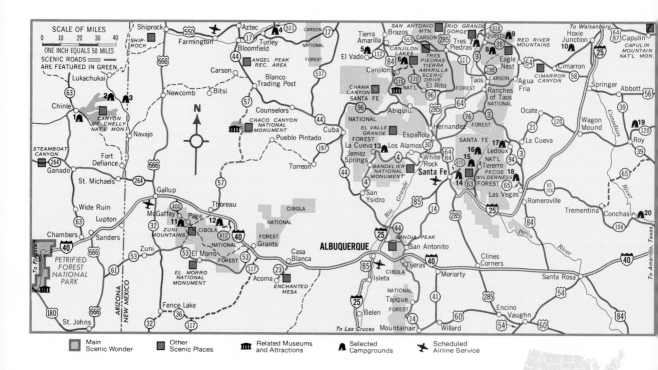

WITHIN A DAY'S DRIVE:

Ancient Indian Strongholds, Snowy Slopes and Dead Volcanoes

Angel Peak Recreation Area, N.M. Angel Peak is at the heart of the rugged Nacimiento Badlands, an area of weathered sandstone shapes colored by minerals in shades of red, yellow, lavender, tan and brown. The summit of the peak itself is a layer of hard dark sandstone. A road with several overlooks leads along the rim of this fantastic region.

Bandelier National Monument, N.M. Here spectacular ruins of New Mexico's last cliff dwellers are preserved. Abandoned about 400 years ago, rooms carved in the yellow tuff canyon walls are reached by trails and ladders. In the canyon bottom a fabulous pueblo of the same period has been excavated. The ruins begin at the end of a paved road.

Canjilon Lakes, N.M. Five beautiful beaver lakes, enlarged by man, are set like jewels among deep green spruce-fir forests and gold of changing aspen near Canjilon. The sparkling waters,

well stocked with trout, are backed by a majestic mountain.

Canyon de Chelly National Monument, Ariz.
(*Picture appears on pages 396–97*)

Capulin Mountain National Monument, N.M.
(*Picture appears on page 396*)

Chaco Canyon National Monument, N.M. Major Indian ruins are scattered throughout 34 square miles of this historic canyon. Pueblo Bonito, one of the most impressive of these, was built over 900 years ago and contained about 800 rooms and several ceremonial chambers. It is located near the base of the cliff that forms one of the canyon walls.

Chama Canyon, N.M. A series of waterfalls gush from side canyons into the Chama; in some places the canyon walls reach 2000 feet above its wide floor. Trout fishing here is excellent, and there are beautiful views of

the surrounding mountains of the Santa Fe National Forest. Lupine, Indian paintbrush, bluebonnets and daisies are among the brilliant wildflowers to be found scattered below the ponderosa pine in spring and summer.

Cimarron Canyon, N.M. This is the gateway to famed Eagle Nest Lake and the Taos-Red River area in the Sangre de Cristo range. U.S. Highway 64 follows the canyon bottom along a beautiful tortuous trout stream, and past austere photogenic palisades. The area is the home of mule deer, elk, bears and wild turkeys.

El Morro National Monument, N.M. The main feature of the area is Inscription Rock, called El Morro (The Headland) by the Spanish. It is a huge sandstone mesa towering 200 feet into the sky. Travelers on the old Acoma–Zuni Trail passed by here for centuries, pausing to carve names and messages into the soft rock. The first legible signature is dated 1605, but there are also Indian petroglyphs many hundreds of years old.

El Valle Grande, N.M. This old, 100,000-acre Spanish land grant embraces one of the world's biggest calderas. Composed of great grassy valleys and cinder cones forested with pine, spruce, fir and aspens, it is a beautiful, and interesting, scenic attraction. Nestling in tuff-cliffed Jemez Mountains, the area supports elk, mule deer, bears and cougars.

Enchanted Mesa, N.M. The summit of this 430-foot-high sandstone butte is reached by steep hiking trails. It is a strenuous climb, but the rewards are views up to 160 miles to the north

Sandia Peak, N.M. *The longest aerial tram ride in North America takes visitors to an elevation of 10,378 feet to enjoy breathtaking views such as this one over the sunlit, snowcapped Sandia Mountains.*

Shiprock, N.M. *This mass of dark lava rock, rising dramatically 1400 feet above the arid surrounding desert, once filled the cone of a volcano, which was later eroded away. Smaller outcrops around it are dikes, injections of igneous material into cracks in the original rock, now exposed by weathering.*

Capulin Mountain National Monument, *N.M. (left). Active as recently as 2000 years ago, Capulin is the highest (1000 feet) and most perfect of a number of volcanic cones in the Raton Basin, many of them visible from its summit. There is a road to the top, and the crater within is 415 feet deep on the high side, and 1450 feet across from rim to rim.*

Canyon de Chelly National Monument, *Ariz. (below). A rim drive with five scenic overlooks skirts the south side of the 130-square-mile area, which was an ancient stronghold of the Navajos and is still Indian territory. Highlights include a beautiful Indian ruin, the White House, reached by a mile-long trail; the Mummy Cave, and the tall, vertical Spider Rock.*

across the desert to Mount Taylor (11,389 feet) and the San Mateo Mountains. Sharing the Acoma Indian reservation, nearby Acoma Pueblo is located atop another tall mesa.

Pecos Wilderness, N.M. This is truly a magnificent Wilderness Area, accessible by trail travel only. Found here are timberline peaks and mosaic patterns of alpine forests dotted with aspen woods, lush meadows, parks and rock slides. Ten alpine lakes and many clear streams provide fishing. Mule deer, elk, bears, cougars, turkeys, blue grouse and bighorn sheep of the timberline type are of esthetic and sport value. Elevations in the area range from 9000 to 13,105 feet.

Red River Mountains, N.M. Mount Wheeler, New Mexico's highest mountain at 13,116 feet, dominates this magnificent section of the Sangre de Cristo range. Ski lifts in the area operate in summer too, to carry visitors up to the peaks for sweeping views over the mountains above Taos and the Red River Pass.

Rio Grande Gorge, N.M. This is a magnificent gorge extending 50 miles south from the Colorado line, with dark volcanic walls up to 1000 feet high. It was designated a "Wild River" by act of

Congress in 1968. The river, which abounds with trout, is accessible by foot trails only from the canyon rim.

San Antonio Mountain, N.M. The grassy slopes of this massive, rounded mountain form a winter sanctuary for herds of elk, and the plains below are home to hundreds of antelope. A wildlife management area was established here in 1965 to improve the rangeland that supports the animals. One of its features is a flourishing prairie dog town.

Sandia Peak, N.M.
(*Picture appears on page 395*)

Shiprock, N.M.
(*Picture appears on page 395*)

Steamboat Canyon, Ariz. Unlike most canyons, carved by rivers in rock, this one is geologically unique: it is cut in a series of clay buttes, and is totally lacking in vegetation. State Highway 264 offers a succession of remarkable views as it traverses the canyon in a westerly direction.

Tres Piedras–Tierra Amarilla Scenic Drive, N.M. Although the road is only partly paved, it is not difficult to drive, and offers one of the most scenic journeys in the state. It crosses Tusas Ridge, passing a series of delightful mountain streams and Hopewell Lake, where there is fine fishing all year round. Approaching Tierra Amarilla, the Brazos Peaks become visible to the north. An

overlook provides views down into the Chama Valley.

Zuni Mountains, N.M. The Continental Divide follows the crest of these ancient, rolling mountains. Several mountain streams have been dammed into lakes by the Zuni Indians, and there are a number of unexcavated Indian ruins in the area.

RELATED MUSEUMS AND ATTRACTIONS

Abiquiu, N.M. Ghost Ranch Museum; natural history.

Bloomfield, N.M. Chaco Canyon National Monument Park Museum.

Petrified Forest National Park, Ariz. Rainbow Forest Museum.

Saguaro National Monument
ARIZONA

A forest of young saguaros covers an Arizona slope.

The Weird World
of the Giant Cactus

Only 17 miles east of Tucson, Arizona, where the Tanque Verde Mountains shimmer in the hot sky above the Santa Cruz Valley, lies the main area of Saguaro National Monument. Named for the giant saguaro cactus that grows here almost as abundantly as trees in a forest, it includes in its 123-square-mile area a spread of desert, the grass and chaparral landscape of the Tanque Verdes and the forested highlands of the Rincon Range.

Since its discovery by Spanish conquistadores in the mid-16th century, the area of the Saguaro National Monument was variously exploited until it was decreed a national monument in 1933. Ever since, careful efforts have been made to protect the cacti and facilitate the growth of these unusual plants.

For a plant so huge and sturdy looking (this cactus may weigh six or seven tons and grow as high as 50 feet), the saguaro is remarkably vulnerable at all stages of life. It is a stem succulent. Highly adapted for the collection and storage of water, stem succulents range in size from tiny button or pincushion cacti weighing only a few ounces to the towering saguaro, the Goliath of the family in this section of the Sonoran desert.

Its structure is ingenious. An inner supporting skeleton of tough, woody ribs fused at the base gives it surprising strength to stay upright despite occasional battering by windstorms. Inside and outside this skeleton is a mass of

pulpy absorbent tissue. The cactus is covered with a heavy, waxy, spiny skin which is vertically grooved in deep, accordionlike pleats that swell with moisture after a rainfall.

The root system of the saguaro is by necessity a highly efficient gatherer of water. A lacelike pattern of tiny rootlets extends in all directions, reaching a few feet down in the soil and outward at least as far as the cactus is tall. This system not only draws up every available drop of water but also anchors the giant and holds it firmly against the elements. When violent thunderstorms bring the rains in the spring or summer, the roots are mighty drinkers: they fill the cactus so full that its skin fairly bulges.

Once full, a saguaro cactus, even after several arid years, has enough stored moisture to survive, but it grows only after summer rains. Every year it puts out the large white flowers that have become the Arizona state symbol. These blossoms appear over a period of several weeks in May and June. Each flower, however, blooms only for a very short time—it usually unfolds a few hours after sunset and closes forever the following afternoon.

This poses an unusual problem in pollination. Like most flowers, the saguaro can reproduce only when its flowers are fertilized by pollen from another plant, which is usually carried by bees as they feed. In the saguaro, with so short a period available for pollination, other agents have also become involved. Among these are birds, notably the white-winged dove that nests in the cactus.

Few plants in nature encounter more critical factors in their reproduction than the saguaro cactus. When its egg-shaped fruit bursts open in June or July, it reveals a deep-red, juicy pulp with a profusion of tiny black seeds. (Indians harvest this fruit in season, eating it like watermelon and also making a potent liquor from its fermented juices.) The saguaro seed cannot fall to the ground just anywhere and take hold; it must have a spot sheltered from the sun to germinate. Only then, having also survived the birds and the rodents and man, it puts out a tiny cactus bud which in two years will grow to be about a quarter of an inch in diameter. It has been calculated that

The extraordinary and often eerie appearance of a saguaro is due largely to its thick, armlike branches, rare in a cactus; as many as 50 grow on one trunk.

A number of birds nest in cacti, including the cactus wren, shown here. Sometimes one of them impales itself fatally on a needle-sharp spine.

only one out of several million saguaro seeds is able to produce a plant.

If a saguaro survives, it may live for 200 years, but the saguaro grows with remarkable slowness; after nine years it may still be only six inches tall. Its growth rate varies greatly, according to the amount of annual rainfall. In its first year especially the baby cactus is a tempting dish for the desert rodents who find much of their needed moisture in its tender, juicy pulp. Birds and digging rodents like ground squirrels may uproot seedlings, and insects may eat them. The few plants that survive their first year of growth are usually those that luckily took root by rocks or other plants: this tends to conceal and protect them from both marauding animals and whatever extremes of climate may beset them.

The cactus is also home to a number of creatures. In its branches nest gilded flickers, Gila woodpeckers, white-winged doves, curved-billed thrashers and occasionally cactus wrens. The woodpeckers and flickers excavate their nests; the holes they make become covered with a hard scar tissue created by dried sap, affording a dry, safe, sheltered refuge from desert heat and rain. The birds actually exca-

The Remarkable Saguaro —and How It Works

The giant saguaro can store sufficient water to enable it to bloom even after several years of desert drought. When the plant takes up water and its pulpy tissue swells with moisture, the skin expands. After a heavy rainfall it becomes an almost smooth cylinder, and its circumference can grow to more than half as much again as when it is dry.

BLOOMING SAGUARO

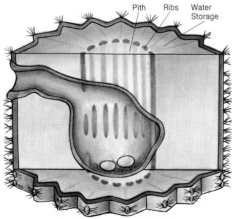

Pith   Ribs   Water Storage

CROSS SECTION WITH GILA WOODPECKER NEST

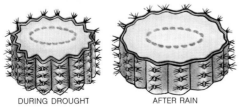

DURING DROUGHT   AFTER RAIN

vate their nests the winter before they are to use them, to allow the sap to harden. Desert insects seek out these nest holes as cool refuges from the midday heat.

The saguaro "forests" in both sections of the national monument can be readily viewed by visitors from their own cars. Desert roadways encompass both areas; there are picnic sites for outdoor lunches, turnouts and short walking trails. Visitors must bring their own water in each case.

The western part of the monument, the Tucson Mountain Section, is easily approached, just beyond the famous Arizona–Sonora Desert Museum where plants and animals native to the area are on view in fascinating displays. Park roads in this section pass through a "nursery," a maze of young saguaros that spread out like a marching army over hills in every direction. There are hiking trails, viewing spots and four picnic areas.

From Tucson a wide, paved highway known as the Old Spanish Trail leads to the main, eastern entrance of the monument and to an air-conditioned visitor center where maps, exhibits and booklets help to explain what the visitor will see.

The mountainous section of the national monument is scarcely less interesting than the desert area, but it is completely wild. No roads lead through it, only a few hiking and horseback trails winding into the Rincon Range. The trails climb 6000 feet through changing environments to the tallest peak in the park, Mica Mountain, 8666 feet high. In the upper Sonoran life zone are cool stands of pine, oak and other trees. Higher up, in the Canadian life zone, the visitor may see whitetail deer, coatimundis, raccoons or, if he is very lucky, a wild turkey. He may hear the distant scream of a mountain lion or occasionally see the lumbering form of a black bear. Such wildlife is unlikely to be encountered along the loop road, however.

Unique in its diversity as well as in its unmatched stand of giant cactus, the Saguaro National Monument is one of the most intriguing of our protected areas. The desert, with its harsh environment and its fierce and adaptable population, is nowhere displayed to greater advantage than here; and above the bizarre shapes of the cacti, at their dramatic best at sunrise and sunset, brood the cool highland beauties of the Rincon Range.

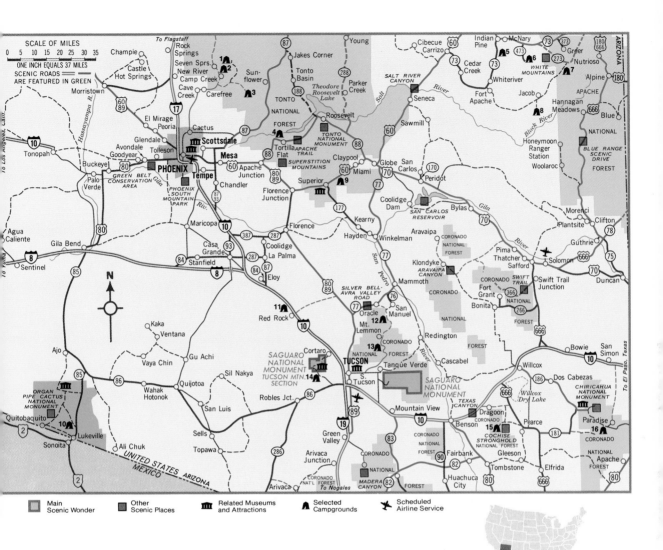

WITHIN A DAY'S DRIVE:

Magnificent Canyons and the Ruins of Ancient Indian Villages

Apache Trail. Justly famous, the drive climbs around the northern edge of the legendary Superstition Mountains, cuts through Fish Creek Canyon with its tall bronze walls, skirts Canyon, Apache and Roosevelt lakes, each a blue oasis in the khaki desert landscape. The 76-mile road, built in 1905 as a supply route for Roosevelt Dam builders, parallels an ancient trail of Apache Indians.

Aravaipa Canyon. The seven-and-a-half-mile gorge is a wilderness dream for naturalists, hikers and backpackers. Most desert bird-life can be spotted in its neigh-

borhood, and it follows the course of a perennially flowing stream, a rare pleasure in this country.

Blue Range Scenic Drive. Steep walls and dense woods keep all but hardy horseback riders and hikers out of the heart of the mountains, but anyone can explore the Blue Range area from this 12-mile drive. From a valley thick with aspens and firs, a steep gravel road switchbacks down to the Blue River, each turn bringing panoramas of wild scenery.

Chiricahua National Monument.
(Picture appears on page 405)

Cochise Stronghold. A campsite, picnic grounds, hiking and horseback trails now quietly grace this region of the Dragoon Mountains, once a place for Apache campfires and the hideout of the great warrior Cochise during violent wars of the 1860s. The Stronghold is a natural fortress, all but one side tightly locked in by towering rock walls.

Green Belt Conservation Area. From a quarter to two miles wide, a green swath of lush vegetation straddles Route 80, which roughly follows the Gila River west of Phoenix. It is a stretch of land

403

Superstition Mountains. *Horseback riders seem to shrink in size before the jagged ramparts of the Superstitions, wild mountains where coyotes* *howl and where a few tough prospectors are still searching for gold—and for the fabled Lost Dutchman Mine, said to be hidden deep in its fastnesses.*

rich in birdlife: whitewing and mourning doves, Gambel quails and roadrunners are among the bird watcher's quarry.

Madera Canyon. Wildlife of every sort—deer, javelinas, mountain lions, rare coatimundis and about 200 species of birds—find a congenial home in this beauty spot of the Santa Rita range, part of the Coronado National Forest.

Organ Pipe Cactus National Monument. In a remote corner of the state, 300,000 acres preserve a unique expanse of the Sonoran desert. It is America's only major stand of the oversize, multispined organ pipe cactus, set picturesquely among ironwood, saguaro, paloverde and ocotillo.

Phoenix South Mountain Park. The world's largest municipal park, nearly 15,000 acres, overlooks the bowl-shaped Phoenix valley from its perch on the Salt River Mountains. Lookout points,

hiking and bridle trails, picnic spots and desert plants all provide touches of wilderness in view of a city.

Salt River Canyon.
(Picture appears on facing page)

San Carlos Reservoir. The waters of the Gila River, checked by the Coolidge Dam, provide excellent bass fishing, with boat and tackle concessions operated by the San Carlos Apache Indian Reservation. Wild pigs are occasionally seen along the shore. Float trips can be made downstream of here.

Silver Bell–Avra Valley Road. From the irrigated Avra Valley the 50-mile road climbs into dry mountain terrain, winding up through dazzling scenery. The final drop into desert lowlands passes close by a magnificent saguaro forest.

Superstition Mountains.
(Picture appears on this page)

Swift Trail. The 31-mile road starts in desert landscapes, then coils up to an alpine setting at Clark Peak in the cloud-shrouded Pinaleno range. Refreshing streams and springs line the trail, and small Riggs Flat Lake is stocked with trout.

Texas Canyon. An excellent highway picnic area here invites drivers to stop and examine leisurely this natural pile of jumbled and weather-worn rock. The weird formations constantly change color as the sun moves across the sky.

Tonto National Monument. A winding path half a mile long climbs 350 feet into history: 14th-century adobe and rock houses built by Salado Indians occupy a natural cave. The ancient rooms survey miles of rough desert country and calm Roosevelt Lake below.

White Mountains. Regarded by many as Arizona's loveliest mountains, they climb 11,500 feet and are heavily forested with ponderosa pines. Some of the state's finest trout-fishing streams are here, as well as about 30 jewel-like artificial lakes. The range is located entirely within the White Mountain Apache Indian Reservation.

RELATED MUSEUMS AND ATTRACTIONS

Ajo. Organ Pipe Cactus National Monument Museum.

Phoenix.
Arizona Mineral Museum.
Desert Botanical Garden of Arizona.

Superior. Boyce Thompson Southwestern Arboretum.

Tucson.
Arizona–Sonora Desert Museum.
University of Arizona Mineralogy Museum.

Willcox. Chiricahua National Monument Museum.

Chiricahua National Monument. *Frozen lava carved by weather into banded pillars is among the strange natural statuary found along the roadside in the park. Rugged mesas and plateaus, as well as an unusual fern forest, harbor wild bears, pigs and a number of rare songbirds.*

Salt River Canyon. *Once Apache Indians used this canyon as a trail and a refuge after hunting raids, but today's visitors come to swim and fish in the river and to picnic along its shores. A paved road through the area drops 2000 feet in five miles, then rises up in a dramatic series of switchbacks.*

405

Olympic National Park

WASHINGTON

The wild Hoh River, lined by rain forest, flows beneath an almost constant downpour.

An Olympian Mix of Rain Forest, Snowy Peaks and a Wild Shore

In the northwestern extremity of the United States, where Washington state thrusts a rocky promontory into the Pacific, lies one of our most excitingly varied national parks. It has tall mountains, eternally snowcapped and overrun with slow glaciers; a 50-mile stretch of some of the wildest beach in the country; and a rain forest as green and dim as an Amazon jungle, dripping beneath the heaviest rainfall in North America. The name of this remarkable park is—justly—Olympic.

The Olympic Peninsula, of which the park's 1400 square miles form a large part, seems almost like another country. Its towns are few and scattered, the waters of the Hood Canal and Puget Sound cut it off from Seattle and the bustling Washington "mainland," and its peaks seem more closely related to the mountains of Vancouver Island, rising just across the Juan de Fuca Strait, than to the mighty Cascade Range 100 miles to the east.

The great jumble of mountains at the heart of the peninsula was first sighted by a Spanish sea captain in 1774, and some 14 years later an English captain named the highest peak Mount Olympus, after the legendary home of the Greek gods. Strangely enough, the heart of these mountains remained unexplored for more than a century after, and not until 1889 and 1890 were the first crossings of the high wilderness made. Almost immediately proposals

Sunlight filters dimly through the moss-draped colonnades to kindle a growing green luminance in the luxuriant depths of the Hoh Rain Forest.

were made that the magnificence of the scenery here, particularly the great forests, should be preserved. A forest reserve was established in 1897, a Mount Olympus National Monument in 1909, and finally, after many long and bitter struggles with some local interests, Olympic National Park was created in 1938.

Driving from Seattle or coming in by ferry from Victoria, Port Angeles, on the north shore of the peninsula, is the natural gateway to the park; it is here that the national park headquarters is found. Here, too, the main highway around the Olympic Peninsula, U.S. 101, passes closest to the high mountain country; and there are three spectacular drives leading from it into the park.

East of Port Angeles is the road to Deer Park. Mostly unpaved, it is a succession of steep hairpin bends, but anyone accustomed to mountain driving should have no trouble making it to the top. There is a magnificent view north and south, across the strait to Vancouver Island and toward the lofty, icy heart of the Olympic Mountains. In the alpine meadows here deer are common, and some delicate plants are found that grow nowhere on earth outside the Olympics, including the piper bellflower and the Flett violet.

The drive to Hurricane Ridge is probably the most popular mountain highway in the park, and it is easy to see why. It is a good road, starting near park headquarters and finishing in flowery meadows right on the edge of the Olympics. In serried ranks the great mountains march off into the distance to the south, a succession of snowy summits with glaciers winding among them, and often with piled masses of cloud scurrying across from the west. In June the first avalanche lilies bloom as the snow withdraws from the meadows, and for the next three months there is a succession of colorful flowers. Deer can be seen browsing against the splendid mountain backdrop, and sometimes mountain goats can be spotted clinging to the steep cliffs above the highway. There is a nature trail here, and regular summer wildflower walks led by park naturalists. You can drive nine miles farther along the ridge to Obstruction Point for a series of wide views, but this road is once again unpaved.

The third climb into the mountains from Route 101 is west of Port Angeles, and leads up the Elwha River valley, along the shore of Lake Mills, to Olympic Hot Springs, at the head of a forested canyon.

Back on Route 101, the next place to stop is Lake Crescent, which is everyone's idea of what a mountain lake should be: a bowl of sparkling blue water reflecting plunging forested slopes, with Mount Storm King looming over the southern shore. There is a lodge here, offering fishing in the lake (it's really too cold for swimming), and a park visitor center with a self-guiding trail through the towering forest on the lower slopes of Storm King.

America's Heaviest Rainfall
–and Why It Happens

Moisture-laden clouds blowing inland from a warm Pacific coastal current are forced to rise by the high barrier of the Olympics. As they ascend, they cool and their moisture condenses into heavy rain or snow. Thus the western slope of the mountains averages 140 inches of precipitation, while the eastern side, lying in what is known as a rain shadow, stays comparatively dry.

Highway 101 now leaves the edge of the park, and at the point where it does so a side road leads south to Sol Duc Hot Springs, along the banks of the Soleduck River. This is a fine place to watch salmon coming up the river to spawn from August to October. At Salmon Cascades they fling themselves desperately out of the water, from one shallow pool to another, trying again and again to make their way against the current to the headwaters where they themselves were spawned.

The rain forests are perhaps the most extraordinary phenomena at Olympic. The term normally applies to tropical forests alone, and these are in fact the only true rain forests in temperate latitudes. They are brought into being by the abnormally high rainfall of the western slopes of the Olympics, ranging from about 80 inches a year near the coast to 150 inches or more along the river valleys in the mountain foothills. (Mount Olympus itself receives about 200 inches of precipitation a year, but this is mostly in the form of snow. Most American cities, by comparison, have less than 50 inches of annual precipitation.) Three river valleys contain most of the rain forests: those of the Hoh, Queets and Quinault rivers. The Hoh River road leads for 19 miles into the park along the riverbank, and as it proceeds the forest around it gradually becomes denser and higher. The road ends at a park visitor center, with several self-guiding trails leading off into the tall green stillness.

Deer are a common sight on Hurricane Ridge, the alpine meadow that is the most popular overlook in the park. On a clear day you can see to Canada.

The rain forest is a magical place. Footsteps on the nearly two feet of duff on the forest floor are muffled; the thickness of the trees keeps out wind; even the rain that falls here so frequently filters down as a sort of green mist. Sun reaches the forest floor only in tiny blurred bright patches, though it lights the upper stories of the great trees far above with halos of fire. In the almost unearthly silence the quietest birdsong seems loud, and occasional deer and elk flit like brown ghosts among the moss-hung trunks.

Some of the giants among American trees live in these woods: the world's largest Douglas fir (14½ feet in diameter and 221 feet tall), the second biggest Sitka spruce (18 feet across, 248 feet high), a western red cedar 20 feet thick, 230-foot western hemlocks, and black cottonwoods of more than 175 feet. In fact, six western tree species reach their maximum height here. Since the debris on the forest floor is so thick, seeds are usually buried without a chance to grow—which is why most of the biggest trees in the forests seem to sprout from nurse logs. These are fallen, decomposing trees which act as fertile hosts to seeds that drop onto them. It is not uncommon to see several great trees growing in a line along one fallen giant, and the prevalence of nurse logs accounts for the occasional effect of colonnades among the trees—as if they had been carefully planted in rows.

As you climb higher into the Olympics, the forest changes, though record-size Pacific silver fir and alpine fir are also found on slopes beyond the park roads. The timberline in these mountains (above which trees do not grow) is about 5500 feet, but long before that the auto traveler has dropped out, and the world is left to the backpacker and climber. This is magnificent climbing country, and the wilderness interior of the park is well provided with trails, shelters and climbers' rest huts. Real alpine climbing is necessary to reach the summit of the higher peaks: Mount Olympus, at nearly 8000 feet, has seven glaciers on its flanks, with ice 900 feet thick in places, and there are more than 50 glaciers in the high country as a whole.

Access to the very best of the Olympic beaches is also for the hiker rather than the driver—and this means access to beaches as wild as any in the country. Drive off Route 101 just north of Forks to an Indian village called La Push, and then hike through the woods to reach Second and Third beaches, rich in sea stacks, and tide pools full of endlessly fascinating marine life. Beyond Teahwhit Head, another hike south of La Push, is the Giants Graveyard, a confused offshore jumble of contorted rock formations which breaks the huge Pacific surges into a smother of foam. Trees along these shores are bent almost flat by the constant push of the battering wind off the sea. Hiking along the beaches of the Olympic strip, head down into the gale while you search in the creamy swash for beautifully shaped driftwood or smoothly polished stones (Rialto Beach, north of La Push, is particularly good for these), is one of the more exhilarating ways to enjoy the park.

For the less energetic, however, there is plenty of access to the ocean along Route 101. Ruby Beach, where the highway meets the shore, offers a series of sea stacks, and good

The handsome Roosevelt elk, at one time in danger of extinction, now roams the park in such numbers (over 5000) that it is also known as the Olympic elk.

The moist, mild climate of the western Olympics encourages rich growth. This falls in the Quinault Rain Forest flows through vivid shades of green.

opportunities for driftwood collecting. All along the highway from here to Queets the beach lies just below a line of wooded cliffs, with parking turnouts for occasional sudden seaside vistas, and trails down to the beach. Scramble down any of these to enjoy the tide pools, or perhaps to see a line of gray whales spouting far out to sea as they swim north on their annual migration from California to Alaska. At Kalaloch there is a wide sand beach, a park lodge and another park naturalist program that offers guided tours of the neighboring tide pools and their rich variety of colorful life daily in summer. Like many of the beaches in the Olympic Strip, Beach Four, near here, is good for clam digging at low tide.

Once Route 101 has left the beach at Queets it only touches the park once again—at Lake Quinault, a beautiful lake with forest drives along either shore that is more heavily developed than most in the park. It is part of an Indian reservation, and it is possible to arrange at the lodge here to take a ride in an Indian dugout canoe up the Quinault River, for a last look at the rain forest. The Quinault Rain Forest, the most southerly stretch, lines the riverbanks above the lake.

Fifty miles south of here you can pick up high-speed highways that will take you to the contemporary bustle of Seattle and Portland in only a couple of hours of actual time— but several centuries in feeling. For the Olympic experience is essentially one of wildness and timelessness. A strange natural phenomenon—great reservoirs of cloud swelled by a broad ocean and broken open on the heads of high mountains—has created the inexorable movement of powerful glaciers among misty peaks, the green dripping hush of the forest cathedrals, and the thunder and smash of the waves on a wild shore. It is a cornucopia of carefully preserved natural riches, strikingly uncrowded even today—a place that thoroughly deserves its Olympic title.

A 50-mile stretch of magnificently wild Pacific beach is included in Olympic Park. Sea stacks, tall and solitary rocks that are the only remains of fallen wave-cut arches, are common along the shore. This sunset glows at a beach near La Push, an Indian fishing village on the Quillayute River.

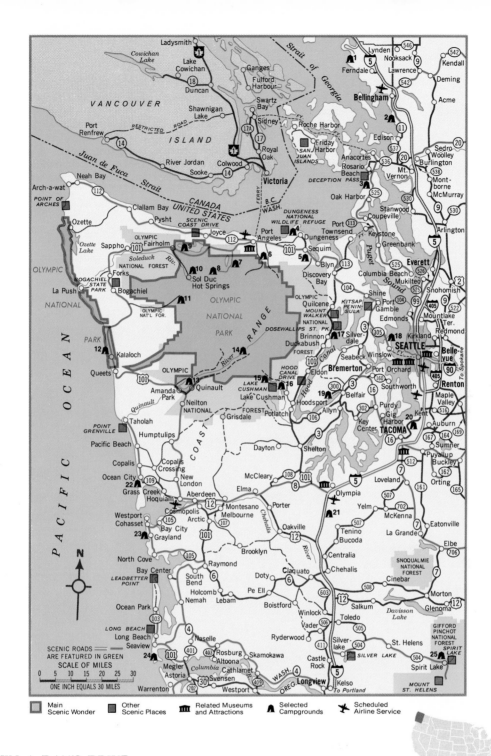

WITHIN A DAY'S DRIVE:

Wooded Valleys and Lonely Beaches

Bogachiel State Park. A fine hiking trail along the densely forested Bogachiel River valley begins here. There is a small area of rain forest, and some great alder trees. The valley is less frequented than the other western valleys, and there is a good chance of seeing deer and elk.

Deception Pass. The channel that divides Whidbey Island from Fidalgo Island funnels one of the most powerful and turbulent currents in the area, and a highway bridge across it is a good place to watch the water rushing through. Whidbey Island itself has miles of fine sandy beaches.

Dosewallips State Park. The tumbling Dose Cascades are a highlight of the magnificent Dosewallips River valley, on the dry side of the Olympic Peninsula. A trail follows the river from the beach up to Dose Meadow, an alpine meadow bright with flowers and ringed by snowy peaks.

415

Dungeness National Wildlife Refuge. A long sandspit that curves out into the strait of Juan de Fuca is largely farmland, with fine views back toward the high Olympics. The waters inside the spit are havens for vast flocks of wintering ducks and geese.

Hood Canal Drive. Despite its name, this is a natural waterway, entered as "canal" on Captain George Vancouver's charts and thus misnamed ever since. U.S. 101 follows the shoreline along most of its length, offering splendid beach views. The drive is brightened with rhododendron and dogwood in late spring, and flaming maples in fall.

Kitsap Peninsula. Lakes and forests dot this pleasantly placid area only a ferry ride away from Seattle. The Hood Canal shore offers magnificent views to the snowy Olympics.

Lake Cushman. A dam has backed up the north fork of the Skokomish River into a lake with a 40-mile shoreline. Mount Washington towers above its north shore, and a short hike beyond the western end of the lake brings you to dashing Staircase Rapids.

Leadbetter Point. An isolated spot that is actually an undeveloped state park, Leadbetter offers sand dunes, good clamming beaches—and a remarkable sense of solitude. Willapa Bay, inside the point, is celebrated for its oysters.

Long Beach. The beach that runs along the ocean side of the North Beach Peninsula is one of the longest hard-sand beaches in the world. Twenty-eight miles in length, most of it can be driven

Mount St. Helens. *Cars can drive up this symmetrical 9677-foot peak as far as the timberline at just over 4000 feet. Above here is a series of shifting pumice slopes that look easy to climb but are not. In fact, only experienced climbers can get right to the top. This view is from across Spirit Lake.*

San Juan Islands. *Pyramid-shaped Mount Baker rises like a misty dream in this twilight view across the San Juan Islands. A wide panorama of* *them can be enjoyed from the lookout tower atop Mount Constitution, on Orcas Island. Or admire them by ferry between Anacortes and Sidney, B.C.*

by car at low tide (though the razor-clam beds near the waterline must be avoided). Waves here are often spectacular, and clamming is a popular pastime.

Mount St. Helens.
(*Picture appears on facing page*)

Mount Walker. Although Mount Walker's summit is only 2800 feet high, the view from here is one of the most striking in the entire Olympic Peninsula. The panorama of the snowy Olympics fills the horizon to the west, and across the Hood Canal and Puget Sound to the east rise the twin cones of Mount Baker and Mount Rainier and the great wall of the Cascade Range. A gravel road leads to the summit.

Point Grenville. From the high cliffs that drop away from the Point Grenville coast guard station there is an incomparable panorama of broad ocean and miles of coast. The beach below can only be reached a mile south of the point, and offers caves, rocky coves and tide pools.

Point of Arches. A dirt road that is impassable in bad weather heads south from Neah Bay to this remarkable collection of jagged offshore rocks, wave-cut arches and sea caves. Drive to Portage Head and then walk along Shi-Shi Beach, a favorite with beachcombers, to get there. It is on private property, and access is sometimes restricted.

San Juan Islands.
(*Picture appears on this page*)

Scenic Coast Drive. State Highway 112 runs along the north shore of the Olympic Peninsula all the way from Port Angeles to Neah Bay. It is a spectacular drive most of the way, sometimes following along at beach level (Agate and Crescent beaches are local favorites), sometimes climbing to high overlooks with views over the Juan de Fuca Strait to Vancouver Island and inland toward the Olympics.

Silver Lake. The fishing for trout, bass and bluegill is excellent here, and there are several islands in

the lake that can be visited by boats available for rent. Nearby Seaquest State Park offers hiking trails and camping.

Spirit Lake. The dominating view from this lovely mountain lake is of proud Mount St. Helens rearing to the south. The lake is ringed with cliffs, forested slopes and small bays, and hiking trails from here open up the alpine wilderness on the lower slopes of nearby Mount Margaret.

**RELATED MUSEUMS
AND ATTRACTIONS**

Olympia. State Capitol Museum; natural history, marine life.

Port Angeles. Olympic National Park Pioneer Memorial Museum; natural history.

Seattle.
Seattle Marine Aquarium.
University of Washington Arboretum.
University of Washington Natural History Museum.

Tacoma. Point of Defiance Park Aquarium and Zoo.

Mount Rainier

NATIONAL PARK, WASHINGTON

The still waters of Lake Eunice reflect Mount Rainier's majestic 14,410-foot peak.

WASHINGTON

Mount Rainier

Mountain Meadows, Lakes and Glaciers—All in Easy Range

Nothing quite prepares a person for a first view of Mount Rainier. There are several higher peaks in the United States, but none that so dominates a surrounding landscape by its sheer towering bulk. You may first catch sight of it from as much as 100 miles away as you gaze southeast from Puget Sound or see it as you approach from the east, looming on the horizon against the setting sun. There it is, a white cone that rears above the horizon like a phantom peak levitated on layers of cloud and hazy distance. Your first reaction is probably to pass it off as a tall buildup of cloud; look again and you realize it is Rainier, brooding over southern Washington just as Kilimanjaro's vastness rules the East African plain. For those who live within sight of it, it is grandly and simply "The Mountain."

It is Rainier's gleaming ice cap that gives the great mountain its shining summit: no American mountain outside of Alaska is topped with more glaciers—a 37-square-mile mass of ice and snow that smooths and conceals all but the most rugged peaks and ridges, so that even from quite close the upper 6000 feet of Rainier looks like the icing on a giant cake, its dazzling whiteness reflecting the brilliant clouds that often plume from the peak.

Rainier is in fact a dormant volcano, though it has not erupted for more than 100 years, and even then only in small outbursts. It seems

There are 27 separate glaciers on Rainier—more than on any American peak outside Alaska. These climbers are 9000 feet up on the Puyallup Glacier.

even larger than it is because it stands apart from the Cascade range to which it belongs: nearly 400 square miles of mountain and surrounding foothills. This corner of the country is generally cool and moist, and it snows or rains a lot on the mountain—about 60 inches on the lower levels and up to 100 inches in the subalpine regions below the summit. Indeed, Paradise, at 5400 feet on the south side of the mountain, gets an *average* of 50 feet of snow a year, and in mid-March 1956 it received the nation's greatest-ever single snowfall—over 30 feet. In the winter of 1972 an incredible 1122 inches—over 93 feet—broke all seasonal records. Packs of snow up to 25 feet are common, and even lower levels bear patches of snow well into July.

The first recorded sighting of the great mountain took place in 1792—though the Indians had known of it for centuries and apparently regarded the summit with fear and awe, despite the excellent hunting available on its slopes. Captain George Vancouver, who made many discoveries in these parts, spotted the snowy peak as he sailed in nearby Puget Sound, and named it for his friend Peter Rainier, a British admiral who was never in fact to see it. Explorers and settlers scaled Rainier's heights in 1852 and 1855, but it was not until 1857 that a widely known assault upon the peak was carried out. Lieutenant August Kautz, climbing with a doctor, two soldiers and a Nisqually Indian guide, reached within a few hundred feet of the 14,410-foot summit, only to be turned back by high winds.

Paradise Ice Caves, reached by a three-mile hike, are well worth the effort to get there. They are hollowed out inside the Paradise Glacier, and *the ice formations are beautifully lit in shades of blue and green as the sun filters in. Some years they are closed because of heavy, late-lying snow.*

In 1870 Hazard Stevens and Philemon Van Trump reached the peak, though they were forced to remain there for the night and might have frozen to death had they not found shelter in snow caves formed by steam vents. James Longmire, who helped guide them and subsequent expeditions on Rainier, and who later completed the ascent himself, knew the mountain better than anyone at this period. It was he who discovered mineral springs on the southwest side of Rainier and who built a hotel and resort there, in an area that still bears his name. Only a few years later, in 1899, the whole mountain and its approaches became America's fifth national park.

Now Longmire is one of the park's four visitor centers, a short drive from the southwest,

or Nisqually, entrance. It is in a pleasant forested setting, with magnificent views of the mighty peak above, and a half-mile nature trail, the Trail of the Shadows, which leads past the springs. On the way to Longmire you pass the scene of the great mudflow down Kautz Creek. Mudflows, rather than volcanic activity, are the most destructive natural events that still punctuate the mountain's quiet life. The Kautz flow in 1947 was caused when a high crest of mud, built up by heavy rain, broke loose from behind a wall of ice and careered down the slope, thrusting huge boulders before it, snapping trees like matchsticks and burying the park road under 50 feet of mud and debris. The whole riverbed was reshaped. Today a nature trail explains the mud's devastation and the rebirth of the forest as it winds past dead stumps and new seedlings.

Beyond Longmire the road zigzags upward to Paradise, where there is a comfortable lodge and a modernistic circular visitor center with a sweeping 360-degree view of the peak and its surrounding alpine meadows and forests. This is probably the most stunning—and comfortable—panoramic viewpoint high on a great mountain anywhere in the world. From Paradise you can take the Nisqually Glacier Vista Trail—which brings a visitor about as close to a glacier as he is likely to get short of a full-fledged climbing expedition—and the Paradise Ice Caves Trail, when open, for a six-mile round trip to the beautiful blue-green caves hollowed out beneath the Paradise Glacier.

All the time, as you have been climbing to Paradise and beyond, the vegetation has been gradually shading from one life zone to another. Rainier, as a giant freestanding mountain in a temperate latitude, bears on its flanks no less than four different zones of characteristic vegetation and wildlife, from the moist deciduous woodland of the lowest hills to the nearly barren alpine tundra of Burroughs Mountain, and on up to the icy slopes below the summit (see diagram on pages 424–425).

But the two features of Rainier that fill most of its 1,750,000 visitors annually with wonder and delight are the multitude of glaciers and the vivid wildflower meadows. The glaciers are visible from all sides of Rainier, great slow-moving rivers of ice spilling off its flanks and pushing steep walls of boulders before them. The only way to the summit for the hundreds of climbers who assault the peak each year is across one or more of them; but it requires considerable know-how and experience, and beginners are urged to enjoy them from a distance. They are full of hidden crevasses, and there is a constant danger of rockfalls from the piles at their snouts.

Rainier, however, is also a mountain on which you can *learn* to climb. Each summer a guide concession, called Rainier Mountaineering, Inc., gives classes and seminars in such matters as rope travel, cramponing and ice-ax arrest. For $55, a two-day escorted climb to the summit can be arranged for those who have satisfied their instructor that they are adequately prepared to follow in his footsteps. And it is no mean climb: the 1963 American Mount Everest expedition practiced on Rainier.

Vivid painted cups and blue lupines decorate the slopes at Unicorn Park, one of Rainier's many flowery high meadows accessible by foot.

But there is plenty to see for people who merely drive around the mountain, or get out only to stretch their legs on short trails at the many parking areas and overlooks. From Paradise you can drive on down Stevens Canyon, past the dizzy view into Box Canyon, by the shores of blue Reflection Lakes, around the east flank of the mountain, with more splendid views toward the summit, then out of the park by Tipsoo Lake. Or you can continue along a spectacular mountain drive to the Sunrise Visitor Center, 1000 feet higher than Paradise, and the closest you can get to the summit by road; here Rainier leans out of the sky almost on top of you. But wherever you drive during the brief Rainier summer (and most roads are open only in summer), be sure to take time for a stroll on a wildflower meadow trail. The trail to the Paradise Ice Caves, and the Emmons Glacier Vista Trail, are particularly rewarding for flowers. Yellow glacier lilies, white avalanche lilies, magenta painted cups, blue lupines, rosy spireas, yellow monkey flowers and red penstemon carpet the meadows in colorful suc-

cession from when the snow leaves in July until it returns in September.

And the park is rich in wildlife too. Birds are less common than animals; most noticeable are the grouse, ptarmigan, larks, finches, ravens, crows and those two tame and noisy birds of the western mountains, Clark nut-

Driving Through Rainier's Life Zones

Arctic-Alpine Zone, 6500 feet to summit. *The top 6000 feet of this great mountain are just barren rock and eternal snow and ice. Immediately below the snow line is alpine tundra. Around 7500 feet the brilliantly colored flowering plants shown here begin to appear. Near 6500 feet cling the first trees; park visitors can drive this high.*

LUPINE

PAINTED CUPS

SITKA VALERIAN

ALASKA SPIREA

Hudsonian Zone, 5000–6000 feet. *Broad meadows of vivid wildflowers dotted with groves of trees girdle the mountain in the upper half of this zone. The lower half is forest, dominated by mountain hemlock. Zones overlap at various elevations; some of the plants shown here, for instance, can also be found in the Arctic-Alpine Zone. And changes in temperature and precipitation cause some differences in the life zones on opposite sides of Rainier.*

RUSTY MENZIESIA

MONKEY FLOWER

AVALANCHE LILY

GLACIER LILY

Canadian Zone, 3000–5000 feet. *This forest zone also contains some of the typical vegetation of zones above and below it. Wildflowers grow here, though not as spectacularly as in the upper meadows. At this level, where the Pacific silver fir dominates, the trees are generally taller than at higher elevations, and the mountainsides thus seem much more heavily forested. This is the most extensive of Rainier's forest zones.*

OREGON GRAPE

TWINFLOWER

VANILLA LEAF

PIPSISSEWA

Humid Transition Zone, below 3000 feet. *The dense forest in this humid zone is the domain of the giant trees: Douglas firs, Western hemlocks (related to the smaller mountain hemlocks of the higher zones) and western red cedars often reach heights of 250 feet, and most are over 200 feet. Lowland-loving deciduous trees also appear here, and lush ferns are common in the moister areas.*

BLACK-BERRY

SALAL

TRILLIUM

WESTERN SKUNK CABBAGE

crackers and Oregon jays. Animals include beavers, blacktail deer, black bears, cougars and mountain goats (actually not goats but rock antelope; about 400 of them are here). Fishing is possible in the icy lake and streams from July to late October.

But however you enjoy the great mountain, there will come a time when you will have to drive down, back to the plains below and the journey home. Then suddenly you will find the mountain changed again, from a closeness of rocks and forests and trails and waterfalls, to that shining vision you first saw, lifting like a cloud mountain, impossibly far away.

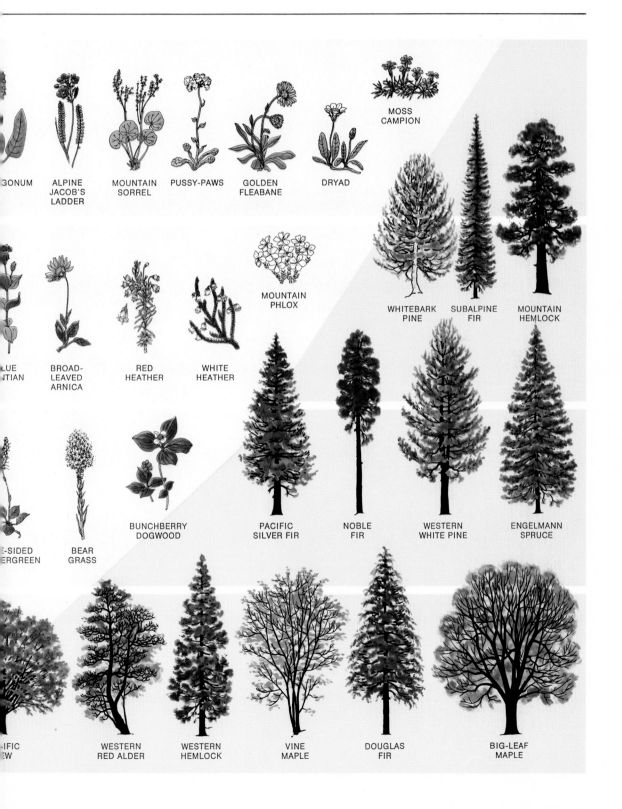

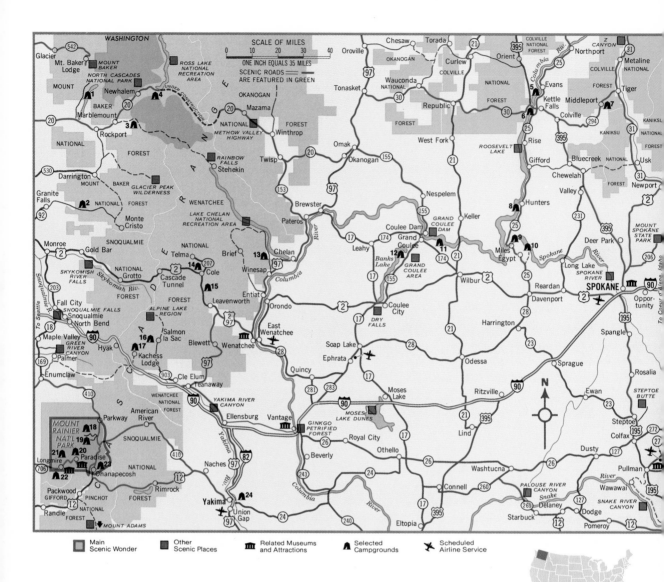

Main Scenic Wonder   Other Scenic Places   Related Museums and Attractions   Selected Campgrounds   Scheduled Airline Service

Tall Cascades, Snowy Wildernesses and Shining Volcanic Peaks

Alpine Lake Region.
(Picture appears on page 428)

Dry Falls. During the last Ice Age the Columbia River, blocked by an ice dam from its usual course, cascaded in torrents over cliffs here in the greatest waterfall ever known. A staggering three and a half miles wide, the fall is estimated to have been 800 feet high at one time but erosion later cut it back to half that. The river left the sheer lava walls dry when it returned to its previous channel.

Ginkgo Petrified Forest. A park here contains more than 200 kinds of colorful petrified trees, once buried in lava, now exposed by erosion. The stands of petrified ginkgo trees are unique: though they survived in China, they have been extinct here for millennia.

Glacier Peak Wilderness. Many lakes, cascading streams, glaciers, alpine meadows and spectacular vistas make this a strikingly scenic area. There are logging and mining roads around the perime-

ter, but some hiking is necessary into the high country dominated by Glacier Peak at 10,541 feet. Other peaks in this impressive range are from 5000 to 9000 feet.

Grand Coulee Area. Derived from a French word used for a flow of lava, a coulee is a steep-sided ravine, usually dry. Both meanings are appropriate here. Swollen by melting glaciers, the Columbia River once raged over the lava plateau and cut deeply into cracks in the lava. When it returned to its normal channel, it left behind many small lakes and the dry coulees whose walls expose successive layers of lava.

Grand Coulee Dam. The largest concrete dam in the world rises 550 feet from bedrock to the spillway and is 4173 feet long. The view from downstream is impressive. In summer the spillway is colorfully illuminated at night.

Green River Canyon. The only typical sandstone gorge in western Washington is deep and narrow, and the river has carved some remarkably shaped formations in its sheer walls.

Lake Chelan National Recreation Area. A passenger boat cruises daily from the more developed southern end of this narrow 55-mile lake up into the North Cascades wilderness through steep-walled canyons. Mountains rise almost from the edge of the lake to a height of 8500 feet.

Methow Valley Highway. Starting in arid land, the highway traverses apple orchards along the Methow River, then winds up the evergreen slopes of the Cascades to cross Harts Pass at over 6000 feet. Three miles from the summit is Slate Mountain Lookout, one of the most magnificent panoramic views in the West.

Moses Lake Dunes. South and east of Moses Lake is a constantly changing area of sand dunes formed by prehistoric torrents of glacial meltwater. Hundreds of interlacing waterways make some dunes into islands.

Mount Adams.
(*Picture appears on page 429*)

Mount Baker. The ice-covered volcanic cone of Mount Baker rises 10,750 feet, and like mounts Rainier and Hood is a landmark for hundreds of miles around. The wildflowers of its alpine meadows make some of its trails particularly rewarding. Kulshan Ridge connects Mount Baker with lower Mount Shuksan, nine miles away in North Cascades National Park. A favorite vantage point is Austin Pass, about midway between the two mountains.

Mount Spokane State Park. For a panoramic view of the lake-studded mountains of eastern Washington and western Idaho, drive the 34 miles from the city of Spokane to the summit of Mount Spokane (5881 feet). The largest state park in Washington (20,000 acres), it has many good hiking trails and ski runs in its rolling pine hills.

North Cascades National Park.
(*Picture appears on page 429*)

Palouse River Canyon. This canyon and its falls are a dramatic surprise in the rolling wheat country. The Palouse River tumbles 300 feet down a sheer wall to a pool, then flows on between steep and rugged canyon walls to join the Snake River.

Rainbow Falls. From Stehekin, in the Lake Chelan National Recreation Area, a bus makes the half-hour trip to the 312-foot falls, whose voluminous spray always

Ross Lake National Recreation Area. *Steep Colonial Peak towers over the glacier-green waters of Thunder Creek Arm on Diablo Lake, one of three lakes created in these mountains by dams on the Skagit River.*

427

Alpine Lake Region. *Typical of the small and lovely lakes in this highlands area above Snoqualmie Pass are these two deep-blue lakes set in glacier-cut* *cairns. The peaks of the Cascade Mountains reach away behind them to the towering, snowy summit of Mount Rainier, looming 50 miles in the distance.*

seems to catch the sun at exactly the right angle to produce a shimmering rainbow.

Roosevelt Lake. The long, winding lake formed by the Grand Coulee Dam extends 151 miles up to the Canadian border. The land near the dam is arid, but farther north meadows full of wildflowers brighten the hilly shoreline, forests grow to the water's edge, and wildlife abounds.

Ross Lake National Recreation Area.
(*Picture appears on page 427*)

Skykomish River Falls. Highway 2 offers a spectacular view of Bridal Veil, biggest of the three falls on the Skykomish River. The water divides into several channels, then plunges 1500 feet over a ravine. The 150-foot drop of Sunset Falls can be seen from a Forest Service road. Eagle Falls, the smallest, is a rushing cascade.

Snake River Canyon. The Snake River's famous Hells Canyon has ended before the river enters Washington, but even here the steep lava walls are an awesome 2000 feet high. Fishing for salmon, steelhead and the enormous prehistoric sturgeon is popular wherever there is river access.

Snoqualmie Falls. The waters of the Snoqualmie River tumble down for 270 feet before racing on through a canyon. A walkway at the canyon edge downstream from the falls provides a good view. The flow is powerful in spring, with misty spray rising high in the gorge, but the falls may dwindle to only a trickle at the end of a dry summer.

Spokane River. This churning, rapids-filled river surges in a series of cascades through the city of Spokane, but is only occasionally visible between the city buildings. The best views into its steep lava gorge are at nearby Riverside State Park.

Steptoe Butte. You can drive to the summit of this 3600-foot, pyramid-shaped mountain for a remarkable view over the Palouse River Canyon, the Rockies foothills to the east and the distant Cascades to the west.

Yakima River Canyon. The old highway between Yakima and Ellensburg runs beside rapids and quiet pools along the bottom of one of the most beautiful canyons in the state. On the dry side of the mountains the overhanging cliffs and rock formations are unsoftened by vegetation, though there are wildflowers in the spring.

Z Canyon. This canyon cut by the Pend Oreille River in the northeast corner of the state is famous for its extreme narrowness. It is 400 feet deep, but for the most part only 18 feet wide.

RELATED MUSEUMS AND ATTRACTIONS

Mount Rainier National Park. Longmire House Museum; natural history. Paradise Visitor Center.

Pullman. Washington State University Charles B. Conner Museum; natural history.

Spokane. John A. Finch Arboretum.

Vantage. Ginkgo Petrified Forest State Park Museum.

Wenatchee. Ohme Gardens; native plants and trees.

North Cascades National Park. *Jagged Liberty Bell Mountain, at the park's eastern entrance, is typical of the multitude of snowy peaks in this wilderness of magnificent alpine scenery. Much of the park is accessible only by hiking trails, but a new road opens up the east end.*

Mount Adams. *The volcanic cone of Mount Adams, capped by nine glaciers, rises above a forest road through a meadow of flame-colored vine maple. The Pacific Crest Trail crosses the primitive area near the 12,307-foot peak. Ice caves are plentiful on the southern slopes.*

Columbia River Gorge
OREGON AND WASHINGTON

Crown Point rises over the Oregon side of the gorge.

WASHINGTON

Columbia
River Gorge

OREGON

A Noble Setting for a Historic Waterway

The mighty Columbia River, second only to the Mississippi in volume, is actually born in Canada. From the Canadian Rockies in the depths of British Columbia it swings on its 1200-mile journey to the sea, watering central Washington and dividing Washington and Oregon on the way. Sometimes savage, sometimes tamed by huge dams, the Columbia is nowhere more spectacular and dramatic than when it flows through the towering 60-mile canyon known as the Columbia Gorge.

The Columbia passed through several phases before reaching its present proud state. Many millions of years ago a river that was only a trickle compared to the present powerful flow carved a modest valley on its way to the ocean. This was a time of great eruptions among the volcanoes that covered so much of the Pacific Northwest, and whose dead cones, like mounts Rainier, Baker and Hood, remain as landmarks. They covered the area around the Columbia with layer upon layer of basaltic lava. Then, perhaps as recently as 300,000 years ago, a series of overpowering deluges swept down from the breakup of vast glacial systems to the northeast. They raced down the modest bed of the Columbia, gouging deep, wide canyons and exposing the successive layers of the lava flows. This mighty torrent too dwindled in time, though its flow remained much greater than that of the old river. This is the Columbia today—a major river flowing down a gorge cut

431

Oneonta Creek and Gorge

Punchbowl Falls

A pageant of quiet creeks and swift falls unfolds along the southern bank of the Columbia River, each small waterway bound for the mighty gorge below. Trails lead to viewing places, including an overlook and bridge at Oregon's tallest falls (left): the upper of the two cascades is 620 feet.

by one of the most powerful torrents the world has ever known.

The Columbia is a river of human as well as geologic history. As the principal Indian highway from the Rockies to the sea, it played an important part in the opening of the Northwest. The explorers Lewis and Clark were the first white men to travel the river's lower reaches, and they were followed by pioneer fur traders. But when settlers began arriving from the East to settle the gentle valleys of Oregon, they found the river section of the Oregon Trail too rough for them, and began carving out routes along the riverbanks. Railroads and highways followed, and now the Columbia Gorge is a major transportation throughway from the mountains to the sea.

You can enjoy many of the splendors of the area without ever leaving your car if you like:

the Columbia River Highway, a fast expressway, follows the gorge for its entire length, mostly at river level, with swelling blue vistas opening up around every curve in the road. But for those who want to make its acquaintance more directly, the old scenic highway from Troutdale is recommended. This climbs up along the cliffs to Crown Point, a rocky promontory 700 feet above the river that offers one of the finest panoramas of the gorge, with breathtaking views stretching away in both directions. The climb is a dramatic series of switchbacks in a masterpiece of early highway engineering.

Along here too is one of the most striking waterfalls in an area rich in them. Multnomah Falls is a sparkling 620-foot leap over a sheer cliff, and a bridge across the creek below the falls yields a fine view. Along this stretch of the Columbia each little creek as it seeks the great river drops in a steep falls or a whitewater cascade, each rocky gorge and glen appearing lovelier than the last. There are at least a dozen major falls.

Back on the main highway now, Bonneville Dam rears 200 feet over the river, the first

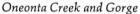

Multnomah Falls

Who's Who in the World of Pacific Salmon

SILVER

The most adaptable salmon, the eight-pound silver thrives in most of Oregon's coastal streams, spawning both near salt water and in fresh headwaters.

CHUM

The 10-pound chum prefers spawning close to salt water, in a lagoon or tide pool fed by a freshwater stream. The young go to sea almost at once.

of many that harness the Columbia's power. The fish ladders here are ideal places to watch the spawning salmon leap upriver. The "ladders" are in fact a series of terraced pools leading from river level to the top of the dam, and salmon as big as 50 pounds hurl themselves from pool to pool against the tumbling water in their fierce urge to return to the river of their birth to spawn. After spawning, exhausted and starving, they will die, but their tiny fry will repeat the remarkable cycle of salmon life. First they grow in fresh water to fingerling size, then they migrate downriver to the Pacific, where they spread out as far as the Bering Sea and the Aleutian Islands. Years later, grown to full size, they return, journeying unerringly back up the Columbia and other western rivers until they reach the waters of the very creek or river inlet where they were born—and where they in turn will spawn, starting up the life cycle once again.

Anglers line both banks of the river below the dam fishing for the salmon, as well as for the other great fish that make the Columbia and a host of northwestern rivers a fisherman's paradise: steelhead, cutthroat, shad and the enormous sturgeon, a prehistoric species which can reach as much as 200 pounds.

Fighting the rushing rapids, a salmon is caught in graceful midleap—one of many it must make in its long, hard struggle to swim upstream to spawn.

Spanning the river just west of Cascade Locks is the historic Bridge of the Gods. Now it seems like an ordinary highway bridge with dramatic views, but according to Indian legend there was once a natural rock bridge across the Columbia at this spot. It was cast down and destroyed by Tyhee Sohole, the Supreme Being, in his rage at his two sons, who had quarreled over a beautiful maiden. All three were killed in the smashing of the bridge, and were later resurrected as mounts Hood, Adams and St. Helens; the debris from the broken bridge created the Cascades.

From Hood River, the end of the most spectacular reach of the gorge, snowcapped Mount Hood can be seen towering on the horizon above the fields and orchards of the pastoral Hood River Valley. The views to the south from here, particularly in springtime when the apple, cherry and pear blossoms are out, are worth a long journey to see.

At Hood River you can cross over to the Washington side and enjoy a more distant view of the landscapes through which you have been traveling. This is a slower, more winding road than the Oregon expressway; a series of overlooks gives some striking panoramas of the high, jagged basalt cliffs and the series of terraces on the Oregon side, and of the many tiny islands in midstream. Sometimes the road shoots into tunnels blasted in the cliffs and emerges again into newly dazzling river vistas.

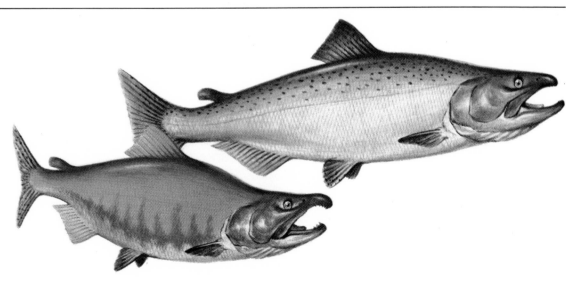

SOCKEYE

The fierce-looking sockeye, up to 12 pounds, spawns only in streams headed by lakes. The young stay there for a year before migrating out to the ocean.

CHINOOK

From 10 to 45 pounds, the chinook or king is the largest of this quartet, the most wide-ranging and the most prolific—a female averages 6000 eggs.

Beacon Rock, a 900-foot monolithic rock rising sheer above the Washington shore, has a steep summit trail that rewards a breathless climb with perhaps the most sweeping views on the entire length of the river.

But there is much more to the Columbia Gorge than just the scenery, striking though it is. The rugged cliffs and glens are host to a remarkable variety of ferns, lichens, mosses and shy pastel-colored wildflowers—some of them found nowhere else in the world. In early June the U.S. Forest Service combines with the Columbia Gorge Garden Club to put together a display of all the flowers and shrubs native to the surroundings of the gorge. For keen botanists this show, which takes place at Wahkeena Falls, is an irresistible introduction to the natural riches of the area.

The flats along the riverbanks, and the gorge walls themselves, abound in wildlife. Game birds and coyotes are common, and even an occasional cougar is seen. In the winter, when snow blankets the tops of the gorge, deer and elk come down almost to the river level to feed. Bald and golden eagles occasionally tilt over the gorge on broad wings.

Despite the ease with which the gorge can be enjoyed from either bank, the closest acquaintance with a great river is usually the most revealing—and on the Columbia you can take a boat from Portland through the gorge as far as Bonneville Dam every Thursday, Friday, Saturday and Sunday in summer. From water level the Columbia Gorge seems even more majestic—a fit setting for the river's royal progress to the ocean.

Pockets of tranquil farmland lie among the wooded hills alongside the Columbia River Gorge. For more than 300 miles highways on either shore follow the course of the stupendous river, passing parks, picnic areas, campgrounds and trails that wind inland to rocky gorges and up to scenic overlooks.

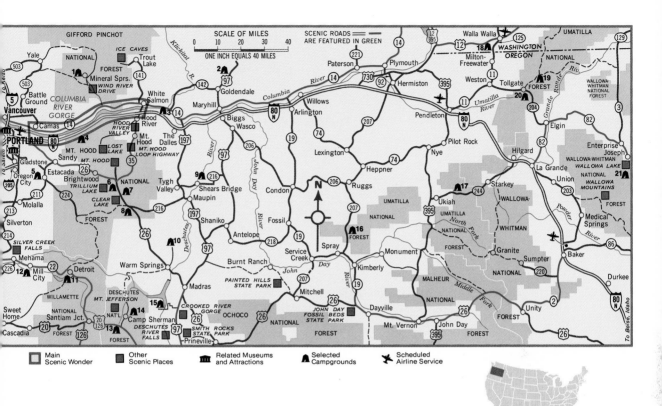

WITHIN A DAY'S DRIVE:

Salmon Streams, Fossils Galore and a Forest Beneath a Lake

Clear Lake, Ore. Centuries ago a lava flow sealed off the upper McKenzie River, and as the waters rose they flooded part of a forested valley. Today visitors can peer an amazing 100 feet down into the translucent lake and see erect tree trunks, preserved by the lake's icy waters.

Crooked River Gorge, Ore. Mountain streams keep the Crooked River full all year, slowly cutting down its bed and heightening its sheer rocky parapets. The abruptness of the chasm is enhanced by the flatness of the surrounding grasslands.

Deschutes River Falls, Ore. Named Rivière des Chutes (river of falls) by French explorers, it lives up to the ancient billing. A series of rapids in the space of a dozen miles includes Steelhead, Odin, Big and Cline falls.

Hood River Valley, Ore. Orchards spangle the upper reaches of the wide valley, creating a springtime froth of pastel blossoms and an autumn bounty of ripe fruits. Wildflowers and lush ferns grow along the riverbank, and along side creeks occasional waterfalls plunge into quiet pools. The snowy cone of Mount Hood rises proudly over all.

Ice Caves, Wash. The wilderness region south of 12,000-foot Mount Adams, a land of wooded slopes below snowfields, is honeycombed with ice caves. Some are known only from the hollow sounds horses' hooves make as they cross them, but several have openings where viewers can enter and admire the elaborate ice architecture.

John Day Fossil Beds State Park, Ore.
(Picture appears on page 439)

Lost Lake, Ore. Not really lost, but splendidly aloof at the end of a steep seven-mile gravel road, the lake surveys the glacier-clad cone of Mount Hood. Anglers, boatmen and campers are drawn to its solitude, and hikers find trails that thread dense forests.

Mount Hood, Ore.
(Picture appears on page 439)

Mount Hood Loop Highway, Ore. The round trip drive from Portland eastward around Mount Hood covers 170 miles and a world of extravagant Oregon scenery. Overlooks command bird's-eye views of the Columbia River; 13 state parks offer trails and picnic facilities, and side roads wind to river valleys, lakes and remote campgrounds.

Mount Jefferson, Ore. Two miles high, the peak is the centerpiece of a wilderness retreat laced with lakes that spill over into dozens of small creeks. The Skyline Trail, the popular superhighway for hikers in the Cascades, loops through the area, providing easy access to secluded pools that lure fishermen to try for trout.

Painted Hills State Park, Ore. Colored like an artist's palette with streaks of green, copper, bronze, red and white, these hills are the place to spend an afternoon picnicking by Bridge Creek and then hunting for fossils: the land covers a trove of prehistoric plants and animals.

Silver Creek Falls, Ore. A state park preserves and protects a wild region of Silver Creek and its tributaries, an area lavishly endowed with 14 waterfalls. Park roads approach some of the cascades, and winding woodland trails edge the creek canyon and link them all.

Smith Rocks State Park, Ore. Sleek rock cliffs, rising to rough-hewn pinnacles, stand here like the background for a Western movie. A fishing stream loops through the park, and picnic spots and trails invite leisurely exploration.

Trillium Lake, Ore. Gravel Forest Service roads lead to this spruce-edged man-made lake, once an oval of meadowland. A launching ramp encourages restful rowing and canoeing—no motors are allowed on the lake. Once called Reflection Lake, its waters are a looking glass for Mount Hood.

Wallowa Lake, Ore. *(Picture appears on this page)*

Wallowa Mountains, Ore. Rivaling any other mountains in North America for primitive grandeur, the Wallowa peaks cut into the skyline with massive cliffs and steeples. More than 60 lakes lie in basins carved by glaciers, some faced with twisted marble in rainbow colors. The Eagle Cap wilderness is ideal country for hikers and horseback riders.

Wind River Drive, Wash. For about 15 miles the road runs northwest from the Columbia Gorge along the Wind River, at one spot crossing the river chasm on a suspension bridge strung 257 feet above the waterway. A side road leads to Goose Lake and a Forest Service lookout point that surveys vast stretches of forest and rugged peaks.

RELATED MUSEUMS AND ATTRACTIONS

Portland, Ore.
Hoyt Arboretum.
Oregon Museum of Science and Industry; natural history.

John Day Fossil Beds State Park, *Ore. (above). The peaked hill and its surroundings are part of a semiarid plateau that once was abundantly watered and wooded. Geologists—and casual visitors— can find signs of the ancient past: fossils of palm, breadfruit and cinnamon trees as well as vivid opals, jasper and petrified wood.*

Wallowa Lake, *Ore. (left). This crescent of water scoured out by glaciers is cupped by the foothills of magnificent Wallowa Mountain peaks, some over 10,000 feet and most bright with snowfields. The alpine landscape is a favorite with hikers and horseback riders, with trails that circle placid lakes and cross high-country passes.*

Mount Hood, *Ore. (right). Even when it appears only as a small triangle on the far horizon, Mount Hood is the special property of all Oregonians. Other peaks in the Cascades climb higher than its 11,235 feet, but none inspires greater affection. Here it rises in double image, mirrored perfectly in the calm waters of Lost Lake.*

Oregon Coast

OREGON

The broad Pacific slides up the golden sands of Crescent Beach, in Oregon's Ecola State Park.

Oregon
Coast

OREGON

Rocky Cliffs and Wide Beaches Line a Tempestuous Shore

Wave-cut arches leading into sun-flecked coves, and lone sea stacks crowned by ragged clumps of evergreen, are typical views along the 350

The elements of the Oregon coast are magnificent: 350 miles of jutting headlands and rocky reefs, sandy beaches, snug coves glittering with mirrorlike tide pools. In the middle of the coast lies a 50-mile swath of golden sand dunes. Behind the entire stretch of shore rises a 4000-foot mountain range, cut westward with 21 rushing white-water streams. Between the mountains and the sea, there is a lush evergreen forest of towering Douglas fir, spruce and hemlock, myrtle and cedar, and an understory of flowering rhododendrons and azaleas; the narrow plains are also dotted lavishly with freshwater lakes. Lakes and rivers contain steelhead and salmon, and the ocean and bays are populated with seals, sea otters, crustaceans, seabirds and waterfowl. And, best of all, this immense stretch of shoreline belongs to all Americans.

Long ago Oregon set aside its beaches as "public highways" to be used in perpetuity by the people of the state and the nation. Recently the state legislature strengthened this common-law concept by decreeing not only the right of the people to the beaches but to all dry sand areas to 16 feet above mean high tide. This secured for all time the public's right of access to the beaches—and barred further commercial development along the coast unless it was in the public interest.

To view this coastline in perspective you must go back to the four great ice ages in history, for it was during the Tertiary period of ice, volcanic flows and erosion that it was formed. The jutting headlands were sculptured by invasions of the sea cutting away at a gradually uplifting coastline. The repeated drowning of river mouths left shallow bays and narrow alluvial plains. Sand dunes formed at the mouths of many streams. The great agate beaches along the midcoast filled up the cavities in the lava flows.

The seas continue to sculpt the Oregon coast. Battered by winter storms, the sandy beaches shift and re-form, new outcroppings appear, and even the massive headlands erode. In our time a majestic arched rock north of Nye Beach called Jump Off Joe was completely swept away. Opposite Jump Off Joe a large

miles of magnificent shoreline that is Oregon's Pacific coast. Highway 101, from which this view was taken, runs the length of the coast, sometimes right above the water atop tall cliffs, sometimes beside broad beaches and sand dunes, sometimes swinging inland into the hills.

block began to slide into the sea about 30 years ago. The sea is still attacking this headland, and within a relatively short time it too will disappear forever.

Highway 101 parallels the full length of the Oregon coast, running past lonely beaches and basaltic headlands, swinging around jutting terraces with sheer, heart-stopping drops to the pounding surf below. Where the terrain proved too rugged for bulldozers, or the terraces are especially beautiful, the road ducks inland. Thirty-six state parks, many stretching for miles along the beachheads and terraces, march down the entire length of the ocean front—and

more are being built. On the rocky headlands and in sandy coves are a multitude of scenic turnouts, rest stops and picnic areas.

Traveling from north to south down the coast brings a rapid succession of outstanding scenes. Astoria, on Oregon's northern border, is steeped in western history. It was here, at the jaws of the Columbia River, that buckskin-clad fur traders established their stronghold. Lewis and Clark, after reaching the Pacific on their epic exploration, wintered at Fort Clatsop, which is now a National memorial to them. The Columbia River, the greatest salmon-producing stream in the world, and its adjacent

Starfish and anemones make a colorful still life at a beach tide pool. Such tide pools, teeming with marine creatures, fill rock hollows at low tide.

offshore waters are the salmon fishing center of the West for both sport and commercial fishermen, whose boats throng the ports.

Clatsop Beach, extending some 20 miles to Tillamook Head, is the first great seascape to the south. Razor clams on the gently sloping beaches draw summer visitors with shovel and pail to work the low tides. Driftwood piles high against the foredunes, left by the winter storms, and nonclammers beachcomb for bits of sculptured flotsam. Just below Seaside the Sunset Highway heads east, and near Necanicum Junction a blacktop side road leads from it up the steep slopes to Saddle Mountain State Park. The mountain's twin peaks form the highest point in the northern Coast Range; from a summit overlook reached by a winding trail there is a breathtaking panorama of the

Sea Lion Caves is a popular stopping place north of Florence. A herd of Steller's sea lions lives in the cave, and they often disport themselves on a ledge just above the sea—sharing it, as seen here, with a flock of cormorants. An elevator takes cave visitors down the cliff for a close-up view.

entire north coast. On a clear day you can see ships as far as 30 miles out at sea, and all the way up to the mouth of the Columbia.

From Tillamook Head to Cape Falcon are the first of a series of great headlands with scenic overlooks, interspersed with rocky coves and tide pools. Ecola and Oswald West state parks are the places for viewing them at close range. The mountains to the east are a haven for black-tailed deer, Roosevelt elk, black bear and a host of other mammals and birds. Winding paths and stairways lead down the rocky cliffs to beaches and tide pools below, or climb to overlooks some 400 feet up the cliffsides. Sea lions and seabirds live on the rocky islands and reefs offshore. Down in the tide pools, sculpins and blennies dart about, searching for morsels of food. Hermit and sand crabs scurry across the tidal floor, and limpets and spiral-shelled snails glide over the rocks. Green and brown seaweeds, some grown to great size, sway with the current, rippling like wheatfields in wind. Starfish and sea anemones splash a rainbow of brilliant colors in the depths.

At the jaws of Tillamook Bay winter storms explode with boiling surf against Kincheloe Point, a four-mile spit that separates the bay from the open sea. Battered spruce and shore pine lean at crazy angles along the spit, exhausted by the long struggle against the ocean. The once-thriving village of Bay Ocean has been all but abandoned, and several times in recent years high tides have seethed clear across the southern end of the spit near Cape Meares. It can only be a matter of time before the sea claims Kincheloe Point and opens a broad new entrance into the bay. South of Tillamook, 101 swings inland and does not touch the coast again until Lincoln City—though side roads flanked by rhododendrons branch off to overlooks at Cape Meares and Cape Lookout state parks.

From Lincoln City, 101 follows the coast through a rich spread of flowering rhododendron and windswept shore pine some 80 miles to Florence, at the mouth of the Siuslaw. The highway traverses high terraces overlooking the sea, with fine vistas of rocky reefs, picturesque coves and inlets. Some of the finest views in this section can be enjoyed at Boiler Bay, Pirate Cove, Otter Crest and Whale Cove. Sea Lion Caves is a favorite haunt of these delightful creatures, which they share with hundreds of cormorants. The underwater marine

Enjoying Oregon's Coast

A surf rider skims the waves below the dramatic silhouette of a rock arch at Cape Kiwanda. The water this far north is rather cold for swimming.

Halfway down the Oregon shore lies a 50-mile stretch of sand dunes, some reaching up to 90 feet. In some spots, as at right, they encroach on forest.

center on the waterfront at Yaquina provides an ideal introduction to the endlessly fascinating life of the coastal tide pools.

This reach of the ocean provides a fantastic display during storms and heavy surf, when the boiling water pounds the rocky reefs and headlands and climbs the steplike cliffs as if to destroy the terraces above. Spouting Horn, south of Yachats, is especially awesome as the seas surge into a rocky cavern and spew geysers of foam and spray into the sky.

Each tide uncovers new treasures for the rock hound along this stretch of coast: sparkling agates in all colors and shapes—the blue, green and gray of the sea, the coral, yellow and purple of a flamboyant Pacific sunset, or

the mysterious black agate, darker than the depths of the sea. The chalk cliffs here tell a vivid story of the many invasions of the sea, for layer upon layer of marine fossil remains are exposed. Fossil shells eroded out of the cliffs are strewn along the beaches or may be easily pried from the rocks. It is not difficult for the amateur paleontologist to add to his collection marine fossils of the Pliocene, Miocene and Oligocene epochs, laid down 12 to 40 million years ago.

Just below Florence the seascape changes character. The jutting headlands soften into a 50-mile reach of low foredunes behind which lie mountains of golden sand dunes extending about three miles inland. The high points in

this constantly shifting desert are the 90-foot rolling dunes just to the west of Woahink and Cleawox lakes. Strong winds continue to move the sands inland, drowning evergreen forests in their path. Shore pine and Sitka spruce stand half buried in mountains of sand, mute evidence of the eastward invasion. Tourist-filled dune buggies roller-coaster over the sand; hikers, emulating desert prospectors, carry canteens in their packs as they trek across the arid landscape toward the sea.

A vast freshwater lake system parallels the dunes on the narrow plain to the east. Shining jewels strung out in a green velvet furrow, from the air the lakes look like many-legged starfish, their arms curling into winding can-

yons and creek bottoms. It is difficult to predict the fate of the Oregon dunes and the freshwater lakes behind them. Recently designated a National Recreation Area, this superb combination of sand and water seems doomed to lose its primitive charm when it is developed to serve large numbers of people.

South of Coos Bay—the West's main lumber port—101 strikes inland across rolling mountains, then rides the high terraces another 30 miles to Port Orford, a snug little harbor sheltered from the north by a hooking cape called The Heads. Loop or side roads, some little more than trails through dense jungles of azaleas and blueblossom, lead to breathtaking vistas several hundred feet above the sea, or to secluded beach and tide-pool sanctuaries. Cape Arago, 200 feet high, overlooks beautiful coves below and Simpson Reef offshore. Sea otters and sea lions play around the reefs, easily observed from headlands. Cliffs, islands and reefs darken at times with a noisy influx of sea and surf birds. The Seven Devils road south from Charleston follows high terraces a mile or so behind the cliff heads, whose bases are cloaked with garnet, zircon, chromite, gold and platinum black sands. Several unimproved roads lead to overlooks with magnificent views of the wild coast at Secchi Beach, Agate Beach and Whiskey Run. The routes were traveled by gold prospectors, and evidence of their mining activities is seen in numerous old diggings, open pits along backcountry roads.

From Gold Beach, where the Rogue River ends its spectacular journey to the sea (and where exciting river trips up to Agness begin), south to the California line is probably the most rugged stretch of the coast. Rocky reefs and jagged headlands prevail, and the countless tiny coves and grottoes hardly ever see a human visitor.

Perhaps the most imposing seascape, as well as the westernmost point on the Oregon coast, is Cape Blanco, a flat, grassy terrace that juts two miles out to sea near Port Orford. From the air it looks like a broad-based steeple with a circular dome on its tip. Two-hundred-foot cliffs drop abruptly to surging surf below. Where the narrow road crosses the knifelike tip to the dome beyond it gives one the feeling of riding a steel beam at the top of a skyscraper. Overlooks provide a view of Blanco Reef directly offshore and Orford Reef to the south. Castle, Gull and Tower rocks, surrounded by reefs, thrust from the foaming sea to the north of the cape.

This stirring vista shows the Oregon coast at its best. And despite the crush of civilization in some areas, most of the coast is like that: primitive and hauntingly beautiful, it remains one of the glories of our West.

On the Oregon coast the sun seems to drop into the sea. Here, at a typical wide beach, it lights a cheerful family scene. Since the land faces westward, it takes the brunt of heavy winter storms whipped up by the prevailing westerly winds. In winter this can be a bleak and lonely shore.

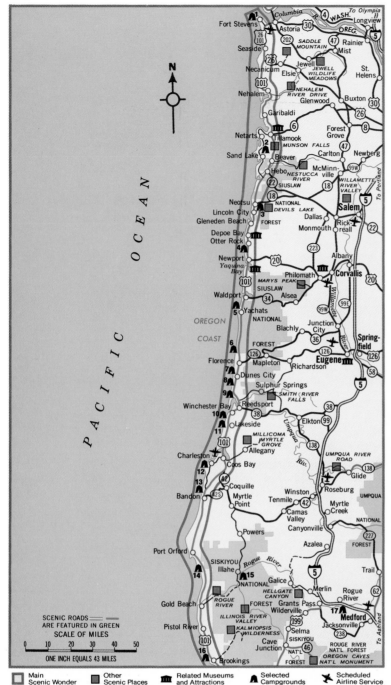

SCENIC ROADS ——
ARE FEATURED IN GREEN
SCALE OF MILES

0 10 20 30 40 50
ONE INCH EQUALS 43 MILES

☐ Main
Scenic Wonder ■ Other
Scenic Places 🏛 Related Museums
and Attractions ▲ Selected
Campgrounds ✈ Scheduled
Airline Service

Illinois River Valley. The rapids of the Illinois River run through Siskiyou National Forest in a deep, narrow canyon before joining the Rogue. A scenic road follows the river from Selma to just below Illinois Falls.

Jewell Wildlife Meadows. Roosevelt elk, black bear and many native birds can all be observed from special vantage points along the nature trails in this outstanding wildlife area near Astoria.

Kalmiopsis Wilderness. This mountainous area in south Oregon is noted for its remarkable abundance of rare flowers. Rarest of all is the Kalmiopsis leachiania, a living fossil from the Tertiary period, which began 65 million years ago. A member of the heath family, its flower resembles a rhododendron.

Marys Peak. At 4097 feet this mountain in Siuslaw National Forest is the highest point in the Coast Range. Its summit, reached by a side road from the Alsea River highway, has a panoramic view of surrounding peaks and toward the distant Pacific.

Millicoma Myrtle Grove. Not far from the city of Coos Bay a small state park preserves a stand of the rare and beautiful Oregon myrtle trees.

Munson Falls.
(*Picture appears on page 450*)

Nehalem River Drive. Deer, elk and other wildlife are often visible from this scenic road, lined with stands of Douglas fir and hemlock, with an understory of fern. The drive runs from the river's mouth to Sunset Highway at Elsie, then down the north fork of the river from Necanicum Junction to Nehalem Bay.

Nestucca River. This fine coastal stream, named for a local Indian tribe, is famed for its superb salmon and steelhead fishing and sea-run cutthroats. A number of hatcheries are open to visitors.

Oregon Caves National Monument.
(*Picture appears on page 451*)

WITHIN A DAY'S DRIVE:

Salmon Runs and Rare Flowers

Devils Lake. This lake at the edge of Siuslaw National Forest has excellent fishing, and a state park on its shore. The shortest river in the world, "D" River, flows the 400 yards between Devils Lake and the Pacific.

Hellgate Canyon. As the Rogue River leaves the mountains, it is forced between high rock walls only 20 to 30 feet apart; their jutting fingers make river navigation a real trial of skill. Jet boats depart from Grants Pass.

449

Rogue River.
(Picture appears on facing page)

Saddle Mountain. This twin-peaked mountain is the highest point in the northern Coast Range. A trail runs to the summit where there is a spectacular view of the Columbia River and the Pacific.

Smith River Falls. Fanning out over a series of steps sculptured in smooth sandstone, the river spills into pools below, which are popular for swimming.

Umpqua River Road. From the town of Wilbur this scenic drive winds up the North Umpqua into the mountains—and ultimately to Crater Lake National Park. The Umpqua River canyon deepens and becomes wilder beyond Idleyld Park.

Willamette River Valley. The wide valley of rolling farm and timberland lies between the Coast Range and the rugged Cascades. Shady Champoeg State Park is typical of several lovely valley parks. A scenic loop drive can be taken along the back roads northwest of Salem.

RELATED MUSEUMS AND ATTRACTIONS

Corvallis. Oregon State University Museum of Natural History.

Depoe Bay. The Aquarium.

Eugene. University of Oregon Museum of Natural History.

Tillamook. Natural History Museum.

Yaquina Bay. Marine Gardens.

Rogue River (*above*). *This swift river of deep canyons, rushing rapids and somber forest walls is best seen by boat. Daily excursions cover the 32-mile trip through increasingly wild country from the river's mouth at Gold Beach up to Agness and back. Boats also go beyond Agness to explore the remote upper reaches.*

Munson Falls (*facing page*). *The waters of Munson Creek spill in a narrow silvery cascade between dark walls of evergreen forest in the foothills of the Coast Range six miles south of Tillamook.*

Oregon Caves National Monument (*right*). *A labyrinthine limestone cave on the slopes of Mount Elijah is the feature here; it is surrounded by nearly 500 acres of forested highlands laced with trails. These formations are in the 60-foot-high Paradise Lost room.*

Crater Lake
NATIONAL PARK, OREGON

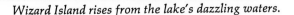
Wizard Island rises from the lake's dazzling waters.

OREGON

Crater
Lake

Sapphire Symmetry in a Flooded Volcano

How blue is blue, and how deep is deep? Both the answers lie in the depths of Crater Lake, which gleams among the wooded slopes of the Cascade Mountains in southern Oregon. If the sun is shining and the sky is clear, the lake's waters take on an almost incandescent blue glow; even under cloudy skies the intensity of the color is still remarkable. Only Switzerland's Lake Lucerne can compare. As for depth, Crater is the deepest lake in the United States. At its lowest point it registers 1932 feet by sonic depth finder—a figure difficult to grasp until you realize that it means the lake is about as deep as the mountainous slopes that surround it are high—2000 feet, or more than a third of a mile.

There is a direct relationship between the lake's brilliant color and remarkable depth. On a clear day the sun's red, orange, yellow and finally green wavelengths are all absorbed, while only blue is ultimately reflected up from the depths. And the purity of the water also contributes to the blueness. It is claimed to be 20 times as pure as most drinking water, and a Crater Lake National Park naturalist urges his audience in an hourly talk high above the lake: "Drink it if you get down there."

Ever since prospector John Wesley Hillman first came upon the lake in 1853 as he searched for a rumored gold mine, man has struggled to describe its remarkable color and symmetry— usually in vain. Hillman tried, but gave up:

"The vast loneliness of the place, the sparkling water so many feet below, the beautiful view . . . are too great to be described; one must see them to appreciate them." He named it Deep Blue Lake, appropriately enough.

William Gladstone Steel was even more reverent. Arriving in 1885, after the lake's name had been changed to Crater, he declared: "It is unique in all the world. The day is coming when people of all nations will arrive to view its grandeur, then return to their homes to wonder that such things can be." He led a 17-year campaign to make the area a national park; and after he succeeded, in 1902, he became one of its first superintendents.

Inevitably, a place as startlingly beautiful as Crater Lake acquired its Indian legends. And Klamath Indian mythology helps shed light on the actual story of the lake's creation. The Indians saw ancient Mount Mazama, the 12,000-foot volcano whose caldera, or collapsed summit, is now filled with the lake, as a passageway between the worlds above and below. Llao, the chief of the underworld, had just retreated inside when his enemies tossed a mountaintop over the passageway to seal his exit forever. The crater left by this huge impact filled with water and became a shrine of peace. Actually, the top of Mazama was demolished by an enormous volcanic eruption about 6000 years ago which covered everything for 35 miles around with pumice and ash and left a caldera five miles across and 4000 feet deep. This eventually filled halfway up with rain and melting snow, and the blue water has stayed at about the same level ever since (see the drawings below).

The name of Crater Lake actually comes from the smaller crater on Wizard Island, which rises from the lake.

William Steel's prophecy of the crowds that would come from everywhere to see the lake has materialized in this age of the jet and the trailer—though the national park's location, a round-trip drive of several hours off the main interstate highway between Canada and California, has kept attendance down to a comfortable level of around 600,000 visitors a year. Although 50 feet of snow fall here every winter, the south and west entrances to the park and the road to the rim are kept open; and the sight of the blue water gleaming amid the snow is perhaps even more thrilling than the summer view. There is even skiing on the park slopes—with trails, but without lifts—and the coffee shop stays open amid the snow, though no winter accommodation is available.

The seasons here are basically an eight-month winter, a brief and delightful summer in July and August, and an even shorter spring and fall. Throughout, the hemlock, fir and pine that cover the pumice slopes around the lake stay green. Much of the park's activity centers upon Rim Village, the cluster of buildings on the southwest slope above the lake near where Hillman first set eyes on it. Anyone who has the time should certainly take the one-way, 33-mile drive all round the rim of the crater. Highlights of the drive include the Watchman, an excellent viewpoint with a museum devoted

This tiny rocky projection jutting steeply from the deep blue water and crowned with bright evergreens is known because of its outline as Phantom Ship.

The Volcano That Exploded

Crater Lake actually occupies a caldera rather than a crater; this is the collapsed cone of a volcano. The volcano containing Crater Lake was once a towering 12,000 feet, and known as Mount Mazama. In a tremendously powerful eruption about 6000 years ago the volcano ejected huge quantities of lava; at the same time cracks opened beneath the volcano and drained away several cubic miles of the molten material inside. Mount Mazama was so emptied out by these ejections and drainings that there was no longer any base to support its cone, which collapsed into the hollow interior, leaving the present great basin. Eventually this filled with water, creating the lake.

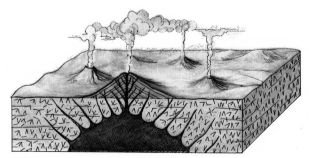

ABOUT A MILLION YEARS AGO MOUNT MAZAMA RISES FROM A VOLCANIC FOUNDATION TO A HEIGHT OF OVER 12,000 FEET.

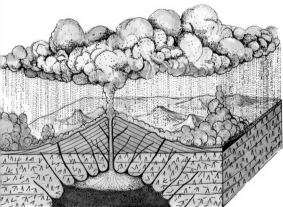

ABOUT 6,000 YEARS AGO MOUNT MAZAMA ERUPTS, COVER-
ING AN AREA OF 350,000 SQUARE MILES WITH PUMICE.

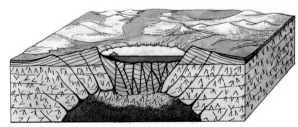

AFTER THE ERUPTION THE VOLCANO'S PEAK COLLAPSES INTO
THE DRAINED MAGMA CHAMBER; A LAKE FORMS IN THE CRATER.

to the park's natural history; Hillman Peak, highest point on the rim at 8156 feet; Cloud-cap, with a remarkable view over the lake's surrounding mountains, including twin-peaked Mount Scott; and the Pinnacles, striking spires of pumice and tuff that rise 200 feet above Wheeler Creek Canyon.

At the Cleetwood Trail, about halfway around the lake, you can walk down just over a mile to Cleetwood Cove, where launch trips go out on the lake several times a day in summer. They stop at Wizard Island, a miniature volcano close to the western shore on which trees 900 years old clothe the slopes.

For people who want to linger in the park —or perhaps wait for a sunny day to see the lake at its shining best—there are three camp-grounds around the caldera rim and lodge accommodation at Rim Village. And even people who just want to make a flying visit and take a wide-eyed look at the lake from the nearest viewpoint will find some beguiling wildlife on hand. Golden-mantled squirrels, often confused with chipmunks, and noisy Clark's nut-crackers are persistent beggars wherever park visitors gather.

Wilder wildlife includes ravens, eagles and falcons, sometimes seen swooping over the lake. Deer and bears can occasionally be glimpsed, usually at a considerable distance. Now and then a Cascade red fox, coyote, pine marten or bobcat shows itself and, even more rarely, a cougar. According to early visitors, the lake contained no fish, but several species have subsequently been introduced. Rainbow and brown trout and kokanee salmon are holding their own, though their numbers have never grown much because of a lack of suitable spawning grounds and adequate food. So pure is the lake water that it can support little life, though aquatic moss has been found at a record depth of 425 feet. Those who wish to try may fish without a license, though there is a daily limit of 10.

But basically the lake is simply a place to look at, and to listen to the remarkable story of its origins, told in regular naturalist talks at the Sinnott Memorial Overlook. The sight of the lake's blue symmetry, and the thought of the awesome fire and destruction that gave it birth thousands of years ago, are a potent mixture for the imagination.

A winter snowfall enhances the vivid color of Crater Lake and the dramatic isolation of Wizard Island, a miniature cone rising in the middle of the watery caldera. Winters in this part of Oregon are long and snowfall in the Cascades is heavy, but one road into the park is kept open all year.

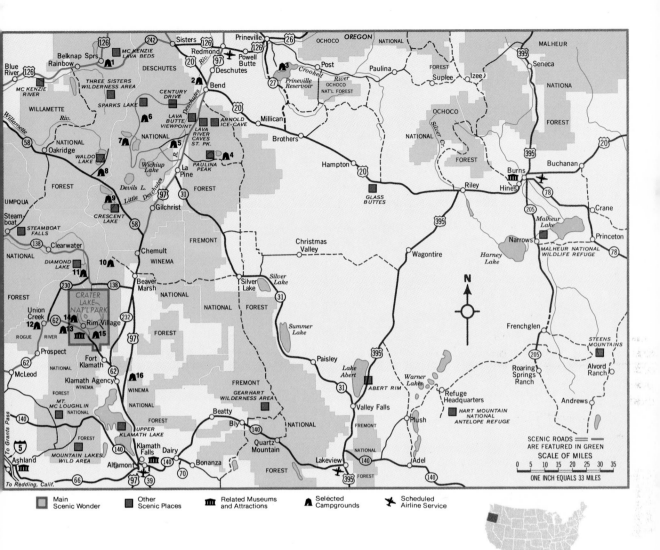

WITHIN A DAY'S DRIVE:

Volcanic Vistas, Clear Lakes and Mountain Highways

Abert Rim. Some geologists regard this ridge, several miles long and 2500 feet high, as one of the largest earthquake faults in the world. It is followed closely by U.S. Highway 395, from which there are many fine views of the rim and Lake Abert, a large saline lake spreading out below the base of the fault.

Arnold Ice Cave. Conifers and sage surround the cave hollowed from an underground river of lava. Its depths, once seething cauldrons of molten basalt, are so cold that the ice inside never thaws, even in summer.

Century Drive. Sparkling lakes, quiet mountain meadows, snow-capped peaks, swift streams and majestic pine forests can be seen along this 100-mile circuit, one of Oregon's most scenic drives. Wildlife, including mule deer and Roosevelt elk, is abundant.

Crescent Lake. This 4000-acre glacial lake is an important habitat for bald eagles and ospreys. Trails lead into the nearby Diamond Peak Wilderness to connect with the Pacific Crest National Scenic Trail and several smaller lakes. Cowhorn Mountain serves as a lofty backdrop.

Diamond Lake. Mounts Thielsen and Bailey flank this crystalline lake—one of the favorite beauty spots in the Oregon Cascades, and more heavily developed than other high-country lakes.

Gearhart Wilderness Area. Spectacular lava formations, including pillars, columns and toadstool rocks, along with impressive 400-foot cliffs, are found in the area's southeast section.

Glass Buttes. Midway between Bend and Burns on Highway 20, a dramatic thrust, comprised mostly of obsidian, rises abruptly

457

above the plateau. Pearly hues and shades of red and green give color accents to the predominantly black buttes.

Hart Mountain National Antelope Refuge. Pronghorn antelope share the 240,000-acre refuge with bighorn sheep, mule deer and over 200 bird species. Hart Mountain itself is a massive volcanic ridge towering out of the plains to more than 8000 feet.

Lava Butte Viewpoint. Many of the major Cascades peaks are visible from the summit of this small cinder cone. Flora and lava formations of the area are identified along a trail around the crater inside the butte.

Lava River Caves State Park. The turbulent volcanic era that produced Crater Lake also formed these caves. Nearly a mile long and 50 feet wide, the main cave is one of the finest examples of a lava tube or tunnel. The walls are glazed with molten lava, and lava drips hang from the ceiling.

McKenzie Lava Beds. Black, contorted lava flows cover a spectacular 65 square miles of mountain slopes, ridges and valleys near McKenzie Pass. Lava gutters, pressure ridges and crevasses are seen from the summit of McKenzie Highway.

McKenzie River. Oregon's most beautiful white-water river is paralleled by Highway 126 and a river trail which both provide excellent river views through the old-growth Douglas firs that line its banks. The upper portion of the river, between Blue River and Clear Lake, is the finest.

Malheur National Wildlife Refuge. One of the great areas of the West for wildlife study, photography and observation, the vast shallow marshes, lakes and sagebrush uplands here have a wide variety of migratory waterfowl, game and shore birds and several species of mammals.

Mountain Lakes Wild Area. The area derives its name from the numerous beautifully colored mountain lakes bounded on all sides by lofty peaks—the highest of them Aspen Butte at 8265 feet. Access is from well-maintained trails restricted to hikers and horseback riders.

Mount McLoughlin. The dominant peak in southern Oregon towers 9495 feet skyward. For the adventurous, a trail leads to the summit for unsurpassed views.

Upper Klamath Lake. *Oregon's largest freshwater lake is noted for its vast tule marshes. Bald eagles and ospreys are often spotted from the highway that skirts the wildlife refuge at the lake's western end.*

Three Sisters Wilderness Area. *The glacial peaks that give the area its name are all over 10,000 feet and are probably the most photographed in Oregon. Here, sunrise gleams on Middle (right) and North Sisters.*

Paulina Peak. At 7985 feet, this is the highest point on the rim of wide Newberry Crater, now filled with Paulina and East lakes. The view from here over the lakes, and an awesome Cascades panorama, is outstanding.

Sparks Lake. Lush meadows that provide forage for mule deer and Roosevelt elk surround the serene 600-acre lake. The view of South Sister Mountain from the southern shore is a favorite one.

Steamboat Falls. The falls are only about 20 feet high, but the interest here is in watching the dramatic leaps of steelhead trout as they climb upriver to spawn. The campground offers the best view of this.

Steens Mountains. The highest land in southeast Oregon, at over 9000 feet, this 100-mile range is a rugged place of sudden dramatic summer storms. A loop road follows the crest from Frenchglen, 5000 feet above the barren potash of Alvord Desert.

Three Sisters Wilderness Area. *(Picture appears on facing page)*

Upper Klamath Lake. *(Picture appears on this page)*

Waldo Lake. Snowcapped Diamond Peak rises on the horizon beyond this pristine lake. Oregon's largest natural high country lake, it offers a rare combination of wildness and accessibility.

RELATED MUSEUMS AND ATTRACTIONS

Ashland. Southern Oregon Museum of Natural Resources; natural history.

Burns. Malheur National Wildlife Refuge Museum.

Crater Lake. National Park Museum.

Klamath Falls. Klamath County Museum; natural history.

Redwood National Park

CALIFORNIA

A back road curves among the towering redwoods.

Our Tallest Trees Survive the Ax

The coast redwood: *Sequoia sempervirens.* No superlative can take the measure of these living giants that connect earth and sky in Redwood National Park. The oldest of them boast as many as 2000 annual rings, and in height they are unsurpassed. One tree, for instance, has been measured at 367.8 feet—already the tallest known living thing in creation and still in its prime, green and growing.

All along the 300-mile drive from San Francisco to the park entrance north of Eureka, starting with the famous Muir Woods just across the Golden Gate, you can find isolated groves of ancient redwoods. For it is only in these lowland hills and valleys between the coastal mountains and the Pacific, moistened by as much as 100 inches of annual rain and heavy fog, that the redwood flourishes.

These scattered redwood parks and preserves are the remnants of a great forest that once blanketed some two million acres—3125 square miles—of the northern California coast, from Big Sur country all the way to the Oregon line. But the arrival of large numbers of settlers in the 19th century inaugurated a period of reckless exploitation. The result was that the two million acres of virgin redwood forest had been reduced to 300,000 acres by 1965. Of these, only 58,000 acres—90 square miles—were given sanctuary in the 46-mile-long strip of Redwood National Park in 1968, after more than 40 years of dedicated effort by

461

Driftwood lies piled on Gold Beach, an idyllic spot for beachcombers. Much of the timber here is from dead trees and limbs washed down coastal creeks to the sea, then cast back up by the tide. Gold Bluff, a line of rugged cliffs, backs the five-mile beach, adjacent to Prairie Creek park.

conservationists. And the remaining redwoods —including some old-growth giants—are still in great demand. So even today, driving on California Route 101, you will share the road with an endless procession of giant trucks heavy-laden with truncated old-growth redwoods on their way to the sawmill.

The fact that the national park does not come close to including all the remaining old-growth redwoods is evidence of the power of the timber industry; in the opinion of many, its efforts have resulted in a park too limited to offer a satisfactory experience of the giant trees to its increasing numbers of visitors. Some foresters also protest that the park is incomplete as an ecological unit, and that the long-term survival of its trees is endangered. From the casual tourist's point of view, however, there are lots of redwoods left to enjoy.

Until federal consolidation of the area is completed, Redwood National Park is simply a collection of three existing state parks, still

Rhododendrons cluster around the massive trunks of redwoods in Del Norte, one of the three state parks that are combined in Redwood National Park.

under state administration, connected and enlarged by formerly private lands on which commercial logging operations and other "nonconforming uses" are being eliminated.

From south to north, the three redwood state parks are Prairie Creek, just north of Orick, and Del Norte Coast and Jedediah Smith, near Crescent City and the Oregon border. Each provides information services, well-equipped campgrounds and miles of clearly marked trails that offer a half hour's stroll, a full day's march or anything in between.

Once in the redwood forest, you will find life on three levels. Far above you the crowns of the redwoods, sometimes mixed with Douglas fir, form an almost unbroken canopy. Below, in clearings or places where the canopy allows the sunlight to filter through, an understory of younger redwoods and firs, tan oak and madrona lives in the shelter of the giants. In the deep, moist duff that carpets the forest floor grow shrubs like huckleberry, salal, blue blossom, wood rose and thimbleberry. In the spring the California rosebay rhododendron gives a display of its red-purple flowers that attracts thousands of tourists. Most spectacu-

463

lar, perhaps, are the ferns, which turn acres of forest floor into a jungle of green. Fern Canyon, in Prairie Creek Park, leads you between 50-foot cliffs bright with ferns, right to the beach.

In this bosky stronghold, craning your neck to gaze upward, it is easy to imagine yourself among the soaring pillars of one of the great cathedrals of Europe. The tree trunks are bare of branches for 150 feet and more, and from below they seem to lean in a sheltering circle far above your head.

You may be surprised to learn from the fallen foliage which litters the ground that the leaf of this giant tree is a tiny half to three quarters of an inch long, arranged in delicate, flat sprays, and that its cones are no larger than a good-sized olive. Despite its size, the cone produces plenty of seeds to perpetuate the species, but they are largely superfluous: the great tree reproduces most readily by sprouting nodes on its wide-spreading roots, or from seed-

ing in the stumps and trunks of fallen trees. Typically, redwood progeny cluster around the parent, forming spectacular groves, or "family circles," of mixed-generation trees.

If undisturbed by man's technology, the redwood forest forms an almost imperturbable ecosystem. Trees topple occasionally when high winds pull at their crowns, levering their shallow roots out of the ground; sometimes one falls under its own immense weight. Otherwise the trees seem indifferent to time itself. Direct hits by lightning may behead a tree repeatedly; ground fires may scar its trunk, even burn a tunnel through it; but the tree lives on. Even the redwood's genetic identity is unchanged in 30 million years.

Other national parks may offer a greater variety of spectacular landscapes and natural curiosities; but Redwood testifies to the persistence of life itself—against the odds of time, the elements and man's destructive ingenuity.

A dramatic reminder of the destruction Redwood National Park was designed to avert: near Prairie Creek, loggers have stripped the area in the fore-ground, while the great trees stand untouched in the background. Only a fifth of our remaining redwoods are protected by inclusion in the park.

Giants of the Western Evergreen Forest

The giant sequoia is the largest living thing in terms of sheer bulk, although it does not grow so tall as the coast redwood; both, incidentally, are members of the Sequoia family. The tallest known coast redwood is 367.8 feet, and still growing. The Douglas fir is one of the most common trees in the great evergreen forests of the West; the coastal form may grow to 300 feet, with a trunk 15 feet in diameter, but the mountain form, found in the Rockies, is only a third that size. The Port Orford cedar (commonly miscalled Lawson's cypress) is a particularly lovely conifer, with typical cedar fronds instead of needles. The Sitka spruce, with stiff, blue-green leaves that project from the twig in all directions, is found only along the West Coast.

GIANT SEQUOIA
Sequoia gigantea

COAST REDWOOD
Sequoia sempervirens

DOUGLAS FIR
Pseudotsuga taxifolia

PORT ORFORD CEDAR
Chamaecyparis lawsoniana

SITKA SPRUCE
Picea sitchensis

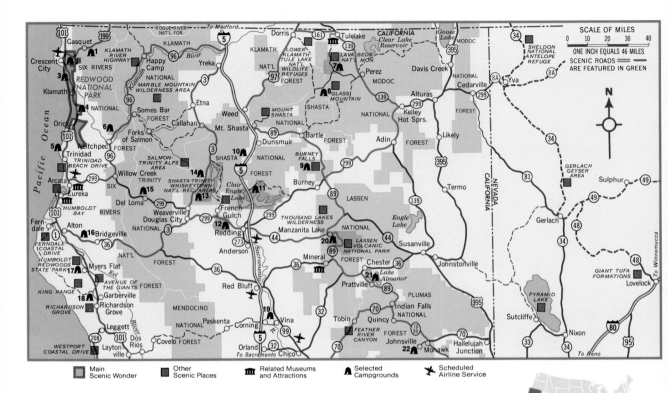

Main Scenic Wonder Other Scenic Places Related Museums and Attractions Selected Campgrounds Scheduled Airline Service

WITHIN A DAY'S DRIVE:

A Wild and Lonely Coast, Fine Forests and a Desert Lake

Avenue of the Giants, Calif. From Garberville north for roughly 30 miles, old Route 101 winds along the Eel River through groves of gargantuan redwoods. A leisurely drive leaves time for exploring turnouts and hiking trails.

Burney Falls, Calif. Burney Creek bubbles up through lava rock, divides in two and cascades 130 feet into an emerald-green pool. Little side falls, amid ferns and mosses, gush from the porous rock, while swifts dart to nests hidden behind the falls.

Feather River Canyon, Calif. *(Picture appears on facing page)*

Ferndale Coastal Drive, Calif. The highway crosses grassy hills to the rockbound shore at Capetown, follows the coast, then climbs inland through mountain forests. It is a ride through unspoiled country, remote enough for abundant wildlife.

Gerlach Geyser Area, Nev. Little known even to local residents, the area is the bizarre province of hot springs and erupting geysers, dramatic visual reminders of the earth's inner turmoil.

Giant Tufa Formations, Nev. These odd outcroppings are one of many clues that a sea once filled this region: rocks are coated with tufa, a deposit formed when warm, salty waters evaporate.

Glass Mountain, Calif. Lava flows and pine forests share the sweeping high-country landscape, but the mountain is best known for its slabs of shiny obsidian, the black glasslike stone Indians used to fashion into arrowheads.

Humboldt Bay, Calif. Mud flats, sandy shorelines, salt marshes and eelgrass beds make the bay a favorite winter home for waterfowl and shorebirds—and rookeries of egrets and herons.

Humboldt Redwoods State Park, Calif. Campgrounds, picnic spots and hiking trails encourage visitors to linger in a noble stand of ancient redwoods. The most imposing grove rises along Bull Creek, in the Rockefeller Forest.

King Range, Calif. Between Shelter Cove and Punta Gorda, mountains meet the sea, creating a backcountry wilderness ideal for outdoor pleasures: beachcombing, surf-fishing and skindiving along the shore; camping, picnicking and bird-watching inland.

Klamath River Highway, Calif. For over 100 miles Route 96 follows the Klamath River, winding through deep canyons and tall forests rich with wildlife. Anglers fish for trout and salmon, and swimmers enjoy secluded pools.

Lassen Volcanic National Park, Calif. *(Picture appears on page 469)*

Feather River Canyon, *Calif. Folds of richly wooded hills line the swift-flowing river in a succession of steep slopes. For close to 50 miles a highway* *runs along this canyon, and drivers can linger at campgrounds and picnic areas or simply admire the river's changes of mood between pools and rapids.*

Lava Beds National Monument, Calif. Trails lead to lava flows and caves, cinder cones, buttes and miniature volcanoes, a fascinating moonscape that also harbors bighorn sheep and coyotes.

Lower Klamath–Tule Lake National Wildlife Refuges, Calif. Thousands of ducks, geese and other waterfowl migrate here in autumn and spring or find refuge all year. Other wildlife includes deer and great horned owls.

Marble Mountain Wilderness Area, Calif. Alpine meadows, forested hills and about 80 trout lakes fill the isolated mile-high landscape. Hikers walk trails through groves of oaks and evergreens, and campers find small lakes they can keep to themselves.

Mount Shasta, Calif.
(*Picture appears on this page*)

Pyramid Lake, Nev.
(*Picture appears on this page*)

Richardson Grove, Calif. In one of the first important redwood parks north of San Francisco, the old forest monarchs grow right up to the highway. The park also offers hiking trails, picnic areas and swimming in the Eel River.

Salmon–Trinity Alps Area, Calif. More than 285,000 acres here encompass soaring granite peaks, high-flung meadows, nearly 90 trout-filled lakes and plenty of clear streams. Ptarmigans, wolverines, fishers and martens are among the rare wild inhabitants to be glimpsed along the trails.

Shasta–Trinity–Whiskeytown National Recreation Areas, Calif. Three huge man-made lakes lie among manzanita-covered hills and pine-forested slopes. Spotted

around each lake are picnic areas, beaches and viewpoints.

Sheldon National Antelope Refuge, Nev. High desert land shelters animals like mule deer, jackrabbits, sage grouse and kangaroo rats, but its main tenants are pronghorn antelopes, the fastest of America's four-footed animals.

Thousand Lakes Wilderness, Calif. Although nobody has ever counted 1000 lakes here, the impression of a vast number persists: lava potholes, bogs, ponds and lakes spangle the roadless 15,515 acres, all laced by trails that thread through gentle wooded valleys and rough lava rock.

Trinidad Beach Drive, Calif. From Trinidad north for 20 miles the coast offers a wealth of wildlife and water sports. Sea lions bark from rocky perches, seals bob in

Mount Shasta, *Calif. Perpetually cloaked in glacial snows, the 14,162-foot peak, an extinct volcano, towers over the misty evergreen forests, jewel-like lakes and lava-covered rocks that surround its foothills. It dominates the countryside for more than 100 miles.*

Pyramid Lake, *Nev. The largest natural lake in Nevada, the royal blue waters are the remains of a prehistoric lake. Two islands break its glossy surface: the small triangle of rock that inspired its name, and a flat, broad island that is a white pelican sanctuary.*

the surf, waterfowl float in lagoons and marshes. A string of coastal lagoons are ideal for water skiers and the beaches for beachcombers.

Westport Coastal Drive, Calif. Windswept rocks, sandy beaches and tide pools fill this coast road with a variety of splendid seascapes. Parks along the way lure hikers and campers.

RELATED MUSEUMS AND ATTRACTIONS

Arcata, Calif. Humboldt State University; fish hatchery, wildlife pens and geology museums.

Eureka, Calif. Clarke Museum; bird collection.

Mineral, Calif. Lassen Volcanic National Park, Loomis Museum.

Tulelake, Calif. Lava Beds National Monument Museum.

Lassen Volcanic National Park, *Calif. A broken tree trunk stands as a reminder that about 50 years ago Lassen Peak exploded and poured out hot lava. Now snowfields and virgin forest blanket its slopes.*

Yosemite National Park

CALIFORNIA

Glowing with autumn colors, trees frame the sheer cliffs of Half Dome above the Merced River.

CALIFORNIA

Yosemite
National
Park

Falls Leap into a High Valley in One of the West's Great Panoramas

Yosemite National Park is one of the proudest treasures of America's national park system. And the seven-square-mile valley secluded in the granite fastness of its western flank is like a rare diamond locked in stone.

For conservationists, the park is historically important because its establishment in 1864 by President Lincoln made it the first of the state preserves that later became part of the national park system. Yosemite is especially revered as the favorite shrine of John Muir, the great Scots-born naturalist and conservationist. He came to the park in 1868, and during the rest of his long life he lived and visited there often. Some say he died of a broken heart in 1914 after an arduous losing battle to save the Hetch Hetchy Valley, one of the park's wonders, from being drowned by a reservoir.

Even as you enter Yosemite Valley, you will understand immediately why Muir claimed for the region "the most songful streams in the world . . . the noblest forests . . . the loftiest granite domes . . . the deepest ice-sculptured canyons." California routes 41, 120 and 140 converge on the western end of the valley, delivering you at one of the world's most astonishing vistas: a wide-screen, three-dimensional panorama of primeval nature that fills the eye and stops the breath. At your left, the sheer granite face of El Capitan dominates the lower valley, rising in monolithic majesty more than

Leaning out like a daredevil over Yosemite Valley, Glacier Point offers high-altitude views of Yosemite Falls, a double drop that plunges 2425 feet.

3600 feet from its floor. At its feet the Merced River—the River of Mercy—flows fast or slow, loud or soft, according to the season, and from the towering valley walls its tributaries hurl themselves from high-hanging streambeds into the abyss.

The picture-postcard panorama is irresistible, drawing you toward it, down into the valley where you can examine each of its marvels separately and from different angles of view in ever-changing perspective. But, as John Muir wrote, "One must labor for beauty as for bread, here as elsewhere," and in the valley your insulated and comfortable automobile will therefore be more hindrance than help. Dividing your attention between the busy roadway ahead and the breathtaking scenery on either side will prove both dangerous and frustrating. Even passengers will find the valley's battlements truncated by the car's low windshield and windows. Stay in your car, then, and you risk missing the very sightseeing experience you have come to enjoy.

Indeed, the automobile and its accompanying roads and services have been a subject of controversy almost since cars were first admitted to the valley in 1914, after a debate that John Muir described as "a prodigious lot of gaseous commercial eloquence." That first year, 127 vehicles came; some 50 years later, on the Fourth of July alone, 54,700 auto-borne visitors crowded into the valley. Meanwhile the valley floor has accumulated a certain amount of urban sprawl, all interconnected by an extensive road network: two grocery and general stores;

Snow bends trees and transforms branches into icy lacework, but El Capitan, a sleek granite fortress, rears straight up, unruffled by seasonal moods.

A golden sunset glow shrouds Yosemite's lofty walls and silhouettes the dark shapes of the trees lining the motionless waters of the Merced River.

two post offices, a photo studio and a hospital; two gas stations and other services; overnight accommodations—hotels, lodges, cabins, campgrounds—for about 4500 tourists.

Recently, however, the Park Service has initiated steps to curtail increasing congestion in the valley, especially in the summer months when campgrounds overflow and traffic is bumper to bumper. While discussions continue about actually moving some of the tourist facilities out of the fragile, overstressed valley altogether, the Park Service has already set up a one-way road system in the valley and banned private cars from the eastern end of the valley, beyond Curry Village.

A recently inaugurated system of free shuttle buses offers a partial solution to the prob-
lems of overcrowding: frequent loop tours run through the most scenic areas. Some of the specially designed buses have open-air seating on the top deck; all have extra-large window openings to give unimpeded views. And they make frequent stops at all points of special interest, providing the opportunity to explore on foot to your heart's content—or your legs' endurance—with the assurance that another bus will be along shortly to take you farther, or return you to the parking lot where you have left your car or to your campsite or hotel.

The floor of Yosemite Valley is a pedestrian's pleasure, even for the inexperienced hiker. It is flat and smooth, in striking contrast to the abrupt and rugged terrain of the surrounding heights. The comfortable foot-

ing of the valley floor is the end result of a geological evolution reaching back more than 30 million years.

The granite of the Sierra Nevada range was originally molten rock that infiltrated older sedimentary layers left by a shallow arm of the Pacific Ocean that covered the area. As these sedimentary layers eroded, the granite was exposed and later tilted toward the west to create the steep eastern flank and the long western slope of the mountain range today. As the tilt increased, the flow of streams like the Merced became more rapid, cutting deep V-shaped valleys in the granite. Then, during the ice ages two to three million years ago, glaciers gouged out the valley until it had the sheer sides and rounded bottom of a U. Finally, the melting

glaciers formed a lake whose bed is the present valley floor.

From this level vantage, you are free to wander at the feet of the valley's wonders of water and stone, "so compactly and harmoniously arranged," Muir wrote, "that the valley, comprehensively seen, looks like an immense hall or temple lighted from above." The lower valley is guarded by El Capitan, that incomparable outcropping sheared off by the glaciers like a loaf of bread cut by a sharp blade. Across the valley from El Capitan—part of the same ridge before the ice intruded—are the Cathedral Spires, reaching a height of 2700 feet above the floor.

Just to the east, the valley is bracketed by another pair of spectacular rock formations.

475

The Three Brothers, on the north side, are a trio of leaning peaks piled on top of each other, the topmost reaching a height of almost 4000 feet. To the south is Sentinel Rock. Beyond, the upper valley widens, backed by a semicircle of granite domes—Sentinel, Half, Basket and North. Some of these curious monoliths were formed by the glaciers; others by exfoliation, a process in which the surface layers of rock released from subterranean pressures peel off like layers of an onion, smoothing and rounding the outcropping.

Yosemite's falling water is the perfect foil for its upstanding rock. Especially in the spring, when the upland snows melt, the valley is baptized by pure, cold streams that seem to issue from heaven. Their ancient channels severed by the glaciers, the streams leap from the palisades, cascading and free-falling until water meets rock. Though it is the water that appears vanquished in the encounter, atomized into gentle mist, over generations it is the solid stone that crumbles gradually under the continuous assault.

The most splendid of the valley's falls is Yosemite, which plunges just beyond the Three Brothers in two suicidal leaps, a total drop of 2425 feet, the height of 13 Niagaras stacked up on top of each other. Bridalveil, Vernal, Nevada and Illilouette falls are all much loftier than Niagara; and the highest single plunge of them all is Ribbon Falls, which spills recklessly 1612 sheer feet. Nowhere else in the country is there so striking a collection of waterfalls in so small an area.

Though there is enough on the valley floor to enchant for many days and most visitors go no farther, the surrounding high country is a spectacle in its own right. From the valley itself, trails lead to the top of the walls, even to the brink of Yosemite Falls, offering a viewing aerie far above the crowd. Away from the valley, there are more than 700 miles of trails of varying difficulty, suitable for trips lasting anywhere from an hour to a week or more, on foot or on the horses or burros available for rental in the park. One of the most rewarding longer treks is the 60-mile High Sierra Loop, six 10-mile days with a comfortable campsite waiting at the end of each evening.

Hub of the high-country trails is the Tuolumne Meadows—the largest alpine meadow in the Sierra Nevadas—on the Tioga Road that bisects the park from east to west (it is open in the summer only). Even if you do not have the time or the inclination for a lengthier stay

Yosemite Has More Than Half of America's Highest Falls

NIAGARA
New York
186 ft.

YELLOWSTONE
(Lower Falls)
Wyoming
308 ft.

VERNAL
(Yosemite)
California
317 ft.

ILLILOUETTE
(Yosemite)
California
370 ft.

NEVADA
(Yosemite)
California
594 ft.

BRIDALVEIL
(Yosemite)
California
620 ft.

in the park, the Tioga Road with its frequent scenic turnouts offers a passing acquaintance with the varied landscape: acres of rock polished by glaciers; boulders—called glacial erratics—stranded by the melting ice; crystal-clear mountain lakes, reflecting the surrounding peaks; cascading streams of sweet icy water; forests of lodgepole pine and hemlock. The road also passes through most of the park's two-mile altitude range, so you will be a transient visitor to many of the ecological communities that coexist here, from the Sequoia forests along the western border to the stunted and twisted juniper and pine thickets that cling to the bare rocky heights. In all, the park is home to some 80 species of mammals, more than 200 species of birds and over 1500 kinds of trees and plants.

With its wealth of wilderness and wildlife, Yosemite's regal treasures are rich and multifaceted enough for a lifetime of visits. But even if you come only once for a short stay in a small part of the park, you may well remember it as the visit of a lifetime.

Half Dome and Liberty Cap tower behind Nevada Falls, a mighty chute of water that thunders down 594 feet between groves of high-rise evergreens.

MULTNOMAH
Oregon
620 ft.

FAIRY
Washington
700 ft.

SILVER
STRAND
California
1170 ft.

RIBBON
(Yosemite)
California
1612 ft.

YOSEMITE
(Upper, Cascades, Lower)
California
2425 ft.

WASHINGTON
MONUMENT
Washington, D.C.
555 ft.

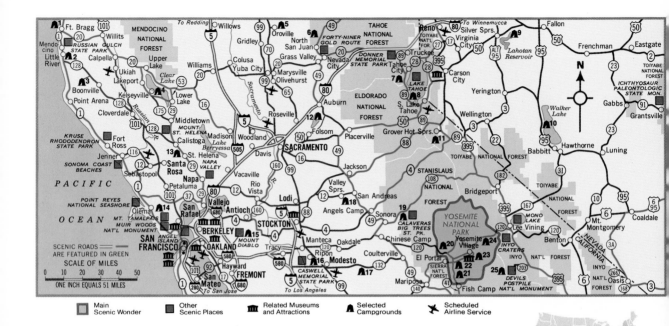

| Main Scenic Wonder | Other Scenic Places | Related Museums and Attractions | Selected Campgrounds | Scheduled Airline Service |

WITHIN A DAY'S DRIVE:

Redwoods, a Primitive Shore and Some Reminders of Gold Rush Days

Angel Island, Calif. The largest island in San Francisco Bay has sheltered a prison, an immigrant station and a missile base. But today it is a park where hikers, picnickers and anglers find a rustic refuge from San Francisco, all in dazzling view of the city and its high-flying bridges.

Calaveras Big Trees State Park, Calif. Stands of Sierra redwoods are the feature attraction here, mighty skyscrapers that dwarf their surroundings. Waterfalls and deep pools in the park's river lure swimmers and picnickers.

Caswell Memorial State Park, Calif. Picnic tables nestle under groves of oaks in a huge preserve of these sprawling trees. The woods line the Stanislaus River, making an outdoor playground complete with swimming holes.

Devils Postpile National Monument, Calif.
(Picture appears on page 481)

Donner Memorial State Park, Calif. Once the tragic site where

pioneers of the Donner party were stranded by snows, this is now one of nature's most hospitable parks: tall pine trees ring cool Donner Lake, where boats calmly glide and anglers try for trout and salmon.

Forty-Niner Gold Route, Calif. Rich in history and gold as well as scenery, aptly numbered Route 49 twists 270 miles from Mariposa to Sattley through picturesque Sierra Nevada foothills. Mining towns like Mount Bullion and El Dorado line the highway like Technicolor scenes from old Western movies.

Ichthyosaur Paleontologic State Monument, Nev. Gigantic reptiles called ichthyosaurs once swam the sea that covered western Nevada. They became extinct when the sea evaporated about 70 million years ago, but some are remarkably preserved in fossilized form here.

Inyo Craters, Calif. A 15-minute hike leads to two funnel-shaped craters, extraordinary because

they cradle lakes, one the color of grass, the other jade green.

Kruse Rhododendron State Park, Calif. There is only one specialty here, but it is a brilliant spectacle from mid-May to mid-June: dazzling blossoms cloak hundreds of rhododendron bushes, some 20 to 30 feet high.

Lake Tahoe, Calif. and Nev. *(Picture appears on page 480)*

Mono Lake, Calif. Blue and apparently inviting, the odorous waters are actually full of minerals and chemicals. Odd rock outcroppings line the shore, and two volcanic islands rise from the lake, one often spewing hot water from springs.

Mount Diablo, Calif. A steep rise from low plains gives Diablo an Olympian outlook; some say the view from the summit reaches farther than any other in North America. On a clear day the claim rings true: vast stretches of coast, inland valleys and mountain ranges amazingly unfold.

Muir Woods National Monument, *Calif. Sunlight splinters through a graceful arcade of tall trees in this redwood park a few miles from San Fran-cisco. Sky-high redwoods and low-growing ferns grow side by side along the park's main trail, where markers identify various trees and shrubs.*

Mount St. Helena, Calif. Oaks dot rolling green foothills, whose folds are occasionally crowded with a line of woods and watered by tiny streams. It is a park perfect for hikers and horseback riders, whose solitude is broken only by occasional grazing herds of shy deer.

Mount Tamalpais, Calif. Within a stone's throw of San Francisco, this 2600-foot height is a popular aerie for wide-angle views of the city and its waters. A network of hiking and riding trails links the top with beaches below.

Muir Woods National Monument, Calif.
(Picture appears on page 479)

Napa Valley, Calif. Hills covered with miles and miles of vineyards form the heart of California's wine country. Route 29 passes most of the famous wineries, where visitors are welcome to learn about the art of winemaking and enjoy samples of some of the wines.

Point Reyes National Seashore, Calif.
(Picture appears on facing page)

Russian Gulch State Park, Calif. A trail-covered promontory juts into the Pacific here, pocked with a lively blowhole, quiet coves and tide pools. One trail goes inland along a canyon forested with redwoods, firs and oaks, all underlaid with ferns—and ends at a refreshing waterfall.

Sonoma Coast Beaches, Calif. Although the waters are too cold and the undertow too dangerous for swimming, these 11 miles of shore parks are a haven for lazy beachcombers and sunbathers.

**RELATED MUSEUMS
AND ATTRACTIONS**

Berkeley, Calif.
Botanical Gardens.
University of California Earth Sciences Building.

Carson City, Nev. Nevada State Museum; natural science.

Mill Valley, Calif. Muir Woods National Monument Park Museum.

Oakland, Calif.
Oakland Museum; natural history.
Rotary Natural Science Center.

San Francisco, Calif.
California Academy of Sciences Museum; natural history.
California Division of Mines and Geology Mineral Museum.

Stockton, Calif. University of the Pacific Herbarium.

Yosemite, Calif. Yosemite National Park Museum.

Point Reyes National Seashore,
*Calif. (above). Phalanxes of surf
endlessly advance and retreat on
the broad triangular granite peninsula that is Point Reyes.
A wild shore laced with trails, it
is often fog-bound in summer, but
offers long views on clear days.*

Lake Tahoe, *Calif. and Nev. (left).
The famous lake and its surroundings is a mecca for vacationers,
but the 71-mile drive that circles it still offers views of
scenic solitude: here a quiet
rocky cove frames the distant
wall of the snowy Sierra Nevadas.*

**Devils Postpile National Monu-
ment,** *Calif. (right). Looking like
organ pipes, the basaltic columns
were formed by an ancient lava
flow, then neatly smoothed and
polished by glacial action. When
weathering cuts off pieces, they
add to a stockpile of stone bricks.*

481

Big Sur Coast
CALIFORNIA

Waves lash the rugged coast above Point Sur.

America's Loveliest Shoreline Drive

Properly speaking, Big Sur in itself is an inconspicuous Pacific shore community about 150 miles south of San Francisco, a small dot on the California road map where the Big Sur (Spanish for "Big South") River meets the sea. But by extension, Big Sur has come to stand for much more: the name refers to the whole 50-mile stretch of California coastline from just below Carmel to a few miles south of the small town of Lucia, between the crest of the Santa Lucia Mountains and the water's edge.

Even more than real estate, Big Sur is a state of mind. On a less than literal map, it is one of the capitals of the California life-style, a landmark in the American imagination. When you venture into Big Sur country, you are on the adopted home ground of writers like Robinson Jeffers, Henry Miller and Jack London; photographers like Edward Weston and Ansel Adams. They found in the remoteness of Big Sur, its relentless exposure to the energy of nature, a context appropriate to their own creative energies. And they, in turn, added their fame and character to the region's own. Inevitably they have been followed by droves of campers, pilgrims, sightseers and soul seekers.

Although Big Sur is too marked by civilization to be eligible for national park status, until quite recently the area was safeguarded by its very ruggedness and inaccessibility. It was not until 1937, after 18 years of literally cliff-hanging labor by convict road gangs, that Cali-

The Evolution of a Coast: Headland into Sea Stack

The drawing at left shows the progression of erosion on a coast very much like that at Point Sur, on the facing page. Three stages can be seen in the carving of the coast by the powerful Pacific waves. Toward the back of the picture a rocky headland projects into the water. In the middle, wave action has cut a hole through a weak part of a headland, creating an arch. In the foreground a much enlarged arch has collapsed, leaving a solitary rock standing in the sea beyond the headland. This is known as a sea stack, and continued battering by the sea will relentlessly wear it down further and slowly but surely increase its distance from shore.

fornia Route 1 opened up the Big Sur country. Now you can be in the heart of it half a day out of San Francisco.

Heading south from the Golden Gate, you soon find yourself on one of the country's—indeed, the world's—most spectacular drives. Route 1 snakes through endless curves, climbing and plunging, leaving your car clinging to the flank of terra firma while the sea lunges hungrily at the foot of the cliffs below. Giant redwoods and fragrant, dark green firs are scattered over the gentle folds of the grass-covered mountains; rivers rush through dark canyons to the sea.

The weather competes with the landscape for your attention, entertaining you with an ever-changing light show. Waves of cottony fog roll in from the ocean, blurring the hard line between land and sea. Sometimes the road is invisible five feet beyond your car. In clear weather a bank of clouds may stand off to sea, tracing the coastline in the sky. In the changing light, both water and rock take on a succession of colors, seeming to change substance as well. There are occasional overlooks where you can pull off the road to enjoy the views at

A crowd of seabirds flash their wings beneath the rocky headlands that swoop down to the Pacific surf at Point Sur. A highway runs along the coast.

your leisure—but since the views are so extraordinary at every turn, never enough.

The entrance to the Big Sur country is the Carmel Valley. As you leave it behind, its broad, green floor sloping right to the sea, you are at the entrance of Point Lobos State Reserve, which has been called "the greatest meeting of land and water in the world."

The view at Point Lobos, with its rough and dangerous coast guarded by offshore rocks, waves and whirling eddies, is typical of most of the Big Sur coast. The rocks are the nesting place for many types of seabirds, including the endangered brown pelican. The headlands that extend into the sea are especially notable for their population of sea mammals. You may well see the playful sea otter floating on its back in a bed of kelp, daintily popping a sea urchin or an abalone into its mouth with its dexterous forefeet. With luck, you may also spot two species of sea lion—the California and the Steller—and the harbor seal.

Farther out to sea, during its November-to-April round-trip migrations, you may see the California gray whale spouting and diving, easing its 40-ton, 50-foot bulk through the water with majestic grace. Around the populous rocks, the predatory, 30-foot killer whale, a member of the porpoise and dolphin family, hunts birds and seals. Since most of Big Sur's offshore life is unapproachable, a pair of binoculars—and a long telephoto lens for your camera—are especially useful.

Some 30 miles south of Point Lobos, after following Route 1's Grand Prix course through the rocky lowlands and clifftop meadows of Big Sur, you take the road inland to Pfeiffer–Big Sur State Park. In total contast to the typical Big Sur landscape, large parts of Pfeiffer are densely wooded with a mixed redwood forest, including also sycamore, maple, cottonwood and alder. The woods shelter a variety of wildlife—among them the wild boar, an ugly customer, best given a wide berth. The park has scenic picnic grounds and is laced with trails and roads. There are a variety of overnight accommodations—from motels to campsites—in the area, but during the tourist season all are crowded and reservations are necessary.

And this makes its own point about the dangers lying ahead for this coast. Only 35 years ago Big Sur was described in the California volume of the Federal Writers' Project as "bleak." Now we cherish its bleak beauty, but, as in the Oscar Wilde poem, "Each man kills the thing he loves." There is talk of turning Route 1 into a four-lane highway, of straightening out its coast-hugging curves. People, fire, pollution, commercialization, cars: all the problems that always beset natural areas could change the Big Sur coast almost beyond recognition. The residents of Big Sur, and conservationists everywhere, will have to fight hard to keep this astonishing stretch of Pacific coast as unspoiled as it is. But it will be a battle well worth the winning.

The magical mellow sunlight of a California afternoon floods the gently rolling, grassy hills above the Little Sur River valley. The green coastal hills, grazed by sheep and spangled with flowers every spring, climb up steeply inland to the 5000-foot crest of the wild, sparsely settled Santa Lucia Range.

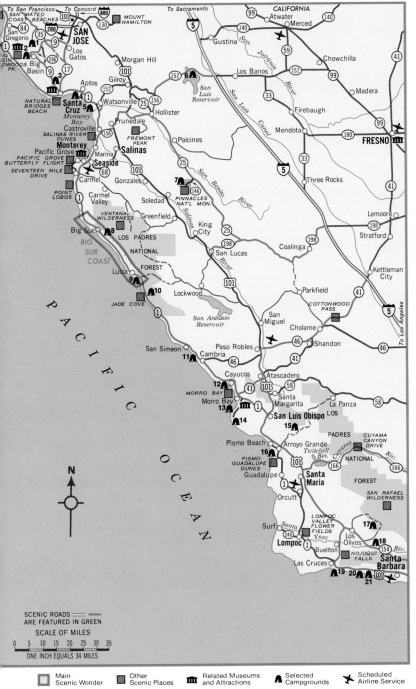

Cuyama Canyon Drive. For 30 miles the road follows the Cuyama River, passing through an impressive high-walled gorge that twists along the northern flanks of the Sierra Madre Mountains.

Fremont Peak. A half-mile trail climbs to the 3169-foot summit, where long vistas of green farmlands stretch to the east and the curving Pacific shoreline is visible to the west. Campers and picnickers enjoy the trails through canyons and over ridges spotted with hardy pines and oaks.

Jade Cove. Beachcombing and skin-diving are popular here, but jade hunting is the specialty: the best finds are along the rocky beaches at low tide. A promontory of almost solid soapstone juts into the sea, a favorite place to stand on the lookout for sea otters and gray whales.

Lompoc Valley Flower Fields. The genial climate and the flat and fertile meadows of the valley floor help make this America's largest center for growing flower seeds. From May to September the fields are a kaleidoscope of dazzling flowers in rainbow colors, growing alongside vegetables, grains and grazing livestock.

Morro Bay. The landlocked bay is dominated by Morro Rock, a Gibraltar-like conical bluff that rears up 576 feet above the sea. The massive volcanic promontory —easily accessible by a causeway—is the nesting territory of many seabirds.

Mount Hamilton. A narrow road winds through flowering meadows and gentle hills to the mountain's 4209-foot summit. On the west peak sit the glistening domes of the Lick Observatory, where —from 1 to 5 P.M.—visitors may enjoy astronomical views through the mammoth 120-inch telescope.

Natural Bridges Beach. A narrow finger of land juts out into the Pacific here and the pounding surf has carved away two perfect arches from the sandstone. Swimmers and picnickers enjoy the beaches and the tide pools, which teem with marine life.

WITHIN A DAY'S DRIVE:

Flower Fields and Butterflies

Big Basin Redwoods State Park. Since 1902 this park—the first in the California system—has protected the mighty trees: some are 18 feet in diameter and 350 feet tall. Picnic sites and hiking trails invite leisurely sight-seeing.

Cottonwood Pass. At 2000 feet, the high road through the barren Diablo Range makes a spectacular approach to the San Joaquin Valley. The summit overlook dramatizes the contrast between the arid heights and the fertile lowlands.

Seventeen Mile Drive. *One of America's most famous scenic roads, the drive winds among pines and scrub oaks and cypresses bent by the wind, past beaches of glittering white sand and along jagged cliffs and ledges. Here sunlight warms crags where a solitary Monterey cypress surveys the sea.*

Nojoqui Falls. A two-mile side road through oak-studded fields leads to the county park that shelters one of California's most graceful waterfalls. The creek plummets in long white ribbons between lofty rock walls and among cascading shrubs.

Pacific Grove Butterfly Flight. The town trees, especially the pines, attract swarms of monarch butterflies that migrate each winter from Canada and Alaska. They are an extraordinary sight as they mass in great clusters on limbs and trunks. A similar phenomenon, but on a smaller scale, takes place at Pismo Beach.

Pinnacles National Monument. (*Picture appears on facing page*)

Pismo–Guadalupe Dunes. A band of fine piled sand approximately a mile wide and five miles long draws beach buffs to this seashore park, which is also popular with bird watchers. An area is set aside for dune buggies.

Point Lobos. (*Picture appears on facing page*)

Salinas River Dunes. The small dunes area where the Salinas River meets the Pacific attracts hikers and beachcombers. In summer, upper reaches of the river are almost dry, but some waters flow underground to re-emerge in shoreside pools.

San Mateo Coast Beaches. About 25 miles of ocean beaches, all within easy reach of the shore highway, Route 1, are part of California's extensive beach and park reserves.

San Rafael Wilderness. Part of the Los Padres National Forest, the mountain-ringed wilderness is unbroken by automobile roads and includes a sanctuary for the rare California condor. Hikers and backpackers find trails through primitive woodlands.

Pinnacles National Monument. *Volcanic upheavals and millions of years of weathering have created these commanding stone monuments. Carved stone spires, ridges, cliffs and canyons cover 10,000 acres.*

Seventeen Mile Drive.
(*Picture appears on facing page*)

Ventana Wilderness. The coastal Santa Lucia Range cradles this refuge for deer and wild pigs; it contains notable trout streams.

RELATED MUSEUMS AND ATTRACTIONS

Big Basin Redwoods State Park. Nature Lodge.

Fresno. Fresno Museum; natural history and botanical gardens.

Morro Bay. Museum of Natural History.

Pacific Grove. Museum of Natural History.

Santa Cruz. Museum of Natural History.

Point Lobos. *A small but carefully protected state reserve includes serene meadows, secluded spots like China Cove and Bird Island and shelters America's last natural stand of rare California cypress.*

489

Sequoia–Kings Canyon

NATIONAL PARKS, CALIFORNIA

The icy wall of the Sierra looms over the parks.

CALIFORNIA

Sequoia-Kings
Canyon National
Parks

Our Biggest Trees Grow Below Lofty Sierra Peaks

Only 50 miles southeast of the bustling city of Fresno, and reaching to the towering majesty of 14,495-foot Mount Whitney, lies a stretch of America's most primeval land, preserved in adjacent national parks: Kings Canyon, a rugged and breathtaking expanse of granite mountains furrowed by mile-deep canyons; and Sequoia, home of the largest living things on earth.

Some 4000 years ago, when the earliest Pharaohs ruled Egypt, a tiny seed fluttered down to a bare patch of ground in what is now Sequoia National Park. The seed took root and flourished. Today the result, the General Sherman Tree, towers 272 feet. By no means the tallest of trees, it is unexcelled for sheer massive bulk. Even a dozen people with arms outstretched could not encircle the trunk. If the unthinkable happened, and the General was cut down, it would provide lumber enough to build 40 five-room houses. Its weight has been estimated to be over 2000 tons, and it would be even taller and heavier if lightning did not repeatedly blast off its top.

So awesome is the overwhelming bulk of a big *Sequoiadendron giganteum* that its beauty often goes unnoticed. Pale shafts of sunlight filter through the lofty branches, and even if a crowd is examining one of these ancient monsters, it is somehow always very quiet beneath it. There is no wind, and the leaf fall of centuries has created a soundproof carpet.

491

A Tilting Block Raised the Sierra

Abrupt mountain ranges are often formed by tilting movements of blocks of the earth's crust along a fault, or cleavage, line. The Sierra Nevada is a perfect example of such a block that rotated, raising a mighty 14,000-foot wall at the eastern edge and sinking on the west. Later, sediments slowly filled the San Joaquin Valley.

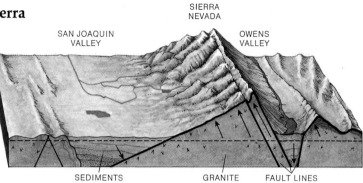

SIERRA NEVADA
SAN JOAQUIN VALLEY
OWENS VALLEY
SEDIMENTS   GRANITE   FAULT LINES

How could this race of giants have survived so long? The secret lies partly in the incredible bark of the sequoia. Its high tannin content protects it from insects, and its thickness of up to two feet makes it proof against the penetration of disease, the gnawing of starved animals —and the ravages of fire. Lightning and man between them have caused many huge fires in the course of most sequoias' lives. But the tree stands up proudly through the blaze, goes slightly black for a few seasons, grows another layer of bark and lives another 1000 years. To a certain extent the fires have been beneficial. A fierce blaze burns up the dry duff of the forest floor, making the germination of fallen seeds possible. On unburned ground a seed's root cannot reach moisture and nutrients in the soil, and so never grows.

For the survival of these trees, and for the still unspoiled beauty of the whole park area, we must thank the dedicated Scots-born naturalist John Muir, who recognized the outstanding features of the area when he first visited it in 1875. Immensely moved by the colossal trees, yet disturbed by the incursions of logging teams, he wrote: "No doubt these trees would make good lumber after passing through a saw mill, as George Washington after passing through the hands of a French chef would have made good food."

In 1890, after 15 years of effort, the trees were preserved in America's second national park. (Adjacent Kings Canyon was added in 1940.) Today hundreds of thousands of people visit the 1320 square miles of the twin parks yearly, mainly to gaze in amazement at the

Nearly as enormous as the General Sherman Tree, the President Tree, a neighbor, presides over the Senate and House groves in the Giant Forest.

giant trees: trees where fire has hollowed out room-sized space within the living trunk, or burned a great hole through it; caves in hollow logs, one large enough to take a man on ponyback; fallen trees a car can be driven through. And John Muir would surely have been delighted to know that thousands of people a year hike or ride the 225 miles of a spectacular mountain trail named for him.

Mountains are the other element of the twin parks—and mountains that are giants among their fellows just as the great trees are. In the last Ice Age, slow glaciers sliced through this corner of California, carving mammoth U-shaped canyons thousands of feet deep. At several points along the majestic Kings River —at Tehipite, South Fork and Middle Fork canyons—the depth is over a mile. From the beetling rims, a tiny moving dot you see far below is probably a fisherman casting in the blue, rushing river for rainbow trout. And in a breathtaking extension of the vertical scale, the jagged ridge of the Sierra Nevada towers magisterially to the east, culminating in the lofty peak of Mount Whitney, the United States' highest spot outside Alaska. The park boundary stretches to its very summit. No mountaineering skills are needed to reach it, since the John Muir Trail leads along a knife-edge to reach the peak. Gazing down the mountain's avalanche-furrowed flanks toward the central California valley, or across into Nevada, you feel on top of the world—and rightly, for there is no higher place for well over 2000 miles in any direction.

For those who prefer to do their sight-seeing by car, the 46-mile drive along the "Generals Highway" is the perfect way to go. Panoramic views, lofty trees, spectacular rocks and immense canyons follow one another in

493

astonishing succession. The General Sherman Tree stands close to the road; a short, narrower road leads up to the vast granite lump known as Moro Rock, with commanding views to the Sierra skyline. A six-mile drive off the main road leads to the weird subterranean growths of the Crystal Cave. You could travel the Generals Highway a dozen times, from its 1700-foot beginning in the Sierra foothills to its 7000-foot summit, and see, with the changing light and seasons, fresh vistas each time.

Such is the great range of altitude and climate in the twin parks that the visitor passes through almost bewildering changes of plant life. The low approaches show extensive oak woods interspersed with scrubby chaparral. As you begin to rise you will see cedars, and through stands of ponderosa pine you will at last glimpse your first mighty sequoia at around 4000 feet. If you climb higher on trails, the timber thins out, and after it disappears altogether, the only growths in the highest alpine meadows are dwarf mountain sorrels, red rock primroses and the white alpine saxifrage.

Almost anywhere in the forest the visitor may find himself face to face with a black bear weighing anything up to 500 pounds—especially in the oak woods during the fall, when the bears go to seek acorns. A more uncommon forest inhabitant is the lumbering porcupine, and one to avoid is the vicious, three-foot-long Pacific fisher, built like a huge weasel, and an enemy of all.

Sequoia–Kings Canyon is a place of superlatives, containing at once America's biggest tree and its second tallest mountain. In the clear, vibrant mountain air the vistas, up to the Great Western Divide and down into the precipitous canyons, are endless—and perpetually surprising. The tall forests are places of wonder and silence, and there are enough flowery meadows, bubbling mountain creeks and steep trails to keep botanists, fishermen and wilderness backpackers happy for weeks on end. It is a beautifully preserved reminder of America's natural magnificence.

The quarter-mile climb to the summit of Moro Rock is not difficult, and benches are strategically placed for viewing and resting along the way. From the top some of the finest panoramas in the park stretch in all directions. This one, of the lower Kaweah River Canyon, shows winter fog sliding in.

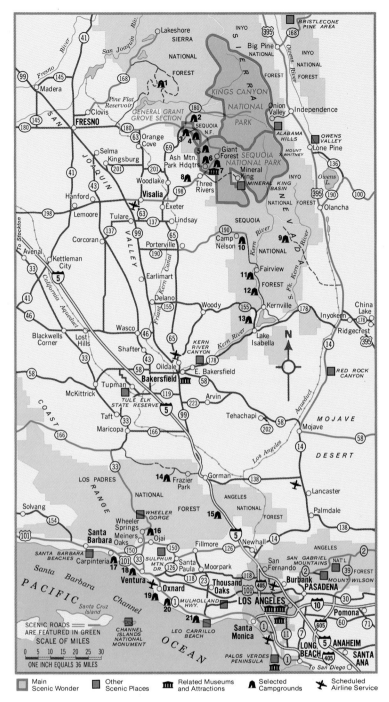

Map legend:

Main Scenic Wonder | Other Scenic Places | Related Museums and Attractions | Selected Campgrounds | Scheduled Airline Service

SCENIC ROADS ARE FEATURED IN GREEN
SCALE OF MILES
0 5 10 15 20 25 30
ONE INCH EQUALS 36 MILES

WITHIN A DAY'S DRIVE:

Scenery from the Movies

Alabama Hills. Between Lone Pine and towering Mount Whitney a dirt road turns off along a canyon leading into the Alabama Hills. These rugged hills surround Movie Flat, an area strewn with oddly shaped boulders,

which has long been a favorite for filming Western movies.

Bristlecone Pine Area. The sequoias are ancient, but the bristlecone pines are the oldest living things—though they may look

dead from their fight to survive above 10,000 feet in the White Mountains. Well-marked roads north of Big Pine, open in summer only, lead to the groves of pines, and to panoramic views into the High Sierra country.

Channel Islands National Monument. Two of the eight Channel Islands in the Pacific south of Santa Barbara preserve rookeries of sea lions and nesting seabirds, as well as unusual land and sea vegetation. It is possible to land small boats on the two, Anacapa and Santa Barbara, and the island hiking is excellent.

Kern River Canyon. High in the Sierras the Kern River twists its way among boulders and between colorful canyon walls. Highway 178 follows the river northwest from Bakersfield to Lake Isabella, passing popular Kern River State Park.

Leo Carrillo Beach. Beautiful sandy beaches carved by jutting headlands into a series of coves are the highlights of this state beach, one of the most spectacular in a chain of fine public beaches along this shore. It is often used for filming movie scenes.

Mineral King Basin. (*Picture appears on page 496*)

Mount Wilson. The Angeles Crest Highway beginning at La Canada traverses most of the highlights of the San Gabriel Mountains, including a turnoff to the 5710-foot-high plateau of Mount Wilson, with its famous observatory near Skyline Park.

Mulholland Highway. Canyon roads lead up the steep sides of the Santa Monica Mountains to the crest, where Mulholland Highway runs along the high mountain spine, offering views over the San Fernando Valley, Los Angeles and the beaches.

Owens Valley. Mountain peaks that rise over 14,000 feet on either side of this long desert trough make it the nation's deepest valley—and one with some of the best mountain vistas. From canyons that line it, trails lead into the High Sierras and into the Panamint Range that looms above Death Valley.

Palos Verdes Peninsula. The 15-mile drive around this comparatively wild Los Angeles peninsula along a 100-foot clifftop provides magnificent views of the sea and broad beaches from turnouts.

Red Rock Canyon. Colorful formations eroded by wind and water line this desert canyon. It has recently been given state park status, but there are no facilities, and visitors should bring their own water. The canyon is bright with wildflowers in the spring.

San Gabriel Mountains. Between the coast and the desert rise the rugged San Gabriel Mountains. The Angeles Crest Highway (State Highway 2) traverses them. Jarvi Memorial Vista offers dizzying views into Devils and Bear canyons, and a four-mile hike up Mount Baden-Powell yields another fantastic view. The wildest terrain is included in the San Gabriel Wilderness Area.

Santa Barbara Beaches.
(*Picture appears on facing page*)

Sulphur Mountain Drive. This little-traveled but highly scenic route rises to only 2700 feet, but it is high enough to provide sweeping views over three surrounding green valleys and even as far out to sea as the distant Channel Islands.

Tule Elk State Reserve. A fenced dry lake bed of about 1000 acres protects a herd of the smallest of the American elks. The Tule elk, once numerous, were thought to be extinct. A herd of about 30 is now maintained here.

Wheeler Gorge. Beyond the serene valley surrounding Ojai lies a spectacular mountain area of forests, canyons and streams. Wheeler Gorge and the high, white sandstone outcrop of Piedra Blanca are the highlights.

RELATED MUSEUMS AND ATTRACTIONS

Bakersfield. Kern County Museum.

Los Angeles.
Ferndell Nature Museum.
Los Angeles County Museum of Natural History.
U.C.L.A. Botanic Garden.

Palos Verdes Estates. Marineland of the Pacific.

Three Rivers. Sequoia–Kings Canyon National Park Museum.

Mineral King Basin. *Below Sawtooth Mountain the former mining town of Mineral King is now a base for pack trips into the back country of the Sequoia park. Beyond Farewell Canyon, above, lies Farewell Gap Pass. The lovely basin is a center of controversy over possible Disney development.*

Santa Barbara Beaches. *The blue waters along this 70-mile stretch of coast are noted for year-round comfortable temperature. Apart from good swim-* *ming, the half-dozen public beaches around Santa Barbara also offer lush semitropical vegetation. Here a Monterey cypress leans over wood sorrel.*

Death Valley
NATIONAL MONUMENT, CALIFORNIA

The vista from Dantes View embraces the Badwater salt flats and 11,000-foot Telescope Peak.

Hottest, Driest, Lowest—All in One

Looking in the bright light like a strange surrealist painting, a giant rock lies in the middle of the flat plain called the Race Track, in the foothills

There is plenty in Death Valley to remind a visitor of the "valley of the shadow of death" in the 23rd Psalm. And anyone who arrives there—as many do—by way of nearby Las Vegas could even imagine the place as a convenient purgatory in which to atone for a luxurious stay in the gambling capital.

In contrast to Las Vegas' prodigal outpouring of water in swimming pools and fountains, Death Valley is so dry that men have died there in search of it. Las Vegas is an indoor town, shadowed and air-conditioned to encourage its special business; Death Valley offers little relief from the relentless sun, and the main business of man and beast is survival. And while Las Vegas is noisy day and night with music and the relentless clatter of gambling machines, Death Valley stuns the ears with the accumulated silence of the ages.

But just within the valley itself (now included in an enormous national monument) there are contrasts enough. Its famous heat, for instance, drove the thermometer to 134 degrees—the second highest temperature ever recorded on earth—on July 10, 1913; and there were two unbroken weeks during that summer when the daily high temperature never failed to top 120. Yet that same winter, the valley recorded its lowest temperature, a chilly 15 degrees. The valley floor descends to 280 feet below sea level near Badwater—the lowest dry land in the Western hemisphere, and one of the lowest spots on earth. But only 15 miles away, in the Panamint Mountains that guard the monument's western flank,

Telescope Peak looms 11,000 feet above sea level—more than two miles above Badwater. The valley is notoriously dry, receiving less rainfall (1.68 inches) in an average year than many nondesert valleys on a single rainy day. Yet many times in its history sudden cloudbursts have dumped enough water in a limited area to cause flash floods of death-dealing force.

Men have feared the valley's extremes ever since a band of settlers stumbled into it in the winter of 1849, searching for a short cut to

of the Panamint Range. The rocks, some weighing as much as 600 pounds, actually slide along the ground after a rain (note the track of this rock).

The phenomenon is attributed to the effect of strong desert winds propelling the rocks over the slippery surface of what was once a lake bed.

the California goldfields. As the last of them scrambled over the mountains on the far side two desperate months later, minus almost everything save their lives, they christened the valley in parting: "Goodbye, Death Valley." Yet from that day to this, generations have found the valley an irresistible lure. Recurrent rumors of gold and silver—most of them false —and the discovery of other valuable minerals induced many to ignore the valley's fearsome reputation. In the flamboyant 1920s one cele-

brated desert rat, known as Death Valley Scotty, even convinced a Chicago millionaire to finance the construction of an ornate, sprawling castle in the wilderness at the northern end of the valley. Scotty's Castle still stands, its richly decorated rooms open to tourists, as the most incongruous landmark in this place of natural wonders.

The common wisdom is that you should plan your Death Valley visit for the winter, when the temperature usually moderates to the

Death Valley is a study in remarkable colors and textures produced by wind, great heat and high evaporation. On the facing page, Zabriskie Point glows gold in the sunrise. The Devils Golf Course, above, is an area of fantastically jagged rock salt; and, right, wind sculpts the dunes at Mesquite Flat.

comfortable 60s and 70s, with refreshingly chilly nights. But if you have the slightest contrary streak in you, and an urge to challenge nature at its most intransigent, come in midsummer. As long as you are prudent—carrying emergency water for yourself and your car, driving only on the main roads and following the Park Service's summer rules—you won't be in any great danger. In fact, although all but one of the campgrounds below sea level are closed in summer, those at more temperate altitudes are open, as are the lodgings at Furnace Creek and Stove Pipe Wells.

As you drive away from one of these outposts of civilization toward the hot spot near Badwater, the official temperature on what the locals insist is a cool day may be 110 degrees or more. In such heat an air-conditioned car is no more than a thin-skinned bubble, offering fragile sanctuary against the inferno. At Bad-

water, if you get out of the car for a moment, the ground temperature may be nearly 200 degrees, and you will feel it through your shoes.

Because the Death Valley basin has been isolated from the rest of the American continent for the last few million years, protected from invasion by high mountains all around, its plant and animal populations are unique. Of the more than 600 plant species that have been identified in the national monument, each restricted to its own climate zone and soil, 21 grow nowhere else on earth. Among the park's special animal inhabitants, three are particularly noteworthy: a snail, a shrimp and the minnowlike pupfish that has adapted to the salt-saturated water of the valley's streams and marshes.

The hot, dry climate has prompted a variety of ingenious mechanisms for survival. Moisture is the critical problem. Some animals, the predators, may derive it from their prey: the kit fox from the grasshopper mouse, the mouse from the grasshopper. Others, vegetarians, draw water from the plants they eat. But the kangaroo rat manages to get all the water it needs from metabolizing the dry seeds that are its diet. So successful is this creature's internal alchemy that it will not drink rain-water even when it is available.

Various plants have evolved their own strategies for resisting heat and absorbing water. The mesquite tree, for instance, uses a root as much as 100 feet long to tap deep-lying moisture. The cholla cactus, by contrast, spreads its shallow root system in a 30-foot diameter to catch as much rain as possible. Most plants here have small leaves to reduce water loss, and the cactus stores moisture in its green stem, insulated by its spines.

You can spend days driving around in the valley, exploring the northern half from a base at Stove Pipe Wells, the southern section from Furnace Creek. Highlights of the northern end include the giant Ubehebe Crater, half a mile across and 500 feet deep, and the Race Track, a perfectly flat plain that was once the floor of an old lake, and where the desert wind pushes large rocks across the even surface when it is wet, making them look as if they were giant snails moving under their own power.

In the south, Dantes View is perhaps the most dramatic panorama in the valley, with an outlook a mile down to the glittering salt plains around Badwater and up to the two-mile-high Panamint Mountains beyond. Here too is the Devils Golf Course, a fantastically eroded rock garden, and Zabriskie Point, where vividly colored slopes blend and mingle like shapes in an abstract painting.

But whether you stay in Death Valley for half a day or a week, summer or winter, a growing awareness of its finely tuned survival systems will soon make you realize how out of place you are there, how dependent on complex technology even for a visit. And then you cannot help but marvel at the creatures of Death Valley, which have so successfully fought to survive in this terrifying but strangely beautiful place.

Badwater, reflecting the crest of Telescope Peak at sunrise, is the lowest point—282 feet below sea level—in the Western hemisphere. It is also one of the hottest places on earth, where summer temperatures between 115 and 120 degrees are by no means uncommon. The record is 134 degrees.

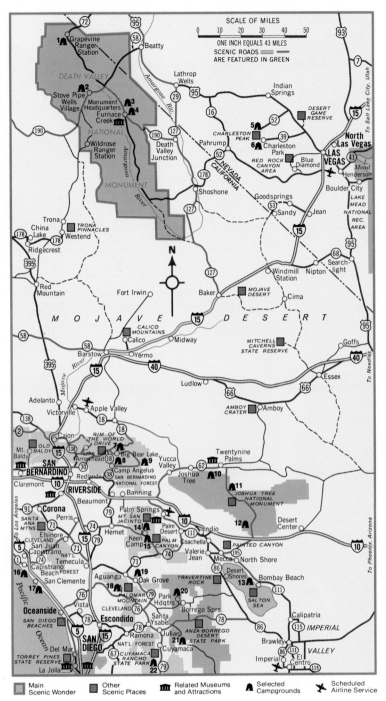

up the canyon, where more than 1000 fan palms border the turbulent stream. Other scenic highlights include Font's Point, Tamarisk Grove and Fish Creek.

Calico Mountains, Calif. Doran Drive, a narrow loop road, leads through high-walled canyons into this colorful mountain range. Hikers can explore gorges bright with desert flowers in the spring.

Charleston Peak, Nev. In the late fall, golden-leaved aspen trees light up the lower slopes of this mountain, which stands like a sentinel (11,919 feet) in the Toiyabe National Forest offering skiing and other sports within a short drive of Las Vegas. A hiking trail heads to Cathedral Rock for a good view of the forest and surrounding desert.

Cuyamaca Rancho State Park, Calif. There are 50 miles of hiking and riding trails within the 20,000-acre park, and one of them leads to Cuyamaca Peak (6515 feet), where on a clear day you can see all the way to Mexico and the Pacific Ocean, with a vast panorama of desert and mountain ranges in between. Birds and other wildlife are commonly seen among magnificent stands of oaks and conifers.

Desert Game Reserve, Nev. Rare desert bighorn sheep are the major attraction at this refuge. A visitor center offers helpful information about how best to see them and the other wildlife that roam here.

Joshua Tree National Monument, Calif.
(*Picture appears on page 507*)

Mitchell Caverns State Reserve, Calif. These are California's only accessible limestone caverns and contain some lovely cave coral. Guided tours are available around Tecopa Cavern, with some remarkable flowstone and dripstone formations. There is a self-guiding nature trail outside the caverns, with excellent views of the Providence Mountains.

Mojave Desert, Calif. and Nev. This enormous desert area occu-

WITHIN A DAY'S DRIVE:

Beaches and Barren Desert

Amboy Crater, Calif. An unmarked sandy side road off Route 66 winds to within about a half mile of the crater's rim. A steep climb leads the rest of the way to the top for views inside the 200-foot-high volcanic cone.

Anza-Borrego Desert State Park, Calif. Almost half a million acres of desert wilderness form a living museum of desert plant and animal life. Park headquarters at Borrego Palm Canyon features a self-guiding nature trail leading

Palm Canyon, *Calif. The palms here reach an impressive height, and form shady groves around sparkling streams. Good trails traverse the canyon.*

Red Rock Canyon Area, *Nev. Ramparts of the tall Spring Mountains emerge from the morning mist above the cactus garden of the Mojave Desert.*

pies most of the southeastern corner of California and is at its most beautiful between February and May, when the wildflowers are out and it is not yet too hot. The Apple Valley area is particularly attractive and offers a variety of resort facilities.

Mount San Jacinto, Calif. One of the sheerest mountains in the world, San Jacinto rises with startling abruptness above Palm Springs to a height of 10,805 feet above the desert floor. An aerial tramway carries passengers 8516 feet up to Mountain Station for magnificent views and an escape from the desert heat.

Old Baldy, Calif. A lift to the summit of 10,064-foot Mount San Antonio (also known as Old Baldy) enables visitors to enjoy panoramic views; a scenic road leads from the floor of Strawberry Canyon up into the surrounding San Gabriel Mountains.

Painted Canyon, Calif. Of the three canyons in the picturesque desert area southeast of Indio, this is the most outstanding. An easy one-mile trail provides the best views of its colorful, eroded walls of sheer rock.

Palm Canyon, Calif.
(Picture appears on this page)

Palomar Mountain, Calif. High atop the mountain is the world-famous Palomar Observatory. The heavily wooded state park nearby has well-developed riding and hiking trails and several good viewpoints. Perhaps the best of these is the tower on Boucher Hill, from which the Pacific is visible on a clear day.

Red Rock Canyon Area, Nev.
(Picture appears on this page)

Rim of the World Drive, Calif. This lovely mountain drive along the crest of the San Bernardino

range goes as high as 7000 feet and passes lakes Arrowhead, Big Bear and Gregory. The Butler Peak Lookout, reached by a road north of Big Bear Lake, is spectacular, and there is another memorable panoramic view at Lakeview Point.

Salton Sea, Calif. Once a dry desert wasteland between the Imperial and Coachella valleys, the sea was formed in 1905 by an overflow of the Colorado River. Today it is a major recreation area and the most popular boating park in southern California.

San Diego Beaches, Calif. The coastal area south of Oceanside is dotted with white sand beaches backed by high bluffs. The surf is generally mild, making it safe for swimming, and surf fishing is good throughout the area.

Santa Ana Mountains, Calif. A scenic route through Santa Ana

Canyon and continuing south on Highway 71 provides good views of this range. Turning west at Lake Elsinore, the road leads past an old mission site and on to Capistrano.

Torrey Pines State Reserve, Calif. The Torrey pine grows only along the ocean in this area and on offshore Santa Rosa Island. Well-marked trails wind through the rare and ancient trees.

Travertine Rock, Calif. The formation is a mound of enormous boulders once partially submerged by Lake Cahuilla, sections of which are now covered with rough limestone. Miles of Coachella Valley farmland can be seen spreading out below the summit (a climb of about 200 feet).

Trona Pinnacles, Calif. This series of strange geological formations makes a good side trip from the Wildrose Canyon route into Death Valley. Ranging in height from 10 to 150 feet, they rise dramatically from the desert.

RELATED MUSEUMS AND ATTRACTIONS

Claremont, Calif. Rancho Santa Ana Botanic Garden.

Death Valley, Calif. Death Valley National Monument Museum.

La Jolla, Calif. University of California (San Diego) T. Wayland Vaughan Aquarium and Museum; oceanography.

Palm Springs, Calif. Palm Springs Desert Museum; desert animals, plants and minerals.

Riverside, Calif. Riverside Municipal Museum; natural history.

San Diego, Calif. San Diego Natural History Museum.

Twentynine Palms, Calif. Joshua Tree National Monument Museum.

Joshua Tree National Monument, *Calif. The Joshua tree or "praying plant" is one of the most spectacular plants of our southwestern deserts. It sometimes reaches a height of 40 feet, and bears clusters of white blossoms. Quartz boulders appear in this view of the Hidden Valley area of the monument.*

507

Mount McKinley National Park
ALASKA

The snow-deep peak of Mount McKinley, rooftop of North America, soars a massive 20,320 feet.

Pristine Wilderness Surrounds America's Mightiest Mountain

About halfway along the single road that threads into the park, drivers climb 3700 feet over the sweeping tundra at Polychrome Pass. Here a bird's-

The park bus jounced along the winding dirt road that penetrates the vast arctic-alpine wilderness of Mount McKinley National Park. It had just left the park entrance on its free journey over the 87-mile-long road, the only one in the park's 3030 square miles.

On this particular trip, typical of many the park buses make every day, June was nearly over but large patches of snow still lay in the hollows of the barren tundra, on the slopes of the foothills and on the peaks obscured by an overcast. This is a good time of year to see the park, despite the mosquitoes, because of the 24 hours of daylight, the flowers and the nesting birds. The bugs would be gone in August but so would the flowers and the birds, and the evenings would be darker.

All eyes were straining for a glimpse of the biggest peak of them all, Mount McKinley. The clouds parted and a glacier-clad summit could be seen, thrusting up into the blue. A passenger asked if that was *the* mountain, but the bus driver shook his head. It was just one of the baby peaks; you don't often see McKinley until you are 60 miles out in the park, he explained, and more often than not you don't see it even then. Denali, "The Great One"—as the Indians call it—creates its own weather around its 20,320-foot peak, and is often cloud-covered.

But he pointed to a patch of yellow and two darker shapes behind: a sow grizzly bear and her two spring cubs. Most of the bus passengers expected to see a dark brown animal, but as the bus stopped they focused binoculars on

a blond mass ambling over the bright green tundra. There is always some apprehension about bears, but in fact there has never been a fatality caused by a bear in McKinley Park. The few maulings—more in the nature of cuffings—have been a warning to photographers that they were getting too bold. These are wilderness bears, not campground scroungers or circus actors begging for handouts.

The sight of grizzlies took the edge off the visitors' disappointment that the highest mountain on the continent might be wrapped in cloud throughout their trip. Now the road dropped down from the tundra uplands to a

eye view into the valley reveals the course of a "braided" river, one of many in the park. When glacial snows melt and streams pour from the moun- *tains, they carry with them silt and sand, often in such quantities that riverbeds overflow and create new side channels, like long braids of hair.*

spruce forest along a braided glacial river. The bus stopped again and passengers scrambled out to take pictures of a bull moose, the largest member of the deer family, browsing on willows. Its antlers, shed annually in early winter, had more growing to do before the animal scraped off their velvet just before the mating season in September. They gave it a majestic appearance compared with the antlerless cow seen feeding in a nearby pond with her small rust-colored calf.

Down on the river gravel a band of caribou was spotted. Apparently they often gather here in the summer. Young males and females

look alike, both with antlers, but the old bulls have much larger and more intricate racks. Now the caribou were scattered in small groups throughout this part of the park, but later they would merge to start their migration to the west and north. Although they graze on a variety of tundra plants in the summer, they depend for winter survival on fragile lichens, which take up to 100 years to regrow. But caribou herds range widely, often changing migration routes, thus allowing the habitats that sustain them to recover.

In Igloo Canyon a passenger caught sight of Dall sheep up on a rocky spire of Cathedral

More than a dozen glaciers creep down from the peaks of Mount McKinley, flowing all the way to the lowland valleys, their front edges often covered with plants. Muldrow Glacier (the right-hand ridge) is the longest in the park: it runs about 40 miles and ends within a mile of the park road.

Glaciers: A Glimpse of Living Geology

Glaciers form when, in the course of centuries, annual snowfall exceeds annual melt. Many forces—pressure and melting are two of them—change the masses of snow into ice, and eventually the bulk is heavy enough to begin moving downward of its own weight. Crevasses form when a glacier meets an obstacle in its progress and must turn aside. Glaciers carry enormous amounts of dirt and rocks along with them, and when they finally reach their stopping place (the snout) and begin to retreat, this debris is deposited in heaps (moraines).

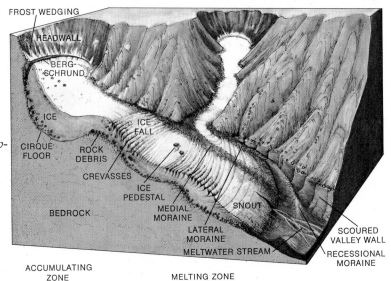

FROST WEDGING
HEADWALL
BERG-SCHRUND
ICE
CIRQUE FLOOR
ROCK DEBRIS
ICE FALL
CREVASSES
ICE PEDESTAL
BEDROCK
MEDIAL MORAINE
SNOUT
LATERAL MORAINE
MELTWATER STREAM
SCOURED VALLEY WALL
RECESSIONAL MORAINE
ACCUMULATING ZONE
MELTING ZONE

512

Mountain. At first hard to distinguish from snow patches, they turned out to be ewes with newborn offspring (the rams keep their own company, usually in more remote areas). The agility of the young lambs as they bound from crag to crag is remarkable—it is their defense against predators.

Then the bus climbed slowly up into Sable Pass. The journey ahead was almost all above the tree line, offering vistas of tundra, talus slopes, ice, snow and braided streambeds draining the glaciers that blended with the low clouds. Tundra is a Finnish word meaning treeless. It is more than a type of plant cover, just as desert is more than sand and prairie is more than grass. Indeed, the tundra, the desert and the prairie have much in common besides an absence of forests: plant and animal communities specific to each, a vastness seemingly dominated by the sky, a special mood that pervades these landscapes.

The bus stopped for passengers to photograph flowers decorating an expanse of green. The land is green only because permafrost—permanently frozen ground—underlies most of the park. It traps rain and meltwater at the surface, creating bogs and muskeg in low depressions. Permafrost forms whenever the average annual temperature is below freezing. Its presence determines the type of vegetation that will grow, which in turn determines how near the permafrost is to the surface. Thick, high ground cover, which grows where there is more moisture, insulates the frozen soil beneath. Short, sparse vegetation, which grows where moisture is less, allows the sun's warmth to penetrate the soil.

Park visitors soon learn how to work out a route over the tundra by looking at the plant cover (man-made trails are few in the park). Ground huggers like dryas, lowbush cranberry, alpine bearberry and lichens mean easy walking. You follow animal trails along ridges, or walk the river bars. In such open country getting lost is rarely a problem, but finding your way around tussocks, across bridgeless streams and up steep mountain slopes is challenging and exhilarating. Away from the road a visitor feels like an explorer.

Many tundra plants have a feature in common with desert ones—a leathery or fuzzy leaf surface that aids in the conservation of moisture. Familiar species are stunted: a plant only two inches high is a willow, a thigh-high bush is a dwarf birch. What they lack in height they make up for in deep root systems that reach down to a microclimate 50 degrees warmer than the 40-below surface temperatures.

Adaptability is the key to survival in the North, whether for plants, animals or humans. Nature calls the shots and those that take heed not only survive but flourish. Those that don't, die. Perhaps that is part of the spell of the tundra world most McKinley visitors become caught up in—they come mostly to see the mountain but find themselves becoming fascinated by arctic life systems.

At last the overcast began to lift and break up into patches of blue sky. More and more snow-covered peaks were unveiled. The braided streams widened as the glaciers flanking the mountains became larger and larger. At the Toklat River the driver braked suddenly. Wolves were loping along the riverbed. Only in Alaska is there room enough for men *and* wolves, and only in a national park are they protected from hunters and trappers. Somehow wolves embody the essence of wilderness. They are predators, like man, but kill only what they need to survive.

At the Eielson Visitor Center the bus stopped for passengers to look at exhibits that explain glaciology and mountaineering on Mount McKinley. Here, as others had done along the road, hikers retrieved their packs from the back of the bus and started off for a four-day trek into the mountains.

Until 1972, access into McKinley Park was available only to those who took the early morning tour bus operated from the hotel near the McKinley Park railroad station and returned at noon, or by private car driven in over the circuitous Denali highway. With the opening of the new Fairbanks-to-Anchorage highway, the National Park Service realized that the narrow park road and the limited camping sites could not accommodate an increase in visitors and that to expand them would destroy the park's wilderness aspect.

The solution seemed to be to allow into the park only enough visitors in private cars to fill the campsites available (about 80 in four different areas), on a reservation basis, then provide free and frequent bus service for others. After a season of operation, even skeptics agree this answers McKinley's access problem.

Now hikers and backpackers can get off anywhere, knowing they will be picked up again by a regular service between 7 A.M. and midnight. Instead of watching for other cars, visitors can let a knowledgeable bus driver point out wildlife and characteristics of landscapes they would otherwise overlook. At the visitor center, the Eielson ranger was talking on a shortwave radio to an expedition that had just reached the summit of McKinley. Already this year three parties had made it to the top and several more were on their way up. Not all climbs are successful: storms, high altitude, supply logistics and physical exhaustion turn back many climbers, and a few have never come back. On this occasion the climbers were reporting blue skies around the peak and thinning clouds below.

At this point some passengers transferred to a bus returning to park headquarters, while others continued to Wonder Lake and the campground there. Other passengers make their way to Camp Denali, a small wilderness resort just outside the park boundary.

Again the scenery was changing. Instead of winding up over passes and down across rivers or threading along steep cliffs, the road now unrolled across an arctic prairie punctuated with pothole ponds. Waterfowl and an occasional beaver broke their smooth surfaces. But to the south of the road, diminishing clouds began to disclose a scene of alpine grandeur: snow-mantled peaks with glaciers tumbling down below the snow line. Could Mount McKinley be higher than these?

Suddenly, there it was.

The bus passengers all craned their necks upward, higher and higher. It was hard to believe. The two summits—the south peak 1000 feet higher and two miles distant from the north—floated above the clouds and far above the neighboring mountains that just a moment ago had been so astonishing.

The rest of the mountain slowly revealed itself as the bus traveled the last 10 miles to Wonder Lake. When the passengers arrived at the campground, Denali itself stood forth in its full incredible bulk and height at last: "The Great One," taller than anything else in North America—and looking every inch its size.

Among the many wonders of the wild arctic world, the misty aurora borealis, or northern lights, may be the most spellbinding. Auroras tend to occur around the earth's magnetic poles—eerie showers of glowing light which are thought to be electrified particles of rare gases lit up by the sun's powerful radiation.

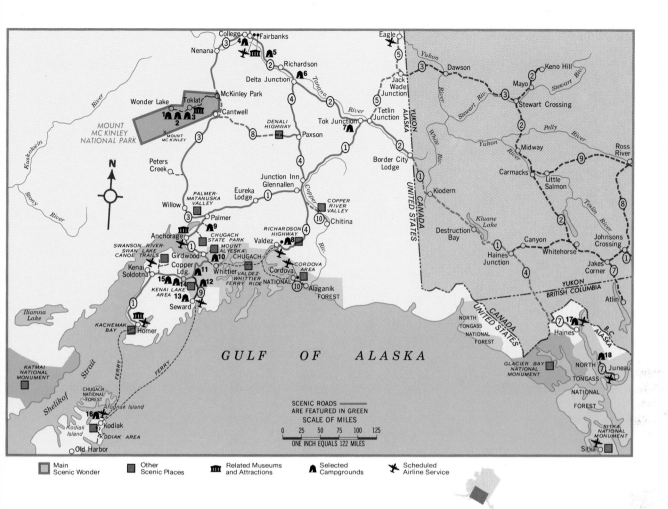

WITHIN A DAY'S JOURNEY:

Mighty Glaciers, Volcanoes, Icebergs and a Rugged Fiord Coast

Chugach State Park. A rugged mountain wilderness laced with glaciers provides a paradise for hikers and climbers within a few miles of Anchorage. Trails lace the area and connect Mount Alyeska with Eagle River.

Copper River Valley. The Edgerton Highway to Chitina passes a spectacular series of waterfalls and wilderness lakes. Above the valley the Wrangell Mountains tower over 16,500 feet.

Cordova Area. The rugged, fiord-like coastline of Prince William Sound is a striking backdrop for the tiny fishing port of Cordova. The remarkable sandbars of the Copper River Delta are a short drive away, and the area is a major waterfowl migration route.

Denali Highway. The approach road to Mount McKinley National Park, open only in summer, offers a series of majestic views of the mighty Alaska Range towering to the north, glaciers winding down the mountain flanks.

Glacier Bay National Monument. (*Pictures appear on pages 516–17*)

Kachemak Bay. Kachemak is a deep fiord 30 miles long. From the highway above Homer there are magnificent views across Cook Inlet toward the volcanic peaks of the Chigmit Mountains.

Katmai National Monument. (*Picture appears on pages 516–17*)

Kenai Lake Area. This is rough mountain country with glacial

rivers and spruce and birch forests. Visitors find campgrounds and hiking trails.

Kodiak Area. Ferries from Homer or Seward serve Kodiak Island, a major center for Alaskan fishing. Scenic shoreline drives north and south of the village of Kodiak lead to a number of pleasant sandy beaches, and most of the island is a national wildlife refuge.

Mount Alyeska. A chair lift here takes skiers up to the Chugach Mountain slopes for more than half the year. At other times it takes hikers to trails through an expanse of alpine tundra.

Palmer–Matanuska Valley. The most developed agricultural area in Alaska grows huge vegetables

515

Glacier Bay National Monument (*left*). *Excursion boats from the Glacier Bay Lodge sail daily from May through September among the islands and up to the edge of glaciers. Seals, whales and mountain goats are among the wildlife to be spotted here—and a host of seabirds. This gull's nest is one of many on Sebree Island.*

Glacier Bay National Monument (*right*). *The face of Muir Glacier is one of the most dramatic sights for most monument visitors. Born high in the Fairweather Range, the river of ice "calves," or forms icebergs, as it meets the water.*

Katmai National Monument (*below*). *The Valley of the Ten Thousand Smokes, ringed by now-extinct volcanoes, is one of the highlights here. Katmai is a remarkable mixture of fire and ice, with ash and lava staining the snow. It can only be reached by air, but fine hikes, and a bus trip to the valley, start from Brooks River.*

in its rich soil, but the wilder aspect of the state is not far away. You can drive close to the Matanuska Glacier, and the Knik River drive provides spectacular views.

Richardson Highway. This scenic route to Valdez climbs into an area of rocky tundra near Thompson Pass, then winds along narrow Keystone Canyon, where waterfalls plunge hundreds of feet.

Sitka National Monument. Totem poles of the Tlingit Indians, who fought against early Russian traders in Alaska, line a trail here, and exhibits outline the area's history. Sitka itself overlooks an island-studded bay.

Swanson River–Swan Lake Canoe Trails. Both trails consist of chains of lakes connected by winding rivers. There is good trout fishing, and camping is permitted along the shores.

Valdez-Whittier Ferry Ride. Prince William Sound is like a large inland sea studded with islands, and this trip takes you along its north shore. At Columbia Glacier, passengers often see ice falling into the water to form icebergs.

RELATED MUSEUMS AND ATTRACTIONS

Anchorage. Anchorage Log Cabin Museum; natural history. Wildlife Museum.

College. University of Alaska Museum; natural history.

Homer. Homer Society of Natural History.

Mount McKinley National Park. Eielson Visitor Center.

Waimea Canyon
KAUAI, HAWAII

Waimea Canyon

HAWAII

Waimea's vivid walls tower above the slender river.

A Dizzying Chasm at the Heart of a Paradise Island

The last thing you expect to see on a lush Pacific island is a sere, gaping chasm—a miniature Grand Canyon cleaving the green peaks. But there it is, cutting across the western side of the Hawaiian island of Kauai: Waimea Canyon. While Waimea's dimensions (10 miles long, a mile wide and half a mile deep) hardly rival those of Arizona's great gorge, its proportions are scarcely less dramatic and certainly its colors, both intense and subtle, are more than a match. But what fixes Waimea securely in one's memory is the surprise of finding such an austere spot in a setting of Pacific beaches and dense rain forests.

Kauai (pronounced *cow-wai*), in fact, specializes in unveiling the unexpected. The fourth largest of the eight major Hawaiian islands, Kauai is 95 miles northwest of Oahu and only 27 minutes by jet from Honolulu. It brims with storybook tropical beauty. Among its other dramatic endowments is the wettest spot on earth, not far from Waimea Canyon's arid slopes. Rising from the center of the island to 5170 feet, Mount Waialeale (which means rippling water) draws almost 500 inches of rainfall a year. In 1947–48 it received a record 624 inches—52 *feet*. Waialeale, which can be seen from the rim of Waimea Canyon when the mists lift, is a source of irrigation for the whole island, supplying water for 100 different falls and at least six main rivers, one of which gouged the canyon itself.

Waimea Canyon is a 40-mile drive from the main airport at Lihue, the island's capital, and the route offers enough scenery and diversion to take up two hours, a half day or as long as you will give it. Along the way you pass gently rolling pineapple and sugarcane fields (which, along with tourism, are the islands' staple industries). A stranger sight is the shimmering green rice paddies, which are not found on any of the other islands. Midwesterners who think the only soil for growing things is velvety black earth will puzzle over the vermilion carpet of mineral-rich volcanic soil near Kaumakani, scene of Hawaii's reddest and most productive farmland. In 1955 Kaumakani turned out 15.52 tons of sugar per acre, a world record.

Nearby, at Waimea Bay, in the winter of 1777–78, Captain James Cook first set foot on the Hawaiian islands. His landing, followed seven years later by another by Captain George Vancouver, was to change forever the simple pattern of Hawaiian life. Waimea was also the scene of the first missionary settlement and a sandalwood trade flourished here before the forests were denuded of those fragrant trees.

Beyond Waimea town, you begin the slow climb to the canyon. After Kekaha, the road quickly departs the dry coastal plain and swings into cool uplands, through forests of koa, their pale, gnarled branches crowned with thick foliage; past silver oak and spicy eucalyptus; past acres of wild native begonias and tree-climbing nasturtiums. One of the strangest trees is the Australian paperbark, which sheds curls of paper-thin bark as it grows. To the left are views of the sea and, 17 miles off the coast, the island of Niihau; its owners prohibit all except invited visitors, and for this reason it is called the "forbidden island." Straight ahead lies Puu Ka Pele (Mountain of Pele), whose 3687-foot summit is often shrouded by mist; to the right, the first hints of Waimea Canyon. At the base of Puu Ka Pele a side road leads to the canyon lookout.

At first, there is nothing to do but stare. It is a half mile straight down, and before you stretch 25 square miles of pinnacled gorge. Feeder canyons join the main chasm in riblike

From the Kalalau Overlook, at the northern end of the canyon, there is an overwhelming vista of sheer green cliffs falling down into the blue Pacific.

The colors at Waimea are startling: orange and red cliffs softened by bright green brush, all in constantly shifting light under a clear tropical sky.

formation. If you have the time, stay through a morning and afternoon to watch the colors change on the canyon walls as the sun moves overhead and clouds flee across the tropic sky. Morning tones are subtle, hard to capture with a camera: delicate blues and greens, dusty rose. By afternoon the reds light up across the canyon as though the gorge were on fire; the blues and greens glow with metallic glints of copper, bronze and gold. Of course you hope for clear weather to sight-see, but there is something haunting and arresting about the sight of fog and mist filtering into the chasm, changing the colors on the canyon walls, then gliding out again, ghostlike.

Waimea Canyon began as a crack in the side of the Great Kauai Volcanic Dome, was eroded over millions of years by river action, sculpted into stunning formations by wind and rain. Its cliffs are nesting places for white-tailed tropical birds that fly out to sea and feed on fish. Elepaio birds—small flycatchers—are abundant in the surrounding woods.

Kauai, the garden island, has some of the most varied and showy plant life in the Pacific, and the most striking around Waimea is the ilihai, which thrives in a narrow belt on the western slope. Its clusters of narrow swordlike leaves rise from single slender stems to a height of from four to 12 feet: it blooms in June and July in towering pagodalike golden tiers. On the drier slopes grows the native white hibiscus tree, producing the only fragrant hibiscus blossom. Mokihana, which provides the sweetest flower lei of them all, further scents this otherworldly scene.

Across from the lookout, a branch canyon enters the main canyon at right angles. This is the Koaie, and five miles up is a large village site with a 180-foot temple which was built in five terraces against the cliff.

Another eye-filling view of the canyon is at Kaana Ridge (which has a parking lot, pavilion and lookout area), and from there you can proceed to the fascinating Kokee district through a tropical rain forest full of mokihana berry, ilihai, silver oak and wild plum trees. Here in a mountain meadow is a state forest reserve

with cabins for rent—a place cool enough at night for woolens. Past Kokee you wind through a dense forest for three miles and then emerge at the Kalalau Lookout.

At Kalalau you stand 4000 feet above the Pacific and look down razor-edged ridges to a green valley, a narrow white sand beach and a savage pounding sea. Here are the famous Na Pali Cliffs, bordering Kalalua Valley, the most rugged and exposed coastline in the islands. In this remote valley Hawaiians lived for many hundreds of years, but today only stray goats, pigs and cattle still roam it, and campers come and go. The only practical way down to the valley for most people is by hired helicopter, which takes you almost within arm's reach of the fluted cliffs, cascading falls and dense woodlands. This is one of James Michener's chosen wonders of Hawaii.

Here, at the end of Kauai, you can look up the coast toward Haena Point, separated from it by seven miles of dense, junglelike growth —22 miles by slick and slippery paths. A visitor can only hope that this unparalleled spectacle of canyon, cliff and sea will remain as splendidly unimpaired as it is today.

Mount Waialeale, which looms high over Waimea, is the wettest spot on earth, its sides covered with virtually impenetrable tropical rain forest.

The Rich and Exotic Flora of Hawaii

Isolated by thousands of miles of ocean from the nearest mainland, and blessed with a warm, moist climate, the Hawaiian islands are a showcase for a largely unique plant life (most of its flora are found nowhere else). The ohia-lehua, for instance, is ubiquitous in the islands, often the first tree to appear on a new lava flow; its red flowers are much used for the lei, or flower garland. The lovely kokia keokeo blooms in rocky ravines. The wiliwili, with flowers ranging from pale yellow to deep orange, is one of the few Hawaiian trees that sheds its leaves. The spectacular flame flower, bright and red as its name, grows on a vine. The glowing torch ginger tops canes 20 feet high.

OHIA-LEHUA
Metrosideros collina

KOKIA KEOKEO (White Hibiscus)
Hibiscus arnottianus

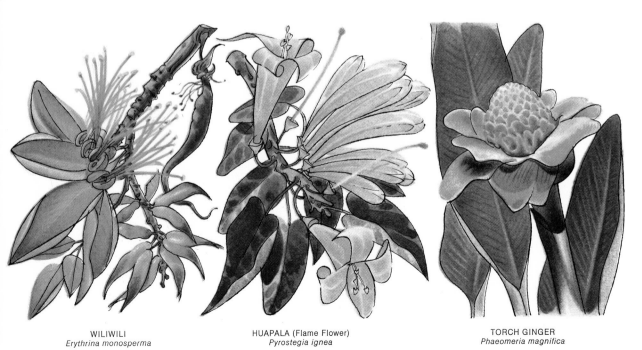

WILIWILI	HUAPALA (Flame Flower)	TORCH GINGER
Erythrina monosperma	*Pyrostegia ignea*	*Phaeomeria magnifica*

523

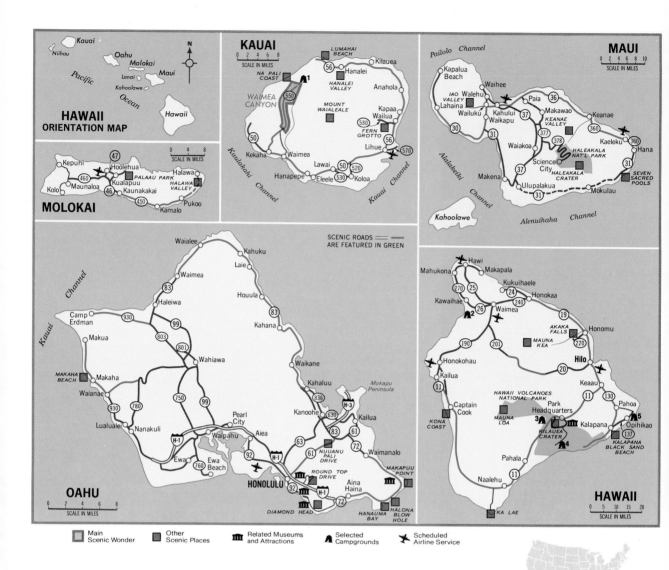

Main Scenic Wonder   Other Scenic Places   Related Museums and Attractions   Selected Campgrounds   Scheduled Airline Service

WITHIN THE ISLANDS:

Black Sands and Live Volcanoes

Akaka Falls, Hawaii. The foot trail to the falls loops through an enchanted forest thick with giant tree ferns, groves of bamboos and climbing orchids, all creating a soft green canopy overhead that sheds only misty shafts of light. But the end of the trail opens up on sunstruck Akaka Falls, a narrow band of water that plunges 420 feet over rocks covered with moss.

Diamond Head, Oahu. Among the world's most famous landmarks, the near-perfect volcanic crater on the edge of Honolulu's Waikiki Beach symbolizes the exotic beauty of all the Hawaiian

islands. A hiking trail in the crater climbs to the seaward cliffs, and below them lies a beach park for water sports.

Fern Grotto, Kauai. A launch ride three miles up the Wailua River, Hawaii's only navigable waterway, takes visitors to this cool cave lavishly festooned with ferns, a natural amphitheater where serenaders eagerly show off the fine acoustics.

Halawa Valley, Molokai. Legend and history cling to this lovely green valley, once settled by Hawaiian farmers and fishermen, now deserted except for a few

houses, an old church and some ancient burial grounds. Jungle overruns taro plots, blankets the valley cliffs and often hides hiking trails to plunging Moaula and Hipuapua waterfalls.

Haleakala Crater, Maui. (*Picture appears on page 527*)

Halona Blow Hole, Oahu. When surging seas crash against the ledges here, water squeezing through an underwater lava tube shoots a dazzling fountain high into the sky.

Hanalei Valley, Kauai. Fluted green mountains, often laced with waterfalls and spanned by rainbows, are the backdrop for a tranquil valley checkered with neat taro patches, some flooded and glistening like quicksilver. Altogether the landscape looks like an authentic Hawaiian Shangri-la.

Hanauma Bay, Oahu.
(*Picture appears on page 526*)

Iao Valley, Maui.
(*Picture appears on this page*)

Ka Lae, Hawaii. Jagged lava cliffs and deep, windswept waters mark the southernmost tip of the United States. The earliest Hawaiians settled here: visitors find ruins over 1000 years old and stones to which canoes were once secured—all in sight of Mauna Loa.

Kalapana Black Sand Beach, Hawaii. When lava flows collided with the ocean, the hot liquid cooled into black ledges and stones or froze into coarse sand that tides grind ever finer. Coconut palms hang over the dusky shore like a lineup of giants' feather dusters carelessly stuck into the sand.

Keanae Valley, Maui. A lookout yields a sweeping panorama: the lush deep valley runs inland to Haleakala volcano and seaward between taro patches and banana groves covering a small peninsula. For more down-to-earth views, hikers can follow a trail that cuts across the valley.

Kilauea Crater, Hawaii. The showpiece of Hawaii Volcanoes National Park, Kilauea Crater is so large and deep that visitors can see its frequent eruptions in close-up. Roads and trails lace the area: even without the fireworks, there are enough gaping chasms, bubbling pits and steam vents to spellbind onlookers for days.

Kona Coast, Hawaii. The 60-mile drive along Hawaii's west coast flanks the slopes of Mauna Loa, surveys languid seascapes, passes exotic coffee plantations, macadamia nut orchards and lava flows. And it is an excursion to historic places where Hawaiian kings once held court and missionaries first built their churches.

Lumahai Beach, Kauai. A dreamlike Pacific paradise, this beach area was in fact the main setting of the movie *South Pacific*. Currents forbid safe swimming, but flowing pandanus trees, curving sands and curling surf make a memorable view.

Makaha Beach, Oahu. Some of the most perfect waves in the world surge to shore here. International surfers meet in December to race their boards and compete for world championships.

Makapuu Point, Oahu. Visitors need Coast Guard permission to drive the narrow road to the lighthouse at the end of this massive headland, but a sweeping view rewards the effort: the entire windward coast of Oahu unfolds below the Koolau Range.

Mauna Kea, Hawaii. Only strong hikers can reach the summit of Mauna Kea, at 13,796 feet the highest point in the state. But auto-borne visitors can drive a steep cinder road—past quails,

Iao Valley, *Maui. Steep forest-clad pinnacles wall in this primeval gorge divided in the middle by the rushing Iao Stream. Footpaths thread down to the waterway and climb up to a lookout point for long-range views into the deeper recesses of this tropical Eden.*

Hanauma Bay, *Oahu (left). Koko Crater looms over the arching bay, once a volcano crater itself. Ages of pounding from heavy surf gradually eroded its ocean wall, creating a popular beach resort with crystal-clear waters for swimming and snorkeling.*

Haleakala Crater, *Maui (right). The vast crater valley lies like a desolate moonscape filled with cinder slopes and rough lava rock. On its slopes live rare wildlife like the nene, Hawaii's state bird, and the silversword plants, which are unique to this volcanic area.*

Na Pali Coast, *Kauai (below). High-rise cliffs dive recklessly straight into the sea, while a graceful wave curls at their feet. This jungled coast, broken by narrow, deep valleys, is a natural fortress accessible only by sea or by helicopter excursions.*

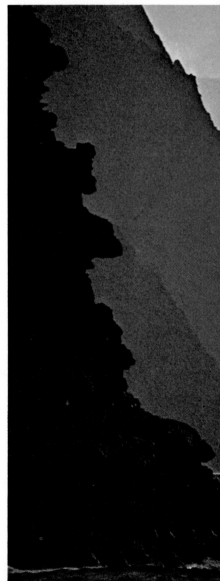

pheasants and other wild game —up to a 9600-foot lookout, a lofty perch for aerial views of the island, including impressive close-ups of Mauna Loa.

Mauna Loa, Hawaii. More than any other place on earth, the landscape here resembles the jagged peaks, ridges and rubble of the moon. The highest drive in the Pacific—it climbs to 11,150 feet—winds up among weird stone sculptures, and lava flows that still spill from the volcano.

Mount Waialeale, Kauai. With around 500 inches of rainfall a year, this cloud-shrouded fastness is the world's wettest spot. An almost inaccessible wilderness of lush gorges and valleys extends below its summit; it can be admired on a helicopter tour.

Na Pali Coast, Kauai.
(Picture appears on this page)

Nuuanu Pali Drive, Oahu. The highway climbs the Koolau Range above Honolulu, passing through a jungle of eucalyptus, bamboo and philodendron. The summit lookout is justly famous: towering palisades drop about 2000 feet to the green coastal strip along graceful Kaneohe Bay.

Palaau Park, Molokai. The 2000-foot lookout draws visitors here: sheer cliffs fall to tiny, triangular Kalaupapa Peninsula, site of a leper colony for 100 years, once succored by the famous Belgian priest Father Damien. Today's settlement welcomes tours of its historic seabound home.

Round Top Drive, Oahu. A short distance from Honolulu, the mountain drive passes through virgin forests and provides bird's-eye views of Oahu's south coast from Pearl Harbor to Diamond Head.

Seven Sacred Pools, Maui. Just before the paved highway ends on Maui's southeast coast, a bridge crosses the series of pools carved out of rock by a cascading stream. They offer cool swimming holes.

RELATED MUSEUMS AND ATTRACTIONS

Hawaii Volcanoes National Park, Hawaii. Park Museum.

Honolulu, Oahu.
Bernice P. Bishop Museum; natural history.
Foster Botanic Gardens.
University of Hawaii Waikiki Aquarium.

Sea Life Park, Oahu.

Campground Directory

This listing of the campgrounds surrounding each of the 50 Scenic Wonders should be used with the map that accompanies each "wonder," on which campgrounds are indicated by a number and a campground symbol. Campgrounds were chosen on the basis of size, type and quality of facilities, attractiveness of setting, and location (proximity to related scenic attractions). All are on public lands.

Here is a sample listing under its heading, followed by instructions on how to read it:

Mount Washington
(Map is on page 32)

8 Wildwood. From ST 25A, E 1 mi., N 1 mi. on local rds. Apr. 15–Oct. 15. 240 tents, 80 trailers (max. 25 ft.). Fee. Resv. required. Elec., sewer hookup. Dumping station. Showers. Cafe. Store 1 mi. Swimming, fishing.

8 is the number of this campground on the map (page 32) where it appears.
Wildwood is its official name. Occasionally the same campground may be known locally by a different name.
From ST 25A, E 1 mi., N 1 mi. on local rds. Only the more important roads are marked on the maps, and wherever local roads or Forest Service roads have to be used to reach the camp, directions and distances are given from the nearest marked road.
Apr. 15–Oct. 15. Many campgrounds are open seasonally, and opening and closing dates are given whenever this is the case. Sometimes, as stated, the campground is open all year.
240 tents, 80 trailers (max. 25 ft.). This is the kind and number of spaces allotted, and the maximum length of trailer allowed in places where there is such a restriction. (In these listings all types of camping vehicles are covered

by the term "trailer.") Some campgrounds simply offer a certain number of spaces to be used by either tents or trailers.
Fee. Whenever there is a charge, either for admission to the park where a campground is located, or for an overnight stay at the campground itself, this is mentioned. The amounts are not given, but such fees on public lands are usually small, averaging $2.00.
Resv. required. Some campgrounds—though not many—require advance reservations for space. Others do not require them but accept them—and particularly when traveling in popular areas in summer it is wise to take advantage of this when possible.
Elec., sewer hookup. Dumping station. Sometimes there is a charge for hookups, and where this is the case it is specified. Such facilities are increasing on state and national lands these days, and some campgrounds whose listings here do not mention hookups or dumping stations may have acquired them recently. All campgrounds offer some sort of toilet facilities —pit toilets in the more primitive places, flush toilets in the others.
Showers are indicated where available.
Cafe. Store 1 mi. If such amenities exist at the campground itself, they are listed without a distance indicated; otherwise distances are given to the nearest mile.
Swimming, fishing and other recreational facilities, such as boat dock, launch or rental, and horseback riding, are listed where available.
National Park Service campgrounds are included in the booklet "Camping in the National Park System" (stock no. 2405-00535). Send 55 cents, by check or money order only, to Superintendent of Documents, U.S. Government Printing Office, Washington, D.C. 20402.

Acadia National Park

(Map is on page 24)

Two campgrounds in the park, with trailer space but no utility connections.

For information on all state campgrounds, write to State Park and Recreation Commission, State House, Augusta, Maine 04330.

For information on U.S. Forest Service campgrounds, write to Eastern Region, Forest Service, Clark Building, 633 W. Wisconsin Ave., Milwaukee, Wis. 53203.

1 Matagamon Lake Wilderness. From ST 159, W 14 mi. on Grand Lake. May 15–Oct. 15. 38 tents or trailers. Fee. No flush toilets. Swimming. Boat launch.

2 South Branch St. Pk. From ST 159, W 35 mi. on Trout Brook Rd. May 5–Oct. 15. 21 tents. Fee. Resv. accepted. No pets. No flush toilets. Swimming, fishing. Boat launch, rental.

3 Roaring Brook. Off ST 11 at Millinocket, NW 26 mi. on Roaring Brook Rd. May 15–Oct. 15. 14 tents. Fee. Resv. accepted. No pets. No flush toilets. Fishing 1 mi.

4 Katahdin Stream. Off ST 11 at Millinocket, NW 26 mi. on Nesowadnehunk Rd. May 15–Oct. 15. 13 tents. Fee. Resv. accepted. No pets. No flush toilets. Swimming, fishing.

5 Newsowadnehunk. Off ST 11 at Millinocket, NW 36 mi. on Ripogenous Rd. May 15–Oct. 15. 12 tents. Fee. Resv. accepted. No pets. No flush toilets. Swimming, fishing.

6 Lily Bay St. Pk. May 15–Oct. 15. 89 tents or trailers (max. 24 ft.). Fee. No flush toilets. Swimming, fishing. Boat launch, rental.

7 Cathedral Pines. May 15–Oct. 15. 56 tents or trailers. Fee. Resv. accepted. Showers. Store 1 mi. Swimming, fishing.

8 Rangeley Lake St. Pk. May 15–Oct. 15. 51 tents or trailers (max. 20 ft.). Fee. Showers. Swimming, fishing. Boat launch, rental.

9 Mt. Blue St. Pk. May 30–Oct. 15. 183 tents or trailers (max. 24 ft.). Fee. No flush toilets. Swimming, fishing. Boat launch, rental.

10 Hastings. June 1–Oct. 15. 24 tents or trailers (max. 22 ft.). Fee. Cafe. Fishing.

11 Crocker Pond. S. 4 mi. at West Bethel. June 1–Oct. 15. 7 tents. Fee. Swimming, fishing. Boat dock.

12 Sebago Lake St. Pk. May 1–Oct. 15. 295 tents or trailers (max. 20 ft.). Fee. Showers. Cafe, store. Swimming, fishing. Boat launch, rental. Riding.

13 Bradbury Mountain. May 1–Nov. 1. 54 tents or trailers (max. 20 ft.). Fee. No flush toilets. Store 1 mi.

14 Winslow Memorial Park. From Hwy. 95, 2 mi. on Staples Pt. Rd. May 31–Aug. 1. 100 tents or trailers. Fee. Dumping station 1 mi. Store 1 mi. Swimming, fishing. Boat launch.

15 Lake St. George St. Pk. May 1–Nov. 1. 31 tents or trailers (max. 24 ft.). Fee.

No flush toilets. Store 1 mi. Swimming, fishing. Boat launch, rental.

16 Camden Hills St. Pk. May 15–Nov. 1. 118 tents or trailers (max. 24 ft.). Fee. Showers. Store 1 mi.

17 Lamoine St. Pk. May 30–Oct. 15. 50 tents or trailers (max. 24 ft.). Fee. No flush toilets. Swimming, fishing. Boat launch, rental.

18 Seawall. May 1–Oct. 30. 230 tents or trailers (max. 22 ft.). Fee. Swimming, fishing 1 mi.

19 Black Woods. May 1–Oct. 30. 290 tents or trailers (max. 22 ft.). Fee. Resv. accepted. Showers 1 mi. Store 1 mi. Swimming, fishing 1 mi. Boats for rent.

20 Machias River. All year. 10 tents or trailers (max. 24 ft.). Fee. No flush toilets. Swimming, fishing.

21 Elsmore Landing. All year. 12 tents or trailers. Fee. No flush toilets. Swimming, fishing. Boat launch.

22 Long Lake. From US 1, W 1½ mi. & S 1 mi. on Peter Dana Pt. Rd. All year. 32 tents or trailers. Fee. Resv. accepted. No flush toilets. Swimming, fishing. Boat launch, rental.

23 Cobscook. May 15–Oct. 15. 128 tents or trailers (max. 20 ft.). Fee. No flush toilets. Fishing. Boat launch.

Mount Washington

(Map is on page 32)

One campground on the mountain, in Tuckerman Ravine.

For information on state campgrounds in New Hampshire, write to Division of Economic Development, P.O. Box 856, Concord, N.H. 03301;
    in New York, to Park Information, Parks and Recreation, Bldg. 2, State Campus, Albany, N.Y. 12226;
    in Vermont, to Department of Forests and Parks, Montpelier, Vt. 05602.

For information on U.S. Forest Service campgrounds, write to Eastern Region, Forest Service, 633 W. Wisconsin Ave., Milwaukee, Wis. 53203.

1 Coles Creek. May 15–Oct. 15. 80 tents, 100 trailers (max. 30 ft.). Fee. Elec., water hookup. Dumping station. Showers. Cafe, store. Swimming, fishing. Boat launch, rental.

2 Jacques Cartier St. Pk. May 15–Oct. 15. 104 tents, 22 trailers. Fee. Elec. hookup. Dumping station. Showers. Cafe, store. Swimming, fishing. Boat launch, rental.

3 Fish Creek. May 6–Dec. 2. 382 tents or trailers (max. 25 ft.). Fee. Dumping station. Store 1 mi. Swimming, fishing. Boat launch, rental.

4 Wilmington Notch. May 1–Sept. 19. 50 tents or trailers (max. 25 ft.). Fee. Dumping station. Fishing.

5 Lake Eaton. May 16–Sept. 12. 142 tents or trailers (max. 25 ft.). Fee. Dumping station. Store 1 mi. Swimming, fishing. Boat launch, rental.

6 Limekiln Lake. From ST 28, S 1 mi. on local rd. May 16–Dec. 2. 274 tents or trailers (max. 25 ft.). Fee. Store 1 mi. Swimming, fishing. Boat launch, rental.

7 Moffitt Beach. May 12–Sept. 12. 257 tents or trailers (max. 25 ft.). Fee. Dumping station. Store 1 mi. Swimming, fishing. Boat launch, rental.

8 Pixley Falls St. Pk. May 1–Oct. 15. 18 tents or trailers (max. 28 ft.). Fee. No flush toilets. Fishing.

9 Woodford St. Pk. May 25–Oct. 12. 71 tents, 40 trailers (max. 18 ft.). Fee. Resv. accepted. Showers. Swimming, fishing. Boat launch, rental.

10 St. Catherine St. Pk. May 25–Oct. 12. 84 tents or trailers (max. 18 ft.). Fee. Resv. accepted. Dumping station. Showers. Cafe. Store 1 mi. Swimming, fishing. Boat launch, rental.

11 Eagle Point. May 16–Sept. 12. 65 tents or trailers (max. 25 ft.). Fee. Cafe 1 mi. Swimming, fishing. Boat launch, rental.

12 Rogers Rock. May 16–Dec. 2. 301 tents or trailers (max. 25 ft.). Fee. Dumping station. Swimming, fishing. Boat launch.

13 Button Bay. From ST 7, W 2 mi., NW 5 mi., S 1 mi. on local rds. May 25–Oct. 12. 70 tents or trailers (max. 18 ft.). Fee. Resv. accepted. Dumping station. Showers. Swimming, fishing. Boating.

14 Little River (Waterbury Dam). May 25–Oct. 12. 64 tents, 45 trailers (max. 18 ft.). Fee. Resv. accepted. Showers. Swimming, fishing. Boat launch, rental.

15 Cumberland Bay St. Pk. May 15–Oct. 15. 220 tents or trailers. Fee. Dumping station. Showers. Cafe. Swimming, fishing.

16 Grand Isle St. Pk. May 25–Oct. 12. 159 tents or trailers (max. 18 ft.). Fee. Resv. accepted. Dumping station. Showers. Cafe, store. Swimming, fishing. Boat launch, rental.

17 North Hero. From ST 2, N 2 mi. on local rd. May 25–Oct. 12. 80 tents or trailers (max. 18 ft.). Fee. Resv. accepted. Showers. Swimming, fishing.

18 Lake Carmi St. Pk. May 25–Oct. 12. 177 tents or trailers (max. 18 ft.). Fee. Resv. accepted. Dumping station. Showers. Cafe. Swimming, fishing. Boat launch, rental.

19 Brighton St. Pk. From ST 105–114, S 3 mi. on local rd. May 25–Oct. 12. 84 tents, 40 trailers (max. 18 ft.). Fee. Resv. accepted. Showers. Cafe. Swimming, fishing. Boat launch, rental.

20 New Discovery. May 25–Oct. 12. 64 tents, 40 trailers (max. 18 ft.). Fee. Resv. accepted. Showers. Swimming 1 mi. Fishing. Boat launch, rental.

21 Moose Brook. June 15–Sept. 4. 42 tents or trailers. Fee. Showers. Cafe, store 1 mi. Swimming, fishing 1 mi.

22 Franconia Notch St. Pk. May 21–Oct. 12. 98 tents or trailers. Fee. Showers. Store 1 mi. Swimming 1 mi.

23 Covered Bridge. From jct. ST 16, 153 and 113, N 1 mi., W 5 mi. on local rds. May 30–Oct. 15. 49 tents or trailers (max.

22 ft.). Fee. Swimming, fishing 1 mi.

24 White Ledge. May 30–Oct. 15. 39 tents or trailers (max. 22 ft.). Fee. Cafe 1 mi. Fishing 4 mi.

25 White Lake St. Pk. May 7–Oct. 12. 185 tents or trailers. Fee. Cafe 1 mi. Store 2 mi. Swimming, fishing 1 mi. Boat launch, rental.

26 Pillsbury St. Pk. June 30–Sept. 15. 20 tents or trailers. Fee. No flush toilets. Fishing 1 mi. Boat launch, rental.

27 Bear Brook St. Pk. May 15–Oct. 12. 90 tents or trailers. Fee. Swimming, fishing 1 mi. Boats for rent.

28 Greenfield St. Pk. May 27–Oct. 12. 252 tents or trailers. Fee. Cafe, store 1 mi. Swimming, fishing 1 mi. Boat launch, rental.

Niagara Falls
(Map is on page 43)

For information on state campgrounds in New York, write to Park Information, Parks and Recreation, Bldg. 2, State Campus, Albany, N.Y. 12226;
in New Jersey, to Division of Parks, Forestry and Recreation, P.O. Box 1889, Trenton, N.J. 08625;
in Pennsylvania, to Bureau of State Parks, Room 601, Feller Bldg., 301 Market St., Harrisburg, Pa. 17101.

For information on U.S. Forest Service campgrounds, write to Eastern Region, Forest Service, 633 W. Wisconsin Ave., Milwaukee, Wis. 53203.

1 Pymatuning. All year. 540 tents, 490 trailers (max. 30 ft.). Fee. Elec. hookup —extra chg. Dumping station. Showers. Cafe, store. Swimming, fishing. Boat launch, rental.

2 Pymatuning. Apr. 15–Dec. 20. 600 tents or trailers (max. 28 ft.). Fee. No pets. Dumping station. Showers. Cafe, store. Swimming, fishing. Boat launch, rental.

3 Atwood Lake Park. All year. 569 tents or trailers (max. 30 ft.). Fee. Elec. hookup—extra chg. Dumping station. No flush toilets. Showers. Cafe, store 1 mi. Swimming, fishing. Boat dock, launch, rental.

4 Salt Fork St. Pk. All year. 212 tents or trailers (max. 30 ft.). Fee. No pets. Elec. hookup. Dumping station. Showers. Swimming, fishing. Boating.

5 Seneca Lake Park. All year. 150 tents, 416 trailers (max. 30 ft.). Fee. Elec. hookup—extra chg. Dumping station. Showers. Cafe, store. Swimming, fishing. Boat launch, rental.

6 Laurel Hill. Apr. 15–Dec. 20. 268 tents or trailers (max. 28 ft.). Fee. No pets. Dumping station. Showers. Cafe, store. Swimming, fishing. Boat launch.

7 Shawnee St. Pk. All year. 335 tents or trailers (max. 28 ft.). Fee. No pets. Showers. Cafe, store 1 mi. Swimming, fishing. Boat launch, rental.

8 Keystone St. Pk. Apr. 15–Dec. 20. 40 tents or trailers (max. 28 ft.). Fee. No

pets. Showers. Cafe, store. Swimming, fishing. Boat launch, rental.

9 Prince Gallitzin St. Pk. Apr. 15–Dec. 20. 437 tents or trailers (max. 28 ft.). Fee. No pets. Showers. Cafe, store. Swimming, fishing. Boat launch, rental.

10 Cook Forest St. Pk. All year. 100 tents or trailers (max. 28 ft.). Fee. No pets. No flush toilets. Cafe, store 1 mi. Swimming, fishing.

11 Twin Lakes. From Hwy. 321, NW 2 mi. on FR 191. June 1–Sept. 7. 5 tents, 45 trailers (max. 22 ft.). Fee. Elec. hookup. Cafe 5 mi. Swimming, fishing.

12 Buckaloons. Apr. 1–Dec. 30. 50 tents, 40 trailers (max. 22 ft.). Fee. Elec. hookup. Showers. Cafe 1 mi. Swimming, fishing. Boat launch.

13 Allegany St. Pk. All year. 146 tents, 157 trailers (max. 32 ft.). Fee. Elec. hookup—extra chg. Showers. Cafe, store. Swimming pool. Fishing. Boat launch, rental. Horseback riding.

14 Lake Erie. May 15–Oct. 15. 146 tents, 157 trailers (max. 32 ft.). Fee. Elec. hookup—extra chg. Dumping station. Showers. Cafe, store. Swimming, fishing. Boat launch, rental. Horseback riding.

15 Letchworth St. Pk. May 15–Oct. 19. 300 tents or trailers (max. 28 ft.). Fee. Elec. hookup. Showers. Cafe, store. Swimming, fishing.

16 Four Mile Creek St. Pk. May 15–Nov. 15. 150 tents, 250 trailers. Fee. Resv. required. Elec. hookup. Dumping station. Showers. Cafe, store 1 mi. Swimming 1 mi. Fishing. Boat launch. Horseback riding.

17 Wellesley Island. May 15–Oct. 15. 260 tents, 130 trailers (max. 30 ft.). Fee. Elec., water, sewer hookup. Dumping station. Showers. Cafe, store. Swimming, fishing. Boat launch, rental.

18 Cedar Point St. Pk. May 15–Oct. 15. 107 tents, 96 trailers (max. 30 ft.). Fee. Elec., water, sewer hookup. Dumping station. Showers. Cafe, store. Swimming, fishing. Boat launch, rental.

19 Sampson St. Pk. May 1–Oct. 15. 245 tents or trailers (max. 30 ft.). Fee. Elec. hookup—extra chg. Showers. Cafe. Swimming, fishing. Boat launch.

20 Taughannock Falls St. Pk. May 1–Oct. 15. 68 tents or trailers (max. 30 ft.). Fee. Elec. hookup—extra chg. Water hookup. Showers. Cafe. Store 1 mi. Swimming, fishing. Boat launch.

21 Buttermilk Falls St. Pk. May 1–Oct. 15. 60 tents, 42 trailers (max. 18 ft.). Fee. Showers. Cafe. Store 1 mi. Swimming pool. Fishing.

22 Robert H. Treman St. Pk. May 1–Oct. 15. 129 tents or trailers (max. 30 ft.). Fee. Elec. hookup—extra chg. Showers. Cafe. Store 1 mi. Swimming pool. Fishing.

23 Watkins Glen St. Pk. May 1–Oct. 15. 100 tents or trailers (max. 30 ft.). Fee. Showers. Cafe. Store 1 mi. Pool.

24 Leonard Harrison St. Pk. All year. 30 tents or trailers (max. 28 ft.). Fee. No pets. No flush toilets. Cafe 1 mi. Store. Fishing.

25 Ricketts Glen St. Pk. All year. 102 tents or trailers (max. 28 ft.). Fee. No pets. No flush toilets. Cafe, store. Swimming, fishing. Boat launch, rental.

26 Caledonia. All year. 206 tents or trailers (max. 28 ft.). Fee. No pets. Cafe, store. Swimming, fishing.

Cape Cod National Seashore
(Map is on page 52)

Four private campgrounds in the Seashore.

For information on state campgrounds in Connecticut, write to State Park and Forest Commission, 165 Capitol Ave., Hartford, Conn. 06115;
in Massachusetts, to Division of Forests and Parks, 100 Cambridge St., Boston, Mass. 02202;
in New York, to Park Information, Parks and Recreation, Bldg. 2, State Campus, Albany, N.Y. 12226;
in Rhode Island, to Rhode Island Development Council, Tourist Promotion Division, Roger Williams Bldg., 49 Hayes St., Providence, R.I. 02908.

For information on U.S. Forest Service campgrounds, write to Eastern Region, Forest Service, 633 W. Wisconsin Ave., Milwaukee, Wis. 53203.

1 Savoy Mountain St. Forest. May 1–Oct. 15. 45 tents, 60 trailers (max. 16 ft.). Fee. Showers. Swimming, fishing, boat launch. Horseback riding.

2 Mohawk Trail St. Forest. May 1–Oct. 30. 58 tents or trailers (max. 16 ft.). Fee. Cafe, store. Swimming, fishing. Horseback riding.

3 D.A.R. St. Forest. May 1–Oct. 15. 50 tents or trailers (max. 20 ft.). Fee. Swimming, fishing. Boat launch. Horseback riding.

4 Burr Pond. From Hwy. 8, W 1 mi. on town rd. May 1–Sept. 30. 50 tents or trailers (max. 35 ft.). Fee. Showers—extra chg. Swimming, fishing.

5 Housatonic Meadows. May 1–Sept. 30. 50 tents or trailers (max. 35 ft.). Fee. Fishing.

6 Kettletown. From US 6 & 202, SE 2 mi. on town rds. May 1–Sept. 30. 120 tents or trailers (max. 35 ft.). Fee. Showers—extra chg. Swimming.

7 Hammonasset Beach. May 1–Sept. 30. 900 tents or trailers (max. 35 ft.). Fee. Dumping station. Showers—extra chg. Cafe. Store 1 mi. Swimming, fishing.

8 Wildwood. From ST 25A, E 1 mi., N 1 mi. on local rds. April 15–Oct. 15. 240 tents, 80 trailers (max. 25 ft.). Fee Resv. required. Elec., sewer hookup. Dumping station. Showers. Cafe. Store 1 mi. Swimming, fishing.

9 Hither Hills. Apr. 15–Oct. 15. 161 tents or trailers (max. 25 ft.). Fee. Resv. required. Showers. Cafe, store. Swimming, fishing.

10 Rocky Neck. May 1–Sept. 30. 250

tents or trailers (max. 35 ft.) Fee. Dumping station. Cafe. Store 1 mi. Swimming, fishing.

11 Burlingame. Apr. 1–Oct. 31. 755 tents or trailers (max. 30 ft.). Fee. Dumping station. Cafe, store. Swimming, fishing.

12 Arcadia. Apr. 1–Oct. 31. 25 tents or trailers (max. 30 ft.). Fee. Swimming, fishing.

13 Hopeville Pond. May 1–Sept. 30. 82 tents or trailers (max. 35 ft.). Fee. Dumping station. Showers—extra chg. Cafe. Store 1 mi. Swimming, fishing. Boat launch.

14 Geo. Washington Memorial St. Forest. Apr. 1–Oct. 31. 40 tents, 26 trailers (max. 30 ft.). Fee. Swimming, fishing. Boat launch.

15 Erving St. Forest. From ST 2, N 2 mi. on forest rd. May 1–Oct. 10. 28 tents or trailers (max. 16 ft.). Fee. Cafe. Swimming, fishing. Boat launch. Horseback riding.

16 Lake Dennison. May 1–Oct. 15. 50 tents or trailers (max. 20 ft.). Fee. Showers. Swimming, fishing. Boat launch.

17 Harold Parker St. Forest. From ST 28, E 2 mi. on forest rd. May 1–Oct. 15. 120 tents or trailers (max. 20 ft.). Fee. Showers. Store. Swimming, fishing. Boats for rent. Horseback riding.

18 Massasoit. May 1–Oct. 15. 130 tents or trailers (max. 25 ft.). Fee. Elec. hookup—extra chg. Water, sewer hookup. Dumping station. Showers. Swimming, fishing.

19 Myles Standish St. Forest. From ST 58, E 3 mi. on forest rd. May 1–Oct. 15. 242 tents or trailers (max. 20 ft.). Fee. Cafe. Swimming, fishing. Boating.

20 Shawme–Crowell St. Forest. May 1–Oct. 15. 230 tents or trailers (max. 20 ft.). Fee. Showers.

Hudson Valley
(Map is on page 63)

For information on state campgrounds in New York, write to Park Information, Parks and Recreation, Bldg. 2, State Campus, Albany, N.Y. 12226;
in New Jersey, to Division of Parks, Forestry and Recreation, P.O. Box 1889, Trenton, N.J. 08625;
in Pennsylvania, to Bureau of State Parks, Room 601, Feller Bldg., 301 Market St., Harrisburg, Pa. 17101.

For information on U.S. Forest Service campgrounds, write to Eastern Region, Forest Service, 633 W. Wisconsin Ave., Milwaukee, Wis. 53203.

1 Little Pond. May 16–Sept. 12. 8 tents, 67 trailers (max. 30 ft.). Showers 1 mi. Swimming, fishing. Boat launch.

2 Beaverkill. May 1–Sept. 12. 105 tents or trailers. Fee. Showers 1 mi. Swimming, fishing.

3 Mongaup Pond Campsite. May 16–Dec. 2. 160 tents or trailers. Fee. Swimming, fishing.

4 Woodland Valley. May 16–Dec. 2. 57 tents or trailers. Fee. Showers.

5 Lake Taghkanic St. Pk. May 14–Oct. 31. 78 tents, 31 trailers (max. 21 ft.). Fee. Resv. required. Showers. Cafe, store 1 mi. Swimming, fishing. Boat launch, rental.

6 Taconic St. Pk. May 14–Oct. 31. 120 tents, 30 trailers (max. 18 ft.). Fee. Cafe, store 1 mi. Swimming, fishing.

7 Clarence Fahnestock St. Pk. May 14–Oct. 31. 83 tents, 55 trailers (max. 30 ft.). Fee. Resv. required. Cafe 1 mi. Fishing. Boat launch. Horseback riding.

8 Lake Welch–Harriman St. Pk. Apr. 15–Oct. 15. 138 tents, 82 trailers (max. 17 ft.). Fee. Resv. required. Dumping station. Showers. Swimming. Boat rental.

9 Stokes St. Pk. All year. 81 tents or trailers (max. 24 ft.). Fee. Resv. accepted. No flush toilets. Swimming, fishing 1 mi. Boat launch.

10 Promised Land St. Pk. All year. 316 tents, 216 trailers (max. 28 ft.). Fee. No flush toilets. Cafe 1 mi. Store. Swimming, fishing. Boat launch, rental.

11 Tobyhanna St. Pk. All year. No tents. 140 trailers (max. 28 ft.). Fee. No flush toilets. Cafe 1 mi. Store. Swimming, fishing. Boat launch, rental.

12 Hickory Run St. Pk. Apr. 15–Dec. 20. 261 tents or trailers (max. 28 ft.). Fee. No pets. No flush toilets. Cafe 1 mi. Store. Swimming, fishing. Boat launch, rental.

13 Worthington St. Pk. From I-80, NE 4 mi. on local rd. All year. 85 tents or trailers (max. 24 ft.). Fee. Resv. accepted. No flush toilets. Fishing. Boat launch.

14 Swartswood St. Pk. All year. 67 tents or trailers (max. 24 ft.). Fee. Resv. accepted. Dumping station. Cafe 1 mi. Swimming 1 mi. Fishing. Boat launch, rental.

15 Jenny Jump St. Pk. Apr. 1–Oct. 31. 20 tents or trailers (max. 24 ft.). Fee. Resv. accepted. No flush toilets.

16 Stephens St. Pk. All year. 40 tents or trailers (max. 24 ft.). Fee. Resv. accepted. No flush toilets. Cafe 1 mi. Swimming 1 mi. Fishing.

17 Voorhees St. Pk. All year. 33 tents or trailers (max. 24 ft.). Fee. Resv. accepted. No flush toilets.

18 Cheesequake St. Pk. All year. 53 tents or trailers (max. 24 ft.). Fee. Resv. accepted. No flush toilets. Cafe 1 mi. Swimming, fishing 1 mi. Riding.

19 Allaire St. Pk. All year. 57 tents or trailers (max. 24 ft.). Fee. Resv. accepted. No flush toilets. Cafe, store 1 mi. Fishing 1 mi. Horseback riding.

20 Turkey Swamp Park. All year. 64 tents or trailers (max. 30 ft.). Fee. Resv. accepted. Elec. hookup—extra chg. Water hookup. Dumping station. Showers—extra chg. Fishing. Boat rental. Riding.

21 Bulls Island St. Pk. Apr. 1–Nov. 30. 50 tents or trailers (max. 24 ft.). Fee. Resv. accepted. Boat launch.

22 French Creek St. Pk. All year. 160 tents, 130 trailers (max. 28 ft.). Fee. No flush toilets. Cafe 1 mi. Store. Swimming, fishing. Boat launch.

23 Baker Park. From Hwy. 23, S .5 mi. on Hwy. 29, near Phoenixville. May 1–Sept. 30. 41 tents or trailers (max. 26 ft.). Fee. Resv. accepted. Dumping station. Showers. Cafe, store 1 mi. Swimming pool—extra chg. Fishing. Boat dock, rental.

24 Parvin St. Pk. All year. 57 tents or trailers (max. 24 ft.). Fee. Resv. accepted. No flush toilets. Cafe 1 mi. Swimming, fishing. Boat launch, rental.

25 Lebanon. All year. 90 tents or trailers (max. 24 ft.). Fee. Resv. accepted. No flush toilets. Swimming 1 mi.

26 Wharton. All year. 55 tents, 20 trailers (max. 24 ft.). Fee. Resv. accepted. No flush toilets. Swimming, fishing 1 mi. Boat launch.

27 Bass River. All year. 157 tents or trailers (max. 24 ft.). Fee. Resv. accepted. Showers. Cafe 1 mi. Swimming 1 mi. Fishing. Boat launch.

28 Egg Harbor City Lake. May 30–Sept. 15. 10 tents, 20 trailers. Fee. Elec. hookup—extra chg. Dumping station. Cafe. Swimming, fishing.

Shenandoah National Park
(Map is on page 72)

Four campgrounds in the park, with trailer space but no utility connections; 21 trailside shelters.

For information on state campgrounds in Delaware, write to Division of Parks, Recreation and Forests, P.O. Box F, Dover, Del. 19901;
in Maryland, to Department of Forests and Parks, State Office Bldg., Annapolis, Md. 21404;
in Virginia, to Division of Parks, State Office Bldg., Richmond, Va. 23219;
in West Virginia, to Division of Parks and Recreation, State Office Bldg., Charleston, W. Va. 25305.

For information on U.S. Forest Service campgrounds, write to Southern Region, Forest Service, 1720 Peachtree Rd. NW, Atlanta, Ga. 30309.

1 New Germany St. Pk. May 15–Oct. 1. 30 tents or trailers (max. 22 ft.). Fee. No pets. Showers. Cafe. Swimming, fishing. Boat launch, rental.

2 Deep Creek Lake St. Pk. May 15–Oct. 1. 56 tents or trailers (max. 23 ft.). Fee. Resv. accepted. No pets. Showers. Cafe. Swimming, fishing. Boat launch.

3 Swallow Falls St. Pk. May 15–Oct. 1. 125 tents or trailers (max. 22 ft.). Fee. No pets. Showers. Fishing.

4 Tygart Lake St. Pk. May 1–Oct. 15. 34 tents or trailers (max. 22 ft.). Fee. Showers. Store. Swimming, fishing 1 mi.

5 Audra St. Pk. May 1–Oct. 30. 40 tents, 47 trailers (max. 22 ft.). Fee. Dumping station. Showers. Cafe, store. Swimming, fishing 1 mi.

6 Blackwater Falls St. Pk. May 1–Oct. 15. 65 tents or trailers. Fee. Elec., water hookup. Dumping station. Showers. Cafe, store. Swimming, fishing 1 mi. Horseback riding.

7 Spruce Knob Lake. Apr. 1–Nov. 1. 43 tents, 30 trailers (max. 22 ft.). Fee. Fishing. Boat dock, launch.

8 Matthews Arm. Apr. 1–Oct. 31. 186 tents, 167 trailers (max. 30 ft.). Fee. Dumping station. Cafe, store 1 mi. Fishing 1 mi.

9 Big Meadows. All year. 263 tents, 200 trailers (max. 30 ft.). Fee. Dumping station. Showers—extra chg. Cafe, store. Fishing.

10 Loft Mountain. Apr. 1–Oct. 31. 231 tents, 167 trailers (max. 30 ft.). Fee. Dumping station. Showers—extra chg. Store.

11 Sherando Lake. Apr. 15–Oct. 1. 66 tents, 31 trailers (max. 22 ft.). Fee. Showers. Cafe. Swimming, fishing. Boat dock, launch, rental.

12 Douthat St. Pk. All year. 120 tents, 140 trailers (max. 26 ft.). Fee. Dumping station. Showers. Cafe. Swimming, fishing. Boat launch, rental. Riding.

13 Peaks of Otter. May–Nov. 80 tents, 62 trailers (max. 30 ft.). Fee. Cafe, Store. Fishing.

14 Cave Mountain Lake. May 15–Oct. 15. 42 tents or trailers (max. 22 ft.). Fee. Elec. hookup. Cafe. Swimming.

15 Otter Creek. May–Nov. 42 tents, 25 trailers (max. 30 ft.). Fee. Cafe, store. Fishing.

16 Bear Creek Lake. All year. 60 tents or trailers (max. 26 ft.). Fee. Showers. Cafe. Swimming, fishing. Boat launch, rental.

17 Pocahontas St. Pk. All year. 80 tents, 40 trailers (max. 26 ft.). Fee. Dumping station. Showers. Cafe, store. Swimming, fishing. Boat launch, rental. Horseback riding.

18 Westmoreland St. Pk. All year. 158 tents or trailers (max. 26 ft.). Fee. Elec. hookup—extra chg. Showers. Cafe. Swimming, fishing. Boat launch, rental.

19 Cedarville St. Pk. Apr. 1–Nov. 1. 90 tents or trailers (max. 22 ft.). Fee. No pets. Showers. Fishing.

20 Prince William Forest Park. All year. 65 tents or trailers (max. 35 ft.). Fee. Elec., water, sewer hookup—extra chg. Dumping station. Showers.

21 Bull Run Regional Park. All year. 125 tents or trailers (max. 30 ft.). Fee. Dumping station. Showers. Cafe. Swimming pool—extra chg. Fishing. Horseback riding.

22 Greenbelt Park. Balto-Wash Pkwy. or Hwy. 201 to Good Luck Rd. Apr. 1–Nov. 30. 178 tents or trailers (max. 22 ft.). Fee.

23 Catoctin Mountain Park. From ST 77, W to Foxville-Deerfield Rd., N 2 mi. Apr. 15–Oct. 31. 50 tents or trailers (max. 22 ft.). Fee. Fishing.

24 Elk Neck St. Pk. All year. 300 tents or trailers (max. 22 ft.). Fee. No pets.

Showers. Cafe, store. Swimming, fishing. Boat launch, rental.

25 Belleplain State Forest. All year. 205 tents or trailers (max. 24 ft.). Fee. Dumping station. Showers. Cafe. Swimming, fishing. Boat launch.

26 Martinak St. Pk. All year. 30 tents or trailers. Fee. No pets. Fishing. Boat launch.

27 Cape Henlopen St. Pk. Apr. 1–Oct. 30. 100 tents, 160 trailers (max. 30 ft.). Fee. Dumping station. Showers. Cafe. Store 1 mi. Swimming, fishing. Boat launch, rental.

28 Delaware Seashore St. Pk. All year. 200 tents, 240 trailers (max. 30 ft.). Fee. Dumping station. Showers. Cafe. Store 1 mi. Swimming, fishing. Boat launch, rental.

29 Trap Pond St. Pk. Apr. 1–Nov. 11. 75 tents, 140 trailers (max. 30 ft.). Fee. Dumping station. Showers. Cafe. Store 1 mi. Swimming, fishing. Boat launch, rental.

30 Assateague St. Pk. All year. 311 tents or trailers (max. 22 ft.). Fee. No pets. Dumping station. Showers. Cafe. Swimming, fishing.

31 Shad Landing St. Pk. All year. 200 tents or trailers (max. 22 ft.). Fee. Resv. accepted. No pets. Dumping station. Showers. Cafe, store. Swimming, fishing. Boating.

32 Janes Island St. Pk. All year. 25 tents or trailers. Fee. No pets. No flush toilets. Swimming, fishing.

Mammoth Cave National Park
(Map is on page 81)

One campground in the park, with trailer space but no utility connections.

For information on state campgrounds in Alabama, write to Bureau of Publicity and Information, State Highway Dept. Bldg., Montgomery, Ala. 36104;

in Illinois, to Tourism Division, Department of Business and Economic Development, 222 S. College St., Springfield, Ill. 62706;

in Indiana, to Division of State Parks, 616 State Office Bldg., Indianapolis, Ind. 46204;

in Kentucky, to Department of Public Information, Travel Division, Capitol Annex Bldg., Frankfort, Ky. 40601;

in Mississippi, to Mississippi Park System, 717 Robert E. Lee Bldg., Jackson, Miss. 39201;

in Tennessee, to Division of State Parks, Department of Conservation, 2611 West End Ave., Nashville, Tenn. 37203.

For information on U.S. Forest Service campgrounds, write to Eastern Region, Forest Service, 633 W. Wisconsin Ave., Milwaukee, Wis. 53203, and Southern Region, Forest Service, 1720 Peachtree Rd., NW, Atlanta, Ga. 30309.

1 Stephen A. Forbes St. Pk. From US 50, N 2 mi. on gravel rd. Open as

weather permits. 10 tents, 70 trailers (max. 30 ft.). Fee. No flush toilets. Cafe. Fishing. Boat launch, rental.

2 Red Hills St. Pk. Open as weather permits. 150 tents, 75 trailers (max. 30 ft.). Fee. Elec. hookup. Dumping station. No flush toilets. Cafe. Fishing. Boat launch, rental. Horseback riding.

3 Spring Mill St. Pk. Apr. 1–Oct. 30. 80 tents or trailers. Fee. Elec. hookup—extra chg. Showers. Cafe, store. Swimming 1 mi. Fishing. Boat launch, rental. Horseback riding.

4 Starve Hollow Beach. Apr. 1–Oct. 1. 200 tents or trailers. Fee. Dumping station. No flush toilets. Showers. Store. Swimming, fishing. Boat launch, rental.

5 Clifty Falls St. Pk. Apr. 1–Oct. 30. 60 tents or trailers. Fee. Elec. hookup—extra chg. Water hookup. Showers. Cafe. Horseback riding.

6 Clark State Forest. Apr. 1–Oct. 1. 45 tents or trailers. Fee. No flush toilets. Fishing. Boat launch. Horseback riding.

7 Harrison–Crawford State Forest. 75 tents or trailers. Fee. No flush toilets. Boat launch. Horseback riding.

8 Ferdinand State Forest. Apr. 1–Oct. 1. 80 tents or trailers. Fee. No flush toilets. Swimming, fishing. Boat launch, rental. Horseback riding.

9 Lake Murphysboro St. Pk. Open as weather permits. 115 tents or trailers (max. 30 ft.). Fee. Elec. hookup. Dumping station. No flush toilets. Fishing. Boats for rent.

10 Pounds Hollow. May 15–Oct. 15. 76 tents or trailers (max. 22 ft.). Fee. Showers 1 mi. Cafe 1 mi. Swimming. Fishing 1 mi. Boat dock, rental.

11 Lake Glendale. Apr. 1–Oct. 1. 60 tents or trailers (max. 32 ft.). Fee. Elec. hookup. Showers. Swimming, fishing. Boat dock, launch, rental.

12 Cave-in-Rock St. Pk. Open as weather permits. 155 tents or trailers (max. 30 ft.). Fee. Elec. hookup. No flush toilets. Cafe. Fishing. Boat launch.

13 Moutardier. All year. 157 tents, 120 trailers. Fee. Dumping station. Store. Swimming, fishing. Boat launch, rental.

14 Mammoth Cave Nat'l Park Headquarters. All year. 145 tents or trailers. Fee. Dumping station. Showers—extra chg. Cafe, store 1 mi. Fishing 1 mi. Boat launch.

15 Barren River Reservoir. Apr. 1–Oct. 31. 102 tents or trailers. Fee. Elec., water, sewer hookup. Dumping station. Showers. Swimming, fishing. Boating.

16 Kentucky Dam Village St. Pk. All year. 220 tents, 30 trailers. Fee. Elec. hookup. Dumping station. Showers. Cafe 1 mi. Store. Swimming, fishing 1 mi. Boat launch, rental. Riding.

17 Hillman Ferry. Apr. 1–Oct. 19. 258 tents, 51 trailers (max. 32 ft.). Fee. Elec. hookup. Dumping station. Showers. Swimming, fishing. Boat launch.

18 Rushing Creek. May 1–Sept. 4. 150 tents, 60 trailers (max. 21 ft.). Fee. Elec. hookup. Showers. Swimming, fishing. Boat launch.

19 Paris Landing. All year. 75 tents or trailers. Fee. Elec., water hookup. Dumping station. Showers. Cafe, store. Swimming, fishing. Boat launch, rental.

20 Reelfoot Lake. All year. 50 tents or trailers. Fee. Elec. hookup. Showers. Cafe 1 mi. Store. Swimming 1 mi.

21 Natchez Trace St. Pk. All year. 80 tents or trailers. Fee. Elec., water hookup. Dumping station. Showers. Cafe, store. Swimming, fishing. Boats for rent.

22 Montgomery Bell St. Pk. All year. 80 tents or trailers. Fee. Elec., water hookup. Dumping station. Showers. Cafe, store. Swimming, fishing. Boating.

23 Cedars of Lebanon St. Pk. All year. 140 tents, 100 trailers. Fee. Elec., water hookup. Dumping station. Showers. Cafe, store. Swimming. Riding.

24 Henry Horton St. Pk. All year. 70 tents or trailers. Fee. Elec. hookup. Dumping station. Showers. Cafe, store. Swimming.

25 David Crockett St. Pk. All year. 85 tents or trailers. Fee. Elec., water hookup. Dumping station. Showers. Cafe. Swimming, fishing. Boats for rent.

26 Chewalla. All year. 42 tents or trailers (max. 22 ft.). Fee. Elec. hookup. Showers. Cafe 4 mi. Swimming, fishing. Boat dock, launch.

27 Davis Lake. From Natchez Trace Pkwy., W 2 mi. on gravel rd. All year. 29 tents or trailers (max. 22 ft.). Fee. Showers. Cafe 5 mi. Swimming, fishing. Boat dock, launch.

28 Joe Wheeler St. Pk. All year. No fixed number of sites (max. 24 ft.). Fee. Swimming, fishing. Boat launch.

29 Corinth. From US 278, S 2 mi. on country rd., 1 mi. on forest rd. All year. 56 tents or trailers (max. 22 ft.). Fee. Cafe 3 mi. Swimming, fishing. Boat dock, launch, rental.

30 Monte Sano St. Pk. All year. No fixed number of sites (max. 24 ft.). Fee. No flush toilets. Horseback riding.

31 Little Mountain St. Pk. Apr. 15–Sept. 15. 16 tents, no fixed number of trailers (max. 29 ft.). Fee. Elec. hookup. Showers. Cafe. Swimming, fishing. Boat launch, rental.

32 DeSoto (Falls Div.) St. Pk. All year. No fixed number of sites (max. 25 ft.). Fee. Showers. Swimming, fishing.

Great Smoky Mountains National Park

(Map is on page 89)

Seven campgrounds in the park, with trailer space but no utility connections (three open all year); several primitive campgrounds and trail shelters; lodge and cottage accommodations available.

For information on state campgrounds in Georgia, write to Department of State Parks, 270 Washington St. SW, Atlanta, Ga. 30334;

in Kentucky, to Department of Public Information, Travel Division, Capitol Annex Bldg., Frankfort, Ky. 40601;

in North Carolina, to Travel and Promotion Division, Department of Conservation, Raleigh, N.C. 27611;

in South Carolina, to Department of Parks, Recreation and Tourism, Box 1358, Columbia, S.C. 29202;

in Virginia, to Division of Parks, State Office Bldg., Richmond, Va. 23219;

in West Virginia, to Division of Parks and Recreation, State Office Bldg., Charleston, West Va. 25305.

For information on U.S. Forest Service campgrounds, write to Southern Region, Forest Service, 1720 Peachtree Rd., NW, Atlanta, Ga. 30309.

1 General Butler St. Pk. All year. 82 tents, 58 trailers. Fee. Dumping station. Elec. hookup. Showers. Cafe, store 1 mi. Swimming, fishing. Boats for rent.

2 Portsmouth St. Pk. All year. 127 tents, 107 trailers (max. 30 ft.). Fee. Dumping station. Showers. Store 1 mi. Swimming, fishing. Boat launch.

3 Kanawha City Interchange. From US 60, S 7 mi. on Louden Heights Rd. May 1–Oct. 30. 45 tents or trailers (max. 19 ft.). Fee. Elec., water hookup. Dumping station. Showers. Cafe, store 1 mi. Swimming.

4 Pipestem St. Pk. Apr. 1–Jan. 30. 20 tents, 50 trailers (max. 28 ft.). Fee. Elec., water, sewer hookup—extra charge. Dumping station. Showers. Cafe, store. Swimming pool—extra charge. Fishing—extra charge. Horseback riding.

5 Hungry Mother St. Pk. All year. 115 tents or trailers (max. 26 ft.). Fee. Elec. hookup—extra charge. Showers. Cafe. Store 1 mi. Swimming, fishing. Boats for rent. Horseback riding.

6 Breaks Interstate St. Pk. Apr.–Nov. 70 tents or trailers (max. 26 ft.). Fee. Elec., water hookup. Dumping station. Showers. Cafe, store. Swimming, fishing. Boat dock, rental. Horseback riding.

7 Buckhorn Lake St. Pk. All year. 50 tents or trailers (max. 25 ft.). No fee. No flush toilets. Store 1 mi. Swimming, fishing. Boat launch.

8 Levi Jackson Wilderness Road St. Pk. All year. 110 tents, 80 trailers. Fee. Elec., water, sewer hookup. Dumping station. Showers. Store 1 mi. Swimming 1 mi. Horseback riding.

9 General Burnside Island St. Pk. March 1–Dec. 1. 100 tents or trailers. Fee. Elec. hookup. Showers. Swimming pool. Fishing. Boat dock, rental.

10 Lake Cumberland St. Pk. Apr. 1–Oct. 31. 150 tents or trailers. Fee. Elec., water hookup. Dumping station. Showers. Cafe, store. Swimming pool. Fishing. Boat dock, rental. Horseback riding.

11 Willow Grove. From Hwy. 52, N 15 mi. on Willow Grove Rd. All year. 57 tents or trailers. No fee. Cafe, store 1 mi. Swimming, fishing.

12 Fall Creek Falls St. Pk. All year. 100 tents or trailers. Fee. Elec., water hookup. Showers. Swimming, fishing. Boats for rent.

13 Cumberland Mountain St. Pk. All year. 150 tents or trailers. Fee. Elec., water hookup. Dumping station. Showers. Cafe, store. Swimming, fishing. Boats for rent.

14 Cove Lake St. Pk. All year. 125 tents or trailers. Fee. Elec., water, sewer hookup. Dumping station. Showers. Cafe, store. Swimming, fishing. Boats for rent.

15 The Pinnacle. May 1–Oct. 31. 165 tents or trailers. Fee. Store 1 mi.

16 Warrior's Path St. Pk. All year. 100 tents or trailers. Fee. Elec., water hookup. Dumping station. Showers. Cafe. Store 1 mi. Swimming, fishing. Boats for rent. Horseback riding.

17 Doughton Park. May–Nov. 96 tents, 28 trailers. Fee. Cafe 1 mi.

18 J. Price Memorial Park. May–Nov. 128 tents, 68 trailers. Fee. Store 1 mi. Fishing. Boat launch.

19 Black Mountain. May 27–Sept. 5. 45 tents or trailers (max. 22 ft.). Fee. Cafe 4 mi. Fishing.

20 Mt. Pisgah. May–Nov. 70 tents or trailers. Fee. Dumping station. Cafe, store.

21 Cosby. May 1–Oct. 31. 219 tents, 230 trailers (max. 25 ft.). Fee. Dumping station. Fishing 1 mi. Horseback riding.

22 Smokemont. All year. 136 tents, 180 trailers (max. 30 ft.). Fee. Dumping station. Showers. Fishing 1 mi. Horseback riding.

23 Elkmont. All year. 34 tents, 310 trailers (max. 25 ft.). Fee. Dumping station. Fishing 1 mi. Horseback riding.

24 Cades Cove. From Hwy. 73, SW 3 mi. on forest rd. All year. 180 tents or trailers (max. 25 ft.). Fee. Dumping station. Store. Fishing 1 mi. Riding.

25 Look Rock. May 1–Oct. 15. 92 tents or trailers (max. 25 ft.). Fee. Dumping station.

26 Tsali. May 27–Sept. 5. 42 tents or trailers (max. 22 ft.). Fee. Fishing. Boat dock, launch, rental.

27 Indian Boundary. May 15–Nov. 1. 100 tents or trailers (max. 22 ft.). Fee. Showers. Swimming, fishing. Boat dock.

28 Harrison Bay St. Pk. From Hwy. 58, N 2 mi. on local rd. All year. 200 tents or trailers. Fee. Elec., water hookup. Dumping station. Showers. Cafe, store. Swimming, fishing. Boat launch, rental.

29 Cloudland Canyon. All year. 50 tents, 35 trailers (max. 17 ft.). Fee. Elec., water hookup. Showers. Cafe.

30 Red Top Mountain St. Pk. All year. 175 tents, 75 trailers (max. 27 ft.). Fee. Elec., water hookup. Dumping station. Showers. Cafe. Swimming, fishing. Boat dock, launch, rental.

31 Amicalola Falls St. Pk. All year. 50 tents, 25 trailers (max. 17 ft.). Fee. Elec., water hookup. Showers. Cafe. Store 1 mi. Fishing. Boat launch, rental.

32 Jackrabbit Mountain. May 27–Sept. 5. 100 tents or trailers (max. 22 ft.). Fee. Showers. Cafe 5 mi. Swimming, fishing. Boat dock, launch, rental.

33 Moccasin Creek St. Pk. All year. 50 tents or trailers (max. 27 ft.). Fee. Elec., water hookup. Showers. Fishing. Boat launch, rental.

34 Oconee St. Pk. All year. 140 tents or trailers. Fee. Elec., water hookup. Dumping station. Showers. Store. Swimming, fishing. Boats for rent.

35 Table Rock St. Pk. All year. 110 tents or trailers (max. 25 ft.). Fee. Elec., water hookup. Showers. Swimming, fishing, swimming pool. Boats for rent.

36 Croft St. Pk. All year. 25 tents, 50 trailers. Fee. Elec., water hookup. Showers. Fishing. Boats for rent.

37 Greenwood St. Pk. All year. 160 tents or trailers (max. 30 ft.). Fee. Elec., water hookup. Showers. Cafe, store. Swimming, fishing. Boat dock, launch, rental.

38 Baker Creek St. Pk. All year. 50 tents or trailers. Fee. Elec., water hookup. Dumping station. Showers. Fishing. Boat launch.

Outer Banks
(Map is on page 100)

Six campgrounds in Cape Hatteras National Seashore, with trailer space but no utility connections. Three are open all year.

*For information on state campgrounds in North Carolina, write to Travel and Promotion Division, Department of Conservation and Development, Raleigh, N.C. 27611;
in South Carolina, to Department of Parks, Recreation and Tourism, Box 1358, Columbia, S.C. 29202.*

For information on U.S. Forest Service campgrounds write to Southern Region, Forest Service, 1720 Peachtree Rd. NW, Atlanta, Ga. 30309.

1 Morrow Mountain St. Pk. All year. 100 tents or trailers (max. 20 ft.). Fee. Resv. required. Showers. Swimming, fishing, 1 mi. Boats for rent.

2 Wm. B. Umstead St. Pk. Apr. 1–Oct. 15. 28 tents or trailers (max. 20 ft.). Fee. Resv. required. Dumping station. Showers. Fishing. Boats for rent.

3 Cliffs of the Neuse. Apr. 1–Oct. 15. 36 tents or trailers (max. 20 ft.). Fee. Resv. required. Dumping station. Showers. Swimming, fishing 1 mi. Boats for rent.

4 Little Pee Dee St. Pk. All year. 45 tents or trailers (max. 30 ft.). Fee. Elec., water hookup. Showers. Swimming, fishing. Swimming pool. Boats for rent.

5 Edisto Beach St. Pk. All year. 50 tents or trailers. Fee. Elec., water hookup. Dumping station. Showers. Swimming, fishing. Boat launch.

6 Huntington Beach St. Pk. All year. 128 tents, 53 trailers. Fee. Elec., water hookup. Showers. Cafe. Swimming.

7 Myrtle Beach St. Pk. All year. 155 tents or trailers. Fee. Elec., water hookup. Dumping station. Showers. Cafe, store. Swimming, fishing. Swim-

ming pool—extra chg.

8 Masonboro St. Pk. Apr. 1–Nov. 1. 70 tents or trailers (max. 20 ft.). Fee. Resv. required. Dumping station. Showers. Fishing. Boat launch.

9 Neuse River. March 1–Dec. 1. 22 tents or trailers (max. 22 ft.). Fee. Elec. hookup. Cafe 3 mi. Swimming, fishing. Boat dock.

10 Oregon Inlet. All year. 120 tents or trailers (max. 30 ft.). Fee. Showers. Cafe, store 1 mi. Swimming, fishing 1 mi. Boat launch, rental.

11 Pea Island. All year. 40 tents or trailers (max. 30 ft.). Fee. Swimming. Fishing 1 mi.

12 Salvo. May–Labor Day. 140 tents or trailers (max. 30 ft.). Fee. Showers. Swimming. Fishing 1 mi.

13 Cape Point. All year. 212 tents or trailers (max. 30 ft.). Fee. Showers. Swimming, fishing 1 mi.

14 Frisco. May–Labor Day. 130 tents or trailers (max. 30 ft.). Fee. Showers. Swimming, fishing 1 mi.

15 Silver Lake. All year. 20 tents or trailers (max. 30 ft.). No fee. Cafe, store 1 mi. Swimming, fishing 1 mi. Boating.

16 Ocracoke Beach. May–Labor Day. 50 tents, 100 trailers (max. 30 ft.). No fee. Swimming, fishing 1 mi.

Okefenokee Swamp
(Map is on page 107)

Camping in two nearby state parks.

*For information on state campgrounds in Florida, write to Department of Natural Resources, Education and Information Division, J. Edwin Larson Bldg., Tallahassee, Fla. 32304;
in Georgia, to Department of State Parks, 270 Washington St. SW, Atlanta, Ga. 30334.*

For information on U.S. Forest Service campgrounds write to Southern Region, Forest Service, 1720 Peachtree Rd. NW, Atlanta, Ga. 30309.

1 Kolomoki Mounds St. Pk. All year. 25 tents or trailers (max. 27 ft.). Fee. Elec., water hookup. Showers. Cafe. Swimming, fishing. Boat launch, rental.

2 Chehaw St. Pk. All year. 50 tents, 25 trailers (max. 17 ft.). Fee. Elec., water hookup. Showers. Cafe. Boat dock.

3 Georgia Veterans Mem. St. Pk. All year. 50 tents, 25 trailers (max. 27 ft.). Fee. Elec., water hookup. Dumping station. Showers. Cafe. Swimming, fishing. Boat launch, rental.

4 Little Ocmulgee St. Pk. All year. 50 tents or trailers (max. 27 ft.). Fee. Elec., water hookup. Dumping station. Showers. Cafe. Swimming, fishing. Boat launch.

5 Gordonia Alatamaha St. Pk. All year. 25 tents or trailers (max. 27 ft.). Fee. Elec., water hookup. Dumping station. Showers. Cafe, store 1 mi. Swimming, fishing. Boat dock, rental.

6 Reed Bingham St. Pk. All year. 25 tents or trailers (max. 27 ft.). Fee. Elec., water hookup. Dumping station. Showers. Cafe. Swimming, fishing. Boat launch.

7 Seminole St. Pk. All year. 25 tents or trailers (max. 27 ft.). Fee. Elec., water hookup. Showers. Cafe. Swimming, fishing. Boat dock, launch.

8 Three Rivers St. Pk. All year. 65 tents or trailers (max. 30 ft.). Fee. Elec. hookup—extra chg. Water hookup. Showers. Cafe, store. Swimming, fishing. Boat dock, launch, rental.

9 Silver Lake. All year. 15 tents, 30 trailers (max. 22 ft.). Fee. Swimming, fishing.

10 Ochlockonee River St. Pk. All year. 30 tents or trailers. Fee. Resv. accepted. Elec. hookup—extra chg. Water hookup. Showers. Swimming, fishing. Boat launch.

11 Suwannee River St. Pk. All year. 40 tents or trailers (max. 20 ft.). Fee. Resv. accepted. Elec. hookup—extra chg. Showers. Cafe. Store 1 mi. Swimming, fishing. Boat launch.

12 O'Leno St. Pk. All year. 65 tents or trailers. Fee. Resv. accepted. Elec. hookup—extra chg. Water hookup. Dumping station. Showers. Swimming, fishing. Boat dock.

13 Laura S. Walker St. Pk. All year. 75 tents, 25 trailers (max. 27 ft.). Fee. Elec., water hookup. Dumping station. Showers. Cafe. Swimming, fishing. Boat dock, launch.

14 Stephen C. Foster St. Pk. All year. 50 tents, 10 trailers (max. 17 ft.). Fee. Elec., water hookup. Showers. Cafe. Fishing. Boat dock, launch, rental.

15 Crooked River St. Pk. All year. 50 tents, 25 trailers (max. 17 ft.). Fee. Elec., water hookup. Dumping station. Showers. Cafe. Swimming, fishing. Boat launch.

16 Fort Clinch St. Pk. All year. 117 tents or trailers. Fee. Resv. accepted. Elec. hookup—extra chg. Water hookup. Dumping station. Showers. Cafe, store. Swimming 1 mi. Fishing. Boat launch.

17 Little Talbot Island St. Pk. All year. 60 tents or trailers (max. 30 ft.). Fee. Resv. accepted. Elec. hookup—extra chg. Water hookup. Dumping station. Showers. Cafe. Swimming 1 mi. Boat dock.

18 Anastasia St. Pk. All year. 135 tents or trailers. Fee. Resv. accepted. Elec. hookup—extra chg. Water hookup. Dumping station. Showers. Cafe, store. Swimming, fishing. Boating 1 mi.

Everglades National Park
(Map is on page 118)

Two main campgrounds in the park with trailer space, but no utility connections; a number of primitive camping places in the back country.

For information on state campgrounds write to Department of Natural Resources, Education and Information

Division, J. Edwin Larson Bldg., Tallahassee, Fla. 32304.

For information on U.S. Forest Service campgrounds write to Southern Region, Forest Service, 1720 Peachtree Rd. NW, Atlanta, Ga. 30309.

1 Manatee Springs St. Pk. All year. 100 tents or trailers. Fee. No pets. Resv. accepted. Elec. hookup—extra chg. Water hookup. Showers. Cafe. Store 1 mi. Swimming, fishing. Boat dock, launch, rental.

2 Flagler Beach St. Pk. All year. 34 tents or trailers. Fee. No pets. Resv. accepted. Elec. hookup—extra chg. Water hookup. Dumping station. Showers. Cafe. Swimming, fishing. Boat launch.

3 Tomoka St. Pk. All year. 112 tents or trailers (max. 30 ft.). Fee. No pets. Resv. accepted. Elec. hookup—extra chg. Dumping station. Showers. Cafe, store. Swimming, fishing. Boat dock, launch, rental.

4 Juniper Springs. All year. 55 tents, 32 trailers (max. 22 ft.). Fee. Elec. hookup. Showers. Cafe. Swimming, fishing. Boat dock, rental.

5 Alexander Springs. All year. 80 tents, 36 trailers (max. 22 ft.). Fee. Elec. hookup. Showers. Cafe. Swimming, fishing. Boat dock, launch, rental.

6 Clearwater Lake. All year. 7 tents, 35 trailers (max. 22 ft.). Fee. Swimming, fishing. Boat dock.

7 Hontoon Island St. Pk. All year. 30 tents or trailers. Fee. No pets. Resv. required. Elec. hookup—extra chg. Water hookup. Showers. Cafe. Fishing. Boat dock.

8 Lake Griffin St. Pk. All year. 47 tents or trailers. Fee. No pets. Resv. accepted. Elec. hookup—extra chg. Water hookup. Dumping station. Showers. Store 1 mi. Fishing. Boat dock, launch.

9 Withlacoochee State Forest (Silver Lake). All year. 120 tents or trailers (max. 20 ft.). Fee. Elec. hookup—extra chg. Showers. Swimming, fishing. Boat launch.

10 Hillsborough River St. Pk. All year. 131 tents or trailers (max. 20 ft.). Fee. No pets. Resv. accepted. Elec. hookup—extra chg. Dumping station—extra chg. Showers. Cafe, store. Swimming, fishing. Boats for rent.

11 Fort De Soto. All year. 85 tents, 75 trailers. Fee. No pets. Elec., water hookup. Dumping station. Showers. Store. Cafe 1 mi. Swimming, fishing. Boat launch, rental.

12 Oscar Sherer St. Pk. All year. 104 tents or trailers (max. 20 ft.). Fee. No pets. Resv. accepted. Elec. hookup—extra chg. Water hookup. Dumping station. Showers. Cafe. Swimming. Fishing 1 mi. Boat dock, rental.

13 Myakka River St. Pk. All year. 76 tents or trailers. Fee. No pets. Resv. accepted. Elec. hookup—extra chg. Water hookup. Showers. Cafe, store. Fishing. Boat dock, launch, rental.

14 Highlands Hammock St. Pk. All year. 165 tents or trailers. Fee. No pets.

Resv. accepted. Elec. hookup—extra chg. Water hookup. Dumping station. Showers. Cafe, store. Fishing 1 mi.

15 Long Point Recreation Park. All year. 92 tents, 58 trailers. Fee. Resv. accepted. Elec., water, sewer hookups—extra chg. Dumping station. Showers. Store, cafe. Swimming 1 mi. Fishing. Boat launch, rental.

16 Jonathan Dickinson St. Pk. All year. 200 tents or trailers. Fee. No pets. Resv. accepted. Elec. hookup—extra chg. Dumping station. Showers. Cafe, store. Swimming, fishing. Boat dock, rental.

17 Pahokee St. Pk. All year. 40 tents or trailers. Fee. No pets. Resv. accepted. Elec. hookup—extra chg. Water hookup. Dumping station. Showers. Cafe, store. Swimming, fishing. Boat dock, rental.

18 Collier Seminole St. Pk. All year. 130 tents or trailers. Fee. No pets. Resv. accepted. Elec., water hookup—extra chg. Dumping station. Showers. Store 1 mi. Fishing. Boat dock, launch.

19 Flamingo. All year. 308 tents, 235 trailers. Fee. Dumping station. Showers 1 mi. Cafe, store 1 mi. Fishing. Boat launch, rental.

20 Long Pine Key. All year. 108 tents or trailers. Fee. Fishing.

21 John Pennekamp Coral Reef St. Pk. All year. 125 tents or trailers (max. 30 ft.). Fee. No pets. Resv. accepted. Elec. hookup—extra chg. Water hookup. Showers. Cafe, store. Swimming, fishing. Boat dock, launch, rental.

22 Long Key St. Pk. All year. 60 tents or trailers (max. 30 ft.). Fee. No pets. Resv. required. Elec. hookup—extra chg. Water hookup. Showers. Swimming, fishing.

23 Bahia Honda St. Pk. All year. 113 tents or trailers. Fee. No pets. Resv. accepted. Elec. hookup—extra chg. Water hookup. Dumping station. Showers. Cafe, store. Swimming, fishing. Boat dock, launch, rental.

Boundary Waters Canoe Area
(Map is on page 129)

Primitive campsites only within Boundary Waters Area.

For information on state campgrounds in Michigan write to Michigan Tourist Council, Suite 102, 300 S. Capitol Ave., Lansing, Mich. 48926;
in Minnesota, to Division of Parks and Recreation, Centennial Office Bldg., St. Paul, Minn. 55101;
in Wisconsin, to Vacation and Travel Service, Department of Natural Resources, Box 450, Madison, Wis. 53701.

For information on U.S. Forest Service campgrounds, write to Eastern Region, Forest Service, 633 W. Wisconsin Ave., Milwaukee, Wis. 53203.

For specific information about Superior National Forest write to Superior National Forest, Federal Bldg., Duluth, Minn. 55801.

1 McCarthy Beach. May 15–Sept. 15. 72 tents or trailers (max. 22 ft.). Fee. No pets. Showers. Cafe, store 1 mi. Swimming, fishing. Boat launch, rental.

2 Bear Head Lake. May 15–Sept. 15. 59 tents or trailers (max. 22 ft.). Fee. No pets. Swimming 1 mi. Fishing. Boat launch, rental.

3 Birch Lake. From Hwy. 1, S 4.5 mi. on forest rd. June 1–Sept. 10. 38 tents or trailers (max. 22 ft.). Fee. Fishing. Boat dock, launch.

4 Fall Lake. From Hwy. 169, E 5 mi. on county rd., NE 2 mi. on forest rd. June 1–Sept. 10. 69 tents or trailers (max. 22 ft.). Fee. Elec. hookup. Cafe 1 mi. Swimming, fishing. Boat dock, launch, rental.

5 Trails End. From US 61, NW 58 mi. on county rd. May 15–Sept. 15. 36 tents or trailers (max. 22 ft.). Fee. Cafe 3 mi. Fishing. Boat dock, launch, rental.

6 Sawbill Lake. From US 61, N 24 mi. on county rd. June 1–Sept. 10. 50 tents or trailers (max. 22 ft.). Fee. Showers. Cafe 1 mi. Fishing. Boat dock, launch, rental.

7 Two Island Lake. From US 61, NW 14 mi. on county rd. June 1–Sept. 15. 39 tents or trailers (max. 32 ft.). Fee. Fishing. Boat dock, launch, rental.

8 Grand Marais. May 1–Oct. 1. 60 tents or trailers (max. 30 ft.). Fee. Elec., water hookups. Sewer hookup—extra chg. Dumping station. Showers. Cafe, store 1 mi. Swimming 1 mi. Fishing. Boat dock, launch.

9 Cascade River St. Pk. May 30–Sept. 1. 50 tents or trailers (max. 22 ft.). Fee. No flush toilets. Fishing.

10 Temperance River St. Pk. May 30–Sept. 1. 62 tents or trailers (max. 22 ft.). Fee. No flush toilets. Fishing.

11 Whiteface Reservoir. From US 53, E 15 mi. on county rd., S 3 mi. on forest rd. June 1–Sept. 10. 59 tents or trailers (max. 22 ft.). Fee. Swimming, fishing. Boat dock, launch.

12 Savanna Portage. May 15–Sept. 30. 60 tents or trailers (max. 22 ft.). Fee. No pets. Showers. Fishing 1 mi. Boat launch.

13 Jay Cooke St. Pk. May 15–Sept. 15. 95 tents or trailers (max. 22 ft.). Fee. Showers. Cafe 1 mi. Fishing.

14 Pattison. Open as weather permits. 80 tents or trailers (max. 25 ft.). Fee. Elec. hookup—extra chg. Cafe, store. Swimming, fishing. Boat launch.

15 Amnicon Falls. Open as weather permits. 40 tents or trailers (max. 25 ft.). Fee. No flush toilets. Cafe 1 mi. Fishing.

16 Burlington Bay Campsites (Two Harbors). May 15–Sept. 15. 60 tents, 52 trailers. Fee. Elec., water hookup. Dumping station. Showers—extra chg. Cafe, store 1 mi. Swimming, fishing 1 mi.

17 Gooseberry Falls. May 15–Sept. 15. 125 tents or trailers (max. 22 ft.). Fee. No pets. Showers. Cafe, store 1 mi.

18 Red Cliff. May 30–Sept. 15. 30 tents or trailers (max. 30 ft.). Fee. Elec. hookup—extra chg. Water hookup. No flush toilets. Swimming. Fishing 1 mi.

Boat dock, launch.

19 Porcupine Mountains (Union Bay & Presque Isle). May–Dec. 183 tents or trailers. Fee. Elec. hookup. Dumping station. Showers. Swimming.

20 F.J. McLain. May–Dec. 90 tents or trailers. Fee. Elec. hookup. Dumping station. Showers. Store. Swimming 1 mi.

21 Fort Wilkins. May–Dec. 163 tents or trailers. Fee. Elec., sewer hookups. Dumping station. Showers. Store. Swimming, fishing. Boat launch.

22 Baraga. May–Dec. 138 tents or trailers. Fee. Elec. hookup. Dumping station. Showers. Swimming, fishing 1 mi. Boat launch.

23 Lake Ste. Kathryn. From ST 28, S 8 mi. on county rd. May 15–Oct. 1. 25 tents or trailers (max. 22 ft.). Fee. No flush toilets. Fishing. Boat launch.

24 Van Riper. May–Dec. 227 tents or trailers. Fee. Elec. hookup. Dumping station. No flush toilets. Showers. Store. Swimming. Fishing 1 mi. Boat launch, rental.

St. Croix River
(Map is on page 139)

For information on state campgrounds in Michigan write to Michigan Tourist Council, Suite 102, 300 S. Capitol Ave., Lansing, Mich. 48926;
in Minnesota, to Division of Parks and Recreation, Centennial Office Bldg., St. Paul, Minn. 55101;
in Wisconsin, to Vacation and Travel Service, Department of Natural Resources, Box 450, Madison, Wis. 53701.

For information on U.S. Forest Service campgrounds, write to Eastern Region, Forest Service, 633 W. Wisconsin Ave., Milwaukee, Wis. 53203.

1 Mille Lacs Kathio St. Pk. May 12–Oct. 1. 45 tents or trailers (max. 22 ft.). Fee. No pets. Showers. Swimming 1 mi. Fishing. Boat launch.

2 Father Hennepin St. Pk. May–Nov. 62 tents or trailers (max. 22 ft.). Fee. No pets. Showers. Swimming 1 mi. Fishing. Boating.

3 St. Croix St. Pk. May 1–Sept. 30. 238 tents or trailers (max. 22 ft.). Fee. No pets. Elec. hookup. Showers. Cafe. Store 1 mi. Swimming, fishing. Boat launch, rental. Horseback riding.

4 Totogatic Park. May 10–Sept. 30. 80 tents or trailers (max. 28 ft.). Fee. Elec. hookup—extra chg. Swimming, fishing. Boat launch, rental.

5 Two Lakes. May 15–Sept. 15. 105 tents, 97 trailers (max. 22 ft.). Fee. Showers 4 mi. Cafe 4 mi. Swimming, fishing. Boat dock, launch, rental.

6 Namekagon Lake. May 15–Sept. 15. 34 tents or trailers (max. 22 ft.). Fee. Cafe 1 mi. Swimming, fishing. Boat dock, launch, rental.

7 Big Lake West. Open as weather permits. 73 tents or trailers (max. 25 ft.). Fee. No flush toilets. Cafe 1 mi. Swimming, fishing. Boating.

8 North Trout Lake. Open as weather permits. 66 tents or trailers (max. 25 ft.). Fee. No flush toilets. Cafe 1 mi. Swimming, fishing. Boat launch, rental.

9 Muskellunge Lake. Open as weather permits. 90 tents or trailers (max. 25 ft.). Fee. No flush toilets. Cafe 1 mi. Swimming, fishing. Boat launch, rental.

10 Spectacle Lake. From ST 17, S 8.5 mi., SE 4 mi. on forest rd. June 1–Sept. 15. 41 tents or trailers (max. 22 ft.). Fee. Swimming, fishing. Boat dock, launch.

11 Franklin Lake. June 1–Sept. 15. 87 tents or trailers (max. 22 ft.). Elec. hookup. Swimming, fishing. Boat dock, launch, rental.

12 Bewabic St. Pk. May–Dec. 52 tents or trailers. Fee. Elec. hookup. Swimming, fishing 1 mi. Boat launch, rental.

13 Lake Antoine. May 30–Sept. 30. 80 tents or trailers. Fee. Elec., water hookup. Dumping station. Showers. Store. Boating. Horseback riding.

14 Bagley Rapids. May 15–Oct. 15. 100 tents or trailers. Fee. Elec. hookup. Store. Swimming, fishing. Boat launch, rental.

15 Spearhead Point. From Hwy. 13, W 10 mi. on county and forest rds. May 15–Sept. 15. 27 tents or trailers (max. 22 ft.). Fee. Showers 1 mi. Cafe 1 mi. Swimming, fishing. Boat dock, launch, rental.

16 Interstate St. Pk. Open as weather permits. 86 tents or trailers (max. 25 ft.). Fee. Showers. Swimming, fishing. Boat launch, rental.

17 William O'Brien St. Pk. May 1–Sept. 15. 125 tents or trailers (max. 22 ft.). Fee. No pets. Elec. hookup. Showers. Cafe 1 mi. Swimming 1 mi. Fishing. Boat launch, rental.

18 Frontenac St. Pk. May 1–Sept. 30. 59 tents or trailers (max. 22 ft.). Fee. No pets. Showers. Swimming, fishing.

19 Nerstrand Woods St. Pk. May 1–Sept. 30. 62 tents or trailers (max. 22 ft.). Fee. No pets. Showers.

20 Helmer Myre St. Pk. May 1–Sept. 30. 141 tents or trailers (max. 22 ft.). Fee. No pets. Swimming, fishing. Boating.

21 Whitewater St. Pk. May 1–Oct. 15. 149 tents or trailers (max. 22 ft.). Fee. No pets. Showers. Swimming 1 mi.

22 Beaver Creek Valley St. Pk. From Hwy. 76, W 3 mi. on local rd. May 1–Oct. 15. 75 tents or trailers (max. 22 ft.). Fee. No pets. Showers. Fishing.

23 Goose Island. May 1–Oct. 31. 20 tents, 140 trailers (max. 30 ft.). Fee. Elec. hookup—extra chg. Dumping station. Showers—extra chg. Store 1 mi. Boat launch, rental.

24 Dexter Park. May 1–Oct. 31. 43 tents or trailers (max. 27 ft.). Fee. Dumping station. Showers. Swimming, fishing. Boat dock, launch.

25 Lake Wazeecha. May 1–Oct. 31. 68 tents or trailers. Fee. Store 1 mi. Swimming, fishing. Boat launch, rental.

26 Roche A Cri St. Pk. Open as weather permits. 45 tents or trailers (max. 25 ft.).

Fee. Swimming, fishing 1 mi.

27 Mirror Lake St. Pk. Open as weather permits. 95 tents, 85 trailers (max. 25 ft.). Fee. Elec. hookup—extra chg. Dumping station. Showers. Swimming, fishing. Boat launch.

28 Mauthe & Long Lake. Open as weather permits. 371 tents or trailers (max. 25 ft.). Elec. hookup—extra chg. Dumping station. Showers. Cafe, store. Swimming, fishing. Boat launch, rental. Horseback riding.

29 Terry Andrae St. Pk. Open as weather permits. 105 tents or trailers (max. 25 ft.). Fee. Elec. hookup. Showers. Cafe. Swimming, fishing. Horseback riding.

Sleeping Bear Dunes
(Map is on page 147)

For information on state campgrounds in Indiana write to Division of State Parks, 616 State Office Bldg., Indianapolis, Ind. 46204;
in Michigan, to Michigan Tourist Council, Suite 102, 300 S. Capitol Ave., Lansing, Mich. 48926;
in Ohio, to Division of Parks and Recreation, 913 Ohio Departments Bldg., Columbus, Ohio 43215.

For information on U.S. Forest Service campgrounds, write to Eastern Region, Forest Service, 633 W. Wisconsin Ave., Milwaukee, Wis. 53203.

1 Willow Slough State Fish & Game Area. Apr. 1–Oct. 30. 50 tents or trailers. Fee. Showers. Cafe 1 mi. Fishing. Boat launch, rental.

2 Jasper–Pulaski State Fish & Game Area. Apr. 1–Oct. 30. 42 tents or trailers. Fee.

3 Tippecanoe River. All year. 90 tents or trailers. Fee. Elec. hookup. Showers. Fishing. Horseback riding.

4 Bass Lake State Beach. May 30–Sept. 12. 95 tents or trailers. Fee. Elec. hookup—extra chg. Showers. Cafe. Swimming, fishing. Boat launch.

5 Indiana Dunes. All year. 300 tents or trailers. Fee. Elec. hookup—extra chg. Showers. Cafe, store. Swimming.

6 Warren Dunes St. Pk. All year. 366 tents or trailers. Fee. Elec. hookup. Dumping station. Showers. Store. Swimming 1 mi.

7 Chain O' Lakes. Apr. 1–Oct. 30. 360 tents or trailers. Fee. Elec. hookup—extra chg. Dumping station. Showers. Cafe, store. Swimming 1 mi. Fishing. Boat launch, rental. Horseback riding.

8 Pigeon River. Apr. 1–Oct. 30. 25 tents or trailers. Fee. No flush toilets. Cafe, store 1 mi. Fishing. Boat launch, rental.

9 Pokagon. All year. 450 tents or trailers. Fee. Elec. hookup—extra chg. Dumping station. Showers. Cafe, store. Swimming 1 mi. Fishing. Boat launch, rental. Horseback riding.

10 Yankee Springs. All year. 320 tents

or trailers. Fee. Elec. hookup. Dumping station. Showers. Store 1 mi. Swimming, fishing. Boat launch, rental.

11 Muskegon St. Pk. All year. 346 tents or trailers. Fee. Elec. hookup. Dumping station. Showers. Store. Swimming. Fishing 1 mi. Boat launch.

12 White Cloud St. Pk. All year. 80 tents or trailers. Fee. Elec. hookup. Dumping station. Showers.

13 Silver Lake St. Pk. All year. 250 tents or trailers. Fee. Elec. hookup. Dumping station. Showers. Swimming. Fishing 1 mi. Boat launch.

14 Charles Mears St. Pk. All year. 179 tents or trailers. Fee. Elec. hookup. Dumping station. Showers. Store. Swimming 1 mi. Boating.

15 Ludington St. Pk. All year. 414 tents or trailers. Fee. Elec. hookup. Dumping station. Showers. Store. Swimming, fishing 1 mi. Boat launch, rental.

16 Orchard Beach St. Pk. All year. 175 tents or trailers. Fee. Elec. hookup. Dumping station. Showers. Swimming 1 mi.

17 Benzie St. Pk. All year. 200 tents or trailers. Fee. Elec. hookup. Dumping station. Swimming. Boat launch.

18 D.H. Day St. Pk. All year. 130 tents or trailers. Fee. Elec. hookup. Dumping station. No flush toilets. Swimming. Boat launch.

19 Traverse City. May–Dec. 333 tents or trailers. Fee. Elec. hookup. Dumping station. Showers. Swimming. Fishing 1 mi. Boating.

20 Interlochen St. Pk. All year. 551 tents or trailers. Fee. Elec. hookup. Dumping station. Showers. Store. Swimming, fishing. Boat launch, rental.

21 William Mitchell St. Pk. All year. 270 tents or trailers. Fee. Elec. hookup. Dumping station. Showers. Swimming, fishing 1 mi. Boat launch.

22 Otsego Lake St. Pk. All year. 203 tents or trailers. Fee. Elec. hookup. Dumping station. Showers. Store. Swimming. Fishing 1 mi. Boat launch, rental.

23 Hartwick Pines St. Pk. All year. 48 tents or trailers. Fee. Elec. hookup. Dumping station. Showers. Store. Fishing 1 mi.

24 South Higgins Lake St. Pk. All year. 510 tents or trailers. Fee. Elec. hookup. Dumping station. Showers. Store. Swimming, fishing 1 mi. Boat launch, rental.

25 Wilson St. Pk. May–Dec. 160 tents or trailers. Fee. Elec. hookup. Dumping station. Showers. Store. Swimming. Fishing 1 mi. Boat launch, rental.

26 Harrisville St. Pk. All year. 229 tents or trailers. Fee. Elec. hookup. Dumping station. Showers. Swimming. Boat launch.

27 Round Lake. May 1–Oct. 31. 33 tents or trailers (max. 22 ft.). Fee. Elec. hookup. Cafe 1 mi. Swimming. Fishing 1 mi. Boat dock, launch.

28 Tawas Point St. Pk. All year. 202 tents or trailers. Fee. Elec. hookup. Dumping station. Showers. Store. Swimming, fishing 1 mi. Boat launch.

29 Albert E. Sleeper St. Pk. May–Dec. 356 tents or trailers. Fee. Elec. hookup. Dumping station. Showers. Store. Swimming, fishing 1 mi.

30 Metamora–Hadley St. Pk. From Hwy. 24, W 2 mi. on local rd. All year. 240 tents or trailers. Fee. Elec. hookup. Dumping station. Showers. Store. Swimming. Fishing 1 mi. Boat launch, rental.

31 Proud Lake St. Pk. All year. 207 tents or trailers. Fee. Elec. hookup. Dumping station. Showers. Swimming, fishing 1 mi. Boat launch.

32 Waterloo St. Pk. From Hwy. 94, exit 150, NW 4 mi. on local rd. All year. 428 tents or trailers. Fee. Elec. hookup. Dumping station. Showers. Store. Swimming. Fishing 1 mi. Boat launch, rental. Horseback riding.

33 Walter J. Hayes St. Pk. All year. 210 tents or trailers. Fee. Elec. hookup. Dumping station. Showers. Store 1 mi. Swimming. Fishing 1 mi. Boat launch, rental.

34 Harrison Lake. All year. 201 tents or trailers (max. 30 ft.). Fee. Elec. hookup. Dumping station. Showers. Cafe, store 1 mi. Swimming, fishing. Boat launch, rental.

35 Sterling St. Pk. All year. 192 tents or trailers. Fee. Elec. hookup. Dumping station. Showers. Store. Fishing. Boat launch.

36 East Harbor. All year. 570 tents or trailers (max. 30 ft.). Fee. Showers. Cafe. Store. Swimming 1 mi. Fishing. Boat launch, rental.

Mississippi Palisades
(Map is on page 155)

Camping in Mississippi Palisades State Park.

For information on state campgrounds in Illinois write to Tourism Division, Department of Business and Economic Development, 222 S. College St., Springfield, Ill. 62706;
in Iowa, to Public Relations, State Conservation Commission, 300 4th St., Des Moines, Iowa 50319;
in Wisconsin, to Vacation and Travel Service, Department of Natural Resources, Box 450, Madison, Wis. 53701.

For information on U.S. Forest Service campgrounds, write to Eastern Region, Forest Service, 633 W. Wisconsin Ave., Milwaukee, Wis. 53203.

1 Clear Lake St. Pk. All year. 350 tents or trailers. Fee. Elec. hookup—extra chg. Dumping station. Showers. Swimming, fishing. Boating.

2 Backbone St. Pk. All year. No fixed number of sites. Fee. Elec. hookup—extra chg. Dumping station. Showers. Swimming, fishing. Boating.

3 Pikes Peak St. Pk. All year. No fixed number of sites. Fee. Elec. hookup—extra chg. Dumping station. Showers. Cafe 1 mi.

4 Wyalusing St. Pk. All year. 74 tents or trailers. Fee. Elec. hookup—extra chg. No flush toilets.

5 Devils Lake, South. All year. 270 tents or trailers (max. 25 ft.). Fee. Elec. hookup—extra chg. Showers. Cafe, store. Swimming, fishing. Boats for rent.

6 Devils Lake, North. All year. 230 tents or trailers (max. 25 ft.). Fee. Elec. hookup—extra chg. Showers. Cafe, store. Swimming, fishing. Boats for rent.

7 Governor Dodge St. Pk. All year. 224 tents or trailers (max. 25 ft.). Fee. Elec. hookup—extra chg. Dumping station. Showers. Cafe 1 mi. Swimming, fishing. Boat launch.

8 Lake Le-Aqua-Na St. Pk. All year. 250 tents or trailers (max. 30 ft.). Fee. Elec. hookup. Showers. Boating.

9 White Pines Forest St. Pk. All year. 300 tents or trailers (max. 30 ft.). Fee. Fishing.

10 Mississippi Palisades St. Pk. All year. 200 tents or trailers (max. 30 ft.). Fee. Elec. hookup. Dumping station. No flush toilets. Cafe 1 mi. Fishing. Boat launch.

11 Bellevue St. Pk. All year. No fixed number of sites. Fee. Dumping station. Showers. Fishing 1 mi. Boating 1 mi.

12 Lake MacBride St. Pk. All year. No fixed number of sites. Fee. Elec. hookup —extra chg. Dumping station. Showers. Swimming, fishing 1 mi. Boating 1 mi.

13 Rock Creek St. Pk. All year. No fixed number of sites. Fee. Elec. hookup —extra chg. Dumping station. Showers. Swimming 1 mi. Fishing. Boating 1 mi.

14 Pine Lake St. Pk. All year. 225 tents or trailers. Fee. Elec. hookup—extra chg. Dumping station. Showers. Swimming 1 mi. Fishing. Boating 1 mi.

15 Dolliver Memorial St. Pk. All year. 44 tents or trailers. Fee. Elec. hookup— extra chg. Dumping station. Showers. Fishing.

16 Black Hawk Lake St. Pk. All year. 225 tents or trailers. Fee. Elec. hookup— extra chg. Dumping station. Showers. Swimming, fishing. Boating.

17 Ledges St. Pk. All year. No fixed number of sites. Fee. Elec. hookup—extra chg. Dumping station. Showers. Store 1 mi. Fishing 1 mi.

18 Spring Brook St. Pk. All year. No fixed number of sites. Fee. Elec. hookup —extra chg. Dumping station. Showers. Swimming, fishing. Boating.

19 Lake Anita St. Pk. All year. No fixed number of sites. Fee. Elec. hookup—extra chg. Dumping station. Showers. Fishing. Boating.

20 Viking Lake St. Pk. All year. No fixed number of sites. Fee. Elec. hookup —extra chg. Dumping station. Showers. Swimming, fishing. Boating.

21 Lake Ahquabi St. Pk. All year. No fixed number of sites. Fee. Elec. hookup —extra chg. Dumping station. Showers. Swimming, fishing.

22 Red Haw Lake St. Pk. All year. No fixed number of sites. Fee. Elec. hookup —extra chg. Showers. Swimming, fishing. Boat launch, rental.

23 Lake Keomah St. Pk. All year. No fixed number of sites. Fee. Showers. Swimming, fishing. Boat launch, rental.

24 Lake Darling St. Pk. All year. No fixed number of sites. Fee. Dumping station. Showers. Swimming, fishing.

25 Geode St. Pk. From US 34, SW 4 mi. on county rd. All year. No fixed number of sites. Fee. Elec. hookup—extra chg. Dumping station. Showers. Cafe 1 mi. Swimming, fishing. Boating 1 mi.

26 Delabar St. Pk. All year. 150 tents or trailers (max. 30 ft.). Fee. Elec. hookup. No flush toilets. Cafe 1 mi. Fishing. Boating.

Flint Hills
(Map is on page 165)

For information on state campgrounds in Kansas, write to State Park and Resources Authority, 801 Harrison, Topeka, Kans. 66612;
in Nebraska, to Nebraskaland, State Capitol, Lincoln, Neb. 68509.

For information on U.S. Forest Service campgrounds, write to Rocky Mountain Region, Forest Service, Federal Center, Bldg. 85, Denver, Colo. 80225.

1 Johnson Lake Rec. Area. All year. No fixed number of sites. No fee. Showers. Store 1 mi. Swimming, fishing.

2 Stolley. All year. No fixed number of sites. Fee.

3 Alexandria Lakes Rec. Area. All year. No fixed number of sites. No fee. No flush toilets. Cafe. Store 1 mi. Swimming, fishing.

4 Lovewell St. Pk. Apr. 15–Nov. 15. 50 tents or trailers. Fee. Showers. Cafe 1 mi. Swimming, fishing. Boat launch, rental.

5 Webster St. Pk. Apr. 15–Nov. 15. 50 tents or trailers. Fee. Showers. Cafe 1 mi. Swimming 1 mi. Fishing. Boat launch, rental.

6 Cedar Bluff St. Pk. Apr. 15–Nov. 15. 30 tents or trailers. Fee. Elec., water, sewer hookup. Showers. Cafe, store 1 mi. Swimming, fishing. Boat launch, rental.

7 Wilson St. Pk. All year. No fixed number of sites. Fee. Dumping station. Showers. Swimming, fishing. Boat dock, launch, rental.

8 Ottawa County. All year. No fixed number of sites. No fee. No flush toilets. Showers. Swimming, fishing. Boat launch, rental.

9 Milford St. Pk. Apr. 15–Nov. 15. 200 tents or trailers. Fee. Dumping station. Showers. Cafe. Swimming, fishing. Boat launch, rental.

10 Tuttle Creek St. Pk. Apr. 15–Nov. 15. 150 tents or trailers. Fee. Elec., water, sewer hookup—extra chg. Showers. Cafe, store 1 mi. Swimming, fishing. Boat launch, rental.

11 Shawnee County State Lake. All year. 125 tents or trailers. Fee. Elec.

hookup—extra chg. Water hookup. Dumping station. Showers. Swimming, fishing. Boat launch, rental.

12 Council Grove. All year. No fixed number of sites. No fee. No flush toilets. Cafe, store 1 mi. Swimming, fishing. Boat launch, rental.

13 Kanopolis St. Pk. Apr. 15–Nov. 15. 150 tents, 165 trailers. Fee. Elec., water, sewer hookup—extra chg. Showers. Cafe, store 1 mi. Swimming, fishing. Boat launch, rental.

14 Cimarron Crossing. May 15–Sept. 15. 30 tents, 20 trailers (max. 26 ft.). Fee. Elec. hookup. Showers. Cafe, store 1 mi. Swimming 1 mi. Fishing. Horseback riding.

15 Cheney St. Pk. Apr. 15–Nov. 15. 150 tents, 10 trailers. Fee. Showers. Cafe 1 mi. Swimming, fishing. Boat launch.

16 Toronto St. Pk. Apr. 15–Nov. 15. 100 tents or trailers. Fee. Elec., water, sewer hookup—extra chg. Showers. Cafe, store 1 mi. Swimming, fishing 1 mi. Boat launch, rental.

17 Fall River St. Pk. Apr. 15–Nov. 15. 150 tents or trailers. Fee. Elec., water, sewer hookup—extra chg. Showers. Cafe, store 1 mi. Swimming, fishing. Boat launch, rental.

Ozark National Scenic Riverways
(Map is on page 174)

For information on state campgrounds in Arkansas write to State Parks, Recreational and Travel Commission, 149 State Capitol, Little Rock, Ark. 72201;
in Missouri, to State Park Board, Box 176, Jefferson City, Mo. 65101;
in Oklahoma, to Tourism Division, 500 Will Rogers Bldg., Oklahoma City, Okla. 73105.

For information on U.S. Forest Service campgrounds in Missouri write to Eastern Region, Forest Service, 633 W. Wisconsin Ave., Milwaukee, Wis. 53203;
in Arkansas and Oklahoma, to Southern Region, Forest Service, 1720 Peachtree Rd. NW, Atlanta, Ga. 30309.

1 Crawford. May 1–Oct. 15. 100 tents or trailers (max. 30 ft.). Fee. Showers. Cafe, store. Swimming, fishing. Boat launch, rental.

2 Pomme de Terre St. Pk. Apr. 15–Oct. 31. 288 tents, 22 trailers (max. 30 ft.). Fee. Elec. hookup—extra chg. Water, sewer hookup. Dumping station. Showers. Cafe, store 1 mi. Swimming, fishing. Boat launch, rental.

3 Lake of the Ozarks St. Pk. Apr. 15–Oct. 31. 205 tents, 16 trailers (max. 30 ft.). Fee. Elec. hookup—extra chg. Dumping station. Showers. Cafe, store. Swimming, fishing. Boat launch, rental. Horseback riding.

4 Meramec St. Pk. Apr. 15–Oct. 31. 194 tents, 56 trailers (max. 30 ft.). Fee. Elec. hookup—extra chg. Water, sewer hookup. Dumping station. Showers.

Cafe, store. Swimming, fishing. Boat launch, rental.

5 Alley Spring. May 1–Oct. 31. 200 tents or trailers (max. 35 ft.). Fee. Showers. Cafe, store 1 mi. Swimming, fishing. Boat launch, rental. Horseback riding.

6 Big Spring. May 1–Oct. 31. 208 tents or trailers (max. 35 ft.). Fee. Showers—extra chg. Cafe, store. Swimming, fishing. Boat launch.

7 Lake Charles St. Pk. All year. 73 tents, 90 trailers. Fee. Elec. hookup—extra chg. Showers. Cafe. Store 1 mi. Swimming, fishing. Boat launch, rental.

8 Heber Springs. All year. 69 tents or trailers. No fee. Showers. Cafe, store 1 mi. Swimming, fishing. Boat dock, launch, rental.

9 Buffalo River St. Pk. All year. 50 tents or trailers. Fee. Elec. hookup—extra chg. Water hookup. Dumping station 1 mi. Showers. Cafe, store. Swimming, fishing. Boat launch, rental. Riding.

10 Bull Shoals St. Pk. All year. 100 tents or trailers. Fee. Elec. hookup—extra chg. Dumping station. Showers. Cafe, store 1 mi. Swimming, fishing. Boat dock, launch, rental.

11 Table Rock St. Pk. Apr. 15–Oct. 31. 229 tents, 22 trailers (max. 30 ft.). Fee. Elec., sewer hookup—extra chg. Water hookup. Dumping station. Showers. Cafe 1 mi. Store. Swimming, fishing. Boat launch, rental.

12 Twin Bridges. All year. 49 tents, 45 trailers. No fee. Elec. hookup. Showers. Cafe. Swimming, fishing. Boat launch, rental.

13 Honey Creek. All year. 69 tents, 60 trailers. No fee. Elec., water hookup. Showers. Cafe. Swimming, fishing. Boat launch.

14 Devil's Den St. Pk. Apr. 1–Nov. 1. 80 tents, 50 trailers (max. 20 ft.). Fee. Elec. hookup—extra chg. Dumping station 1 mi. Showers. Cafe, store. Horseback riding.

15 Lake Tenkiller St. Pk. All year. 88 tents, 250 trailers. No fee. Elec., water, sewer hookup. Dumping station. Cafe. Store 1 mi. Swimming, fishing. Boat launch, rental.

16 Petit Jean. All year. 100 tents or trailers. Fee. Elec. hookup—extra chg. Water hookup. Dumping station. Showers. Cafe, store. Swimming, fishing. Boat launch. Horseback riding.

17 Lake Wister St. Pk. All year. 90 tents or trailers. No fee. Elec., water, sewer hookup. Dumping station. Showers. Cafe, store. Swimming, fishing. Boat launch, rental.

18 Beavers Bend St. Pk. All year. 75 tents, 80 trailers (max. 20 ft.). No fee. Elec., water hookup. Dumping station. Showers. Cafe, store. Swimming, fishing. Boats for rent.

19 Daisy St. Pk. All year. 50 tents or trailers. Fee. Elec. hookup—extra chg. Water, sewer hookup. Showers. Cafe, store 1 mi. Swimming, fishing. Boats for rent.

20 Lake Ouachita St. Pk. All year. 227 tents or trailers. Fee. Elec. hookup—extra chg. Showers. Cafe, store. Swimming, fishing. Boat launch, rental.

21 Lake Catherine St. Pk. All year. 100 tents or trailers. Fee. Elec. hookup—extra chg. Water hookup. Sewer hookup 1 mi. Showers. Cafe, store. Swimming, fishing. Boat dock, launch, rental.

Wichita Mountains
(Map is on page 185)

For information on state campgrounds in Oklahoma, write to Oklahoma Tourism Division, 500 Will Rogers Bldg., Oklahoma City, Okla. 73105; in Texas, to Parks and Wildlife Department, John H. Reagan Bldg., Austin, Tex. 78701.

For information on U.S. Forest Service campgrounds, write to Southern Region, Forest Service, 1720 Peachtree Rd. NW, Atlanta, Ga. 30309.

1 Black Mesa St. Pk. All year. 10 tents or trailers (max. 20 ft.). No fee. Swimming, fishing. Boats for rent.

2 Sanford–Yake. All year. 105 tents or trailers. No fee. Cafe, store. Fishing. Boat dock, launch, rental.

3 Palo Duro Canyon St. Pk. All year. 34 tents, 20 trailers. Fee. Elec., sewer hookups—extra chg. Water hookup. Showers. Cafe, store. Horseback riding.

4 Quartz Mtn. St. Pk. All year. 201 tents, 200 trailers. No fee. Elec., water, sewer hookups. Dumping station. Showers. Cafe, store. Swimming pool, swimming, fishing. Boat launch, rental.

5 Fort Cobb. All year. 102 tents, 100 trailers. No fee. Elec. hookup. Showers. Cafe. Swimming, fishing. Boat launch, rental.

6 Red Rock Canyon St. Pk. All year. 49 tents, 50 trailers (max. 20 ft.). No fee. Elec., water, sewer hookup. Dumping station 1 mi. Showers. Cafe. Store 1 mi. Swimming pool, swimming.

7 Foss Reservoir. All year. 79 tents, 80 trailers. No fee. Elec. hookup. Showers. Store. Swimming, fishing. Boat launch.

8 Roman Nose St. Pk. All year. 178 tents, 175 trailers. No fee. Elec., water, sewer hookup. Showers. Cafe. Swimming, fishing. Boat launch, rental. Horseback riding.

9 Boiling Springs St. Pk. All year. 116 tents, 200 trailers. No fee. Elec., water, sewer hookup. Showers. Swimming pool, swimming.

10 Alabaster Caverns St. Pk. All year. 23 tents, 25 trailers. No fee. Elec. hookup. Showers. Cafe. Horseback riding.

11 Little Sahara. All year. 20 tents, 25 trailers. No fee. Elec., water hookup. Showers.

12 Great Salt Plains St. Pk. All year. 88 tents, 90 trailers. No fee. Elec. hookup. Showers. Cafe, store. Swimming, fishing. Boat launch, rental.

13 Keystone St. Pk. All year. 67 tents or trailers. No fee. Elec. hookup. Showers.

Swimming, fishing. Boats for rent.

14 Little River St. Pk. All year. 225 tents or trailers. No fee. Elec. hookup. Dumping station. Showers. Cafe, store. Swimming, fishing. Boat launch, rental. Horseback riding.

15 Rock Creek. All year. 106 tents or trailers (max. 25 ft.). Fee. Dumping station. Cafe, store 1 mi. Swimming.

16 Lake Murray St. Pk. All year. 250 tents, 200 trailers. No fee. Elec., water, sewer hookup. Dumping station. Showers. Cafe, store. Swimming pool, swimming, fishing. Boat launch, rental. Horseback riding.

17 Lake Texoma St. Pk. All year. 266 tents, 250 trailers. No fee. Elec., water, sewer hookup. Dumping station. Showers. Cafe, store. Swimming pool, swimming, fishing. Boat launch, rental. Horseback riding.

18 Eisenhower St. Pk. All year. 88 tents, 50 trailers. Fee. Elec., sewer hookup—extra chg. Water hookup. Showers. Cafe, store. Swimming, fishing. Boat launch.

Bayou Country
(Map is on page 194)

For information on state campgrounds in Alabama write to Bureau of Publicity and Information, State Highway Department Bldg., Montgomery, Ala. 36104; in Florida, to Department of Natural Resources, Education and Information Division, J. Edwin Larson Bldg., Tallahassee, Fla. 32304; in Louisiana, to State Parks and Recreation Commission, P.O. Drawer 1111, Baton Rouge, La. 70821; in Mississippi, to Mississippi Park System, 717 Robert E. Lee Bldg., Jackson, Miss. 39201.

For information on U.S. Forest Service campgrounds, write to Southern Region, Forest Service, 1720 Peachtree Rd. NW, Atlanta, Ga. 30309.

1 Chemin-A-Haut St. Pk. All year. 25 tents, 24 trailers. Fee. Elec., water, sewer hookup. Dumping station. Showers. Cafe. Swimming pool—extra chg. Swimming, fishing. Boat launch.

2 Holmes County St. Pk. All year. 10 tents, 20 trailers (max. 30 ft.). Fee. Elec., water hookup—extra chg. Dumping station. Showers. Store 1 mi. Swimming, fishing. Boat launch, rental.

3 Payne Lake. All year. 19 tents or trailers (max. 22 ft.). Fee. Showers. Cafe 1 mi. Swimming, fishing. Boat dock, launch, rental.

4 Lock 7. All year. 27 tents or trailers (max. 18 ft.). Fee. No flush toilets. Swimming, fishing 1 mi. Boat launch.

5 Chickasaw St. Pk. All year. No fixed number of sites (max. 24 ft.). Fee. No pets. No flush toilets.

6 Marathon Lake. From Hwy. 501, E 4 mi. on FR 506, S 3 mi. on FR 520. All year. 36 tents or trailers (max. 22 ft.).

Fee. Showers. Swimming, fishing. Boat dock, launch.

7 Roosevelt St. Pk. All year. 20 tents, 30 trailers (max. 30 ft.). Fee. Elec., water hookup—extra chg. Dumping station. Showers. Store 1 mi. Swimming, fishing. Boat launch, rental.

8 Lake Bruin St. Pk. All year. 82 tents or trailers. Fee. Elec., water hookup. Dumping station. Showers. Cafe. Swimming, fishing. Boat launch, rental.

9 Clear Springs. All year. 23 tents or trailers (max. 22 ft.). Fee. Elec. hookup. Showers. Swimming, fishing. Boat dock.

10 Chicot St. Pk. All year. 60 tents, 36 trailers. Fee. Elec., water, sewer hookup. Dumping station. Showers. Cafe, store. Swimming pool—extra chg. Swimming, fishing. Boat launch, rental.

11 Longfellow-Evangeline St. Pk. All year. 12 tents, 10 trailers. Fee. Elec., water hookup. Dumping station. Showers. Cafe. Store 1 mi. Swimming pool—extra chg. Swimming 1 mi. Boat launch.

12 Percy Quin St. Pk. All year. 70 tents, 50 trailers (max. 30 ft.). Fee. Elec., water hookup—extra chg. Dumping station. Showers. Store. Swimming, fishing. Boat launch, rental.

13 Fairview Riverside St. Pk. All year. 60 tents, 20 trailers. Fee. Elec., water hookup. Dumping station. Showers. Swimming, fishing. Boat launch, rental.

14 Fontainbleau St. Pk. All year. 100 tents, 72 trailers. Fee. Elec., water hookup. Dumping station. Showers. Cafe, store. Swimming pool—extra chg. Swimming. Boat launch, rental.

15 Paul B. Johnson St. Pk. All year. 80 tents, 40 trailers. Fee. Elec., water, sewer hookup—extra chg. Dumping station. Showers. Cafe, store. Swimming, fishing. Boat launch, rental.

16 Magnolia St. Pk. All year. 50 tents, 20 trailers (max. 30 ft.). Fee. Elec., water hookup—extra chg. Dumping station. Showers. Cafe, store 1 mi. Swimming, fishing 1 mi. Boat launch, rental.

17 Gulf St. Pk. All year. 64 tents, 30 trailers (max. 29 ft.). Fee. No pets. Elec., water, sewer hookup. Showers. Cafe 1 mi. Swimming, fishing. Boat launch, rental.

18 Fort Pickens St. Pk. All year. 203 tents or trailers. Fee. Resv. required. No pets. Elec. hookup—extra chg. Dumping station. Showers. Cafe, store. Swimming, fishing. Boat dock, launch.

19 Munson. All year. 58 tents or trailers (max. 20 ft.). Fee. No pets. Elec. hookup—extra chg. Showers. Swimming, fishing.

20 Fred Gannon Rocky Bayou St. Pk. All year. 50 tents or trailers. Fee. Resv. required. No pets. Elec. hookup—extra chg. Water hookup. Dumping station. Showers. Swimming, fishing. Boat dock, launch.

21 Grayton Beach St. Pk. All year. 36 tents or trailers (max. 30 ft.). Fee. Resv. required. No pets. Elec. hookup—extra chg. Water hookup. Dumping station. Showers. Cafe, store. Swimming, fishing. Boat launch, rental.

Padre Island National Seashore

(Map is on page 203)

Camping permitted on the beaches. One official campground with facilities, trailer space but no utility connections.

For information on state campgrounds write to Parks and Wildlife Department, John H. Reagan Bldg., Austin, Tex. 78701.

For information on U.S. Forest Service campgrounds, write to Southern Region, Forest Service, 1720 Peachtree Rd. NW, Atlanta, Ga. 30309.

1 Inks Lake. All year. 183 tents, 14 trailers. Fee. Elec. hookup—extra chg. Water hookup. Dumping station. Showers. Cafe. Store. Swimming, fishing. Boat launch, rental.

2 Bastrop St. Pk. All year. 48 tents, 25 trailers. Fee. Elec., sewer hookup—extra chg. Water hookup. Showers. Cafe. Swimming pool—extra chg.

3 Stubblefield Lake. From I-45, W 10 mi. on forest rds. 1374 and 208. March 15–Oct. 1. 22 tents or trailers (max. 22 ft.). Fee. Showers. Fishing.

4 Huntsville St. Pk. All year. 178 tents, 27 trailers. Fee. Elec., sewer hookup—extra chg. Water hookup. Dumping station. Showers. Cafe, store. Swimming, fishing. Boat launch, rental. Horseback riding.

5 Double Lake. From Hwy. 2025, E 20 mi. on FR 210. March 15–Oct. 1. 55 tents or trailers (max. 22 ft.). Fee. Showers. Cafe. Swimming, fishing. Boat dock.

6 Stephen F. Austin St. Pk. From I-10, E 3 mi. to pk. rd. 99, N 2½ mi. to pk. rd. 38. All year. 40 tents or trailers. Fee. Elec., sewer hookup—extra chg. Water hookup. Showers. Cafe. Store 1 mi. Swimming pool—extra chg. Fishing.

7 Goliad St. Pk. All year. 25 tents, 20 trailers. Fee. Elec., sewer hookup—extra chg. Water hookup. Showers. Store.

8 Goose Island St. Pk. From Hwy. 30 NE to pk. rd. 13. All year. 76 tents, 63 trailers. Fee. Elec., sewer hookup—extra chg. Water hookup. Showers. Cafe, store 1 mi. Swimming, fishing. Boat launch, rental.

9 Lake Corpus Christi St. Pk. From Hwy. 359, NW 2 mi. on pk. rd. 25. All year. 155 tents, 40 trailers. Fee. Elec., sewer hookup—extra chg. Water hookup. Dumping station. Showers. Cafe, store 1 mi. Swimming, fishing. Boat launch.

10 Padre Island Nat'l. Seashore. All year. No fixed number of sites. No fee. Dumping station. Showers. Cafe. Swimming, fishing.

11 Bentsen–Rio Grande St. Pk. From US 83, SW 2 mi. on pk. rd. 43. All year. 90 tents, 80 trailers. Fee. Elec., sewer hookup—extra chg. Water hookup. Showers. Fishing.

12 Isla Blanca Trailer Park. From Pt. Isabel, 3 mi. on pk. rd. 100, S at end of causeway ½ mi. All year. 60 trailers

(max. 30 ft.). Fee. Resv. accepted. Elec., water, sewer hookup. Dumping station. Showers. Cafe 1 mi. Swimming, fishing 1 mi. Boat launch, rental.

Devils Tower National Monument

(Map is on page 213)

One campground in the monument, with trailer space but no utility connections.

For information on state campgrounds in Wyoming write to Wyoming Travel Commission, 2320 Capitol Ave., Cheyenne, Wyo. 82001;
in South Dakota, to Travel Division, Department of Highways, Pierre, S.D. 57501;
in North Dakota, to Travel Division, State Highway Bldg., Capitol Grounds, Bismarck, N.D. 58501;
in Montana, to Advertising Department, Montana Highway Commission, Helena, Mont. 59601.

For information on U.S. Forest Service campgrounds in North Dakota and Montana write to Northern Region, Forest Service, Federal Bldg., Missoula, Mont. 59801;
in South Dakota and Wyoming, to Rocky Mountain Region, Forest Service, Federal Center, Bldg. 85, Denver, Colo. 80225.

1 Cartside Lake. All year. 50 tents, 100 trailers. No fee. No flush toilets. Store 1 mi. Swimming, fishing.

2 Theodore Roosevelt Nat'l. Mem. Pk., North Unit. From US 85, W 5 mi. on pk. rd. All year. 18 tents, 15 trailers (max. 35 ft.). Fee.

3 Fort Stevenson Rec. Area. May 1–Sept. 15. 400 tents or trailers. Fee. Elec., water hookup—extra chg. Sewer hookup. Dumping station. Showers. Cafe, store. Swimming, fishing. Boat launch, rental.

4 Lake Sakakawea St. Pk. May 1–Oct. 30. 500 tents, 75 trailers (max. 22 ft.). Fee. Elec., water hookup. Dumping station. Showers. Cafe 1 mi. Store. Swimming, fishing. Boat dock, launch, rental.

5 Downstream. May 30–Oct. 31. 25 tents or trailers. Fee. Elec. hookup. Dumping station. Showers. Swimming pool—extra chg. Fishing. Boat dock, launch.

6 Sibley Island. May 1–Oct. 30. 100 tents, 43 trailers. Fee. Elec. hookup—extra chg. Dumping station. Showers. Fishing.

7 Fort Lincoln St. Pk. May 1–Oct. 30. 62 tents, 48 trailers (max. 22 ft.). Fee. Elec. hookup. Dumping station. Showers. Fishing.

8 Cottonwood. From I-94, N 6 mi. on pk. rd. All year. 51 tents or trailers (max. 35 ft.). Fee. Horseback riding.

9 Medicine Rocks St. Pk. May 1–Oct. 1. 10 tents or trailers (max. 25 ft.). No fee. No flush toilets.

10 Butte View. May 15–Sept. 15. No fixed number of tents. 55 trailers. Fee. Elec., water hookup. Dumping station. Showers.

11 Haley Rec. Area. May 1–Oct. 30. No fixed number of sites (max. 22 ft.). Fee. Resv. accepted. Elec. hookup. Dumping station. Showers.

12 Shadehill Reservoir Rec. Area. All year. No fixed number of sites. Fee. No flush toilets. Showers. Cafe, store. Swimming, fishing. Boat launch, rental.

13 Belle Fourche. May 15–Sept. 30. 51 tents or trailers (max. 32 ft.). Fee. Dumping station 1 mi. Cafe, store 1 mi. Swimming 1 mi.

14 Keyhole St. Pk. May 1–Sept. 1. 50 tents or trailers. No fee. No flush toilets. Cafe, store. Swimming, fishing. Boat launch, rental.

15 Reuter Canyon. From US 14, N 2 mi. on FR 838. June 1–Oct. 1. 12 tents or trailers (max. 22 ft.). Fee. Cafe 4 mi. Fishing 4 mi.

16 Indian Creek. May 30–Oct. 31. 42 tents or trailers. Fee. Elec. hookup. Dumping station. Showers. Fishing. Boat launch.

Badlands National Monument

(Map is on page 224)

Two campgrounds in the monument, one primitive, neither with utility connections.

For information on state campgrounds write to Travel Division, Department of Highways, Pierre, S.D. 57501.

For information on U.S. Forest Service campgrounds write to Rocky Mountain Region, Forest Service, Federal Center, Bldg. 85, Denver, Colo. 80225.

1 Timon. From US 14A, SW 4 mi. on FR 222. June 1–Dec. 1. 12 tents or trailers (max. 22 ft.). Fee. Cafe 4 mi.

2 Pactola. June 1–Oct. 1. 36 tents, 26 trailers (max. 22 ft.). Fee. Cafe 1 mi. Fishing. Boat dock, launch, rental.

3 Southside. June 1–Oct. 1. 21 tents, 88 trailers (max. 22 ft.). Fee. Cafe 2 mi. Swimming, fishing. Boat dock, launch, rental.

4 Sylvan Lake. May 15–Oct. 1. 35 tents or trailers. Fee. Showers—extra chg. Cafe, store 1 mi. Swimming, fishing. Boats for rent. Horseback riding.

5 Grizzly Bear. June 1–Oct. 1. 20 tents, 16 trailers (max. 22 ft.). Fee. Cafe 2 mi. Fishing.

6 Center Lake. May 15–Oct. 1. 35 tents or trailers. Fee. Showers—extra chg. Swimming, fishing. Boat launch, rental.

7 Legion Lake. May 15–Oct. 1. 35 tents or trailers. Fee. Showers—extra chg. Cafe, store 1 mi. Swimming. Fishing 1 mi. Boat launch, rental. Riding.

8 Stockade Lake. May 15–Oct. 1. 160

tents or trailers. Fee. Showers—extra chg. Cafe, store 1 mi. Swimming, fishing. Boat launch, rental.

9 Blue Bell. May 15–Oct. 1. 35 tents or trailers. Fee. Showers—extra chg. Cafe, store 1 mi. Fishing 1 mi. Horseback riding.

10 Elk Mountain. May 15–Oct. 1. 54 tents, 46 trailers (max. 26 ft.). Fee. Showers. Cafe, store 1 mi.

11 Cedar Pass. All year. 140 tents or trailers (max. 27 ft.). Fee. Cafe 1 mi.

Scotts Bluff National Monument
(Map is on page 234)

No camping in the monument.

For information on state campgrounds write to Nebraskaland, State Capitol, Lincoln, Neb. 68509.

For information on U.S. Forest Service campgrounds write to Rocky Mountain Region, Forest Service, Federal Center, Bldg. 85, Denver, Colo. 80225.

1 Lodgepole. All year. No fixed number of sites. No fee. No flush toilets. Swimming, fishing.

2 Bridgeport. All year. No fixed number of sites. No fee. No flush toilets. Swimming, fishing.

3 Wildcat Hills. All year. No fixed number of sites. No fee. No flush toilets.

4 Lake Minatare. Jan. 15–Sept. 30. No fixed number of sites. No fee. No flush toilets. Cafe, store. Swimming, fishing. Boats for rent.

5 Fort Robinson St. Pk. All year. No fixed number of sites. Fee. Resv. required. Elec. hookup—extra chg. Showers. Cafe. Fishing.

6 Chadron St. Pk. All year. No fixed number of sites. Fee. Resv. required. Cafe. Store 1 mi. Fishing 1 mi. Swimming pool—extra chg. Boats for rent.

7 Walgren Lake. All year. No fixed number of sites. No fee. No flush toilets. Fishing.

8 Smith Lake. All year. No fixed number of sites. No fee. No flush toilets. Swimming, fishing.

9 Cottonwood Lake. All year. No fixed number of sites. No fee. No flush toilets. Swimming, fishing.

10 Merritt Reservoir. All year. No fixed number of sites. No fee. No flush toilets. Swimming, fishing.

11 Big Alkali. All year. No fixed number of sites. No fee. No flush toilets. Fishing. Boats for rent.

12 Ballards Marsh. All year. No fixed number of sites. No fee. No flush toilets.

13 Long Lake. All year. No fixed number of sites. No fee. No flush toilets. Swimming, fishing.

14 Lake Ogallala. All year. No fixed number of sites. No fee. No flush toilets.

Cafe. Swimming, fishing. Boats for rent.

15 Victoria Springs. All year. No fixed number of sites. Fee. Swimming, fishing. Boats for rent.

Rocky Mountain National Park
(Map is on page 243)

Seven campgrounds in the park, some with trailer space, but none with utility connections.

For information on state campgrounds in Colorado write to Colorado Travel Development, 602 State Capitol Annex, Denver, Colo. 80203;
in Wyoming, to Wyoming Travel Commission, 2320 Capitol Ave., Cheyenne, Wyo. 82001.

For information on U.S. Forest Service campgrounds in Colorado and Wyoming write to Rocky Mountain Region, Forest Service, 1250 Federal Center, Bldg. 85, Denver, Colo. 80225.

1 Gates of Lodore. May 15–Oct. 15. 18 tents or trailers (max. 30 ft.). No fee. No flush toilets. Fishing.

2 Rio Blanco. All year. 10 tents or trailers. Fee. Swimming, fishing. Boating.

3 Colorado National Monument. All year. 81 tents or trailers (max. 30 ft.). Fee.

4 Island Acres. All year. 32 tents or trailers (max. 22 ft.). Fee. Dumping station 1 mi. No flush toilets. Cafe, store 1 mi. Swimming, fishing.

5 Cottonwood Lake. June 15–Sept. 15. 42 tents or trailers (max. 22 ft.). Fee. Fishing 1 mi. Boat dock.

6 Vega St. Rec. Area. All year. 45 tents or trailers (max. 18 ft.). Fee. Cafe, store 1 mi. Swimming, fishing. Boat dock, launch. Horseback riding.

7 Lake Irwin. May 15–Nov. 4. 27 tents or trailers (max. 32 ft.). Fee. Fishing. Boat dock.

8 Lakeview. May 15–Nov. 4. 32 tents or trailers (max. 22 ft.). Fee. Cafe 3 mi. Fishing 1 mi. Boat dock, launch, rental.

9 Dinner Station. May 15–Nov. 4. 22 tents or trailers (max. 32 ft.). Fee.

10 Cottonwood Lake. From ST 306, SW 3.5 mi. on FR 210. June 1–Oct. 15. 28 tents, 25 trailers (max. 16 ft.). Fee. Swimming 1 mi.

11 Collegiate Peaks. From ST 306, W 2.4 mi. on FR 209. June 1–Oct. 10. 29 tents or trailers (max. 16 ft.). Fee. Fishing. Boats for rent.

12 Perry Mountain. May 25–Oct. 25. 9 tents, 21 trailers (max. 16 ft.). Fee. Cafe 3 mi. Fishing. Boat dock, launch, rental.

13 Difficult. June 1–Oct. 15. 46 tents or trailers (max. 22 ft.). Fee. Cafe 4 mi. Fishing.

14 Maroon Lake. June 1–Oct. 15. 46 tents or trailers (max. 22 ft.). Fee.

15 Bogan Flats. May 1–Oct. 31. 34 tents or trailers (max 32 ft.). Fee. Fishing.

16 Redstone. May 1–Oct. 31. 34 tents or trailers (max. 22 ft.). Fee. Fishing.

17 Chapman. June 1–Oct. 15. 21 tents or trailers (max. 32 ft.). Fee. Cafe 5 mi. Fishing.

18 Green Mountain. All year. 50 tents or trailers. Fee. Cafe, store 1 mi. Swimming, fishing. Boat dock, launch. Horseback riding.

19 Trappers Lake. June 1–Nov. 10. 51 tents or trailers (max. 22 ft.). Fee. Showers. Cafe. Swimming, fishing. Boating.

20 North Fork. June 1–Nov. 10. 49 tents or trailers (max. 22 ft.). Fee. Fishing.

21 Meadows. July 1–Sept. 8. 32 tents or trailers (max. 22 ft.). Fee. Fishing.

22 Steamboat Lake. All year. 20 tents or trailers (max. 22 ft.). Fee. No flush toilets. Cafe, store 1 mi. Swimming, fishing. Boat dock, launch.

23 Seed House. June 15–Sept. 8. 25 tents, 22 trailers (max. 22 ft.). Fee.

24 Big Creek Lakes. June 15–Sept. 8. 45 tents, 25 trailers (max. 22 ft.). Fee. Swimming, fishing. Boat dock.

25 Lakeview. June 15–Sept. 15. 29 tents or trailers (max. 22 ft.). Fee. Fishing. Boat dock, launch.

26 Lost Creek. June 15–Sept. 15. 14 tents or trailers (max. 22 ft.). Fee. Fishing.

27 French Creek. June 1–Oct. 1. 15 tents or trailers (max. 32 ft.). Fee. Fishing.

28 Ryan Park. May 15–Oct. 15. 48 trailers (max. 32 ft.). Fee. Resv. required.

29 Bow River. June 15–Sept. 15. 13 tents or trailers (max. 32 ft.). Fee. Fishing.

30 Lake Owen. May 15–Oct. 30. 33 tents or trailers (max. 22 ft.). Fee. Fishing. Boat dock, launch.

31 Browns Park. June 10–Sept. 20. 28 tents or trailers (max. 32 ft.). Fee. Fishing 1 mi.

32 West Lake. June 1–Sept. 30. 26 tents, 28 trailers (max. 32 ft.). Fee. Showers 2 mi. Cafe 2 mi. Swimming, fishing. Boat dock, launch.

33 Fort Collins Mtn. Park. May 1–Sept. 30. 43 tents or trailers (max. 32 ft.). Fee. Fishing.

34 Chambers Lake. June 10–Sept. 20. 53 tents or trailers (max. 32 ft.). Fee. Swimming, fishing. Boat dock.

35 Timber Creek. May 30–Oct. 15. 101 tents or trailers (max. 25 ft.). Fee. Dumping station. Fishing. Horseback riding.

36 Moraine Park. May 30–Oct. 15. 263 tents or trailers (max. 25 ft.). Fee. Dumping station. Fishing 1 mi. Horseback riding.

37 Glacier Basin. May 30–Oct. 15. 236 tents, 183 trailers (max. 25 ft.). Fee. Dumping station. Fishing. Horseback riding.

38 Olive Ridge. June 1–Sept. 30. 39 tents or trailers (max. 32 ft.). Fee. Showers 2 mi. Cafe 2 mi. Fishing 2 mi.

39 Stillwater. May 15–Oct. 15. 160 tents or trailers (max. 15 ft.). Fee. Dumping station. Showers 1 mi. Store 1 mi. Swimming, fishing. Boat launch.

40 Camp Dick. May 15–Sept. 30. 34 tents or trailers (max. 32 ft.). Fee.

41 Idlewild. June 1–Sept. 15. 24 tents or trailers (max. 32 ft.). Fee. Cafe 1 mi. Fishing.

42 Cold Springs. June 15–Sept. 15. 57 tents or trailers (max. 22 ft.). Fee. Showers 5 mi. Cafe 5 mi. Fishing 5 mi.

43 Kelly Dahl. May 1–Oct. 31. 21 tents or trailers (max. 32 ft.). Fee. Showers 1 mi. Cafe 1 mi.

44 Golden Gate Canyon. From ST 119, E 4 mi. on gravel rd. All year. 20 tents or trailers (max. 22 ft.). Fee. No flush toilets. Fishing.

45 Cherry Creek. All year. 100 tents or trailers. Fee. Elec., sewer hookup. Dumping station. Showers. Cafe. Store 1 mi. Swimming, fishing. Boat launch, rental. Horseback riding.

46 Tenderfoot Mountain. May 30–Sept. 30. 32 tents or trailers (max. 16 ft.). Fee. Cafe 1 mi.

47 Jefferson Creek. June 10–Sept. 10. 17 tents or trailers (max. 22 ft.). Fee. Fishing. Boat launch.

48 Buffalo. May 20–Sept. 10. 41 tents or trailers (max. 16 ft.). Fee. Showers 3 mi. Fishing 2 mi.

49 South Meadows. May 15–Oct. 1. 56 tents or trailers (max. 22 ft.). Fee. Showers 2 mi. Fishing 3 mi.

50 Colorado. May 15–Oct. 1. 62 tents or trailers (max. 22 ft.). Fee. Showers 3 mi. Fishing 2 mi.

51 Clyde. From ST 67, E 8 mi. on FR 370. May 15–Nov. 1. 10 tents or trailers (max. 22 ft.). Fee. Fishing.

Black Canyon of the Gunnison National Monument
(Map is on page 253)

Two campgrounds in the monument with trailer space but no utility connections.

For information on state campgrounds write to Colorado Travel Development, 602 State Capitol Annex, Denver, Colo. 80203.

For information on U.S. Forest Service campgrounds write to Rocky Mountain Region, Forest Service, Federal Center, Bldg. 85, Denver, Colo. 80225.

1 South Rim. All year. 102 tents or trailers (max. 21 ft.). Fee. No flush toilets. Cafe 1 mi. Store.

2 Elk Creek. All year. 175 tents or trailers (max. 30 ft.). Fee. Dumping station. Store 1 mi. Swimming, fishing 1 mi. Boat dock, launch, rental.

3 Big Cimarron. From US 50, S 20 mi. on county rd. June 1–Sept. 5. 16 trailers (max. 22 ft.). Fee. Fishing.

4 Amphitheatre. From US 550, E 5 mi. on forest rd. May 25–Sept. 5. 15 tents, 12 trailers (max. 22 ft.). Fee. Showers 1 mi. Cafe 1 mi.

5 Priest Gulch. May 1–Nov. 1. 14 tents, 16 trailers (max. 32 ft.). Fee. Fishing.

6 Mesa Verde National Park. May 1–Oct. 15. 498 tents, 250 trailers (max. 20 ft.). Fee. Dumping station. Showers—extra chg. Cafe, store. Horseback riding.

7 Thompson Park. June 1–Nov. 1. 51 tents or trailers (max. 22 ft.). Fee.

8 Haviland Lake. June 15–Sept. 15. 43 tents or trailers (max. 32 ft.). Fee.

9 Transfer Park. From US 160, NW 24 mi. on county rd. May 15–Sept. 15. 25 tents or trailers (max. 22 ft.). Fee. Cafe 4 mi. Fishing. Boat dock, launch.

10 Vallecito. June 15–Sept. 15. 44 tents or trailers (max. 22 ft.). Fee. Cafe 3 mi. Fishing. Boat dock, launch, rental.

11 Pine Point. From US 160, N 14 mi. on county rd., NE 4 mi. on forest rd. June 15–Sept. 15. 31 tents or trailers (max. 22 ft.). Fee. Cafe 4 mi. Fishing. Boat dock, launch, rental.

12 Navajo. All year. 30 tents or trailers. Fee. Cafe, store. Swimming, fishing. Horseback riding.

13 Thirty-Mile. From Hwy. 149, SW 11 mi. on FR 520. June 1–Nov. 1. 33 tents, 30 trailers (max. 32 ft.). Fee. Fishing.

14 Williams Creek. From US 160, NW 22 mi. on FR 631, N .5 mi. on FR 640. June 1–Oct. 31. 30 tents or trailers (max. 32 ft.). Fee. Showers. Fishing. Boat dock, launch, rental.

15 Wolf Creek. June 15–Oct. 30. 26 tents or trailers (max. 16 ft.). Fee. Fishing 1 mi.

16 Echo Canyon. All year. No fixed number of sites (max. 22 ft.). Fee. No flush toilets. Showers. Swimming.

Great Sand Dunes National Monument
(Map is on page 262)

One campground in monument with trailer space but no utility connections.

For information on state campgrounds write to Colorado Travel Development, 602 State Capitol Annex, Denver, Colo. 80203.

For information on U.S. Forest Service campgrounds write to Rocky Mountain Region, Forest Service, Federal Center, Bldg. 85, Denver, Colo. 80225.

1 Monarch Park. From US 50, S 9 mi. on FR 235. June 1–Oct. 11. 24 tents, 36 trailers (max. 22 ft.). Fee. Cafe 4 mi. Fishing.

2 Big Meadows. From US 160, SW 2 mi. on forest rd. June 1–Sept. 15. 40 tents, 38 trailers (max. 22 ft.). Fee. Fishing. Boat dock.

3 Spectacle Lake. From Hwy. 17, NW 5 mi. on FR 250. June 1–Sept. 1. 22 tents,

20 trailers (max. 22 ft.). Fee. Fishing.

4 Elk Creek. June 1–Sept. 1. 31 tents, 29 trailers (max. 22 ft.). Fee. Fishing.

5 Aspen Glade. June 1–Sept. 1. 28 tents, 24 trailers (max. 16 ft.). Fee. Cafe 5 mi. Fishing.

6 Pinyon Flat. Apr. 1–Nov. 1. 121 tents or trailers (max. 30 ft.). Fee. Dumping station.

7 Alvarado. May 18–Oct. 25. 14 tents, 44 trailers (max. 16 ft.). Fee. Cafe 1 mi. Fishing 1 mi.

8 Lake Isabel. May 25–Sept. 30. 15 tents or trailers (max. 22 ft.). Fee. No flush toilets. Store. Boating.

9 Lathrop St. Pk. All year. 77 tents or trailers. Fee. Elec. hookup. Showers. Cafe, store. Swimming, fishing. Boat launch. Horseback riding.

10 Cuchara. May 18–Nov. 1. 7 tents, 20 trailers (max. 16 ft.). Fee. Cafe 4 mi. Fishing.

Carlsbad Caverns National Park
(Map is on page 272)

No camping in the park.

For information on state campgrounds in New Mexico write to State Park and Recreation Commission, Box 1147, Santa Fe, N.M. 87501 and Tourist Division, Department of Development, 113 Washington Ave., Santa Fe;
*   in Texas, to Parks and Wildlife Department, John H. Reagan Bldg., Austin, Tex. 78701 and Texas Highway Department, P.O. Box 5064, Austin.*

For information on U.S. Forest Service campgrounds in New Mexico write to Southwestern Region, Forest Service, 517 Gold Ave. SW, Albuquerque, N.M. 87101;
*   in Texas, to Southern Region, Forest Service, 1720 Peachtree Rd. NW, Atlanta, Ga. 30309.*

1 Mesa. Apr. 1–Oct. 30. 24 tents or trailers (max. 22 ft.). Fee. Fishing 1 mi. Boat dock, launch, rental.

2 Iron Creek. Apr. 1–Nov. 30. 15 tents or trailers (max. 22 ft.). Fee.

3 City of Rocks St. Pk. All year. 56 tents or trailers. Fee. No flush toilets.

4 Rockbound St. Pk. All year. 20 tents or trailers. Fee. Water hookup. No flush toilets.

5 Pancho Villa St. Pk. All year. 25 tents or trailers. Fee. Showers. Cafe, store 1 mi.

6 Caballo Lake St. Pk. All year. 24 tents or trailers. Fee. Showers. Store. Swimming, fishing. Boat launch, rental.

7 Elephant Butte Lake St. Pk. All year. 78 tents or trailers. Fee. Elec. hookup—extra chg. Water hookup. Showers. Cafe, store 1 mi. Swimming, fishing. Boat launch, rental.

8 South Fork. Apr. 1–Sept. 30. 60 tents,

42 trailers (max. 16 ft.). Fee. Cafe 3 mi. Fishing.

9 Ruidoso. May–Sept. 20 tents, 30 trailers (max. 14 ft.). Fee. No flush toilets. Swimming 1 mi. Fishing.

10 Silver. Apr. 1–Oct. 30. 32 trailers (max. 32 ft.). Fee. Cafe 4 mi.

11 Bottomless Lakes St. Pk. From US 380, S 7 mi. on paved rd. All year. 60 tents or trailers. Fee. Elec. hookup—extra chg. Water hookup. Showers. Cafe, store. Swimming pool—extra chg. Fishing. Boats for rent. Riding.

Big Bend National Park
(Map is on page 283)

One lodge and four campgrounds in the park, two with utility connections.

For information on state campgrounds write to Parks and Wildlife Department, John H. Reagan Bldg., Austin, Tex. 78701, and Texas Highway Department, P.O. Box 5064, Austin.

For information on U.S. Forest Service campgrounds write to Southern Region, Forest Service, 1720 Peachtree Rd. NW, Atlanta, Ga. 30309.

1 Davis Mountains St. Pk. All year. 54 tents, 27 trailers. Fee. Elec., sewer hookup—extra chg. Water hookup. Showers. Cafe, store 1 mi. Swimming pool—extra chg.

2 Balmorhea St. Pk. All year. 18 tents, 12 trailers. Fee. Elec. hookup—extra chg. Water hookup. Dumping station. Showers. Cafe 1 mi. Swimming pool—chg.

3 Riverside Park. All year. No fixed number of sites. No fee. Cafe. Store 1 mi. Fishing.

4 Chisos Mountain Basin. All year. 72 tents or trailers (max. 30 ft.). Fee. Dumping station. Showers 1 mi. Cafe, store 1 mi. Horseback riding.

5 Rio Grande. All year. 100 tents or trailers (max. 35 ft.). Fee. Dumping station. Store 1 mi. Fishing 1 mi. Boat launch.

Glacier National Park
(Map is on page 294)

Hotels, lodges and cabins in the park, plus 17 campgrounds, with trailer space but no utility connections.

For information on state campgrounds write to Advertising Department, Montana Highway Commission, Helena, Mont. 59601.

For information on U.S. Forest Service campgrounds write to Northern Region, Forest Service, Federal Bldg., Missoula, Mont. 59801.

1 Bowman Lake. June 1–Oct. 1. 48 tents or trailers (max. 26 ft.). Fee. No pets. No flush toilets. Swimming, fishing 1 mi. Boat launch.

2 Avalanche Creek. June 1–Oct. 1. 140 tents or trailers (max. 26 ft.). Fee. No pets. Dumping station. Fishing 1 mi.

3 St. Mary Lake. June 1–Oct. 1. 156 tents or trailers (max. 26 ft.). Fee. No pets. Dumping station. Cafe, store 1 mi. Fishing 1 mi. Boat launch, rental. Horseback riding.

4 Two Medicine Lake. June 1–Oct. 1. 99 tents or trailers (max. 26 ft.). Fee. No pets. Dumping station. Cafe, store 1 mi. Swimming, fishing 1 mi. Boat launch, rental. Horseback riding.

5 Apgar. June 1–Oct. 1. 200 tents or trailers (max. 26 ft.). Fee. No pets. Dumping station. Cafe, store 1 mi. Boat launch, rental. Horseback riding.

6 Hungry Horse. June 1–Sept. 15. 27 tents or trailers (max. 22 ft.). Fee. Showers 1 mi. Cafe 1 mi. Swimming, fishing. Boat dock.

7 Elmo State Rec. Area. May 1–Sept. 30. 35 tents, 40 trailers (max. 20 ft.). Fee. Swimming, fishing. Boat launch.

8 Holland Lake. From Hwy. 209, E 3 mi. on FR 44. June 1–Sept. 15. 35 tents or trailers (max. 22 ft.). Fee. Swimming, fishing. Boat dock, launch, rental.

9 River Point. June 15–Sept. 15. 26 tents or trailers (max. 22 ft.). Fee. Showers 2 mi. Swimming, fishing. Boat dock, launch, rental.

10 Blackfoot. June 1–Sept. 30. 2 tents, 23 trailers (max. 22 ft.). Fee. Fishing.

11 Bean Lake. All year. 50 tents or trailers. Fee. No flush toilets. Swimming, fishing.

12 Choteau Park. All year. 35 tents or trailers. No fee. Dumping station. Cafe, store 1 mi. Swimming pool 1 mi.

13 Tiber Reservoir Rec. Area. May 1–Oct. 1. 50 tents or trailers. Fee. No flush toilets.

14 Dry Wolf. June 1–Oct. 15. 13 tents, 26 trailers (max. 32 ft.). Fee. Fishing.

15 Many Pines. June 15–Oct. 15. 19 tents, 23 trailers (max. 22 ft.). Fee. Cafe. Fishing.

16 Canyon Ferry Rec. Area. May 1–Oct. 1. 50 tents or trailers. Fee. No flush toilets. Cafe. Swimming, fishing. Boat launch, rental.

17 Lost Creek St. Pk. May 1–Oct. 1. 35 tents or trailers (max. 20 ft.). No fee. No flush toilets.

18 Indian Trees. June 1–Sept. 1. 18 tents or trailers (max. 22 ft.). Fee. Fishing 1 mi.

19 Grasshopper. July 1–Sept. 15. 23 trailers (max. 16 ft.). Fee. Showers 1 mi. Cafe 1 mi. Swimming, fishing 3 mi.

20 Lewis and Clark Cavern St. Pk. May 1–Oct. 1. 25 tents, 35 trailers. Fee. Cafe.

21 Red Mountain. May–Oct. 22 tents or trailers (max. 24 ft.). Fee. No flush toilets. Fishing.

22 Woodbine. May 1–Oct. 15. 43 tents or trailers (max. 32 ft.). Fee. Fishing.

23 Afterbay. All year. 35 tents or trailers (max. 20 ft.). No fee. No flush toilets.

Cafe, store 1 mi. Swimming, fishing. Boat dock, launch.

Hells Canyon
(Map is on page 304)

The Idaho Power Co. maintains several campgrounds in the area, with utility connections.

*For information on state campgrounds in Idaho write to Department of Commerce and Development, Room 108, State Capitol Bldg., Boise, Idaho 83707;
   in Montana, to Advertising Department, Montana Highway Commission, Helena, Mont. 59601.*

*For information on U.S. Forest Service campgrounds in Idaho write to Pacific Northwest Region, Forest Service, Box 3623, Portland, Ore. 97208;
   in Montana, to Northern Region, Forest Service, Federal Bldg., Missoula, Mont. 59801.*

1 Indian Creek St. Pk. May–Oct. 75 tents, 50 trailers (max. 20 ft.). Fee. Elec., water sewer hookup—extra chg. Showers. Cafe, store 1 mi. Swimming, fishing. Boat launch.

2 Yaak. May 1–Sept. 30. 37 tents, 42 trailers (max. 22 ft.). Fee. Showers 5 mi. Fishing. Boat dock.

3 McGillivray. May 20–Sept. 30. 52 tents or trailers (max. 32 ft.). Fee.

4 Samowen. June 1–Sept. 15. 44 tents, 40 trailers (max. 22 ft.). Fee. Cafe 5 mi. Swimming, fishing. Boat docks, rental.

5 Round Lake St. Pk. May–Oct. 25 tents or trailers (max. 20 ft.). Fee. Showers. Swimming, fishing. Boat launch.

6 Bells Bay. From US 95A, W 3 mi. on FR 545. May 15–Sept. 30. 18 tents, 19 trailers (max. 22 ft.). Fee. Elec. hookup. Cafe 5 mi. Fishing. Boat dock.

7 Heyburn St. Pk. May–Nov. 50 tents or trailers (max. 20 ft.). Fee. Elec., water, sewer hookup—extra chg. Showers. Cafe, store. Swimming, fishing. Boat launch, rental.

8 Quartz Flat. Apr. 15–Oct. 15. 52 trailers (max. 32 ft.). Fee. Elec. hookup. Fishing.

9 Lewis and Clark. May 20–Sept. 30. 17 tents or trailers (max. 32 ft.). Fee.

10 Powell. June 1–Sept. 15. 35 tents, 34 trailers (max. 22 ft.). Fee. Cafe 1 mi. Fishing.

11 Wendover. June 1–Sept. 15. 27 tents, 25 trailers (max. 16 ft.). Fee. Cafe 3 mi. Fishing.

12 Winchester St. Pk. May 1–Nov. 1. 31 tents or trailers (max. 20 ft.). Fee. No flush toilets. Cafe, store 1 mi. Fishing. Boat launch.

13 Seven Devils. From US 95, SW 16.5 mi. on FR 517. July 4–Oct. 8. 8 tents or trailers (max. 16 ft.). Fee. Fishing.

14 Corn Creek. March 1–Oct. 31. 22 tents or trailers (max. 32 ft.). Fee. Fishing. Boat dock, launch.

Yellowstone–Grand Teton National Parks

(Map is on page 320)

Hotels, lodges and campgrounds in Yellowstone, one campground with utility connections; lodges and campgrounds in Grand Teton, one campground with utility connections.

For information on state campgrounds write to Wyoming Travel Commission, 2320 Capitol Ave., Cheyenne, Wyo. 82001.

For information on U.S. Forest Service campgrounds write to Rocky Mountain Region, Forest Service, Federal Center Bldg. 85, Denver, Colo. 80225.

1 Mammoth. Apr. 15–Oct. 31. 91 tents or trailers. Fee. Showers 1 mi. Cafe, store 1 mi. Fishing 1 mi. Horseback riding.

2 Indian Creek. June 1–Sept. 1. 78 tents or trailers (max. 24 ft.). Fee. No flush toilets. Fishing 1 mi.

3 Norris. June 1–Sept. 10. 116 tents or trailers. Fee. Fishing 1 mi.

4 Madison Junction. June 1–Sept. 15. 292 tents or trailers. Fee. Dumping station. Fishing 1 mi.

5 Lewis Lake. June 1–Oct. 31. 100 tents or trailers. Fee. No flush toilets. Fishing 1 mi. Boat launch.

6 Grant Village. June 1–Sept. 30. 399 tents or trailers. Fee. Dumping station. Showers 1 mi. Fishing 1 mi. Boat dock, launch, rental.

7 Bridge Bay. June 1–Oct. 15. 440 tents or trailers. Fee. Dumping station. Fishing 1 mi. Boat dock, launch, rental.

8 Fishing Bridge. June 1–Sept. 15. 317 tents or trailers. Fee. Dumping station. Cafe, store 1 mi. Fishing 1 mi.

9 Canyon. June 1–Sept. 15. 340 tents or trailers. Fee. Dumping station. Showers 1 mi. Cafe, store 1 mi. Horseback riding.

10 Tower Fall. June 1–Sept. 15. 53 tents or trailers (max. 24 ft.). Fee. No flush toilets. Cafe, store 1 mi. Fishing. Horseback riding.

11 Pebble Creek. June 1–Sept. 15. 36 tents or trailers. Fee. No flush toilets. Fishing.

12 Buffalo Bill St. Pk. May 1–Sept. 1. 30 tents or trailers. No fee. No flush toilets. Cafe, store. Fishing. Boat launch, rental.

13 Horseshoe Bend. All year. 120 tents, 210 trailers (max. 25 ft.). Fee. Dumping station. Cafe. Swimming, fishing. Boat dock, launch.

14 Tie Flume. From US 14, E 2 mi. on forest rd. June 15–Sept. 30. 25 tents or trailers (max. 22 ft.). Fishing.

15 Sitting Bull. June 15–Oct. 15. 43 tents or trailers (max. 22 ft.). Fee. Cafe 2 mi. Fishing. Boat dock, launch, rental.

16 Thermopolis Hot Springs St. Pk. May 1–Sept. 1. 20 tents, 40 trailers (max.

16 ft.). No fee. Sewer hookup. Showers. Cafe. Store 1 mi. Swimming, fishing.

17 Lizard Creek. June 15–Sept. 15. 60 tents or trailers. Fee. Fishing.

18 Colter Bay. May 15–Oct. 15. 525 tents or trailers. Fee. Dumping 1 mi. Showers 1 mi. Cafe, store 1 mi. Swimming, fishing 1 mi. Boat launch, rental. Horseback riding.

19 Signal Mountain. June 1–Sept. 15. 86 tents or trailers. Fee. Dumping station. Cafe, store 1 mi. Swimming, fishing. Boat launch, rental.

20 Gros Ventre. May 1–Sept. 30. 410 tents or trailers. Fee. Dumping station. Fishing.

21 Alpine. June 1–Sept. 30. 43 tents or trailers (max. 22 ft.). Fee. Showers. Cafe 1 mi. Swimming. Fishing 1 mi. Boat dock, launch, rental.

22 Granite Creek. From Hwy. 189, NE 8 mi. on FR 30029. June 15–Sept. 15. 72 tents, 53 trailers (max. 22 ft.). Fee. Showers. Cafe 1 mi. Swimming, fishing.

23 Green River Lake. July 1–Sept. 30. 23 tents or trailers (max. 22 ft.). Fee. Swimming. Fishing 1 mi. Boat dock.

24 Fremont Lake. May 15–Oct. 1. 62 tents or trailers (max. 32 ft.). Fee. Cafe 1 mi. Swimming. Fishing 1 mi. Boat dock, launch, rental.

25 Ayer's Park. Apr. 1–Nov. 1. 20 tents, 16 trailers (max. 30 ft.). No fee. No flush toilets.

Craters of the Moon National Monument

(Map is on page 329)

One campground in the monument, with trailer space but no utility connections.

For information on state campgrounds write to Department of Commerce and Development, Room 108, State Capitol Bldg., Boise, Idaho 83707.

For information on U.S. Forest Service campgrounds write to Pacific Northwest Region, Forest Service, Box 3623, Portland, Ore. 97208.

1 Ponderosa St. Pk. May–Oct. 170 tents or trailers (max. 20 ft.). Fee. Elec., water hookup. Dumping station. Showers. Cafe, store 1 mi. Swimming, fishing. Boat launch, rental.

2 Lola Creek. From Hwy. 21, NW 2 mi. on forest rd. June 30–Sept. 15. 24 tents or trailers (max. 16 ft.). Fee. Fishing.

3 Redfish. From US 93, SW 2 mi. on forest rd. June 15–Sept. 15. 46 tents or trailers (max. 32 ft.). Fee. Showers 1 mi. Cafe 1 mi. Swimming. Fishing 1 mi. Boat dock, launch, rental.

4 Henry's Lake St. Pk. June–Oct. 32 tents or trailers (max. 20 ft.). Fee. Showers. Swimming, fishing. Boat launch.

5 Buttermilk. June 1–Oct. 30. 66 tents or trailers (max. 32 ft.). Fee. Cafe 1 mi. Swimming, fishing. Boat dock, launch, rental.

6 Buffalo. June 1–Oct. 30. 127 tents or trailers (max. 32 ft.). Fee. Elec. hookup. Showers 4 mi. Cafe 1 mi. Swimming, fishing. Boat dock, launch.

7 Calamity. From US 26, W 15 mi. on FR 20076. May 15–Oct. 31. 36 tents, 44 trailers (max. 32 ft.). Fee. Cafe 3 mi. Swimming, fishing. Boat dock, launch.

8 Lava Flow. Apr. 15–Oct. 15. 51 tents or trailers. Fee.

9 Bruneau Dunes St. Pk. All year. 50 tents or trailers (max. 22 ft.). Fee. Elec., water hookup—extra chg. Dumping station. Showers. Swimming, fishing. Boat launch.

10 Three Island Crossing St. Pk. March 1–Oct. 31. 50 tents or trailers (max. 20 ft.). Fee. Elec., water hookup. Dumping station. Showers. Cafe, store 1 mi.

11 Shoshone Falls. From US 93, E 3 mi. on Falls Ave., N 1 mi. on local rd. All year. 30 tents or trailers (max. 35 ft.). No fee. Cafe. Swimming 1 mi. Boat dock.

12 Father and Sons. From Oakley, W 21 mi. on FR 70500. June 1–Oct. 15. 16 tents, 22 trailers (max. 16 ft.). Fee. Fishing 1 mi.

13 Massacre Rocks St. Pk. May–Oct. 52 tents or trailers (max. 20 ft.). Fee. Elec., water hookup—extra chg. Dumping station. Showers. Fishing. Boat launch.

14 Indian Rocks St. Pk. May 1–Oct. 15. 50 tents or trailers (max. 20 ft.). Fee. Elec., water hookup—extra chg. Dumping station. Showers. Cafe, store 1 mi.

15 Willow Flats. From Hwy. 91, NE 10 mi. on county rd., NE 6 mi. on FR 30006. June 15–Sept. 15. 27 tents or trailers (max. 22 ft.). Fee. Elec. hookup. Fishing.

Great Salt Lake Desert

(Map is on page 342)

No camping in the desert.

For information on state campgrounds in Utah write to Utah Travel Council, Council Hall, Capitol Hill, Salt Lake City, Utah 84114;
in Nevada, to Nevada State Park System, Room 221, Nye Bldg., 201 S. Fall St., Carson City, Nev. 89701.

For information on U.S. Forest Service campgrounds write to Intermountain Region, Forest Service, 324 25th St., Ogden, Utah 84401.

1 Thomas Canyon. From Hwy. 46, SE 7 mi. on forest rd. June 1–Oct. 1. 28 tents or trailers (max. 16 ft.). Fee. Fishing.

2 Payson Lakes. June 1–Sept. 30. 4 tents, 30 trailers (max. 22 ft.). Fee. Swimming, fishing.

3 Utah Lake St. Pk. From I-15, W 2 mi. March–Nov. 40 tents or trailers (max. 30 ft.). Fee. Elec. hookup. Showers. Cafe. Fishing. Boat launch, rental.

4 Lodgepole. June 15–Sept. 30. 42 tents or trailers (max. 32 ft.). Fee. Fishing.

5 Wasatch Mountain St. Pk. May–Oct. 86 tents or trailers (max. 30 ft.). Fee. Resv. accepted. Elec., water, sewer hookup—extra chg. Dumping station. Showers—extra chg. Cafe. Swimming, fishing 1 mi. Horseback riding.

6 Aspen Grove. From Hwy. 35, NW 3 mi. on forest rd. June 1–Oct. 31. 29 tents, 26 trailers (max. 22 ft.). Fee. Cafe 3 mi. Fishing.

7 Mirror Lake. July 1–Sept. 15. 84 tents or trailers (max. 16 ft.). Fee. Cafe. Swimming, fishing. Boat dock, launch, rental.

8 Rockport Lake St. Pk. Apr.–Nov. 75 tents or trailers (max. 30 ft.). Fee. Showers—extra chg. Swimming, fishing. Boat dock, launch.

9 East Canyon Lake St. Pk. May–Nov. 50 tents or trailers (max. 30 ft.). Fee. No flush toilets. Cafe. Swimming, fishing. Boat dock, launch, rental.

10 Great Salt Lake St. Pk. All year. 30 tents or trailers (max. 30 ft.). Fee. No flush toilets. Cafe. Swimming. Boat dock, launch.

11 Willard Bay Lake St. Pk. Apr.–Dec. 20 tents or trailers (max. 30 ft.). Fee. Cafe. Swimming, fishing. Boat dock, launch, rental.

12 Hyrum Lake St. Pk. Apr.–Oct. 20 tents or trailers (max. 30 ft.). Fee. Elec. hookup. Showers. Swimming, fishing. Boat dock, launch.

13 Monte Cristo. June 20–Sept. 9. 43 tents or trailers (max. 22 ft.). Fee.

14 Buckboard Crossing. From Hwy. 530, E 2 mi. on forest rd. Apr. 15–Oct. 31. 68 tents or trailers (max. 22 ft.). Fee. Elec. hookup. Cafe. Fishing. Boat dock, launch, rental.

15 Antelope Flat. Apr. 15–Oct. 31. 122 tents or trailers (max. 22 ft.). Fee. Elec. hookup. Swimming, fishing. Boat dock, launch.

16 Lucerne Valley. From Hwy. 530, SE 4.5 mi. on forest rd. Apr. 15–Oct. 31. 153 tents or trailers (max. 22 ft.). Fee. Elec. hookup. Cafe 1 mi. Swimming, fishing. Boat dock, launch, rental.

17 Mustang Ridge. From Hwy. 260, S 3 mi. on forest rd. May 1–Oct. 31. 73 tents or trailers (max. 22 ft.). Fee. Cafe 5 mi. Swimming, fishing. Boat dock, launch.

18 Steinaker Lake St. Pk. May–Oct. 30 tents or trailers (max. 30 ft.). Fee. Swimming, fishing. Boat dock, launch.

19 Split Mountain Gorge. All year. 35 tents or trailers (max. 20 ft.). Fee.

20 Green River. May 15–Oct. 15. 100 tents, 94 trailers (max. 20 ft.). Fee. Dumping station. Fishing.

Arches–Canyonlands National Parks
(Map is on page 355)

Three campgrouds in the parks, with trailer space but no utility connections.

For information on state campgrounds write to Utah Travel Council, Council Hall, Capitol Hill, Salt Lake City, Utah 84114.

For information on U.S. Forest Service campgrounds write to Intermountain Region, Forest Service, 324 25th St., Ogden, Utah, 84401.

1 Ferron Reservoir. June 15–Nov. 1. 29 tents or trailers (max. 22 ft.). Fishing. Boat dock, launch, rental.

2 Green River St. Pk. Apr.–Dec. 14 tents, 30 trailers (max. 30 ft.). Fee. Showers—extra chg. Swimming. Fishing 1 mi. Boat launch, rental.

3 Arches National Monument. Apr. 1–Oct. 30. 52 tents or trailers (max. 20 ft.). Fee.

4 Warner. June 15–Sept. 30. 20 tents or trailers (max. 22 ft.). Fee.

5 Dead Horse Point St. Pk. All year. 18 tents, 30 trailers (max. 30 ft.). Fee.

6 Needles. All year. 27 tents or trailers (max. 20 ft.). Fee. No flush toilets.

7 Bowery. June 1–Oct. 15. 53 trailers (max. 22 ft.). No fee. Cafe 1 mi. Swimming, fishing. Boat dock, launch, rental.

8 Mackinaw. June 1–Oct. 15. 64 trailers (max. 22 ft.). No fee. Cafe 1 mi. Swimming, fishing. Boat dock, launch, rental.

9 Capitol Reef National Monument. Apr. 2–Nov. 30. 53 tents, 32 trailers (max. 30 ft.). Fee. Cafe 1 mi. Fishing.

10 Posy Lake. June 15–Sept. 15. 4 tents, 19 trailers (max. 16 ft.). Fee. Swimming, fishing. Boat dock, launch.

11 Bullfrog Basin. All year. 90 tents or trailers (max. 25 ft.). Fee. Cafe, store 1 mi. Swimming, fishing 1 mi. Boat launch, rental.

12 Hall's Crossing. All year. 25 tents, 50 trailers (max. 25 ft.). Fee. No flush toilets. Store 1 mi. Swimming, fishing 1 mi. Boat launch, rental.

13 Devils Canyon. May 15–Oct. 25. 30 tents or trailers (max. 22 ft.). Fee.

Bryce Canyon–Zion National Parks
(Map is on page 369)

Four campgrounds in the parks, with trailer space but no utility connections. Inn and lodge at Bryce.

For information on state campgrounds write to Utah Travel Council, Council Hall, Capitol Hill, Salt Lake City, Utah 84114.

For information on U.S. Forest Service campgrounds write to Intermountain Region, Forest Service, 324 25th St., Ogden, Utah 84401.

1 Ward Mountain. May 15–Oct. 15. 22 tents or trailers (max. 16 ft.). Fee. Resv. accepted.

2 Lehman Creek. From Hwy. 74, W 3 mi. on forest rd. May 15–Oct. 15. 23 tents or trailers (max. 22 ft.). Fee. Resv. accepted. Fishing.

3 Echo Canyon. All year. 34 tents or trailers (max. 20 ft.). Fee. No flush toilets. Fishing. Boat launch.

4 Eagle Valley Reservoir. All year. 24 tents or trailers (max. 20 ft.). Fee. Swimming 1 mi. Fishing. Boat launch.

5 Minersville Lake St. Pk. Apr.–Oct. 18 tents, 20 trailers (max. 30 ft.). Fee. Swimming. Fishing. Boat dock, launch.

6 Cedar Breaks National Monument. Apr. 2–Nov. 30. 53 tents, 32 trailers (max. 30 ft.). Fee. Cafe 1 mi. Fishing.

7 Navajo Lake. From Hwy. 14, SW 3 mi. on forest rd. June 15–Sept. 15. 28 trailers (max. 22 ft.). Cafe 2 mi. Swimming, fishing. Boat dock, launch, rental.

8 Duck Creek. June 1–Sept. 15. 74 tents, 72 trailers (max. 32 ft.). Fee. Cafe 2 mi. Fishing. Boat dock, launch, rental.

9 North. May 1–Nov. 15. 59 tents, 52 trailers (max. 35 ft.). Fee. Showers—extra chg. Cafe, store 1 mi. Riding.

10 South. May–Sept. 145 tents, 152 trailers (max. 40 ft.). Fee. Dumping station. Cafe, store.

11 Watchman. All year. 229 tents, 280 trailers (max. 40 ft.). Fee. Dumping station. Cafe, store.

12 Coral Pink Sand Dunes St. Pk. Apr.–Nov. 20 tents or trailers (max. 30 ft.). Fee. Showers—extra chg.

Grand Canyon National Park
(Map is on page 383)

Five campgrounds with trailer space on the South Rim, one with utility connections; one campground with trailer space but no utility connections at North Rim, and primitive campground at the bottom of the canyon. Hotel, lodges and inn at South Rim, lodge and inn at North Rim.

For information on state campgrounds in Arizona write to Travel Information Section, Department of Economic Planning, Suite 1704, 3003 N. Central Ave., Phoenix, Ariz. 85012;
in Nevada, to Nevada State Park System, Room 221, Nye Bldg., 201 S. Fall St., Carson City, Nev. 89701.

For information on U.S. Forest Service campgrounds write to Southwestern Region, Forest Service, 517 Gold Ave. SW, Albuquerque, N.M. 87101.

1 Overton Landing. All year. 20 tents or trailers. Fee. Elec., water, sewer hookup. Showers. Cafe, store. Swimming, fishing. Boat dock, launch, rental.

2 Echo Bay. All year. 203 tents or trailers (max. 25 ft.). Fee. Dumping station. Showers 1 mi. Cafe, store 1 mi. Swimming, fishing 1 mi. Boat launch, rental.

3 Temple Bar. All year. 178 tents or trailers (max. 25 ft.). Fee. Dumping station. Cafe, store 1 mi. Swimming, fishing 1 mi. Boat launch, rental.

4 Bright Angel Point. May 15–Oct. 1. 78 tents or trailers. Fee. Dumping station. Showers—extra chg. Cafe, store 1 mi. Horseback riding.

5 Mather. All year. 350 tents or trailers. Fee. Showers—extra chg. Cafe, store 1 mi. Horseback riding.

6 Ten X. Apr. 1–Nov. 30. 57 tents, 70 trailers (max. 22 ft.). Fee. Cafe 3 mi.

7 Desert View. May 15–Oct. 1. 50 tents or trailers. Fee. No flush toilets. Cafe, store 1 mi.

8 Cottonwood Cove. All year. 165 tents or trailers (max. 25 ft.). Fee. Dumping station. Showers 1 mi. Cafe, store 1 mi. Swimming, fishing 1 mi. Boat launch, rental.

9 Katherine. All year. 184 tents or trailers (max. 25 ft.). Fee. Dumping station. Cafe, store 1 mi. Swimming, fishing 1 mi. Boat launch, rental.

10 Lake Havasu St. Pk. All year. 100 tents or trailers (max. 22 ft.). Fee. Showers. Cafe, store 1 mi. Swimming, fishing. Boat launch, rental.

11 Granite Basin. Apr. 1–Nov. 30. 23 tents or trailers (max. 22 ft.). Fee. Fishing. Boat dock.

12 White Spar. May 1–Oct. 31. 66 tents or trailers (max. 22 ft.). Fee. Cafe 2 mi.

13 Kaibab Lake. Apr. 15–Oct. 31. 59 tents or trailers (max. 22 ft.). Fee. Showers 4 mi. Cafe 4 mi. Fishing. Boat dock, launch.

14 Bonito. May 30–Sept. 4. 44 tents or trailers (max. 22 ft.). Fee.

15 White Horse Lake. May 15–Oct. 31. 78 tents or trailers (max. 22 ft.). Fee. Fishing. Boat dock, launch, rental.

16 Pine Flat. Apr. 1–Nov. 1. 59 tents or trailers (max. 32 ft.). Fee. Cafe 1 mi. Swimming, fishing.

17 Cave Spring. May 15–Sept. 15. 79 tents or trailers (max. 32 ft.). Fee. Cafe 1 mi. Swimming, fishing.

18 Lakeview. May 30–Sept. 5. 44 tents or trailers (max. 32 ft.). Fee. Showers 5 mi. Cafe 5 mi. Swimming. Fishing 1 mi. Boat dock, launch.

19 Ashurst Lake. May 30–Sept. 5. 51 tents or trailers (max. 32 ft.). Fee. Swimming, fishing. Boat launch.

20 Pine Grove. May 1–Sept. 15. 46 tents or trailers (max. 32 ft.). Fee. Swimming. Fishing 2 mi. Boat dock, launch.

21 Rock Crossing. May 15–Sept. 15. 35 tents or trailers (max. 22 ft.). Fee. Fishing 1 mi.

22 Canyon Point. May 15–Oct. 1. 78 tents or trailers (max. 22 ft.). Fee. Fishing 3 mi. Boat dock.

Petrified Forest National Park

(Map is on page 394)

No camping in the park.

For information on state campgrounds in Arizona write to Travel Information Section, Arizona Department of Economic Planning and Development, Suite 1704, 3003 N. Central Ave., Phoenix, Ariz. 85012;
in New Mexico, to State Park and Recreation Commission, Box 1147, Santa Fe, N.M. 87501 and Tourist Division, Department of Development, 113 Washington Ave., Santa Fe.

For information on U.S. Forest Service campgrounds write Southwestern Region, Forest Service, 517 Gold Ave. SW, Albuquerque, N.M. 87101.

1 Cottonwood. Apr. 1–Oct. 31. 60 tents, 35 trailers (max. 16 ft.). No fee. Cafe, store 1 mi. Horseback riding.

2 Tsaile. All year. 100 tents or trailers. No fee. No flush toilets. Fishing. Boat launch. No drinking water.

3 Wheatfield. All year. 20 tents or trailers. No fee. No flush toilets. Fishing. Boat launch.

4 Navajo Lake St. Pk. All year. 61 tents or trailers. Fee. Elec. hookup—extra chg. Water hookup. Showers. Store. Swimming, fishing. Boat launch, rental.

5 El Vado Lake St. Pk. All year. 55 tents, 44 trailers. Fee. No flush toilets. Swimming, fishing. Boat launch.

6 Canjilon Lakes. June 15–Sept. 15. 28 tents, 36 trailers (max. 22 ft.). Fee. Swimming, fishing. Boat dock.

7 Rio Grande Gorge St. Pk. All year. 47 tents or trailers. No fee. No flush toilets. Fishing. No drinking water.

8 Columbine. May 15–Sept. 15. 20 tents, 27 trailers (max. 32 ft.). Fee. Cafe 5 mi.

9 Fawn Lakes. May 15–Sept. 15. 22 tents or trailers (max. 32 ft.). Fee. Showers. Cafe 3 mi. Fishing.

10 Cimarron Canyon. May 1–Nov. 30. 260 tents or trailers (max. 16 ft.). Fee. No flush toilets. Store. Fishing.

11 McGaffey. Apr. 1–Oct. 31. 29 tents or trailers (max. 22 ft.). Fee. Fishing.

12 Bluewater Lake St. Pk. All year. 79 tents, 21 trailers. Fee. Elec. hookup—extra chg. Water hookup. Showers. Cafe, store. Swimming, fishing. Boat launch, rental. Horseback riding.

13 Redondo. May 1–Oct. 31. 25 tents, 28 trailers (max. 22 ft.). Fee.

14 Black Canyon. May 1–Oct. 31. 35 tents, 25 trailers (max. 32 ft.). Fee. Fishing 2 mi.

15 Holy Ghost. From ST 63, NW 2.3 mi. on FR 10122. May 1–Oct. 31. 22 tents or trailers (max. 16 ft.). Fee. Fishing.

16 Jacks Creek. From ST 63, N 3 mi. on forest rd. May 1–Oct. 31. 47 tents, 41 trailers (max. 16 ft.). Fee. Cafe 2 mi. Fishing 1 mi.

17 Morphy Lake St. Pk. Jan.–Oct. 20 tents or trailers. Fee. No flush toilets. Fishing. No drinking water.

18 Storrie Lake St. Pk. All year. 21 tents or trailers. Fee. Showers. Swimming, fishing. Boat launch.

19 Chicosa Lake St. Pk. May–Dec. No fixed number of sites. Fee. No flush toilets. Boat launch.

20 Conchas Lake St. Pk. All year. 134 tents, 60 trailers. Fee. Elec. hookup—extra chg. Water, sewer hookup. Cafe. Store. Swimming, fishing. Boat launch, rental.

Saguaro National Monument

(Map is on page 403)

Camping in the Tucson Mountain section of the park, with trailer space and utility connections.

For information on state campgrounds write to Travel Information Section, Department of Economic Planning and Development, Suite 1704, 3003 N. Central Ave., Phoenix, Ariz. 85012.

For information on U.S. Forest Service campgrounds write Southwestern Region, 517 Gold Ave. SW, Albuquerque, N.M. 87101.

1 Horseshoe. All year. 20 tents or trailers (max. 16 ft.). Fee.

2 Seven Springs. All year. 23 tents or trailers (max. 16 ft.). Fee.

3 Riverside. All year. 20 tents or trailers. Fee. No flush toilets. Fishing.

4 Tortilla. All year. 77 tents or trailers (max. 22 ft.). Fee. Dumping station. Cafe 1 mi. Swimming. Fishing 2 mi. Boat dock, launch.

5 Lower Log Road. Apr.–Oct. 50 tents or trailers. Fee. No flush toilets. Swimming, fishing.

6 Hawley Lake. Apr.–Oct. 100 tents or trailers. Fee. Elec., water, sewer hookup. Showers. Cafe, store. Swimming, fishing. Boat launch, rental. Riding.

7 Big Lake. June 1–Sept. 15. 137 tents or trailers (max. 32 ft.). Fee. Showers 1 mi. Swimming. Fishing 1 mi. Boat dock, launch, rental.

8 Tonto Lake. Apr.–Oct. 25 tents or trailers. Fee. No flush toilets. Store. Fishing. Boat launch, rental.

9 Oak Flat. All year. 27 tents or trailers (max. 22 ft.). Fee. Cafe 4 mi.

10 Organ Pipe Cactus National Monument. All year. 208 tents or trailers (max. 30 ft.). Fee. Dumping station.

11 Picacho Park. All year. 11 tents, 26 trailers (max. 22 ft.). Fee. Elec., water hookup—extra chg. Dumping station 1 mi. Showers. Cafe, store 1 mi.

12 Peppersauce. All year. 31 tents or trailers (max. 22 ft.). Fee.

13 Rose Canyon. Apr. 1–Nov. 30. 98 tents or trailers (max. 22 ft.). Fee.

14 Palo Verde. All year. 118 tents or trailers. Fee. Resv. accepted. Elec. hookup. Dumping station. Store.

15 Cochise Stronghold. All year. 21 tents or trailers (max. 22 ft.). Fee.

16 Rustler Park. May 15–Nov. 30. 25 tents or trailers (max. 16 ft.). Fee.

Olympic National Park

(Map is on page 415)

Lodges at Kalaloch, Lake Crescent, Lake Quinault, and 15 campgrounds in the park, none with utility connections.

For information on state campgrounds write to Visitor Information Bureau, General Administration Bldg., Olympia, Wash. 98501.

For information on U.S. Forest Service campgrounds write to Pacific Northwest Region, Forest Service, Box 3623, Portland, Ore. 97208.

1 Birch Bay St. Pk. All year. 179 tents, 52 trailers (max. 20 ft.). Fee. Elec., water hookup. Dumping station. Showers. Store 1 mi. Swimming, fishing. Boating.

2 Larrabee St. Pk. All year. 75 tents, 26 trailers (max. 20 ft.). Fee. Elec., water, sewer hookup. Showers. Swimming, fishing. Boat launch.

3 Deception Pass St. Pk. All year. 267 tents, 360 trailers. Fee. Showers. Cafe, store 1 mi. Swimming, fishing. Boat dock, launch.

4 Dungeness Rec. Area. All year. 65 tents or trailers. Fee. Dumping station. Showers—extra chg. Swimming, fishing 1 mi. Boat launch.

5 Sequim Bay St. Pk. All year. 69 tents, 26 trailers (max. 20 ft.). Fee. Elec., water, sewer hookup. Dumping station. Showers. Swimming, fishing. Boat launch.

6 Heart O' the Hills. Apr. 1–Oct. 30. 100 tents or trailers (max. 20 ft.). Fee.

7 Elwha. All year. 23 tents or trailers (max. 20 ft.). Fee. Fishing 1 mi.

8 Olympic Hot Springs. June 15–Sept. 30. 50 tents or trailers (max. 15 ft.). No fee. Fishing.

9 Fairholm. Apr. 1–Oct. 30. 90 tents or trailers (max. 30 ft.). Fee. Cafe, store 1 mi. Swimming, fishing. Boat launch.

10 Soleduck. Apr. 1–Oct. 30. 84 tents or trailers (max. 30 ft.). Fee. Cafe, store 1 mi. Swimming 1 mi. Fishing.

11 Hoh. All year. 95 tents or trailers (max. 30 ft.). Fee. Fishing.

12 Kalaloch. All year. 163 tents, 178 trailers (max. 30 ft.). Fee. Dumping station. Cafe, store 1 mi.

13 Falls Creek. May 30–Sept. 10. 5 tents, 21 trailers (max. 16 ft.). Fee. Elec. hookup. Cafe 1 mi. Swimming, fishing. Boat dock, launch, rental.

14 Graves Creek. Apr. 1–Oct. 30. 45 tents or trailers (max. 15 ft.). Fee.

15 Staircase. Apr. 1–Oct. 30. 50 tents or trailers (max. 20 ft.). Fee. Fishing.

16 Lake Cushman St. Pk. All year. 50 tents, 30 trailers (max. 20 ft.). Fee. Elec., water, sewer hookup. Showers. Cafe 1 mi. Swimming, fishing. Boat launch.

17 Dosewallips St. Pk. All year. 75 tents, 40 trailers (max. 20 ft.). Fee. Elec., water, sewer hookup. Showers. Cafe 1 mi. Swimming, fishing.

18 Fay Bainbridge St. Pk. All year. 27 tents or trailers (max. 20 ft.). Fee. Elec., water, sewer hookup. Showers. Swimming, fishing. Boat launch.

19 Belfair St. Pk. All year. 147 tents, 47 trailers (max. 20 ft.). Fee. Elec., water, sewer hookup. Showers. Cafe, store 1 mi. Swimming, fishing.

20 Dash Point St. Pk. All year. 110 tents, 28 trailers (max. 20 ft.). Fee. Elec., water, sewer hookup. Showers. Swimming, fishing.

21 Millersylvania St. Pk. All year. 189 tents, 52 trailers (max. 20 ft.). Fee. Elec., water hookup. Dumping station. Showers. Cafe, store 1 mi. Swimming, fishing. Boat launch. Horseback riding.

22 Ocean City St. Pk. All year. 151 tents, 29 trailers (max. 20 ft.). Fee. Elec., water, sewer hookup. Showers. Swimming, fishing.

23 Twin Harbors St. Pk. All year. 370 tents, 49 trailers (max. 20 ft.). Fee. Elec., water, sewer hookup. Showers. Cafe, store 1 mi. Swimming, fishing. Horseback riding.

24 Fort Canby Historic St. Pk. All year. 60 trailers (max. 20 ft.). Fee. Cafe, store 1 mi. Swimming, fishing. Boat launch.

25 Spirit Lake. June 15–Sept. 15. 114 tents, 29 trailers (max. 22 ft.). Fee. Cafe 1 mi. Swimming, fishing. Boat dock, launch, rental.

Mount Rainier National Park

(Map is on page 426)

Two hotels and nine campgrounds in the park, with trailer space but no utility connections.

For information on state campgrounds write to Visitor Information Bureau, General Administration Bldg., Olympia, Wash. 98501.

For information on U.S. Forest Service campgrounds write to Pacific Northwest Region, Forest Service, Box 3623, Portland, Ore. 97208.

1 Horseshoe Cove. Apr. 20–Oct. 20. 28 tents or trailers (max. 22 ft.). Fee. Cafe 1 mi. Swimming. Fishing 1 mi. Boat dock, launch, rental.

2 Gold Basin. Apr. 1–Nov. 30. 55 tents, 45 trailers (max. 32 ft.). Fee. Cafe 5 mi. Fishing.

3 Marble Creek. Apr. 15–Nov. 15. 27 tents or trailers (max. 16 ft.). Fee.

4 Colonial Creek. Apr. 15–Nov. 1. 87 tents or trailers (max. 22 ft.). Fee. Swimming, fishing. Boat launch.

5 Evans. May–Oct. 67 tents or trailers (max. 26 ft.). Fee. Swimming, fishing. Boat dock, launch.

6 Kettle Falls. May–Oct. 74 tents or trailers (max. 26 ft.). Fee. Dumping station. Cafe, store 1 mi. Swimming, fishing. Boat dock, launch.

7 Lake Gillette. May 1–Oct. 31. 30 tents or trailers (max. 32 ft.). Fee. Swimming, fishing. Boat dock, launch, rental.

8 Hunters Park. May–Oct. 25 tents or trailers (max. 26 ft.). No fee. Swimming, fishing. Boat dock, launch.

9 Fort Spokane. May–Oct. 60 tents or trailers (max. 26 ft.). Fee. Store 1 mi. Swimming, fishing. Boat dock, launch.

10 Porcupine Bay. May–Oct. 31 tents or trailers (max. 20 ft.). Fee. Store 1 mi. Swimming, fishing. Boat dock, launch.

11 Spring Canyon. May–Oct. 100 tents or trailers (max. 26 ft.). Fee. Dumping station. Cafe. Swimming, fishing. Boat dock, launch.

12 Steamboat Rock St. Pk. All year. 50 trailers (max. 20 ft.). Fee. Elec., water hookup. Showers. Swimming, fishing. Boat launch.

13 Lake Chelan St. Pk. All year. 176 tents, 25 trailers (max. 20 ft.). Fee. Elec., water hookup. Dumping station. Showers. Cafe, store 1 mi. Swimming, fishing. Boat dock, launch.

14 Nason Creek. May 1–Oct. 31. 27 tents, 40 trailers (max. 32 ft.). Fee. Showers 1 mi. Cafe 4 mi. Swimming, fishing. Boat dock, launch, rental.

15 Tumwater. May 1–Oct. 31. 29 tents, 25 trailers (max. 22 ft.). Fee. Fishing.

16 Salmon La Sac. May 30–Oct. 1. 52 tents, 63 trailers (max. 22 ft.). Fee. Cafe. Swimming, fishing.

17 Kachess. May 30–Oct. 1. 115 tents, 135 trailers (max. 22 ft.). Fee. Swimming, fishing. Boat dock, launch, rental.

18 Sunrise. July 1–Oct. 1. 63 tents or trailers (max. 20 ft.). Fee. Cafe 1 mi.

19 White River. July 1–Oct. 15. 125 tents or trailers (max. 20 ft.). Fee.

20 Paradise. July 15–Sept. 15. 65 tents or trailers (max. 25 ft.). Fee. Cafe.

21 Cougar Rock. June 15–Oct. 15. 200 tents or trailers (max. 30 ft.). Fee. Dumping station. Fishing 1 mi.

22 Sunshine Point. All year. 28 tents or trailers (max. 25 ft.). Fee. No flush toilets. Fishing.

23 Ohanapecosh. May 1–Nov. 1. 230 tents or trailers (max. 30 ft.). Fee. Dumping station. Fishing.

24 Yakima St. Pk. All year. 28 tents, 36 trailers (max. 20 ft.). Fee. Elec., water, sewer hookup. Showers. Cafe, store 1 mi. Fishing.

Columbia River Gorge

(Map is on page 437)

For information on state campgrounds in Oregon write to Travel Information Section, State Highway Division, Salem, Ore. 97310; in Washington, to Visitor Information Bureau, General Administration Bldg., Olympia, Wash. 98501.

For information on U.S. Forest Service campgrounds, write to Pacific Northwest Region, Forest Service, P.O. Box 3623, Portland, Ore. 97208.

1 Government Mineral Springs. May

15–Sept. 30. 40 tents, 18 trailers (max. 32 ft.). Fee. Fishing.

2 Brooks Memorial St. Pk. All year. 23 tents or trailers (max. 20 ft.). Fee. Elec., water, sewer hookup. Showers. Cafe, store 1 mi. Swimming 1 mi. Fishing.

3 Memaloose St. Pk. Apr. 15–Oct. 31. 67 tents, 48 trailers. Fee. Elec., water hookup. Dumping station. Showers. Fishing. Boat launch.

4 Ainsworth St. Pk. May–Oct. 45 trailers (max. 35 ft.). Fee. Elec., water, sewer hookup. Dumping station. Showers.

5 Milo McIver St. Pk. Apr. 15–Oct. 31. 42 tents or trailers. Fee. Elec., water hookup. Dumping station. Showers. Fishing. Boat launch.

6 Trillium Lake. June 1–Sept. 30. 12 tents, 28 trailers (max. 32 ft.). Fee. Cafe 4 mi. Swimming, fishing. Boat dock, launch.

7 Clackamas Lake. From US 26, S 8 mi. on FR S42. May–Oct. 26 tents, 21 trailers (max. 16 ft.). Fee. Swimming. Fishing 1 mi. Boat dock.

8 Rock Creek Reservoir. Apr. 15–Nov. 24. 30 tents or trailers (max. 32 ft.). Fee. Fishing. Boat dock.

9 Beaver Tail. All year. 33 trailers (max. 26 ft.). Fee. Fishing.

10 Kah-Nee-Ta. All year. 50 tents, 38 trailers. Fee. Resv. accepted. Elec., water, sewer hookup. Dumping station. Showers. Cafe. Swimming pool—extra chg. Horseback riding.

11 Detroit Lake. Apr. 12–Oct. 1. 214 tents, 106 trailers (max. 35 ft.). Fee. Resv. accepted. Elec., water, sewer hookup. Showers. Swimming, fishing. Boat launch.

12 Fishermen's Bend. Apr. 10–Oct. 31. 40 tents or trailers (max. 20 ft.). Fee. Showers. Fishing.

13 South Shore. May–Oct. 42 tents, 37 trailers (max. 22 ft.). Fee. Store 1 mi. Swimming, fishing. Boat dock, launch, rental.

14 Smiling River. May–Oct. 37 tents or trailers (max. 32 ft.). Fee. Showers 1 mi. Cafe, store 1 mi. Fishing.

15 Cove Palisades St. Pk. Apr. 12–Oct. 1. 185 tents, 87 trailers (max. 35 ft.). Fee. Resv. accepted. Elec., water, sewer hookup. Dumping station. Showers. Cafe, store. Swimming, fishing. Boat dock, launch, rental.

16 Bull Prairie. From Hwy. 207, NE 3 mi. on FR S642. May 1–Nov. 30. 26 tents or trailers (max. 32 ft.). Fee. Swimming. Fishing 1 mi. Boat dock, launch.

17 Frazier. May 15–Nov. 30. 30 tents or trailers (max. 22 ft.). Fee. Showers 2 mi. Cafe 2 mi. Swimming. Fishing 1 mi.

18 Fort Walla Walla Park. May 1–Oct. 1. 100 tents, 44 trailers (max. 25 ft.). Fee. Elec. hookup—extra chg. Water hookup. Dumping station 1 mi. Showers. Cafe, store 1 mi. Swimming 1 mi.

19 Jubilee Lake. June 15–Nov. 15. 47 tents or trailers (max. 22 ft.). Fee. Swimming. Fishing 1 mi. Boat dock, launch.

20 Woodward. June 1–Oct. 15. 10 tents,

20 trailers (max. 22 ft.). Fee. Cafe 3 mi.

21 Wallowa Lake St. Pk. May–Oct. 89 tents, 121 trailers (max. 35 ft.). Fee. Resv. accepted. Elec., water, sewer hookup. Dumping station. Showers. Cafe, store 1 mi. Swimming, fishing. Boat launch, rental. Horseback riding.

Oregon Coast
(Map is on page 449)

For information on state campgrounds write to Travel Information Section, State Highway Division, Salem, Ore. 97310.

For information on U.S. Forest Service campgrounds, write to Pacific Northwest Region, Forest Service, P.O. Box 3623, Portland, Ore. 97208.

1 Fort Stevens St. Pk. All year. 379 tents, 224 trailers (max. 35 ft.). Fee. Resv. accepted. Elec., water, sewer hookup. Showers. Cafe 1 mi. Swimming, fishing.

2 Cape Lookout St. Pk. All year. 193 tents, 53 trailers (max. 35 ft.). Fee. Resv. accepted. Elec., water, sewer hookup. Showers. Cafe 1 mi. Swimming, fishing.

3 Devils Lake St. Pk. Apr. 12–Oct. 1. 68 tents, 32 trailers (max. 35 ft.). Fee. Elec., water, sewer hookup. Showers. Cafe, store 1 mi. Swimming, fishing. Boat launch.

4 Beverly Beach St. Pk. All year. 151 tents, 127 trailers (max. 35 ft.). Fee Resv. accepted. Elec., water, sewer hookup. Showers. Cafe, store.

5 Tillicum Beach. All year. 7 tents, 40 trailers (max. 20 ft.). Fee. Elec. hookup. Cafe 4 mi. Swimming, fishing. Boat dock, launch, rental.

6 Sutton Creek. May 15–Oct. 15. 63 tents or trailers (max. 32 ft.). Fee. Elec. hookup. Cafe 3 mi. Swimming, fishing. Boat dock, launch, rental.

7 Honeyman St. Pk. All year. 313 tents, 66 trailers (max. 35 ft.). Fee. Resv. accepted. Elec., water, sewer hookup. Dumping station. Showers. Swimming, fishing. Boat launch.

8 Siltcoos. All year. 24 tents, 56 trailers (max. 22 ft.). Fee. Elec. hookup. Cafe 2 mi. Swimming, fishing. Boat dock, launch, rental.

9 Tahkenitch Lake. Apr. 15–Sept. 15. 4 tents, 32 trailers (max. 22 ft.). Fee. Elec. hookup. Cafe 1 mi. Fishing 1 mi. Boat dock, launch, rental.

10 Umpqua Lighthouse St. Pk. Apr. 12–Oct. 1. 41 tents, 22 trailers (max. 35 ft.). Fee. Elec., water, sewer hookup. Showers. Swimming, fishing.

11 Eel Creek. All year. 17 tents, 85 trailers (max. 22 ft.). Fee. Elec. hookup. Cafe 1 mi. Swimming. Fishing 1 mi. Boat dock, launch, rental.

12 Sunset Bay St. Pk. Apr. 12–Oct. 1. 108 tents, 29 trailers (max. 35 ft.). Fee. Resv. accepted. Elec., water, sewer hookup. Showers. Cafe 1 mi. Swimming, fishing. Boat launch.

13 Bullards Beach St. Pk. Apr. 15–Oct. 30. 64 tents, 128 trailers (max. 35 ft.). Fee. Elec., water, sewer hookup. Showers. Cafe, store 1 mi. Swimming, fishing. Boat launch.

14 Humbug Mountain St. Pk. Apr. 12–Oct. 1. 70 tents, 30 trailers (max. 35 ft.). Fee. Resv. accepted. Elec., water, sewer hookup. Showers. Cafe 1 mi. Swimming, fishing. Boat launch.

15 Illahe. May 25–Oct. 15. 46 tents or trailers (max. 32 ft.). Fee. Elec. hookup. Swimming, fishing. Boat dock.

16 Harris Beach St. Pk. All year. 128 tents, 34 trailers (max. 35 ft.). Fee. Resv. accepted. Elec., water, sewer hookup. Dumping station. Showers. Swimming, fishing.

17 Valley of the Rouge St. Pk. Apr. 12–Oct. 1. 77 tents, 97 trailers (max. 35 ft.). Fee. Elec., water, sewer hookup. Dumping station. Showers. Cafe 1 mi. Swimming, fishing. Boat launch.

Crater Lake National Park
(Map is on page 457)

Three campgrounds in the park with trailer space, but no utility connections. Open from June to October.

For information on state campgrounds write to Travel Information Section, State Highway Division, Salem, Ore. 97310.

For information on U.S. Forest Service campgrounds, write to Pacific Northwest Region, Forest Service, P.O. Box 3623, Portland, Ore. 97208.

1 Paradise. May 1–Oct. 31. 42 tents, 22 trailers (max. 22 ft.). Fee. Cafe 3 mi. Fishing.

2 Tumalo St. Pk. Apr. 12–Oct. 1. 68 tents, 20 trailers (max. 35 ft.). Fee. Elec., water, sewer hookup. Showers. Cafe, store 1 mi. Swimming 1 mi. Fishing.

3 Prineville Reservoir St. Pk. Apr. 12–Oct. 1. 47 tents, 22 trailers (max. 35 ft.). Fee. Resv. accepted. Elec., water, sewer hookup. Showers. Swimming, fishing. Boat launch.

4 Cinder Hill. From US 97, E 18 mi. on county rd. May 25–Oct. 30. 105 tents or trailers (max. 32 ft.). Fee. Showers 1 mi. Cafe 1 mi. Fishing. Boat dock, launch, rental.

5 La Pine St. Pk. May–Oct. 50 tents, 95 trailers (max. 35 ft.). Fee. Elec., water, sewer hookup. Dumping station. Showers. Swimming, fishing.

6 Lava Lake. May 30–Sept. 30. 3 tents, 35 trailers (max. 22 ft.). Fee. Swimming, fishing. Boat dock, launch, rental.

7 Quinn River. Apr. 20–Oct. 15. 40 tents or trailers (max. 22 ft.). Fee. Fishing. Boat dock.

8 Shadow Bay. From Hwy. 58, NE 6.5 mi. on FR 204, NW 2 mi. on FR 204D. July 1–Oct. 15. 49 tents, 32 trailers (max. 22 ft.). Fee. Swimming, fishing.

Boat dock, launch.

9 Crescent Lake. Apr. 20–Oct. 31. 47 tents or trailers (max. 22 ft.). Fee. Cafe 1 mi. Swimming, fishing. Boat dock, launch, rental.

10 Digit Point. From US 97, W 12 mi. on FR 2731. June 1–Oct. 1. 37 tents or trailers (max. 22 ft.). Fee. Swimming, fishing. Boat dock, launch.

11 Diamond Lake. May 15–Nov. 15. 244 tents, 201 trailers (max. 22 ft.). Fee. Elec. hookup. Showers 1 mi. Cafe 1 mi. Swimming, fishing. Boat dock, launch, rental.

12 Union Creek. June 1–Oct. 20. 63 tents or trailers (max. 16 ft.). Fee. Cafe 1 mi. Fishing.

13 Huckleberry. From Hwy. 62, S 4 mi. on FR 311. June 25–Oct. 15. 25 tents or trailers (max. 22 ft.). Fee.

14 Rim. July 15–Sept. 15. 54 tents or trailers (max. 30 ft.). Fee. Cafe, store.

15 Mazama. July 1–Oct. 15. 200 tents or trailers (max. 30 ft.). Fee. Dumping station.

16 Collier Memorial St. Pk. May 1–Oct. 1. 18 tents, 50 trailers (max. 35 ft.). Fee. Elec., water, sewer hookup. Showers. Fishing.

Redwood National Park

(Map is on page 466)

Four campgrounds in the park, with trailer space but no utility connections.

For information on state campgrounds in California write to Office of Tourism and Visitor Services, 1400 Tenth St., Sacramento, Cal. 95814;
in Nevada, to Nevada State Park System, Room 221, Nye Bldg., 201 S. Fall St., Carson City, Nev. 89701.

For information on U.S. Forest Service campgrounds in California write to California Region, Forest Service, 630 Sansome St., San Francisco, Cal. 94111;
in Nevada, to Intermountain Region, Forest Service, 324 25th St., Ogden, Utah 84401.

1 Panther Flat. All year. 41 tents, 31 trailers (max. 22 ft.). Fee. Cafe 2 mi. Swimming, fishing.

2 Jedediah Smith Redwoods St. Pk. All year. 107 tents or trailers (max. 26 ft.). Fee. Resv. required. Showers. Swimming, fishing. Horseback riding.

3 Del Norte Redwoods St. Pk. All year. 142 tents or trailers (max. 26 ft.). Fee. Resv. required. Showers. Fishing.

4 Prairie Creek Redwoods St. Pk. All year. 100 tents or trailers (max. 26 ft.). Fee. Resv. required. Showers. Fishing. Horseback riding.

5 Patrick's Point St. Pk. All year. 123 tents or trailers (max. 30 ft.). Fee. Resv. required. Showers. Fishing.

6 Aikens. May 1–Nov. 15. 29 tents or trailers (max. 22 ft.). Fee. Swimming, fishing.

7 Lava Beds National Monument. All year. 40 tents, 20 trailers (max. 25 ft.). Fee.

8 Medicine Lake. From Hwy. 139, W 4.8 mi., S 17 mi. on county rd. SW 11.5 mi. on FR 47N75. June 15–Oct. 15. 44 tents or trailers (max. 22 ft.). Fee. Cafe. Swimming, fishing. Boat dock, launch, rental.

9 McArthur-Burney Falls St. Pk. April 10–Oct. 31. 118 tents or trailers (max. 30 ft.). Fee. Resv. required. Dumping station. Showers. Cafe, store. Swimming, fishing. Boat launch.

10 Castle Crags. Apr. 1–Oct. 31. 64 tents or trailers (max. 22 ft.). Fee. Resv. required. Showers. Swimming, fishing.

11 Point McCloud. From I-5, NE 16 mi. on county rd., SE 3 mi. on forest rd. May 1–Oct. 15. 36 tents or trailers (max. 32 ft.). Fee. Showers. Cafe. Swimming, fishing. Boat dock, launch, rental.

12 Oak Bottom. All year. 105 tents, 30 trailers. Fee. Dumping station. Cafe. Swimming, fishing. Boat dock, launch, rental.

13 Tannery Gulch. May 1–Oct. 1. 87 tents, 38 trailers (max. 22 ft.). Fee. Cafe 5 mi. Swimming, fishing. Boat dock, launch, rental.

14 Preacher Meadows. May 1–Oct. 1. 45 tents or trailers (max. 16 ft.). Fee. Cafe 2 mi. Swimming. Fishing 3 mi. Boat dock, launch, rental.

15 Hayden Flat. May 1–Oct. 31. 30 tents, 41 trailers (max. 22 ft.). Fee. Swimming, fishing.

16 Grizzly Creek Redwoods St. Pk. All year. 30 tents or trailers (max. 30 ft.). Fee. Resv. required. Showers. Swimming, fishing.

17 Hidden Springs Unit. Apr. 1–Sept. 30. 155 tents or trailers (max. 26 ft.). Fee. Resv. required. Showers. Swimming, fishing.

18 Richardson Grove St. Pk. All year. 185 tents or trailers (max. 24 ft.). Fee. Resv. required. Dumping station. Showers. Cafe, store. Swimming, fishing. Horseback riding.

19 Woodson Bridge St. Pk. All year. 46 tents or trailers (max. 30 ft.). Fee. Resv. required. Showers. Swimming, fishing. Horseback riding.

20 Manzanita Lake. May 1–Oct. 15. 273 tents or trailers (max. 25 ft.). Fee. Showers—extra chg. Cafe, store 1 mi. Swimming, fishing 1 mi. Boat launch, rental.

21 Almanor. June 1–Oct. 1. 102 tents, 45 trailers (max. 22 ft.). Fee. Cafe 1 mi. Swimming. Fishing 1 mi. Boat dock, launch, rental.

Yosemite National Park

(Map is on page 478)

Hotels, lodges and cabins in the park, including tent cabins, and 18 campgrounds, all with trailer space but none with utility connections.

For information on state campgrounds in California write to Office of Tourism and Visitor Services, 1400 Tenth St., Sacramento, Cal. 95814;
in Nevada, to Nevada State Park System, Room 221, Nye Bldg., 201 S. Fall St., Carson City, Nev. 89701.

For information on U.S. Forest Service campgrounds in California write to California Region, Forest Service, 630 Sansome St., San Francisco, Cal. 94111;
in Nevada, to Intermountain Region, Forest Service, 324 25th St., Ogden, Utah 84401.

1 MacKerricher St. Pk. All year. 147 tents or trailers (max. 30 ft.). Fee. Resv. required. Dumping station. Showers. Fishing. Boat launch.

2 Van Damme St. Pk. All year. 82 tents or trailers (max. 30 ft.). Fee. Resv. required. Showers. Fishing.

3 Hendy Woods St. Pk. All year. 95 tents or trailers (max. 24 ft.). Fee. Resv. required. Dumping station. Swimming, fishing. Horseback riding.

4 Clear Lake St. Pk. All year. 80 tents or trailers (max. 24 ft.). Fee. Resv. required. Dumping station. Showers. Swimming, fishing. Boat launch.

5 Oroville St. Pk. All year. 136 tents or trailers (max. 30 ft.). Fee. Resv. required. Dumping station. No flush toilets. Showers. Swimming, fishing. Boat dock, launch, rental.

6 Schoolhouse. Apr. 1–Oct. 31. 67 tents or trailers (max. 22 ft.). Fee. Cafe 5 mi. Swimming. Fishing 1 mi. Boat dock, launch.

7 William Kent. June 15–Oct. 15. 55 tents, 40 trailers (max. 22 ft.). Fee. Cafe 1 mi. Swimming. Fishing 1 mi. Boat dock, launch, rental.

8 Emerald Bay St. Pk. June 1–Labor Day. 100 tents or trailers (max. 26 ft.). Fee. Resv. required. Showers. Swimming, fishing. Boat dock.

9 Lahontan Reservoir. All year. No fixed number of sites (max. 20 ft.). Fee. Dumping station. No flush toilets. Cafe 1 mi. Swimming, fishing. Boat launch.

10 Tamarack Point. All year. 20 tents or trailers (max. 22 ft.). No fee. No flush toilets. Store 1 mi. Swimming 1 mi. Fishing. Boat launch.

11 Grover Hot Springs St. Pk. June 1–Labor Day. 76 tents or trailers (max. 30 ft.). Fee. Resv. required. Showers. Swimming, fishing.

12 Folsom Lake St. Pk. All year. 150 tents or trailers (max. 30 ft.). Fee. Resv. required. Cafe, store. Swimming, fishing. Boat dock, launch, rental. Horseback riding.

13 Bothe–Napa Valley St. Pk. All year. 35 tents or trailers (max. 24 ft.). Fee. Resv. required. Showers. Swimming. Horseback riding.

14 S. P. Taylor St. Pk. All year. 72 tents or trailers (max. 24 ft.). Fee. Resv. required. Showers. Store. Swimming, fishing. Horseback riding.

15 Mount Diablo St. Pk. All year. 80 tents or trailers (max. 26 ft.). Fee. Resv.

required. Horseback riding.

16 Caswell Memorial St. Pk. All year. 65 tents or trailers (max. 30 ft.). Fee. Resv. required. Showers. Swimming, fishing.

17 Turlock Lake St. Pk. All year. 65 tents or trailers (max. 21 ft.). Fee. Resv. required. Showers. Swimming, fishing. Boat dock, launch, rental.

18 New Hogan Lake, North Shore. All year. 121 tents or trailers (max. 20 ft.). Fee. Cafe. Store 1 mi. Swimming 1 mi. Fishing. Boat launch, rental.

19 Calaveras Big Trees St. Pk. May 1– Labor Day. 129 tents or trailers (max. 30 ft.). Fee. Resv. required. Dumping station. Showers. Store. Swimming.

20 Crane Flat. May–Oct. 164 tents or trailers (max. 35 ft.). Fee. No pets.

21 Wawona. May–Oct. 187 tents or trailers (max. 35 ft.). Fee. Cafe, store 1 mi. Swimming 1 mi. Fishing. Horseback riding.

22 Camp 11. May 15–Oct. 15. 241 tents or trailers. Fee. No pets. Dumping station. Cafe, store 1 mi. Swimming.

23 Camp 14. May 15–Oct. 30. 250 tents or trailers (max. 35 ft.). Fee. No pets. Dumping station 1 mi. Cafe 1 mi. Store. Swimming, fishing. Horseback riding.

24 Tuolumne Meadows. May–Oct. 600 tents or trailers (max. 35 ft.). Fee. Cafe, store 1 mi. Fishing. Horseback riding.

25 Devils Postpile National Monument. June 15–Sept. 15. 50 tents or trailers (max. 35 ft.). Fee. Fishing.

Big Sur Coast
(Map is on page 487)

Along this stretch there are several state parks with camping facilities, such as the large Pfeiffer–Big Sur with trailer space but no utility connections, and a number of private campgrounds.

For information on state campgrounds, write to Office of Tourism, 1400 Tenth St., Sacramento, Cal. 95814.

For information on U.S. Forest Service campgrounds, write to California Region, Forest Service, 630 Sansome St., San Francisco, Cal. 94111.

1 Portola St. Pk. All year. 60 tents or trailers (max. 26 ft.). Fee. Resv. required. Showers. Swimming, fishing.

2 Big Basin Redwoods St. Pk. All year. 260 tents or trailers (max. 30 ft.). Fee. Resv. required. Dumping station. Showers. Cafe, store. Swimming. Horseback riding.

3 Henry Cowell Redwoods St. Pk. May 1–Dec. 31. 51 tents or trailers (max. 22 ft.). Fee. Resv. required. Dumping station. Showers. Swimming, fishing. Horseback riding.

4 New Brighton Beach St. Pk. All year. 100 tents or trailers (max. 30 ft.). Fee. Resv. required. Showers. Swimming, fishing.

5 Sunset Manresa Beach St. Pk. All year. 90 tents or trailers (max. 30 ft.). Fee. Resv. required. Showers. Fishing.

6 San Luis Reservoir St. Pk. All year. 34 tents or trailers (max. 30 ft.). Fee. Resv. required. No flush toilets. Swimming, fishing. Boat launch.

7 Chalone Creek. All year. 44 tents or trailers (max. 30 ft.). Fee.

8 Pfeiffer–Big Sur St. Pk. All year. 218 tents or trailers (max. 30 ft.). Fee. Resv. required. Dumping station. Showers. Cafe, store. Swimming, fishing. Horseback riding.

9 Kirk. All year. 33 tents or trailers (max. 16 ft.). Fee. Cafe 4 mi. Fishing.

10 Plaskett. All year. 44 tents or trailers (max. 16 ft.). Fee. Cafe 3 mi.

11 San Simeon Beach St. Pk. All year. 69 tents or trailers (max. 26 ft.). Fee. Resv. required. No flush toilets. Fishing.

12 Atascadero St. Pk. All year. 104 tents or trailers (max. 25 ft.). Fee. Resv. required. Swimming, fishing.

13 Morro Bay St. Pk. All year. 115 tents or trailers (max. 30 ft.). Fee. Resv. required. Elec., water hookups. Dumping station. Showers. Fishing. Boat dock, rental.

14 Montana de Oro St. Pk. All year. 50 tents or trailers (max. 20 ft.). Fee. Resv. required. No flush toilets. Swimming, fishing.

15 Lopez Lake Rec. Area. All year. 218 tents, 144 trailers (max. 35 ft.). Elec., water, sewer hookups. Dumping station. Showers. Cafe, store. Swimming, fishing. Boat launch, rental. Horseback riding.

16 Pismo Beach St. Pk. All year. 143 tents or trailers (max. 30 ft.). Fee. Resv. required. Elec., water hookups. Dumping station. Showers. Swimming.

17 Figueroa. March 15–Nov. 15. 34 tents or trailers (max. 22 ft.). Fee.

18 Cachuma Lake Rec. Area. All year. 426 tents or trailers (max. 30 ft.). Fee. Dumping station. Showers. Cafe, store. Swimming pool—extra chg. Fishing. Boat launch, rental.

19 Gaviota St. Pk. All year. 59 tents or trailers (max. 30 ft.). Fee. Resv. required. Store. Swimming, fishing. Boat launch. Horseback riding.

20 Refugio St. Beach. All year. 65 tents or trailers (max. 30 ft.). Fee. Resv. required. Elec., water hookup. Showers. Store. Swimming, fishing.

21 El Capitan Beach St. Pk. All year. 25 tents or trailers (max. 30 ft.). Fee. Resv. required. Showers. Store. Swimming, fishing.

Sequoia–Kings Canyon National Parks
(Map is on page 495)

Eight campgrounds in Kings Canyon, six with trailer space, but no utility connections; nine campgrounds in Sequoia, seven with trailer space, but no utility connections. Three lodges with varying types of accommodations in the parks.

For information on state campgrounds, write to Office of Tourism, 1400 Tenth St., Sacramento, Cal. 95814.

For information on U.S. Forest Service campgrounds, write to California Region, Forest Service, 630 Sansome St., San Francisco, Cal. 94111.

1 Lower Dinkey Creek. June 1–Oct. 15. 135 tents or trailers (max. 22 ft.). Fee. Cafe. Swimming, fishing.

2 Hume Lake. May 1–Nov. 15. 85 tents or trailers (max. 22 ft.). Fee. Cafe 2 mi. Swimming. Fishing 1 mi. Boat dock, rental.

3 Azalea. May 1–Oct. 31. 64 tents, 50 trailers (max. 30 ft.). Fee. Dumping station. Showers. Cafe, store 1 mi. Horseback riding.

4 Sunset. May 1–Oct. 31. 125 tents, 100 trailers (max. 30 ft.). Fee. Cafe, store 1 mi. Horseback riding.

5 Dorst Creek. June–Oct. 157 tents, 100 trailers (max. 30 ft.). Fee. No flush toilets. Fishing 1 mi.

6 Lodgepole. June–Oct. 217 tents, 100 trailers (max. 30 ft.). Fee. Dumping station. Store. Fishing 1 mi. Riding.

7 Potwisha. All year. 20 tents, 24 trailers (max. 30 ft.). Fee. Fishing 1 mi.

8 Lake Kaweah. All year. 100 tents or trailers. Fee. Swimming 1 mi. Fishing. Boat launch, rental.

9 Troy Meadow. From US 395, NW 23.6 mi. on county rd. 152, NW 10 mi. on FR 21S02. May 1–Nov. 15. 64 tents or trailers (max. 22 ft.). Fee. Fishing.

10 Quaking Aspen. May 1–Oct. 31. 53 tents or trailers (max. 22 ft.). Fee. Cafe 2 mi. Fishing 1 mi.

11 Gold Ledge. All year. 37 tents or trailers (max. 22 ft.). Fee. Cafe 5 mi. Fishing.

12 Headquarters. All year. 44 tents or trailers (max. 22 ft.). Fee. Cafe 4 mi. Fishing.

13 Live Oak. All year. 96 tents or trailers (max. 20 ft.). Fee. Dumping station 1 mi. Cafe, store 1 mi. Swimming, fishing 1 mi. Boat launch, rental.

14 McGill. May 13–Oct. 31. 64 tents or trailers (max. 16 ft.). Fee.

15 Oak Flat. All year. 44 tents or trailers (max. 32 ft.). Fee.

16 Wheeler Gorge. All year. 62 tents or trailers (max. 16 ft.). Fee. Swimming, fishing.

17 Carpinteria Beach St. Pk. All year. 77 tents or trailers (max. 30 ft.). Fee. Resv. required. Elec., water hookups. Showers. Cafe, store. Swimming.

18 Emma Wood Beach St. Pk. All year. 200 tents or trailers (max. 30 ft.). Fee. Resv. required. No flush toilets. Swimming, fishing.

19 McGrath Beach St. Pk. All year. 174 tents or trailers (max. 30 ft.). Fee. Resv.

required. Showers. Swimming, fishing.

20 Point Mugu St. Pk. All year. 98 tents or trailers (max. 24 ft.). Fee. Resv. required. No flush toilets. Swimming, fishing.

21 Leo Carrillo Beach St. Pk. June 1– Sept. 30. 140 tents or trailers (max. 30 ft.). Fee. Resv. required. Dumping station. Showers. Cafe, store. Swimming, fishing.

Death Valley National Monument

(Map is on page 505)

Eleven campgrounds in the monument, five are open all year. All but two have trailer space, though none have utility connections.

For information on state campgrounds in California write to Office of Tourism, 1400 Tenth St., Sacramento, Cal. 95814; in Nevada, to State Park System, Room 221, Nye Bldg., 201 S. Fall St., Carson City, Nev. 89701.

For information on U.S. Forest Service campgrounds, write to California Region, Forest Service, 630 Sansome St., San Francisco, Cal. 94111.

1 Mesquite Springs. All year. 60 tents or trailers. Fee. Dumping station.

2 Stovepipe Wells. All year. 200 tents or trailers. Fee. Dumping station. Cafe, store 1 mi.

3 Sunset. Nov.–May. 500 tents or trailers. Fee. Dumping station 1 mi. Showers 1 mi. Cafe, store 1 mi. Swimming 1 mi. Horseback riding.

4 Texas Spring. Nov.–Apr. 85 tents or trailers. Fee. Dumping station 1 mi. Cafe, store 1 mi. Swimming 1 mi. Horseback riding.

5 McWilliams. May 1–Oct. 15. 63 tents or trailers (max. 32 ft.). Fee. Cafe 1 mi.

6 Mary Jane Falls. May 1–Oct. 15. 50 tents or trailers (max. 16 ft.). Fee.

7 Hanna Flats. May 15–Oct. 1. 88 tents or trailers (max. 22 ft.). Fee. Cafe 3 mi. Fishing 1 mi. Boat dock, launch, rental.

8 Green Valley. All year. 56 tents or trailers (max. 16 ft.). Fee. Showers 1 mi. Cafe 1 mi. Swimming. Fishing 1 mi. Boat dock, launch, rental.

9 Heart Bar St. Pk. May 1–Oct. 31. 100 tents or trailers (max. 30 ft.). Fee. Resv. required. No flush toilets. Horseback riding.

10 Indian Cove. All year. 114 tents, 75 trailers (max. 27 ft.). Fee. No flush toilets. No drinking water.

11 Jumbo Rocks. All year. 130 tents or trailers (max. 27 ft.). Fee. No flush toilets. No drinking water.

12 Cottonwood. All year. 62 tents or trailers (max. 27 ft.). Fee.

13 Salton Sea St. Pk. All year. 214 tents or trailers (max. 30 ft.). Fee. Resv. required. Dumping station. Showers. Cafe,

store. Swimming, fishing. Boat dock, launch, rental.

14 Mount San Jacinto St. Pk. Apr. 1– Oct. 31. 83 tents or trailers. Fee. Resv. required. Showers. Horseback riding.

15 Lake Hemet. Feb. 15–Dec. 15. 250 tents or trailers. Fee. Elec. hookup—extra chg. Water hookup. Dumping station. Showers. Cafe 1 mi. Store. Fishing. Boat launch, rental.

16 Doheny Beach St. Pk. All year. 115 tents or trailers (max. 30 ft.). Fee. Resv. required. Dumping station. Showers. Swimming, fishing.

17 San Clemente Beach St. Pk. All year. 83 tents or trailers (max. 30 ft.). Fee. Resv. required. Elec., water, sewer hookups. Showers. Swimming, fishing.

18 Palomar Mountain St. Pk. All year. 51 tents or trailers (max. 21 ft.). Fee. Resv. required. Showers. Fishing. Horseback riding.

19 Oak Grove. All year. 68 tents or trailers (max. 32 ft.). Fee. Cafe 1 mi.

20 Anza-Borrego Desert St. Pk. All year. 103 tents or trailers (max. 30 ft.). Fee. Resv. required. Elec., water, sewer hookups. Showers. Horseback riding.

21 Aqua Caliente County Pk. All year. 56 tents, 117 trailers. Fee. No pets. Elec., water, sewer hookup. Showers. Store.

22 Cuyamaca Rancho St. Pk. All year. 179 tents or trailers (max. 30 ft.). Fee. Resv. required. Showers. Fishing. Horseback riding.

Mount McKinley National Park

(Map is on page 515)

Seven campgrounds in the park, five with trailer space but none with utility connections.

For information on state campgrounds write to Department of Economic Development, Alaska Travel Division, Pouch E, Juneau, Alaska 99801.

For information on U.S. Forest Service campgrounds, write to Alaska Region, Forest Service, P.O. Box 1628, Juneau, Alaska 99801.

1 Teklanika. From Denali Hwy, W 29 mi. on forest rd. June 1–Sept. 10. 20 tents, 50 trailers (max. 25 ft.). Fee. No flush toilets.

2 Savage River. June 1–Sept. 10. 24 tents or trailers (max. 25 ft.). Fee.

3 Riley Creek. June 1–Sept. 10. 75 tents, 100 trailers (max. 25 ft.). Fee. Store 1 mi.

4 Chena River. June 1–Sept. 10. 33 tents or trailers. Fee. No flush toilets. No drinking water.

5 Harding Lake. June 1–Sept. 10. 89 tents or trailers (max. 30 ft.). Fee. Dumping station. No flush toilets. Cafe, store. Swimming, fishing. Boat launch, rental.

6 Big Delta. May 1–Oct. 15. 24 tents or

trailers (max. 20 ft.). Fee. No flush toilets. Showers 1 mi. Cafe, store 1 mi.

7 Eagle Trail. June 1–Sept. 10. 40 tents or trailers (max. 30 ft.). No fee. No flush toilets. No drinking water.

8 Valdez Glacier. June 1–Sept. 10. 40 tents or trailers (max. 20 ft.). No fee. No flush toilets. Fishing 1 mi.

9 Eklutna Basin Rec. Area. June 1–Sept. 10. 30 tents or trailers. No fee. No flush toilets. Swimming. Boat launch. No drinking water.

10 Williwaw. May 25–Sept. 5. 36 tents or trailers (max. 16 ft.). Fee. Showers 1 mi. Cafe 1 mi.

11 Granite Creek. May 25–Sept. 5. 24 tents or trailers (max. 16 ft.). Fee.

12 Trail River. May 25–Sept. 5. 85 tents or trailers (max. 32 ft.). Fee. Cafe 2 mi. Fishing. Boat dock.

13 Seward Municipal Small Boat Harbor. All year. 100 tents or trailers. Fee. Dumping station. Showers—extra chg. Cafe. Store 1 mi. Fishing. Boat launch, rental.

14 Russian River. May 25–Sept. 5. 80 tents or trailers (max. 32 ft.). Fee. Showers 4 mi. Cafe 1 mi. Fishing.

15 Hidden Lake. From Sterling Hwy, E 20 mi. on Skilak Rd. All year. 30 tents or trailers (max. 20 ft.). No fee. No flush toilets. Swimming, fishing. Boat launch.

16 Fort Abercrombie. June 1–Sept. 10. 8 tents or trailers (max. 20 ft.). No fee. No flush toilets.

17 Chilkoot Lake. June 1–Sept. 10. 32 tents or trailers. No fee. No flush toilets. Fishing. No drinking water.

18 Mendenhall. May 25–Sept. 5. 65 tents or trailers (max. 22 ft.). Fee. Resv. required. Cafe 5 mi. Swimming. Fishing 3 mi. Boat dock.

Waimea Canyon

(Map is on page 524)

Camping at Kokee State Park near the Canyon.

For information on state campgrounds write to Division of State Parks, P.O. Box 621, Honolulu, Hawaii 96809.

1 Kokee Park. All year. 24 tents or trailers. No fee. Resv. required. Showers. Cafe. Fishing 1 mi. Horseback riding.

2 Hapuna Beach St. Pk. All year. No fixed number of tents, 8 trailers. No fee. Resv. required. Showers. Swimming, fishing.

3 Namakani Paio. All year. 6 tents, 4 trailers (max. 15 ft.). No fee.

4 Kipuka Nene. All year. 4 tents or trailers (max. 15 ft.). No fee. No flush toilets.

5 MacKenzie St. Pk. All year. 6 tents or trailers. No fee. Resv. required. No flush toilets. Swimming 1 mi. Fishing.

PRECAMBRIAN 600—4,500 *

BACTERIA

BLUE-GREEN ALGAE

FLAGELLATES

GRAPTOLITE

SEGMENTED WORM

BRACHIOPOD

RED ALGAE

500 ORDOVICIAN ▶

TRILOBITE

ECHINODERM

Adirondack Mountains rising

CORAL

TETRAPOD
Ancestral Amphibian

EARLY TREE FERN

PRIMITIVE
LEAFLESS PLANT

CROSSOPTERYGIAN
Primitive Amphibian

HORSETAIL BRUSHES

New England
mountains
building
up

345 MISSISSIPPIAN ▶

PRIMITIVE SHARK

GONIATITES

CRINOID GARDEN

◀ TRIASSIC 230

TRIASSOCHELYS

Extensive deserts of deep sand

GINKGO

BENNETTITALEA

CYCAD

COELOPHYSIS

180 JURASSIC ▶

Pacific mountains
formed by block tilting

CYNOGNATHUS

PLESIOSAURUS

MAPLE

PTERANODON

ANDROMEDA
First flowering plant

SEQUOIA

TRICERATOPS

TYRANNOSAURUS

65 PALEOCEN

CREODONT
Early Carnivorous
Mammal

◀ MIOCENE 25

SYNDYOCERAS
Four-horned Antelope

DINOHYUS
Giant Pig

AGRIOCHOERUS
Even-toed Mammal

BALUCHITHERIUM
Giant Hornless
Rhinoceros

CYNODICTIS
Small Primitive D

Volcanic activity
widespread in West

13 PLIOCENE ▶

Shaping of modern landscapes

MERYCHIPPUS
Ancestral Horse

AGRIOTHERIUM
Ancestral Bear

The Ages that Shaped the American Earth

The geological story of the earth is almost inconceivably long. Current estimates put earth's age at about 4½ billion years, and of that incredible span, only the last 600 million years—from the Cambrian period to the present—can be traced with any accuracy. On this diagram of geological periods, designed to show the principal events as they affected the North American land mass, the dimly known pre-Cambrian period recedes into the distant past, and the emphasis is on more recent times. The geological time track shows some of the more important events, including the first appearance of different forms of life. It must be remembered that the geological occurrences shown here did not take place suddenly, but over vast spans of time; some of the more recent disturbances, indicated by earthquakes and volcanic activity, continue to shape the earth to this day.

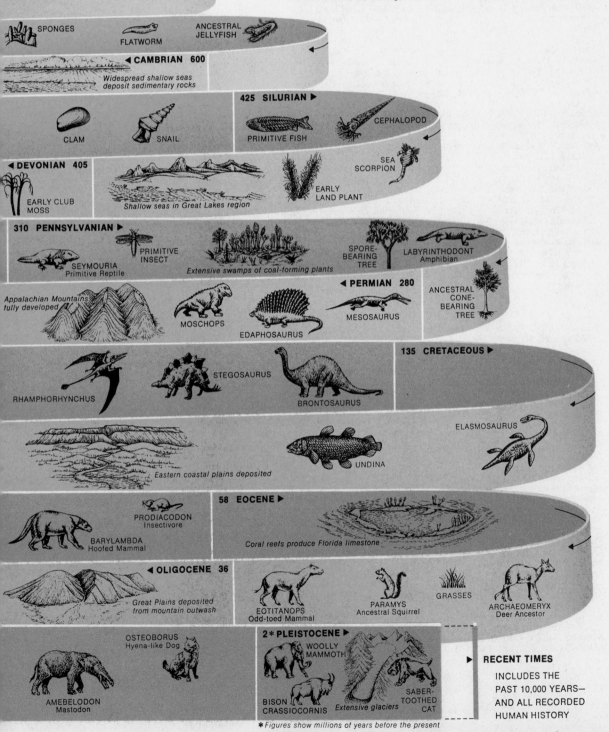

SPONGES

FLATWORM

ANCESTRAL JELLYFISH

◀ CAMBRIAN 600

Widespread shallow seas deposit sedimentary rocks

425 SILURIAN ▶

CLAM

SNAIL

PRIMITIVE FISH

CEPHALOPOD

SEA SCORPION

◀ DEVONIAN 405

EARLY CLUB MOSS

Shallow seas in Great Lakes region

EARLY LAND PLANT

310 PENNSYLVANIAN ▶

PRIMITIVE INSECT

SPORE-BEARING TREE

LABYRINTHODONT
Amphibian

SEYMOURIA
Primitive Reptile

Extensive swamps of coal-forming plants

Appalachian Mountains fully developed

◀ PERMIAN 280

ANCESTRAL CONE-BEARING TREE

MOSCHOPS

EDAPHOSAURUS

MESOSAURUS

135 CRETACEOUS ▶

RHAMPHORHYNCHUS

STEGOSAURUS

BRONTOSAURUS

ELASMOSAURUS

Eastern coastal plains deposited

UNDINA

58 EOCENE ▶

PRODIACODON
Insectivore

BARYLAMBDA
Hoofed Mammal

Coral reefs produce Florida limestone

◀ OLIGOCENE 36

Great Plains deposited from mountain outwash

EOTITANOPS
Odd-toed Mammal

PARAMYS
Ancestral Squirrel

GRASSES

ARCHAEOMERYX
Deer Ancestor

OSTEOBORUS
Hyena-like Dog

2 ✳ PLEISTOCENE ▶

WOOLLY MAMMOTH

SABER-TOOTHED CAT

AMEBELODON
Mastodon

BISON CRASSIOCORNIS

Extensive glaciers

RECENT TIMES

INCLUDES THE PAST 10,000 YEARS— AND ALL RECORDED HUMAN HISTORY

✳ Figures show millions of years before the present

Index

The page numbers in regular type face are references to the text; in italics, to maps; and in boldface, to pictures.

Abajo Mountains, Utah, 355, *355*, **357**
abalones (shellfish), 485
Abbeville, La., 193, *194*
Abert, Lake, Ore., 457
Abert Rim, Ore., 457, *457*
Absaroka Wilderness Area, Wyo., 320–322, *320*
Academy of Natural Science, Philadelphia, Pa., 65
Acadia National Park, Me., 18–25, **18–19**, *24*
  Nature Center, 21, 25
Acoma Pueblo, N.M., 396
Acoma–Zuni Trail, N.M., 394
Adams, Mount, N.H., 29
Adams, Mount, Wash., 426, **429**, 435, 437
Adirondack High Peaks, N.Y., 34, 35
Adirondacks (mountains), N.Y., 10, 33, 34, 59
Adirondack Museum, Blue Mountain Lake, N.Y., 35
Agate Beach, Ore., 448
Agate Beach, Wash., 417
Agate Fossil Beds National Monument, Neb., 234, *234*, 235
Agness, Ore., 448, **451**
air plants, **116**, 118
Akaka Falls, Hawaii, Hawaii, 524, *524*
Alabama–Coushatta Indian Reservation, Tex., 203
Alabama Hills, Calif., 495, *495*
Alabaster Caverns State Park, Okla., 185, *185*
Alamosa, Colo., 260, *262*
Alaska Range, 515
Albany, N.Y., 59
alders, 486
  Western red, **425**
Aleutian Islands, 435
alewives (fish), 25
Allagash River, Me., **25**
Allagash Wilderness Waterway, Me., *24*, **25**
Allegany State Park, N.Y., 43, *43*
Allegheny National Forest, Pa., 43, *43*
Alley Springs, Mo., 171, *172*
alligators, 106, 112–113, **117**, **121**, 190
Alpine, N.J., 61
Alpine–Big Bend Scenic Drive, Tex., *283*, **284**
Alpine Garden, N.H., 31
Alpine Lake Region, Wash., 426, **428**
Alsea Bay, Ore., 445
Alsea River, Ore., 449
Alum Cove Natural Bridge, Ark., 174, *174*
Alvord Desert, Ore., 459
Alyeska, Mount, Alaska, 515, *515*
Amboy Crater, Calif., 505, *505*
American Falls, *see* Niagara Falls
American Flats, Colo., 254
American Meteorite Museum, Sedona, Ariz., 387
American Museum of Natural History, New York, N.Y., 65
Amicalola Falls, Ga., 89, *89*
Amistad, Lake, Tex., *283*, 284

Amnicon Falls, Wis., 129, *129*
Anacapa Island, Calif., 495
Anacortes, Wash., **417**
Anchorage, Alaska, 17, 513, 515, *515*
  Anchorage Log Cabin Museum, 516
  Wildlife Museum, 516
Andrews Glacier, Colo., 239
Anemone Cave, Me., 21
Angel Arch, Utah, 353, 354
Angeles Crest Highway, Calif., 495, 496
Angel Island, Calif., 478, *478*
Angel Peak Recreation Area, N.M., 394, *394*
Angels Landing, Utah, 364
Angel's Window, Ariz., 378
anhingas (birds), **117**
Anhinga Trail, Fla., 116
Animas River, Colo., 254, **257**
Animas River Overlook, Colo., 253, **253**
anis (birds), 112
Anse, La., 190
antelope, *see* pronghorns
Antelope Island State Park, Utah, 337–339, **338–339**
Anthony's Nose (mountain), N.Y., **61**
Anticline Overlook, Utah, 355
Antonito, Colo., 263
Anza–Borrego Desert State Park, Calif., 505, *505*
Apache Lake, Ariz., 403
Apache Trail, Ariz., 403, *403*
Apostle Islands, Wis., 129, **130**
Appalachian Chain, 29, **66–67**, 68, 71, 86
Appalachian Gap, Vt., 32, *32*
Appalachian Trail, **25**, 71, 72, 88, 89
Apple River, Wis., 135
Apple River Canyon, Ill., *155*, **157**
apples, custard (trees), 115
Apple Valley, Calif. and Nev., 506
Aquarium, Depoe Bay, Ore., 450
Aquarium and Turtle Kraals, Key West, Fla., 120
Aquatarium, St. Petersburg, Fla., 120
Aransas National Wildlife Refuge, Tex., **201**, 202, *203*, 205
Arapaho Glacier, Colo., 243, *243*
Aravaipa Canyon, Ariz., 403, *403*
Arbor Lodge State Park, Neb., 165, *165*
Arbuckle Recreation Area, Okla., 187
Arcadia Bird Sanctuary, Easthampton, Mass., 55
Arcadia Scenic Turnout, Mich., **147**, *147*
Arches National Park, Utah, 346–359, **350–351**, **353**, *355*
  Visitor Center, 359
Arco, Idaho, 330
Arethusa Falls, N.H., 32
Arizona Mineral Museum, Phoenix, Ariz., 405
Arizona–Sonora Desert Museum, Tucson, Ariz., 402, 405
Arkansas Game and Fish Commission, Little Rock, Ark., 177
Arkansas River, Colo., 262
armadillos (animals), 183

Arnaudville, La., 190
Arnold Arboretum, Boston, Mass., 55
Arnold Ice Cave, Ore., 457, *457*
Arrowhead, Lake, Calif., 506
ashes (trees), 118, 135, 234, 367
  pop, 115
Ash Hollow State Historical Park, Neb., 234, *234*
Ashokan Reservoir, N.Y., 63, *63*
Ashton, Idaho, 332
Ashumet Holly Reservation, East Falmouth, Mass., 55
Aspen Area, Colo., 243, **244–245**, 247
Aspen Butte, Ore., 458
aspens, 125, 128, 135, 241, 242, 297, 321, 367, 380, 383, 394, 403, 505
  quaking, 210, 251, **256**
Assateague Island National Seashore, Md. and Va., 72, **73**
asters, 171, 378
Astoria, Ore., 443, *445*, 449, *449*
Atchafalaya Basin, La., 190, *194*, **194**
Atchafalaya Swamp, La., 194
Athabasca Lake, Minn., 128
Atlantic Ocean, 21, *24*, 30, 59, 63, **94–95**, 96, **96–97**, 100, *100*, 106
Audubon, John James, 81
Audubon Center of Greenwich, Conn., 65
Audubon State Park, Ky., *81*, 81–82
Ausable Chasm, N.Y., 32, *32*
Au Sable River, Mich., *147*, 148, **148**
Ausable River, N.Y., 32, 35
Austin Pass, Wash., 427
Avenue of the Giants, Calif., 466, *466*
Avery Island, La., **190–191**, 192–193, *194*
avocets (birds), **201**, 202
Avon, N.C., 98
Avra Valley, Ariz., 404
Awosting State Park, N.Y., 64
azaleas, 72, 101, 190, 442, 447
  flame, 86, 88
  Indian, 119

Backbone State Park, Iowa, 155, *155*
Baden–Powell, Mount, Calif., 496
badgers, 162, 167, **252**, 282, 289–290, 302
Badlands National Monument, S.D., 216–227, **216–217**, **218**, **220–221**, **222–223**, *224*
  Museum, 226
Bad River, Wis., 129
Badwater Salt Flats, Calif., **498–499**, 500, 504, **504**
Bahia Honda, Fla., *118*, **119**
Bailey, Mount, Ore., 457
Baker, Mount, Wash., 417, *417*, 426, 427, 431
Bakersfield, Calif., 495
Balanced Rock, Idaho, 329, *329*
Balanced Rock, Tex., 204
Balance Rock, Wis., **156–157**
Bald Eagle Creek, Pa., 43
Bald Eagle Lookout, Pa., 43, *43*

Bald River Falls, Tenn., 89, *89*
Balmorhea State Park, Tex., 283, *283*
bamboos, **190–191**, 524, 526
bananas, 525
Bandelier National Monument, N.M., 394, *394*
Baraboo Bluffs, Wis., 155
Bar Harbor, Me., 21, *24*
Barkley, Lake, Ky. and Tenn., 82
Barnstable Bay, Mass., 52, *52*
barracudas (fish), 113
Bartholomews Cobble, Ashley Falls, Mass., 55
Bartram, William, 105–106
Basket Dome, Calif., 476
bass, 129, 176, 195, 272, 417
  largemouth, 101, 103, 119
  lunker, 175
  red, 171
  smallmouth, 136, 171, 302
  white, 175
Bass Harbor, Me., 23
Bass Harbor Head, Me., 23
Basswood Lake, Minn., 128
Basswood River, Minn., 128
Bat Cave, Carlsbad Caverns, N.M., 268–269, 269
bats, Mexican freetail, 268–271, **268–269**
Battie, Mount, Me., 24
Battle Hollow, Wis., 137
Baxter State Park, Me., 24, *24*, **25**
Bay Ocean, Ore., 445
Bayou Country, La., 188–195, **188–189**, **190–191**, **192**, *194*
bayberries, **51**, 54
bay trees, 119
  red, 113
Beach Drive, Fla., 194, *194*
Beach Four, Wash., 414
beach grasses, 145
Beacon Rock, Wash., 436
bearberries, **51**
  alpine, 513
Bear Canyon, Calif., 496
Bear Creek Falls, Colo., 253, *253*
bear grasses, **425**
Bear Lake, Colo., **236–237**
Bear Lake, Idaho and Utah, 342, *342*
Bear Mountain, N.Y., **56–57**, 59–60, 65
  Trailside Museum, 65
Bear River, Utah, 337, *339*
  Migratory Bird Refuge, 337
bears, 69, 103, 104, 129, 302, 320, 405, 456
  black, 88, 89, 107, 126, 136, 251, **252**, 290–291, **293**, 318, 396, 402, 425, 445, 449, 494
  brown, 291
  grizzly, **252**, 290, 292, **293**, 510
Beartooth Highway, Mont., 294, *294*
Beartooth Pass, Mont., 294
Beartooth Plateau, Mont., 294
Beaver Creek, Ind., 81
Beaver Meadows, Colo., 239, 241
beavers, 64, 126, **126–127**, 128, 136, 141, 162, 182, 242, 289, 302, 425, 514
Beavers Bend State Park, Okla., 174, *174*
Beaver Scenic Drive, Utah, 369, *369*
beeches, 54, 80, 174
Bee Mountain, Tex., **284**
bees, 377
beggarticks (plants), **172**
begonias, 521
Belknap, Mount, Utah, 369
Belle Fourche River, Wyo. and S.D., **212**, 224
Bellevue, Iowa, 152, *155*
Bellevue State Park, Iowa, 154
bellflowers, piper, 409

Bend, Ore., 457
Bennett Spring State Park Nature Center, Lebanon, Mo., 177
Bentsen–Rio Grande Valley State Park, Tex., 203, *203*
Benzie State Park, Mich., 146
bergamots (plants), 164
Bering Sea, 435
Berkeley Springs, W.Va., 72, *72*
Berkeley Springs State Park, W.Va., 72
Berkshire Hills, Mass., **53**, 54
Berkshire Museum, Pittsfield, Mass., 55
Bernard, Me., 23
Bernheim Forest, Ky., 81, **81**
  Nature Center and Natural History Museum, 83
Bernice P. Bishop Museum, Honolulu, Oahu, Hawaii, 526
Betatakin, Ariz., 386
Big Basin Redwoods State Park, Calif., 487
  Nature Lodge, 489
Big Bear Lake, Calif., 506
Big Belt Range, Mont., 296, 297
Big Bend National Park, Tex., 15, 276–285, **276–277**, **278**, **280–281**, **282**, *283*
  Museum, 285
Big Cataloochee Knob, N.C. and Tenn., 88
Big Cinder Butte, Idaho, 326
Big Cottonwood Canyon, Utah, 344
Big Creek Lakes, Colo., 243, *243*
Big Cypress Swamp, Fla., 118, *118*
Big Duck River Falls, Tenn., 81, *81*
Big Eddy Falls, Wis., **140**
Big Falls, Ore., 437
Bighorn Canyon National Recreation Area, Wyo., *294*, **295**, 320, *320*
Bighorn Lake Reservoir, Wyo., 320
Bighorn National Forest, Wyo., 320, *320*
Bighorn River, Mont. and Wyo., **220**, **295**
Big Meadows, Va., 70, 71
Big Mountain Ski Resort, Mont., 297
Big Pine, Calif., 495
Big Pocono Overlook, Pa., 63, *63*
Big Rock Candy Mountain, Utah, 371–372
Big Room, N.M., 268
Big Shell Beach, Tex., 200
Big Smoky Falls, Wis., **140**
Big Southern Butte, Idaho, 325, 330
Big Spring State Park, Mo., **168–169**, 169, 171, 172
  Museum, 177
Big Sur, Calif., 461, 482–489, **482–483**, **484**, **486**, 487
Big Thicket Scenic Area, Tex., 203, *203*
Big Thompson Canyon, Colo., 243, *243*
Big Thompson River, Colo., 239
Billy's Lake, Okefenokee, Ga., 106
Biloxi, Miss., 194, 195
Biological Laboratory Aquarium, Woods Hole, Mass., 55
birches, 21, 29, 35, **53**, 125, 154, 170, 330, 515
  dwarf, 513
  white, 35, 135, 224
  yellow, 86
Bird City, La., 192
Bird Island, Calif., **489**
Bird Island, Utah, 339
Bird Woman Falls, Mont., **288**
bison, *see* buffalo
bitterns (birds), 105
bitterbrush, 328
Bitterroot Range, Idaho and Mont., 294, *294*, 328, *328*
Bitterroot River, Mont., 294

blackberries, **424**
blackbirds, redwing, 51, 153
blackbrushes, 380
Black Canyon of the Gunnison National Monument, Colo., 248–257, **248–249**, 250, **251**, *253*, 299, **301**
Black Hills National Forest, S.D. and Wyo., 209, 213, *213*, 214, 224, 226, **226**
Black Kettle National Grasslands, Okla., 185
Black Mesa State Park, Okla., 185, *185*
Black River, Mich., 130
Black River, N.M., **268**
Black River Harbor, Mich., 130
Black Rock Summit, Nev., 371
Blackwater National Wildlife Refuge, Md., 72, *72*
bladderworts (plants), **105**
Blanca Peak (Mount Blanca), Colo., 260, *262*, **263**
Blanco Reef, Ore., 448
blazing stars (flowers), **172**
blennies (fish), 445
Block Island, R.I., *52*, **55**
Blowing Rock, N.C., 89, *89*
bluebells, 145, **241**
bluebirds, mountain, 328
blueblossoms, 447, 463
bluebonnets, 394
bluegills (fish), 129, 171, 195, **333**, 417
blue grama grasses, **163**
Bluegrass Country, Ky., *81*, **83**
Blue Hole, Ohio, 147, *147*, 149
blue jays, 112, 380
Blue Mesa, Ariz., **388–389**, **390**, 391
Blue Mesa Dam, Colo., 249
Blue Mesa Lake, Colo., 254
Blue Range Scenic Drive, Ariz., 403, *403*
Blue Ridge Mountains, Va., 68, **70**, 71, 73
Blue Ridge Parkway, Va., 71, 72, *72*, **84–85**
  Visitor Center, 74
Blue River, Ariz., 403
Blue River, Ore., 458
bluestem grass, 161, **163**
Bluestone Gorge, W. Va., 92
Boardman State Park, Ore., *445*
boars, wild, 486
  Russian, 89
Bobby Hole, Utah, 354
bobcats, 69, 126, 171, 183, 226, 261, **274**, **275**, 282, 302, 328, 368, 392, 456
Bob Marshall Wilderness, Mont., 297
bobolinks, 214
Bodie Island, N.C., 97–98
  Visitor Center, 101
Bogachiel River, Wash., 415
Bogachiel State Park, Wash., 415, *415*
Boiler Bay, Ore., 445, *445*
Bombay Hook National Wildlife Refuge, Del., 72, **75**
Bonner County Museum, Sandpoint, Idaho, 307
Bonners Ferry, Idaho, 304–305, 306
Bonneville, Capt. Benjamin, 326
Bonneville Dam, Ore., 433, 435, 436
Bonneville Salt Flats, Utah, **340–341**, *341*
Boone, Daniel, 14, **14–15**
Boquillas Canyon, Tex., **280–281**
Borah, Mount, Idaho, *329*, 330–331
Borrego Springs, Calif., 505
Bosque del Apache National Wildlife Refuge, N.M., 272, *272*
Boston Mountains, Ark., 175
Botanical Gardens, Berkeley, Calif., 480

555

Bottomless Lakes, N.M., 272, 272
Boucher Hill, Calif., 506
Boundary Waters Canoe Area, Minn., 122–131, **122–123, 124, 127,** *129*
bowfins (fish), 342
Bowman's Hill State Wildflower Preserve, Washington Crossing, Pa., 65
Box Canyon, Colo., *253,* 253–254
Box Canyon, Neb., 233
Box Canyon, Wash., 423
Boyce Thompson Southwestern Arboretum, Superior, Ariz., 405
Boysen Reservoir, Wyo., 320, *320*
Bozeman Pass., Mont., **297**
Bradbury Mountain State Park, Me., 24, *24*
Brahma Temple, Ariz., 378
Brasstown Bald Mountain, Ga., *89,* 90
Brazos Peaks, N.M., 397
bream (fish), 103, 119, 176
Breaux Bridge, La., 192, *194*
Bretton Woods, N.H., **26–27**
Brewster Natural History Museum, Mass., 55
Bridalveil Falls, Calif., 476, **476**
Bridal Veil Falls, Colo., 245
Bridal Veil Falls, Utah, *342,* **343**
Bridal Veil Falls, Wash., 428
Bridge Creek, Ore., 438
Bridgeport, Wis., 156
Bridger Range, Mont., 294
Bridger's Pass, Wyo., *243,* 244
Brigantine National Wildlife Refuge, N.J., 63, *63*
Brigham City, Utah, 337, 340, *342*
Brigham Young University Geology Museum, Provo, Utah, 345
Bright Angel Point, Ariz., 378
Bristlecone Pine Area, Calif., *495,* **495**
Brockway Mountain Drive, Mich., **129,** *129*
Broken Bow Reservoir, Okla., 174
Bronson Museum, Attleboro, Mass., 55
Brooks Lake, Wyo., 320, *320*
Brooks Range, Alaska, 31
Brooks River, Alaska, **516–517**
Broussard, La., 190
Brownlee Dam, Idaho, 301
Brown's Park National Wildlife Refuge, Colo., *243,* 244
Bruce Lake Natural Area, Pa., *63,* 63–64
Brule, S.D., 219
Brule River, Minn., 137, 138
Brule River Valley, Minn., 135–136
Bruneau Canyon, Idaho, 329, *329*
Bruneau Dunes, Idaho, *329,* **333**
Bryce, Ebenezer, 364, 368
Bryce Canyon National Park, Utah, 360–373, **360–361,** *362, 363,* 379
   Visitor Center, 372
Buck Hill Falls, Pa., 64
buckwheat
   dwarf, 327
   wild, 378
buffalo, 136, 162, 166, 180–181, **180–181,** 221, **223, 225,** 226, 234–235, 262, **295, 338–339,** *339*
Buffalo, N.Y., 39
   Museum of Science, 45
buffalo berries, 221
Buffalo Bill Reservoir, Wyo., 322
Buffalo River, Ark., *174,* **175**
Buffalo Track Canyon, Kan., 166
Bull Creek, Calif., 466
Bullfrog Basin Scenic Highway, Utah, 355, *355*
Bull Island, S.C., *100,* **101**
Bull Shoals Lake, Ark. and Mo., 174–175, *174*
bunchgrass, 259

Burlington, Vt., 33
Burney Creek, Calif., 466
Burney Falls, Calif., 466, *466*
Burning Coal Vein, N.D., *213,* **215**
Burns, Ore., 457
Burroughs Mountain, Wash., 423
Bushkill Falls, Pa., 64
Butler Peak Lookout, Calif., 506
Butte–Livingston Scenic Drive, Mont., *294,* **297**
buttercups, 367
butterflies, 117
   monarch, 488
   White Mountain, 29
Buxton, N.C., 98

Cache la Poudre Canyon, Colo., *243,* 244
cactuses, 116, 272, **274–275,** 279, 381, 392
   cholla, 504
   organ pipe, 404
   pincushion, 399
   prickly pear, 210, **384**
   saguaro, **398–399,** *399–402,* **400, 401, 402,** 404
Cactus Flats, S.D., 219
Cades Cove, Tenn., **86–87,** 88
Cadillac Mountain, Me., **18–19,** 21, 23, 25
Cahuilla, Lake, Calif., 507
Caladesi Island State Park, Fla., 118, *118*
Calaveras Big Trees State Park, Calif., 478, *478*
Calico Mountains, Calif., *505,* 505
California Academy of Sciences Museum, San Francisco, Calif., 480
California Division of Mines and Geology Mineral Museum, San Francisco, Calif., 480
Camas Prairie, Idaho, 306
Cambridge, Idaho, 301, 306
Camden Hills State Park, Me., 24, *24*
Camel, Utah, 367
camellias, **101**
Campbell Falls State Park, Conn., 52, *52*
Canadian River Valley, Tex., 187
Canjilon Lakes, N.M., *394,* *394*
Cannon Mountain, N.H., 32
Canon City, Colo., 262
   Municipal Museum, 263
Canyon de Chelly National Monument, Ariz., *394,* **396–397**
Canyon Creek Falls, Colo., 253
Canyon Ferry Reservoir, Mont., 295, 297
Canyon Lake, Ariz., 403
Canyonlands National Park, Utah, 346–359, **346–347, 348, 352,** 355
Canyon Reservoir, Tex., *203,* 204
Cape Arago, Ore., *445,* 448
Cape Blanco, Ore., *445,* 448
Cape Cod Canal, Mass., 49
Cape Cod National Seashore, Mass., 46–55, **46–47, 48–49, 50,** 52
   Visitor Center, 49
Cape Elizabeth, Me., 24–25, *24*
Cape Falcon, Ore., 445
Cape Hatteras, S.C., **96–97,** *97,* 100
Cape Henlopen State Park, Del., 72, *72*
Cape Kiwanda, Ore., **446**
Cape Lookout, N.C., *96,* 100
Cape Lookout State Park, Ore., 445, *445*
Cape May, N.J., 72
Cape May Point, N.J., 72, *72*
Cape Meares, Ore., *445, 445*

Cape Romain, N.C., **101**
Cape Royal, Ariz., 378
Capetown, Calif., 466
Capistrano, Calif., 507
Capitol Reef National Park, Utah, *355,* **356**
   Visitor Center, 359
Capote Waterfall, Tex., *283,* **284**
Capulin Mountain National Monument, N.M., *394,* **396**
caracaras (birds), 205
cardinal flowers, 152, **172**
Caribbean Gardens, Naples, Fla., 120
caribou, 511
Carl Etling, Lake, Okla., 185
Carlsbad Caverns National Park, N.M., 264–275, **264–265,** *266,* **268–269,** *270,* **271,** 272
Carlsbad Municipal Museum, Carlsbad, N.M., 275
Carmel, Calif., *483,* **487**
Carmel Valley, Calif., *485,* **487**
Carnegie Institute Natural History Museum, Pittsburgh, Pa., 45
Carolina Sandhills National Wildlife Refuge, S.C., 100, *100*
Carter County Museum, Ekalaka, Mont., 215
Casa Grande, Tex., 282
Cascade Canyon, Wyo., **313**
Cascade Head, Ore., *445*
Cascade Locks, Ore., 435
Cascade Range, Wash., 409, 417, 421, 427, **428,** 437, 450, 453, **457–459**
Cascades, N.H., 32
Casco Bay, Me., 24, *24*
Cassoday, Kan., 164
Castle Gardens Scenic Area, Wyo., *320,* **322**
Castle of the Gods, Wyo., 323
Castle Peak, Idaho, *329,* **332**
Castle Rock, Kan., *165,* *165*
Castle Rock, Ore., 448
Castolon, Tex., 280
Castolon Peak, Tex., **282**
Caswell Memorial State Park, Calif., 478, *478*
Catahoula, Lake, La., *194, 194*
Cataract Canyon, Utah, 354
catfish, 136, 272, 342
   black bullhead, **105**
   brown bullhead, *105*
Cathedral, Tex., **284**
Cathedral Caverns, Ala., *81,* *81*
Cathedral Gorge State Park, Nev., *369,* **372**
Cathedral Ledge, N.H., 33
Cathedral Mountain, Alaska, 511–513
Cathedral Rock, Calif., 505
Cathedral Rock, Okla., 186
Cathedral Spires, Calif., 475
cat's-claws (plants), 380
Catskill Mountains, N.Y., 59, 63, *63,* 64
cattails (plants), 51, 149
cattle, **158–159,** 161, **162–163**
   Brangus, *183*
   Charolais, *182*
   Hereford, *183*
   longhorn, 181–183, **182,** 234
   Santa Gertrudis, **183**
   shorthorn, **182**
Cave Hills, S.D., 213, *213*
Cave-in-Rock State Park, Ill., *81,* *81*
Cave Island Nature Trail, Ky., **80**
Cave of the Mounds, Wis., 155, *155*
Caverns of Sonora, Tex., *283,* *283*
Cave Spring, Mo., *173*
Cave of the Winds, N.Y., **40–41**
Cayuga Lake, N.Y., 43, *43,* 45
Cedar Bluff State Park, Kan., *165,* *165*
Cedar Breaks National Monument,

Utah, *369*, **373**
Cedar Canyon, Okla., 185
Cedar City, Utah, 367, *369*
Cedar Key, Fla., 118, *118*
Cedar Lake, Okla., 177
Cedar Mountain, Wyo., 322
Cedar Pass, S.D., **218**, 222–223, 224
Cedar River, Iowa, 156
cedars, 49, 74, 97, 130–131, 170, **215**, 234, 305, 442
  Port Orford, **465**
  red, 221, 289
  Western red, 304, 413
Center Lake, S.D., 224, *224*
Central Florida Museum, Orlando, Fla., 120
Century Drive, Ore., 457, *457*
chachalacas (birds), 205
Chaco Canyon National Monument, N.M., 394, *394*
  Park Museum, 397
Chadron, S.D., 219
Chadron State Park, S.D., 234
Chain O'Lakes, Ind., 147, *147*
Chair Mountain, Colo., **247**
Chalk Cliffs, Colo., 245
Chama, N.M., 262, 263
Chama Canyon, N.M., 394, *394*
Chama Valley, N.M., 397
Chamber of Commerce and Mines Museum, Ely, Nev., 372
Chamber of Commerce Museum, Wallace, Idaho, 307
Champlain, Lake, N.Y. and Vt., *32*, 33
Champoeg State Park, Ore., 450
Channel Islands National Monument, Calif., 495, *495*, 496
chaparrals (trees), 494
Charenton, La., 190
Charles Mound, Ill., **157**
Charleston, Ore., 448
Charleston Museum, Charleston, S.C., 101
Charleston Peak, Nev., 505, *505*
Chasm View, Colo., 251
Chasm Wall, Colo., 251
Chatcolet, Lake, Idaho, 304
Chatham, Mass., 49
Chattahoochee National Forest, Ga., 90
Chattahoochee River, Ga., **108**
Chattanooga, Tenn., *89*, 92
Chautauqua Lake, N.Y., 43–44, *43*
Checkerboard Mesa, Utah, **368**
Cherokee, N.C., 87
cherries
  black, **51**, 174
  wild, 175
Chesapeake Bay, Md., 74
Chesapeake Biological Laboratory, Solomons, Md., 74
Chesapeake and Ohio Canal, Md. and Va., **75**
Chesler Park, Utah, 354
Cheyava Waterfall, Ariz., 377
Cheyenne Bottoms Wildlife Refuge, Kan., 165, *165*
Cheyenne River, S.D., 219, 224
chickadees
  black-capped, 211
  mountain, 251
Chigmit Mountains, Alaska, 515
Chihuahuan Desert, N.M. and Tex., 267
Chimney Rock, Colo., 253, *254*
Chimney Rock, Neb., 233, 234, *234*
Chimney Rock, N.C., *89*, 90
Chimney Rocks State Park, Utah, 369 *369*
Chimney Tops Mountain, N.C. and Tenn., 88
China Cove, Calif., **489**
Chinese Temple, Mammoth, Ky., **79**

Chinese Wall, Wyo., 322
Chinle Formation, Ariz., **393**
chipmunks, 69, 211, 221, 368
  least, *252*
Chippewa River, Minn., 139, *139*
Chiricahua National Monument, Ariz., *403*, **405**
  Museum, **405**
Chisos Basin, Tex., 280, 282
Chisos Mountains, Tex., **276–277**, 283
Chitina, Alaska, 515
chokecherries, 229, 243, 261
Chugach Mountains, Alaska, 515
Chugach State Park, Alaska, 515, *515*
cicadas, 171
Cimarron Canyon, N.M., 394, *394*
Cimarron River, Okla. and N.M., 186, 394
cinquefoils (flowers), 210
ciscoes (fish), 342
Citadel Mountain, Mont., **286–287**
City of Rocks State Park, N.M., 272, *272*
Clam River, Wis., 135
clams, 416
  razor, *417*, 444
Clark, William, 14–15, 296, 301, 305, 433, 443
Clark Landing, Mont., 296
Clark Peak, Ariz., 404
Clarke Museum, Eureka, Calif., 469
Clarks Fork Canyon, Wyo., 320–321, *320*
Clarkston, Wash., 301
Clatsop Beach, Ore., 444
Clatsop Plains Beaches, Ore., *445*
Clay, Mount, N.H., 29
Clear Lake, Ore., 437, *437*, 458
Clearwater River, Idaho, 301, 304, *304*, 306
Cleawox Lake, Ore., 447
Cleetwood Cove, Ore., 456
Cleetwood Trail, Ore., 456
Clements Mountain, Mont., **290–291**
Clepsydra Geyser, Wyo., 317
Cliffs of Beaver Creek, Ind., 81, *81*
Cliffs of Calvert, Md., 72, *72*
Cliffs of the Neuse, N.C., 100, *100*
Clifty Falls State Park, Ind., 81, *81*
Cline Falls, Ore., 437
Clingmans Dome, N.C. and Tenn., 87
Clinton, Mount, N.H., 29
Cloisters, New York, N.Y., 61
Cloudcap Mountain, Ore., 456
Cloudland Canyon, Ga., 10, *89*, **92**
Cloud Peak Primitive Area, Wyo., 320, 323
Clouds, Lake of the, Mich., **130**
clover, prairie, 164
Coachella Valley, Calif., 506, 507
coachwhips, western (snakes), **281**
Coal Canyon, Ariz., 383, *383*
Coast Range, Ore. and Wash., *415*, 444, 449, 450, **450**
coatimundis (animals), 402, 404
Cob Cave, Ark., 177
Cobscook Bay State Park, Me., *24*, 25
Coconino National Forest, Ariz., 386
Coeur d'Alene Lake, Idaho, 304, *304*, **305**, 306
Coeur d'Alene National Forest, Idaho, 304
Colburn Mineral Museum, Asheville, N.C., 92
Cold Spring, N.Y., 62
Cold Spring, Tex., 203
College of Southern Utah Museum of Natural History, Cedar City, Utah, 372

Collegiate Range, Colo., 245
Collier–Seminole State Park, Fla., 118, *118*
Collins, Floyd, 78
Colonial Peak, Wash., **427**
Colorado College Museum, Colorado Springs, Colo., 247
Colorado National Monument, Colo., *243*, **246–247**
  Natural History Museum, 247
Colorado Petrified Forest, Colo., 244
Colorado Plateau, 13, 349
Colorado River, 11, *203*, 204, 242, 299, 349, 353–354, *355*, 357, **358–359**, 364, **376**, 377, **380–381**, 382, *383*, 385, **386–387**, 506
Colorado River Road, Utah, 355–356, *355*
Colorado School of Mines Geology Museum, Golden, Colo., 247
Colorado Springs, Colo., *243*, **244**
Colter Bay, Wyo., 312
Colton Point State Park, Pa., 44
Colt State Park, R.I., 52, *52*
Columbia Glacier, Alaska, 516
Columbia River, Ore. and Wash., 14, 299, 426, 431, 437, 443, 445, 450
Columbia River Gorge, Ore. and Wash., 430–439, **430–431**, *432*, **433**, **436**, *437*
Columbia River Highway, Ore., 433
columbines, 156, 241, 367
  blue, 368
Columbus, Christopher, 14, 15
condors, California, 488
Connecticut River, Conn., 52, *52*, 53
Connecticut River Valley, **34**
Connors Pass, Nev., 369
Constitution, Mount, Wash., **417**
Continental Divide, **238**, 242, 243, *243*, 244, 245, 255, 262, 263, **263**, 292, 297, 318, **321**, 329, 397
Cook, Captain James, 521
Cook Inlet, Alaska, 515
Coolidge Dam, Ariz., 404
Coos Bay, Ore., *445*, 447, 449
coots (birds), black, 337
Copper Falls, Wis., 129, *129*
Copper Falls State Park, Wis., 129
Copper River Delta, Alaska, 515
Copper River Valley, Alaska, 515, *515*
Coquille Point, Ore., *445*
Coral Pink Sand Dunes, Utah, *369*, **373**
Cordova Area, Alaska, 515, *515*
Core Bank, N.C., 99
Corkscrew Swamp Wildlife Sanctuary, Fla., *118*, **121**
cormorants, 21, 214, **444**, 445
cornflowers, 164
Cornwall Bridge, Conn., 53
Coronado National Forest, Ariz., 404
Corps of Engineers Mississippi River Test Mockups, Vicksburg, Miss., 195
Corpus Christi, Tex., 199–200, *203*
  Museum, 205
Cortes, Hernando, 14
Cottonwood Canyon, Utah, *369*, *369*
Cottonwood Creek, Utah, 369
Cottonwood Falls, Kan., 164
Cottonwood Pass, Calif., 487, *487*
cottonwoods, 145, 225, **247**, 261, **274**, 297, 323, 357, 367, 486
  black, 413
cougars, 251, 261, 280, 293, 302, 339, 367, 377, 402, 404, 425, 436, 456
Courtebleu, Bayou, La., **188–189**, 190
Courthouse Rock, Neb., *234*, **235**
Cowhorn Mountain, Ore., 457
Cowhouse Island, Ga., 106
coyotes, 126, 136, 167, 183, 184, 202,

221, **252**, 261, 280–282, 289, 302, 328, 339, 377, 381, 436, 456, 468
crabs, 16
  blue, 74
  hermit, 445
  sand, 445
Craggy Gardens Visitor Center, Asheville, N.C., 92
cranberries, 64
  lowbush, 513
cranes
  sandhill, 106, 234
  whooping, **201**, 202, **205**
crappies (fish), 176, 195, 302
Crater Lake National Park, Ore., 450, 452–459, **452–453**, **455**, **456**, *457*
  Park Museum, 459
Craters of the Moon National Monument, Idaho, 324–333, **324–325**, **326–327**, **328**, *329*
  Museum, 332
Crawford Notch State Park, N.H., 32, *32*
Crazy Mountains, Mont., 294, *294*
Crescent, Lake, Wash., 410
Crescent Beach, Ore., **440–441**
Crescent Beach, Wash., 417
Crescent Beach State Park, Me., 25
Crescent City, Calif., 463, *466*
Crescent Lake, Ore., 457, *457*
Crescent Lake National Wildlife Refuge, Neb., 234, *234*
Crescent Rocks, Va., 70
crocodiles, 112
Crooked Lake, Minn., 128
Crooked River, Fla., 107, *107*
Crooked River Gorge, Ore., 437, *437*
Crook Point, Ore., 445
Crown Point, N.Y., 33
Crown Point, Ore., **430–431**, 433
crows, 69, 185, 424
Crystal Cave, Calif., 494
Crystal Cave, Ky., 78
Crystal Cave, Wis., 139, *139*
Crystal Geyser, Utah, 355, *357*
Crystal Ice Caves, Idaho, *329*, **331**
Crystal River, Colo., **247**
Cuba, Mo., 169
Cuchara Pass, Colo., 262, *262*
cuckoos, mangrove, 112
Cumberland Caverns, Tenn., 81, *81*
Cumberland Gap, Ky., Tenn. and Va., 90
Cumberland Head, N.Y., 33
Cumberland Island, Ga., 107, *107*
Cumberland Mountains, Ala. and Tenn., 81, 195
Cumbres Pass, Colo., 262 *262*
Curecanti Dams, Colo., 251, 254
Curecanti National Recreation Area, Colo., 254, 256
curlews, long-billed, 234
currants, 210
  wax, 251
Current River, Mo., **168–169**, 169–172, **170–171**, **173**, *174*
Curry Village, Yosemite, Calif., 17, 474
Cushman, Lake, Wash., 415, 416
Custer National Forest, S.D., 213
Custer State Park, S.D., 226
  Historical Museum and Zoo, 226
Cuyama Canyon Drive, Calif., 487, *487*
Cuyamaca Peak, Calif., 505
Cuyamaca Rancho State Park, Calif., 505, *505*
Cuyama River, Calif., 487
Cylburn Park Natural History Museum, Baltimore, Md., 74
cypresses, 82, 101, **101**, 105–107, **110–111**, 112, 118, 120, **188–189**, 190, 195, **488**, **489**

bald, 74, **105**, **121**
  Monterey, **497**
  pond, 105
Cypress Gardens, S.C., *100*, **101**, 103
Cypress Gardens, Winter Haven, Fla., 120

Daisies, 394
Dakota Zoo, Bismarck, N.D., 215
Dallas Divide, Colo., *253*, **254–255**, *257*
Dalles Gorge, Wis., 135–136, **137**, 137–138
Damariscotta River, Me., 25
Daniel Boone National Forest, Ky., 92
Dantes View, Calif., **498–499**, 504
Danville, Ark., **176**
Dardanelle, Lake, Ark., 176
Dark Hollow Falls, Va., 71
Dartmouth College Natural History Museum, Hanover, N.H., 35
Davenport Public Museum, Davenport, Iowa, 157
Davis Mountains State Park, Tex., 283, *283*, 285
Dead Horse Mountains, Tex., 282
Dead Horse Point, Utah, *355*, 357
  State Park Visitor Center, 359
Dead Indian Hill, Wyo., 321
Dead Man's Cave, Okla., 185
Death Valley National Monument, Calif., 496, 498–507, **498–499**, **500–501**, **502**, **503**, **504**, *505*
  Museum, 507
Deception Pass, Wash., 415, *415*
Deep Creek Canyon Drive, Mont., 294–295, *294*
deer, 21, 69, 71, 81, 88, 89, 106, 129, **134**, 153, 171, 190, 224, 226, 234, 261, 283, 293, 295, 404, 409, 410, **410–411**, 415, 436, 456, 468, 480, 489
  blacktailed, 425, 445
  kaibab, 383
  mule, 211, 221, 233, 242, **252**, 274, 280, 290, 302, 320, 328, 339, 367, 378, 395, 457–459
  Rocky Mountain mule, 396
  white-tailed, 88, **117**, 128, 136, 170, 180, 183, 184, 211, 280, 290, 297, 302, 320, 396, 402
Deer Creek Reservoir, Utah, 344
Deer Park, Wash., 409
Deerfield River, Mass., **54**
Deershelter Rock, Wis., 155
Delabar State Park, Ill., 155, *155*
Delano Peak, Utah, 369
Delaware Bay, N.J. and Del., 72
Delaware River, Del. and Pa., *63*, 64, **65**
Delaware Water Gap, Pa. and N.J., *63*, **65**
Delicate Arch, Utah, 351, **353**
Del Norte, Colo., 262
Del Norte Coast State Park, Calif., **462**, 463
Denali, Camp, Alaska, 514
Denali Highway, Alaska, 513, 515, *515*
Denver, Colo.
  Botanic Gardens, 247
  Museum of Natural History, 247
  Red Rocks Park, *243*, 244
Denys Bay, Me., 25
Depoe Bay, Ore., 445
Deschutes River Falls, Ore., 437, *437*
Deseret Peak, Utah, 342, *342*
Desert Botanical Garden of Arizona, Phoenix, Ariz., 405
Desert Game Reserve, Nev., 505, *505*
Desert View, Ariz., 385
Des Moines River, Iowa, 155
De Soto, Hernando, 14, 82, 90

De Soto Falls, Ala., *81*, **82**
De Soto Falls, Ga., *89*, 90
Destin, Fla., 194
Deva Temple, Ariz., 378
Devil's Backbone Road, Tex., *203*, 204
Devils Canyon, Calif., 496
Devil's Chair, Okla., 185
devil's-claw vines, 112
Devil's Coffin, Okla., 185
Devils' Den, Okla., 185, *185*
Devil's Den State Park, Ark., **174**, 175
Devil's Garden, Utah, **350–351**
Devil's Gate, Utah, 342
Devils Golf Course, Calif., **503**, 504
Devils Lake, Ore., 449, *449*
Devils Lake, Wis., *155*, **156–157**
Devils Orchard, Idaho, 326, 327
  Nature Trail, 328
Devils Postpile National Monument, Calif., 11, *478*, **481**
Devil's Punch Bowl, Iowa, 157
Devils River, Tex., 284
Devil's Slide, Utah, 342, *342*
Devil's Stair Steps, Colo., 262
Devils Tower National Monument, Wyo., 11, 206–215, **206–207**, **208**, **209**, **212**, *213*
  Park Museum, 215
D. H. Day State Park, Mich., 145
Diablo, Mount, Calif., 478, *478*
Diablo Lake, Wash., **427**
Diablo Range, Calif., 487
Diamond Head, Oahu, Hawaii, 524, *524*, 526
Diamond Lake, Ore., 457, *457*
Diamond Peak Wilderness, Ore., 457, 459
Diamond Shoals, N.C., 98
Diamondville, Wyo., 342
Dighton Rock State Park, Mass., *52*, 52
Dillon Reservoir, Colo., *243*, 244
Dingmans Falls, Pa., 64
Dinosaur National Monument, Colo. and Utah, *243*, **247**, 342, **344–345**
  Quarry Visitor Center, 247
dippers, *see* ouzels
Dixville Mountains, N.H., 32
Dixville Notch, N.H., 32, *32*
Dodge, Col. Richard I., 209–210
Doe River, N.C. and Tenn., **93**
dogwoods, 71, 80, 86, 88, 105, 171, 175, 416
  bunchberry, **425**
Dolliver Memorial State Park, Iowa, 155, *155*
Dolly Sods Scenic Area, W.Va., 72–73, *72*
Dolores River, Colo., 254
Dolores River Overlook, Colo., *253*, 254
dolphins, 117, 194
Donner Lake, Calif., 478
Donner Memorial State Park, Calif., 478, *478*
Door Trail, S.D., 222, **222–223**
Doran Drive, Calif., 505
Dose Cascades, Wash., 415
Dose Meadow, Wash., 415
Dosewallips River, Wash., 415
Dosewallips State Park, Wash., 415, *415*
doves, 368
  ground, 282
  mourning, 69, 404
  rock, 233
  white-winged, 401, 404
Dragoon Mountains, Ariz., 403
"D" River, Ore., 449
Drive Through the Ages, Utah, 342, *342*
dryads (flowers), **425**
dryas (plants), 513
Dry Diggins Lookout, Idaho, **300**, 301, 302, 307
Dry Falls, Wash., 426, *426*

Dubuque, Iowa, 154, *155*
Duchesne River, Utah, 345
Duck Creek, Utah, 371
Ducknest Falls, Wis., 140
Duck Rock, Fla., **117**
ducks, 100, 101, **108**, 125, 153, 185–187, 205, 214, 416, 468
  black, 136
  mallard, 136
  wood, 136
Duluth, Minn., 135, 137
Dunderberg Mountain, N.Y., 59
Dunedin, Fla., 118
Dungeness National Wildlife Refuge, Wash., *415*, 416
Durango, Colo., **257**
  Public Library Museum, 256
dusty millers (plants), 51
Dworshak Dam and Fish Hatchery, Idaho, 304, *304*

Eagle Cap Wilderness, Ore., 438
Eagle Falls, Wash., 428
Eagle Lake, Me., **22**, 23
Eagle River, Alaska, 515
eagles, 125, 242, 291, 456
  bald, **53**, 64, 149, 153, 186, 302, 311, 436, **459**
  golden, 186, 251, 261, 293, 302, 345, 367, 436
Earthquake Area Visitor Center, Mont., 332
Earthquake Lake, Mont., 329, *329*
East Central State College Museum, Ada, Okla., 187
Eastham, Mass., 49
East Lake, Ore., 459
East Temple, Utah, 367
Echo Lake, Me., 23
Echo Lake State Park, N.H., 32, 33
Ecola State Park, Ore., **440–441**, 445, *445*
Edgerton Highway, Alaska, 515
Edisto Beach State Park, S.C., 100, *100*
eelgrass, 466
Eel River, Calif., 466, 468
Effigy Mounds National Monument, Iowa, 152, *155*
Egg Island, Utah, 338
egrets (birds), 192, 466
  American, 119
  cattle, 119, **190–191**
  reddish, 205
  snowy, **110–111**, 112, 119, **190–191**
Eielson Visitor Center, Alaska, 513, 516
Eisenhower, Mount, N.H., 29
Elbert, Mount, Colo., 245
El Camino del Rio, Tex., *283*, **285**
El Capitan, Yosemite, Calif., 11, 473, **474**, 475
El Capitan Mountain, Tex., 267
El Dorado, Calif., 478
Elephant Butte Reservoir, N.M., 272, 272
Elephant Hill, Utah, 354
Elephant Rocks, Mo., *174*, 175
Eleven Point National Scenic River, Mo., *173*, *174*, 175
Elijah, Mount, Ore., **451**
Elk River, Mo., 176
elks, 166, 180–183, 224, 234–235, 242, **252**, 261, **274–275**, 290–291, 293, 295, 297, 302, 306, 311, 318, 320, 394, 397, 415
  Roosevelt, **413**, 445, 449, 457, 459
  Tule, 496
Ellensburg, Wash., 428
Elmer Thomas, Lake, Okla., 184
El Morro National Monument, N.M.,

394–395, *394*
elms, 51
Eloise Butler Wildflower Garden, Theodore Wirth State Park, Minneapolis, Minn., 141
Elsie, Ore., 449
Elsinore, Lake, Calif., 507
El Valle Grande, N.M., *394*, 395
Elwha River Valley, Wash., 410
Ely, Minn., 128
Ely Scenic Drive, Nev., 369, *369*
Emerald Falls, Tenn., 91
Emerald Mound, Miss., 194
Emerald Pool, Utah, 367
Eminence, Mo., 172, *174*
Emmons Glacier Vista Trail, Wash., 424
Emporia, Kan., 164, *165*
Enchanted Mesa, N.M., *394*, 395–396
Enchanted Rock, Tex., *203*, 204
Endless Mountains, Pa., 45
Engineer Mountain, Colo., 255
Englewood, N.J., 61
Enterprise, Ore., 302
Erie, Lake, 42, *43*, 44
Erie Canal, 62
Ernie's Country, Utah, 353
Escambia River, Fla., *194*, 195
Estes, Joel, 239, 242
Estes, Lake, Colo., 239
Estes Park, Colo., 239, 242, 243, *243*
  Village, 239
eucalyptuses, 52, 526
Eunice, Lake, Wash., **418–419**
Eureka, Calif., 461
Eureka, Kan., 162–164, *165*
Evangeline Oak, La., 191
Evans, Mount, Colo., *243*, 245
Evans Notch, Me., 24, 25
Evansville Museum of Arts and Sciences, Evansville, Ind., 83
Everett, Mount, Mass., 52, 54
Everglades City, Fla., 115, *118*
Everglades National Park, Fla., 17, 110–121, **110–111**, **112–113**, **114**, **115**, **116**, **117**, *118*
Everglades Wonder Gardens, Bonita Springs, Fla., 120
Everhart Museum of Natural History, Science and Art, Scranton, Pa., 65

Fairbanks, Alaska, 17, 513
Fairbanks Museum of Natural History, St. Johnsbury, Vt., 35
Fairchild Tropical Garden, Fla., 119
Fairweather Range, Alaska, **517**
Fairy Falls, Wash., 477
Fairyland–Tower Bridge–Bryce Trail, Utah, 367
falcons, 456
  peregrine, 202, 251
  prairie, 233
Fall River, Colo., 239, 241, 242
Fall River Pass, Colo., 241, 242
Fall River Road, Colo., 242
Falls Creek Falls State Park, Tenn., *89*, 90–91
Falls View Bridge, N.Y., 40
Farewell Canyon, Calif., **496**
Farewell Gap Pass, Calif., **496**
Fargo, Ga., 106, *107*
Farnsworth Park, Ohio, 149
Farview Curve Overlook, Colo., 242
Feather River Canyon, Calif., *466*, **467**
Federal Aquarium, Guttenberg, Iowa, 157
fendlerbushes, cliff, 378
Fenske Lake, Minn., **122–123**
Fern Canyon, Calif., 464

Ferndale Coastal Drive, Calif., 466, *466*
Ferndell Nature Museum, Los Angeles, Calif., 496
Fern Grotto, Kauai, Hawaii, 524, *524*
ferns, 33, 70, 82, **116**, 153, 156, **302–303**, 304–305, 367, 385, **405**, 449, 464, 466, **479**, 480
  leather, 113
  oak, 251
  strap, 118
  tree, 524
ferrets, black-footed, 210
Fidalgo Island, Wash., 415
figs, strangler, 112, 119
finches, 424
Finger Lakes, N.Y., 43
Firehole River, Wyo., 316
Fire Island, N.Y., *52*, 53
firs, 21, 86, **93**, 378, 480, 485
  alpine, 413
  balsam, 29, 71, 86, 91, 125
  Douglas, 241, 251, 289, 368, 380, 413, **425**, 442, 449, 458, 463, **465**
  noble, **425**
  Pacific silver, 413, **425**
  subalpine, 289, **425**
Fish Creek, Calif., 505
Fish Creek Canyon, Ariz., 403
Fish Creek Falls, Colo., *243*, 244
fishers (animals), 289, 468
  Pacific, 494
Fisher's Cave, Mo., 176
Fisher's Gap, Va., 71
Fisher Towers, Utah, *355*, 357
Flag Rock, Va., *89*, 91
Flagstaff, Ariz., 378, *383*
Flaming Gorge National Recreation Area, Utah and Wyo., *342*, **345**
Flamingo, Fla., 116, *118*
flamingos, 116, 119
  pink, 118
Flanders Nature Center, Woodbury, Conn., 55
Flathead Lake, Mont., **294**, **296–297**
Flathead River Drive, Mont., *294*, 295
Flathead Valley, Mont., **295**
Flattop Mountain, Wyo., **323**
flickers (birds)
  gilded, 401
  red-shafted, 328
Flint Hills, Kan., 158–167, **158–159**, **160**, **162–163**, **164**, *165*
Florence, Ore., **444**, 445, *445*, 446, 449
Florida Mountains, N.M., 274
Florida's Gulfarium, Fort Walton Beach, Fla., 195
Florida State Museum, Gainesville, Fla., 120
Florissant Fossil Beds National Monument, Colo., *243*, 244
Flume, The, N.H., 32, *32*
Flume Brook, N.H., 32
Flume Cascade, N.H., 32
flycatchers
  elepaio, 522
  scissor-tailed, 183
  Western, 211
Folkston, Ga., 106, *107*
Font's Point, Calif., 505
Forest Canyon, Colo., **238**, 242
Forest Capital Center, Perry, Fla., 109
Forks, Wash., 413
Fort Clatsop, Ore., 443
Fort Cobb Crow Roost, Okla., 185, *185*
Fort Cobb Reservoir, Okla., 185
Fort Hays Kansas State College Museum, Hays, Kan., 167
Fort Niobrara National Wildlife Refuge, Neb., 234, *234*
  Natural History Museum, 235
Fort Tryon Park, New York, N.Y., 61

Fort Wilkins State Park Museum, Copper Harbor, Mich., 131
Forty Mile Bend, Fla., 115
Forty-Niner Gold Route, Calif., 478, *478*
Fossil Fish Beds, Wyo., 342, *342*
Fossil Forest, Wyo., 318
fossils, 152–153, 154, 162, 165, 219, **221**, 226, 233–235, 292, 382, 383
Foster Botanic Gardens, Honolulu, Oahu, Hawaii, 526
Fountain Paint Pots, Wyo., 317
Four Corners Museum, Cortes, Colo., 256
foxes, 21, 126, 136, 182, 226, 392
 Cascade red, 456
 gray, 69, 104, 162, 368
 kit, 503
 red, 233, **252**
Franconia Notch, N.H., 32–33, *32*
Franconia State Park, N.H., 32
Franklin, Mount, N.H., 29
Franklin Cliffs, Va., 70
Franklin and Marshall College North Museum, Lancaster, Pa., 45
Fredonia, Ariz., 369
Fremont Island, Utah, **338**
Fremont Lake, Wyo., *320*, 321
Fremont Peak, Calif., 487, *487*
Fremont River, Utah, 367
Frenchglen, Ore., 459
French King Bridge, Mass., *52*, 53
Frenchman Bay, Me., 21
Fresno, Calif., 491, *495*
 Museum, 489
frigate birds, 120
frogs
 green tree, **105**
 pig, **105**
Frontenac State Park, Minn., 139
Frozen Niagara, Mammoth Cave, Ky., 80
Furnace Creek, Calif., 503, *504*
Fur Trade, Wildlife and Indian Museum, Medora, N.D., 215
Fusillade Mountain, Mont., **286–287**

Galena, Ill., 154
Galena Summit, Idaho, 329, *329*
Gallatin Range, Wyo., 318
Gallatin Valley, Mont., *294*, 295–296
Galveston, Tex., 200, *203*
Galveston Beach, Tex., *203*, **204**
Galveston Island, Tex., **204**
Gannett Peak, Wyo., **321**, 323
Garberville, Calif., 466
Garden in the Woods, Framingham, Mass., 55
Garden of the Gods, Colo., 241, *243*, **244**
Garden Wall, Mont., 292
Garrison, N.Y., 62, *62*
Garrison Dam, N.D., 214
Gaston Museum of Natural History, Gastonia, N.C., 92
Gate, The, Colo., *253*, 256
Gates of the Mountains, Mont., *294*, 296
Gatlinburg, Tenn., 87
Gay Head Cliffs, Mass., *52*, **55**
Gearhart Wilderness Area, Ore., 457, *457*
geese, 153, 186–187, 205, 234, 416, 468
 Canada, 75, 100, 101, 108, 129, 139, 244
Gem Village Museum, Bayfield, Colo., 256
General Sherman Tree, Calif., 491, **494**
Generals Highway, Calif., 493–494

Genesee Gorge, N. Y., *43*, 44
Genesee River, N.Y., 44
Gene Stratton Porter State Memorial, Ind., 147
Geneva State Park, Ohio, *43* 44
gentians (plants), 149
 blue, **425**
Geographical Center of North America, N.D., 213, *213*
George, Lake, N.Y., *32*, 33, *35*
Georgetown Lake Area, Mont., *294*, 296
George Washington Bridge, N.Y. and N.J., 61
Gerlach Geyser Area, Nev., *466*, *466*
Ghost Forest, Colo., 260
Ghost Ranch Museum, Abiquiu, N.M., 397
Giantess Geyser, Wyo., 316
Giant Forest, Calif., **492**
Giants Graveyard, Wash., 413
Giant Springs, Mont., 296
Giant Sycamore Tree, Mass., *52*, 53
Giant Tufa Formations, Nev., *466*, *466*
Gila Cliff Dwellings National Monument, N.M., 272, *272*
Gila River, Ariz., 403, 404
gilias (herbs), 378
gingers, torch, **523**
Ginkgo Petrified Forest, Wash., 426, *426*
 State Park Museum, 429
Glacier Bay National Monument, Alaska, *515*, **516–517**
Glacier National Park, Mont., 286–297, **286–287**, 288, 290–291, 292, 294
 Museum, 297
Glacier Peak Wilderness, Wash., 426, *426*
Glacier Point, Calif., **472**
Glass Buttes, Ore., 457–458, *457*
Glass Mountain, Calif., 466, *466*
Glass Mountain, Okla., 185–186, *185*
Glen Arbor, Mich., 146, *147*
Glen Canyon Dam, Utah, **358–359**, 381
 Visitor Center, 359
Glen Ellis Falls, N.H., *32*, 33
Glen Haven, Mich., 145, 146
Glen Lake, Mich., 145, 146
Glenwood Canyon, Colo., *243*, 245
Goat Island, N.Y., **38–39**, 39, 40
goats, mountain, 290–291, **293**, 295, 302, 306, **306**, 410, 425
goat's rue (plants), **172**
Goblin Valley, Utah, *355*, 357
Gogebic, Lake, Mich., 129, *129*
Going-to-the-Sun Highway, Mont., 291
Gold Beach, Calif., 463
Gold Beach, Ore., 448, **451**
Gold Camp Road, Colo., *243*, 245
Golden Gate, Calif., 461, **485**
Golden Spike National Historic Site, Utah, 340–341
Good Harbor Bay, Mich., 146
gooseberries, 251
Goose Lake, Wash., 438
Goosenecks of the San Juan River, Utah, *355*, 357
gophers, 202
Gordonsville Turnpike, Va., 71
Goshen Pass, Va., *72*, 73
Gotham, Wis., 156
Grabens, Utah, 354
Grafton Notch State Park, Me., 24, *25*
grama grasses, **163**
Granby, Colo., 242, *243*
Grand Canyon, Ariz., 10, 16, 299, **301**, 362–363, 374–387, **374–375**, **376**, **378–379**, **380–381**, **382**, *383*
 National Park Tusayan Museum, 387
Grand Canyon Caverns, Ariz., 383, *383*
Grand Canyon of the Yellowstone,

Wyo., 317, **319**
Grand Coulee Area, Wash., 426, *426*
Grand Coulee Dam, Wash., 426, 427, 428
Granddad Bluff, Wis., **140–141**
Grandfather Mountain, N.C., *89*, 91
Grand Island, Neb., 166–167
Grand Isle, La., 194, *194*
Grand Isle, Vt., 33
Grand Lake, Colo., 242
Grand Lake, Me., 24, 25
Grand Lake o' the Cherokees, Okla., *174*, 175
Grand Loop Road, Wyo., 318
Grand Mesa, Colo., *243*, 245
Grand Portage National Monument, Minn., 128, 129, *129*
Grand Prismatic Hot Spring, Wyo., 318
Grand Prix, Calif., 486
Grand Rapids Public Museum, Mich., 149
Grand River, Okla., 175
Grand Sable Banks, Mich., 129
Grand Sable Dunes, Mich., 129, *129*
Grand Teton National Park, Wyo., 308–323, **308–309**, 310, **312–313**, *320*
 Museum, 323
Grandview Point, Utah, **346–347**, 351
Granite Dells, Ariz., 383, *383*
Granite Park Chalet, Mont., 292
Granite Peak, Mont., 296
Gran Quivira National Monument, N.M., 272, *272*
Grantsburg River, Wis., 136
Grants Pass, Ore., 449
Grant, Ulysses, 15
Granville Gulf, Vt., 34
grapes
 Oregon, **424**
 sea, 118
Grasshopper Glacier, Mont., *294*, 296
grasshoppers, 503
Grasslands Trail, Tex., 202
Great Arch, Utah, 367
Great Falls of the Missouri River, Mont., *294*, 296
Great Falls of the Potomac, Md. and Va., *72*, **75**
Great Gulf Wilderness, N.H., **28–29**, 31
Great Kauai Volcanic Dome, Kauai, Hawaii, 521
Great Lakes, 62, 128
 see also Erie; Huron; Michigan; Ontario; Superior
Great Marathon Basin, Tex., 283, *283*
Great Rift, Idaho, 325–326, **326–327**
Great River Road, Ill. and Iowa, 154
Great Salt Lake, Utah, **336**, **338–339**, 342, *342*, 364
Great Salt Lake Desert, Utah, 334–345, **334–335**, **340–341**, *342*
Great Salt Lake State Park, Utah, 337
Great Salt Plains National Wildlife Refuge, Okla., *185*, 186
Great Sand Dunes National Monument, Colo., 258–263, **258–259**, 260, 261, *262*
 Park Museum, 263
Great Smoky Mountains National Park, N.C. and Tenn., 72, 84–93, **84–85**, **86–87**, *89*
 Museum, 92
Great Swamp National Wildlife Refuge, N.J., *63*, 64
Great Swamp Wilderness, R.I., *52*, 53
Great West Wall, Utah, 367
Great White Throne, Utah, 367, **367**
Green Belt Conservation Area, Ariz., 403–404, *403*
Green Mountain National Forest, Vt., 34

Green Mountains, Vt., 11, 33
Green River, Ky., 80, **80**
Green River, Utah and Wyo., **247**, *320*, **322**, **344–345**, 349, 353, *355*
Green River Canyon, Wash., *426*, 427
Green River Lakes, Wyo., *320*, **323**
Green Spring, Mo., 175
Green Swamp, Fla., 118, *118*
Greenwood Ice Caves, Me., *24*, 25
Gregory Lake, Calif., 506
Gregorys Bald, N.C., and Tenn., 88
Greylock, Mount, Mass., *52*, **53**
Greysolon, Daniel, 137
Grinnell Glacier, Mont., 289
Grosvenor Arch, Utah, 369
Gros Ventre Range, Wyo., 321
Grote's Landing, N.Y., 34
Grotto Geyser, Wyo., 316
grouse, 234, 291, 424
    blue, 302
    Franklin, 302
    ruffed, 69, 129, 302
    sage, 468
    sharp-tailed, 136
Guadalupe Mountains, Tex., 267
Guadalupe Mountains National Park, Tex., *272*, **274–275**
Guadalupe Peak, Tex., **274–275**
Guadalupe River, Tex., 204
Gulf of Mexico, 12, 14, *107*, *118*, 120, 151, 183, 190, 193, 194, *194*, 199, 200
Gulfport, Miss., *194*, 195
Gull Rock, Ore., 448
gulls, 21, 51, 153, 214, 337
    California, 338–339
gumbo-limbo trees, 112
gums (trees)
    black, 53, 105, 174
    red, 174
Gunnisonian-Quaker Hill Museum of Natural History, Pawling, N.Y., 65
Gunnison Island, Utah, 339
Gunnison Point, Colo., 251
Gunnison River, Colo., **248–249**, 249, 253

Hackberries, 112, 162
Haddam Meadows State Park, Conn., 52
Haena Point, Kauai, Hawaii, 522
Hagerman National Wildlife Refuge, Tex., 187
Halawa Valley, Molokai, Hawaii, 524, *524*
Haleakala Crater, Maui, Hawaii, *524*, 525, **527**
Half Dome, Yosemite, Calif., 11, **301**, **470–471**, 476, **477**
Halona Blow Hole, Oahu, Hawaii, 524, *524*
Hamilton, Mount, Calif., 487, *487*
Hamlin Beach State Park, N.Y., *43*, 44
Hammocks Beach, N.C., 100, *100*
Hampton Museum of Marine Life, Morehead City, N.C., 101
Hanalei Valley, Kauai, Hawaii, 524–525, *524*
Hanauma Bay, Oahu, Hawaii, *524*, **526**
Hanging Boulder, N.H., 34
Hanging Lake, Colo., 245
Hanover College Geology Museum, Hanover, Ind., 83
hares, 128
Harney Peak, S.D., 224, *224*
Harpers Ferry, W.Va., 72, 73
Harriman, N.Y., 60
Harris Beach State Park, Ore., *445*
Harrisburg, Pa., 45
Harrison State Park, Pa., 44
Hart Mountain National Antelope Ref-

uge, Ore., *457*, 458
Harts Pass, Wash., 427
Hartwick Pines, Mich., *147*, **148**
Harvard, Mount, Colo., 245
Harvard University Geological Museum, Boston, Mass., 55
Hatch Point, Utah, 355
Hat Point, Ore., 302
Hatteras Inlet, N.C., 98
Hatteras Island, N.C., 98–99
Hatteras Light, N.C., 98
Havasu, Lake, Ariz., *383*, **386–387**
Havasu Creek, Ariz., **381**
Havasu Waterfall, Ariz., 377, **382**
Haverstraw, N.Y., 60
Hawaii Island, Hawaii, 524–526, *524*
Hawaii Volcanoes National Park, Hawaii, 525
    Museum, 526
Hawk Falls, Pa., 64
Hawk Mountain, Pa., *43*, 44
hawks, 44, 136, 242, 291, 302, 368
    marsh, **201**, 202
    night, 162, 328
    red-tailed, 251
    sharp-shinned, 69
    sparrow, 233, 261
Hawksbill, N.C., 91
Hawksbill Mountain, Va., 71
Hawks Nest, W.Va., *89*, 91
Hayden, Mount, Colo., **257**
Haystack Mountain, Vt., *32*, 33
hazelnuts, 51
Hazens Notch, Vt., 33
Heads, The, Ore., 447
Headwall, N.H., 31
Hearts Content Scenic Area, Pa., 43
heath, 449
heather, 54
    beach, **51**
    red, **425**
    white, **425**
Heaven's Gate Observation Point, Idaho, 302, 306–307
H. E. Bailey Turnpike, Okla., 183
Hebgen Lake, Idaho, 329
Heceta Beach, Ore., *445*
He Devil Peak, Idaho, 299
Hegman Lake, Minn., **128**
Helena, Mont., 297
Helena National Forest, Mont., 295
Hellgate Canyon, Ore., 449, *449*
Hells Canyon, Idaho and Ore., **298–307**, **298–299**, **300**, **302–303**, *304*, 428
Hells Canyon Dam, Idaho, 301, 303
Hell's Half Acre, Tex., 283
Hell's Half Acre, Wyo., *320*, 321
hemlocks, 21, 29, 43, 54, 64, 69, 80, 82, 86, 289, 442, 449, 477
    mountain, **425**
    western, 413, **425**
Hennepin, Louis, 38–39, 137
Henry Mountains, Utah, 352, 355, *355*, 357
Henry's Fork, Idaho, 330
Herbert C. Bonner Bridge, N.C., 98
herons, 107, 119, **190–191**, 466
    blue-crowned night, **117**
    great blue, 136, 162, 170, **201**, 202, 337, 339, 367
    little blue, **117**
herring, 342
Hetch Hetchy Valley, Calif., 473
Heyburn State Park, Idaho, 304, *304*
Hiawatha National Forest, Mich., 130
hibiscuses, 522, **522**
hickories, 69, 118, 170, 174
Hickory Run State Park, Pa., *63*, 64
Hidden Lake, Mont., 292
Hidden Valley, Calif., **507**
Hidden Valley, Colo., 242

Higgins Hollow, Mass., **50**
High Cliff State Park, Wis., 139, *139*
High Falls, Minn., 129
High Falls Gorge, N.Y., 35
High Head, Mass., 49
High Knob Mountain, Va., 91
Highland Lakes Chain, Tex., *203*, 204
Highland Light, Truro, Mass., 49
Highland Recreation Area, Mich., *147*, 148
Highlands, Hudson, N.Y., 11, 59
High Point, Colo., 251
High Point State Park, N.J., *63*, 64
High-Rollway Overlook, Mich., *147*, **148**
High Sierra Loop, Calif., 476
High Tor, N.Y., 60
High Trail Ridge, Okefenokee, Ga., 103–104
High Uintas Primitive Area, Utah, *342*, **345**
Hillers, Mount, 355
Hillman, John Wesley, 453–454
Hillman Peak, Ore., 456
Hindu Temples, Utah, 367
Hipuapua Waterfall, Molokai, Hawaii, 524
Hiram Blauvelt Wildlife Museum, Oradell, N.J., 65
Hither Hills State Park, N.Y., 54
Hobart and William Smith Colleges Museum, Geneva, N.Y., 45
Hobo Cedar Grove, Idaho, 304, *304*
Hoh Rain Forest, Wash., 16, **408**
Hoh River, Wash., **406–407**, 411
Holden Arboretum, Mentor, Ohio, 45
hollies, 53, 97, 100, 119
Holy City, Okla., 184
Holy City, Wyo., 322
Homer, Alaska, 515
    Homer Society of Natural History, 516
Homestead, Fla., 116, *118*
Homosassa Springs, Fla., 118, *118*
Honey Creek, Okla., 187
Honey Creek State Park, Iowa, 156
Honolulu, Oahu, Hawaii, 519, 524, *524*, 526
Hood, Mount, Ore., 427, 431, 435, 437, *437*, 438, **439**
Hood Canal, Wash., 409, *415*, 416, 417
Hood Canal Drive, Wash., *415*, 416
Hood River, Ore., 435
Hood River Valley, Ore., 437, *437*
Hoover Dam, Ariz. and Nev., 385
Hopewell Gap, W.Va., 74
Hopewell Lake, N.M., 397
Hord Lake Recreation Area, Neb., *165*, **166–167**
Horicon National Wildlife Refuge, Wis., 139, *139*
horsemint (flowers), **172**
horses, wild, 320, 338
Horseshoe Canyon, Utah, **352**, 354
Horseshoe Falls, *see* Niagara Falls
Horseshoe Park, Colo., 241, 242
Hot Springs, Mont., 304, *304*
Hot Springs National Park, Ark., *174*, 175–176
    Museum, 177
Housatonic Meadows State Park, Conn., 53
Housatonic River, Conn., *52*, 53
House on the Rock, Wis., 155, *155*
Hovenweep National Monument, Colo., 253, 254
Hoyt Arboretum, Portland, Ore., 438
huapalas (flowers), **523**
huckleberries, **51**, 463
Hudson River, 34, **56–57**, *58*, 59–62, *61*, *63*
Hudson Valley, 56–65

Hueco Tanks, Tex., 272, 274
huisache trees, 282
Hulls Cove, Acadia, Me., 21
Humboldt Bay, Calif., 466, *466*
Humboldt Redwoods State Park, Calif., 466, *466*
Humboldt State University, Arcata, Calif., 469
Humbug Mountain State Park, Ore., *445*
hummingbirds, 242
Humphreys Peak, Ariz., 378
Hungry Horse Reservoir Area, Mont., 294, 296–297
Huntington Beach State Park, S.C., 100–101, *100*
Huron, Lake, Mich., 148
Huron Mountains, Mich., 129
Huron National Forest, Mich., *147*, 148
Huron River Falls, Mich., 129, *129*
Hurricane Ridge, Wash., 409, **410–411**
Hurricane Scenic Drive, Ariz. and Utah, 369, *369*
Hyner View, Pa., *43*, **44**

Iao Valley, Maui, Hawaii, *524*, **525**
ibises (birds)
    scarlet, 112
    white, **117**, 118
Ice Age National Scientific Reserve, Wis., 139
Ice Caves, Wash., 437, *437*
Ichetucknee Springs State Park, Fla., 107, *107*
Ichthyosaur Paleontologic State Monument, Nev., 478, *478*
Idaho Falls, Idaho, 330
Idleyld Park, Ore., 450
Igloo Canyon, Alaska, 511
Ile des Cannes, La., 190
ilihais (trees), 522
Illilouette Falls, Calif., 476, **476**
Illinois Falls, Ore., 449
Illinois River, Okla., 177
Illinois River Valley, Ore., 449, *449*
Imperial Valley, Calif., 506
Independence, Mo., **232**
Indiana Dunes National Lakeshore, Ind., *147*, **148–149**
Indian grasses, 161, **163**
Indian Head, Ill., 152–153
Indian Lake, N.Y., **34**
Indian paintbrushes (flowers), 241, 368, **394**
Indian pipes (plants), 88
Indian River, N.Y., *32*, **34**
indigo, wild, 164
    white-stem, 202
Indio, Calif., 506
Inks Lake, Tex., 204
Inner Gorge, Ariz., 377, **378**, 380, 381–382
Inscription House, Ariz., 386
Inspiration Point, Utah, **360–361**
Intermittent Spring, Wyo., *320*, 321
Interstate Park, Wis., **137**
Intracoastal Waterway, 193, 202
Inyo Craters, Calif., 478, *478*
Iowa State Museum, Des Moines, Iowa, 157
ipecac (plants), **172**
irises
    Georgia, **105**
    Rocky Mountain, 241
Iron Mountain Road, S.D., 224, *224*
ironwood (trees), 404
Isabella, Lake, Calif., 495
Island Beach State Park, N.J., *63*, 64
Island Park, Utah, 247

Island in the Sky, Utah, 349, 353
Isle au Haut, Me., 21, 24
Isle Royale National Park, Mich., *129*, **131**
    Park Museum, 131
Izatys, Wis., 137

Jack Diehm Museum of Natural History, Fort Wayne, Ind., 149
Jacks Fork River, Mo., 169, 172, **173**, *174*
Jackson, Mount, Mont., 292
Jackson, Mount, N.H., 29
Jackson Hole, Wyo., 311–312, *320*, 322
Jackson Hole Highway, Wyo., 313
Jackson Lake, Wyo., 311, 312
Jacob Lake, Ariz., 380, 383, *383*
Jacob's ladders, alpine (herbs), **425**
Jade Cove, Calif., 487, *487*
Jamaica Bay Wildlife Refuge, New York, N.Y., *63*, 64
James River, Va., 71, 72
Jam Up Cave, Mo., 169
Jarbidge Wilderness, Nev., 342, *342*
Jarvi Memorial Vista, Calif., 496
jasmine, 105
javelinas (wild pigs), 282, 404
Jay Cooke State Park, Minn., 129, *129*
Jay Peak, Vt., *32*, 33
jays
    blue, 112, 380
    Canada, 302
    green, 205
    Oregon, 425
    scrub, 251
    Steller's, 302, 380
Jeanerette, La., 190, **194**
Jedediah Smith State Park, Calif., 463
Jefferson, Mount, N.H., **28—29**, 29
Jefferson, Mount, Ore., 437, *437*
Jefferson Island, La., 192
Jefferson Rock, W.Va., 73
Jefferson, Thomas, 14
Jekyll Island, Ga., 107, *107*
Jemez Mountains, N.M., 395
Jennison Trailside Museum, Bay City, Mich., 149
Jenny Lake, Wyo., 312
Jerktail Landing, Mo., 169
Jewel Cave, Tenn., 81, *81*
Jewel Cave National Monument, S.D., 224, *224*
Jewell Wildlife Meadows, Ore., 449, *449*
jimsonweeds, 377
J. N. ("Ding") Darling National Wildlife Refuge, Sanibel, Fla., **121**
Jockey Ridge, N.C., 97, **99**
John A. Finch Arboretum, Spokane, Wash., 429
John Day Fossil Beds State Park, Ore., 437, **439**
John Muir Trail, Calif., 493
John Pennekamp Coral Reef State Park, Fla., *118*, **121**
Johnson Sauk Trail State Park, Ill., 155, *155*
Johnson's Shut-ins State Park, Mo., *174*, **177**
Joliet, Louis, 14, **14–15**
Jonas Ridge, N.C., 91
Jordan Pond, Acadia, Me., 21, **22**
Jordan River, Utah, 339
Jordan Valley, Mich., *147*, 148
Jordan Valley Wilderness Area, Mich., 148
Joseph, Ore., 302
Joshua Tree National Monument, Calif., *505*, **507**

    Museum, 507
Joshua trees, **507**
Juan de Fuca Strait, Wash., 409, *415*, 416, 417
Jump Off Joe, Ore., 442–443
juncos (birds), 251
Jungle Gardens, La., **190**, 192
junipers, 145, 210, 221, **244**, 368, 378, 477
    piñon, 251
    Rocky Mountain, 233, 368
Juniper Springs, Fla., *118*, 119

Kaana Ridge, Kauai, Hawaii, 522
Kabob Terrace, Utah, 367
Kachemak Bay, Alaska, 515, *515*
Kaibab National Forest, Ariz., 383, *383*
Kaibab Plateau, Ariz., **376**, 378, **378–379**, 382
Kalaloch, Wash., 16, 414, *415*
Ka Lae, Hawaii, Hawaii, *524*, 525
Kalalau Overlook, Kauai, Hawaii, **520**, 522
Kalalau Valley, Kauai, Hawaii, 522
Kalamazoo Nature Center, Mich., 149
Kalamazoo River, Mich., *147*, 148
Kalapana Black Sand Beach, Hawaii, Hawaii, *524*, 525
Kalaupapa Peninsula, Molokai, Hawaii, 526
Kalmiopsis Wilderness, Ore., 449, *449*
Kanab, Utah, 380
Kanab Scenic Drive, Utah, 369, 370
Kancamagus Highway, N.H., *32*, 33
Kaneshe Bay, Oahu, Hawaii, 526
Kanopolis State Park, Kan., 165–166, *165*
Kansas Forestry Fish and Game Commission exhibits, Pratt, Kan., 167
Kansas State Teachers College Biology Museum, Emporia, Kan., 167
Kansas State University Herbarium and Zoological Museum, Manhattan, Kan., 167
Katahdin, Mount, Me., **24**, **25**
Katmai National Monument, Alaska, *515*, **516–517**
Kauai Island, Hawaii, 519, 522, *524*–526, *524*, **526–527**
Kauffman Museum, Bethel College, North Newton, Kan., 167
Kaumakani, Kauai, Hawaii, 521
Kautz, Lieutenant August, 421
Kautz Creek, Wash., 422
Kaweak River Canyon, Calif., **494**
Keanae Valley, Maui, Hawaii, *524*, 525
Keet Seel (Indian ruins), Ariz., 386
Kekaha, Kauai, Hawaii, 521
Kelleys Island, Ohio, *147*, 148
Kellogg Bird Sanctuary of Michigan State University, Richland, Mich., 149
Kenai Lake Area, Alaska, 515, *515*
Kennebec River, Me., **24**, 25
Kensington Park Nature Center, Milford, Mich., 149
Kent Falls, Conn., 10, *52*, **54**
Kentucky Lake, Ky. and Tenn., 82
Kentucky State Game Farm, Frankfort, Ky., 92
Kern County Museum, Bakersfield, Calif., 496
Kern River Canyon, Calif., 495, *495*
Kern River State Park, Calif., 495
Keshena Falls, Wis., 140
Kettle Moraine State Forest, Wis., 139, *139*
Kettle Rapids, Wis., 135, 137
Keystone Canyon, Alaska, 516

Key West, Fla., 119
Kiamichi Mountains, Okla., 174
Kilauea Crater, Hawaii, Hawaii, *524*, 525
killdeer (birds), 162
Killdeer Mountains, N.D., 213–214, *213*
Kill Devil Hills, N.C., 98
killifish, 103
Kincheloe Point, Ore., 445
kingfishers, 136
Kingman Museum of Natural History, Battle Creek, Mich., 149
King Mountain Scenic Drive, Tex., 283–284, *283*
King Ranch, Tex., *203*, 204
King Range, Calif., *466*, *466*
Kings Canyon National Park, Calif., 490–497, **494**, *495*
King's Peak, Utah, **345**
Kings River, Calif., 493
Kingston, N.Y., 59, *63*
Kingsville, Tex., 204
Kirwin Reservoir National Wildlife Refuge, Kan., *165*, 166
Kitchen Creek, Pa., 44
kites, white-tailed (birds), 205
Kitsap Peninsula, Wash., *415*, 416
Kittatinny Mountains, N.J. and Pa., **65**
Kittatinny Point, N.J., **65**
Kitty Hawk, N.C., 97, *100*
Kiwanda Beach, Ore., *445*
Klamath County Museum, Klamath Falls, Ore., 459
Klamath River Highway, Calif., *466*, *466*
Knife Lake, Minn., 128
Knif River, Alaska, 516
knots (birds), 202
Koaie Canyon, Kauai, Hawaii, 522
koa trees, 521
Kodachrome Basin, Utah, 369
Kodiak Area, Alaska, 515, *515*
Kokee, Kauai, Hawaii, 522
kokia keokeos (flowers), **522**
Koko Crater, Oahu, Hawaii, **526**
Kolob Canyons, Utah, *369*, 370–371
Kona Coast, Hawaii, Hawaii, *524*, 525
Koolau Range, Oahu, Hawaii, 525, 526
Kootenai River, Idaho, 306
Kruse Rhododendron State Park, Calif., 478, *478*
Kulshan Ridge, Wash., 427

La Canada, Calif., 495
La Croix, Lake, Minn., 128
lady's slippers, 51, 88
Lafayette, La., 190–191, *194*
    Natural History Museum, 195
Lafourche, La., 190
Laguna Atascosa National Wildlife Refuge, Tex., *203*, 204–205
Laguna Madre, Tex., 200, **200–201**, 202, *203*
Lajitas, Tex., **285**
Lake Chelan National Recreation Area, Wash., *426*, 427
Lake Fork, Colo., 256
Lake Havasu City, Ariz., 387
Lakes of the Clouds, N.H., **30**
Lakeside, Utah, 339
Lakeview Point, Calif., 506
Lamar, Tex., 205
Lamar River, Wyo., 318
Lame Johnny Creek, S.D., 226
Lanagan, Mo., 176
Land Between the Lakes, Ky. and Tenn., *81*, 82
Landscape Arch, Utah, 350–351, **350–351**

Land of Standing Rocks, Utah, 353
La Push, Wash., 413, **414**, *415*
Laramie Peak, Wyo., 233
larches, 289
larks, 424
    horned, 162
larkspur, 164, 367
La Sal Mountains, Utah, 353, **353**, 355, *355*, 357
Lassen Volcanic National Park, Calif., *466*, 469
Las Vegas, Nev., 500, 505
lather bushes, 104
Lathrop State Park, Colo., 262, *262*
Laughing Pig, Wyo., 322
Laughing Whitefish Falls, Mich., 129–130, *129*
Laughing Whitefish River, Mich., 129
laurel, mountain, 71, 86, 88
Laurel Caverns, Pa., *43*, 44
Lava Beds, Idaho, 329–330, *329*
Lava Beds, Utah, *369*, 371
Lava Beds National Monument, Calif., *466*, 468
    Museum, 469
Lava Butte Viewpoint, Ore., *457*, 458
Lava Falls, Ariz., 380–381
Lava River Caves State Park, Ore., *457*, 458
La Ventana, Tex., 282
Lawtonka, Lake, Okla., 183
Layton, Utah, 337
Leadbetter Point, Wash., *415*, 416
Lebanon State Forest, N.J., *63*, 64
Le Conte, Mount, N.C. and Tenn., 87
Lee Canau Peninsula, Mich., 143, 146
Lee's Creek, Ark., 175
Lee's Ferry, Ariz., **381**, 382
Left Hand Tunnel, N.M., **266**
"Legend of Sleepy Hollow, The," 62
Lehman Caves National Monument, Nev., *369*, 370
    Visitor Center, 372
Leland, Mich., 146
Leo Carillo Beach, Calif., **495**, *495*
Letchworth State Park, N.Y., 44
Lewis, Captain Meriwether, 14, **14–15**, 296, 301, 305, 433, 443
Lewis and Clark Caverns State Park, Mont., **294**, 297
Lewis and Clark Expedition, 14, **14–15**
Lewis and Clark Highway, Idaho, *304*, 307
Lewis River Canyon, Wyo., 311
Lewiston, Idaho, 300, 303, *304*, 306
Liberty Bell Mountain, Wash., 429
Liberty Cap, Calif., **477**
Liberty Gorge, N.H., 32
lichens, 210, 233, **241**, 242, **292**, 344, 371, 511–513
    arctic, 30
Lick Observatory, Calif., 487
Liers Otter Sanctuary, Homer, Minn., 141
lignum vitae (trees), 119
Lihue, Kauai, Hawaii, 521
lilies
    avalanche, 424, **424**
    glacier, 424, **424**
    sego, 368
Limberlost Region, Va., 69
Lime Creek, Colo., 254
Lime Creek Canyon, Colo., *253*, 254
Lime Lake, Mich., 146
limpets (shellfish), 445
Lincoln, Abraham, 15
Lincoln City, Ore., 445
Lincoln National Forest, N.M., 275
Lindsey Peak, Colo., **262–263**
Linville Falls and Gorge, N.C., *89*, 91
Linville Mountain, N.C., 91

Linville River, N.C., 91
Litchfield Nature Center and Museum, Litchfield, Conn., 55
Little Bitterroot River, Mont., 304
Little Black Peak, N.M., 275
Little Carp River, Mich., **131**
Little Chief Mountain, Mont., **286–287**
Little Colorado River Gorge, Ariz., *383*, 385
Little Cottonwood Canyon, Utah, 344
Little Duck River, Tenn., 81
Little Missouri Bay, N.D., 214
Little Missouri River, N.D., 214
Little Pigeon River, N.C. and Tenn., 88
Little River, Ala., **82**
Little Rocky Mountains, Mont., **294**, 297
Little Sahara State Park, Okla., *185*, 186
Little Stony Man, Va., 70
Little Sur River Valley, Calif., **486**
Little Wyandotte Cave, Ind., **83**
liverworts (plants), 210
lizards, **274**, 380, 392
    alligator, **281**
    gecko, 112
    western collared, **281**
Llano River, Tex., 285
Lochsa River, Idaho, **307**
Locke, Mount, Tex., 284–285
locust trees, black, 69
Loda Lake Scenic Area, Mich., 149
Lodgepole Creek, Neb., 235
Logan Canyon, Idaho and Utah, 342, *342*
Logan Pass, Mont., 292
Lolo Pass, Idaho, 305
Lompoc Valley Flower Fields, Calif., **487**, *487*
London Bridge, Ariz., 387
Lone Pine, Calif., 495
Long Beach, Wash., *415*, 416–417
Longfellow Mountains, Me., 25
Longhorn Cavern, Tex., *203*, 205
Long Lake, Mich., 149
Longmire, James, 422
Long Pine Key, Fla., 116
Long Pond, Me., 23
Longs Peak, Colo., 240
Long Valley Junction, Utah, 370
Looking Glass Rock, Utah, *355*, 358
Lookout Mountain, Tenn., 89, **90**, **92**
Lookout Tower, Iowa, 156
Loomis Museum, Mineral, Calif., 469
Loon Mountain, N.H., 33
loons (birds), 126
Los Angeles, Calif., 495
    Los Angeles County Museum of Natural History, 496
Los Padres National Forest, Calif., 488
"Lost Bridge Road," N.D., 213–214
Lost Creek Falls, Mont., 297
Lost Creek State Park, Mont., **294**, 297
Lost Lake, Ore., 437, *437*, **439**
Lost River, Idaho, 330, 332
Lost River, W.Va., 72, 73
Lost River Nature Garden, North Woodstock, N.H., 35
Lost Sea, Tenn., 89, 91
Long Trail, Vt., 33
Lost Valley State Park, Ark., *174*, **177**
Louisiana State University Museums of Geoscience and Natural Science and Herbarium, Baton Rouge, La., 195
Louisiana Wildlife Museum, New Orleans, La., 195
Loveland, Colo., 239, *243*
Loveland Pass, Colo., 243, *243*
Lover's Leap, Tenn., **90**
Lower Falls, N.H., 33

Lower Falls of the Yellowstone, Wyo., 317, **319**
Lower Geyser Basin, Wyo., 316
Lower Klamath–Tule Lake National Wildlife Refuges, Calif., *466*, **468**
Lower Slide Lake, Wyo., *320*, 321
Lower Souris National Wildlife Refuge, N.D., *213*, 214
Lucia, Calif., 483, *487*
Lucin Cutoff, Utah, 338
Lumahai Beach, Kauai, Hawaii, *524*, 525
Luman Nelson Museum of New England Wildlife, Marlboro, Vt., 35
Lunar Crater, Nev., *369*, 371
lupines (flowers), 378, 394, **423**, 424, **424**
Luray Caverns, Va., 72, 73
Lure, Lake, N.C., 90
Lyndon B. Johnson Lake, Tex., 204

MacDonald Pass, Mont., *294*, 297
Mackay, Idaho, 331
mackerel, 118
king, **204**
Maclay Gardens State Park, Tallahassee, Fla., 109
Madera Canyon, Ariz., *403*, 404
Madera Canyon, Tex., 285
Madison, Mount, N.H., 29
Madison Canyon, Idaho, 329
Madison River, Idaho, 329
Mad River Glen, Vt., 32
Magador Valley, Mich., *147*, 148–149
Magnolia Gardens and Nurseries, John's Island, S.C., 101
magnolias, 82, 119
giant, 107
swamp, 74
mahoganies
Madeira, 119
mountain, 261
West Indian, 112
Mahogany Hammock, Fla., 116
Mahtotopa Mountain, Mont., **286–287**
Makaha Beach, Oahu, Hawaii, *524*, 525
Makapuu Point, Oahu, Hawaii, *524*, 525
Makoshika State Park, Mont., *213*, 214
Malaquite Beach, Tex., 199, 202
Malheur National Wildlife Refuge, Ore., *457*, 458
Museum, 459
Mal Pais Lava Beds, N.M., 275
Mammoth Cave National Park, Ky., 76–83, **76–77**, 79, **80**, *81*
Mammoth Dome, Ky., 80
Mammoth Hot Springs, Wyo., **316**
manatees (animals), 113
Manchester College Natural History Museum, North Manchester, Ind., 149
manchineel trees, 115
mangroves, **112–113**, 114, 118
Manhattan, Mont., 297
Manistee National Forest, Mich., *147*, 149
Manitou Islands, Mich., 144–145, 146
Manitou Springs, Colo., 246
Mansfield, Mount, Vt., 34
Mansfield Channel, Tex., 199
manzanitas (plants), 468
maples, 29, **34**, 51, 80, 112, 135, 154, 155, 170, 175, 416, 486
big-leaf, **425**
sugar, 86, 183
vine, **425**
Maquoketa Caves State Park, Iowa, *155*, 156

Maquoketa River, Iowa, 155
Marathon, Tex., 279, 282
Marble, Colo., **247**
Marble Canyon National Monument, Ariz., *383*, 385
Marble Mountain Wilderness Area, Calif., *466*, 468
Marconi Station, Mass., 49
Marcy, Mount, N.Y., 34, 59
Margaret, Mount, Wash., 417
Marie Lake, Wyo., 246
Marine, Minn., 138
Marine Gardens, Yaquina Bay, Ore., 450
Marine Institute, University of Georgia, Sapelo Island, Ga., 108
Marineland of Florida, Marineland, Fla., 120
Marineland of the Pacific, Palos Verdes Estates, Calif., 496
Mariposa, Calif., 478, *478*
Mark Twain National Forest, Mo., 175
marlin (fish), 194, **204**
marmots (animals), 242, 290
hoary, **293**
yellowbellied, *252*, 368
Maroon Bells, Colo., **244–245**
Marquette, Father Jacques, 14, **14–15**
Marquette, Iowa, 152
marram grass, **51**
Marshall University Geology Museum, Huntington, W.Va., 92
Marshes of Glynn, Ga., 107, **109**
marsh grass, **48–49**, 75, 192
martens (animals), 289, 468
pine, 456
Martha's Vineyard, Mass., *52*, 53–54, **55**
martins, purple (birds), 139, 202
Marys Peak, Ore., 449, *449*
Massachusetts Audubon Society Sanctuary, Wellfleet, Mass., 51
Massanutten Mountain, Va., **68–69**
Matanuska Glacier, Alaska, 516
Mather, Stephen, 16
Matheson Hammock, Fla., *118*, 119
Mattamuskeet, Lake, N.C., *100*, 101
Maui, Hawaii, *524*, 525–526, **525**, 527
Maumee River Parkway, Ohio, *147*, 149
Mauna Kea, Hawaii, Hawaii, *524*, 525–526
Mauna Loa, Hawaii, Hawaii, *524*, 525, 526
Maury River, Va., 73
Maxwell Game Preserve, Kan., *165*, 166
mayflowers, 51
Maymount Park Wildlife Exhibit, Richmond, Va., 74
Mazama, Mount, Ore., 454, **454–455**
Maze District, Utah, 349, 353, 354
McCamey, Tex., 284
McDonald Lake, Mont., 292
McDonald Lodge, Mont., 292
McGregor, Iowa, **150–151**, 154, 155
McKee Jungle Gardens, Vero Beach, Fla., 120
McKenzie, Donald, 301
McKenzie Lava Beds, Ore., *457*, 458
McKenzie River, Ore., 437, *457*, 458
McKinley, Mount, National Park, Alaska, 17, 508–517, **508–509**, 510–**511**, 512, **514**, *515*
McLoughlin, Mount, Ore., *457*, 458
Mead, Lake, National Recreation Area, Ariz. and Nev., **381**, *383*, 385
Meadowlark Lake, Wyo., 321
meadowlarks, 202, 233
Meanders of the Mississippi, Miss., *194*, **195**
Medano Creek, Colo., 261
Medano Pass, Colo., 259, 260

Medicine Bow National Forest, Wyo., 244
Medicine Creek Reservoir, Neb., *165*, 166
Medicine Park, Okla., 183
Medicine Rocks State Park, Mont., *213*, **215**
Megunticook, Mount, Me., 24
Menominee River, Mich., 140–141
menziesias, rusty (flowers), **424**
Meramec Caverns, Mo., 176
Meramec River, Mo., 176
Meramec State Park, Mo., *174*, 176
Nature Museum, 177
Merced River, Calif., **470–471**, 473, **474–475**, *475*
Meredith, Lake, Tex., 187
Merritt Reservoir, Neb., 235
Mesa Falls, Idaho, *329*, 330
Mesa Verde National Park, Colo., **12–13**, 13, *253*, **254–255**
Park Museum, 256
Mescalero Apache Reservation, N.M., 272, 274
Mesquite Flat, Calif., **503**
mesquites (plants), 279, 282, 380, 504
Meteor Crater, Ariz., *383*, 385
Methow River, Wash., 427
Methow Valley Highway, Wash., *426*, 427
Metropolitan Museum of Art, New York, N.Y., 61
Miami, Fla., 115, **115**, *118*
Miamus River Gorge, N.Y., 63, 64
Mica Mountain, Ariz., 402
mice, 145, **274**
grasshopper, 503
jumping, 261
pocket, 380
white-footed, 128
Michigamme National Forest, Mich., 130
Michigan, Lake, **142–143**, 143–146, **144**, **145**, *147*, 149
Michigan State University Museum, East Lansing, Mich., 149
Michigan Technological Museum, Houghton, Mich., 131
Mid-Cape Highway, Mass., 49
Middle Fork, Utah, 371
Middle Fork Canyon, Calif., 493
Middle Park, Colo., 244
Middle Sister Mountain, Ore., **458**
Milford Reservoir, Kan., *165*, 166
Milford State Park, Kan., 166
Mill Creek Canyon, Utah, 344
Mille Lacs Lake, Minn., 139, *139*
Millicoma Myrtle Grove, Ore., 449, *449*
Million Dollar Highway, Colo., 253, 255
Mills, Lake, Wash., 410
Milner Pass, Colo., 242
Mineopa State Park, Minn., 139, *139*
Mineral King Basin, Calif., *495*, **496**
Mineral Point Historical Society Museum, Mineral Point, Wis., 157
Mineral Ridge Scenic Area, Idaho, 304, *304*
Miner's Falls, Mich., **130**
Minerva Terrace, Wyo., **316**
minks, 64, 128, 136, 167, 289, 302
Minneapolis, Minn., *139*, 140
Minnehaha Falls, Minn., 139–140, *139*
Minnesota Caverns, Min., 140
Minnetonka Cave, Idaho, *329*, 330
Minnewaska, Lake, N.Y., 63, 64
Minnie's Lake, Okefenokee, Ga., 106
Minnie's Run, Ga., 106
Mirror Lake, Idaho, 307
Mirror Lake, Utah, 342, *342*
Mirror Lake, Wyo., 246
Missionary Island, Ohio, 149

Mission Range, Mont., **295, 296–297,** 297
Mississippi Palisades, Ill., Iowa and Wis., 150–157, **150–151, 152–153,** *155*
Mississippi Palisades State Park, Ill., 151–154, **152–153**
Mississippi River, 10, 14, **14–15,** 137, 138, *139,* 151, 155, 189, *193, 194,* **195**
Missouri River, 14, 165, *165,* 214, 296–297
Mitchell Caverns State Reserve, Calif., 505, *505*
Mitchell Pass, Neb., **228–229,** 231, 234
Moab, Utah, 350–354, *355*
Museum, 359
Moaula Waterfall, Molokai, Hawaii, 524
Mobridge, S.D., 214
moccasin flowers, 156
moccasins, cottonmouth (snakes), 106
Mohawk River, N.Y., 59
Mohawk Trail, Mass., *52,* **54**
Mohegan Bluffs, R.I., **55**
Mojave Desert, Calif. and Nev., 505–506, *505,* **506**
mokihana flowers, 522
Molly Stark Mountain, Vt., 32
Molokai, Hawaii, 524, *524,* 526
Monahans Sandhills State Park, Tex., *283,* 284
Monarch Pass, Colo., *262,* 263
monkey flowers, 424, **424**
monkeys, 118
Mono Lake, Calif., 478, *478*
Monongahela National Forest, W.Va., 72–73
Monroe, Mount, N.H., 29, **30**
Montana College of Mineral Science Museum, Butte, Mont., 297
Montana State University Herbarium, Bozeman, Mont., 297
Montauk Point, N.Y., *52,* 54
Montauk Springs, Mo., 171
Montauk State Park, Mo., 169–170
Montezuma Castle National Monument, Ariz., *383,* 386
Monticello, Utah, 354
Montrose, Colo., 251, *253*
Montville Trail, Colo., 260
Monument Basin, Utah, **346–347**
Monument Rocks, Kan., *165,* **166**
Monument Valley, Utah, *355,* **359**
Moore Park, Tex., 285
moose, 126, 131, 136, 290–291, **293,** 306, 311, 318, 320, 511
Moose, Wyo., 312
Moosehead Lake, Me., 25
Moran, Mount, Wyo., 311, 312
Morgan's Museum of Natural History, Winfield, W.Va., 92
Mormon Island Recreation Area, Neb., *165,* 166–167
Moro Rock, Calif., 494, **494**
Morro Bay, Calif., 487, *487*
Museum of Natural History, 489
Morro Rock, Calif., 487
Morrow Mountain, N.C., *100,* 101
State Park Natural History Museum, 101
Mosca Dune, Colo., 259, 260, *262*
Moses Lake Dunes, Wash., *426,* 427
mosquitoes, 510
moss campions (flowers), **425**
mosses, **33,** 53, 157, 210, 241–242, **292,** 367, 466, 524
juniper, 157
sphagnum, 105
"mosses," Spanish, 97, 100, 108, **121,** **188–189,** 190, **190**

Moss Glen Falls, Vt., *32,* 34
Mountain Fork River, Okla., 174
Mountain Lake Sanctuary, Fla., *118,* 119
Mountain Lakes Wild Area, Ore., *457* 458
mountain lions, *see* cougars
Mountain Station, Calif., 506
Mount Bullion, Calif., 478
Mount Desert Island, Me., **20,** 21–22
Mount Evans Highway, Colo., 245
Mount Hood Loop Highway, Ore., 437, *437*
Movie Flat, Calif., 495
Moxie Falls, Me., *24,* 25
Moyie Falls, Idaho, 304–305, *304*
Moyie River, Idaho, 305
Mud Lake, Idaho, 329
Muir, John, 16, **16–17,** 473, 475, 493
Muir Glacier, Alaska, **517**
Muir Woods National Monument, Calif., 461, *478,* 479
Park Museum, 480
Muldrow Glacier, Alaska, **512**
Mulholland Highway, Calif., 495, *495*
Mullica River, N.J., 64
Multnomah Falls, Ore., **432,** 433, **477**
Mummy Cave, Ariz., **396–397**
Munising Falls, Mich., *129,* **130**
Munson Creek, Ore., **450**
Munson Falls, Ore., *449,* **450**
Museum of the Cornwall Countryside, Cornwall, N.Y., 65
Museum of the Great Plains, Lawton, Okla., 187
Museum of History and Science, Waterloo, Iowa, 157
Museum of Natural Science, Houston, Tex., 205
Museum of North Carolina Minerals, Spruce Pine, N.C., 92
Museum of Northern Arizona, Flagstaff, Ariz., 387
Museum of Rocks and Minerals, Murfreesboro, Ark., 177
Museum of Science, Boston, Mass., 55
Museum of Science, Miami, Fla., 120
Museum of Science and History, Louisville, Ky., 83
Museum of Science and Natural History, Tampa, Fla., 120
Museum of the Sea, Cape Hatteras, N.C., 101
mushrooms, morel, 153
Mushroom State Park, Kan., 166
Music Pass, Colo., 259
Muskegon Lake, Mich., 149
Muskegon River, Mich., 148
Muskegon State Park, Mich., *147,* 149
muskrats, 136, 289
Myakka River State Park, Fla., *118,* 119
Myrtle Beach State Park, S.C., *100,* 101
myrtles (trees), 97, 100, 105, 113, 442
Oregon, 449
Mystery Cave, Minn., *139,* 140

Nacimiento Badlands, N.M., 394
Nags Head, N.C., 97, 98, **99,** *100*
Nankin Mills Nature Center, Garden City, Detroit, Mich., 149
Nantucket Island, Mass., *52,* 54
Nantucket Maria Mitchell Association, 55
Na Pali Cliffs, Kauai, Hawaii, 522
Na Pali Coast, Kauai, Hawaii, *524,* **526–527**
Napa Valley, Calif., *478,* 480
Narragansett Bay, R.I., 52
Narrows, Utah, 364–365, 367

Narrows Aquatic Farm, Mo., 175
nasturtiums, 521
Natchez, Miss., 194
Natchez Trace Parkway, Miss., *81,* 82, 194, *194*
National Bison Range, Mont., *294,* **295**
Natural Arch, Colo., 262, *262*
Natural Area, Vt., 33
Natural Bridge, Ala., *81,* 82
Natural Bridge, Ky., *89,* **91**
Natural Bridge, Va., 72, **73**–74
Natural Bridge Caverns, Tex., *203,* 205
Natural Bridge and Caves, N.Y., *32,* 34
Natural Bridges Beach, Calif., 487, *487*
Natural Bridge Scenic Area, Ark., 174
Natural Bridges National Monument, Utah, *355,* **357**
Natural Chimneys, Va., 72, **73**
Natural History Museum, Evansville, Ind., 83
Natural History Museum, Mammoth, Ky., 83
Natural History Museum, Tillamook, Ore., 450
Natural Tunnel, Va., *89,* 91–92
Navajo Lake, Utah, *369,* 371
Navajo Loop Trail, Utah, 367
Navajo Mountain, Utah, *355,* 358
Navajo National Monument, Ariz., *383,* 386
Museum, 387
Neah Bay, Wash., 417
Nebo, Mount, State Park, Ark., *174,* 176
Nebraska National Forest, Neb., 234, *234*
Necanicum Junction, Ore., 444, 449, *449*
Nedonna Beach, Ore., *445*
Needles, Utah, 349, 353, 354
Needles, The, S.D., 224, **227**
Needles Highway, S.D., *227*
Needles Overlook, Utah, 355
Nehalem Bay, Ore., *445,* 449, *449*
Nehalem River Drive, Ore., *449, 449*
Nelson and Kennedy Ledges State Park, Ohio, *43,* **45**
Nemakagan River, Wis., 135
nenes (birds), 527
Neptune State Park, Ore., *445*
Nesika Beach, Ore., *445*
Nestucca River, Ore., *449, 449*
Neuse River, N.C., 100
Nevada Falls, Calif., 476, **476, 477**
Nevada State Museum, Carson City, Nev., 480
Never Summer Mountains, Colo., 242
Neville Public Museum, Green Bay, Wis., 141
Newberry Crater, Ore., 459
Newburgh, N.Y., 59, *63*
New England Aquarium, Boston, Mass., 55
Newfound Gap Road, N.C. and Tenn., 87
New Glarus Area, Wis., *155,* 156
New Glarus Woods and Roadside Park, Wis., 156
New Iberia, La., 191–192, *194*
New Jersey State Museum, Trenton, N.J., 65
New London Public Museum, Wis., 141
New Market Gap, Va., **68–69**
New Meadows, Idaho, 306
New Orleans, La., 189–190, *194*
New River Canyon, W.Va., 91
Newspaper Rock State Historic Monument, Utah, *355,* 358
New York City, N.Y., 59, 61, *63,* 64
Aquarium, 65
Botanical Garden, 65
Niagara Cave, Minn., *139,* 140

565

Niagara Falls, N.Y., 36–45, **36–37**, **38–
39**, **40–41**, **42**, *43*, 476, **476**
Niagara River, N.Y., 39, 42
Niagara Suspension Railway Bridge,
N.Y., 39
Nicholet National Forest, Wis., 141
Niihau, Hawaii, 521
Nine Mile Pond, Fla., 116
Niobrara River, Neb., *234*, 235
Nisqually, Wash., 422
Nisqually Glacier Vista Trail, Wash.,
423
Nitanee, Lake, Pa., 44
Noel, Mo., 176
Nojoqui Falls, Calif., *487*, 488
No Man's Land Historical Museum,
Goodwell, Okla., 187
nopals, *see* cactus, prickly pear
Norfolk, Va., 96
Norman Bird Sanctuary, Portsmouth,
R.I., 55
Norris Geyser Basin, Wy., *314*, 316
North Beach Peninsula, Wash., 416
North Carolina State Museum, Raleigh,
N.C., 101
North Cascades National Park, Wash.,
426, *427*, **429**
North Dome, Calif., 476
Northeast Harbor, Me., 23
North Fork River, Colo., 249
North Fork River, W.Va., 74
North Fork Valley, W.Va., 74
North Platte, Neb., 167
North Platte River, Neb., 231, 233, 234,
234
North Rim of the Grand Canyon, Ariz.,
377–378, **378**, 380, 383, *383*
North Sister Mountain, Ore., **458**
North Turkey Foot Creek, Ohio, 149
North Umpqua River, Ore., 450
Northwestern State College Natural
History Museum, Alva, Okla., 187
Norton, Va., 91
Norton Reservoir, Kan., 167
Noxon Reservoir, Mont., 307
nutcrackers, Clark's (birds), 302, 424–
425, 456
nuthatches (birds)
brown-headed, 104
white-breasted, 378
nutrias (animals), 192
Nuuanu Pali Drive, Oahu, Hawaii, *524*,
526
Nye Beach, Ore., 442

Oahe, Lake, N.D. and S.D., *213*, 214
Oahu, Hawaii, 519, 524–526, *524*, **526**
Oak Creek Canyon, Ariz., *383*, **387**
Oakland Museum, Oakland, Calif., 480
Oak Openings, Ohio, *147*, 149
oaks, 34, 51, 69, 108, 119, 135, 153, 155,
170, 175, 191, 284, 380, 402, 468,
480, 487, 488, 494, 505
gambel, 251
live, 97, 105, 118, 183, 190, 195, 202
madrona, 463
scrub, 224, **488**
silver, 521, 522
tan, 463
water, 105
white, 69, 174
Oberlin, Mount, Mont., **288**
Observation Point, Utah, 366
Observatory Drive, Tex., *283*, 284–285
Obstruction Point, Wash., 410
Ocala National Forest, Fla., 119
Ocean Drive, Acadia, Me., **20**, 21
Oceanside, Calif., 506
Ochlockonee River, Fla., 107, *107*

ocotillos (plants), 279, 404
Ocracoke Island, N.C., 98–99
Odessa Meteor Crater, Tex., *283*, 285
Museum, 285
Odin Falls, Ore., 437
Ogden, Utah, 338
Ogden River, Utah, 339
Ogeechee River, Ga., 108
Oglala National Grasslands, Neb., 234,
234
ohia-lehuas (trees), **522**
Ohiopyle Falls, Pa., *43*, 44
Ohio River, *43*, 44, 81
Ohio River Coral Reef, Ky., *81*, 82
Ohme Gardens, Wenatchee, Wash., 429
Ojai, Calif., 496
Okeechobee, Lake, Fla., **115**, *118*, 119
Okefenokee Swamp, Ga., 102–109, **102–
103**, **104**, **105**, **106**, *107*, 120
Park, 106
Park Museum, 109
Oklahoma State University Natural
History Museum and Herbarium,
Stillwater, Okla., 187
Oklawaha River, Fla., *118*, 119
Okoboji Lakes, East and West, Iowa,
156
Old Baldy, Calif., *505*, 506
Old Faithful Geyser, Wyo., 17, 311, 315,
315
Visitor Center, 316
Old Man of the Mountains, N.H., 32,
54
Old Spanish Trail, Ariz., 402
Oliver Reservoir, Neb., *234*, 235
Olmsted, Frederick Law, 15, **16–17**
Olympic Hot Springs, Wash., 410
Olympic National Park, Wash., 15, 16,
17, 406–417, **406–407**, **408**, **410–411**,
412, **414**, *415*
Pioneer Memorial Museum, 417
Olympic Peninsula, Wash., 409, 415,
415
Olympic Strip, Wash., 414
Olympus, Mount, Wash., 409, 411, 413
Oneonta Creek and Gorge, Ore., **433**
Ontario, Lake, 42, *43*, 44, 45
Ophir, Colo., **256**
opossums, 74, 106, 170, 183
oranges, 108, 119
mock, 251
orchids, 53, 64, 70, 74, 108, 115, **116**,
118, **121**, 524
ghost, 112
Oregon Caves National Monument,
Ore., *449*, **451**
Oregon Coast, 440–451, **440–441**, *442–
443*, *444*, *445*, **446–447**, *448*, *449*
Oregon Inlet, N.C., 98
Oregon Museum of Science and Indus-
try, Portland, Ore., 438
Oregon State University Museum of
Natural History, Corvallis, Ore.,
450
Oregon Trail, 14, **228–229**, 231, **232**,
234, 322, 433
Orford Reef, Ore., 448
Organ Pipe Cactus National Monument,
Ariz., **403**, 404
Museum, 405
Orick, Calif., 463, *466*
osage trees, 162
Oshkosh Public Museum, Oshkosh,
Wis., 141
ospreys, *75*, 107, **117**, 125, 302, **459**
Oswald West State Park, Ore., 445, *445*
Ottauquechee River, Vt., **33**
Ottawa National Forest, Mich., 130, 141
Ottawa National Wildlife Refuge,
Mich., *147*, 149
Otter Creek Park, Ky., *81*, 82

Otter Crest, Ore., 445
Otter Point, Acadia, Me., 21
otters, 106, 112, 136, 289, 302
Ouachita, Lake, Ark., *174*, 176
Ouachita Mountains, Ark., *174*, **176**
Ouachita National Forest, Okla., 177
Ouray, Colo., 253–254
Outer Banks, N.C., 94–101, **94–95**, **96–
97**, **99**, *100*
ouzels (birds), 242, 291, 367
Overhanging Bluff Drive, Mo., *174*, 176
Overland Trail, **322**
Overseas Highway, Fla., **119**
Owachomo Bridge, Utah, **357**
Owen, Mount, Wyo., **310**, 311, **312–313**
Owens Valley, Calif., **493**, 495–496, *495*
Owl Creek Mountains, Wyo., 323
owls, 136, 302, 368
great horned, 136, 202, 261, 282, 468
hoot, 171
screech, 171, 261
Oxbow Dam, Idaho, 301, 302
oysters, 108, 416
Ozark Mountains, Ark. and Mo., 175,
176
Ozark National Forest, Ark., 174
Ozark National Scenic Riverways, Mo.,
168–177, **168–169**, **170–171**, *173*, 174

Pacific Crest National Scenic Trail,
Ore. and Wash., **429**, 457
Pacific Grove Butterfly Flight, Calif.,
487, 488
Pacific Grove Museum of Natural His-
tory, Pacific Grove, Calif., 489
Pacific Ocean, 14–15, 16, 414, **414**, *415*,
435, 443, *449*, 475, 480, **481**, *505–
506*
Packer Meadow, Idaho, *304*, 305
Packsaddle, Tex., **284**
Pactola Lake, S.D., 224–225, *224*
Padre Island National Seashore, Tex.,
10, **10–11**, 196–205, **196–197**, **198**,
200–201, **202**, *203*
Pahayokee Hammock, Fla., 116
painted buntings (birds), 282
Painted Canyon, Calif., *505*, 506
painted cups (flowers), **423**, 424, **424**
Painted Desert, Ariz., *383*, 386, 387,
389, 391, **393**
Painted Hills State Park, Ore., *437*, 438
Painted Rocks Lake, Mont., 294
Painted Wall, Black Canyon, Colo.,
248–249, 251
Palaau Park, Molokai, Hawaii, *524*, 526
Palisade Head, Minn., 130
Palisades, Mississippi, *see* Mississippi
Palisades
Palisades, N.J. and N.Y., **58**, 59, **60–61**
Palisades Interstate Park, N.J. and N.Y.,
60
Palisades–Kepler State Park, Iowa, *155*,
156
Palisades Parkway, N.J., 61
Palm Canyon, Calif., **505**, *505*, **506**
Palmer–Matanuska Valley, Alaska,
515–516, *515*
palmettoes (trees), 195
Palmetto State Park, Luling, Tex., 205
palms, 108, **119**
cabbage, 115
coconut, 113, 120, 525
fan, 505
royal, 115, 118
sabal, 100
Palm Springs, Calif., 506
Desert Museum, 507
Palo Duro Canyon, Tex., *185*, **186–187**
Palomar Mountains, Calif., *505*, 506

Palomar Observatory, Calif., 506
Palos Verdes Peninsula, Calif., *495*, *496*
Palouse River Canyon, Wash., *426*, *427*, *428*
paloverde (plants), 404
Panama City, Fla., 194
Panamint Range, Calif., 496, 500, **500–501**, 504
pandanus trees, 525
panthers, 103, 107, 116, **117**
paperbark trees, 521
paperflowers, 378
Pappy's Pasture, Utah, 354
Paradise Visitor Center, 429
Paradise Glacier, Wash., **422**, 423
Paradise Ice Caves, Wash., **422**, 424
Paradise Ice Caves Trail, Wash., 423
Paradise Lost Room, Oregon Caves, Ore., **451**
Paradise Valley, Mass., 51
Paria River, Utah, 367
Parker Dam, Ariz., **386–387**
parrot fishes, 113
partridges, 136
  chukar, 302
  Hungarian, 302
Pascagoula River, Miss., 194–195, *194*
pasque flowers, 241
Pass Creek Gorge, Idaho, *329*, 331
Pasture Wash, Ariz., 378
Paulina Lake, Ore., 459
Paulina Peak, Ore., *457*, 459
paurotis (trees), 115
Paurotis Pond, Fla., 116
Payette Lake, Idaho, *329*, 331
Payne's Prairie, Fla., *118*, 119
Peabody Museum of Natural History, New Haven, Conn., 55
Pea Island National Wildlife Refuge, N.C., 98
Peak-to-Peak Highway, Colo., 243
Peale, Mount, Utah, 353
pea plants, 261
Pearl Harbor, Oahu, Hawaii, 526
Pearl River, Miss., 195
Peattie, Donald Culross, 377
Peavy Falls, Wis., 140
pecans, wild, 190
Pecos River, Tex. and N.M., **268**, 284, 285
Pecos River Overlook, Tex., *283*, 285
Pecos Valley, Tex., 284
Pecos Wilderness, N.M., *394*, 396
Pedernales Falls State Park, Tex., 205
Pedernales River, Tex., *203*, 205
Pee Dee River, N.C., 101
Peekaboo Loop, Utah, 367
Peekskill, N.Y., 62, *63*
pelicans, 214
  brown, 485
  white, 120, **201**, 311, 339, **468–469**
Pemaquid Peninsula, Me., 24, *25*
Pemetic Mountain, Acadia, Me., 21
Pemigewasset River, N.H., 32
Pend Oreille, Lake, Idaho, *304*, 306, **306**
Pend Oreille River, Wash., 428
Penn's Cave, Pa., *43*, 44
Penn State Forest, Pa., 64–65
Pennyrile Forest State Park, Ky., *81*, 82
Penobscot Bay, Me., 24, *24*
Penobscot Mountain, Acadia, Me., 21
Pensacola Bay, Fla., *194*, 195
penstemons (flowers), 241, 424
Pepin, Lake, Minn., 139, *139*
peppermint, 172
perch, 25, 129, 302
Perrot State Park, Wis., *139*, **140–141**
Persimmon Gap, Tex., 279
persimmons, 69
Petit Jean State Park, Ark., *174*, 176
Petrified Forest National Park, Ariz.,
318, 386, 388–397, **388–389**, 390, 391, 392, *394*
Petrified Wood Park, S.D., *213*, 214
  Museum, 215
Pettigrew State Park, S.C., *100*, 101
Pfeiffer–Big Sur State Park, Calif., 486
phalaropes, Wilson's (birds), 214
Phantom Ship, Crater Lake, Ore., **455**
pheasants, 167, 526
Phelps, Lake, N.C., 101
Philadelphia, Pa., *63*, 64
philodendrons, 526
phlox, mountain, 149, 425
phoebes, Say's (birds), 328
Phoenix, Ariz., 403
  South Mountain Park, *403*, 404
Pichot, Mount, Okla., 183
pickerel, 103
Pictured Rocks National Lakeshore, Mich., 129, *129*, 130
Piedra Blanca, Calif., 496
Piedra River, Colo., 254
Pierre, S.D., 214
Piers Gorge, Mich., *139*, 140–141
Pigeon River, Minn., 129
Pigeon River State Forest, Mich., 148
pigeons, white-crowned, 112
pigs, wild, 282, 404, **405**, 489
pikas (animals), 242, 290, 293
pike, 214
  golden walleyed, 129
  northern, 136, 156, 214
  sauger, 214
  walleyed, 136, 156, 214
Pike, Zebulon, 154, 260
Pikes Peak, Colo., *243*, 245–246, 260
Pikes Peak, Iowa, 154
Pilgrim Lake, Mass., 47
Pilot Knob, Iowa, *155*, 156
Pinaleno Range, Ariz., 404
Pine Barrens, N.J., 64
Pine Creek, Ariz., 387
Pine Creek Gorge, Pa., *43*, 44
Pine Creek Tunnel, Utah, 365–367
Pine Island Wildlife Refuge, Fla., *118*, 120
Pineland Trail, Fla., 116
Pine and Oak Alley, La., 191
pines, 21, 29, 35, 51, 53, **53**, 97, 104, 108, 116, **124**, 126, 129, 135, 149, 191, 225, 234, 239, 321, 377, 402, 466, 468, 487, **488**
  Australian, 118
  bristlecone, 368, **370**, 495
  limber, 241, 289, 328, 368
  loblolly, 72
  lodgepole, 241, 289, 477
  longleaf, 101
  pitch, 51, 64
  piñon, **244**, 251, 261, 368, 378, 380, 381
  ponderosa, 210, **225**, 233, 241, **302–303**, 342, 368, 380, 383, 386, 394, 395, 405, 494
  red, 125, 148
  shore, 445, 447
  shortleaf, 170
  Torrey, 507
  Western white, **425**
  white, 125, 130, 148, 155, 157
  whitebark, **425**
Pink Cliffs, Utah, 367
Pinkham Notch, N.H., 33
Pinnacle, The, Cumberland Gap, Ky., Tenn. and Va., 90
Pinnacle Mountain, S.C., 93
Pinnacles, Ore., 456
Pinnacles National Monument, Calif., *487*, **489**
Pinnacles Overlook, S.D., **216–217**
piñons, *see* pines, piñon
Pioneer Mountains, Idaho, 325
Pipe Spring National Monument, Ariz., *383*, **384**
Pipestem State Park, W.Va., *89*, 92
pipsissewas (plants), **424**
Pirate Cove, Ore., 445
Pismo Beach, Calif., 488
Pismo–Guadalupe Dunes, Calif., *487*, 488
pitcher plants, **105**
Pittsburg Landing, Idaho, 302
Pittsburg Saddle, Idaho, 302
Placid, Lake, N.Y., *32*, 34
Platte River, Kan. and Neb., **232–233**
Platte River, Mich., 146
Platt National Park, Okla., *185*, 187
  Museum, 187
Pleasant Valley Wildlife Sanctuary, Lenox, Mass., 55
plovers, upland, 214
plums, 112
  beach, **51**, 54
  wild, 162, 522
Point of Arches, Wash., *415*, 417
Point Betsie, Mich., 146
Point Defiance Park Aquarium and Zoo, Tacoma, Wash., 417
Point of Gap, Pa., 65
Point Grenville, Wash., *415*, 417
Point Imperial, Ariz., 378
Point Lobos State Reserve, Calif., 485–486, *487*, **489**
Point Lookout, Md., 72, 74
Point Reyes National Seashore, Calif., *478*, **481**
Point Sur, Calif., **482–483**, 484
poison ivy, 51
Polar Caves, N.H., *32*, 34
Polychrome Pass., Alaska, **510–511**
polygonums (herbs), **425**
Ponca, Ark., *175*
Ponce de Léon, Louis, 14
pond lilies, 149
ponies, wild, 99
  Chincoteague, *73*
Pontchartrain, Lake, La., *194*, **195**
Pony Express Route, 322
Pool, The, Franconia, N.H., 32
Popham Beach State Park, Me., 24, *25*
poplars, tulip, 69
Popo Agie River, Wyo., 323
poppies, 367
  prickly, 378
Porcupine Mountains State Park, Mich., *129*, **131**
porcupines, 128, 261, 302, 494
porpoises, 113
Portage Head, Wash., 417
Portage River, Mich., 149
Port Angeles, Wash., 409, 410, *415*, 417
Port Gibson, Miss., 194
Port Kent, N.Y., 33
Portland, Ore., 414, 436, *437*, 445
Portland Society of Natural History, Portland, Me., 25
Port Orford, Ore., 447, 448
Portsmouth Island, N.C., 99
Potawatomi Gorge and Falls, Mich., *129*, 130
Potomac River, 72–74, **75**
poverty grass, **51**
Powder Mill Ferry, Mo., 169, 172
Powder River Pass, Wyo., *320*, 321
Powell, Lake, Utah, 354, *355*, 358, **358–359**
Powell, Major John Wesley, 326, 364, 377, **380**, 382
prairie chickens, 167
Prairie du Chien, Wis., 154, *155*
Prairie Creek, Iowa, 155
Prairie Creek State Park, Calif., 463,

463, 464
prairie dock (plants), **172**
Prairie Dog River, Kan., 167
prairie dogs, 210–211, **210–211**, 397
  Gunnison's, 378
  see also squirrels, ground
Prairie Dog State Park, Kan., *165,* 167
Prairie Dog Town, Okla., 183
Prescott, Ariz., 383, *383*
Presidential Range, N.H., 29, 33
President Tree, Calif., **492**
Presidio, Tex., 279, *283,* **285**
Presque Isle, Wis., **130**
Presque Isle Peninsula, Pa., *43,* 44
Prickly Pear Creek, Mont., 297
prickly pears, *see* cactus
Priest Lake, Idaho, *304,* 305
primroses, **172**
  Missouri, 171
  red rock, 494
  yellow evening, 368
Prince, W.Va., 91
prince's-plumes (flowers), 367
Princeton, Mount, Colo., *243,* 245
Prince William Sound, Alaska, 515, 516
Profile Lake, N.H., 32
Profile Rock, Mass., *52,* 54
Promised Land State Park, Pa., 63
Promontory Mountains, Utah, 338
Promontory Point, Utah, *336,* 338
pronghorns, 162, 221, 234, 261, 283,
  311, 318, 397, 458, 468
Prospect Peak, W.Va., 72
Prospect Point, N.Y., 39
Providence Canyons, Ga., *107,* **109**
Providence Mountains, Calif., 505
Providence Natural History Museum,
  Providence, R.I., 55
Provincetown, Mass., 51, *52*
Provo Canyon, Utah, **343**
Provo River, Utah, 344–345
ptarmigans (birds), 242, 424, 468
puccoons, Indian (flowers), 145
Pueblo Bonito, N.M., 394
Puffer Lake, Utah, 369
Puget Sound, Wash., 409, *415,* 417, 421
Pulltite Branch, Mo., 170
Pulltite Spring, Mo., 169–170
Pumpkin Creek Valley, Neb., 235
Punchbowl Falls, Ore., **433**
Punderson State Park, Ohio, *43,* 44
Punta Gorda, Calif., 466
pupfish, 503
Purgatoire River, Colo., 262
Purgatory Chair Lift, Colo., *253,* 255
Purgatory Chasm, Mass., *52,* 54
pussypaws (flowers), **425**
Puuka Pele Mountain, Kauai, Hawaii,
  521
Puyallup Glacier, Wash., **420**
Pymatuning Waterfowl Museum,
  Linesville, Pa., 45
Pyramid Lake, Nev., *466,* **468–469**
Pyramid Peak, Colo., **244–245**

Quails, 162, 525
  bobwhite, 171, 183
  California, 302
  Gambel, 367, 404
  mountain, 302
Quartz Mountain State Park, Okla.,
  185, 187
Quechee Gorge, Vt., *32,* **33**
Queen Anne's lace, 164
Queen's Chamber, N.M., **270**
Queen Wilhelmina State Park, Ark.,
  174, 176–177
Queets, Wash., 414, *415*
Queets River, Wash., 411

Quillayute River, Wash., **414**
Quinault, Lake, Wash., 414
Quinault Rain Forest, Wash., 412, 414
Quinault River, Wash., 411, 414, *415*
Quivira National Wildlife Refuge, Kan.,
  165, 167
Quoddy Head, Me., *24, 25*

Rabbit brushes, 220, 259, 328
rabbits, 105, 162, 167, 171, 226, 251, 392
  black-tailed jack, 339
  cottontail, 128, 183, 211, 261, 339
  jack, 183, 468
  marsh, 106
raccoons, 69, 81, 105, 112, 128, 136, 145,
  170, 274–275, **302,** 402
Race Track, Death Valley, Calif., **500–
  501,** 504
Radium Springs, Ga., 107, *107*
railroad vines, 202
Rainbow Bridge National Monument,
  Utah, *355,* **357**
Rainbow Curve, Colo., 242
Rainbow Falls, Wash., *426,* 427–428
Fainbow Falls, Wis., **140**
Rainbow Forest Museum, Ariz., 397
Rainbow Lake, Mont., 304
Rainbow Springs, Fla., *118,* **120**
Rainbow Terrace, Wyo., 323
Rainier, Mount, National Park, Wash.,
  16, 417, 418–429, **418–419,** 420, 422,
  423, 424–425, *426,* **428,** 431
  Longmire House Museum, 429
  Longmire Visitor Center, 422–423
  Paradise Visitor Center, 429
Rainy Lake, Minn., 128
Rancho Santa Ana Botanic Garden,
  Claremont, Calif., 507
Rangeley Lake, Me., *24, 25*
Ranger Peak, Tex., 274
  Aerial Tramway, *272,* 274
Rathbun, Lake, Iowa, 155–156, *155*
Raton Basin, N.M., **396**
rats, 251
  kangaroo, 202, 261, 468
  wood, 106
Rattlesnake Falls, Tenn., *81,* 82
rattlesnakes, 108, **200–201,** 202, 282,
  367, 392
  black-tailed, **281**
  diamondback, 104
  Grand Canyon, 380
ravens, 69, 377, 424, 456
Ravine Gardens, Palatka, Fla., 120
Raymondville, Tex., 204
Red Bluffs of the Escambia River, Fla.,
  194, 195
redbud trees, 71, 80, 86, 88, 171
Red Canons Park, Colo., 262, *262*
Red Canyon, Utah, *369,* 371
Red Canyon Trail, Utah, 342–344, *342*
redfish, 118
Redfish Lake, Idaho, *329,* **333**
Red Lodge, Mont., 294
Red Mountain Pass, Colo., *253,* 255
Red River, La., Okla. and Tex., **10–11,**
  186, **186**
Red River Mountains, N.M., *394,* 396
Red River Pass, N.M., 396
Red Rock, Lake, Iowa, *155,* 156
Red Rock Canyon, Calif., *495,* 496
Red Rock Canyon Area, Nev., *505,* **506**
Red Rock Canyon State Park, Okla.,
  185, **187**
Red Rock Dam, Iowa, 156
Red Rocks Park, Colo., 240
Redstone, Colo., **247**
Redwood National Park, Calif., 460–
  469, **460–461,** *462, 463, 464,* 466

redwoods, **462,** 463–464, **465,** 466, 478,
  479, 480, 485, 486
Reelfoot Lake, Tenn., *81,* 82
Reflection Lakes, Wash., 423
Regan, Mount, Idaho, **330–331**
Republican River, Kan., 166
Reva Gap, S.D., *213,* 214
rhododendrons, 54, 72, 86, 88, 92, **93,**
  416, 442, 445, 449, **462,** 478
  California rosebay, 463
Rialto Beach, Wash., 413
Ribbon Falls, Calif., 476, **477**
Rib Mountain State Park, Wis., **139,**
  141
Richardson Grove, Calif., *466,* 468
Richardson Highway, Alaska, *515,* 516
Richmond Hill State Park, Ga., 107–
  108, *107*
Rich Mountain, Ark., 177
Ricketts Glen, Pa., *43,* 44
Riggins, Idaho, 302, *304,* 306, 307
Riggs Flat Lake, Ariz., 404
Rim Drive, Bryce Canyon, Utah, 368
Rim Rock Drive, Colorado National
  Monument, Colo., **246–247**
Rim Village, Ore., 454, 456, *457*
Rim of the World Drive, Calif., *505,*
  506
Rincon Range, Ariz., 399, 402
Rio de las Animas Perdidas, Colo., 253
Rio Grande Gorge, N.M., *394,* 396–397
Rio Grande National Forest, Colo., 263
Rio Grande Reservoir, Colo., *253,* 255
Rio Grande River, 203, *203,* 205, 255,
  272, **278,** 279, **280–281,** 282, *283,*
  284, **285**
Riverside Geyser, Wyo., 316
Riverside Municipal Museum, River-
  side, Calif., 507
Riverside State Park, Wash., 428
roadrunners (birds), 282, 367, 404
Roan Mountain, N.C. and Tenn., *89,*
  93
Roanoke Island, N.C., 98
Roaring Fork Valley, Colo., **244–245**
Roark Bluff, Ark., **175**
Rockchuck Peak, Wyo., **312–313**
rockchucks (animals), 368
Rock City, Kan., *165,* 167
Rock City Gardens, Tenn., 90
Rock City Park, N.Y., *43,* 44
Rock Creek Park, Wash., D.C., 72, 74
Rock Cut, Colo., 242
Rockefeller Forest, Calif., 466
Rock Hound State Park, N.M., *272,* 274
Rockpile Roadside Park, Tex., 285
Rocky Gorge, N.H., 33
Rocky Mountain National Park, Colo.,
  10, 12–13, 14, 219, 236–247, **236–
  237,** **238,** 240, **241,** 242, **243,** 262,
  263, **263,** 294, 297, **322,** 329, 428
  Moraine Park Visitor Center,
  241
  Natural History Museum, 247
Rogue River, Ore., *445,* 448, 449, *449,*
  451
Rollins Pass, Colo., *243,* 246
Rollins Sanctuary, Fla., *107,* 108
Roosevelt, Theodore, 16, **16–17,** 209,
  214, **214**
Roosevelt Dam, Ariz., 403
Roosevelt Lake, Ariz., 403, 404
Roosevelt Lake, Wash., *426,* 428
Roosevelt National Forest, Colo., 244
rosemary, wild, 108
roses
  cliff, 378
  meadow, 221
  rugosa, **51**
  wild, 164, 251
  wood, 463

Ross Barnett Reservoir, Miss., *194*, 195
Ross Creek Scenic Area, Mont., *304*, 305
Ross Lake National Recreation Area, Wash., *426*, **427**
Rotary Natural Science Center, Oakland, Calif., 480
Roughlock Falls, S.D., *224*, 225
Round Spring, Mo., 170–172
Round Top Drive, Oahu, Hawaii, *524*, 526
Royal Gorge, Colo., 262, *262*, **301**
Royal Palm Hammock, Fla., 116
Ruby Beach, Wash., 413
Ruby Mountain Scenic Area, Nev., *342*, 344
Rushmore, Mount, S.D., 224, *224*, **225**
Russell Cave Natural History Museum, Bridgeport Ala., 83
Russian Gulch State Park, Calif., *478*, 480
Rutgers University Geology Museum, New Brunswick, N.J., 65
Rye Nature Center, Rye, N.Y., 65

Sabbaday Falls, N.H., 33
Sable Pass, Alaska, 513
Sacramento Pass, Nev., 369
Saddle Creek, Idaho, 301
Saddle Mountain State Park, Ore., 444, *449*, 450
Saddle Rock Hiking Trail, Neb., 233
sage, 457
sagebrush, 210, 259, 320–321, 329, 368
Sage Creek Rim Road, Badlands, S.D., 223
Saguaro National Moument, Ariz., 398–405, **398–399**, *400*, *403*
sailfish, 194, **204**
St. Augustine Alligator Farm, Fla., 109
St. Clair Lake, Mo., 176
St. Croix, Lake, Wis., 135, 136, **138**
St. Croix Falls, Wis., **132–133**
St. Croix River, Minn. and Wis., 132–141, **132–133**, **134**, **137**, **138**, *139*
St. Croix Valley, Wis., 135, 137–138
St. Elmo, Colo., 245
St. George Island, Fla., *107*, 108
St. Helena, Mount, Calif., *478*, 480
St. Helens, Mount, Wash., *415*, **416**, 417, 435
St. Joe National Forest, Idaho, 304–305
St. Joe River, Idaho, *304*, 305
St. John, Mount, Wyo., **312–313**
St. Johns River, Fla., *107*, 108
St. Lawrence River, 45
St. Mark's Wildlife Refuge, Fla., *107*, 108
St. Martinville, La., 191, *194*
St. Mary, Mont., 291
St. Mary Lake, Mont., **286–287**, 291
St. Mary's River, Ga., 106, *107*
Saint Simons Island, Ga., *107*, 108
Sakakawea, Lake, N.D., *213*, 214
Sakonnet River, Mass., 52
salals (plants), **424**, 463
Salamonie River State Forest, Ind., 149
Salem, Mo., 169
Salem, Ore., *449*, 450
Salinas River, Calif., 488
Salinas River Dunes, Calif., *487*, 488
salmon, 25, 411, 428, **434**, 435, 442–444, *449*, 466
  chinook, 302, **435**
  chum, **434**
  coho, 146
  kokanee, **296–297**, 456
  silver, **434**
  sockeye, **435**

Salmon, Idaho, 329
Salmon Cascades, Wash., 411
Salmon Falls Creek, Idaho, 329
Salmon River, Idaho, 302, *304*, 306, **306**
Salmon–Trinity Alps Area, Calif., *466*, 468
Saltair, Utah, 340
Salt Creek Bed, Utah, **353**
Salt Creek Canyon, Utah, 354
Salt Lake Canyons, Utah, *342*, 344
Salt Lake City, Utah, 337, 340, **341**
Salton Sea, Calif., *505*, 506
Salt River Canyon, Ariz., *403*, **405**
Salt River Mountains, Ariz., 404
saltworts (plants), 114
Sam Houston National Forest, Tex., 203
San Antonio, Mount, Calif., 506
San Antonio Mountain, N.M., *394*, 397
San Antonio River, Tex., *203*, 205
San Bernardino Range, Calif., 506
San Carlos Apache Indian Reservation, Ariz., 404
San Carlos Reservoir, Ariz., *403*, 404
Sand Beach, Acadia, Me., 21
Sand Cave, Ky., 78
sanderlings (birds), 202
Sand Hills, Neb., 10, 234–235, **235**
Sand Hills Lakes, Neb., *234*, **235**
Sandhills Region, N.C., 101
Sandia Mountains, N.M., **395**
Sandia Peak, N.M., *394*, **395**
San Diego Beaches, Calif., *505*, 506
San Diego Natural History Museum, San Diego, Calif., 507
Sand Pebble, Utah, 340
sandpipers (birds), 51
San Felipe Springs, Tex., *283*, 285
San Fernando Valley, Calif., 495
Sanford National Recreation Area, Tex., *185*, 187
San Francisco, Calif., 461, 478, *478*, 485
San Francisco Mountains, Ariz., 378, *383*, 385, 386
San Gabriel Mountains, Calif., 495, *495*, *496*, 506
San Gabriel Wilderness Area, Calif., 496
Sangre de Cristo Range, Colo. and N.M., **258–259**, 259, 261, **261**, 262, **262–263**, 396
Sanibel Island, Fla., *118*, **121**
San Jacinto, Mount, Calif., *505*, 506
San Joaquin Valley, Calif., 487, **493**, *495*
San Juan Basin, Colo., 256
San Juan Islands, Wash., *415*, **417**
San Juan Mountains, Colo., 253, **254**
San Juan National Forest, Colo., 255, 263
San Juan River, Utah, 357
San Luis Valley, Colo., 259, **261**, 262
San Marcos, Tex., 204
San Mateo Coast Beaches, Calif., *487*, 488
San Mateo Mountains, N.M., 396
San Miguel Range, Colo., *253*, **256**
San Rafael Swell, Utah, *355*, 358
San Rafael Wilderness, Calif., *487*, 488
Santa Ana Mountains, Calif., *505*, 506–507
Santa Ana National Wildlife Refuge, Tex., *203*, 205
Santa Barbara, Calif., 495, *495*
Santa Barbara Beaches, Calif., *495*, **497**
Santa Barbara Island, Calif., 495
Santa Cruz Museum of Natural History, Santa Cruz, Calif., 489
Santa Cruz Valley, Ariz., 399
Santa Elena Canyon, Tex., **278**, 280
Santa Fe National Forest, N.M., 394
Santa Fe Trail, 14, **232**

Santa Lucia Range, Calif., 483, **486**, 489
Santa Monica Mountains, Calif., 495
Santa Rita Range, Ariz., 404
Santa Rosa Island, Calif., 507
Santa Rosa Island, Fla., *194*, 195
San Solomon Springs, Tex., 283
Sapelo Island Research Foundation, Ga., 109
Sapelo Lighthouse Wildlife Refuge, Ga., *107*, 108
Sapphire Mountains, Mont., 296
Sarasota Jungle Gardens, Sarasota, Fla., 120
Sargent Drive, Acadia, Me., 23
sassafras (plants), 69
Sattley, Calif., 478
Saugatuck, Mich., *147*, 148
Savanna, Ill., 151–152, **152–153**
Savannah, Ga., 107–108, *107*
saw grasses, 113, **114**, 115, 116, **116**
Sawtooth Lake, Idaho, *329*, **330–331**
Sawtooth Mountain, Calif., **496**
Sawtooth Peaks, Idaho, 329, 332, **333**
Sawtooth Primitive Area, Idaho, **330–331**, **333**
saxifrage, alpine (plants), 494
scallops, bay, 108
Scenic Coast Drive, Wash., *415*, 417
Scenic Drive, Idaho, *304*, 306
Scenic Narrow Gauge Railroad, Silverton, Colo., *253*, **257**
Scenic Wisconsin River Drive, Wis., *155*, 156
Schoodic Point, Me., 21
Schoolroom Glacier, Wyo., **313**
Science Museum of St. Paul Institute, St. Paul, Minn., 141
Scott, Hiram, 233
Scott, Mount, Okla., 183–184, **184**
Scott, Mount, Ore., 456
Scotts Bluff National Monument, Neb., 228–235, **228–229**, 230, 232, *234*
  Visitor Center, 235
Scotty's Castle, Death Valley, Calif., 501
Scriver's Wildlife Museum, Browning, Mont., 297
sculpins (fish), 445
sea anemones, 16, 21, **444**, 445
Sea Arama Marine World, Galveston, Tex., 205
sea cows, 113
Sea Island, Ga., 107
Sea Life Park, Oahu, Hawaii, 526
Sea Lion Caves, Ore., **444**, 445, *445*
sea lions, 445, 448, 468, 495
  California, 485
  Steller's, **444**, 485
Seal Rock, Ore., *445*
seals, 442, 468–469
  harbor, 485
Seaman Mineralogical Museum, Houghton, Mich., 131
sea oats, 202
sea otters, 442, 448, 485, 487
Seaquest State Park, Wash., 417
Sears Falls, Neb., *234*, 235
Seaside, Ore., 444, *449*
Seattle, Wash., 414, *415*, 416
  Marine Aquarium, 417
sea urchins, 485
Seawall, Me., 23
seaweeds, 445, 485
Sebago Lake State Park, Me., *24*, 25
Sebree Island, Alaska, **516**
Secchi Beach, Ore., 448
Second Beach, Wash., 413
Secor Park Nature Center, Berkey, Ohio, 149
sedges (plants), 149
See 'Em Alive Zoo, Red Lodge, Mont., 297

Selma, Ore., 449
Selway–Bitterroot Wilderness, Idaho and Mont., 294, *304*, 306
Selway Falls, Idaho, *304*, 306
Selway River, Idaho, 306
Seminole, Lake, Ga., *107*, **108**
Seneca Caverns, Ohio, 147, *147*, 149
Seneca Rocks, W.Va., 72, 74
Sentinel Butte, N.D., *213*, 214
Sentinel Dome, Calif., 476
Sentinel Mountain, Utah, 367
Sentinel Rock, Calif., 476
Sentinel Rock, Ill., 152
Sequoia–Kings Canyon National Park Museum, Three Rivers, Calif., 496
Sequoia National Park, Calif., 490–497 **492**, *495*
sequoias, 244, 461, **465**, 477, 491–493
Serra, Father Junipero, 14
serviceberries, 53, 210
Seven Devils, Ore., 448
Seven Devils Range, Idaho, 299, **300**, *304*
Seven Devils Scenic Area, Idaho, 302, *304*, 306–307
Seven Sacred Pools, Maui, Hawaii, *524*, 526
Seventeen Mile Drive, Calif., *487*, **488–489**
Sevier Canyon Scenic Drive, Utah, *369*, 371–372
Sevier Dry Lake, Utah, *369*, 372
Sevier River, Utah, 371
Seward, Alaska, 515
Shackleford Bank, N.C., *99*
shad (fish), 435
Shadow Mountain National Recreation Area, Colo., 242, *243*, 246
Shark Valley observation tower, Everglades, Fla., 17, 115
Shasta, Mount, Calif., *466*, **468**
Shasta–Trinity–Whiskeytown National Recreation Areas, Calif., *466*, 468
Shavehead Lake, Mich., 149
Shavers Fork Creek, W.Va., 72, **74**
Shawangunck Mountains, N.Y., 64
Sheeder Prairie, Iowa, *155*, 156
sheep
    Barbary, 394
    bighorn, 242, 251, 261, 290–291, **293**, 318, 320, 377, 395, 458, 468, 505
    Dall, 511–513
Sheep Creek Geological Area, Utah, *342*, 344
Sheep Mountain, Wyo., 321
Shelburne Birches, N.H., *32*, 34
Sheldon National Antelope Refuge, Nev., *466*, 468
Shell Canyon, Wyo., *320*, 321
Shell Falls, Wyo., 321
Shelter Cove, Calif., 466
Shenandoah National Park, Va., 66–75, *68–69*, **70**, 72
    Visitor Center, 74
Shenandoah River, Va. and W. Va., 73
Shenandoah Valley, Va., 68, *68–69*
Sheridan Lake, S.D., *224*, 225
Shields River, Mont., 294
Ship Island, Miss., *194*, 195
Shiprock, N.M., *394*, **395**
Shiprock Mountain, Colo., 254
Shi-Shi Beach, Wash., 417
shortgrasses, 161, **163**, 183
Shoshone Canyon, Idaho, 320, *320*, 321
Shoshone Falls, Idaho, *329*, 331
shrews, 128
shrimps, 503
    brine, 338
Shuksan, Mount, Wash., 427
side oats grama (grass), **163**
Sierra Blanca Mountains, N.M., 272,

274, 275
Sierra del Carmen, Tex., **280–281**
Sierra Madre Mountains, Calif., 487
Sierra Nevada Range, Calif., 475, 476, 478, **480**, **490–491**, **493**, 495–496
Sieur de Monts Spring, Acadia, Me., 21
Signal Mountain, Ga., *89*, 92
Signal Mountain, Wyo., 312
Silent City of Rocks, Idaho, *329*, 331–332
Siletz Bay, Ore., *445*
Silver Bell–Avra Valley Road, Ariz., *403*, 404
Silver Cascade, N.H., 32
Silver Creek Falls, Ore., *437*, 438
Silver Lake, Wash., *415*, 417
Silver Lake, Wyo., 246
Silver Sands, Utah, 340
Silver Strand Falls, Calif., **477**
silverswords (plants), **527**
Silverton, Colo., **257**
Simpson Reef, Ore., 448
Singletary Lake, N.C., *100*, 101
Sinking Creek, Mo., 172
Sinks, The, Wyo., *320*, 323
Sinnott Memorial Overlook, Ore., 456
siren fishes, **105**
Siskiyou National Forest, Ore., 449
Sitka National Monument, Alaska, *515*, 516
Sitting Bear, N.C., 91
Sitting Bull Falls, N.M., 272, **273**
Siuslaw National Forest, Ore., 449
Siuslaw River, Ore., 445, *445*
Skagit River, Wash., **427**
Skillet Glacier, Wyo., 312
skimmers, black (birds), **117**, **200**, 202
Skokomish River, Wash., 416
Skull Valley, Utah, 342
skunkbrushes, 221
skunk cabbages, Western, **424**
skunks, 69, 105, 162, 183, 282, 302, 368
Skykomish River Falls, Wash., *426*, 428
Skyline Drive, Shenandoah, Va., 68, **70**, 72, *72*
Skyline Drive, Wasatch Mountains, Utah, *342*, 344
Skyline Park, Calif., 495
Skyline Trail, Mount Jefferson, Ore., 437
Skyway Motorway, Ala., *194*, 195
Slate Mountain, Wash., 427
Sleeping Bear Dunes, Mich., 142–149, *142–143*, **144**, *145*, **146**, *147*
Sleeping Bear Point, Mich., **145**
Sleeping Ute Mountain, Colo., *253*, 254–256
Slide Mountain, N.Y., *63*, 64
Slim Buttes, S.D., 214
Slumgullion Pass., Colo., *253*, 256
smilax vines, 104–105
Smith, Jedediah, 220, 363–364, 368
Smith River Falls, Ore., *449*, 450
Smith Rocks State Park, Ore., *437*, 438
Smithsonian Institution Natural History Museum, Washington, D.C., 74
Smoke Hole Canyon, W.Va., 72, 74
Smoky Mountains, *see* Great Smoky Mountains
Smuggler's Notch, Vt., *32*, 34
snails, 503
    freshwater, 115
    spiral-shelled, 445
    tree, 115
    Zion, 367
Snake River, Idaho, Ore., and Wyo., 298–303, *298–299*, 300, 302–303, *304*, 306, **308–309**, 311, 313, 325, *329*, 330, 331, 332, 427
Snake River, Neb., *234*, 235
Snake River, Wis., *135*, 137

Snake River Canyon, Wash., *426*, **428**
Snake River Falls, Neb., *234*, 235
snakeroot, white, **172**
snakes
    black, 112
    blue racer, 104
    canebrake, 104
    gopher, 392
    king, 104, 392
    pigmy, 104
    red ringneck, 281
    see also rattlesnakes
snakeweed, broom, 378
snappers
    mangrove, 113
    red, **204**
Sneffels, Mount, Colo., 255
snooks (fish), 113
Snoqualmie Falls, Wash., *426*, 428, **428**
Snoqualmie River, Wash., 428
Snow Bowl, Ariz., 386
Snow Canyon, Utah, *369*, 372
    State Park, 372
Snowy Range, Wyo., 246
Snowy Range Pass, Wyo., *243*, 246
Sol Duc Hot Springs, Wash., 411, *415*
Soleduck River, Wash., 411, *415*
Solomon River, Kan., 167
Solon Springs, Wis., 135, 138
Somes Sound, Me., 23
Somesville, Me., 23
Sonoma Coast Beaches, Calif., *478*, 480
Sonora, Tex., 283, *283*, 285
Sonora Desert, Ariz., 380, 399, 404
Sonora–Junction Scenic Drive Tex., *283*, 285
sorrel
    mountain, **425**, 494
    wood, **497**
Soule, La., 190
Souris River, N.D., 214
South Dakota School of Mines and Technology Geology Museum, Rapid City, S.D., 226
Southern Illinois University Natural History Museum, Carbondale, Ill., 83
Southern Oregon Museum of Natural Resources, Ashland, Ore., 459
South Fork Canyon, Calif., 493
South Manitou Island, Mich., 146
South Rim Drive, Black Canyon, Colo., 251
South Rim of the Grand Canyon, Ariz., 377–378, **378**, 380, *383*
South Sister Mountain, Ore., 549
Southwest Harbor, Me., 23, 24
Spanish Bottom Canyon, Utah, 354
Spanish daggers (plants), 279
Spanish Peaks, Colo., 262
Sparks Lake, Ore., *457*, 459
sparrows
    desert, 380
    white-throated, 125
spatterdocks (plants), 149
Spaulding Lake, N.H., 31
Spearfish Canyon, S.D., *213*, 214
Spearfish Creek, S.D., 214
Spider Rock, Ariz., **396–397**
spireas (plants), 424
    Alaska, **424**
    rock, 251
Spirit Lake, Iowa, *155*, 156
Spirit Lake, Wash., *415*, **416**, 417
Split Mountain, Colo. and Utah, **344–345**
Split Rock Lighthouse, Minn., *129*, 130
Spokane, Mount, State Park, Wash., *426*, 427
Spokane, Wash., 428
Spokane River, Wash., *426*, 428

spoonbills, roseate, **117**
Sportsman's Park Museum, Idaho Falls, Idaho, 332
Spouting Horn, Ore., 446
spring beauties (flowers), **173**
Springfield Science Museum, Springfield, Mass., 55
Spring Mountains, Nev., **506**
Spruce Knob, W.Va., 74
spruces, 21, 29, 35, 86, 126, 239, 321, 380, 383, 442, 445, 511, 515
  black, 125
  blue, 241
  Engelmann, 241, 289, **425**
  red, 29, 71, 74, 91
  Sitka, 413, 447, **465**
  white, 125
Squaw Flat, Utah, 354
squirrels, 69, 145, 171, 183, 381
  Florida flying, 105
  flying, 74, 153
  golden-mantled, **252**, 378, 456
  ground, 202, 211, 251, 289, 368
    see also prairie dogs
  Kaibab, 380, 383
  red, 128
  rock, 380
  tassel-eared, 380
Staircase Rapids, Wash., 416
Stamford Museum and Nature Center, Stamford, Conn., 55
Stanislaus River, Calif., 478
Stanley Basin, Idaho, 329, *329*, 332
Stanley Lake, Idaho, *329*, 332
Stansbury Island, Utah, 339
starfish, **444**, 445
Stark Mountain, Vt., 32
State Capitol Museum, Olympia, Wash., 417
State University Museum, Pocatello, Idaho, 332
State University Museum of Natural History, Iowa City, Iowa, 157
State Wildlife Exhibits, Boone, Iowa, 157
State Wildlife Museum, Jackson, Miss., 195
Steamboat Canyon, Ariz., *394*, 397
Steamboat Falls, Ore., *457*, 459
"Steamboat Rock," Iowa, 157
Steelhead Falls, Ore., 437
Steens Mountains, Ore., *457*, 459
Stephen C. Foster State Park, Fargo, Ga., 106
Steptoe Butte, Wash., *426*, 428
Stevens Canyon, Wash., 423
Stillwater, Minn., 138, *139*
Stockton Island, Wis., **130**
Stonewall, Colo., 262, *262*
Stonewall Gap, Colo., 262, *262*
Stonewall Valley, Colo., 262
Stony Man Mountain, Va., 70
Storm King, Mount, Wash., 410
Storm King Mountain, N.Y., 60
Stove Pipe Wells, Calif., 503, 504
Stowe, Vt., 34
Strawberry Canyon, Calif., 506
sturgeon, 136, 428, 435
  white, 302–303
sugar cane, 193
Sugar Loaf Mountain, Mich., 146
Sugar Loaf Mountain, Wis., **140–141**
Sulphur Mountain Drive, Calif., *495*, 496
sumacs, 154
Sumner, Mount, Ill., **157**
Sunbury, Pa., 45
sunflowers, 261, **261**
Sunken Forest, N.Y., 53
Sunken Gardens, St. Petersburg, Fla., 120

Sunrise River, Minn., 135, 137
Sunrise Visitor Center, Wash., 423
Sunset Beach, Utah, 340
Sunset Crater, Ariz., 383, *385*, 387
Sunset Falls, Wash., 428
Sunset Highway, Ore., 444, 449
Sunset Point, Utah, **379**
Sunset View, Colo., 251
Sun Valley, Idaho, 329, *329*, 332
Superior, Lake, 128, 129, *129*, 130, 135, 137, 138
Superstition Mountains, Ariz., 403, *403*, **404**
Susquehanna River, Pa., *43*, 45
Suwanee Canal Recreation Area, Ga., 106
Suwanee River, Fla. and Ga., 106, *107*, *118*, 120
swallows
  Bahama, 112
  cliff, 221
  violet-green, 328, 378
Swamp Trail, Va., 71
Swan Range, Mont., 297
swans, 101
Swansboro, N.C., 100
Swanson River–Swan Lake Canoe Trails, Alaska, *515*, 516
Swan Valley Highway, Mont., 294, 297
sweet peas, 145
sweet Williams (flowers), 171, **173**
Swift Creek Canyon, Wyo., 321
Swiftcurrent Mountain, Mont., 292
Swift Trail, Ariz., *403*, 404
switch grasses, 161, **163**
sycamores, 53, 170, 175, 485
Sylacauga Quarries, Ala., *194*, 195
Sylvan Lake, Ind., 147
Sylvan Lake, S.D., 224, **227**
Syracuse, Utah, 337

Table Rock Lake, Mo., *174*, 177
Table Rock Mountain, S.C., *89*, **93**
Taconic Mountains, N.Y., 59, 64
Tahoe, Lake, Calif. and Nev., *478*, **480**
Talimena Skyline Drive, Okla., *174*, 177
Talledega National Forest, Ala., 195
tallgrasses, 161, **163**
Tamalpais, Mount, Calif., *478*, 480
Tamarisk Grove, Calif., 505
tamarisks, 357
Tamiami Trail, Fla., 17, 115
Tanque Verdes, Ariz., 399
Taos, N.M., 396
Tappan Zee, N.Y., 59, 60
Tappan Zee Bridge, N.Y., 60
Targhee National Forest, Idaho, 330
taros (plants), 524–525
tarpons (fish), 113
Tarrytown, N.Y., 60
tasajillos (plants), 279
Tates Hell Swamp, Fla., *107*, 108
Taughannock Creek, N.Y., 45
Taughannock Falls, N.Y., *43*, 45
Taylor, Mount, N.M., 396
Taylors Falls, Wis., 135, **137**, *139*
Tear of the Clouds, Lake, N.Y., 59
Teche, La., 190
Tecopa Cavern, Calif., 505
Teeple Lake, Mich., 148
Teewinot, Mount, Wyo., **310**, **312–313**
Tehipite Canyon, Calif., 493
Telescope Peak, Calif., **498–499**, 500, 504
Telluride, Colo., **256**
Telos, Lake, Me., *24*, **25**
Temperance River, Minn., *129*, 130
Temperance River State Park, Minn., 130

Temple of Osiris, Utah, 367
Temple of the Sun, N.M., **264–265**
Tenkiller Lake, Okla., *174*, 176
Tennessee River, Tenn., 92
Tennessee State Museum, Nashville, Tenn., 83
Tensleep Canyon, Wyo., *320*, 322
Tensleep Creek, Wyo., 322
Ten Thousand Smokes, Valley of, Alaska, **516–517**
terns, 51
  Caspian, 339
Terry Peak, S.D., *224*, 225–226
Teton Basin, Idaho, *329*, 332
Teton National Forest, Wyo., 321
Teton Pass, Wyo., *320*, 322–323
Teton Range, Wyo., **308–309**, **310**, 311–313, **312**, **313**, 323
Texas Canyon, Ariz., *403*, 404
Texas Falls, Vt., 34
Texas Parks and Wildlife Departments Marine Laboratories, Rockport, Tex., 205
Texoma, Lake, Recreational Area, Tex. and Okla., *185*, 186
Theodore Roosevelt National Memorial Park, N.D., *213*, 214, **214**
  Visitor Center, 215
Thermopolis Hot Springs State Park, Wyo., *320*, 323
Thielsen, Mount, Ore., 457
thimbleberries, 463
Third Beach, Wash., 413
Thompson Falls, Mont., *304*, 307
Thompson Pass, Alaska, 516
Thor's Hammer, Utah, 367
Thousand Island Lake, Mich., *139*, 141
Thousand Islands, N.Y., *43*, 45
Thousand Lakes Wilderness, Calif., *466*, 468
Thousand Springs, Idaho, *329*, 332
Thrall, Kan., 164
thrashers
  curved-billed, 401
  sage, 380
Three Brothers, Calif., 476
Three Lakes Area, Wis., *139*, 141
Three Rivers Petroglyphs, N.M., *272*, 275
Three Sisters Wilderness Area, Ore., *457*, **458**
Three Wise Men, Utah, 367
thrushes, hermit, 377
Thunder Creek Arm, Wash., **427**
Thunder Hole, Acadia, Me., 21
Tierra Amarilla, N.M., 397
tiger lilies, 145
Tigre, La., 190
Tillamook Bay, Ore., 445
Tillamook Head, Ore., 444–445, **450**
Timber of Ages Petrified Forest, S.D., *224*, 226
Timber of Ages Wood Museum, Piedmont, S.D., 226
Timpanogos, Mount, Scenic Area, Utah, **343**
Timpanogos Cave National Monument, Utah, 345
Tinicum Wildlife Refuge, Pa., *63*, 64
Tioga Road, Calif., 476–477
Tionesta Scenic Area, Pa., 43
Tipsoo Lake, Wash., 423
Tishomingo National Wildlife Refuge, Okla., *185*, 187
Titan Tower, Utah, 357
titmice (birds), 251
Toadstool Geologic Park, Neb., *234*, 235
Toiyabe National Forest, Calif., *505*
Toklat River, Alaska, 513
Toledo Museum of Health and Natural

History, Toledo, Ohio, 149
Toltec Scenic Train Ride, Colo. and
    N.M., *262, 263*
Tomaski Mountain, Utah, 353
Tongue River Canyon, Wyo., *320,* 323
Tonto National Monument, Ariz., *403,*
    404
Tonto Natural Bridge, Ariz., *383, 387*
Tonto Platform, Ariz., 382
Tooth, The, Utah, **353,** 354
Tornillo Creek, Tex., 280
Torreya State Park, Fla., *107,* 108
Torrey Pines State Reserve, Calif., *505,*
    507
Totem Pole, N.M., **271**
Totogatik River, Wis., 135
Towaoc, Colo., 256
Tower Rock, Ore., 448
Towers of the Virgin, Utah, **364–365**
Trail Ridge Road, Colo., *240,* 241, 242
Trail of the Shadows, Wash., 422
Trailside Museum, Springfield, Mass.,
    55
Trailside Nature and Science Center,
    Mountainside, N.J., 65
Trappers Lake, Colo., *243,* 246
Traverse City, Mich., 146, *147*
Travertine Creek, Okla., 187
Travertine Rock, Calif., *505,* 507
Trempealeau River, Wis., **140–141**
Tres Piedras–Tierra Amarilla Scenic
    Drive, N.M., *394,* 397
Trillium Lake, Ore., *437, 438*
trilliums (flowers), 88, **424**
Trinidad Beach Drive, Calif., *466,* 468–
    469
Triple Divide Peak, Mont., 291
Trona Pinnacles, Calif., *505,* 507
trout, 25, 54, 89, 118, 242, 244, 306, 344,
    396–397, 404, 417, 438, 466, 468
    brook, 136, 302
    brown, 136, 456
    cutthroat, **296–297,** 302, 435, 449
    Dolly Varden, **296–297,** 302
    German brown, 251
    lake, **296–297**
    Mackinaw, 305, 320, 322
    rainbow, 251, **306,** 320, 456, 493
    steelhead, 302, 304, 428, 435, 442,
        449, 459
Troutdale, Ore., 433
Troy, N.Y., 59
trumpet vines, 119
Truro, Mass., 49, **50,** 51
Trussum Pond, Del., 72, 74
Tuckerman's Ravine, N.H., 31
Tucson, Ariz., 402
Tukuhnikivatz Mountain, Utah, 353
Tule Elk State Reserve, Calif., *495,* 496
tuna, 194
turkeys, wild, 81, 88, 170, 183, 185, 234,
    235, 396, 402
Turner Falls, Okla., *185,* 187
turtles, 432
    Eastern mud, **105**
    Florida cooter, **105**
    green, 190
    sea, 101, 113
    snapping, **105**
Tusas Ridge, N.M., 397
Tushar Mountains, Utah, 369
Tuttle Creek Reservoir, Kan., *165,* 167
Twin Buttes, Idaho, 330
twinflowers, **424**
Twin Sisters, Ill., 152–153

Ubehebe Crater, Calif., 504
Uinta Mountains, Utah, 342
Umpqua River Road, Ore., *449,* 450

Uncompahgre National Forest, Colo.,
    255
Uncompahgre Plateau, Colo., **254–255**
Unicorn Park, Wash., **423**
United States Fish Cultural Station,
    Gainesville, Fla., 120
United States Fish Hatchery and
    Aquarium, Boothbay, Me., 25
United States Military Academy, West
    Point, N.Y., 60
University of Alabama Museum of
    Natural History, Tuscaloosa, Ala.,
    195
University of Alaska Museum, College,
    Alaska, 516
University of Arizona Mineralogy Mu-
    seum, Tucson, Ariz., 405
University of Arkansas Museum, Fay-
    etteville, Ark., 177
University of California Earth Sciences
    Building, Berkeley, Calif., 480
University of California at Los Angeles
    Botanic Garden, Los Angeles,
    Calif., 496
University of California T. Wayland
    Vaughan Aquarium and Museum,
    San Diego, Calif., 507
University of Colorado Museum,
    Boulder, Colo., 246
University Geological Museum, Hous-
    ton, Tex., 205
University of Hawaii Waikiki Aquar-
    ium, Honolulu, Oahu, Hawaii, 526
University of Maine Herbarium, Orono,
    Me., 25
University of Michigan Exhibits Mu-
    seum, Ann Arbor, Mich., 149
University of Minnesota Landscape
    Arboretum, Excelsior, Minn., 141
University of Minnesota Museum of
    Natural History, Minneapolis,
    Minn., 141
University Museum of Natural History,
    Princeton, N.J., 65
University of Nebraska Natural Science
    Museum, Lincoln, Neb., 167
University of Nebraska Trailside Mu-
    seum, Crawford, Neb., 235
University of North Carolina, Coker
    Arboretum, Chapel Hill, N.C., 101
University of Oregon Museum of
    Natural History, Eugene, Ore., 450
University of the Pacific Herbarium,
    Stockton, Calif., 480
University of Pennsylvania Herbarium
    and Arboretum, Philadelphia, Pa.,
    65
University of Texas Marine Science
    Institute, Port Aransas, Tex., 205
University of Texas McDonald Obser-
    vatory, Mount Locke, Tex., 284
University of Utah Earth Science Mu-
    seum, Salt Lake City, Utah, 345
University of Washington Arboretum,
    Seattle, Wash., 417
University of Washington Natural His-
    tory Museum, Seattle, Wash., 417
University of Wyoming Geological
    Museum, Laramie, Wyo., 247
Upheaval Dome, Utah, 353
Upper Geyser Basin, Wyo., 316
Upper Iowa River, Iowa, *155,* 157
Upper Klamath Lake, Ore., *457,* **459**
Upper Mississippi National Wildlife
    Refuge, Ill., 153
Upper St. Croix Lake, Wis., 138
Utah Field Museum of Natural History,
    Vernal, Utah, 345
Ute Pass, Colo., 246
Uwharrie Mountains, N.C., 101

Valdez, Alaska, 516
Valdez–Whittier Ferry Ride, Alaska,
    515, 516
Valentine National Wildlife Refuge,
    Neb., 234, 235
valerians, Sitka (flowers), **424**
Vallecito Lake, Colo., *253,* 256
Valley of Fires, N.M., *272,* 275
Valley of Fire State Park, Nev., *383,*
    384
Van Buren, Mo., 169–170, *172*
Vancouver, Captain George, 416, 421,
    521
vanilla leaves, **424**
Vaseys Paradise, Ariz., 385
Ventana Wilderness, Calif., *487,* 489
Vermilion Chasm, Idaho, 326, **328**
Vernal Falls, Calif., *476,* **476**
Victor, Idaho, 332
violets, 70
    Flett, 409
Virgin River, Utah, 363–365, **364–365,**
    366, 368
voles (animals), 128
Voyageurs National Park, Minn., 125
vultures
    black, 282
    turkey, 69, 251, 282

Wabash River, Ind., 147, *147,* 149
Wacissa River, Fla., *107,* 108
Wacissa Springs, Fla., 108
Wagon Wheel Gap, Colo., 263
Wahconah Falls, Mass., *52,* 54
Waialeale, Mount, Kauai, Hawaii, **519,**
    523, *524,* 526
Waikiki Beach, Oahu, Hawaii, 524
Wailua River, Kauai, Hawaii, 524
Waimea Bay, Kauai, Hawaii, 521
Waimea Canyon, Kauai, Hawaii, 518–
    527, **518–519,** 520, **521,** *524*
Wakulla Springs, Fla., *107,* 109
Walden Pond, Mass., *52,* 54–55
Waldo Lake, Ore., *457,* 459
Walker, Mount, Wash., *415,* 417
Wallowa Lake, Ore., *437,* **438**
Wallowa Mountains, Idaho, 302, *304*
Wallowa Mountains, Ore., *437,* 438,
    438
Wall Street, Utah, 367
Wall of Windows, Utah, 367
Walnut Canyon National Monument,
    Ariz., *383, 387*
    Museum, 387
walnuts, 162
Walsenburg, Colo., 262
Wapsipinicon River, Iowa, 157
Wapsipinicon State Park, Iowa, *155,*
    157
warblers, 69, 108, 282, 381
    Audubon, 211
    Cuban golden, 112
    Kirtland's, 148
Ward Mountain, Nev., *369,* 372
Wasatch Mountains, Utah, 337, **341,**
    342
Wasatch Mountain State Park, Utah,
    342, 344
Washington, Mount, N.H., 26–35, **26–**
    27, 28–29, 30, *32*
    Observatory, 28, **31**
Washington, Mount, Wash., 416
Washington Oaks Gardens, Marine-
    land, Fla., 120
Washington State University, Charles B.
    Conner Museum, Pullman, Wash.,
    429
watercress, 153

water hyacinths, 119
water lettuce, 115, **121**
water lilies, **105**, 106, **106**, **122–123**, 153–154
Waterloo Recreation Area, Mich., *147*, 149
Waterpocket Fold, Capitol Reef National Park, Utah, 355, **356**
Watkins Glen, N.Y., *43*, **45**
Waycross, Ga., 106, *107*
weasels, 162, 261
    Alabama, 106
Weber Canyon, Utah, 342
Weber River, Utah, 339
Webster, Mount, N.H., 29
Weiser, Idaho, 306
Wellesley Island State Park, N.Y., 45
Wellfleet, Mass., 51, *52*
    Wellfleet Bay Wildlife Sanctuary, 55
Wendover, Utah, 341, *342*
Werner, Mount, Colo., 244
West Barnet, Vt., *32*, **34**
West Cornwall, Conn., 53
Western Mountain, Me., 23
West Point, N.Y., 60
Westport Coastal Drive, Calif., *466*, **469**
West Tensleep Creek, Wyo., *320*, **323**
West Tensleep Lake, Wyo., 323
West Virginia University Arboretum and Natural Wildlife Museum, Morgantown, W.Va., 74
Weymouth Woods, N.C., *100*, 101
Whale Cove, Ore., 445, *445*
whales
    California gray, 485
    gray, 414, 485
    killer, 485
Wharton State Forest, N.J., *63*, 64
Wheeler, Mount, N.M., 396
Wheeler Creek Canyon, Ore., 456
Wheeler Geologic Area, Colo., *262*, **263**
Wheeler Gorge, Calif., *495*, **496**
Wheeler Peak, Nev., 369, **370–371**
    Scenic Area, *369*, **370–371**
Whidbey Island, Wash., 415
whippoorwills, 171
Whiskey Run, Ore., 448
White Bird, Idaho, 302, *304*, 306
White Butte, N.D., 215
White Cloud Mountains, Idaho, 329, **332**
Whiteface Mountain, N.Y., *32*, **34**
Whitefish Lake State Park, Mont., *294*, 297
White House, Canyon de Chelly National Monument, Ariz., **396–397**
White Lake Wildlife Refuge, N.D., 215
White Mountain National Forest, N.H., 33
White Mountains, Ariz., *403*, **404–405**
White Mountains, Calif., 495
White Mountains, N.H., 10, 24, 29
White Mountains, N.M., 275
Whiteoak Canyon, Va., *69*, 70
White Rim, Canyonlands, Utah, **346–347, 348,** 352
White River, Ark., and Mo., 175
White River, Ind., 81
White River, S.D., 219, 224
White River National Forest, Colo., 246
White Sands National Monument, N.M., 272, **274**
    Park Museum, 275
Whitewater Canyon, N.M., 272, 275
Whitewater State Park, Minn., 141
Whitewater Wildlife Area, Minn., *139*, 141
Whiting Bay, Me., 25
Whitney, Mount, Calif., 491, 493, *495*
Wichita, Kan., 162, *165*

Wichita Mountains National Wildlife Refuge, Okla., 178–187, **178–179,** 180–181, 184, *185*
Wilbur, Ore., 450
Wildcat Den State Park, Iowa, *155*, 157
Wildcat Hills, Neb., *234*, 235
    Recreation Area, 235
    State Game Refuge, 235
wildcats, 104–105
Wilderness Fishing Trail, Center Lake, S.D., 224
Wilderness Overlook, Cumberland Gap, Ky., Tenn. and Va., 90
Wilderness Waterway, Everglades, Fla., 115
Wild Horse Reservoir, Nev., 342
Wildlife Exhibits, Paris, Mich., 149
Wildlife Loop Road, Custer State Park, S.D., *224*, 226
Wildrose Canyon, Calif., 507
wiliwilis (plants), **523**
Willamette River Valley, Ore., *449*, 450
Willapa Bay, Wash., 416
Willard Bay State Park, Utah, 337
Willard Peaks, Utah, 337
willets (birds), 200, 202
Williams Island, Tenn., 92
William T. Davis Wildlife Refuge, Staten Island, N.Y., 65
willows, 242, 297, 357, 367
    dwarf, 513
Wilmington Notch, N.Y., *32*, 34
Wilson, Mount, Calif., 495, *495*
Wilson Arch, Utah, *355*, 358
Wimberly, Tex., 204
Wind Cave National Park, S.D., 224, **225,** 226
Wind River, Wyo., 323
Wind River Canyon, Wyo., *320*, 323
Wind River Drive, Wash., *437*, 438
Wind River Range, Wyo., *320*, 321, **321**
Winnebago Lake, Wis., 139, *139*
Winnipeg, Lake, Minn., 128
Winnipeg River, Minn., 128
Winona Falls, Pa., 64
wintergreen, one-sided, **425**
wire grasses, 104
Wisconsin Dells, Wis., *139*, **141**
Wisconsin Gardens, Minocqua, Wis., 141
Wisconsin River, Wis., 156, **156–157**
Wise Man, Utah, 367
Witch's Tomb, Okla., 185
Witch Tree, Minn., *129*, 130–131
Witte Memorial Museum, San Antonio, Tex., 205
Wizard Island, Crater Lake, Ore., **452–453,** 454, 456
Woahink Lake, Ore., 447
Wolf Creek Canyon Drive, Mont., *294*, 297
Wolf Creek Pass, Colo., *262*, 263
Wolf Creek Pass, Utah, *342*, **344–345**
Wolf River Falls, Wis., *139*, **140**
wolverines, 293, 468
wolves, 126, 136, 289, 293, 513
    timber, **131**
Wometco Miami Seaquarium, Miami, Fla., 120
Wonder Lake, Alaska, 514, *515*
woodbine, 51
woodchucks, 69, 242
woodcocks, 136
woodpeckers, 69
    gila, 401, *402*
    hairy, 210
    ivory-billed, 106
    pileated, 88, 105, 136, 176
    red-bellied, 116
    red-headed, 105

Woods, Lake of the, Minn., 128
woodsia (plants), 251
Worcester Science Museum, Worcester, Mass., 55
Worden Pond, R.I., 53
Wrangell Mountains, Alaska, 515
wrens
    cactus, 282, 401, **401**
    canyon, 211, 377
Wright Memorial Bridge, N.C., 97
Wupatki National Historical Monument, Ariz., *383*, 387
Wyalusing Rocks, Pa., *43*, 45
Wyalusing State Park, Wis., 154
Wyandotte Cave, Ind., *81*, **83**
Wyoming State Museum, Cheyenne, Wyo., 246
Wyoming Valley, Wis., 155

Yachats State Park, Ore., *445*, 446
Yahoo Creek, Ky., 92
Yahoo Falls Scenic Area, Ky., *89*, 92
Yakima, Wash., 428
Yakima River Canyon, Wash., *426*, **428**
Yale, Mount, Colo., 245
Yampa River, Utah, **247**
Yankee Doodle Lake, Colo., 246
Yaquina Head, Ore., *445*, 446
yarrow (plants), 210
yaupons (hollies), 97, 100
Yavapai Point, Ariz., **301**
Yazoo River, Miss., *194*, 195
Yebechei Rocks, Monument Valley, Ariz. and Utah, *359*
Yellow River, Wis., 135
Yellowstone Falls, Wyo., 17, 317, **319,** 476
Yellowstone National Park, Wyo., 10, 15, 17, 308–323, **308–309, 314, 315, 316, 318, 319,** *320*, 329
    Museums, 323
Yellowstone River, Wyo., **220,** 317, **319,** 320
Yellowtail Dam, Mont., **295**
yellowtails (fish), 113
yews
    Florida, 108
    Pacific, **425**
Yosemite Falls, Calif., **472, 476, 477**
Yosemite National Park, Calif., 11, 15–16, **16–17,** 470–481, **470–471, 472, 474–475, 476–477,** 478
    Museum, 480
Yosemite Valley, Calif., 17, **301, 472,** 473–474
Youghiogheny River, Pa., 44
yucca (plants), **116,** 233, **274,** 380, 392

Zabriskie Point, Calif., **502,** 504
Z Canyon, Wash., *426*, 429
Zion–Mount Carmel Highway, Utah, 365, 367
Zion National Park, Utah, 301, **341,** 360–373, **364–365, 366, 367,** *369*, **379**
    Visitor Center, 372
Zoroaster Temple, Ariz., 378
Zuni Mountains, N.M., *394*, 397

Picture Credits

Photographers

These are arranged in order by page. Where more than one picture appears on a page, read the names in order from left to right, top to bottom. Pictures that occupy two full pages are so indicated. Pictures that extend to a second page are credited on the page where most of the picture appears.

2–3, Robert Walch; 10–11, both NASA; 12–13 middle, Dennis Stock/Magnum; 12–13 bottom, Museum of the American Indian, N.Y., N.Y.; 16–17 top, Culver Pictures, Inc.; 18–19, Robert Walch; 20, Paul A. Knaut, Jr.; 22, Lawrence R. Lowry, Robert Walch; 25, both Charles Steinhacker; 26–27, Dick Smith; 28, Jerome Wyckoff; 30, Dick Smith; 31, Arnout Hyde, Jr.; 33, Thase Daniel; 34, Lawrence Pringle, Carsten W. Johnson; 35, 36–37, Charles E. Rotkin/PFI; 38, Photo Trends; 40–41, 41, 42, 44, all Susan McCartney; 45, Susan McCartney, Ben Waterman; 46–47, Edward S. Barnard; 48, Grant Heilman; 49, Jay Good; 50, Anthony Wolff; 53, Alan Linn; 54, Alan Linn, E. R. Degginger; 55, Donna Harris, Lawrence R. Lowry; 56–57, Donna Harris; 58, Gene Ahrens; 61, Donna Harris; 62, Carroll C. Calkins; 64, Susan McCartney; 65, Robert W. Carpenter; 66–67, Grant Heilman; 69, Jerome Wyckoff; 70, R. Allan Mebane; 73, M. E. Warren, Yeager and Kay; 74, Arnout Hyde, Jr.; 75, Holger Harvey, Fred Maroon/Lou Mercier; 76, W. Ray Scott; 79, 80, National Park Concessions; 82, R. A. Hessler; 83, Richard L. Powell, Bradley Smith/Photo Researchers; 84–85, 87, Kenneth W. Fink; 90, David Muench; 91, Bill Strode/Black Star; 92, John Earl; 93, Roger W. Barbour, Frank J. Miller; 94–95, H. W. Kitchen/Photo Researchers; 96, Frank J. Miller; 97, Jean Anderson; 99, Frank J. Miller/Photo Researchers; 101, Nicolas Foster, Frank J. Miller; 102, 104, Grant Heilman; 106, Max Hunn; 108, Ted Borg; 109, Max Hunn, Charles E. Rotkin/PFI; 110–111, Lawrence R. Lowry; 113, Grant Heilman; 114, David Muench; 116, Walter J. Kenner; 117 (clockwise from top left), Walter J. Kenner, Walter J. Kenner, Caulion Singletary, Kenneth W. Fink, Grant Heilman, Kenneth W. Fink, Caulion Singletary, Grant Heilman; 119, Zigmund Leszczynski/Photo Trends; 120, Ed Cooper; 121, George Leavens/Photo Researchers, Charles Steinhacker, Max Hunn; 122–123, Joseph Fire; 124, Donna Harris; 126, Franklin Institute; 127, 128, Donna Harris; 130, both Charles Steinhacker; 131, Ron Winch, H. Charles Laun; 132–133, Joseph Fire; 134, Tom Algire; 137, 138, Michael R. Burk; 140, Ken Dequaine, Tom Algire; 141, Joseph Fire; 142, Robert W. Carpenter; 144, Michigan Tourist Council; 145, Grant Heilman; 146, Dr. John W. McGee; 148, Michigan Tourist Council, Fred Ragsdale/Freelance Photographers Guild; 150, 152, 153, Tomas Sennett; 156, Ken Dequaine; 157, Tomas Sennett; 158–159, Robert Phillips; 160, Grant Heilman; 162–163, 164, Robert Phillips; 166, Jerome Wyckoff; 167, Fred Maroon/Photo Researchers; 168, 171, Larry Nicholson; 173, Richard Raber; 175, Kenneth L. Smith; 176, DeWys, Inc.; 177, Stephen Green-Armytage, Larry Nicholson; 178–179, John Douglas Bulger; 181, Dean G. Graham; 182, John Douglas Bulger; 184, 186, 187, Pat Faris/Photo Trends; 188, James Steinke; 190, 191, Thase Daniel; 192, Fritz Henle/Photo Researchers; 195, Ted Borg, William A. Garnett; 196–197, Dick Philips; 198, Grant Heilman; 201, 202, National Park Service; 204, Pat Faris/Photo Trends; 205, Henry and Vera Bradshaw; 206, Gene C. Frazier; 208, David Muench; 209, Carl Iwasaki/LIFE magazine © Time Inc.; 211, Ron Winch; 212, Ila Bromberg, Marc Keltner; 214, Wilford Miller; 215, Wilford Miller, Margaret and Bill Jensen; 216–217, 218, David Muench; 220, Willis Peterson; 221, both National Park Service; 222, David Muench; 225, David Muench, Ila Bromberg; 226, Josef Muench; 227, David Muench; 228–229, Jack Zehrt; 230, Bob Clemenz; 232, Ernst Peterson; 233, Henry and Vera Bradshaw; 235, Kenneth W. Fink, Grant Heilman; 236–237, Grant Heilman; 238, David Muench; 240, Willis Peterson; 241, David Muench; 242, Willis Peterson; 244, Ken Dequaine; 245, Ed Cooper; 246, Richard H. Petzold; 247, 248, 250, all David Muench; 251, W. S. Keller; 254, Grant Heilman; 255, 256, David Muench; 257, Jack Zehrt, David Muench; 258, David Muench; 260, Grant Heilman, Lud Munchmeyer; 261, Gene Ahrens; 263, both Jack Olson; 264–265, Bob Clemenz; 266, Peter G. Sanchez; 268, Anthony Wolff; 269, both Peter G. Sanchez; 270, Dick Kent; 271, Josef Muench; 273, Nelson T. Bernard; 274, Ed Cooper; 275, Josef Muench; 276–277, Jack Zehrt; 278, Grant Heilman; 280, David Muench; 282, Jerome Wyckoff; 284, Jerome Wyckoff, Peter Koch; 285, Jack Zehrt; 286–287, Grant Heilman; 288, David Muench; 290, 292, Kenneth W. Fink; 293 top pictures, Thomas F. Myers, all remaining, Kenneth W. Fink; 295, Robert C. Fields, William E. Jensen; 296, David Muench; 297, Ben Strickland; 298, Ernst Peterson; 300, Ray Atkeson; 303, Harald Sund; 305, David Muench; 306, Ray Atkeson; 307, Kyle Walker, James Tallon; 308–309, Hal Rumel; 310, 312, David Muench; 313, R. Allan Mebane; 314, David Muench; 315, Kenneth W. Fink; 316, David Muench; 318, 319, Bob Clemenz; 322, Shostal Agency; 324, Shostal Agency, Tom Algire; 323, David Muench; 324, 326, Peter G. Sanchez; 327, James L. Papadakis; 328, David Muench, Peter G. Sanchez, Peter G. Sanchez; 330, David Muench; 331, James L. Papadakis; 332, Charles E. Rotkin/PFI; 333, David Muench, Daniel D. Sullivan; 334–335, 336, 338, 339, all Robert Phillips; 340, David Muench; 343, Jerome Wyckoff; 344, David Muench; 345, Ray Atkeson, Helen C. Norton; 346–347, Bob Clemenz; 348, David Muench; 350, Willis Peterson; 352, Donna Harris; 353, David Muench, Donna Harris; 354, Donna Harris; 356, David Muench; 357, David Muench, Parker Hamilton; 358, 359, 360–361, 362, David Muench; 363, Willis Peterson; 365, Hildegard Hamilton; 366, Vivian Pfleiderer; 367, David Muench; 368, Bob Clemenz; 370, Willis Peterson; 371, Josef Muench; 372, David Muench; 373, David Muench, Willis Peterson; 374–375, 376, David Muench; 379, Bob Clemenz; 380, 381, all Donna Harris; 382, David Muench; 384, Don Wright, David Muench; 385, David Muench; 386, Josef Muench; 387, Dana C. Morgenson; 388, David Muench; 390, Josef Muench; 391, David Muench; 393, Bob Clemenz; 395, Stephen Green-Armytage, David Muench; 396, James L. Papadakis; 397, Alan Pitcairn/Grant Heilman; 398, David Muench; 400, Josef Muench; 401, John V. Young; 404, Robert Phillips; 405, David Muench, Dana C. Morgenson; 406–407, Edward S. Barnard; 408, Bob Clemenz; 410, Kenneth W. Fink; 412, Edward S. Barnard; 413, 414, Josef Muench; 416, David Muench; 417, Ray Atkeson; 418–419, David Muench; 420, Bob and Ira Spring; 422, 423, David Muench; 427, Ray Atkeson; 428, Ed Cooper; 429, Ed Cooper, Ray Atkeson; 430, Jack Zehrt; 432, David Muench; 433, Ray Atkeson, David Muench; 434, National Park Service/Glenn Gallison; 436, 438, Ray Atkeson; 439, E. R. Degginger, David Muench; 440–441, Ray Atkeson; 443, Josef Muench; 444, Thomas F. Myers, Harald Sund; 446, Thomas F. Myers; 447, Ray Atkeson; 448, Thomas F. Myers; 450, 451, all Ray Atkeson; 452, Philip Hyde; 455, David Muench; 456, Charles Steinhacker; 458, Ed Cooper; 459, Steve Crouch; 460, Josef Muench; 462, David Muench/Van Cleve Photography; 463, 464, Thomas F. Myers; 467, 468, 469, all David Muench; 470–471, Josef Muench; 472, David Muench; 474, Ed Cooper; 475, Thomas F. Myers; 477, 479, David Muench; 480, Philip Hyde; 481, Josef Muench, David Muench; 482, 484, David Muench; 486, Steve Crouch; 488, Josef Muench; 489, Dennis Brokaw, Steve Crouch; 490, 492, 494, David Muench; 496, 497, Josef Muench; 498–499, David Muench; 501, Josef Muench; 502, 503, all David Muench; 504, Josef Muench; 506, 507, all David Muench; 508–509, Dean Brown; 511, Malcolm Lockwood; 512, Emil Muench; 514, Peter G. Sanchez; 516, Dean Brown; 517, Josef Muench, Dean Brown; 518, David L. Pearson; 520, David Muench; 521, Wallace Litwin/Photo Trends; 523, 525, 526, David Muench; 527, Eric L. Ergenbright/Lenstours, Ray Atkeson.

PICTURE EDITOR: Robert J. Woodward.

Artists

10–11, Jerome Wyckoff; **12–13,** Northern Natural Gas Co. Collection at the Joslyn Art Museum, Omaha, Neb. Museum of the American Indian, N.Y., N.Y.; **14–15,** The Bettmann Archive, Inc., The Bettmann Archive, Inc., Culver Pictures, Inc., The New York Historical Society; **16–17,** Culver Pictures, Inc., National Park Service; **23,** Howard Berelson; **31,** Lee J. Ames; **41,** Enid Kotschnig; **50–51, 60,** Howard Berelson; **71, 79, 88,** Lee J. Ames; **98–99,** Dennis R. Fritz; **105,** Howard Berelson; **115,** Frank Schwarz; **126–127, 136, 144,** Howard Berelson; **154,** Matt Greene; **163,** Howard Berelson; **172–173,** Eva Cellini; **182–183,** Joseph Cellini; **193,** Matt Greene; **201–202,** Eva Cellini; **210–211,** Howard Berelson; **223,** Cal Sacks; **232,** Cal Sacks; **241,** Howard Berelson; **252,** Richard Grossenheider; **261,** Lee J. Ames; **269,** Darrell Sweet; **281,** Eva Cellini; **291, 300–301,** Howard Berelson; **317,** Frank Schwarz; **341,** Cal Sacks; **351,** Howard Berelson; **378–379,** Frank Schwarz; **392,** Howard Berelson; **402,** Eva Cellini; **411,** Frank Schwarz; **424–425,** Victor Kalin; **434–435,** Darrell Sweet; **445,** Wesley B. McKeown; **454–455,** Howard Berelson; **465,** Victor Kalin; **476–477,** Darrell Sweet; **485, 493, 512,** Howard Berelson; **522–523, 528,** James Alexander; **552–553,** Eva Cellini and George Kelvin.

All Maps by THE H.M. GOUSHA COMPANY
A SUBSIDIARY OF THE TIMES MIRROR COMPANY